International Finance and Open Economy Macroeconomics

International Finance and Open Economy Macroeconomics

Francisco L. Rivera-Batiz
Indiana University

Luis Rivera-Batiz
University of Chicago

MACMILLAN PUBLISHING COMPANY
NEW YORK

Collier Macmillan Publishers
London

Macmillan Publishing Company
866 Third Avenue, New York, New York 10022

Collier Macmillan Canada, Inc.

Library of Congress Cataloging in Publication Data

Rivera-Batiz, Francisco L.
    International finance and open economy macroeconomics.

    Includes index.
    1. International finance. 2. International economic
relations. 3. Macroeconomics. I. Rivera-Batiz, Luis.
II. Title.
HG3881.R527 1985   332'.042   84–19406
ISBN 0–02–401620–9

Printing: 6 7 8   Year: 9 0 1 2

ISBN 0-02-401620-9

TO OUR PARENTS

Ada and Luis

Preface

We have written this book with the goal of providing a comprehensive but integrated introduction to modern international finance and open economy macroeconomics. With this in mind, the most important recent developments in the area—particularly those relating to flexible exchange rates—and the most advanced, frontier-level research in the field have been gathered and simplified into a form that is accessible to a wide, general audience. The major common thread running throughout the book is our concern with domestic and international policy issues. This is a policy-oriented textbook. Major policy controversies are thus analyzed in their historical context and in light of the latest theoretical developments in the field.

International economics is not an easy discipline. There are many alternative economic environments and topic areas to consider in this diverse and growing field. An adequate treatment of the subject must avoid falling into a fragmented approach to the area and instead provide an integrated view of its complexities. This book follows such a route. We start by providing simple frameworks showing basic principles and then we gradually build a more sophisticated analysis by introducing additional elements into the discussion. The end product is still a highly flexible product that can be easily adapted to the reader's preferences. The more difficult material is left to optional sections or appendixes that can be used by the more knowledgeable reader or set aside without any disruption of continuity.

This book offers an up-to-date discussion of the anatomy of inflation and business cycles in open economies and the related policy issues, the performance of past international monetary regimes such as the gold standard and the gold exchange standard, the why of the collapse of the Bretton Woods system, the economics of managed floating and of Central Bank intervention in foreign exchange markets, the European monetary system and monetary unions, and the changing role and future prospect of gold, the dollar, and other international reserve currencies in world monetary arrangements. We also analyze in detail the external debt crisis of the developing countries in the 1980s, the current role of the International Monetary Fund (IMF) in the world economy, the effects of IMF-sponsored macroeconomic adjustment programs in developing countries, the nature of balance of payments crises, and alternative policy responses to oil price hikes. By the end of the book the reader should have a thorough understanding of these policy issues, the controversies that have surrounded them, and the available evidence on the matter. Our discussion of recent events in the world economy will also update the reader on the current state of international economic affairs.

Our approach is to state the main issues in a down-to-earth manner. No calculus or advanced mathematics is required; only simple algebra is utilized when necessary. A course in introductory economics—and particularly macroeconomics—would be extremely helpful and is recommended by the authors. Those readers with more background will benefit from the rich discussion of recent events and theoretical developments in the area. The abundance of references—and our emphasis in being consistent with the literature—means that the book can be utilized as an initial stepping-stone for advanced study and research in the field. It can thus serve as a handy sourcebook. Working out the problems at the end of each chapter will ensure that understanding of the material has been reached. Adopters of the textbook may obtain a solutions manual for these problems directly from Macmillan.

One may ask what are the main elements in the writing of a textbook. Three key aspects are involved. First must be a supply of comments and suggestions from colleagues and readers of the manuscript. Luckily, we have been provided with highly valuable comments. We want to thank Professors Luis Akle (Instituto Tecnológico Autónomo de Mexico), Robert Z. Aliber (University of Chicago), Victor Canto (University of Southern California), Betty Daniel (State University of New York at Albany), Eusebio Diaz (University of Puerto Rico), Steven Husted (University of Pittsburgh), Marie Thursby (Ohio State University), and José Viñals (Stanford University) for their suggestions at the various stages of our project. Their suggestions and the revisions they induced have made the present version a much improved and polished product compared to the initial drafts. Also, scores of undergraduate and graduate students in the Economics departments at Indiana University, the University of Massachusetts—Amherst, Instituto Tecnológico Autónomo de Mexico (ITAM), and at the graduate schools of business of the University of Southern California and the University of Puerto Rico have given feedback on previous drafts. Their support is therefore immensely appreciated. We also thank our editor at Macmillan, Chip Price, and our production supervisor, Elaine Wetterau, for their suggestions, encouragement and, above all, patience during the long march to the completion of the manuscript.

A second requirement for successful book writing is the availability of a supporting staff. We must first express gratitude to our excellent research assistants for bearing with us through many tedious revisions and updating of figures and tables. They were Larry Krause, Aquiles A. Almansi, Cathy Bonser, and Gary Dymski. The efficient typing of Maggie Newman, Nancy Ferrer, Linda Steinwachs, and Angélica Caraballo, made it all really possible. We are also grateful to Mari Ramirez for her thorough proofreading. A grant from the National Research Council of the National Academy of Sciences, which financed a Postdoctoral Fellowship in International Economics at the Department of Economics of the University of Chicago during 1982–1983, provided financial resources and released time sorely needed by Francisco Rivera-Batiz.

A third requirement for the writing of a textbook is, of course, a strong background in the field and a familiarity with the recent literature and developments in the area. As graduate students at M.I.T. and the University of Chicago we have had the benefit of taking classes from outstanding figures in international economics, to whom we owe an intellectual debt: Rudiger Dornbusch, Jagdish N. Bhagwati, Jacob A. Frenkel, Milton Friedman, Arnold Harberger, the late Harry Johnson, Charles P. Kindleberger, Arthur Laffer, Rachel McCulloch, and Paul Samuelson. The most difficult task, however, has been to keep up with a literature that has been growing as fast or even faster than our waistlines. If this book can make current international economics literature accessible to wider audiences and aid in analyzing international economic problems intelligently, its main objective will have been fulfilled.

F. R-B.
L. R-B.

Brief Contents

xi

Detailed Contents

PART II Introduction to International Macroeconomics

PART III Income, Trade, and Capital Flows: Fixed and Flexible Exchange Rates

PART **IV**   Inflation, Unemployment, and Economic Policy in the Open Economy

PART V   Asset Markets, the Balance of Payments, and the Exchange Rate

PART **VI**   Interdependence in the World Economy

International
Finance and
Open Economy
Macroeconomics

Introduction

It has become a cliché to say that we live in an interdependent world and that all economies are open, that is, they trade with each other. This means that countries are not self-sufficient but rather specialize in producing and exporting the goods and services in which they enjoy a comparative advantage, while at the same time importing from other countries the raw materials, equipment, and consumption goods they cannot produce competitively in international markets. International trade has some clear gains. You personally benefit when buying cheap Taiwanese-manufactured shirts and Japanese-made Toyotas or when your company sells more home computers or refrigerators in Europe. There are, however, some constraints imposed by participating in the international trade game: You have to play by the rules, and most of the time—except in cases where countries impose barriers to trade—this means buying or selling your products at terms heavily influenced by international market forces. Free trade implies the crude fact that foreign producers can sell their products in the United States and thus undercut (and take some consumers away from) American producers selling at higher prices. But it also means that competitive U.S. products can undercut more expensive foreign products in Europe and other world markets. This general interdependence makes the whole (non-Communist) world a single market for many commodities, placing constraints on the extent to which prices can diverge across borders.

But how open are economies in the world? U.S. trade with the rest of the world has expanded enormously since World War II. Exports and imports of goods and services have increased drastically over the past four decades, with an average rate of growth exceeding 10% per annum. This expansion is partly accounted for by economic growth—a larger economy—and general inflation that raise the value of exports and imports. But increased international trade also represents a general trend toward greater openness of the economy. Indeed, the growth of U.S. exports and imports has surpassed that of national income since World War II. This phenomenon is not unique to the United States. It has been characteristic of the world economy overall. The worldwide aggregate of exports has increased steadily since World War II and currently exceeds $2 trillion per year, notwithstanding the shrinking world trade accompanying global recession during the early eighties. In an effort to quantify precisely this trend toward greater openness, we shall examine various indexes or measures

1

of the degree of openness of an economy and apply them to some countries for purposes of comparison.

MEASURING OPENNESS OF THE ECONOMY

The volume of an economy's international trade is usually measured by the value of its exports, imports, or their sum. In 1983, the United States exported $200.2 billion and imported $260.8 billion, making it the economy with the largest volume of trade. This large volume of trade, however, is mostly attributable to the size of the U.S. economy. It should thus not be deduced that the United States is the economy with the highest degree of openness in the world. In order to correct for size, the degree of openness of an economy is commonly determined by comparing the ratio of international trade in goods to the size of the economy, as measured by the value of output produced domestically, called the gross domestic product (GDP). This ratio shows the relative importance of trade in goods in the open economy. Table 1 shows exports and imports relative to GDP for a selected group of countries. In general, it does not matter very much whether exports or imports are used as the numerator, since the

TABLE 1. Indexes of Openness of the Economy

Country	Exports/ GDP[a]	Imports/ GDP
Bahamas	85	65
Brazil	7	8
Belgium	50	52
Canada	26	26
Egypt	20	34
Finland	31	27
France	21	20
Germany	25	25
India	7	8
Israel	44	62
Hong Kong	88	91
Hungary	47	58
Japan	11	9
Korea	33	36
Saudi Arabia	60	42
United Kingdom	29	29
United States	9	10
Uruguay	18	21

Source: Yearbook of National Accounts Statistics, United Nations (1980). Figures are in percentages.
[a] GDP, gross domestic product.

ratio to GDP is similar with both alternatives. A substantial difference in the ratios can be observed, though, in countries showing a large excess of imports over exports—such as Israel—or enjoying a huge excess of exports over imports—such as Saudi Arabia. Table 1 also shows that, roughly speaking, large countries tend to be more self-sufficient than small countries, in the sense that they have a lower degree of openness in their external trade in goods. This can be observed by comparing the ratios for the United States and Japan with those for the Bahamas and Belgium. There are exceptions, though. For instance, Uruguay, with a population of about 3 million and a gross domestic product of less than $10 billion in 1984, is a small economy with a relatively low degree of openness, as measured in Table 1.

As measured by the volume of its trade in goods relative to GDP, the U.S. economy is indeed relatively closed by world standards. This fact is sometimes quoted to allege that the openness of the U.S. economy is not significant and that, consequently, one can safely neglect open economy factors when analyzing it. One should be very cautious, however, against overstating this case. First of all, even if overall exports and imports constitute a small part of GDP, certain sectors in the economy are markedly dependent on their export sales and on products that are heavily imported. U.S. exports are prominent in such industries as civilian aircraft, construction machinery, oil field machinery, and audio equipment, in which more than one-third of production is exported. On the other hand, U.S. imports of oil are equal to 40% of U.S. oil consumption, while about two-thirds of all motorcycles and bikes and more than one-third of all radios and TV sets sold in the United States are imported. Second, since World War II, U.S. exports and imports have gradually, but significantly, risen relative to GDP. The export:GDP ratio has increased from less than 5% during the late forties to about 10% in recent years. The U.S. economy has become increasingly open. In addition, U.S. residents engage in considerable trade in services—in the form of financial services, insurance, tourism, and so forth—with the ratio of trade in goods *and* services to GDP exceeding 10% consistently.

Furthermore, the ratios of exports to GDP and imports to GDP underestimate the degree of openness of the economy. This is so since many goods never actually pass through frontiers, that is, they are never exported or imported, but are potentially tradable. This is the case of Chevys and Fords produced and sold domestically. Part of U.S. automobile production is sold locally and part is exported, but the U.S. automobile industry as a whole is an international one, competing with foreign firms both in international markets and locally. When measuring openness, then, it is relevant to consider the importance of *tradable goods,* not just of actually traded goods, such as exports or imports. Although the United States does not allocate a large fraction of its production to exports, and imports as a fraction of GDP are not significant, a large share of U.S. production and consumption consists of goods potentially tradable and subject to direct international competition. Openness, then, is much more prevalent in the United States than is shown by its relatively small import:GDP and export:GDP ratios.

An adequate measure of openness requires us to determine the relative importance of tradable and *nontraded goods*, which are to be interpreted as being *internationally* nontraded goods, since they may be bought and sold in local markets within each country. Whether it is because of their nature or because of high transport costs, high tariffs, or other restrictions on their international trade, these goods and services are not traded in world markets and, as a result, they are neither exported nor imported. The most important nontraded goods include building and construction, power generation and transportation, as well as some manufacturing industries and most services. Their importance in most economies, both developed and developing, can be easily discerned from Table 2, which shows the share of gross domestic product accounted for by the nontraded goods sector in a selected sample of countries. Nontraded goods are defined to include wholesale and retail trade; transportation and communication; insurance, real estate, and business services; community, social, and personal services; public administration; and defense. The construction sector has thus been excluded from the definition of nontraded goods, although it is often considered to be one. Its inclusion would increase the shares quoted below by 4 to 7 percentage points. In the case of the United States, the figure is 63%, suggesting that tradable goods compose 37% of GDP, a far more important figure than indicated by the statistics for exports and imports. The bottom line is that we should beware of treating the United States as a closed economy. There are crucial linkages—both direct and indirect—between the United States and the rest of the world that can only be ignored at the cost of a serious distortion. At the same time, one should not forget that the U.S. economy is not that of

TABLE 2. **Production of Nontraded Goods as a Fraction of GDP for Selected Countries, 1981**

Country	Percent	Country	Percent
Argentina*	53	Malaysia	41
Canada	64	Mexico	55
Chile	58	Morocco*	52
France	61	Pakistan	44
German Federal Republic	49	Peru	50
India	37	Spain	57
Israel	59	Sweden	66
Italy	53	United Kingdom	65
Japan	53	United States	63
Korea, Republic of	44	Venezuela	49

Source: World Bank, *World Development Report* (1983). Copyright © 1983 by the International Bank for Reconstruction and Development/The World Bank. Reprinted by permission of Oxford University Press, Inc.

* Data for Argentina and Morocco is for 1980.

a small country heavily dependent on, and completely subject to, the vagaries of international markets, nor is it perfectly integrated to world markets in goods and services.

INTERNATIONAL FACTOR MOVEMENTS AND THE DISTINCTION BETWEEN GNP AND GDP

Openness of the economy means not only that domestic residents can buy and sell products in world markets, but also that they can migrate abroad and produce in foreign countries. That is, Mexican workers can move to the United States and be employed in the production of fruits and vegetables in the Sunbelt area, while U.S. multinational firms can move their capital to produce in Brazil or Mexico. Openness thus means that productive factors and financial resources can search internationally for the highest return on their services. These international factor movements give rise to a distinction between gross national product (GNP) and gross domestic product (GDP). GNP represents the value of output *produced by domestic residents* and, in a closed economy, corresponds to the value of output *produced domestically,* which is GDP. This correspondence breaks down in an open economy. For instance, consider the case of temporary Turkish migrants employed as guest workers in Germany. Clearly, some of the production generated by Germany (some of its GDP) is due to this temporary migrant labor and not to Germany's residents. The income received by Turkish workers in Germany, then, is part of Germany's domestic product but not of its national product. In order to calculate GNP, then, we have to subtract the payments to foreigners from the value of GDP. These include wages and salaries (like those earned by Turkish migrant workers in Germany), interest and dividends distributed to foreigners, and profits obtained by branches of foreign companies investing domestically. Of course, to be symmetric, we would also have to *add* to GDP the income received by domestic residents on account of labor or other incomes accruing from their own contributions to production abroad. Symbolically,

$$GNP = GDP + R \tag{1}$$

where R represents net factor income from abroad. A country's GNP exceeds GDP if the country is a net provider of services abroad and falls below GDP if it is a net importer of services.

The divergence between GNP and GDP is significant for many countries. For instance, Pakistan receives substantial amounts of income from its workers abroad in Kuwait and Saudi Arabia and has been a net exporter of services, with its GNP generally exceeding GDP by over 7%. A rich, oil-exporting country like Kuwait, on the other hand, imports foreign workers but receives huge interest payments from its heavy international lending of oil revenues, which more than offsets it. In 1982 the Kuwait GNP exceeded its GDP by over 20%. Examples of countries in which GNP falls short of GDP are Brazil and Costa Rica, countries that became heavy borrowers during the 1970s and thus have to incur a substantial debt service burden. Although the United States is a net creditor and, indeed, is the main international lender, net interest and other payments actually received from abroad are not a significant share of its GNP; as a result, GNP and GDP do not diverge much. In recent years, U.S. GNP and GDP have diverged by about 2% or less.

INTERNATIONAL FINANCE

International trade in goods and services is only one aspect of openness. A complete picture of the openness of the economy should explicitly consider the economy's international trade in financial assets and its financial openness.

The internationalization of financial markets is one of the major developments of the post-World War II period. The United States has been at the forefront of this multifaceted development. For instance, U.S. multinational corporations' financial dealings and operations extend over dozens of countries, while foreign investors and Central Banks allocate a vast amount of funds to purchasing U.S. Treasury bills and bonds (representing short and long-term debt of the U.S. Treasury). U.S. banks have also spread worldwide as bank overseas operations surged during the 1970s. Whereas in 1970 international operations accounted for less than 20% of the total earnings of the largest U.S. banks (Citicorp's extensive overseas operations at the time were an exception), in the early 1980s over 50% of the earnings of Citicorp, Chase Manhattan, the Bank of America, and J. P. Morgan derived from their international operations. The shift is even more dramatic for the large number of other banks that had insignificant foreign operations in the early 1970s, but now obtain 20 or 30% of their earnings and profits from overseas activities.

The openness of an economy to international trade in financial assets provides its residents with some clear-cut benefits. International capital markets complement domestic financial markets by making available funds with which to finance the projects of local firms and government. They thus provide domestic residents with needed funds not accessible in the local capital markets. In addition, world financial markets allow investors to search for a higher return and minimize risks by engaging in international portfolio diversification. They thus provide lenders with investment alternatives not available locally. An economy's integration into world financial markets, however, also imposes severe constraints on some of its basic economic variables and on the effectiveness of some of the most crucial national economic policies. As we shall repeatedly stress in the ensuing chapters, international capital mobility places stringent boundaries on the extent to which domestic interest rates can diverge from those prevailing in world markets, makes the task of controlling the money supply of an economy under fixed exchange rates very difficult, and can be a source of exchange rate turbulence under flexible exchange rates. In a modern environment, then, international financial markets are essential in determining the macroeconomic behavior of open economies, a major theme of this book.

Macroeconomics studies aggregate phenomena in the economy; it is concerned with issues such as the determination of the level of output and its rate of growth, unemployment, inflation, and interest rates. It is also interested in how government policies can—or cannot—affect the aggregate behavior of the economy. Can expansionary fiscal policy really lift the economy out of a recession? And is it true that when the government steps on the monetary bandwagon, inflation picks up? These are problems that macroeconomics tries to answer. It is perhaps unfortunate that macroeconomics is so often cast in a closed-economy context, that is, in a setting where the country's interactions with the rest of the world are ignored. In reality, only the "world" is a closed economy. All national economies, as we have seen, are open, trading with each other at various levels encompassing trade in goods and services, international movements in labor and capital and international finance, that is, trade in financial claims.

OPEN ECONOMY MACROECONOMICS

The field of *open economy macroeconomics* deals with the macroeconomic aspects of economies that trade with each other. As such, it integrates the study of issues involving the balance of payments, exchange rates, foreign trade, and international capital movements into the area of macroeconomics. There are multiple reasons for studying and understanding open economy macroeconomics. First, openness implies that economies are subject to external events which strongly affect their performance. The United States, for instance, has been the subject of intense import competition from an increasing number of foreign countries in recent years. This has had enormous influence on the stagnation of such pillars of U.S. industrial activity as the steel and automobile industries. The soaring oil prices of the 1970s have also greatly affected the United States and the world economy. Rising oil and gasoline prices have caused our rent payments to increase, our driving sprees to diminish, and our winter room temperature to become rather chilly. It is thus clear that we live in a closely interdependent world and, consequently, foreign events will influence us deeply.

A second reason for studying open economy macroeconomics lies in the fact that the impact of macroeconomic policies is very much affected by the openness of the economy. When domestic variables such as domestic interest rates and prices are closely linked to their foreign counterparts, one wonders what effects governments policies can have on them. One can ask for instance, whether monetary policy can really affect domestic interest rates in a world of highly interconnected financial markets. Or can exchange rate changes affect the international competitiveness of our products? These are issues that we try to answer in open economy macroeconomics. It is crucial that we, as consumers, producers and policymakers, understand how openness affects the role of government policies: Standard closed-economy policy prescriptions seldom stand without modifications or qualifications in the open economy.

THE PLAN OF THE BOOK

The first part of the book starts with a detailed analysis of the foreign exchange, eurocurrency, and international money markets. We go over the traditional material on these topics in addition to recent areas of interest and research, such as new developments in foreign exchange futures markets, the growth of offshore banking systems and their interdependency with onshore banking systems, and recent evidence on interest rate arbitrage and the integration of international money markets. A description of balance of payments accounting and an explanation of alternative exchange rate concepts is illustrated by examining actual U.S. data in Part II. The third and fourth parts of the book present full coverage of the state of the art in open economy macroeconomics, both under fixed and flexible exchange rates. Part III introduces the open economy version of the standard *IS-LM* analysis, and Part IV integrates aggregate supply considerations and flexible price macromodeling into an international framework. This includes a discussion of the so-called rational expectations revolution in macroeconomics, the role of wage contracts and expectations on the effectiveness of macroeconomic policy, and the effects of supply side shocks on the open economy.

The monetary approach to the balance of payments and the asset market approach to the exchange rate figure prominently in Part V, which integrates international financial theory and macroeconomic analysis in explaining the balance of payments and the exchange rate. Finally, the last part of the book is devoted to the history and evolution of the international monetary system. The book ends with a policy-oriented chapter that presents an up-to-date discussion of managed floating, the European Monetary System and optimum currency areas, the problem of the external debt of developing countries, and the current role of the International Monetary Fund.

HOW TO USE THIS BOOK

This book is aimed at undergraduate and graduate courses in economics as well as M.B.A. courses in international finance and open economy macroeconomics. Chapters 1 to 9, together with Chapters 15 to 17, comprise a basic one-term course that is fully accessible to undergraduate and graduate students in economics and business administration. The book is quite flexible regarding the subjects to be stressed in particular courses. Undergraduate courses in economics can emphasize open economy macroeconomics whereas M.B.A. courses may concentrate on Chapters 1 to 3, 15, and 17, which stress financial subjects. Graduate courses would surely focus on Chapters 10 to 15 in Parts IV and V, leaving much of the descriptive material as background reference for the students.

The book's organization also offers wide flexibility with respect to the sequence of subjects, since each part can be covered independently of the others. For instance, some instructors may prefer to start with balance of payments accounting and open economy macroeconomics (Parts II to III), studying just the basic international finance concepts required for, or utilized in, the development of the macro-analysis. Others may choose to discuss the monetary and asset market approach to the balance of payments and exchange rates (Chapters 15 and 16) before tackling the Keynesian approach. The book allows this sequence, since Chapters 15 and 16 can be read independently of the rest of the book, as well as of each other.

The International Financial System

PART I

CHAPTER 1

The Foreign Exchange Market

In any open economy, it is always possible to observe some domestic residents engaging in international transactions. American car dealers, for example, buy Japanese Toyotas and Datsuns, while American computer companies sell pocket calculators to entrepreneurial Mexican businessmen. Similarly, some Americans open Swiss bank accounts, while American real estate companies sell houses and condominiums to wealthy Arab sheiks. Most of these international transactions have one special characteristic that distinguishes them from purely domestic transactions: They require the acquisition of a foreign currency on the part of one or more of the participants in the transaction. If a Saudi sheik wants to buy property in the United States, for example, he will have to sell his riyals in exchange for dollars in order to acquire the property. If an American buys a Toyota and pays the Japanese Toyota dealer in dollars, the latter will have to exchange the dollars for yens in order to have the local currency with which to pay his workers and local suppliers. Since most countries have national, sovereign currencies—Germany has the deutsche mark, France the French franc, England the pound sterling, Japan the yen—and their residents deal locally in these currencies—the prices of food, materials, domestic securities, and so on are all denominated in the local currency—some exchange of currencies is necessary. The foreign exchange market, to put it simply, permits buyers and sellers of currencies to exchange one currency for another. If there were only one world currency, say, Esperanto, there would be no foreign exchange market—and clearly no need for this chapter.

1–1 INTRODUCTION TO THE FOREIGN EXCHANGE MARKET

What do we mean by foreign exchange, and which individuals and institutions participate in the foreign exchange market? The term *foreign exchange*, broadly speaking, includes bank deposits denominated in a foreign currency, foreign currency itself (bills and coins), and other short-term claims on foreigners ex-

13

pressed in foreign currencies. Most foreign exchange transactions, however, involve purchases and sales of bank deposits denominated in foreign currencies.

The main participants in the foreign exchange market are retail customers, commercial banks, foreign exchange brokers and Central Banks.

1. *Retail customers.* These participants buy and/or sell foreign currencies for transaction purposes (to engage in the purchase and/or sale of goods, services, and securities across nationalities) or in order to adjust their portfolios, increasing the amount of a given foreign currency held (buying foreign exchange) or decreasing the amount of the foreign currency held (selling foreign exchange). Retail customers usually do not transact directly with each other. Nor do they send orders to buy or sell to a centralized market. In the process of exchanging currencies, retail customers transact with commercial banks.

2. *Commercial banks.* The most important institution involved in the operation of the foreign exchange market is the commercial bank, which buys and sells foreign exchange for its clients. In order to carry out these transactions, the banks hold foreign exchange inventories in the form of working balances (deposits) with banks in foreign countries. If a retail customer wants to purchase foreign exchange, the bank withdraws it from its inventory; if the customer sells foreign exchange, the bank's holdings of foreign exchange will increase. Given the continuous flow of purchases and sales of foreign exchange that commercial banks engage in, they sometimes find themselves holding an excess of foreign exchange reserves, while at other times having a shortage of foreign exchange. As a result, an active market in foreign exchange has arisen among commercial banks, by means of which foreign exchange short banks buy it from banks wishing to dispose of their excess holdings.

3. *Foreign exchange brokers.* In the United States, banks utilizing the foreign exchange market usually do not transact directly with each other but rather interchange currencies (or, more precisely, deposits denominated in different currencies) through the use of foreign exchange brokers, which function as interbank intermediaries. The main function of the brokers is to bring together banks that are trying to buy foreign exchange with those that are selling. It should be noted that the broker's role or function is to arrange a transaction between two parties without at any time actually owning the commodity involved, in this case foreign exchange. In contrast to the commercial bank, the foreign exchange broker does not assume a position in foreign exchange, since he or she never owns the foreign exchange that is being traded. Brokers, then, do not face the risks of exchange rate fluctuations. Commercial banks, on the other hand, in their role as dealers of foreign exchange, own foreign exchange balances and thus bear the risks of their transactions in those currencies.

4. *Central Banks.* Foreign exchange brokers may also serve as agents for the economy's *Central Bank*—a quasi-public institution in charge of regulating and controlling the economy's banking system—in the Bank's foreign exchange dealings. If the Federal Reserve, the U.S. Central Bank, wants to support the

dollar by selling foreign exchange, it will place its sale offer by means of one or more foreign exchange brokers. The actions and role of the Central Bank in the foreign exchange market depend crucially on the type of exchange rate system or regime under which the country's payments system operates. We shall discuss Central Bank intervention in the foreign exchange market later on in this chapter.

The foreign exchange market is the market in which national currencies are traded. As in any other market, a price must exist at which trade can occur. An *exchange rate* is the price of one currency vis à vis another currency. There is, of course, the problem of deciding which of the two currencies is going to be used to express the value of the other. For example, take the case of the pound sterling and the dollar. On July 17, 1981, approximately $2.00 could be traded for £1 in the foreign exchange market. We could then calculate the exchange rate as either the price of a pound in terms of dollars, which is $2.00 per pound ($/£), or the price of a dollar in terms of pounds, which is 0.50 pounds per dollar (£/$), where 0.50 = 1/2.00. We shall be looking at the exchange rate as the *domestic currency price of a foreign currency*. If we adopt the point of view of the United States as the domestic economy, the exchange rate between any currency and the dollar would be expressed in terms of *dollars required to buy the foreign currency*. In the dollar–pound sterling case just referred to, the exchange rate would then be $2.00/£.

An increase in the exchange rate between the dollar and the pound sterling (say, from $2.00/£ to $2.50/£) means that the pound sterling has become more expensive in terms of dollars. This implies that the value of the pound has increased, since the amount of dollars required to buy a pound has increased. In other words, the pound has *appreciated* (in value) in terms of the dollar. By the same token, the dollar is cheaper in terms of the pound sterling. This means that the dollar has *depreciated* in terms of the pound (from £0.50/$ to £0.40/$).

To summarize, and to avoid confusion, the reader should remember that we have defined the exchange rate between a domestic and a foreign currency as the amount of domestic currency needed to buy the foreign currency.[1] If the exchange rate increases, then, the domestic currency depreciates and the foreign currency appreciates. Similarly, a decrease in the exchange rate would imply an appreciation of the domestic currency and a depreciation of the foreign currency.

---

[1] In practice, when the dollar price of a foreign currency is small, it is more convenient to express it as its reciprocal, that is, as the foreign currency price of the dollar. Accordingly, one often finds in the literature the yen–dollar exchange rate quoted as, say, 220 yen per dollar rather than as 0.0045 cents per yen. The reader should thus be aware that uniform conventions regarding exchange rate quotations are not generally followed.

1–2 SPOT AND FORWARD MARKETS

The foreign exchange market is the largest market in the world, with a daily trading volume often above the $100 billion level, about 50 times the volume on the New York Stock Exchange. Foreign exchange markets can be classified as *spot* markets and *forward* markets. The distinction between spot and forward lies essentially in the type of contract involved in the exchange of currencies. In spot markets currencies are bought and sold for immediate delivery and payment; in practice, there may be a 1- or 2-day delay in delivery. This is the type of transaction that would occur if you were to ask your bank to sell you $250 worth of deutsche marks (DM) on the spot. It is not, however, the only type of foreign exchange transaction. The reader may not be familiar with markets for future delivery, since most commodities are traded only on spot markets and lack well-developed forward, or futures, markets. For some commodities, however, these markets do exist along with the usual spot markets. Such is the case with gold, wheat, sugar, pork bellies, and foreign exchange, among others. In forward foreign exchange markets, currencies are bought or sold for future delivery and payment. When an American buys pounds 30-day forward, he or she effectively makes a contract today to buy pounds in 30 days. The seller agrees to deliver and receive payment for the foreign exchange at that date (1 month from now) at an exchange rate specified at the time the contract is negotiated (today). The main difference between spot and forward contracts, then, is that in a spot market the price at which a currency is traded (the spot exchange rate) is set concurrently with the payment and delivery of the currency (today), while in a forward market traders determine the price today (which is called the forward exchange rate) for future delivery and payment.

Why would anyone engage in contracts to buy or sell currency through the forward exchange market? Even though this will be discussed in detail later on in this and the next chapter, it is easy to come up with some examples. A U.S. record company engaging in a contract to purchase British records in 30 days may want to ensure today the rate at which it is going to buy pounds in the future to pay for the records. Otherwise, it would have to pay the spot price for the pound prevailing at this future time, which is uncertain and could possibly be very high. To avoid risks, and to be able to plan its revenues and costs ahead more accurately, the firm may then decide to buy pounds forward, for delivery in 30 days, at the corresponding forward exchange rate quoted today. Suppose, on the other hand, that a British appliance dealer has made a contract to buy some Hotpoint refrigerators in 30 days, for which it has to pay in dollars. In this case, the British firm may want to sell a certain number of pounds (in exchange for dollars) in the forward market. This will ensure the firm the rate at which it is going to sell its pounds for dollars in 30 days, when it has to pay for the refrigerators. The importance of the forward exchange market in international finance should not be underestimated, since most customer transactions in foreign exchange indeed involve forward transactions.

Table 1–1 reproduces the foreign exchange rate quotations for March 6, 1984, as published by *The Wall Street Journal*. The first column gives the quotes as defined in this book, in terms of units of domestic currency ($) required to buy the foreign currency. As can be seen, the spot exchange rate between the dollar and the pound sterling at 3 PM, U.S. Eastern Standard Time (EST) was 1.4855 dollars per pound ($/£). Similarly, the spot exchange rate for West Germany's mark was 0.3922 dollars per deutsche mark ($/DM). We can also observe the forward exchange rates for various currencies, depending on the maturity of the forward contract (in days). For example, the 30-day forward exchange rate for the pound sterling was 1.4868 ($/£). This means that a commercial bank, at 3:00 PM on that day, would have agreed to sell pounds for delivery in 30 days at the rate of 1.4868 dollars per pound.

The Forward Premium

Table 1–1 shows that forward exchange rate quotes generally differ from spot exchange rates. The difference between the forward and the current spot exchange rates, in proportional terms, is called the *forward premium,* symbolically represented as follows:

$$\text{Forward premium} \equiv f_N = \frac{F_N - e}{e}$$

where F_N refers to the forward exchange rate for the delivery of a foreign currency N days from today, and e is the current value of the spot exchange rate for that currency. Often, the forward premium is multiplied by 100 to express it in percentage terms. A foreign currency with a positive value of f_N is referred to as being at a forward premium, while a negative value is called a forward discount. That is, if there is a premium (discount) on the value of the currency forward relative to the value of the currency spot, you have to pay more (fewer) dollars for the delivery of the currency in the future (N days forward) than if you were to ask for delivery today.

Forward contracts usually have maturities of 30, 90, and 180 days. Maturities of up to 1 year are also common. Given this maturity structure, it is often convenient to compute forward premiums and discounts on a standardized yearly basis. This annualized form of the forward premium or discount is called a *standard premium or discount* and is usually expressed as a percentage. It is defined by

$$\text{Standard forward premium (discount)} \equiv P_N = \frac{F_N - e}{e} \cdot \frac{360}{N} \cdot 100$$

TABLE 1–1. **Foreign Exchange Rate Quotations**

Tuesday, March 6, 1984

The New York foreign exchange selling rates below apply to trading among banks in amounts of $1 million and more, as quoted at 3 P.M. Eastern time by Bankers Trust Co. Retail transactions provide fewer units of foreign currency per dollar.

Country	U.S. $ equiv.		Currency per U.S. $	
	Tues.	Mon.	Tues.	Mon.
Argentina (Peso)	.03489	.03489	28.665	28.665
Australia (Dollar)	.9557	.9560	1.0464	1.0460
Austria (Schilling)	.05540	.05522	18.05	18.11
Belgium (Franc)				
Commercial rate	.01908	.01899	52.405	52.660
Financial rate	.01849	.01844	54.070	54.230
Brazil (Cruzeiro)	.0008264	.0008264	1210.00	1210.00
Britain (Pound)	1.4855	1.4852	.6732	.6733
30-Day Forward	1.4868	1.4864	.6726	.6728
90-Day Forward	1.4903	1.4898	.6710	.6712
180-Day Forward	1.4961	1.4957	.6684	.6686
Canada (Dollar)	.7965	.7985	1.2555	1.2523
30-Day Forward	.7966	.7987	1.2553	1.2521
90-Day Forward	.7969	.7989	1.2548	1.2517
180-Day Forward	.7975	.7995	1.2539	1.2508
Chile (Official rate)	.01135	.01135	88.14	88.14
China (Yuan)	.4922	.4898	2.0315	2.0417
Colombia (Peso)	.01084	.01084	92.29	92.29
Denmark (Krone)	.1064	.1058	9.3980	9.4480
Ecuador (Sucre)				
Official rate	.01737	.01737	57.57	57.57
Floating rate	.01129	.01129	88.55	88.55
Finland (Markka)	.1799	.1794	5.5590	5.5730
France (Franc)	.1273	.1260	7.8525	7.9350
30-Day Forward	.1269	.1256	7.8815	7.9640
90-Day Forward	.1255	.1243	7.9650	8.0450
180-Day Forward	.1238	.1228	8.0775	8.1450
Greece (Drachma)	.009980	.009980	100.20	100.20
Hong Kong (Dollar)	.1286	.1285	7.7790	7.7810
India (Rupee)	.0935	.0935	10.6952	10.6952
Indonesia (Rupiah)	.001007	.001007	993.00	993.00
Ireland (Punt)	1.1980	1.1935	.8347	.8379
Israel (Shekel)	.007124	.007232	140.38	138.27
Italy (Lira)	.0006297	.0006240	1588.00	1602.50
Japan (Yen)	.004481	.004473	223.15	223.55
30-Day Forward	.004495	.004488	222.46	222.83

TABLE 1–1. Foreign Exchange Rate Quotations (cont.)

Country	U.S. $ equiv. Tues.	Mon.	Currency per U.S. $ Tues.	Mon.
90-Day Forward	.004525	.004516	220.99	221.43
180-Day Forward	.004573	.004562	218.69	219.21
Lebanon (Pound)	.1706	.1706	5.86	5.86
Malaysia (Ringgit)	.4380	.4382	2.2830	2.2820
Mexico (Peso)				
Floating rate	.005848	.005865	171.00	170.50
Netherlands (Guilder)	.3472	.3442	2.8800	2.9055
New Zealand (Dollar)	.6730	.6730	1.4859	1.4859
Norway (Krone)	.1349	.1345	7.4125	7.4331
Pakistan (Rupee)	.07547	.07547	13.25	13.25
Peru (Sol)	.0004040	.0004040	2475.02	2475.02
Philippines (Peso)	.07133	.07133	14.02	14.02
Portugal (Escudo)	.007686	.007686	130.10	130.10
Saudi Arabia (Riyal)	.2851	.2852	3.5070	3.5060
Singapore (Dollar)	.4838	.4824	2.0670	2.0730
South Africa (Rand)	.8420	.8398	1.1876	1.1908
South Korea (Won)	.001261	.001261	793.30	793.30
Spain (Peseta)	.006776	.006743	147.57	148.30
Sweden (Krona)	.1309	.1298	7.6390	7.7040
Switzerland (Franc)	.4748	.4703	2.1060	2.1265
30-Day Forward	.4777	.4731	2.0935	2.1138
90-Day Forward	.4830	.4781	2.0704	2.0916
180-Day Forward	.4912	.4858	2.0358	2.0584
Taiwan (Dollar)	.02489	.02489	40.17	40.17
Thailand (Baht)	.04351	.04351	22.985	22.985
Uruguay (New Peso)				
Financial	.02120	.02120	47.18	47.18
Venezuela (Bolivar)				
Official rate	.1695	.1695	5.90	5.90
Floating rate	.07764	.07764	12.88	12.88
W. Germany (Mark)	.3922	.3888	2.5500	2.5720
30-Day Forward	.3937	.3903	2.5400	2.5619
90-Day Forward	.3967	.3932	2.5210	2.5434
180-Day Forward	.4014	.3977	2.4914	2.5146
SDR	1.07099	1.06955	.933719	.934970

Special Drawing Rights are based on exchange rates for the U.S., West German, British, French and Japanese currencies. Source: International Monetary Fund.

where N is the maturity of the forward rate in days.[2] It is known as a premium if it is positive and as a discount if negative. If you look back at the actual exchange rates for 1-month ($N = 30$) *forward* market contracts on March 6, 1984, as quoted by *The Wall Street Journal* and appearing in Table 1-1 under the items called 30 day forward, you can calculate the standard forward premiums or discounts for the major currencies at that time:

$$\text{French franc} \quad P_{30}^{Fr} = \frac{0.1269 - 0.1273}{0.1273} \cdot \frac{360}{30} \cdot 100 = -3.77$$

$$\text{Canadian dollar} \quad P_{30}^{C} = \frac{0.7966 - 0.7965}{0.7965} \cdot \frac{360}{30} \cdot 100 = 0.15$$

$$\text{British pound sterling} \quad P_{30}^{£} = \frac{1.4868 - 1.4855}{1.4855} \cdot \frac{360}{30} \cdot 100 = 1.05$$

$$\text{German mark} \quad P_{30}^{DM} = \frac{0.3937 - 0.3922}{0.3922} \cdot \frac{360}{30} \cdot 100 = 4.59$$

$$\text{Swiss franc} \quad P_{30}^{SF} = \frac{0.4777 - 0.4748}{0.4748} \cdot \frac{360}{30} \cdot 100 = 7.33$$

Similarly, you could calculate the standard forward premiums for other maturities (e.g., 90 days, 180 days).

What is the meaning of the forward premium, that is, why do forward and spot exchange rates diverge? We shall explain in later sections. For the moment, we shall return to Table 1-1 in order to clarify some further aspects of the foreign exchange market.

A look at the small typescript at the top of the display on foreign exchange rate quotations in Table 1-1 shows that the quotations refer to *selling* prices for *bank transfers* in the United States as quoted at 3 PM Eastern standard time (in dollars). Terms and phrases that we consider important are italicized throughout this discussion.

The exchange rate quotes in the first column of Table 1-1 refer to quotes for the sale of foreign exchange in the interbank foreign exchange market in New York. These are, then, wholesale quotes, which differ from the rates banks quote at their retail level. In the retail market, banks charge a higher price for the sale of foreign exchange. The additional amount charged compensates the banks for the services they provide at this level. As a consequence, the exchange rates you would face as a retail customer would exceed those quoted in Table 1-1.

---

[2] Term $(F_N - e)/e \cdot 1/N$ shows the N-day forward premium on a daily basis. The term $(F_N - e)/e \cdot (1/N)$ 360 then shows it on a yearly basis, and we multiply by 100 to express it in percentage terms.

A second aspect of foreign exchange transactions that has to be clarified is that these transactions do not generally involve a physical exchange of currencies across geographic borders. They generally involve only changes in debits and credits at different banks in different countries. The notion of foreign currencies actually being flown across the Atlantic does not make any sense in a highly integrated and developed international economy. Foreign exchange transactions, then, do not have to be carried out through physical exchange of actual currency. The main instruments of foreign exchange transactions include cable bank deposit transfers and bank drafts, bills of exchange, and a whole array of other short-term instruments expressed in terms of foreign currency, such as international money orders. This wide range of foreign exchange instruments has arisen out of centuries of international trading and is tailored to the varying circumstances and risks faced by traders. The primary instrument traded in foreign exchange markets, and the only one to be discussed here, is the *bank deposit transfer* made by cable—the telegraphic transfer. A bank deposit transfer occurs when a seller of foreign currency makes a transfer of deposits from its bank account to the account of the buyer of the currency. For example, suppose that General Electric, which is assumed to accept payments in pounds and has a bank account in London, receives a payment in pounds from a London customer. General Electric now holds excess pound sterling deposits in London and desires to sell them to a New York bank; that is, it wants to sell foreign exchange. Usually, G.E. would cable its bank in London to transfer the ownership of, say, £20,000 to the New York bank purchasing the foreign exchange. If G.E. holds an account at this New York bank, the latter can credit G.E.'s account immediately for the corresponding amount of dollars; alternatively, it can issue a cashier's check for the appropriate amount on G.E.'s behalf. The whole process is completed quickly, taking no more than 1 or 2 days.

To take another example, suppose that G.E. has to pay a certain amount of pounds to a British supplier of parts and materials. In this case, G.E. has to buy foreign exchange, which it can do through its New York bank. General Electric purchases the necessary pounds from the bank; it orders the bank to debit the corresponding amount of dollar deposits out of its account at New York and to transfer the pounds purchased with those dollars to G.E.'s bank in London. Then G.E. will cable its London bank to debit its own account and provide the London supplier with the appropriate amount of pounds. Again, all these transactions occur very quickly.

Returning to Table 1–1, one can now understand that the exchange rates quoted apply to bank transfers similar to those just discussed, except that they specifically involve large-scale foreign exchange trading among banks so that both the buyer and the seller are banks.

The foreign exchange market is a truly international market. Commercial banks in different financial centers are interconnected by a fast communications system involving telex and computer links as well as telephone lines. Exchange rate quotes from different financial centers can be obtained immediately at the touch of a telex terminal or through a telephone call. Because of this close interconnection, a demand for dollars in London by a British firm importing goods from the United States can easily be transmitted into a supply of sterling in New York. The main financial centers, including New York, London, Brussels, and Zurich, are all really part of one international market for foreign exchange. In most of these large financial centers, one can quickly buy or sell virtually any currency. The reason is that these centers have attracted banks from almost everywhere in the world, either through branches established there or through working relationships with major banks at the centers. Note that one does not have to be in a large financial center to have access to foreign exchange. Local banks can provide foreign exchange by purchasing it in turn from major banks.

Returning to Table 1–1, one must now realize that the statement that the quotes were for 3:00 PM Eastern standard time does not imply at all that the foreign exchange market closed at that time. The foreign exchange market never—or almost never—closes. Foreign exchange can be found in most international financial centers in the world. If the New York market closes at 3:00 PM, this corresponds to 12:00 PM in San Francisco so that trading in foreign exchange can be carried out through that market. When the San Francisco market closes, trading can move to Tokyo, and later on to Singapore and London. The financial center at which the foreign exchange transaction occurs, then, might move from place to place, but the foreign exchange market never closes.

1–3 TRACING OUT A TYPICAL FOREIGN EXCHANGE TRANSACTION

How does a typical foreign exchange transaction take place? We now follow through the main actions involved in one such typical transaction. Suppose, then, that Acme Importers has to pay £1 million to Royal Exporters in London. The foreign exchange transaction begins when Acme's international financial manager calls the international banking department of, say, Goodbuck Bank. The bank receives the call in its foreign exchange division, where orders to buy and sell foreign exchange from both retail customers and correspondent banks are taken. Here, the bank has several foreign exchange traders who are usually linked through telephone, cable, and computer links to major customers, brokers, and domestic and foreign correspondents.

The first thing that Acme's manager wants from the bank is the current price of the pound sterling, that is, the (spot) exchange rate between the dollar and the pound. He or she would probably receive an answer consisting of two different exchange rates, say 1.5000 and 1.4985.

What this means is that the bank will sell pounds at the price of 1.5000 dollars per pound ($/£) and that it will buy pounds at the price of $1.4985/£.[3]

---

[3] The gap between 1.5000 and 1.4985 is 0.15 cents. This difference will generally be referred to as being 15 basis points, with each point corresponding to 1/100 cents, or 0.01 cents.

In order to profit from buying and selling foreign exchange, commercial banks buy the foreign exchange at a certain price and sell it at a higher price. Otherwise, they would not engage in the activity at all. The percentage difference between the bank's buy (bid) and sell (ask, offer) prices for any given currency is known as the *spread* or *trading margin,* which is generally on the order of about 0.1%. In this particular case, we have the following spread:

$$\text{Spread} = \frac{P_A - P_B}{P_A} \times 100 = \frac{1.5000 - 1.4985}{1.5000} \times 100 = 0.1$$

where P_A represents the ask (sell) price and P_B means the bid (buy) price; we multiply by 100 in order to express the spread as a percentage. The spread for any given currency is affected by the amount of currency traded (the smaller the quantities, the greater the margin), the size of the financial center (if in a major international center, such as New York or London, the margin is smaller), the turbulence or price variability of the currency (the larger the turbulence, the greater the margin), the thinness of the currency market (if it is the New Zealand dollar, then the margin is larger), and the type of instrument traded (e.g., bank notes, bank drafts, require a larger margin).

We have already mentioned that the primary instrument traded in the foreign exchange market is the bank transfer. It is precisely one of these transfers that Acme wishes to make to Royal. After receiving the quote on the spot exchange rate, Acme's financial manager asks to make a transfer of £1 million from its own account, to be deposited in Royal's account at Barclays Bank in London. This concludes the transaction between the bank and its customer, but it does not end the foreign exchange transaction.

After Acme hangs up, one of Goodbuck's foreign exchange traders examines the bank's current *position statement* in terms of the pound. A bank's position statement in a foreign currency shows the bank's assets and liabilities denominated in that foreign currency. Since the bank may hold some pound-denominated deposits in a London branch or at a London correspondent, these appear as assets in the position statement. On the other hand, the bank may owe foreign exchange to customers, appearing as a liability in the position statement. Goodbuck's transaction with Acme, regarding Acme's payment to Royal, generates a liability in Goodbuck's position statement. A *closed or balanced position* of a bank—as related to its position statement—occurs when assets denominated in a given foreign currency, arising from foreign exchange purchases over time, match the amount of liabilities denominated in that currency arising from foreign exchange sales of the bank. Otherwise, a bank is said to have an *open position* in the currency. A positive open position means that assets denominated in a given currency exceed liabilities in that currency. It is often referred to as *being long* in a currency. Conversely, a bank (or any trader, for that matter) is *short* in a currency if it registers a negative balance on its position statement. That is, its liabilities exceed its assets denominated in the given foreign currency.

Goodbuck's foreign exchange trader observes the bank's current position statement and then proceeds in the following manner. Suppose that the bank is long on the pound, as it would be if it had £1 million available as deposits in its account at a London branch or correspondent bank. Then, Goodbuck's foreign exchange trader, or his or her clerical staff, will proceed to cable the London bank and order it to debit Goodbuck's account on the amount of £1 million and credit it to the account of Royal Exporters at Barclays. On the other hand, if Goodbuck has a short position on the pound, the foreign exchange trader will place an order to buy £1 million through a foreign exchange broker in New York.

Major trading centers, such as New York and London, have a small number of foreign exchange brokers. Their number varies, but in most cases you can count them on the fingers of your hands. The main work of a broker is to exchange currencies among the major commercial banks dealing in foreign exchange. Brokers charge only a small margin to carry out any transaction (approximately $0.001 per pound sold) because of the large quantities they deal with. They compete keenly with each other, sometimes by means of rate cutting but more often through a melée of nonprice mechanisms, which include providing selected customers with inside information, better-quality services, and personal gifts. One bank trader claimed that one Christmas he received more than $1000 worth of presents from brokers. Another one recalls that when his wife had a child, a broker called him at the hospital and offered to pick up the hospital bill!

Returning to our specific foreign exchange example, suppose that Goodbuck is short £1 million. One of Goodbuck's foreign exchange traders will then call a broker, placing an order to buy £1 million. The broker may then either quote the rate at which he has offers to sell pounds, or if he does not have any, he may put the trader on hold. The broker will then proceed to call the other major banks in New York that deal in foreign exchange and get their offers to sell pounds (their ask prices). He will then inform Goodbuck's trader of the existing ask prices and, if the trader accepts, as is usually done, the transaction concludes. In some cases, the trader may not accept the ask prices in the New York market and proceed to place bids for purchase of pounds in other financial centers. Whenever pounds are purchased, the foreign exchange trader proceeds to deposit the £1 million purchased on Goodbuck's account at a London branch or correspondent and then asks the branch to transfer the deposit to Royal's account, concluding the transaction.

1–4   SPATIAL AND TRIANGULAR ARBITRAGE

Although the foreign exchange market is spatially dispersed across the major cities and countries, it is unified by keen competition among the highly sophisticated market participants, which count with the most modern information and communications network and face low transaction costs, usually well below 1% of the value of transactions. A powerful force keeping exchange rate quotations in different places in line with each other is the search on the part of market participants for foreign exchange arbitrage opportunities.

Arbitrage is the simultaneous purchase and sale of a commodity or asset in different markets with the purpose of obtaining a sure profit from the differential between the buying and selling price. For instance, if the dollar–pound sterling exchange rate is $2.00 per pound in London, while it is only $1.50 in New York, one could buy pounds in New York and simultaneously sell them in London, obtaining a net gain of 50 cents (minus the tiny transaction costs) for each pound purchased and sold. Of course, *spatial arbitrage* opportunities of this sort—entailing the purchase and sale of a given currency in different locations—would be quickly eliminated as investors rush to profit from them, pulling together the New York and London exchange rate quotations, as is usually observed in practice. That spatial arbitrage opportunities are quickly eliminated is attributable to the low transaction costs and high operational efficiency of the market. It is also a reflection of the fact that exchange rate quotations in different locations are widely available and traders are efficient in using this information to exploit profit opportunities.

A more complicated arbitrage operation is *three-point,* or *triangular, arbitrage.* Suppose that New York's dollar–pound sterling and dollar–deutsche mark exchange rates are $2.00 and $0.50, respectively, while the deutsche mark is worth one-fifth of a pound (0.20 pounds) in West Germany. Under these conditions, one can indeed show that there are effectively two different dollar–deutsche mark exchange rates in the market. The first one is the dollar–deutsche mark rate quoted in New York, by means of which you can buy 1 deutsche mark for $0.50, referred to as the direct exchange rate. A second exchange rate, called a cross-exchange rate, can be obtained by acquiring deutsche marks indirectly through first exchanging dollars for pounds and then using those pounds to buy deutsche marks. Since each deutsche mark costs one-fifth of a pound (0.20 pounds) and each pound is equivalent to $2.00, the dollar–deutsche mark cross-exchange rate is, then, $0.40 per deutsche mark. We can observe that deutsche marks acquired directly in New York are more expensive relative to those obtained through the cross-exchange rate, or

$$\frac{\$0.50}{DM} = e\left(\frac{\$}{DM}\right) > e\left(\frac{\$}{\pounds}\right) e\left(\frac{\pounds}{DM}\right) = \frac{\$0.40}{DM}$$

where e ($/DM) represents the direct dollar–deutsche mark exchange rate, e ($/£) is the dollar–pound sterling direct exchange rate, and so forth. Triangular arbitrage profits can then be easily obtained. For instance, each pound bought in the United States at $2.00 per pound sterling can be exchanged for marks in Germany at 5 deutsche marks per pound. If one were then to sell these deutsche marks in the United States at the rate of $2.50 for each 5 deutsche marks sold, there would be a net profit of $0.50 each time the operations were undertaken. And a sure profit this is, at least in principle, since simultaneously buying and selling currencies entails no open positions in particular currencies. Note again, however, that if foreign exchange market traders make efficient use of the information available, triangular arbitrage profits should quickly disappear. The forces of triangular arbitrage ensure the consistency between direct and cross exchange rates, or

$$e\left(\frac{\$}{\text{DM}}\right) = e\left(\frac{\$}{£}\right) e\left(\frac{£}{\text{DM}}\right)$$

Summarizing, neither spatial nor triangular arbitrage should yield profits in a market in which information is cheaply available and efficiently used by participants in the market. In practice, exchange rates in different locations are closely related, and direct and cross-exchange rates are approximately consistent with each other. The relations tend to break down, however, during periods of great turbulence, or volatility, in foreign exchange markets, suggesting perhaps that the degree of risk entailed in trading currencies soars during those turbulent periods, or that turbulence increases transaction costs and reduces the efficiency of the foreign exchange markets. Finally, the forces of arbitrage cannot operate in the presence of so-called exchange controls that block or restrict the transactions entailed by arbitrage operations. Under those circumstances, one should not expect consistency of exchange rates across locations or between direct and cross-exchange rates.

We have examined arbitrage operations undertaken by selling and purchasing currency in spot foreign exchange markets. Since opportunities for profit from arbitrage disappear rapidly, firms do not frequently engage in such operations. Instead, more habitual types of foreign exchange market operations involve hedging and speculation.

1–5 THE FORWARD MARKET IN FOREIGN EXCHANGE: HEDGING AND SPECULATION

The forward market is the market in foreign exchange contracts that provides deliveries of currencies at a future time. Similarly to spot market traders, forward market traders neither deal directly with each other nor through a centralized market; rather, each usually deals with a commercial bank. To discuss the details and nature of the forward market, let us refer to our earlier example involving the foreign exchange transaction of a U.S. firm called Acme that had to pay in pounds to a London firm called Royal Exporters, Ltd. It was assumed that Acme had to pay Royal instantly—so that Acme ordered pounds on the spot. It is often the case, however, that a firm will know that it will have to pay a certain amount in a foreign currency before the actual payment has to be made. For example, Acme may make a contract specifying the amount of pounds to be paid in 3 months for the import of some equipment from Royal at that time. This transaction leaves Acme open to substantial exchange rate risk because during those 3 months the dollar may depreciate relative to the pound (a depreciation of the dollar is an increase in the dollar price of foreign exchange), forcing Acme to spend a larger amount of dollars to satisfy its import commitment. Acme can avoid this risk by purchasing the pounds in the forward market, for delivery in 90 days, at a price specified today. At the end of the 90-day wait, Acme pays for the pounds at the prespecified price in dollars and uses the pound proceeds to pay for the imports. This procedure, which permits Acme to know in advance the exact amount of dollars it will need to settle the deal with Royal, is called *hedging, or covering*. It refers to a transaction that occurs in order to close an open position in a given currency. In this case, Acme, before covering, had a *negative open position* on the pound, in the sense that it had a commitment to pay a given amount of pounds at a certain date (*a positive open position* indicates an excess of pounds, and it could have arisen if Acme had been holding pounds or if it had been expecting to receive pound payments in 90 days). After Acme covers itself by purchasing pounds forward, its negative position is closed or eliminated. Acme still has a 90-day commitment to pay pounds, but this liability is offset by a pound-denominated asset—the forward contract—which also matures in 90 days and which eliminates the risk arising from possible changes in the dollar–pound sterling exchange rate. This example suggests a basic function of forward markets: They allow traders to insure themselves against exchange rate uncertainties and thereby facilitate international trade.

The meticulous reader will notice that there has to be a counterpart to Acme's forward purchase of pounds. Who is the seller of those pounds? The immediate seller would be a commercial bank, as in the spot market. But remember that the bank only acts as an intermediary between Acme and an ultimate seller. This ultimate seller of forward pounds may be another hedger, like Acme, but with a position just opposite that of Acme. Suppose, for example, that an American firm or individual has invested in 3-month British securities, which it wants to convert back into dollars after the end of the 3 months. The investor may decide to sell the pound proceeds forward in order to assure itself of the rate at which the pounds are to be converted back into dollars after the 3 months. This is precisely the counterpart to Acme's purchase of forward pounds. We see, then, that depending on their special circumstances, some hedgers enter the forward market as buyers and others as sellers of foreign exchange. The forward market permits them to get together and engage in mutually beneficial transactions. In its presence, both the seller and the buyer of forward exchange are able to insure against the exchange rate uncertainty present in their transactions.

Another type of investor may be providing the forward contract bought by Acme. This is the *speculator,* who attempts to profit from changes in exchange rates. Depending on their expectations, speculators may enter the forward market either as sellers or as buyers of forward exchange. We shall now discuss in detail an example of the mechanics of speculation through forward markets by letting you be a fictitious speculator investing in the forward exchange market. We assume that the 3-month forward rate for the pound is $2.10 per pound, and that the current spot rate is $2.00 per pound. We also assume that, based on a subjective evaluation of future possibilities, you expect the spot rate to remain at $2.00 per pound 3 months from today. If these expectations were to be realized, then you, as a speculator, could profit by selling pounds forward at the current forward rate of $2.10 per pound. Why? If the spot rate remains at $2.00 per pound 3 months from today, you could buy pounds spot at that time (at $2.00 per pound) so as to satisfy the commitment you have made to deliver pounds in 3 months. But the forward contract has specified that the sale of pounds is to be made at $2.10 per pound, so that you would obtain a profit of $0.10 per pound sold forward. In general, then, a speculator deliberately makes a commitment to sell pounds forward, assuming an open position in pounds, on the expectation that some profits can be earned from it. Observe, however, that the speculator's expectations could turn out to be incorrect, as they would in our example if the spot exchange rate does not stay constant at $2.00 per pound but increases over the next 3 months to, say, $2.50 per pound. In this case, you would be forced to buy pounds spot at $2.50 per pound at the time in order to deliver the pounds you have agreed to sell 3 months forward at $2.10 per pound. You would lose $0.40 per pound sold forward. In conclusion, the speculator assumes a risky position and faces the risk of exchange rate uncertainty. As a consequence, whenever speculators provide the forward contracts desired by hedgers (such as *Acme*), the forward market serves as a mechanism for transfering risk from hedgers to speculators. Both will be satisfied with their transaction since the hedgers are able to reduce their exchange rate risk, and the speculators hope to profit from the transaction.

1–6 Forecasting Exchange Rates: Forward Markets and Foreign Exchange Advisory Services

The previous section examined the case in which speculation on the basis of differences between the exchange rate anticipated to prevail in the future ($2.00 per pound) and the forward exchange rate ($2.10 per pound) could be expected to provide substantial profits. This looks quite easy at this point, but you should be aware that it actually is not. Generally, the forward exchange rate tends to reflect the spot exchange rate that most investors anticipate will prevail at the point of maturity of the forward contract. This means that when you expect a future exchange rate different from the forward rate, you are leaning against the wind in the sense that your expectations differ from those of most participants in the market.

Why does the forward exchange rate tend to reflect the expected future spot exchange rate? This topic will be discussed in more detail in Chapter 2. At this point we shall only provide a heuristic explanation. Suppose that we take our earlier example, in which it was assumed that your expectation of the future exchange rate differs from the forward rate. If you have based your estimate or expectation of the future spot rate on public information and knowledge as well as on well-known forecasts about the future of the United States and British economies, one might expect that most other investors and speculators would arrive at an estimate of the future spot exchange rate similar to yours. Let us assume, then, that most investors have the same expectations as you do and that, as a consequence, they expect the spot exchange rate between the dollar and pound to remain constant over the next 3 months, at $2.00 per pound. This approach implies, by our own earlier calculations, that all these investors could expect to profit by selling pounds 3 months forward. As a result, there would be a massive increase in the sale of pounds in the three-month forward market. The exchange rate on 3-month forward pounds (the price of forward pounds in terms of dollars) would then decline below $2.10 in response to the increased supply of forward pounds. This decrease in the forward exchange rate would continue until it moves close to the expected exchange rate ($2.00 per pound). At that point, most investors would stop drawing contracts to sell pounds forward, since they could not expect to realize any more profits once the forward exchange rate moves close to the expected exchange rate. When expected profits are eliminated, then, the forward exchange rate will tend to reflect the expected exchange rate on the part of most investors in the market.

This suggests that a forward premium for a given currency (over a given contract period, N) implies that most investors expect the currency to appreciate with respect to the dollar over the period of the contract (since $F_N > e$). Similarly, if the currency is at a forward discount, the currency is expected to depreciate, vis à vis the dollar (since $F_N < e$). In conclusion, a forward premium for a given currency reflects the expected rate of appreciation of that currency relative to the dollar, and a forward discount the expected rate of depreciation of the currency vis à vis the dollar over the period of the contract. At this point, you might find it useful to return to Table 1–1 and specify what the present discussion suggests about the market's assessments of the future exchange rates of the U.S. dollar against the Canadian dollar, French franc, and so forth.

If, as we assumed above, your expectation about the future exchange rate is different from the forward rate, you would be leaning against most investors' expectations of what the future exchange rate is going to be. You would thus be trying to beat the market by guessing better than other investors. Can you do that? Of course, as a matter of chance you can probably do it at some point in your lifetime if you keep trying. The real question, however, is whether you could systematically assemble a more accurate forecast of future exchange rate changes than that of the consensus of market participants as embodied in the forward exchange rate.

This question has been a controversial one in international finance for many years and relates to the question of whether foreign exchange markets are efficient. A market is considered informationally efficient if prices fully reflect available information.[4] In the present context, market efficiency implies that forward exchange rates would fully reflect all available information relevant for future exchange rate determination and would therefore yield as accurate a prediction of future spot exchange rate changes as anybody else's.

Figure 1–1 shows forward exchange rates for 3-month delivery of pounds and the corresponding spot exchange rates prevailing at the time of maturity of the forward contract. As can be observed, the forward exchange rate is not a highly accurate predictor of future spot exchange rates, being in error by as much as 30% or more repeatedly. This failure of forward rates to predict future exchange rates is due to the extreme volatility and unpredictability of the dollar–pound sterling exchange rate during the period.

The inaccurate predictions of the forward market have induced many investors to use the services of foreign exchange advisory services, which offer forecasts and make recommendations as to which currency to hold. Since foreign exchange advisors are generally highly knowledgeable experts on foreign markets who derive their income from these activities, one can expect them to provide informed advice. The question arises as to whether they can beat the market. Of course, foreign exchange advisors can always do that by chance, so the real question is whether they can do it systematically. If they can, this might imply that the forward exchange market is not efficient in fully reflecting available information.

The evidence suggests that most foreign exchange advisory services indeed do not actually do better than the forward market in predicting future exchange rates, but that some have a consistently superior performance difficult to attach to chance.[5] This means that a speculative investment strategy following the advisor's forecasts would yield positive profits. The interpretation of this result is ambiguous, however. On the one hand, it can be taken to imply that experts can systematically beat the market. On the other hand, in order to benefit from foreign exchange advisors' forecasts you would have to hold open positions in certain currencies. The profits obtained may then just reflect a compensation for the risk taken by the investor in holding risky open positions. The notion that profits in foreign exchange markets can merely be a compensation for risk taking—and not an evidence of superior performance on a risk-adjusted basis—can be illustrated by the following example.

Suppose that the 30-day forward exchange rate on the pound is equal to

[4] For details of the concept of foreign exchange market efficiency, see R. Levich, "On the Efficiency of Markets for Foreign Exchange," in R. Dornbusch and J. Frenkel, eds., *International Economic Policy* (Baltimore: Johns Hopkins University Press, 1979).

[5] See R. M. Levich, "Analyzing the Accuracy of Foreign Exchange Advisory Services: Theory and Evidence," in R. Levich and C. Wihlborg, eds., *Exchange Risk and Exposure* (Lexington, Mass.: D. C. Heath Company, 1980).

$1.50 per pound and that holding open positions in pounds is very risky for you perhaps because of the relatively high uncertainty about future exchange rate changes. In such a situation, assume also that you require $0.04 per pound held in compensation for the heart-stopping and stomach-upsetting effects of the additional risks involved in holding open positions in pounds. Suppose, then, that your foreign exchange advisor—whose forecast has been right on average in the past—gives you a forecast of $1.46 on the dollar–pound sterling exchange rate to prevail in 30 days. On this basis, you agree to sell pounds 30 days forward at $1.50 per pound, which could be expected to yield $0.04 per pound (since the spot rate that you expect to prevail 30 days from now is $1.46). Assuming that, this time, the advisor's expectation was exactly right and a dollar–pound sterling exchange rate of $1.46 actually prevails in 30 days, you would then make a profit of $0.04 per pound. Such a profit, however, is merely equal to the amount required to compensate you for the risks taken in holding an open position in pounds. In other words, the risk-adjusted profit obtained from the advisor's service would be zero, in accord with market efficiency, even if the advisor's forecasts do better than the forward market and yield profits on average.[6] The source of ambiguity in the interpretation of this and other[7] empirical evidence regarding market efficiency is the fact that the studies are really testing the joint hypothesis that markets are efficient *and* that compensation for exchange risk—the so-called exchange risk premium— is absent. This is referred to as the joint hypothesis problem in testing market efficiency. A rejection of the forward premium as the "best" predictor of future exchange rate changes can either mean that the forward exchange market is inefficient or that risk premia cannot be ignored, or both—or perhaps neither if the tests used are not well constructed.

In conclusion, the solution to the difficulties of testing market efficiency has not been achieved yet; this is a subject of active current research. The evidence available suggests, however, that the forward exchange rate (the forward premium) might still be looked at as being the most accessible, yet highly unbeatable, forecast of future exchange rates. The inaccuracy of the forward exchange rate in predicting future spot exchange rate changes should thus not be taken to mean that it could be easily beaten by other forecasts, since it is connected to the general unpredictability of future exchange rates—something to which all forecasts are subject. Furthermore, it may appear to the reader that engaging in speculation is very simple in the sense that it may not even require that the speculator tie up some of his or her funds. Actually, if a speculator were

---

[6] For more details, see John Bilson, "The Evaluation and Use of Foreign Exchange Rate Forecasting Services," in R. J. Herring, ed., *Managing Foreign Exchange Risk* (New York: Cambridge University Press, 1983), pp. 149–179.

[7] For a survey and bibliography of the voluminous literature on this topic, see Richard M. Levich "Empirical Studies of Exchange Rates: Price Behavior, Rate Determination, and Market Efficiency" in *Handbook of International Economics*, Vol. 2, Peter B. Kenen and Ronald I. McKinnon, eds. (Amsterdam: North-Holland Publishing Company, 1984).

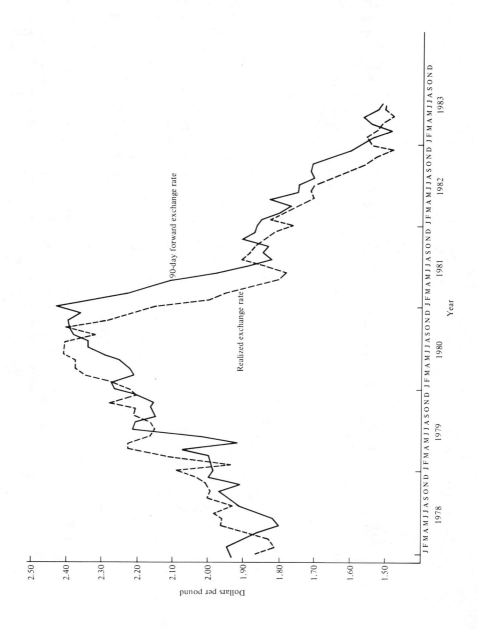

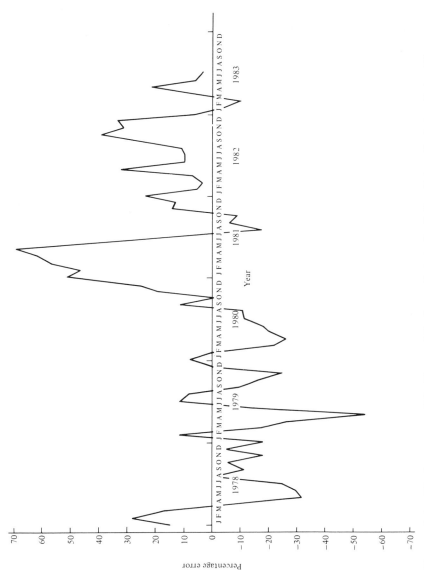

FIGURE 1-1. The Inaccuracy of the Forward Exchange Rate in Predicting Future Exchange Rates. The error is given by: error = (forward rate − realized rate)/realized rate. It is annualized and expressed in percentage form by multiplying by 100. The forward rate is the rate on 90-day delivery of sterling. The realized rate is the spot rate prevailing at the maturity of the forward contract. (From *The Wall Street Journal*, various issues.)

33

to try to engage in a contract to buy or sell pounds 30 days forward, the commercial bank with which he or she deals will probably set a *margin requirement*. That is, it would request that its client deposit an amount, say, 20%, of the total value of the forward transaction as a partial guarantee in case of default. In order to satisfy the margin requirements, the speculator has to set aside part of his or her capital. Credit worthiness and good financial standing are also essential for an individual or institution to engage in transactions through the forward market. This answers a question that may have arisen above: Given the possibility that speculation will lead to losses, what protects banks from contract defaults on the part of speculators? Margin requirements and customer screening are set so as to insure the banks against this risk.

1-7   FUTURES TRANSACTIONS AND THEIR ROLE IN THE FOREIGN EXCHANGE MARKET

A relatively recent innovation in U.S. foreign exchange markets for future delivery is the International Monetary Market (IMM) of the Chicago Mercantile Exchange. It was founded in 1972 by the Chicago Mercantile Exchange, which is an established market for futures commodities contracts. The IMM is an example of what is technically called a *futures market,* which deals in futures transactions. Although sometimes they are used interchangeably, there is a difference between a forward and a futures contract. A *forward* foreign exchange contract, for example, occurs between a bank and an individual. It usually involves the identity of the individual in an essential way (financial standing and credit worthiness are crucial as a guarantee that the contract will be honored) and requires specific arrangements and negotiations between the bank and the person involved. By contrast, a transaction in the *futures* foreign exchange market occurs through an organized, centralized exchange (the IMM), which deals in standardized contracts. The IMM itself guarantees all contracts by being a party to every purchase or sale, standing before the contracts and guaranteeing their fulfillment even if some customer defaults. This implies that the identity of the ultimate seller or buyer of the forward contract loses importance as a guarantee that the contract will be honored, since the Exchange itself (and its financial standing) guarantees the contracts. Any buyer (or seller) using the exchange is thus assured that the contract will be honored, independent of whether some ultimate sellers (or buyers) fail to honor their contracts. This makes futures contracts much more liquid than forward contracts, which has given rise to the statement that "a futures contract is to a forward contract as payment in currency is to payment by check."[8] In most essential respects,

---

[8] As remarked by Lester Telser and Harlow Higinbotham in their article, "Organized Futures Markets: Costs and Benefits," *Journal of Political Economy,* 696 (October 1977).

then, a futures market is very similar to a forward market, but it provides a mechanism for increasing the liquidity of the contract.

To protect itself against customer default, the International Monetary Market imposes some minimum margin requirements on all contracts. This tends to make the IMM relatively unattractive for hedging transactions since commercial banks, depending on their knowledge and previous contact with a customer, set zero or very low margin requirements on this type of transaction. As a result, most hedging transactions are usually made through the forward markets operated by commercial banks. Speculators, on the other hand, use the IMM more frequently, since commercial banks often reject or impose high margins on speculative transactions. In fact, the IMM has practically become a market of speculative transactions in foreign exchange.

Table 1–2 shows *The Wall Street Journal*'s price quotations for futures traded in the International Monetary Market. At first sight, futures price quotations might appear esoteric, so, we shall explain them in detail. First, the quotes for foreign exchange futures appear under the heading of *financial*. As shown, the IMM provides futures for only a limited number of currencies. Let us look closely at the figures on the British pound. All the quotations refer to contracts of a standard size of £25,000 for delivery at the specific dates stated, which are the third Wednesday of the months of September, December, March, and June. The IMM allows only a limited range for the choice of delivery dates. This is because in terms of volume the IMM is a small market, compared to, for example, the commercial banks' forward market. It thus tries to avoid the excessive thinning and the corresponding price instability that would arise in the event of a much larger choice of maturity dates for a given currency. The IMM contracts differ from forward contracts in that the latter specify the delivery dates of the currency in terms of days after the contract is drawn (say, 90 days), rather than as specific dates in the future.

Customers can buy or sell futures in the International Monetary Market by placing their orders with firms that have access to the IMM. These firms employ individuals who are members of the IMM and who are the only ones permitted to trade on the floor. Customer orders are then placed on the floor in accordance with the customer's instructions, with biddings and offers being literally shouted in. A trade occurs when the price at which some seller is willing to sell is matched by the bid price indicated by some other customer(s). These trading prices are almost instantly recorded and used to obtain the prices quoted in Table 1–2 as opening, highest, lowest, and settlement prices for the day (settlement price is a representative price established for the end of the day).

Table 1–2 also provides information on the change in the settlement price from the previous day and about the lifetime high and low prices for a contract. Trading in contracts for a given delivery date may begin up to 18 months and last up to a week before that date. This period is the lifetime of the contract.

TABLE 1–2. Foreign Exchange Futures in the International Monetary Market

Tuesday, March 6, 1984
Open Interest Reflects Previous Trading Day

| | | | | | | Lifetime | | Open |
	Open	High	Low	Settle	Change	High	Low	Interest
				—FINANCIAL—				
BRITISH POUND (IMM)—25,000 pounds; $per pound								
Mar	1.4845	1.4870	1.4800	1.4860	− .0015	1.6010	1.3930	14.697
June	1.4895	1.4930	1.4855	1.4915	− .0015	1.5520	1.3950	14.436
Sept	1.4950	1.4990	1.4900	1.4980	− .0005	1.5240	1.3980	407
Dec	1.4980	1.5040	1.4960	1.5030	− .0010	1.5100	1.3990	87
Mar85	....	....	....	5095	....	1.5170	1.4000	64
Est vol 4,203; vol Mon 8,850; open int 29,791, +102.								
CANADIAN DOLLAR (IMM) − 100,000 dirs.; $ per Can $								
Mar	.7967	.7969	.7950	.7952	− .0032	.8169	.7950	2,007
June	.7970	.7973	.7952	.7955	− .0032	.8168	.7952	3,057
Sept	.7980	.7980	.7959	.7963	− .0032	.8147	.7959	343
Dec	.7980	.7980	.7964	.7968	− .0032	.8040	:7964	160
Mar85	.7990	.7993	.7952	.7969	− .0036	.8038	.7952	75
Est vol 1,895; vol Mon 1,496; open int 5,642, +251.								
JAPANESE YEN (IMM) 12.5 million yen; $ per yen (.00)								
Mar	.4466	.4497	.4451	.4495	+ .0013	.4497	.4125	19,756
June	.4516	.4542	.4498	.4541	+ .0014	.4542	.4180	25,835
Sept	.4561	.4588	.4551	.4588	+ .0013	.4588	.4354	1,051
Dec	.4607	.4637	.4595	.4633	+ .0015	.4637	.4395	342
Est vol 33,793; vol Mon 34,944; open int 46,984, +3,382.								
SWISS FRANC (IMM) − 125,000 francs-$ per franc								
Mar	.4739	.4763	.4726	.4762	+ .0038	.5230	.3702	12,809
June	.4818	.4846	.4807	.4844	+ .0039	.5045	.3742	19,280
Sept	.4904	.4930	.4890	.4915	+ .0041	.5020	.3782	351
Dec	.4980	.5000	.4980	.4994	+ .0042	.4960	.3818	104
Mar85		....	....	.5010	+ .0010	.4962	.4755	10
Est vol 36,643; vol Mon 32,514; open int 32,554, −1,046.								
W. GERMAN MARK (IMM) − 125,000 marks; $ per mark								
Mar	.3908	.3939	.3901	.3938	+ .0047	.4552	.3537	16,892
June	.3954	.3985	.3946	.3984	+ .0047	.4628	.3568	22,414
Sept	.4005	.4030	.3998	.4030	+ .0045	.4695	.3602	757
Dec	.4050	.4065	.4044	.4075	+ .0045	.4755	.3640	283
Mar85		....	....	.4120	+ .0045	.4040	.3699	8
Est vol 29,685; vol Mon 22,812; open int 40,354, −486.								

One can then compute the highest and lowest prices that have prevailed during the lifetime of the contract, all the way from the initial moment of trading up to the present. These are the so-called lifetime high and low prices quoted in Table 1–2.

The last number observed on any given column in Table 1–2 refers to *open interest*. Open interest is the number of contracts outstanding and not already liquidated (canceled) by an offsetting contract (or by delivery of the commodity). A customer can cancel any contract (say, a purchase of foreign exchange for September delivery) by just taking an opposite position (say, a sale of foreign exchange for delivery in September). The IMM then clears these offsetting positions, liquidating the contracts and paying (or collecting from) the customer any difference between the purchase and sale prices. A dramatic case of gains through the futures market is reflected by the experience of mid-1981, when the pound sterling sank from a value of about $2.00 in June to a value of $1.80 three months later. An individual, for example, could have agreed in August 1, 1981 to sell pounds for delivery on September 1981 at a price of $2.0250 per pound. By late August, however, the price of a pound had declined to $1.8400. If the individual had liquidated its future contract to sell pounds, it would have gained an amount equal to $0.1850 per pound sold initially. In fact, most futures contracts are liquidated in the way we have just described rather than actually delivered. The ease with which any contract can be liquidated at any time and any gain or loss collected immediately simply by engaging in an opposite transaction provides them with significant liquidity.

1–8   CENTRAL BANKS AND EXCHANGE RATE REGIMES

We shall now proceed to discuss the role of central banks in the foreign exchange market. Central Banks, such as the Federal Reserve System in the United States, West Germany's Bundesbank, and the Bank of England in Great Britain are government or quasi-government banks. They regulate banks and are the main institution in charge of monetary control in the economy. Central Bank intervention in the foreign exchange market depends on the foreign exchange regime under which the nation is governed. We shall distinguish among three basic types of foreign exchange regimes. There are various historical versions of each regime and, in general, it will not be possible to classify all countries and periods in terms of these three basic types. The reader can refer to Chapters 16 and 17 on the international monetary system for more detailed historical and analytical aspects of different exchange rate regimes.

A *freely flexible (or free-floating) exchange rate regime* exists whenever exchange rates (currency prices) are freely determined by the demand and supply of currencies by private parties. This regime assumes the absence of any systematic government intervention in the foreign exchange market. The exchange rate moves freely in response to market forces.

Under a *fixed* (or *pegged*) *exchange rate regime,* the government intervenes in foreign exchange markets through its Central Bank in an effort to maintain the exchange rate vis à vis different currencies within prescribed limits. The Central Bank in this regime will buy and sell currencies in order to limit the variations of the exchange rate. To carry out its foreign exchange operations, the Central Bank will then hold inventories (or *international reserves*) of foreign exchange. The central value of the exchange rate, around which the government maintains narrow limits, is called a peg for the currency. The Haitian gourde, for example, has been pegged to the U.S. dollar at an exchange rate or peg of $0.20 per gourde since 1907—a remarkable example of a truly pegged exchange rate. The careful reader will observe that there must exist exchange rates between any given national currency and all other foreign currencies traded in foreign exchange markets. A national currency may then be floating in value with respect to some foreign currencies and fixed in value with respect to others. The Haitian gourde, for instance, fluctuates in value with respect to the French franc but has a fixed peg vis à vis the dollar. In the interest of analytical simplicity, the ensuing discussion deals only with cases involving either across-the-board fixed or flexible exchange rates but not both. In fact, most of the following discussion is conducted in terms of just two currencies, which we will call domestic and foreign currencies.

A third type of foreign exchange regime is the *managed* or *controlled floating exchange rate regime.* In contrast to the free floating regime, a controlled floating regime exists when government intervenes in the foreign exchange market in order to influence the exchange rate but does not commit itself to maintaining a certain fixed exchange rate, or some narrow limits around it. The Central Bank "gets its hands dirty" by manipulating the market place for foreign exchange, but it does not intervene to fix the price of foreign exchange as it would in a system of fixed exchange rates.

In order to visualize more clearly the difference between fixed and floating exchange rate regimes, it is useful to think of the market for foreign exchange in terms of traditional supply and demand curves.[9] The private sector's demand for foreign exchange arises from the needs of domestic residents to acquire foreign currencies. These needs may derive from many sources. The prices of

---

[9] The supply and demand analysis we are about to pursue constitutes a partial equilibrium analysis in the sense that it concentrates on one particular market—the foreign exchange market—and ignores the simultaneous interrelationships between all markets in the economy. It would be inconsistent with some general equilibrium theories of exchange rate determination. For a specific case in which this analysis is consistent with some general equilibrium considerations, see R. Dornbusch, "Exchange Rates and Fiscal Policy in a Popular Model of International Trade," *American Economic Review* (December 1975). The reader should be aware, then, that the analysis presented in this section is not applicable to every situation and is only valid under special assumptions. Parts III–V treat complete, general equilibrium theories in full detail. See also P. Kouri, "Balance of Payments and the Foreign Exchange Market: A Dynamic Partial Equilibrium Model," in J. S. Bhandari and B. H. Putnam, eds., *Economic Interdependence and Flexible Exchange Rates* (Cambridge, Mass.: M.I.T. Press, 1983).

foreign goods and assets are denominated in foreign currency, and to buy them requires the purchase of foreign exchange. This gives rise to a demand for foreign exchange. In addition, the demand of the private sector for foreign exchange may come not from immediate transaction needs but from currency diversification decisions made by economic agents (mainly corporations and banks), which hold deposits denominated in various currencies so as to maximize expected returns and to minimize the risk of holding foreign exchange. A rumor that a currency may depreciate (i.e., a "weak" currency) may generate diversions of deposits away from that currency and into "strong" currencies, a phenomenom called currency substitution.

The private sector's demand curve for foreign exchange is represented in Figure 1–2 by the downward-sloping *DD* curve. In order to simplify the exposition, it is assumed that there are only two currencies under consideration: a domestic currency and a foreign currency. The price of the foreign currency in terms of domestic currency is, then, the exchange rate *e*. The demand curve for foreign exchange shows the quantity demanded of foreign exchange as a function of the exchange rate. It is downward sloping on the assumption that, as the price of foreign exchange increases, the quantity demanded will show a decline. How can we rationalize this assumption? Suppose, for example, that domestic (U.S.) residents are buying British punk-rock albums. If the price quoted by the British suppliers is £4.0 and the exchange rate is $2.5 per pound, the price of one album in U.S. dollars is $10.00. Some punk-rock fans are then willing to pay the price, buying the records and creating a given demand for pounds. Suppose now that the exchange rate between the dollar and the pound increases to $3.00 ($/£). If the British suppliers keep their price at £4.0, the price of an album in terms of dollars will now be $12.00. As a consequence, the number of punk-rock albums demanded will tend to decline; at a fixed price of records in pounds, this decline will result in a reduction in the total amount of pounds that U.S. residents wish to spend on British records. This represents a decrease in the quantity demanded of foreign exchange. An increase

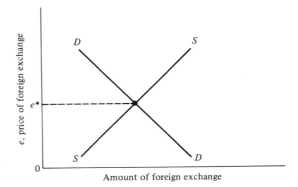

FIGURE 1–2. Equilibrium Under Flexible Exchange Rates

in the exchange rate, e, then induces a reduction in the quantity demanded of foreign exchange by the private sector.

The supply of foreign exchange by the private sector arises from the desires of foreign residents to acquire domestic currency. In order to do so, they have to sell their own currencies, creating the supply of foreign exchange. As such, the supply of foreign exchange is implicitly a demand for domestic currency. Foreigners may wish to acquire domestic currency for transaction purposes (to buy domestic goods, services and assets the prices of which are denominated in domestic currency) or for currency diversification purposes (e.g., to hold domestic currency, in the expectation of a depreciation of the foreign currency).

The private sector supply curve of foreign exchange is represented in Figure 1–2 by the upward-sloping SS curve. This curve shows the quantity supplied of foreign exchange as a function of the exchange rate. The upward slope of the supply curve assumes that, as the price of foreign exchange increases, the quantity supplied of foreign exchange increases. How can we rationalize this assumption? Suppose that a domestic producer of jazz records can sell any desired amount of records at a price of £4.0 in the British market. At that price, and with an exchange rate equal to $2.5 per pound, the domestic currency price of a record sold in England would be $10.00. Given this price, the domestic producer may decide to sell, that is, to export a certain number of jazz records to England. The British buyers of these records will then sell their pounds to acquire U.S. dollars with which to pay for the records, generating a supply of pounds in the foreign exchange market. What happens now if the exchange rate increases to $3.00 per pound sterling? At this new exchange rate, and assuming that jazz records can still be sold at a price of £4.0 per record, the dollar receipts from selling a record in England would increase to $12.00 (£4.00 × $3.00/£). Given this new higher price, the U.S. producer may then decide to increase its exports of jazz records. As foreign residents buy these records, they sell pounds to acquire U.S. dollars with which to buy them, and the supply of pounds increases. That is, as the exchange rate e increases, the quantity supplied of foreign exchange increases.[10]

Under a freely flexible exchange rate regime, the private demand and supply of foreign exchange must be equal in order to have equilibrium in the market.

---

[10] This process assumes that the exporter is small in the British market for records in the sense that it can sell all the records it wants at the given market price; an alternative assumption is that our exporter can only sell more records by decreasing the price in pounds. In this case we have an ambiguity: As the exchange rate increases, the quantity of records exported increases but at a lower price in pounds. As a result, the total supply of pounds could either increase or decrease. This suggests that the supply curve could be upward or downward sloping. We do not examine this case, since our purpose in utilizing the supply–demand framework in Figure 1–2 lies only in its usefulness as a tool in describing the main differences between fixed and flexible exchange rate regimes, and not as a rigorous formal analysis of the determination of exchange rates, which it is not.

Obviously, government authorities could possibly buy or sell foreign exchange. Our definition of the freely flexible exchange rate system, however, assumes that under this regime government interventions in the foreign exchange market are rather unsystematic and negligible in determining the exchange rate. As a consequence, one can safely ignore them.

The exchange rate at which the demand and supply of foreign exchange are equal is the equilibrium exchange rate e^*, determined in Figure 1–2 by the intersection of the DD and SS curves. At that point, algebraically,

$$D(e^*; D_0) = S(e^*; S_0) \tag{1}$$

where D represents the demand for foreign exchange and S is the supply of foreign exchange. Note that we represent the demand for foreign exchange as a function of the exchange rate e and of D_0, which represents a number of other variables affecting D but that are assumed fixed in deriving the demand curve DD. Similarly, the supply of foreign exchange depends not only on the exchange rate, but on other variables as well, represented here by S_0. In deriving the supply curve, we assume these variables to be fixed. The variables that may affect S_0 and D_0 include interest rates, income levels, and expectations about future events. Changes in these variables will tend to shift the demand or supply curves of foreign exchange and will thus change the equilibrium exchange rate. Since we have not yet explained how all these variables affect the DD and SS curves, it should be realized that we have not fully specified the analytics behind the determination of the exchange rate e^*. Such an analysis must wait until Chapter 8. In any case, whatever the factors affecting the demand and supply of foreign exchange, the equilibrium exchange rate under a regime of flexible exchange rates would be determined by the equality shown in equation (1).

The foreign exchange market equilibrium under a fixed exchange rate regime is portrayed in Figure 1–3, where we show our usual DD and SS curves. Figure 1–3(a) assumes that the government is pegging the exchange rate at a level equal to $\underline{e}$, which is below the private sector equilibrium exchange rate e^*. In general, governments will permit some variation of e within a small band around its peg $\underline{e}$. For the sake of simplicity, our diagrammatic analysis assumes that the exchange rate is absolutely fixed at $\underline{e}$, with no band around it. At that fixed exchange rate, there is an excess demand for foreign exchange on the part of the private sector. This excess demand is represented by the horizontal distance between the private demand and supply curves for foreign exchange, which is numerically equal to $\underline{D} - \underline{S}$. At the given exchange rate, demanders of foreign exchange wish to buy more than what suppliers are willing to offer. This excess demand for foreign exchange is filled by the Central Bank, which sells foreign exchange to the private sector in order to prevent the exchange rate from moving above the level of the peg at $\underline{e}$. This means that, during the period of concern, the Central Bank loses (sells) an amount of international

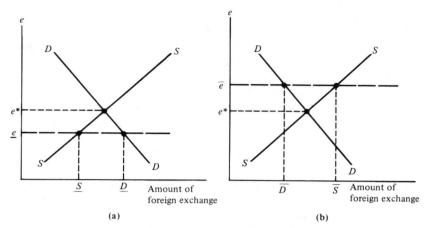

FIGURE 1–3. Pegging the Exchange Rate

reserves (foreign exchange) equal to $\underline{D} - \underline{S}$. As noted above, under a regime of fixed exchange rates, the Central Bank must hold international reserves to maintain exchange rates at peg levels.

Suppose that the exchange rate is pegged at a level equal to $\bar{e}$, which is higher than the equilibrium exchange rate e^*, as shown in Figure 1–3 (b). At that exchange rate, there would be an excess supply of foreign exchange on the part of the private sector, as quantity supplied ($\bar{S}$) exceeds quantity demanded ($\bar{D}$). At the given peg, suppliers of foreign exchange wish to supply more than the demanders of foreign exchange wish to demand. This excess supply of foreign exchange by the private sector is purchased by the Central Bank, as it tries to prevent the exchange rate from dropping below the peg at $\bar{e}$. This example shows that the fixed exchange rate regime, as compared with the flexible exchange rate regime, is one in which the government intervenes to set the price in the market. As in any other market in which the government fixes prices, there will generally be discrepancies between the private sector's demand and supply. In this case, the Central Bank fills these gaps by buying or selling foreign exchange reserves. By contrast, under a freely flexible exchange rate regime, the government does not intervene in the market so that the private sector's demand and supply for foreign exchange will be equal in equilibrium. Therefore, the Central Bank does not have to buy or sell foreign exchange reserves; in theory, it does not have to hold any at all. In short, under fixed exchange rates, shifts in the private sector's demand and supply curves of foreign exchange produce changes in the amount of foreign exchange reserves. This differs from the situation under freely flexible exchange rates, in which the opposite holds: Shifts in the private sector's demand and supply curves of foreign exchange produce changes in the exchange rate but do not affect the amount of foreign exchange reserves. In general, however, Central Banks do intervene in foreign exchange markets, even if they are not committed to a regime of fixed exchange rates. This is, of course, the dirty floating regime mentioned earlier.

Under fixed exchange rates, Central Banks systematically intervene to fix the exchange rate around a certain peg value. Nothing prevents them, however, from changing the parity value at which they buy or sell foreign exchange. The determination of these peg values, as we shall see in Parts III to VI, involves a variety of economic and political considerations. Changes in any of these may lead Central Banks to change parities. If the exchange rate peg is increased, the price of foreign currency in terms of domestic currency is increased and the domestic currency is said to be *devalued*. If the exchange rate peg is decreased, the domestic currency price of foreign currency is decreased and the domestic currency is said to be *revalued*. Note that a devaluation corresponds to a depreciation of the domestic currency, and a revaluation corresponds to an appreciation of the currency. The different terminology arises from the different exchange rate regimes. Devaluation and revaluation refer to adjustments in fixed exchange rate regimes. Depreciation and appreciation, on the other hand, refer to changes in the exchange rate under a system of flexible exchange rates. The pound sterling, for example, was devalued in November 1967 from $2.80 per pound to $2.40 per pound, which means that monetary authorities in England decided to change the peg of the pound vis à vis the dollar. On the other hand, during the month of April 1981, the pound sterling depreciated vis à vis the dollar, from $2.23 (April 1) to $2.14 (May 1), which means that the value of the pound sterling decreased, as determined in the foreign exchange markets. The reader should realize that the difference between devaluation (revaluation) and depreciation (appreciation) is terminological and that the terms are often used interchangeably.

1–9   THE INTERNATIONAL MONETARY SYSTEM: AN INTRODUCTION

The history of the international monetary system shows a pattern of shifts between a number of variants and combinations of fixed and flexible exchange rate regimes. During the late nineteenth century and up to 1914, the *gold standard* predominated in the international monetary system. A gold standard can be classified as a fixed exchange rate regime. Any country participating in the system would peg its currency to gold at a mint parity. This meant that dollar bills, for example, had a value in gold and could be exchanged for gold through the nation's monetary authorities. The official exchange rate between any two currencies then had to equal the ratio of their mint parities. The U.S. dollar had a mint parity equivalent to $20.67 per ounce of gold, and the mint parity of the pound sterling was about £4.25 per ounce of gold; then the dollar–pound sterling official exchange rate was equal to $4.87 per pound sterling.

The onset of World War I in 1914 led to the breakdown of the gold standard. During the interwar years, the international monetary system underwent a time of disarray, with the major industrial countries swinging between periods of flexible exchange rate regimes (as in the period 1919 to 1925 and during 1933 to 1934) and periods of return to the gold standard. In 1944, representatives from the major industrial nations met in Bretton Woods, New Hampshire, and agreed to constrain their countries' actions so as to develop a more consistent and less variable international monetary system. The *International Monetary Fund* (IMF)—a country membership organization—was then created as an international agency coordinating and operating the agreements of what became known as the *Bretton Woods System.* The Bretton Woods agreements imposed a set of rules or constraints mainly oriented toward restricting the freedom of the member countries to change their exchange rate parities. It differed from the gold standard in that most exchange rates were pegged in terms of the dollar, which was used as a vehicle currency—that is, as a medium of transaction and as a means of obtaining other currencies—and served as an international reserve asset. The dollar also had the role of intervention currency, being the currency that central banks bought and sold to support their currencies. Gold still maintained an important role in the system in the sense that it continued to serve as a means of settling international transactions and because the United States stood ready to exchange gold for dollars at the fixed price of $35.00 per ounce. For this reason, the Bretton Woods system is usually referred to as a *gold-exchange standard.*

The Bretton Woods system was in operation during the 1950s and 1960s, although some countries did not enter into the agreement and were able to maintain independent flexible exchange rate regimes, as Canada had from 1950 to 1962. During the sixties, Bretton Woods began to experience difficulties. A glut of U.S. dollars and a shortage of gold gradually eroded confidence in the dollar and its convertibility into gold at a fixed price. An attempt was thus made to create a new international reserve asset that would supplement gold and the U.S. dollar. The outcome was the creation by the IMF in 1969 of *special drawing rights* (SDRs), which Central Banks can use to settle transactions among themselves and with the IMF.[11]

The creation of SDRs as well as many other patch-up arrangements did not prevent further difficulties. In 1971 another major crisis of the international monetary system occurred as most European countries and Japan permitted their currencies to float freely with respect to the U.S. dollar. Even though this flexibility was short-lived (lasting from August to December 1971), and parities and pegs were reestablished for a while longer, since 1973 the currencies

---

[11] SDRs are allocated to member countries according to a formula that depends on such factors as the economic size of the country. The value of an SDR was originally set to equal that of the dollar, but after the emergence of floating exchange rates in 1973 it has been based on a basket of major currencies, which currently include the U.S. dollar, the British pound sterling, the French franc, the Japanese yen, and the West German mark.

of most of the industrial countries have been free to fluctuate vis à vis the dollar. Central Banks, however, have intervened quite frequently in the foreign exchange market so that the current international monetary arrangements among industrial countries can be categorized as a dirty floating regime.[12] Actually, and perhaps paradoxically, Central Bank intervention in foreign exchange markets under the current system has been much greater than that under the Bretton Woods system. The rationale used by Central Banks to justify intervention in the markets is that they intervene in order to smooth out fluctuations in exchange rates. Some empirical evidence tends to indicate, however, that government intervention in foreign exchange markets may have increased, rather than decreased, the turbulence in the market in recent years.[13]

Even though most industrial economies did move during the early seventies to a dirty floating regime, most developing countries have maintained fixed exchange rates with their major trading partners. Nevertheless some do make quite frequent, if small, changes or adjustments in their exchange rates. Such a system, in which the exchange rate is pegged for short periods of time but adjusted frequently, is called the *crawling-peg regime,* experienced by Brazil, Chile, and Portugal recently.

Another current international monetary arrangement regards the *European Monetary System* (EMS). Introduced in March 1979, the main goal of the EMS is to promote European monetary cooperation. It has worked, in particular, to create an area of exchange rate stability among European Community countries and has given birth to a new international currency, the *European currency unit* (ECU), a composite currency defined in terms of a basket of European currencies plus gold. The EMS involves a joint currency float, in which participating countries agree to peg their currencies to each other and to let their currencies float vis à vis those of nonparticipating countries. In effect, a participating country has a fixed exchange rate regime vis à vis other participating countries and a flexible exchange rate regime against nonparticipating countries. The exchange rate of the French franc, for instance, fluctuates with respect to the British pound (Britain and Greece, by the way, are the only countries in the European community that do not participate in the exchange rate mechanisms of the EMS, though the pound sterling, but not the drachma, forms part of the ECU) and the U.S. dollar but is fixed with respect to the deutsche mark.

---

[12] One should be very careful in applying this statement to specific countries and periods. Some countries intervene more frequently and heavily than other countries do, and even the same country shifts from periods of heavy to periods of light intervention in foreign exchange markets.

[13] See Robert P. Flood, "Explanations of Exchange-Rate Volatility and Other Empirical Regularities in Some Popular Models of the Foreign Exchange Market," *Carnegie-Rochester Conference Series on Public Policy, 15* (Autumn 1981). A detailed discussion of the arguments and evidence on the effects of government intervention in foreign exchange markets can be found in Chapter 17.

1–10 SUMMARY

1. The foreign exchange market is the market in which national currencies are traded. Its basic function is to provide the means of payment required for the smooth operation of international transactions. As in any market, a price must exist at which trade occurs; the exchange rate is the price of one currency in terms of another.

2. In this book, we shall look at the exchange rate as the domestic currency price of a foreign currency. Adopting a U.S. vantage point, we quote exchange rates in terms of the dollars required to buy foreign currency.

3. An increase in an exchange rate means that the domestic currency price of a foreign currency increases; that is, the foreign currency becomes more expensive in terms of domestic money. This is referred to as a domestic currency depreciation. Similarly, a reduction in a given exchange rate means that the foreign currency becomes relatively cheap or that the domestic currency appreciates (increases) in value.

4. Foreign exchange markets can be differentiated into two types: spot and forward. In spot markets currencies are bought and sold for immediate delivery and payment; in forward (futures) markets, contracts are provided for the delivery of currencies at some future date. The crucial difference between the spot and forward markets is that in a spot transaction the price at which a currency is traded (the spot exchange rate) is set concurrently with the payment and delivery of a currency, while in forward markets traders determine the price today (the forward exchange rate) for future delivery and payment. The forward market is used by investors to cover their open positions in foreign currencies and thus hedge against unpredictable exchange rate fluctuations. Open positions in a given currency mean that the value of assets and liabilities denominated in that currency do not match. In order to close (or cover) the position, one must then hold equal assets and liabilities denominated in the same currency.

5. The forward exchange rate tends to reflect the spot exchange rate that most participants in the market anticipate will prevail at the point of maturity of the forward contract. Even though the forward rate does not generally predict actual future exchange rates with any degree of accuracy, it still provides the most accessible and yet highly unbeatable forecast of future exchange rates. The inaccuracy of the forward exchange rate in predicting future spot rates is connected to the general unpredictability of future exchange rates, something to which all forecasts are subject.

6. The proportional difference between the forward and the current spot exchange rates of domestic currency against a foreign currency is called the forward premium. A positive value of the forward premium means that the foreign currency is worth more, in terms of domestic currency, for future than for current delivery. A positive value of the forward premium tends to reflect an expected depreciation of domestic currency against the foreign currency. When negative, the forward premium (referred to as being at a discount) suggests that participants in the foreign exchange market anticipate the domestic currency will appreciate relative to the foreign currency.

7. A free-floating exchange rate regime exists whenever exchange rates are freely determined by the supply and demand of currencies by private parties. It presumes the absence of government intervention in the foreign exchange market. Changes in the private demand and supply of foreign exchange can then alter exchange rates but not the country's international reserves.

8. Under a fixed (or pegged) exchange rate regime, the government, through its Central Bank, intervenes in foreign exchange markets in order to maintain the exchange rate against different currencies within prescribed limits. To carry out its foreign exchange operations, the Central Bank holds inventories of foreign exchange, referred to as international reserves. Changes in the private demand and supply of foreign exchange will then alter the level of the country's international reserves.

9. A controlled (or managed) floating exchange rate regime exists when governments intervene in foreign exchange markets to influence the exchange rate but do not commit themselves to maintaining a fixed exchange rate. Depending on Central Bank intervention, changes in the private demand and supply of foreign exchange might then be associated with changes in exchange rates and/or changes in international reserves.

PROBLEMS

1. Describe the process through which someone living in a small town can make a payment in deutsche marks. How does a local bank obtain the foreign exchange? Explain the mechanics involved.

2. Find *The Wall Street Journal*'s foreign exchange rate quotes for today, and calculate the 90-day forward market premiums of the pound sterling, deutsche mark and French franc against the U.S. dollar. How do these forward premiums (discounts) compare with those determined from Table 1–1? What do they suggest about the market's assessment of the future behavior of the exchange rates examined?

3. Using *The Wall Street Journal*'s daily quotes, find today's implicit or cross deutsche mark–pound sterling exchange rate. Then check a British financial periodical to determine the actual exchange rate between the deutsche mark and pound sterling in England for the corresponding date. Are these two quotes strictly comparable?

4. Do you expect forward markets to develop in a fixed exchange rate system? What is the role of the forward market in that system?

5. Countries under pegged exchange rates tend to have forward exchange rates that diverge from the peg. For instance, during the period before the August 1976 devaluation of the Mexican peso in terms of the U.S. dollar, the peso was consistently quoted at a discount on the forward market. This means that if one were to take the forward rate as the predictor of future exchange rates one would be committing clear, consistent errors, except perhaps when the country changes its peg value. Does this mean that the forward rate cannot be looked at as a predictor of future exchange rates in a fixed exchange rate regime? How do you interpret the forward rate in this case? This issue is referred to as the "peso problem" in the literature.

6. The exchange rate of the French franc against the West German mark in April 1982 was pegged at 0.39 deutsche marks per French franc with a 2.25% margin of variation allowed by the European Monetary System around that value. A quote for the 90-day forward rate at the time was 0.38 deutsche marks per French franc. What does this suggest about the market's assessment regarding the prospects of a change in the bilateral French franc–Deutsche mark exchange rate? (Hint: Check whether the forward rate falls within or outside the band.)

7. You are told that the private demand for British pounds can be represented by the following equation:

$$Q_D = 10 - 3e$$

where Q_D represents the quantity demanded of pounds (in millions), and e represents the exchange rate of the dollar against the pound. You are also given the private supply curve of pounds, which is represented by

$$Q_S = 5 + 2e$$

where Q_S is the quantity supplied by pounds (in millions).

(a) Suppose that the United States and Britain are under a system of flexible exchange rates. What would be the equilibrium exchange rate during the period of concern? How many pounds (in millions) would be traded during this period?

(b) Given the situation in part (a), suppose now that the Federal Reserve Board in the United States decides to intervene in the foreign exchange market by purchasing £3 million. What would be the effects of this operation in numerical terms? Explain why and illustrate diagrammatically.

(c) Imagine that the United States and Britain were under a system of fixed exchange rates and that the exchange rate was given at $2.00 per pound. What would be the U.S. Central Bank's gain (loss) of foreign exchange reserves, given the private supply and demand curves of part (a) and assuming that the United States is the country in charge of foreign exchange market intervention? Explain.

CHAPTER 2

International Money Markets

In Chapter 1 we presented an introduction to the mechanics behind the operation of foreign exchange markets and stressed that the basic function of foreign exchange markets is to provide the means of payment required for the smooth operation of international transactions. With this purpose, agents engaging in international transactions purchase foreign currencies and transferable or checkable deposits denominated in foreign currencies. One must recognize, however, that foreign exchange is not generally acquired for its own sake, to be held indefinitely. Just as tourists acquire foreign currency in order to spend it abroad—and have little use for the spare foreign coins left over after their travels—most foreign exchange is acquired in order to be transferred to someone else either as payment for goods and services purchased or to be invested in interest-yielding foreign financial assets. When foreign exchange is acquired in order to engage in international transactions involving the purchases of goods and services, it is said that *international trade* in goods and services has taken place. When international transactions involve the purchase or sale of financial assets, they are referred to as *international financial transactions.*

The arena of international finance is an unusually broad and dynamic one, encompassing such disparate activities as those of Italian investors smuggling lira notes into Switzerland to avoid local taxes, OPEC members choosing in which location and in which foreign assets to invest their wealth, and major U.S. banks setting up foreign branches at a rate faster than that of new international finance textbooks. In Chapters 2 and 3 we shall systematically examine the nature of these transactions and the key variables behind them. The discussion will focus mostly—though not exclusively—on the operation of international markets for short-term financial instruments. Parts V and VI will then address a broad range of economic issues relating to the operation of international financial markets in general.

49

2–1   INTRODUCTION TO CAPITAL AND MONEY MARKETS

Financial markets are commonly classified into capital and money markets. *Capital markets* deal in financial claims having a maturity longer than 1 year, usually referred to as long-term claims. Such claims include stocks (which represent ownership claims and bear no maturity dates), bonds, and long-term loans, among others. *Money markets*, on the other hand, deal in short-term claims, with maturities of less than 1 year.[1] These include marketable government securities (like Treasury bills, which are available in 30-day, 6-month, and other short-term maturities), large-denomination certificates of deposit (CDs) issued by banks, commercial paper (representing short-term corporate debt), and many others. In spite of the wide range of money market instruments, which vary according to the type of issuing institution, term to maturity, and other factors, they share some basic common traits: They are short-term assets that can be bought and sold quickly at low transaction costs (i.e., they are liquid). For these reasons, they are a convenient investment outlet, especially for funds available only for short periods of time. Because of their liquidity, money market assets are regarded as close substitutes for money and are often referred to as *near moneys.*

The money market is a highly competitive market, with information about the interest rates available on alternative instruments readily within reach of a telephone call. Even if laid back, one can easily follow the major money market rates by reading their quotes in the daily newspapers. There is also a broad diversity of investors participating in the money market, ranging from individuals and government institutions to large corporations, all of which can choose from a whole menu of domestic money market instruments. They can also choose to invest in money market instruments abroad, that is, go international. The decision may be made, for instance, to buy Swiss franc-denominated certificates of deposit (CDs) issued by a Swiss bank, dollar CDs issued by the same Swiss bank (called Eurodollar deposits), U.K. Treasury bills, or commercial paper issued by a Canadian multinational company.

The decision to "go international" poses some problems that do not arise when you invest domestically. For instance, when investments in sterling-denominated assets (say, U.K. Treasury bills or sterling-denominated CDs) are made, how do you protect yourself against a sudden depreciation of the pound sterling? In addition, how do you compare rates of return between dollar and sterling-

---

[1] Maturity as used here refers to the remaining term to maturity of the financial instruments. Accordingly, if the instrument has an *original* term to maturity longer than 1 year (say, 10 years) but its *remaining* term is shorter than 1 year (say, 6 months), it is considered a money market claim. By implication, Treasury notes and bonds and other claims with original medium-term and long-term maturity are transformed into money market instruments when their remaining time to maturity becomes less than 1 year. For an extensive discussion of money market instruments and the money market in general, see Marcia L. Stigum, *The Money Market* (Homewood, Ill.: Dow Jones-Irwin, 1983).

denominated CDs? In order to answer these questions, one has to understand the particular procedures and problems of investing in international money markets. This chapter begins with a discussion of investments involving assets denominated in different currencies, such as dollar and sterling certificates of deposit. Chapter 3 then proceeds to a comparative analysis of investments involving financial assets denominated in the same currency but issued or located in different national jurisdictions, such as dollar certificates of deposit issued by New York and London banks.

2–2 INVESTING ON A COVERED BASIS

We shall now focus on the problems associated with investing in assets denominated in different currencies. International investing can be as fascinating and profitable as it can be discouraging and woeful. The intricacies of covering, arbitrage, and speculation absorb the minds of financial managers and executives just as much as they perplex the newcomers. Still, the present sophistication of high international finance requires taking a hard look at the elements of international investing, lest we be oblivious of its idiosyncrasies and waste away our employer's funds or our own fortunes.

Suppose that you are the international financial manager of a large American corporation that has investment funds available for 1 year and is interested in obtaining the highest return subject to the least possible risk. The international finance division in which you work is considering the choice between investing in American and British 1-year Treasury bills, since both U.S. and U.K. Treasury bills are among the safest assets available in the market (due to their negligible default risk, which means that both the amount invested and the attached interest are default-free). You are asked to determine whether the corporation should invest in U.K. or U.S. Treasury bills and are told that the advice provided must be top-notch; otherwise, heads will roll. What would your advice be? In which asset should the company invest?

If the corporation were to invest in American Treasury bills, it would receive $R_{U.S.}$ dollars back after 1 year per dollar invested, where

$$R_{U.S.} = 1 + i \tag{1}$$

with i representing the 1-year interest yield on U.S. Treasury bills. In other words, after 1 year the firm would receive back the dollar invested plus its interest return.

The alternative investment involves U.K. Treasury bills, which yield an interest return equal to i^*. Each *pound* bought and invested in U.K. Treasury bills then generates $1 + i^*$ pounds 1 year in the future. Given that corporate funds are going to be shifted back to dollars (picturesquely described as the firm's preferred habitat), a problem arises when you think (perceptively) about investing in U.K. Treasury bills. If pound-denominated assets are purchased today and the pound depreciates relative to the dollar during the year, the firm may end up with fewer dollars than it started with, even if the yields on U.K. Treasury bills are very high.

The risk involved in the chance that the value of the currency in which the assets held are denominated will fluctuate is called *exchange risk*. This type of risk can be substantial; it means that exchange rate fluctuations can completely offset any interest advantage offered by a given foreign currency-denominated asset. It must thus be realized that a strategy that involves buying pounds, investing in 1-year U.K. Treasury bills, waiting until they mature, and exchanging the pound proceeds for dollars involves exchange risk. While buying U.K. Treasury bills avoids default risk, this merely means that the amount of *pounds* to be received at the end of the year is without risk but that the *dollar* equivalent of those pounds is still subject to exchange risk. Since your assumed financial objectives involve minimizing risks, how do you proceed in order to avoid exchange risk? As discussed in Chapter 1, it is precisely this type of risk that the forward market can insure against. In order to be fully covered, you should sell pounds forward by an amount corresponding to the proceeds of your U.K. Treasury bill investment (including both the pounds invested and the interest to be received on them). This *covered* investment strategy, then, involves the following simultaneous steps:

1. Buy pounds in the spot market. At a spot exchange rate of e dollars per pound, you obtain $1/e$ pounds for each dollar invested.
2. Invest the pounds obtained in the spot market in 1-year U.K. Treasury bills. This will give you $(1/e)\,(1 + i^*)$ pounds at the end of 1 year (per dollar invested).
3. Sell forward the future pound proceeds from the investment. At a forward exchange rate of F dollars per pound, for each pound you sell for delivery 1 year hence, you will receive F dollars at that time; since you will have $(1 + i^*)/e$ pounds available to transfer back to dollars, you would then receive $[(1 + i^*)/e]\,F$ dollars 1 year from now.

The proceeds from the covered investment strategy, in terms of the dollars you end up with after a period of 1 year—per dollar initially invested abroad—are represented by $R_{U.K.}$ and given by

$$R_{U.K.} = \frac{F}{e}\,(1 + i^*) \tag{2}$$

where F and e represent the U.S. dollar–pound sterling forward and spot exchange rates. Note that this covered investment strategy avoids both default and exchange risk. This was achieved, first, by investing in a very safe asset with negligible default risk and, second, by selling forward the future pound proceeds so that exchange risk is eliminated.

We have examined two alternative investment strategies, both of which lack default and exchange risk. Equation (1) represents the dollar proceeds from an investment in U.S. Treasury bills, whereas equation (2) represents the dollar proceeds from an alternative covered investment in U.K. Treasury bills. Which is the superior investment strategy? A complete answer to this question requires us to account for a host of elements, including an analysis of the transaction costs involved, applicable taxes, and forward market margin requirements. To highlight the essentials of the discussion, however, we shall abstract from these issues momentarily.

When investment alternatives are similar in terms of the explicit objective to minimize risk, a maximizing investor would choose whatever investment provides a higher dollar return after 1 year. As long as $R_{U.S.} > R_{U.K.}$, then, you should invest in the United States and, if $R_{U.S.} < R_{U.K.}$ you should invest in the United Kingdom. Note that if $R_{U.S.} = R_{U.K.}$, then *ceteris paribus* there is no clear incentive to choose one alternative over the other. The existence of incentives to invest in one or the other country is therefore measured by the differential between $R_{U.K.}$ and $R_{U.S.}$—the *covered interest differential (CD)*:

$$CD = R_{U.K.} - R_{U.S.} = \frac{F}{e}(1 + i^*) - (1 + i) \qquad (3)$$

A positive value of CD is referred to as a covered differential in favor of London, that is, there would be incentives to invest in the United Kingdom relative to the United States. A negative value of CD is referred to as a covered differential in favor of the United States because there are incentives to invest in the United States. Subjecting equation (3) to some approximation and manipulation, one can easily derive a simple expression that highlights the essential elements involved in evaluating competing investment strategies, with the following result:[2]

---

[2] The derivation of equation (4) is

$$CD = \frac{F}{e}(1 + i^*) - (1 + i) = \left(\frac{F}{e} - 1\right) - i + \frac{e}{e}i^* - \frac{e}{e}i^* + \frac{F}{e}i^* = \frac{F - e}{e} - i + i^* + \frac{F - e}{e}i^*$$

$$\cong \frac{F - e}{e} - i + i^*$$

where the last expression is an approximation, since it ignores the term $[(F - e)/e]\, i^*$. This last term represents the foreign exchange gain or loss on the interest received from investing abroad and, since it is usually a product of two fractions, it yields a very small number. As a matter of fact, for sufficiently (infinitesimally) small investment periods, the term becomes negligible and can be ignored.

$$CD \cong \frac{F - e}{e} + i^* - i$$

$$= f + i^* - i$$

(4)

where the symbol f denotes $(F - e)/e$.

Equation (4) presents a convenient form of the covered interest differential, expressing in a simple way the sources of the returns associated with different investment strategies and facilitating their evaluation. We examine it in some detail to discern its economic significance. The first two terms, $f + i^*$, represent the return from engaging in a *covered* investment in U.K. Treasury bills. To visualize this, recall that the covered investment strategy involving U.K. Treasury bills consists of three *simultaneous* transactions: (1) buy pounds, (2) invest in U.K. Treasury bills, and (3) sell forward the pound proceeds. One can then decompose the return from this investment strategy into two basic components. One component arises from transaction (2), which just represents the interest earned on the investment in U.K. Treasury bills, i^*, the so-called *interest gain*. The second component, $f = (F - e)/e$, arises from transactions (1) and (3) and reflects the return—or loss—from purchasing pounds spot and simultaneously selling pounds forward, the so-called *exchange gain*—or loss. This return (loss) is equal to the difference between the price at which one sells pounds forward (the forward exchange rate, F) and the price one can currently buy pounds spot (the spot exchange rate, e). Expressed in percentage terms, this exchange gain (loss) is precisely equal to $f = (F - e)/e$, which as we saw in Chapter 1 is the *forward premium or discount* on the pound. The third—and final—term in equation (4) represents the gain from investing in U.S. Treasury bills, i. Since the U.S. Treasury bills are denominated in dollars and are not involved in any international transactions, they require no forward covering; for that reason, the exchange cost of investing in the United States is zero.

With the first two terms in equation (4) representing the return obtained from covered investments in U.K. Treasury bills and the interest rate i depicting the return on U.S. Treasury bills, it is clear that the covered interest differential CD represents the difference between the returns on these two investments.

Consider the following hypothetical example, involving a current spot exchange rate for the pound of $e = \$2.00/\pounds$, a 1-year forward rate of $F = \$1.90/\pounds$, a yearly interest rate on U.K. Treasury bills equal to $i^* = 0.12$ and a 1-year return on U.S. Treasury bills of $i = .10$. In this case, the first component of the rate of return on U.K. investments is the 12% rate of interest. The second component involves the gain or loss from having to purchase pounds spot and selling them forward to cover the foreign investment. In the present example, this second component is equal to

$$f = \frac{F - e}{e} = \frac{1.90 - 2.00}{2.00} = -0.05$$

The negative value (−0.05) of f obtained implies pounds are at a discount in the forward market, meaning that one can only sell pounds for 1-year delivery at a price *lower* than that at which one can currently buy pounds spot ($1.90 per pound as compared with $2.00 per pound). This reduces the attractiveness of investing in pound-denominated assets, since part of the interest returns is, in a sense, used up in the forward covering transactions.

Since the return on covered investments in U.K. Treasury bills is the sum of the interest earned and the forward premium (discount), that is, $f + i^*$, the return in the present example is equal to 0.07 (since $f = −0.05$ and $i^* = 0.12$). In other words, the 1-year return on covered investing in U.K. Treasury bills is 7%. Given that the 1-year return on U.S. Treasury bills is assumed to be equal to $i = 0.10$ (or 10%), the rate of return on U.K. Treasury bills as calculated is clearly smaller. There is thus an incentive to invest in U.S. Treasury bills. This is exactly what equation (4) tells us. By substituting the specific values for f, i^*, and i used in our example, the covered interest differential in this case would be given by

$$CD \cong f + i^* - i$$
$$= -0.05 + 0.12 - 0.10$$
$$= -0.03$$

A covered interest differential in favor of the U.S. (negative CD) thus exists.

The concept of a covered interest differential involves comparing the returns of two assets that are similar or equivalent in their risk characteristics. After one finds such alternative investment strategies providing the same risk characteristics, the choice is obvious: Select the one with highest return. Observe, however, that choosing the investment strategy with highest return does not imply that one should choose the investment with the highest interest rate. The appropriate comparison is between the returns from different investment strategies after one covers so as to eliminate exchange risk. As a matter of fact, in our numerical example involving U.S. Treasury bills and covered U.K. Treasury bills, the highest return was provided by the U.S. investment (10% relative to the 7% provided by the covered U.K. investment). Still, the investment offering the highest rate of interest was the U.K. Treasury bill, which earned 12% compared with the 10% provided by U.S. Treasury bills. The reason for the difference in return favoring the U.S. Treasury bills in spite of the interest rate differential favoring the U.K. Treasury bills is that the covered interest differential favors the former. In order to cover the U.K. investments, you would have to sell forward pounds at a discount, which results in an exchange loss large enough to offset the interest rate gain from U.K. investments. As a consequence, the U.K. Treasury bills become an inferior investment strategy. In conclusion, the international investor should guard against investing just on the basis of the relative interest rates (yields) available on comparable instruments in different countries.

2–3 THE COVERED INTEREST PARITY CONDITION

We shall now move beyond the simple analysis of covered investment strategies toward an examination of the market forces governing international interest rate linkages. First we shall look at the main ideas behind the so-called covered interest parity condition, which establishes a rigid connection between international interest rate differentials and forward premia. Later on, we shall look at actual data on covered interest differentials and observe how they are influenced by real-world factors.

By adding some economic reasoning, we can easily transform our discussion of covered investment strategies in the previous section into a theory of international money market equilibrium establishing how international interest rates relate. In order to carry out this task initially at the maximum level of simplicity, we continue to ignore transaction costs, taxes, and so forth.

Note, first, that as long as the covered interest differential is different from zero, there will be incentives for the movement of funds from one country to another because profits can be made from such an undertaking. Equilibrium is defined as a situation in which there are no profit opportunities to be made from the movement of funds across borders. In other words, there are no unexploited opportunities for profit in the simple act of moving funds across borders. This implies that, in equilibrium, the covered interest differential, *CD*, is zero. Or, from equation (4) above, $f + i^* = i$. Rearranging,[3] we find that

$$f \equiv \frac{F - e}{e} = i - i^* \tag{5}$$

That is, the forward premium, *f*, must be equal to the interest rate differential, $i - i^*$. This is what is known as the *covered interest parity condition,* often called the (covered) interest parity theorem.

The interest parity condition is basically a statement about the law of one price, which asserts that a single price should prevail all over the market for any given commodity. In international money markets, the analogy to the law of one price is that securities or assets that share the same characteristics (e.g., have the same risks and liquidity) should yield the same return in equilibrium.

---

[3] For simplicity, equation (5) states the equality of the forward premium and the interest rate differential, even though it should be remembered, from the derivation of equation (4), that in general it is an approximate—not exact—equality. The precise equilibrium condition is derived by setting $CD = 0$ in footnote 2

$$CD = 0 = \frac{F - e}{e} - i + i^* + \frac{F - e}{e} i^*$$

$$= \frac{F - e}{e} (1 + i^*) + i^* - i$$

which yields $f = [(F - e)/e] = [(i - i^*)/(1 + i^*)]$.

In other words, interest rates should be *in line* or *in parity* with each other. If U.S. T-bill investments and covered U.K. T-bill investments are similar in terms of risk and other characteristics, we would expect them to yield the same return. From a slightly different perspective, the interest parity condition can also be interpreted as representing the absence of profits to be made from undertaking the operation of interest arbitrage in international money markets. This can perhaps be best visualized by considering a situation in which the covered returns from U.K. T-bill investments exceed the cost of borrowing in the United States, that is, $i* + [(F - e)/e] - i > 0$. Smart investors could then borrow in the United States and invest in the United Kingdom, which yields a sure profit with no commitment of personal funds, since the operation is credit-financed. Furthermore, the amount of profits is only limited by the borrowings the arbitrageurs manage to obtain. Obviously, from this viewpoint, covered differentials should quickly disappear as hordes of arbitrageurs jump on the bandwagon of easy profits. A zero-profits-from-arbitrage equilibrium condition thus ensues.

The equality between the forward premium and the interest rate differential in equilibrium is represented graphically in Figure 2–1 by line *IP*. Point *A*, for instance, shows that, in equilibrium, a 5% forward premium on the pound sterling (a discount on the dollar) would have to be associated with a 5%

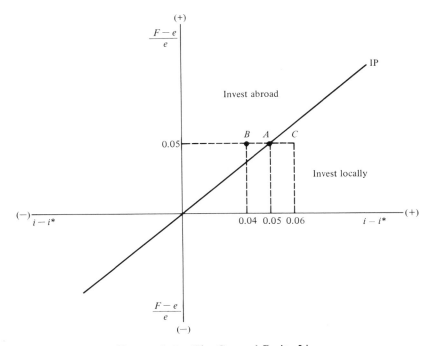

FIGURE 2–1.   The Covered Parity Line

equilibrium interest rate differential favoring dollar assets. In the event that the forward premium on the pound were to exceed the interest differential—such as at point *B*, where a 5% forward premium is coupled with a 4 percent interest differential favoring U.S. investments—this would suggest that profits could be made by investing in sterling-denominated assets, a situation defined earlier as inconsistent with financial equilibrium within the present framework. Conversely, if the forward premium on the pound were less than the interest differential—as at point *C* in Figure 2–1, where a 5% forward premium is associated with a 6% interest differential in favor of U.S. investments—profits could be made by shifting funds to the United States, again inconsistent with equilibrium. Interest parity, then, is represented by points along the line *IP*, where $f = (F - e)/e = i - i^*$.

Note that covered interest parity establishes an equilibrium relationship between a set of interdependent economic variables but does not specify the particular equilibrium values of each of these variables. In a more specific context, what one would like to know is exactly how the variables composing the covered interest parity equation (interest rates, spot and forward exchange rates) move to their equilibrium values so as to maintain interest parity. This will be the subject of Part III, where it will be shown how the general equilibrium values of F, S, i, and i^* are established so as to maintain condition (5).

At first sight, condition (5) looks like a rather innocuous and perhaps obvious condition. But the meticulous reader must have already noticed that, in our discussion, we have neglected a host of real-world complications (say, transaction costs) that might preclude condition (5) from holding. The empirically minded reader might also wonder about the empirical validity of (5). Does interest parity actually hold in financial markets? These questions are addressed in the following sections.

2–4 Deviations from Covered Interest Parity

Figure 2–2 shows the interest differential between U.S. and U.K. Treasury bills during the period 1978 to 1983, as well as the corresponding forward premium or discount on the pound sterling versus the U.S. dollar during those years. It can be observed that deviations from the covered interest parity condition do occur and appear to persist, with covered interest differentials differing from zero at some points by a margin of more than 5%. This was the case during early 1983, when the deviation from a zero covered differential slightly exceeded 6%. Going further back in time, deviations of over 5% also arose during early 1974 and late 1976. Why these divergences from covered interest parity?

A variety of factors may preclude covered interest parity from holding:

1. Transaction costs.
2. Costs of gathering and processing information.

3. Government intervention and regulation.
4. Financial constraints and capital market imperfections.
5. Noncomparability of assets.

We now proceed to discuss in detail how each of these factors influences deviations from covered interest parity. We start by examining transaction costs.

Transaction Costs

There are basically two elements in the cost of transactions: (1) the cost of transacting in the foreign exchange markets (spot and forward), and (2) the cost of transacting in the securities markets (domestic and foreign). Consider, for example, the transactions involved when a U.S. resident holding cash initially engages in covered foreign investments, that is, in capital outflows. In this case, the transactions involved[4] are (1) the purchase of foreign currency (spot), (2) the purchase of foreign securities, and (3) the sale of foreign currency (forward). Each of these transactions involves transaction costs and reduces the net revenues from investing abroad. Investing at home (locally), however, requires only one transaction—the purchase of domestic securities. As a result, investments in domestic assets require a smaller number of transactions and tend to involve lower transaction costs than investments in foreign currency-denominated assets. The implication is that an individual or institution holding dollars will invest in assets denominated in foreign currency only if there is a covered interest differential favoring foreign assets large enough to offset the higher transaction costs involved. In the presence of transaction costs, then, the interest gain from investing abroad relative to investing domestically must offset not only any exchange loss arising from covering the investment but also the higher transaction costs they require.

The effects of transaction costs on covered interest parity are illustrated in Figure 2–3. Line *IP* shows the parity line, as derived in Figure 2–1. What modifications are introduced by transaction costs? Transaction costs generate a neutral band—the entire shaded area in Figure 2–3—representing no profit opportunities from moving funds across countries and currencies. This means that nonzero covered interest differentials do not imply the existence of unexploited profit opportunities. Transaction costs would absorb any apparent profits suggested by such differentials.

Consider first the shaded area demarcated by lines *IP* and *IP'* in Figure 2–3. Points lying within this area depict cases in which the covered interest differential favors foreign securities but in which foreign investments are still not profitable because transaction costs absorb the gain from investing abroad.

---

[4] An additional cost is incurred if the securities are sold before they mature. This would be the case, for instance, when a 180-day Treasury bill is purchased and then sold in 60 days, before maturity.

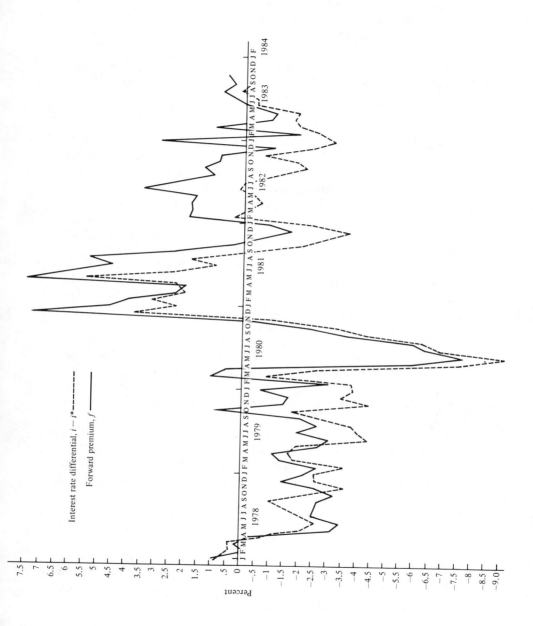

Interest rate differential, $i - i^*$ ----------

Forward premium, f ——————

Percent

60

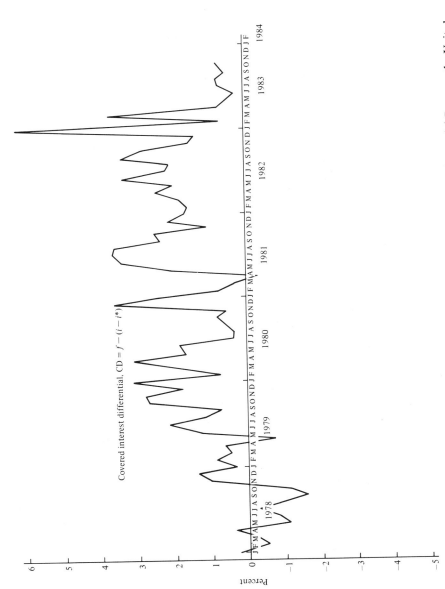

Figure 2-2. Interest Rate Differential, Forward Premium, and Covered Interest Differential Between the United States and the United Kingdom. The forward premium, f, is the 90-day forward premium on the pound vis-à-vis the U.S. dollar; the interest rates i and i^* are the 3-month U.S. and U.K. Treasury bill rates, respectively. All variables have been annualized and expressed in percentage form.

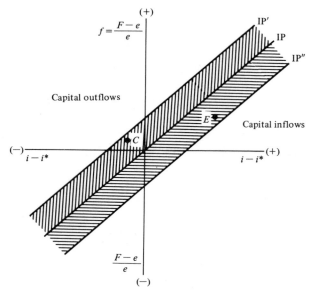

FIGURE 2–3.   Transaction Costs and the Covered Interest Parity Band

Note that cases like this, such as point *C,* are consistent with financial equilibrium because, in spite of the deviation from parity, there are no profits to be made from interest arbitrage. Geometrically, the set of all points enclosed by, and including, lines *IP* and *IP'* is consistent with equilibrium in international financial markets. What about points within the *IP* and *IP''* lines? Let us turn to this question.

We have been describing the plight of an individual investor or institution initially holding dollars, and thus evaluating possible capital outflows from the United States. Consider, on the other hand, the case of a foreign investor who is holding pounds and is evaluating whether to place funds in dollar-denominated assets for a specific period of time, after which they are to be withdrawn and converted back to pounds.

Just as investors initially holding dollars find the transaction costs of purchasing foreign currency-denominated assets higher than for U.S. assets, the transaction costs of dollar investments are higher than those of pound assets for the individual holding pounds initially. Foreign investors will then invest in dollar-denominated assets only if the covered interest differential favoring the dollar is high enough to offset the higher transaction costs involved. This situation is illustrated by means of the *IP''* line in Figure 2–3. Points such as *E,* lying within the area enclosed by the *IP* and *IP''* lines, represent situations wherein the covered interest differential favors U.S. assets, but these investments are still not profitable because transaction costs more than offset the covered interest gains. Since these points are consistent with the absence of unexploited profit opportunities from arbitrage, they are also compatible with international financial equilibrium.

In conclusion, the set of all points enclosed by and including lines *IP* and *IP″* is consistent with equilibrium in international financial markets. This poses a problem in testing whether interest parity holds in practice; that is, one has to account for transaction costs in order to obtain a meaningful test of the existence of arbitrage opportunities. From this viewpoint, only points lying *outside* the neutral band suggest the presence of profit opportunities.

How important are transaction costs in determining deviations from interest parity in the real world? Not too much. Recent available evidence[5] suggests that about 20–30% of the discrepancies from covered interest parity—between U.S. and U.K. Treasury bills—can be explained by transaction costs (assuming that investors hold cash initially; if they were holding U.S. securities the percentage explained by transaction costs increases, but minimally). Actually, this conclusion is what one would expect from a casual look at the foreign exchange and securities markets. The foreign exchange market, for example, involves such a huge volume of transactions that the resultant economies of scale, taken in conjunction with the relatively small number of currencies and instruments traded, give rise to high transacting efficiency, hence small costs. As a matter of fact, the banks and other large-scale institutions and corporations that constitute the core of the international money market face transaction costs frequently below one-tenth of 1%, a negligible amount.[6] Other factors also affect the low costs of foreign exchange transactions, such as market conventions and the lack of government intervention. Most contracts in the foreign exchange market can be (and are) made initially through simple—although legally binding—verbal agreements, and they do not necessitate filling out or satisfying any constraining government requirements and regulations.

Costs of Gathering and Processing Information

A second factor generating divergencies from interest parity involves the costs of gathering and processing information. In deriving the interest rate parity condition, it was implicitly assumed that the investor had free access to all necessary information about interest and exchange rates and that this information

---

[5] See Frank McCormick, "Covered Interest Arbitrage: Unexploited Profits? Comment," *Journal of Political Economy* (April 1979).

[6] See Robert Z. Aliber "Transaction Costs in the Foreign Exchange Market," unpublished manuscript (1984). Alternative estimates of transaction costs range from less than 0.1% to more than 1% of the value of the transaction. The reader should be aware that there is no unique measure of transaction costs in foreign exchange markets. These vary according to the type of transaction, the specific currencies being traded, and the amount exchanged. For instance, transactions costs are higher for individuals and commercial firms engaging in international trade than for large international banks. The lower costs faced by banks, however, are particularly relevant for interest parity, since banks are a predominant force in international money markets and interest arbitrage.

could be processed in a timely fashion in order to profit from investment opportunities. Information costs will introduce a gap between the returns made in different countries, depending on the differential availability and price of information. Nevertheless, one suspects that information costs will not affect the parity condition significantly, since the data processing and telecommunications technological revolution has made information very cheap. It simply does not cost much to acquire and process information from all of the world's markets very rapidly. This is especially true of banks and large organizations, which are the day-to-day participants in the market.

Government Intervention and Regulation

Government intervention and regulation is a third factor influencing capital flows and generating deviations from covered interest parity. Government intervention comes in all forms and devices—through regulation of financial transactions, exchange controls restricting foreign exchange transactions, differential tax treatment of types of income, and so forth. A common form of government intervention involves domestic interest rate ceilings, which prevent domestic interest rates from rising above a certain level. Such regulations tend to create a gap between domestic and foreign rates of return and are thus frequently associated with covered differentials in favor of foreign currencies. The massive capital outflows such differentials would encourage are then avoided through the imposition of exchange controls, which limit purchases of foreign exchange and consequently restrict investing abroad. In this way, government intervention sustains deviations from covered interest parity.

Differential taxation can also explain deviations from covered interest parity. For instance, U.S. tax laws consider interest income as ordinary income for tax purposes. Foreign exchange gains obtained from covering transactions, on the other hand, are catalogued under the separate category of asset capital gains and taxed at the capital gains tax rate. Since the capital gains rate (about 20%) is far lower than the income tax bracket applying to a large corporation (about 50%), a corporate taxpayer would prefer to receive its income in the form of capital gains. This will tend to generate deviations from covered interest parity. Consider the case of a U.S. corporation that is evaluating whether to invest in U.S. or Canadian assets. If the Canadian dollar is at a forward premium with respect to the U.S. dollar, this means that part of the returns from covered Canadian investments would be obtained in the form of foreign exchange (currency) gains taxable at the lower capital gains rate. Since the domestic—and foreign—interest gains are taxable at the higher corporate income tax rate, the American corporation would prefer to invest in Canadian securities, even if Canadian covered yields are lower than U.S. yields, as long as the tax benefit is sufficiently high.[7] In conclusion, when applicable taxes are explicitly consid-

---

[7] This would give rise to abnormal capital flows out of the United States and toward Canadian securities. See M. D. Levi, "Taxation and 'Abnormal' International Capital Flows," *Journal of*

ered, deviations from interest parity can very well be consistent with equilibrium in international money markets, with the relatively low covered returns observed in one country being offset by tax benefits.

Financial Constraints and Capital Market Imperfections

The presence of margin requirements forces investors to set aside some funds when engaging in forward market transactions. As explained in Chapter 1, these margin requirements help ensure that investors satisfy their commitments in the forward market. At the same time, they impose an additional cost, since the funds set aside cannot be optimally invested in interest-yielding assets. A covered interest differential in favor of foreign assets would not then be necessarily associated with unexploited profits, since it may be offset by the cost of margin requirements associated with covered foreign investments. As a result, and similarly to transaction costs, forward market margin requirements give rise to a neutral band around the covered parity line.

Other factors may also work by preventing or restricting entry of investment funds into areas with favorable covered differentials. The unavailability of liquid funds for investment purposes, for instance, may prevent traders from exploiting potential profit opportunities. Capital market imperfections, on the other hand, may result in exuberant profits for those enjoying monopoly power. These will then be associated with persistent deviations from covered interest parity. Among major industrial countries, however, one expects imperfections in the capital market and the availability of investment funds to be relatively unimportant because (1) there is a large amount of funds available to investors both in national markets and through the Eurocurrency market (discussed in Chapter 3) ready to be shifted to the most profitable and/or less risky venture, and (2) given the size of both the securities and the foreign exchange markets in these countries, any investor is very small and, consequently, cannot influence or manipulate prices to any significant extent. Of most markets, both the foreign exchange and the securities markets of industrial countries are among the most perfectly competitive.[8]

Noncomparability of Assets

The empirical evidence available suggests that the factors discussed to this point leave substantial unexplained deviations from covered interest parity. As it turns out, there is indeed a crucial source of measured deviations from interest parity

---

Political Economy (June 1977), for an explanation of the intricacies of U.S. and Canadian tax laws. One should be aware that capital gains realized on the sales of assets held for more than a specific period, say 6 months, are generally treated preferentially for tax purposes, but this is not so for short-term capital gains.

[8] See J. Frenkel and R. Levich, "Covered Interest Arbitrage: Unexploited Profits?", *Journal of Political Economy* (April 1975).

that we have not yet mentioned. To introduce this factor, let us recall that when the covered parity condition was derived, it was made explicit that the rates of interest, i and $i*$, should be for comparable domestic and foreign assets. This means they must be in the same category in regard to liquidity, maturity, risk class, and so forth. A major source of measured deviations from covered parity arises precisely because of the existence of differences among the assets being compared. Risk factors such as default and political risk are particularly significant in generating differences among otherwise identical assets.

Default risk represents the chance that the issuer of the asset under consideration will not satisfy all its commitments—such as not being able to pay interest or repay the principal on time or even at all. Of course, the higher the default risk of an asset, the higher the interest rate it would have to offer in order to compensate investors for the associated risk bearing. Consequently, a covered interest differential in favor of a given asset may just reflect the higher default risk class of that asset relative to the one being compared with, and not any unexploited profit opportunities. In order to evaluate whether the covered interest parity condition holds, care must then be taken to ensure that the assets compared are strictly similar in terms of their default-risk category. If, for instance, one takes relatively safe assets such as U.K. and U.S. Treasury bills, the default-risk problem is not important. By contrast, when comparing CDs issued by U.S. banks relative to those issued by foreign banks, the relative default risks involved must be carefully evaluated, and the judgement as to whether there is any covered differential in returns among them should be based on risk-adjusted interest rates.

Even in the absence of issuer's default risk, political risk is unavoidable in a world of sovereign countries. In the next section we discuss the subject of political risk, which is essential for a correct interpretation of observed deviations from covered interest parity.

2–5 POLITICAL RISK AND INTERNATIONAL MONEY MARKETS

Political risks are those arising from the exercise of political sovereignty by the government of a given country. As such, they are linked to the political jurisdiction under which the assets are issued or held. Perhaps the first thing that comes to mind when political risks are mentioned is the possibility of outright expropriation, such as when U.S. assets abroad are nationalized, or the threat of an asset freeze, as when Iranian assets in the United States were frozen by the Carter Administration in 1979 (the freeze meant that Iranian deposits held in the United States or with U.S. banks abroad could not be used to pay debts or be exchanged for other assets; the value of the assets frozen amounted to more than $12 billion). Although expropriations and freezes are a widely talked-about form of government intervention, political risks need not reflect any dramatic political events. Rather, investors need only be concerned about whether the pertinent authorities will impose exchange controls between the date on which a foreign investment is made and the date of expected repatriation. Exchange controls are intended to impede or restrict foreign exchange transactions and block the transfer of funds across borders through legal sanctions. As a result of the imposition of exchange controls, many an investor has been stuck with foreign assets denominated in foreign currency that cannot be repatriated. Changes in tax legislation and the restrictive regulation of internal financial transactions are still further sources of uncertainty related to political events.

Political risks arising from the possibility of expropriation, asset freeze, exchange controls, and other forms of government intervention and regulation cannot generally be eliminated in a world of sovereign countries, since each reserves the right to engage in any of these activities. The extent to which firms are actually subject to these risks, however, varies widely from one country to another. Consequently, varying degrees of risk are associated with different political jurisdictions. It is clearly not a matter of indifference whether our assets are located in the United States, Switzerland, Britain, or Italy.

How can investors protect themselves against political risk? The most obvious response is to diversify by investing in many countries and to avoid investing in those countries that pose a serious threat or uncertainty to financial transactions. Indeed, it is a crucial prerequisite for the development of any financial center not to impose undue restrictions on its guest investors and to prevent fears of restrictive government regulations or of major impediments to financial transactions. Multinational corporations hedge against political risk by purchasing political risk insurance. They spend hundreds of millions of dollars annually in political risk premiums, usually paid to government insurance plans like the U.S. government Overseas Private Investment Corporation (OPIC), which offers insurance against currency inconvertibility, expropriations, wars, and other adverse insurable events. Still, some residual political risk is unavoidable, and the best the investor can hope for is to acquire or purchase the best information and data available regarding the political climate and potential risks of alternative locations or jurisdictions. Indeed, a whole array of political risk-assessment firms has arisen to provide such services to investors.

The implications of political risk for the analysis of international money market equilibrium are clear. Since political risks vary across political jurisdictions, assets such as CDs issued by New York and London banks are not strictly comparable. Similarly, U.S. and U.K. Treasury bills are not strictly comparable, since they are, again, issued in financial centers that differ in political risk. This means that the traditional covered interest parity comparison involving dollar assets and foreign currency-denominated assets is not strictly valid. Covered interest rate differentials in favor of some asset may just imply that the asset carries political risk and bears a compensatory premium to attract investors.

In the face of political risks, how can one devise a valid test of the covered interest parity condition? The trick consists in comparing assets issued in the same political jurisdiction but which are denominated in different currencies.[9] This test permits a comparison of assets similar in terms of political risk but differing in terms of currency of denomination. The available evidence based on this comparison indicates that political risk can account for most of the observed gaps between the forward premium and interest differentials remaining after taking into account transaction costs, and so forth. If one compares dollar-denominated deposits and sterling-denominated deposits in a given financial center, say, Paris, one finds that the discrepancies between forward premia and interest rate differentials are much smaller than when U.S. dollar-denominated and U.K. sterling-denominated deposits are compared. The minor discrepancies from covered interest parity remaining can then be accounted for by transaction costs.[10] These results suggest that political risks are a crucial factor in international money markets and are indispensable to a correct analysis of international investments.

Summarizing, the available data indicate that once we adjust for political risk and account for transaction costs, the covered interest rate parity condition does tend to hold approximately. There is thus evidence that the covered parity condition is a key equilibrium relationship in international money markets. As such, it will be basic to our analysis in the rest of this book. We should also stress two obvious, but easily forgotten, points. First, there are substantial observed deviations from covered interest parity when no adjustment is made for transaction costs and political risks. Second, the above analysis is concerned only with widely traded international money market instruments. Because of the latter qualification, it should be clear that international return equalization does not apply to sheltered or nontraded assets, that is, to assets that are domestic in nature and not significantly traded internationally, such as housing equity.[11] Our analysis does not imply that the rate of return on all local assets are linked to foreign rates of return in a rigid manner, but only that there is a tendency for internationally traded assets to conform to the covered parity condition once the latter is adjusted for transaction costs and political risk.

---

[9] The importance of political risk can also be examined by comparing the returns offered by assets denominated in the same currency but located in different financial centers, such as the interest rates on dollar-denominated CDs offered in New York, London, and Paris. A full discussion of such comparisons is presented in Chapter 3, on the Eurodollar market.

[10] See Robert Z. Aliber, "The Interest Rate Parity Theorem: A Reinterpretation," *Journal of Political Economy* (November/December 1973); and Frank McCormick, "Covered Interest Arbitrage: Unexploited Profits? Comment," *Journal of Political Economy* (April 1979).

[11] As a matter of fact, claims on houses, such as mortgages and equity ownership, are traded internationally, since foreigners participate in the mortgage market and buy domestic houses. Nevertheless, these assets, and particularly housing equity ownership, lack the liquidity and the low information costs of the assets heavily traded in international money markets.

2–6 INTEREST RATES, EXCHANGE RATE EXPECTATIONS, AND UNCOVERED INTEREST PARITY

Up to this point, we have focused on an analysis of covered international investments, allowing us to show in full view the connection between forward exchange premia and interest rate differentials. We shall now examine uncovered international investments. Since uncovered investments involve taking open positions in foreign currencies, they are subject to—exposed to—the possible effects of exchange rate movements on their returns. Such exposure to foreign exchange rate movements must be clearly understood, as apparently profitable foreign investments may actually not be so if the effects of exchange rate changes are taken into account. A depreciation of the currency in which assets are denominated, for example, can completely offset any advantageous yields they might offer.

The basic nature and dangers of widespread exposure to foreign exchange rate changes were made crystal clear to international money markets when, between June and October 1974, two major multinational banks, the Franklin National Bank of New York and Bankhaus I.D. Herstatt of Germany, went under due to losses suffered from their open positions in foreign currencies. Franklin National, at that time the twenty-third largest bank in the United States, had an outstanding foreign exchange exposure of nearly $2 billion. Herstatt's was equal to $200 million. This massive exposure, combined with unanticipated exchange rate fluctuations, resulted in massive foreign exchange losses and subsequent bank failure. Less drastic and more frequent examples of exchange-related losses can be found in the day-to-day operations of participants in international money markets, whether bank traders, corporate executives, or individual investors. It should be clear, however, that, just as there are major losers from foreign exchange exposure, there are also those who have profited substantially. It has been estimated that between 1967 and 1983, foreign exchange market speculators have made more than $20 billion in net profits.[12]

The analysis of uncovered investments can best be introduced by abstracting initially from risk considerations. One might thus pretend that the investors under consideration are risk-neutral in the sense that they have neither an aversion nor any preference toward risk taking and therefore base their investment decisions on factors other than risk. We shall return to examine the questions of exchange risk and the plight of the risk-averse investor later on in this chapter.

Suppose that a U.S. investor is considering whether to engage in uncovered foreign investments or to invest in comparable (i.e., same maturity) domestic

---

[12] Commercial banks and corporations usually do not admit publicly that they engage in foreign exchange market speculation. Because of that, speculation is often referred to as being undertaken by the Gnomes of Zurich. See Robert Z. Aliber, *The International Money Game* (New York: Basic Books, Inc., 1983), Chapter 4.

assets. The return on domestic assets is given by the domestic interest rate, *i*.
On the other hand, the return that the investor can anticipate to obtain from
foreign assets is composed of two parts: the foreign rate, *i**, and the expected
rate of foreign currency appreciation—which corresponds to the rate of domestic
currency depreciation, *x*. To visualize this, consider the following example involving dollar and pound-denominated assets. Suppose that the spot exchange
rate between the dollar and the pound is given by *e* = \$2.0/£. If the 1-year
interest rate in the United Kingdom is 5% and you invest \$200.00 (£100) in
a pound-denominated asset, at the end of 1 year you would then receive £105
(100 of principal plus 5 interest). In order to compare this return with what
could be earned on a U.S. asset, however, you have to convert the pounds
into U.S. dollars. If you expect the exchange rate to remain unchanged at its
current spot level of *e* = \$2.0/£, the pound proceeds would be converted into
\$210.00 (£105 multiplied by \$2.0/£). There would then be a 5% return on
the U.K. investment. But suppose instead that a variety of information sources
have pointed to a depreciation of the dollar against the pound by 3% over
the next year. This suggests that the exchange rate at which you can expect
to convert pounds back to dollars in 1 year is *e* = \$2.06/£. As a result, the
dollar proceeds from the U.K. investment would be \$216.30 (2.06 × 105). This
corresponds to about an 8% increase above the original investment of \$200.00
and represents the sum of the 5% interest gain plus the 3% anticipated foreign
exchange gain connected to the expected depreciation of the dollar. The implication is that the return on uncovered foreign assets involves the sum of the
nominal interest rate abroad, *i**, plus the anticipated depreciation of the domestic
currency, *x*.

   As long as the rate of return on domestic investments exceeds the expected
rate of return on foreign assets—risk considerations aside—the investor will
shift funds toward domestic assets. Similarly, whenever expected foreign returns
exceed domestic returns, funds will be shifted abroad. Incentives for the movement of funds across borders are then absent only when domestic and foreign
assets have equal expected returns. In other words, equilibrium in international
financial markets suggests that differences in the expected returns obtainable
from domestic currency-denominated investments and similar foreign currency-
denominated investments will be arbitraged away and therefore cannot be sustained in any systematic way. Equality of rates of return then implies

$$i = i^* + x \qquad (6)$$

where *i* and *i** represent domestic and foreign interest rates on comparable
assets, and *x* is the anticipated rate of depreciation of the domestic currency.[13]

---

[13] Equation (6) involves a small approximation. To visualize this, consider the following example
involving 1-year investments. For each dollar invested in domestic assets, the return after 1 year
would be given by $(1 + i)$, where *i* is the domestic rate of interest (annual). The return on foreign
investment, on the other hand is $(1 + i^*)\bar{e}/e$ per dollar invested. The latter is determined by the

Equation (1) is called the *uncovered interest parity condition*. It can be transformed into

$$i - i^* = x \qquad (6a)$$

indicating that interest rate differentials among comparable assets denominated in different currencies represent anticipated exchange rate movements. Assets denominated in currencies that are expected to depreciate will have higher interest rates in order to compensate for the expected (currency) loss associated with the anticipated currency depreciation. If, for example, the foreign interest rate, i^*, is equal to 5% and there is an expected depreciation of the domestic currency, x, of 3%, then equation (6a) implies that the domestic interest rate, i, would have to equal 8%. There would thus be an interest differential in favor of domestic assets to compensate asset holders for their anticipated foreign exchange loss associated with the expected domestic currency depreciation.

2–7 PITFALLS IN THE TESTING OF UNCOVERED INTEREST PARITY

The discussion in Section 2–6 suggests that interest rate differentials are associated with anticipated exchange rate movements. What is the evidence on this matter? Are interest rate differentials between domestic and foreign assets equal to anticipated rates of depreciation of the domestic currency? In order to answer these questions, one must first find a measure of what the anticipated exchange rate changes in the money market are at any given moment in time—a very difficult task.

As a starting point, one could hypothesize that people have perfect foresight and can correspondingly accurately predict exchange rate movements. In this case, anticipated exchange rate changes would be measured by the actual ex-

---

fact that each dollar will yield $1/e$ units of foreign currency which, when invested abroad for 1 year, provide a return of $(1 + i^*)/e$ in foreign currency. When it is exchanged back into dollars, the expected dollar return from the foreign investment would be given by $(1 + i^*)\bar{e}/e$, where $\bar{e}$ is the exchange rate (in dollars per unit of foreign currency), which is anticipated to prevail 1 year in the future. In equilibrium, the expected return abroad must equal the domestic rate of return, or $(1 + i) = (1 + i^*)\bar{e}/e$, which implies that $i = i^* + x + i^*x$, where $x \equiv (\bar{e} - e)/e$ is the anticipated rate of change of the domestic currency during the next year.

The derivation of this last formula is similar to that in footnote 2 above. Observe that equation (6) is an approximation, since it neglects the term i^*x. This last term represents the anticipated foreign exchange gain or loss on the interest received from investing abroad and, since it is usually the product of two small fractions, it yields a very small number. Its insignificance was seen in the U.S.–U.K. investment example wherein the approximation involved in equation (6) meant that the $216.30 return on the $200 invested abroad was not exactly an 8% rate of return (the sum of the foreign interest rate, i^*, and the forward premium x). The clearly minor difference is accounted for by the term under discussion. As a matter of fact, for a sufficiently small investment period, the term becomes negligible and can be ignored.

change rate movements that occur over time. The uncovered interest parity condition could then be tested by examining how closely interest rate differentials and actual exchange rate changes move together. An interest rate differential in favor of domestic assets would be associated with domestic currency depreciation while a differential in favor of foreign assets would be linked to domestic currency appreciation. Figure 2–4 shows this experiment for the case of U.S.–U.K. Treasury bills and U.S. dollar–pound sterling exchange rate changes. As observed, interest rate differentials fail to predict actual exchange rate changes accurately. During 1978 and 1979, for instance, the U.S. dollar generally depreciated in value relative to the pound. Still, over these 2 years, U.S. interest rates, i, generally remained below U.K. interest rates, i^*. According to the uncovered interest parity condition, an interest differential favoring the United Kingdom would be linked to an anticipated dollar appreciation. Similar results can also be found in other time periods and for other countries. What explains these prediction errors?

One basic reason for the failure of interest rate differentials to predict actual exchange rate changes lies in that people simply cannot be expected to have perfect foresight. A substantial part of exchange rate movements are completely unanticipated, hence unpredictable. This unpredictability arises from the fact that exchange rates respond to changes in a variety of economic variables that cannot be perfectly anticipated in advance. Loosely speaking, and as was noted in Chapter 1, in a floating exchange rate regime the exchange rate will adjust to changes in the demand and supply of domestic and foreign currency associated with international trade in goods, services, and assets. Factors that affect these transactions, such as changes in the relative foreign and domestic asset supplies, income growth, and fluctuations in inflation, will all influence the exchange rate. Since it is generally impossible to forecast accurately how these factors change over time (try forecasting what the inflation rate will be next year and then compare with the actual outcome!), there will clearly be a substantial degree of uncertainty as to the behavior of future exchange rates. Actual exchange rate changes thus consist of a systematic component, which is predictable, and a random component, which is unpredictable. Symbolically, this idea can be expressed as

$$\hat{e} = x + \hat{e}_u \qquad (7)$$

where $\hat{e}$ represents actual (proportional) exchange rate changes, x is anticipated currency depreciations, and $\hat{e}_u$ is unanticipated exchange rate movements, all expressed in proportional terms.

In this situation, it is apparent that even if interest differentials do coincide with anticipated currency depreciations—as given by uncovered interest parity—they will not necessarily be closely associated with actual currency depreciations. Substitution of the anticipated rate of depreciation of domestic currency, x, from equation (6a) into equation (7) yields

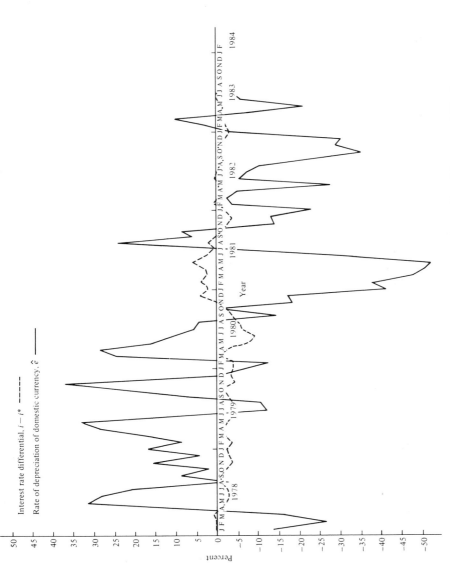

FIGURE 2-4. Do Interest Rate Differentials Forecast Actual Exchange Rate Movements? The interest rates i and i^* are the 3-month U.S. and U.K. Treasury bill rates, respectively; the rate of domestic currency depreciation is the actual rate of depreciation of the dollar vis-à-vis the pound over the 3-month period corresponding to that of the Treasury bills considered. All variables have been annualized and expressed in percentage form.

$$\hat{e} = (i - i^*) + \hat{e}_u \tag{8}$$

which clearly shows how actual exchange rate changes, $\hat{e}$, and interest differentials, $i - i^*$, diverge by the presence of unanticipated exchange rate movements, $\hat{e}_u$, even if uncovered parity holds. In conclusion, in order to test adequately whether uncovered interest parity holds, one must be able to measure anticipated exchange rate changes. The use of actual exchange rate changes as a measure of anticipated currency value changes is incorrect, since there is a substantial degree of uncertainty in future exchange rate movements and participants in money markets can thus not be expected to be endowed with perfect foresight. We are then back to the problem of measuring anticipated exchange rate movements.

2–8   ANTICIPATED EXCHANGE RATE CHANGES, THE FORWARD MARKET, AND EXCHANGE RISK PREMIA

An often-used measure of the anticipated rate of depreciation of domestic currency over a certain time period in the future is the corresponding forward premium. The implication is that, if the forward premium accurately represents the expected rate of change of the domestic currency, uncovered interest parity reduces to the covered interest parity condition. As we saw in previous sections, once one adjusts for transaction costs and political risk, the covered parity condition does tend to hold approximately, suggesting that the uncovered parity condition would hold as well. This inference is highly misleading. The forward premium does not generally present an accurate picture of the anticipated rate of change of the domestic currency, since it also reflects the existence of a risk premium, which we have so far ignored in this discussion.

The existence of an exchange risk premium (or discount) deeply influences forward market equilibrium and thus the determination of the forward premium. Because they bear different risks, there will generally be a discrepancy between the return on uncovered foreign investments, $i^* + x$, and the return from covered foreign investments, $i^* + f$. If the uncovered investments increase (reduce) portfolio risks, the expected returns on the uncovered foreign investments will have to be higher (lower) than returns from covered investments by the amount of the risk premium (discount), to compensate risk-averse investors for increased (reduced) risk taking. But the interest gains from holding foreign assets, i^*, are the same for both covered and uncovered investments. As a consequence, the difference in expected returns between the two will arise from a divergence between the expected exchange gains (losses) of the two strategies. The expected exchange gain from holding foreign assets uncovered is the anticipated rate of depreciation of the domestic currency, x, and the exchange gain from holding foreign assets covered is the forward premium, f. The implication is that financial market equilibrium will occur at a point where the anticipated rate of depreciation, x, exceeds (or is exceeded by) the forward premium, f, by the amount of the risk premium (discount). Symbolically, this relation is represented by

$$x = f + R \tag{9}$$

where R represents the risk premium or discount attached to the acquisition of foreign assets in the absence of covering. This foreign exchange risk premium is positive if foreign investments increase investor portfolio risk. In that case, the expected exchange gain from uncovered foreign investments, x, must exceed the exchange gain from covered investments, f, by the risk premium R so as to compensate (risk-averse) investors for their increased risk taking. A negative value of R, on the other hand, suggests that uncovered foreign investments reduce the investors' portfolio risk. As a result, the exchange gain from covered investments, f, will be larger than the anticipated exchange gain from uncovered foreign investments, x, by the risk discount. Finally, if the foreign investments do not add or substract from investor portfolio risk, the exchange risk premium, R, will be zero and the forward premium will equal the anticipated rate of depreciation of the domestic currency.

The presence of a foreign exchange risk premium or discount means that forward premia and anticipated rates of depreciation will not be equal and, as a result, the first cannot be used as a proxy for the second. The validity of covered interest parity thus cannot be used to infer the validity of uncovered interest parity. The problem in comparing the two is easily visualized by substituting equation (9) into the covered parity condition, which results in

$$i - i^* = f = x - R \tag{10}$$

Equation (10) implies that uncovered interest parity, $i - i^* = x$, is not a general condition in a risky world; that is, deviations from uncovered parity may be associated with the existence of a risk premium or discount.

The problem is then reduced to finding whether a risk premium or discount does exist. The nature of foreign exchange risk premia is a subject of much current research but the available empirical evidence has not yielded consistent results uncovering exchange risk premia.[14] It is apparent that the foreign exchange risk premium is closely associated with the relative riskiness of assets denominated in different currencies. Because the relative riskiness of assets and their associated risk premia change over time, however, a currency bearing a risk premium this year might be at a discount in 2 years, making the estimation

[14] See Jeffrey Frankel's "A Test of Perfect Substitutability in the Foreign Exchange Market," *Southern Economic Journal* (October 1982), and his "In Search of the Exchange Risk Premium: A Six-Currency Test Assuming Mean-Variance Optimization," *Journal of International Money and Finance* (December 1982).

of risk premia extremely difficult. Furthermore, specifying the determinants of risk premia is a highly complex economic problem, making it difficult to specify adequate proxies that could be used in empirical work.[15]

2–9 SUMMARY

1. International money markets are the markets in which short-term claims are traded among countries.

2. Investing in foreign vis à vis domestic assets brings forth the issue of exchange risk, that is, the risk involved in the chance that the value of the currency in which assets are denominated will fluctuate unpredictably. Investors can insure against such fluctuations by covering in the forward market.

3. The returns on covered foreign investments have two components: the nominal interest rate on the foreign assets purchased, i^*, and the gain (or loss) from purchasing foreign currency spot and selling it forward, which corresponds to the forward premium (or discount) on the foreign currency, f, and is referred to as exchange gain (or loss).

4. Since covering foreign investments results in possible exchange gains (or losses) aside from interest gains, when determining whether to invest in covered investments abroad or in domestic investments—with the same risk attached to each—one must choose that investment strategy with the highest return, which does not necessarily imply the one with the highest interest rate.

5. The difference between the return on covered foreign investments and the return on domestic investments is called a covered interest differential, CD. If the nominal interest return on domestic assets is i, then $CD = i^* + f - i$. A positive (or negative) value of CD is referred to as a covered differential in favor of (or against) the foreign country and suggests there are incentives to invest abroad (or domestically) relative to domestically (or abroad).

6. Equilibrium in international money markets will occur when covered differentials are equal to zero, representing the absence of unexploited profit opportunities in the movement of funds across borders. This implies that the forward premium on a foreign currency must be equal to the interest rate differential between domestic assets and the assets denominated in the foreign currency, that is, if $CD = 0$, then $f = i - i^*$. This is called the covered interest parity condition.

7. Significant deviations from the covered interest parity condition can be observed. Such factors as transaction costs, costs of gathering and processing information, government intervention and regulation, and financial constraints

---

[15] See R. J. Hodrick, "International Asset Pricing with Time-Varying Risk Premium," *Journal of International Economics* (November 1981), and L. P. Hansen and R. J. Hodrick, "Forward Exchange Rates as Optimal Predictors of Future Spot Rates: An Econometric Analysis," *Journal of Political Economy* (October 1980). For an analysis of the determinants of the risk premium, see Chapter 15.

and capital market imperfections all explain some of these deviations but not nearly all.

8. Noncomparability of assets, especially political risk differentials, is a significant factor generating measured deviations from covered parity. Political risks arise from the exercise of political sovereignty by the government of a given country and might involve the possibility of asset expropriations or freezes and the unexpected imposition of exchange controls and other government regulations. An observed covered interest rate differential in favor of some asset might just imply that the asset carries political risk and bears a compensatory premium to attract investors.

9. In the absence of extensive government regulation, covered interest parity condition tends to hold approximately, once one adjusts for political risk and transaction costs.

10. The uncovered interest rate parity condition states the equality of international interest rate differentials between domestic and foreign assets and the expected rate of depreciation of domestic currency. The presence of an exchange risk premium invalidates the uncovered interest parity as a general condition of international money markets.

PROBLEMS

1. Suppose that the U.S. dollar–pound sterling exchange rate equals $1.60, while the 1-year forward rate is $1.64 per pound. The yields on 1-year U.S. and U.K. Treasury bills are 9% and 8%, respectively. Calculate the covered interest differential, using the exact formula and the approximation represented by equation (4). What is the difference between the two calculations? On the basis of these results, which country would you expect to face capital outflows? Capital inflows?

2. Using the data provided in Problem 1, suppose that an American investor is considering covered investments in U.K. Treasury bills that can be financed by borrowing at the U.S. prime rate of 10%. Would she be able to obtain net profits from her covered operations? Suppose that in addition to the borrowing costs, this investor also faces transaction costs that further reduce the gains from investing abroad by 0.75%. Would there now be net gains or losses from engaging in covered interest arbitrage? Explain. Use approximations in this exercise, if you wish).

3. Consider the case of a British investor holding pounds initially and evaluating whether to invest in U.K. Treasury bills or in covered U.S. Treasury bills. Using the definitions presented in the text discussion, that is, F is the forward exchange rate of the sterling in dollars, e is the spot exchange rate in dollars per pound, i is the U.S. interest rate, and i^* is the U.K. interest rate, determine the U.K. returns and the covered U.S. returns per pound invested by the Englishman. Show that, if U.S. and U.K. returns are equal, you would obtain the same expression as the covered interest parity condition derived in the text.

4. Consider a U.S. firm deciding whether to invest pounds locally or to undertake covered investments in Canada. Suppose that the Canadian dollar is worth $0.80, the 1-year forward exchange rate is $0.84, and the U.S. and Canadian annual interest rates are 14% and 7%, respectively. The applicable tax rate on the corporation's income is 50%, while that on the firm's capital gains is 25%. Compute the post-tax returns on local (U.S.) investments (per U.S. dollar invested). Compute the post-tax returns on covered Canadian investments (per U.S. dollar invested). Which alternative investment yields the highest post-tax return? Would there be any difference if the investments being considered are 30-day rather than yearly investments? (Hint: Check whether there are any differences in the tax rates applicable to short-term and long-term capital gains.)

5. You are told that the annual interest rate of U.S. Treasury bills is 12%, while that of Canadian Treasury bills is 6%. The U.S.–Canadian dollar exchange rate at the time is equal to 0.80 U.S. dollars per Canadian dollar. Assuming that the uncovered interest parity condition holds, what do you think is the market's assessment of the U.S.–Canadian dollar exchange rate 1 year in the future? Do you see any problems with this calculation? Explain.

CHAPTER 3

Eurocurrencies and Euromarkets: External Financial Markets

Chapter 2 dealt with international money markets involving assets denominated in different currencies. This chapter focuses instead on international money markets involving assets denominated in the same currency but issued in different political jurisdictions. We move on, so to speak, from an examination of the markets for dollar and sterling certificates of deposit (CDs) to an exploration of the linkages between the New York and London markets for dollar CDs.

Our present interest in alternative locations extends the scope of the analysis in a major way, since it incorporates an important development in financial markets during the sixties and seventies—the remarkable growth of the Eurodollar market. Eurodollars are dollar deposits held outside the United States (offshore), such as dollar deposits in London, Zurich, or Paris. The development of a large and active market for offshore dollar deposits has added a new dimension to international financial management. A multinational corporation holding investable dollar funds can now place them in New York, London, or elsewhere. This means that financial executives are required to undertake decisions regarding both the currency of denomination and the location of assets.

The Eurodollar market is not circumscribed to Eurodollar deposits. A large market in dollar-denominated loans made by banks outside the United States is easily accessible to corporations and governments. This Eurodollar loan market provides a source of dollar funds alternative to the domestic U.S. financial market and has assumed a particularly significant role in meeting the financial needs of the public sector in many developing countries. This chapter examines the reasons for the development of the Eurodollar market, its main institutional and economic aspects, and its practical implications for both investors and borrowers. Our discussion goes beyond the Eurodollar market in that it also covers the Euromark, Eurosterling, and other so-called Eurocurrency markets.

79

3-1 EUROCURRENCIES, EURODOLLARS, AND MONEY

A Eurocurrency deposit is a deposit denominated in a currency that is different from the currency of the financial center in which the deposit is held. Deutsche mark deposits in London banks or in Luxembourg are Eurocurrencies, as are sterling deposits in Paris. One must be aware, however, that the term Eurocurrency is misleading, since what is usually referred to as a Eurocurrency deposit may not necessarily involve deposits in Europe at all. For instance, what is traditionally called a Eurodollar is a dollar deposit held outside the United States, regardless of whether it is held in a European, Asian, or Caribbean bank. Therefore, dollar deposits in Asian financial centers such as Hong Kong and Singapore are, paradoxically, Eurodollars. The reader should not be confused by this terminology, which derives from the historical evolution of the Eurocurrency market as a primarily European one during the fifties and sixties, acquiring its present worldwide scope during the seventies. The prefix "Euro" has been retained despite its lack of accuracy. In fact, the terms *external* or *offshore deposits* are more precise, since they portray more accurately the idea of dollar deposits located outside the United States, sterling deposits outside Britain, and so on. By the same token, Eurocurrency loans refer to external (offshore) loans in general and are not necessarily obtained from European banks.

The Eurodeposit market is composed essentially of time deposits, with maturities varying from 1 week or less (overnight deposits are common) to about 3 years. Similarly, Euroloans extend over the short-term and medium-term maturity range. The vast majority of both Eurodeposits and loans, however, are concentrated in the short end of the maturity spectrum, with most maturities being shorter than 6 months. The Eurocurrency market should thus be envisioned as forming part of the international money market. As such, the London dollar market interacts and competes with the U.S. dollar money market as well as with the U.K. pound sterling money market and the German and Swiss money markets.

Should we then consider Eurocurrencies to be money? That is, should Eurodollars be counted as part of the U.S. money supply? The answer to this controversial question hinges on how broad a concept of money we wish to adopt. Inasmuch as the offshore system offers only short-term time deposits (in large part CDs), it is basically a market in near-monies, that is, it deals mainly with short-term liquid instruments very similar to money but not usually included in a narrow definition or concept of money. Eurodollar deposits rarely consist of demand deposits (checking accounts) and therefore would be excluded from a narrow definition of money consisting of currency and checkable deposits. We should point out that the distinction is somewhat arbitrary; in fact, Eurodollars should be included in broad concepts of the U.S. money supply. Actually, the Federal Reserve Board of the United States, in its recent definitions of money, has included overnight Eurodollars as forming part of what it has called *M2*. What should be stressed is thus that what distinguishes the Eurodeposit money market from domestic money markets is not so much the type of financial instruments traded but the fact that they are externally traded.

3–2   AN INTRODUCTION TO EXTERNAL FINANCIAL MARKETS

Commercial banks constitute the core of the Eurocurrency market. Accordingly, in examining the banking system of the United States or any other economy having a Eurocurrency, it becomes critical to make a distinction between the *domestic* and *external* banking systems. The U.S. banking system is an extensive network including thousands of banks operating all over the country. It embraces all dollar deposits accepted and loans made by domestic banks and by domestic branches or subsidiaries of foreign banks operating in the United States.[1] The dollar external banking system, on the other hand, consists of dollar deposits held in—and loans obtained from—the whole array of foreign banks and foreign branches and subsidiaries of U.S. banks that participate in the Eurodollar market. These banks accept Eurodollar deposits, which they then lend to borrowers such as large multinational corporations or governments in developing countries. The dollar external banking system is dominated by the activities of foreign branches and subsidiaries of major U.S. banks (e.g., Bank of America, Chase, and Citibank) whose tentacles extend worldwide. These are joined by the major British, German, and Swiss banks, among many other so-called *Eurobanks,* that issue external dollar deposits and make external dollar loans. These banking activities effectively create a banking system that operates outside the boundaries of the domestic banking system, that is, an external banking system.

One of the key points to remember about Eurobanks, however, is that they are not special or independent banks specializing in the issuance of external deposits and loans, but are rather a part (branches, subsidiaries) of major national banks that have, as only one of their many activities, the issuance of external deposits and loans. For instance, Eurobanking is just one activity among many others for an American bank office in London. Since the bank might be issuing deposits and loans in pounds sterling, this also suggests that banks are frequently simultaneously a part of the British domestic banking system and of the U.S. external (Eurodollar) banking system.

Eurobanking operations are concentrated in a limited number of financial centers that attract external transactions in various Eurocurrencies. The most

---

[1] The distinction between a branch and a subsidiary is a legal one. A U.S. subsidiary of a foreign company is incorporated in the United States and has a legal identity apart from that of the parent company. A U.S. branch of a foreign company is not incorporated in the United States and is considered to be an extension of the parent company. A similar distinction applies to foreign branches and subsidiaries of U.S. firms. The U.S. branches and subsidiaries of foreign-owned banks account for approximately 15% of U.S. banking assets and have a visible presence in major U.S. cities, as a walk through New York's or Chicago's financial districts will quickly reveal. A wide range of nationalities are represented in U.S. banks, including Israel's Bank Leumi, Japan's Mitsubishi Bank, the United Kingdom's Barclays, and many others.

active Eurocurrency center is located in London. The City of London, featuring a rich international banking tradition and enjoying a supportive regulatory environment, has attracted banks from many nationalities engaged mostly in Eurodollar transactions but also transacting in the main Eurocurrencies and in sterling (which is obviously not an external currency in London). Although the London market remains the center of the Eurocurrency market, its traditional historical predominance has been declining in relative terms as a consequence of the rapid deployment of alternative centers. For example, the North American Eurocurrency Market, which includes Euromarket dealings channeled mainly through the Bahamas and Cayman Islands, has been closing in on London's activity; by some measures, in fact, its size may be more than two-thirds that of London. An Asian dollar market centered in Singapore and Hong Kong has also grown rapidly, operating mainly as a regional market servicing the Far East. Other major financial centers with significant Eurocurrency dealings are located in Switzerland, Luxembourg, Panama, and Bahrain. Note that New York (or Chicago, or any other U.S. financial center) is not mentioned in the list. This is because U.S. monetary authorities use various means to discourage the issuance in the United States of deposits denominated in currencies other than the dollar. Their amount is therefore insignificant.

Who uses the Eurocurrency market? Eurobanking activities are a segment of the wholesale international money market. The vast majority of Eurocurrency transactions fall in the above $1 million value range, frequently reaching the hundreds of millions (or even billion) dollar value. Accordingly, the customers of Eurobanks are almost exclusively large organizations,[2] including non-Eurobank institutions—such as multinational corporations, governments, and international organizations—as well as Eurobanks themselves. Multinational corporations form a large and active part of the Eurodeposit market, as they search for the highest rate of return and move liquid funds around to maximize interest receipts. Actually, hundreds of millions of dollars in corporate funds lie deposited at Eurobanks, in the form of certificates of deposit. As borrowers, large multinational corporations—by virtue of their size and credit reputation—can obtain access to external credit with a minimum of documentation or investigation by the banks, and at quite attractive prime rates.[3]

The competitive interest rates offered by Eurodeposits, on the other hand, have also attracted government funds. Central Banks, in particular, maintain a substantial share of their countries' international reserves in the form of high-yielding Eurodeposit holdings. Government borrowing in the Euroloan market is also substantial, arising mostly from the dramatic rise of Eurobank loans to developing countries during the seventies, a subject to which we shall return later on in this chapter. International institutions, like the World Bank, also

---

[2] The Eurocurrency market is, however, easily accessible to affluent individuals and to small firms.

[3] The prime rate is the interest rate charged by banks for short-term loans to corporations and other creditors with high financial standing.

borrow in the Eurocurrency market and lend the proceeds to developing countries. Finally, a substantial share of Eurobanking activities are in fact interbank activities in which banks trade among themselves by mutual lending and borrowing.

The interbank market constitutes a major part of Eurobanking activities. In fact, most transactions in the London market are wholesale interbank transactions. By means of the interbank lending market, a Eurobank holding surplus funds, and with no commercial customers immediately available, can lend its excess reserves to other Eurobanks with clients (borrowers) available but no loanable funds at the moment. The interest rates charged by Eurobanks lending through the interbank market are referred to as *interbank offered rates*. The widely publicized London interbank offered rate (LIBOR) is an average of interbank-offered rates often used as a basis for setting non-Eurobank customer lending rates. The latter are usually above the LIBOR, and the margin between the two is referred to as the Eurolending *spread*. The size of the spread is dependent on the credit-worthiness of the borrowers and might vary over time.

The symbiotic relationship between Eurobanks implied by interbank lending gives rise to a question of interpretation regarding the size of the Eurocurrency market. The interbank network generates Eurodeposits when banks enjoying surplus funds deposit them with another Eurobank. Interbank depositing constitutes a transfer of funds from one bank to another within the same network and does not increase the capacity of the Eurobanking system to lend to commercial customers. What the interbank market does is to allow Eurobanks to achieve a more efficient use of existing funds by making them immediately available where they are needed the most.

Since the size of the Eurocurrency market is frequently measured by including all Eurodeposits—both non-Eurobank and interbank deposits—one must distinguish this measure, referred to as a *gross* measure of the Eurocurrency market, from the so-called *net* measure, which excludes interbank deposits. What measure—net or gross—one uses depends on the purpose for which the size calculations are carried out. The interbank market is a very active and important part of Euromarket trading and, if a measure of the overall activity of the Eurocurrency market is desired, the gross measure is more appropriate. A net measure, on the other hand, is more useful if one is measuring the capacity of Eurobanks as a whole to create deposits and credit vis à vis the nonbank public. This distinction should be kept in mind when assessing figures provided on the size of the Eurocurrency market, such as those presented in Section 3–3.

3–3 HOW EUROCURRENCY DEPOSITS ARE CREATED

The growth of Eurocurrency deposits ever since the early sixties has been simply astonishing. This explosion is clearly visualized from the figures in Table 3–1, which shows both the gross and net measures of the size of the Eurocurrency market. Whereas in 1961, for example, gross Eurocurrency deposits totaled about $1 billion, by the end of 1983 they were more than $2000 billion. This growth has been associated with an increased importance of international financial activity. The external deposits of the major currencies now compose a substantial part of total deposits, as is evident from the data in Table 3–2. Note that Eurodollar deposits still represent most of the Eurocurrency market, with as much as 75% of gross liabilities in Eurocurrencies. Other Eurocurrency deposits, however, grew substantially during the seventies as is reflected in Table 3–2.

The basic reasons for the growth of external deposits will be examined in Section 3–4. At this point, we shall try to answer the more elementary question of how Eurocurrency deposits are actually created. Consider the example of an American firm called Acme, which decides to transfer $1 million out of the account it holds at Goodbuck Bank (in the United States) to a Eurodollar account at Barclays of London.

The first step in the process occurs when Acme draws a $1-million check on its account at Goodbuck payable to Barclays. Barclays then deposits the $1 million received from Acme in its own account at Goodbuck (assuming, for the sake of this example, that Barclays holds some deposits at Goodbuck, which means Goodbuck is a *correspondent bank* to Barclays). The following changes occur in terms of the participants in the transaction, Acme and the two banks, where traditional T accounts have been used to show the changes in the financial statements of each participant:

Acme

Change in Assets		Change in Liabilities
(in millions of dollars)		
Deposits		
Goodbuck (New York)	−1	
Barclays (London)	+1	

Barclays (London)

Change in Assets		Change in Liabilities	
(in millions of dollars)			
Reserves		*Deposits*	
Goodbuck (New York)	+1	Acme	+1

TABLE 3–1. Growth in the Size of Eurocurrency Market (billions of dollars)

Estimated Size	1974	1975	1976	1977	1978	1979	1980	1981	1982	1983 June	1983 December
Gross	395	485	595	740	950	1235	1525	1860	2060	2055	2153
Net	220	255	320	390	495	590	730	890	960	970	n.a.

Source: Morgan Guaranty Trust Company, *World Financial Markets*, December 1983, June 1984. Based on foreign currency liabilities and claims of banks in major European countries, the Bahamas, Bahrain, Cayman Islands, Netherlands Antilles, Panama, Canada, Japan, Hong Kong, Singapore. Reprinted by permission. n.a.: Not available.

TABLE 3–2. External and Domestic Deposits in Dollars and Other Currencies[a]

Currency	Billions of U.S. Dollars					Average Annual Compounded Growth, Percent		
	1965	1970	1975	1980	1981	1965–1970	1970–1975	1976–1981
Dollars								
External	11.4	58.7	189.5	548.4	631.5	38.7	26.2	22.3
Internal	282.1	410.1	704.9	1183.1	1325.5	7.7	11.4	11.5
Deutsche marks								
External	0.9	8.1	39.3	125.3	117.3	54.9	36.8	20.0
Internal	43.3	80.9	191.3	367.2	332.0	13.1	18.8	7.7
Swiss francs								
External	0.9	5.7	15.9	51.6	68.1	44.3	22.5	33.2
Internal	11.5	18.5	37.5	80.7	87.8	10.0	15.2	14.9
Pounds sterling								
External	0.7	0.9	3.1	23.8	18.3	5.2	27.8	35.2
Internal	14.6	15.1	23.4	49.6	48.5	0.7	9.2	16.8
Yen								
External	n.a.	n.a.	n.a.	11.2	16.1	—	—	56.1[b]
Internal	—	—	—	943.4	970.7	—	—	12.9[b]

Source: External bank deposits: Bank for International Settlements, *Annual Report.* Internal deposits: International Monetary Fund, *International Financial Statistics Yearbook,* 1983.   [a] n.a., Not available.   [b] 1977–1981.

Goodbuck (New York)

Change in Assets	Change in Liabilities
(in millions of dollars)	

	Deposits	
	Acme	−1
	Barclays	+1
	(London)	

The transfer of dollars by Acme out of the U.S.-based Goodbuck to the Eurobank Barclays does not decrease the dollars deposited in the U.S. banking system. All that is involved is a bookkeeping operation requiring neither an actual physical movement of dollars nor the $1 million to leave the U.S. banking system.[4] What the transfer of funds does is to give Barclays the claim, or right of ownership, over the domestic deposits previously held by Acme. Total deposits at Goodbuck are not affected; only the ownership of its deposit liabilities has changed.[5] Note, however, that U.S. deposits held by the public have decreased, as Acme shifts its funds toward the Eurodollar market. What happens to Barclays? Its total deposit liabilities are increased, that is, a Eurodollar deposit has been created. But the process does not necessarily end here. Since Barclays' dollar reserves—in the form of deposits at Goodbuck—have simultaneously increased, this means Barclays can loan out or invest part of the newly acquired funds.

Suppose, then, that Barclays lends its dollars to Bozo, Inc., a firm that makes cosmetics for clowns. Bozo then goes out and deposits its dollars at Ballantine Bank (in London). Ballantine in turn holds its reserves in the form of dollar deposits at Goodbuck (in New York). What has happened, in terms of our T accounts? The changes are as follows:

---

[4] This point has been forcefully argued by Milton Friedman in "The Eurodollar Market: Some First Principles," *Morgan Guaranty Survey,* 4–14, October 1969. That the physical transfer of dollars abroad is not required for Eurodollar deposits to be created is not often realized by investors. For example, in his book *The Money Lenders* (New York: Viking Press, 1981), A. Sampson states that he was told by a lawyer that some of his clients often demand insurance against possible losses arising in the event of a Cuban invasion of the Bahamas and the corresponding potential nationalization of assets located there. "I have to explain," the lawyer says, "that Castro wouldn't find any Eurodollars in the safe. They're all really held in New York or London" (p. 228).

[5] The reader may ask: What if Goodbuck is not a correspondent bank to Barclays? The answer is that Goodbuck's total deposits will indeed be affected; that is, they will go down by the amount of Acme's withdrawal. Nevertheless, as long as Barclays maintains its reserves in another U.S. bank, deposits in the U.S. (onshore) banking system as a whole will not be affected.

Barclays (London)

Change in Assets		Change in Liabilities
(in millions of dollars)		

Change in Assets		Change in Liabilities
Reserves Goodbuck (New York)	−1	
Loans and Investments		
Loan to Bozo	+1	

Ballantine (London)

Change in Assets		Change in Liabilities	
(in millions of dollars)			
Reserves Goodbuck (New York)	+1	*Deposits* Bozo	+1

Goodbuck (New York)

Change in Assets		Change in Liabilities	
(in millions of dollars)			
		Deposits Barclays (London)	−1
		Ballantine (London)	+1

As can be observed, the total dollar deposits in New York (at Goodbuck) have not changed, but the total Eurocurrency deposits have increased from $1 million to $2 million. This is because the deposits of Acme at Barclays are still outstanding, as are the deposits of Bozo at Ballantine. This creation of dollars outside the United States is called the *multiple* (or *multiplier*) expansion of Eurodollars because the original $1-million deposit by Acme at Barclays generates new additional deposits as Barclays concedes loans to Bozo. Note, however, that the expansion of Eurodollar deposits does not have to stop at $2 million. As seen from Ballantine's T account in the above example, this bank now has extra reserves that it could loan. As long as some of the proceeds of this loan are deposited back into Ballantine, Barclays, or any other Eurobank, the total amount of Eurodollars would again increase (up to $3 million, if Ballantine were to loan out all its reserves).

The implication is that the multiple expansion of Eurodollars could be infinite. Although it is a theoretical possibility, this outcome would be highly unlikely. The reason is that our example above is based on two unrealistic assumptions. First, we assumed that Barclays lends all its newly acquired dollar reserves ($1 million to Bozo) and that Ballantine does exactly the same. Second, it was supposed that Bozo deposited all its loan proceeds into another Eurobank (Ballantine) and that Ballantine's borrower also deposited all its loan proceeds into another Eurobank. These are unrealistic assumptions. If, for example, Barclays believes that it must have some reserves—in the form of, say, deposits at other banks—in order to meet any withdrawals from its accounts, it will lend Bozo less than $1 million. In the event that the bank believes it needs 10% of those deposits as reserves (a reserve:deposit ratio of 0.10), it will lend only $900,000 and hold $100,000 as reserves. When Bozo—or whichever firm receives the final proceeds of the loan when spent—deposits all its funds in Ballantine, total Eurodeposits would increase by $1.9 million (the sum of Acme's $1 million plus Bozo's $900,000 outstanding), which is less than $2 million. But this is not all. If Bozo is an important multinational company, it would probably deposit only a fraction of its loan in Europe. It would deposit the rest directly in the United States, in which case those dollars would leave the Eurodollar system (i.e., they would leak out of the system). If Bozo deposits 80% of its funds at some bank in New York and the rest (20%) at Ballantine (in London), Eurodollars would increase by only $1,180,000 (which is the sum of Acme's $1 million plus the 20% of Bozo's loan receipts of $900,000 redeposited in the Euromarket). In conclusion, one can expect the multiple expansion of Eurodollars—given a transfer of funds out of the United States—to decrease with increases in bank reserve:deposit ratios and with increases in the leakages out of the Eurodollar system.

What is the empirical evidence on this matter as it relates to the actual operation of Eurocurrency markets? A quantitative approach to this question must pinpoint precisely the connections between the multiplier expansion of Eurodeposits and actual reserve:deposit ratios and Eurodollar leakages. As shown in the Appendix to this chapter, the evidence indicates that a shift of deposits from the domestic to the external banking system results in a total dollar deposit increase of about 1.22 times the original shift. This number provides us with the *Eurodollar multiplier* effect of a shift in deposits from the domestic to the external banking system, meaning that any million-dollar shift of deposits from the United States to the Eurodollar market would increase total dollar deposits by $1,220,000 (this figure consists of the original dollars deposited in the Euromarket plus $220,000 of additional deposits created through the multiplier expansion mechanism). The implication is that the major component in the creation of Eurodollar deposits is the original shift in deposits from domestic to external markets and not so much the multiple expansion of these deposits once in the Eurocurrency system. The actual shifts of funds that have occurred from the United States to external banking facilities are explained in the next section.

3–4   THE ECONOMIC RATIONALE OF EUROCURRENCY MARKETS

The Eurocurrency market started out as, and is still predominantly, a Eurodollar market. The origin of the term *Eurodollar* is assigned to the Russians. During the late fifties and early sixties, a number of Soviet-bloc countries found themselves holding a large stock of dollars, a result of their trade in gold and commodities with both the United States and other European countries. At the time, however, there was a strong anti-Soviet and anti-Communist sentiment in the United States. As a result, the Soviets were afraid of investing their dollars in U.S. assets because of the possibility that they could be seized by the U.S. government. The Soviets consequently decided to deposit their funds in France in a bank whose cable and telex address was EURO-BANK. In time, the dollars deposited in that bank were referred to as Eurodollars, from which all offshore dollars later gathered their name. Whether or not this is the actual etymological explanation of the name Eurodollar, it illustrates dramatically a basic trait of Eurocurrency markets: In large part they are outside the range of national government intervention and regulation. This single fact provides a basic underlying rationale for the growth of the Eurocurrency market overall and a common thread across the large number of empirical regularities, particular financial procedures and practices, and histories of the various Eurocurrencies. Although its importance will be emphasized here within the context of the Eurodollar market, it clearly extends to other Eurocurrencies as well.

The key immediate reason for the growth of the Eurodollar market during the sixties was the ability of Eurobanks to offer higher interest rates on deposits and lower interest rates on loans than were offered by banks in the domestic system. In so doing, they were able to lure customers away—both depositors and borrowers—from domestic commercial banks. That Eurobanks were able to sustain a persistently lower loan-deposit interest rate differential was specifically the result of the presence and imposition of a variety of U.S. government regulations at the time. One of these policies was the Interest Equalization Tax (IET) introduced by the United States in July 1963. The IET taxed foreign borrowings in the United States with the intention of reducing the acquisition of dollars by foreigners; this imposition emerged from the fear of a dollar glut in the hands of foreign residents. As a result of the imposition of the IET, the foreign branches of U.S. banks started immediately to float dollar-denominated bonds, or *Eurobonds,* which could carry lower interest than that available in the suddenly more expensive New York credit market. Foreign borrowers jumped on the opportunity. The real effect of the IET and of other capital controls imposed in its aftermath—such as the voluntary credit restraints—was, consequently, that instead of the foreigners following the dollar into the United States, the dollar followed the foreigners by going abroad. The number of U.S. bank foreign branches and subsidiaries ballooned after this period. At the end of 1964, only 11 banks had established branches abroad; by the end of 1974, when the restrictions were repealed, there were close to 130 banks with a total of 737 foreign branches.

The shift of international banking toward the Eurodollar system was given a second boost by the invocation of Regulation Q by the Federal Reserve in 1966 to prevent domestic interest rates from rising. Regulation Q imposed a ceiling on how high domestic deposit rates, including interest rates on CDs, could rise. With their ability to attract deposits severely curtailed, U.S. banks proceeded to counteract the credit crunch by raising their interest rates on Euro-CDs. The higher Eurodollar interest rates attracted the escaping corporate funds to their branches and subsidiaries abroad. The Eurobanks could then lend to their U.S.-based parent banks, providing the latter with a much-needed source of funds that was not otherwise available. Note that these international banking operations are not especially cumbersome to manage. In fact, all they involve are changes of bookkeeping entries in bank records, allocating credits and debits between the parent company and their foreign branches and/or subsidiaries. The discussion thus makes clear the importance that the integration of the external and domestic banking systems has had in the development of the Eurodollar market. The close relationship between domestic parent banks and their Eurodollar branches and/or subsidiaries means that one cannot separate their decision making, either in terms of whom they lend to or in terms of the interest rates they set. In any case, the effect of Regulation Q was to provide a further incentive for the growth of the Eurodollar market during the late sixties and early seventies.

In addition to controls on interest rates, other government regulations on U.S. banking gave Eurobanks a competitive edge over domestic banks. For instance, the U.S. Federal Reserve Board requires that all member banks with demand deposits above $400 million hold a ratio of non-interest-yielding reserves to total deposits equal to about 16%—the well-known reserve requirement, which varies according to the type of deposit (i.e., demand, savings). Eurobanks are not subject to U.S. reserve requirements; consequently, they can hold their reserves in the form of interest-bearing deposits at other banks. They can also hold a smaller fraction of their assets in the form of reserves, resulting in a larger amount of interest-yielding investments. Eurobanks can also avoid the requirement faced by U.S. domestic banks as to the purchase of deposit insurance from the government, which raises costs for banks located in the United States and yields a relative advantage to Eurobanks. In effect, these regulations amount to a tax imposed by the government on domestic banks. By setting up Eurobank branches and subsidiaries, U.S.-based banks could then avoid the implicit taxation associated with U.S. location.[6]

The main government regulations associated with the growth of the Eurodollar market during the sixties and early seventies have been partly phased out, particularly those relating to interest rate controls. The late seventies and early eighties became a period of heavy deregulation of the U.S. domestic banking industry, though reserve and deposit insurance requirements have been maintained. Still, as shown in Figure 3–1, Eurodollar loan-deposit interest rate differentials have generally remained below those in domestic banks up to the present time. Furthermore, the growth of the Euromarket continued unabated until mid-1982. What explains this sustained expansion of the Eurodollar market? One major explanation is associated with changing investors' perceptions of the political risk attached to the Eurodollar market, as will now be explained.

The expansion of multinational business and finance during the sixties and seventies, as well as the growth of petroleum-derived revenues in the hands of Arab countries after the oil price hikes of the seventies, gave rise to a substantial pool of investment funds seeking placement in international financial markets. The Eurodollar market has served well as a haven for these funds. This is partly the result of the flexibility that Eurodollars allow the firm or individual engaged in international transactions. When funds are urgently needed to complete a deal late in the day in Hong Kong, you just cannot wait until your New York bank opens the next day. A worldwide network of dollar deposits thus makes multinational business more efficient. In addition, investors—whether Arab sheiks or multinational conglomerates—generally seek to diversify their portfolios so as to maximize returns with a minimum of risk. That is, they try to avoid placing all their eggs in the same basket. Toward that end, they hold a range of assets denominated in different currencies and located in various countries. Eurodollar deposits have become a major component in the portfolios of international investors.

In general, dollar deposits abroad are subject to a number of risks not generally faced if one holds domestic deposits. The possibility of exchange controls blocking the withdrawal of funds from Eurobanks, the potential imposition of taxes on the repatriation of Eurodollars, and even the chance of severe regulation of Eurobank activities—something many countries have flirted with—create an environment subject to substantial political risk as compared with domestic deposits. To compensate investors for their increased risk taking, Eurodeposits

[6] Tax avoidance has been a major motivating factor in setting up foreign branches and subsidiaries, not only in terms of the avoidance of the implicit tax of government regulations, but also with regard to circumventing explicit domestic taxes. Domestic banks often search for foreign locations with low corporate income tax rates in order to legally shift income gains to those locations and reduce tax brackets. Similarly, investors seek to deposit their income in low-tax areas, shifting their funds to Eurobanks located in those areas. Switzerland has been particularly successful in attracting deposits on this account. Within the legal jurisdiction of the United States, the Commonwealth of Puerto Rico attracts dollar deposits on the basis of federal income tax exemption.

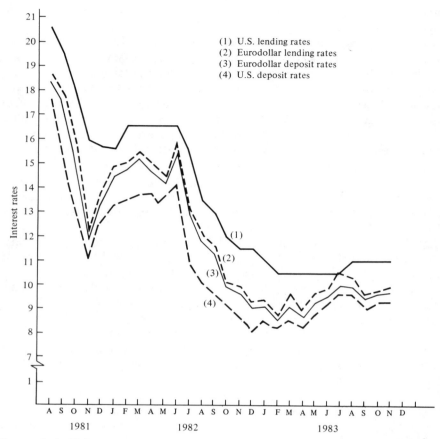

FIGURE 3–1   U.S. and Eurodollar Interest Rates, 1981–1983. *Source:* U.S. lending rates are for commercial bank lending rates to prime borrowers; U.S. deposit rates are for 3-month certificates of deposit issued by Morgan Guaranty; Eurodollar deposit and lending rates are prime banks' bid and offer rates for deposit in London. All from *World Financial Markets,* Morgan Guaranty Trust Company, New York, selected issues (reproduced by permission).

generally offer higher interest rates compared with domestic deposits. These higher deposit rates—and the associated lower loan–deposit interest differential—can be sustained through the competitive edge and flexibility Eurobanks can attain relative to domestic banks. In this way, they can attract funds even when they bear higher political risks.

   The perception of the political risks associated with Eurodollar deposits relative to onshore deposits has, however, changed over time. As a matter of fact, the growth of Eurodollars during the 1970s and very early 1980s can be associated with a general reduction in the perceived political risk of holding

Eurodollars. This increased confidence made Eurodollars relatively attractive to many investors, especially at the higher deposit interest rates they offered. Of course, a substantial number of investors maintained their domestic deposits in fear of the still high comparative risks involved in investing abroad, but the relative growth of the Euromarket can certainly be associated with the reduction of perceived political risks[7] over time. A reversal of this trend relates to the recent difficulties of many developing countries in repaying their debts to Eurobanks. The so-called debt crisis of the 1980s has cast a dark cloud on the continued health of Eurobanks and Eurolending and might have been a factor in the stagnation of Eurocurrency market growth after 1982. The subject of Eurolending will be addressed in Section 3–5.

3–5   EXTERNAL FINANCIAL INTERMEDIATION

One of the major functions of the Eurocurrency market is to funnel funds, mostly Eurodollars, from lending countries to borrowing countries. The United States and several oil-exporting countries have figured prominently as net lenders of Eurodollar funds while the Soviet Union, Eastern European countries, and developing countries in general have predominated as net borrowers. In bringing together lenders and borrowers, the Eurodollar market performs a global financial intermediation task, a task whose scope and delicate nature are best appreciated by looking at its recent history.

The dramatic oil-price hikes of the 1970s[8] were associated with a massive redistribution of wealth from oil-importing to oil-exporting countries. Over the period of 1974 to 1981, for instance, Organization of Petroleum Exporting Countries (OPEC) members increased their wealth by an average of $50 billion per year. Associated with this transfer of wealth were ballooning oil bills faced by the oil-importing countries. The oil-import bill of non-oil-producing developing

---

[7] For more details on the association of shifting risk and the growth of the Eurodollar market, see Robert Z. Aliber, "The Integration of Offshore and Domestic Banking Systems," *Journal of Monetary Economics* (October 1980). Note that shifting perceptions on the political risk of *domestic* currency holdings in anticipation of possible government controls on domestic financial transactions can also influence the relative attractiveness of Eurocurrencies. For instance, widespread capital controls were imposed in Germany during 1970 to 1974 to impede the inflow of funds into German bank deposits, leading to a general anticipation that further controls would be imposed. As a result, to compensate investors in Germany for their higher political risk, the West German mark deposit interest rate rose relative to the Euromark deposit rate. See M. P. Dooley and P. Isard, "Capital Controls, Political Risk and Deviations from Covered Interest Parity," *Journal of Political Economy* (April 1980).

[8] The price of oil (Saudi quotes) increased from $1.30 per barrel in 1970 to $33.50 in 1982. Associated with this general increase in oil prices were the sharp oil price shocks of 1973—when crude petroleum rose from $2.75 to $12.50 a barrel—and 1979, when oil prices more than doubled. These price increases were possible largely because of the tight control of the Organization of Petroleum Exporting Countries over oil prices. The 1973 and 1979 shocks, however, were precipitated by major political events taking place in the Middle East.

countries alone increased from $10 billion in 1973 to $120 billion in 1980. As a result, there were great fears at the time that the failure of oil-importing countries to foot the bills for their oil purchases would result in a collapse of the international monetary system. The collapse did not turn out to materialize, a reflection of the ability of the international financial community to match the dollar revenues of the OPEC giants with the demands for financing required by the oil-importing countries. This so-called *recycling* of oil-related (petro) dollars from the oil czars to the oil paupers was substantially realized precisely through the Eurodollar market. Because of the existence of Eurodollars, for example, a country such as Brazil could arrange within a regulation-free environment to obtain multimillion-dollar loans from a consortium of American, German, and Japanese banks and thereby finance its oil imports.

By financing their huge import bills, Eurolending allowed developing countries to sustain their levels of consumption and investment. Eurodollars thus aided in supporting the ambitious development projects of Brazil, the red-ink deficits of government corporations in Mexico (such as Petróleos Mexicanos), and the privatization of enterprises previously nationalized by Salvador Allende's government in Chile. This dynamic lending activity paved the way for the debt problems of the eighties, during which the difficulties of developing countries in repaying their debts finally made the headlines.

The Third World's debt to the Western banking system has risen above the $0.5-trillion mark. Mexico and Brazil alone owe over $80 billion each to Western banks. In addition, the Soviet Union jointly with East European countries owe more than $65 billion. The debt problem of the eighties arises from the inability, and sometimes unwillingness, of many developing countries to finance their loan repayments, either principal or interest. The response of the developing countries has generally been to attempt to continue their borrowing in order to finance the payments on previous debts, to seek the aid of international organizations such as the International Monetary Fund, or, when default looms ahead, to renegotiate or reschedule their debts. Debt rescheduling usually involves a stretching of the maturities attached to loans. The problems are particularly chilling for the Eurobanks, which due to their earlier lending practices, find themselves holding a vast amount of morose and prospectively defaulted debts. This wide exposure on the part of Eurobanks has caused much public concern, especially regarding the possibility that a default by one or more major developing country borrowers could trigger a sudden withdrawal of funds from the Euromarket and cause a string of Eurobanks to go under, with disastrous repercussions for the international financial system. To what extent are these worries valid?

That the fears, though legitimate, are somewhat exaggerated can be understood by recalling the integrated character of domestic and external banking. The fact that Eurobanks are branches and subsidiaries of domestic banks means that the parent banks can back them up in the event of any serious difficulties. As a matter of fact, those Eurobanks that are branches of domestic banks cannot fail independently of their parent companies. And even though subsidiaries could, in principle, fail independently of their associated domestic banks, the latter would presumably back them up by absorbing any losses or providing them with liquid funds to continue operations. The implication is that unless the failure of their foreign branches and subsidiaries is connected to a failure of domestic banks, short-term difficulties on the part of Eurobanks would not disturb the market for long. Consequently, for an international crisis to be associated with Eurobanking activities would require that governments and monetary authorities stand still and allow the failure of their major commercial banks—an unlikely possibility.

The case of the failure of the Franklin National and I.D. Herstatt banks in mid-1974 provides a clear example of the issues involved. Both banks had borrowed heavily from Eurobanks. As a consequence, the announcement of Herstatt's closing and Franklin National's losses resulted in fears of Eurobank failures and in a sudden withdrawal of deposits out of Eurocurrency markets. The overall size of the London market fell temporarily as a result. The associated instability generated a rapid response from the Central Bank Governors of the Group of Ten countries and Switzerland, indicating their willingness to intervene in the event of a crisis. In September 1974 they reported:[9]

> At their regular meeting in Basle on 9th September, the Governors also had an exchange of views on the problem of the lender of last resort in Euro-markets. They recognized that it would not be practical to lay down in advance rules and procedures for the provision of temporary liquidity. But they were satisfied that means are available for that purpose and will be used if and when necessary.

After this move, and by early 1975, the Eurocurrency market returned to stability. In conclusion, given that Eurobanks are closely connected to domestic banks and since it is unlikely that Central Banks will allow major domestic bank failures to occur without their intervention, a Eurobank-related international monetary crisis does not seem imminent.

Another stabilizing force concerns the variety of financial practices that Eurobanks have developed in order to minimize their risk exposure. Even though Eurobanks are often visualized as taking excessive risks because of their unregulated nature, the Eurocurrency market has been at the forefront of financial innovations intended to deal with exposure to risky ventures. The technique of *syndicated credit* is a feature that allows a group (syndicate) of banks to pool funds together for the concession of very large loans. By providing only part of the financing, the risks of default on the loan are spread among the banks participating in the syndicated loan. Since frequently the banks are from

---

[9] As quoted by R. B. Johnston, *The Economics of the Euro-Market: History, Theory, and Policy* (New York: St. Martin's Press, Inc., 1982), p. 30. The group of 10 countries includes Belgium, Britain, Canada, France, Italy, Japan, the Netherlands, Sweden, the United States, and West Germany. Switzerland is a limited member.

different nationalities, the default risk is effectively spread among different countries, reducing the prospect of a crisis in the event that default actually occurs.

From the bankers' perspective, another stabilizing factor in the Eurodollar market concerns the maturity structure of its deposits and loans. Table 3–3 breaks down Eurobank claims (Euroloans) and liabilities (Eurodeposits). The striking features of the figures shown are (1) most of the claims and liabilities are short-term, and (2) the maturity structure of deposits and loans do not differ that much. The close matching of the maturities of deposits and loans in the Eurocurrency market forms the basis of a crucial difference from domestic banks. The latter usually accept short-term deposits and invest in long-term loans and assets. As a result, Eurobanks are not subject to the risk that domestic banks often face of having interest rates rise while holding old, low-yielding long-term loans. Euroloans are due on a short-term basis and can be reissued at rates commensurate with prevailing interest rates. These adjustable, short-term interest rates allow Eurobanks to shift the risk associated with interest rate variability to the borrower.

Even though Euroloans are effectively made on a short-term basis, long-term and medium-term lending engaging Eurobank participation in syndicated credit (Eurocredit) is a frequent undertaking. In effect, the banks commit themselves to reissue, that is, roll over, a succession of short-term loans over the term to maturity of the medium-term or long-term loan. The institutional procedure used is to agree before hand on the long-term duration of the loan and on the interest rate spread to be charged above the prevailing LIBOR, which is partially determined by an assessment of the risk attached to the long-term loan. Once the duration of the long-term lending and the spread are specified, an agreement is made on a short-term period during which the interest charged remains fixed. Each time the loan is rolled over, however, the interest rate is

TABLE 3–3. **Maturity Structure of Eurocurrency Claims and Liabilities**[a]

Maturity	Total Percent	
	Claims	Liabilities
Less than 8 days	15.6	21.6
8 days to less than 1 month	16.7	20.6
1 month to less than 3 months	23.5	28.2
3 months to less than 6 months	14.8	18.8
6 months to less than 1 year	6.2	5.8
1 year to less than 3 years	7.2	2.7
3 years and over	16.0	2.3
All maturities	100.0	100.0
All maturities, billions of dollars	621.3	616.2

Source: The Bank of England, *Quarterly Bulletin* (December 1983).
[a] Data are for U.K.-based positions in nonsterling currencies as of August 17, 1983.

adjusted to equal the prevailing LIBOR plus the fixed spread. Spreads are not altered during the time in which the long-term loan agreement is in effect but, if a loan has to be renegotiated, spreads will frequently change, depending on reassessments of credit-worthiness. For instance, Brazil generally borrowed in Euromarkets for years at a spread equal to a small fraction above LIBOR. Once Eurobanks recognized the mounting debt problems of this country in 1980, the spreads quickly rose to 2%.

In conclusion, a wide variety of safeguards exists, running from the financial mechanisms installed by the Eurobanks themselves up to the level of Central Bank support, suggesting that fears of a Eurodollar-induced international monetary crisis might be largely unfounded.

3–6 OFFSHORE MARKETS AND THE EFFECTIVENESS OF MONETARY CONTROL

The Eurodollar market has been accused of all sorts of maladies. It has been blamed for world inflation, implicated in speculative behavior destabilizing the value of the dollar, and singled out as undermining government control over the economy. These charges presuppose the notion that the Eurodollar market has substantial macroeconomic significance, that is, a strong role in the overall behavior of national economies. This section examines the macroeconomic implications of the Eurodollar market, stressing the issues bearing on the ability of policymakers to attain public policy goals.

We have seen how the Eurodollar market operates as a kind of monetary haven, that is, a jurisdiction in which banks are subject to minimal regulation. The close integration of Eurobanking with domestic banks then implies that, by shifting activities among their domestic and foreign locations, banks can avoid the controls and regulations imposed by national monetary authorities. This severely constrains the ability of the latter to execute policies. For instance, consider the case of reserve requirements. As noted earlier, member banks of the U.S. Federal Reserve System are subject to the requirement that they hold non-interest-bearing reserves against deposits. These reserve requirements were imposed to ensure the liquidity of domestic banks in the presence of an unexpected large withdrawal of deposits. Since they are crucial in influencing the amount of loanable funds available to banks, reserve requirements are also instrumental in the ability of domestic Central Banks to control credit and the money supply in the economy. With the presence of Eurobanks, however, domestic banks can in effect reduce their reserve requirement burden by shifting deposits to the unregulated offshore banking system, which is not subject to the requirements. Given that national monetary authorities can control only domestic reserve requirements, they cannot effectively influence the reserve:deposit ratios that banks hold. What is worse, Central Banks might even find themselves unable to calculate accurately the effective reserve:deposit ratios held by banks, since the relative amounts of Eurodeposits and domestic deposits vary unpredictably from week to week.

It is easy to understand why domestic policymakers are so concerned about the Eurocurrency market: Its existence and affinity to domestic banking severely undermine the ability of monetary authorities to effectively regulate and control domestic banks and their credit activities. Even though, as we saw earlier, the Eurodollar market does not lead to a massive, frenzied expansion of dollar deposits,[10] it makes the dollar money supply more difficult to manage and adjust. This means the efforts of Central Bank policies become more uncertain and the economy even more difficult to steer. Restrictive domestic monetary policy, for instance, might fail in curtailing credit, since, in the face of any upward pressures on domestic interest rates, domestic banks could shift funds from the Eurodollar to the domestic market, resulting in increased credit and preventing domestic interest rates from rising relative to rates abroad. The short-term capital flows associated with the integration of domestic and external money markets mean that local interest rates become closely linked to Euromarket rates and cannot significantly diverge from them. Government control of the economy is thus undermined. The sting of this fact on policymakers has resulted in renewed calls for regulation of the offshore banking system.

3–7   THE REGULATION OF EUROMARKET ACTIVITIES

Domestic banking systems have traditionally been subject to various forms of regulatory constraints intended to promote a stable monetary environment. Reserve requirements, for instance, limit deposit expansion, while mandatory deposit insurance serves to protect depositors against bank bankruptcies, and so on. The fact that a significant segment of the world banking system—the Eurocurrency market—remains largely unregulated has been the source of much public concern. As a matter of fact, one may wonder why the Eurocurrency market has been able to operate under a minimal-regulation environment for so long. This is a perplexing situation indeed, since there is reasonable consensus among policymakers regarding the need for some regulation. Nevertheless, a look at the alternative means by which regulations might be introduced clearly reveals the reasons for their absence. Suppose, for example, that the United States places regulatory trappings on its Eurobanks in the form of restrictive reserve and deposit insurance requirements.[11] This action on the part of U.S.

---

[10] That this is so must appease the fears of those who have, mistakenly, believed that the Eurodollar market can give rise to an explosion of the supply of dollars in the world and, therefore, to rampant world inflation. The stagnation of the Eurodollar market during 1983–1984 should further relieve our fears that the Eurodollar market ignite world inflation.

[11] The most obvious way of eliminating the loopholes from government intervention provided by offshore markets is to establish uniform requirements for both domestic and Eurobanks. Imposing

authorities would not affect foreign Eurobanks, which are outside the reach of U.S. regulatory constraints. Hence a major part of the Eurodollar market would remain effectively uncontrolled. The main impact of U.S. regulatory measures would then be to increase the costs of U.S. banks, reduce their competitive edge and shift clients toward foreign banks. It is thus apparent why U.S. authorities have not taken such actions. Alternatively, U.S. authorities can attempt to limit U.S. residents' transactions with Eurobanks by means of exchange controls and other restrictions on capital mobility. Although these restrictions may keep a New York firm from purchasing Eurocertificates of deposit or obtaining Eurodollar loans, foreign subsidiaries of U.S. firms could still use the Euromarket freely. And, of course, U.S. government supervision does not extend at all to foreign residents and foreign banks. In conclusion, the possibility of a unilateral introduction of effective controls on the part of any single country over the Euromarket system is questionable.

An alternative route in regulating the Euromarket is through the initiative of the financial centers in which Eurobank activities locate. The impracticality of this route, however, is obvious from the fact that attempts to regulate Euromarket activity in a given financial center will simply move it to less rigidly regulated regions. Actually, there is keen competition among countries for Eurobanking business. Some of these countries, such as Panama, have developed a booming Eurobanking sector, generating welcomed employment and income. From the point of view of individual countries, the major incentives are toward attracting Eurobanking business, not discouraging it. Since 1981, the Federal Reserve has allowed banking offices located in the United States to set up international banking facilities (IBFs), which are free of deposit reserve requirements and interest ceilings on deposits and loans made to foreigners. Since they deal only with foreign customers, IBFs are in the nature of entrepôt business, which accept deposits and lend to foreigners but do not compete with domestic banking activities. The establishment of IBFs shows clear recognition by the Federal Reserve that when other countries maintain Eurobusiness, individual countries gain nothing by restrictive measures. Only multilateral measures on the part of all the major countries involved would assure effective regulation. One cannot rule out for certain, however, that such measures may actually be imposed sometime in the near future, given the heightened fears and worries about the performance of the Eurodollar market to which the so-called debt crisis of the developing countries has given rise.

In this chapter we have discussed in detail the basic aspects of the Eurocur-

---

reserve and deposit insurance requirements on Eurodeposits is an obvious way to establish uniformity. The outright extension of regulation to offshore banking, however, implies an overall increase in government regulation of the economy and has therefore been opposed by some. An alternative suggestion has been to attain uniformity of regulatory constraints by coupling increased Euromarket regulation, say, the establishment of reserve requirements, with reduced domestic regulation, such as reduced reserve requirements on domestic banks. See Robert Z. Aliber, "Monetary Aspects of Offshore Markets," *Columbia Journal of World Business,* (Fall 1979).

rency markets. One of our main observations has been the central role that the Eurocurrency markets have in promoting international capital flows and the integration of domestic and international financial markets. We have not specified the precise influence of the Eurodollar market on U.S. international transactions and on the economy's macroeconomic performance. To do so would first require a discussion of the principles involved in measuring transactions with the rest of the world, that is, of the balance of payments accounts. This is the task of Chapter 4.

3–8 SUMMARY

1. The Eurocurrency market comprises deposits and loans denominated in currencies different from that of the financial center where the deposits are held or loans made. A gross measure of the Eurocurrency market includes all Eurodeposits, while a net measure excludes interbank deposits.

2. The central role of the Eurocurrency market has been to promote international capital flows and to integrate domestic and international financial markets. One of its major functions has been to funnel funds (mostly Eurodollars) from lending to borrowing countries. In particular, the recycling of petrodollars has been carried out to a substantial extent through the Eurodollar market.

3. Eurodollar deposits can be created by transferring funds out of the United States. This results in a multiple expansion of Eurodollars depending on bank reserve holdings and leakages out of the Eurodollar system. The major component in the creation of Eurodollar deposits seems to be the original shift in deposits from domestic to external markets rather than the multiplier expansion of these deposits.

4. Eurobanks are not independent entities specialized in accepting Eurodeposits and issuing Euroloans. They are rather foreign branches and subsidiaries of national banks whose Eurobanking operations are just one among multiple bank activities. Eurobanking activities are a segment of the wholesale international money market, since they overwhelmingly involve large transactions in short-term Eurodeposits and Euroloans.

5. An interbank offered rate is the short-term lending rate Eurobanks charge other banks in the interbank market. Euroloan rates are frequently at a spread of 1 to 2% above the London interbank offered rate (LIBOR).

6. A major factor behind the development of Eurocurrency markets has been the minimal regulation of Eurobanks as compared with domestic banks. This factor, combined with the integration of Eurobanking to domestic banking, undermines the ability of monetary authorities to effectively regulate and control domestic banks and their credit activities.

7. Even though Eurobanks are often visualized as taking excessive risks because of their unregulated nature, the Eurocurrency market has been at the forefront of financial innovations intended to deal with exposure to risky ventures.

8. Medium-term Euroloans are frequently rolled over and interest rates readjusted periodically (say, every 6 months) to reflect changes in market interest rates (LIBOR). The spread remains fixed during the term of the loan, however.

9. The marked growth of the Eurocurrency market during the sixties and seventies slowed down during 1983 to 1984, a phenomenon associated with the dark cloud that the so-called debt crisis of the eighties has cast over the continued health of Eurobanks and Eurolending.

PROBLEMS

1. Contrast Eurobanks and domestic banks in terms of the maturity transformation they carry out, the degree of government regulation they are subject to, the reserve deposit ratios chosen, and the spread between lending and borrowing rates.

2. Why do Eurodollars rarely consist of demand deposits?

3. Are the liabilities of foreign-owned banks operating in the United States included in Federal Reserve Board concepts of the money supply, say M2? Why? Are these liabilities Eurodollars? Are offshore deposits included in M1? In M2?

4. "As long as they renounce or are unable to regulate Euromarkets, domestic authorities will be incapable of affecting credit conditions in Euromarkets." Evaluate this statement.

5. The U.S. banking system has experienced substantial deregulation during the eighties. For instance, a gradual phase out of interest rate controls on U.S. deposits is scheduled to be completed by 1986. Discuss the likely impact that this deregulation process will have on the Eurodollar market.

6. Suppose that there is a general increase in interest rates. How would such a disturbance affect the relative competitiveness of Eurobanks vis-à-vis U.S. onshore banks? Would you expect the Eurodollar market to expand or contract?

7. Suppose that a large Euromarket borrower, say a country like Argentina, defaults on its Euroloan repayment commitments. Can that create a massive Eurobanking and international monetary crisis? Explain why or why not, and then specify possible alternative scenarios regarding the effects of a major debt default on the international financial system and the Eurocurrency market.

8. Define the following concepts and indicate their relationship to the Eurocurrency market:

(a) Floating rate loans and notes

(b) LUXIBOR

(c) Eurobonds

(d) Edge Act

APPENDIX: THE EURODOLLAR MULTIPLIER

This appendix develops the Eurodollar multiplier approach to the analysis of deposit expansion in the Eurodollar market. The multiplier approach specifies algebraically the Eurodollar market expansionary capacity (i.e., its ability to create deposits) and the effect of Eurobank reserves and deposit leakages out of the Eurodollar system on this capacity. This quantitative approach provides empirical estimates of how large the expansionary capacity of the Eurodollar market actually is.

To begin with, the total supply of dollars in the hands of the nonbank public, $M^\$$, is defined as

$$M^\$ = M^{U.S.} + ED - RE \qquad \text{(A-1)}$$

where $M^{U.S.}$ represents the U.S. supply of dollars (a measure of the U.S. money supply which includes currency and coins plus demand deposits located in the United States), and ED denotes Eurodollar deposits. Note that if we were to add together the U.S. dollar supply and Eurodollar deposits, $M^{U.S.} + ED$, we would obtain the world supply of dollars, except that when Eurobanks deposit their reserves in U.S. banks there would be double-counting of some dollar deposits. On the assumption that all Eurobank reserves, RE, are held in the form of deposits at U.S. banks, these would have to be netted out to obtain the world dollar supply in the hands of the public. This is why RE is subtracted in equation (A-1).

As mentioned earlier, Eurodeposits are not subject to legal reserve requirements. Still, banks will voluntarily hold some reserves against Eurodeposits as a precautionary measure. The reserves, RE, that banks choose to hold as a proportion of Eurodollar deposits, ED, can be represented by

$$RE = reED \qquad \text{(A-2)}$$

where $re = RE/ED$ represents the bank's reserve:deposit ratio. As noted before, re is an important variable in the determination of the multiplier expansion of Eurodollars. The second factor that our textual analysis posits as crucial in understanding Eurodollar creation is Eurodeposit leakages, which arise from the fact that individuals do not keep all their deposits in the Euromarket but rather allocate them among both the domestic and offshore banking systems. For the sake of simplicity, we assume that Eurodollar deposits, ED, are related to the total supply of dollars in the hands of the public, $M^\$$, in the following linear fashion:

$$ED = \alpha + \epsilon M^\$ \qquad \text{(A-3)}$$

where α denotes the preferences for Eurodollar deposits on the part of the public (i.e., the higher α is, the more Eurodollar deposits the nonbank public will hold), and ϵ represents that fraction of every additional dollar available to the public that is deposited in the Eurodollar market. The smaller ϵ is, the larger the leakages from the Eurodollar market are in the sense that individuals will deposit only a small fraction of their additional dollars in the Euromarket.

Equation (A-2) represents the needs that Eurobanks have to hold reserves on their Eurodollar deposits, while equation (A-3) expresses the demand for Eurodollar deposits on the part of the public. How do these two basic relationships affect the Eurodollar market capacity to expand? By substituting equations (A-2) and (A-3) into (A-1), we obtain the following formula, specifying the determination of $M^\$$:

$$
\begin{aligned}
M^\$ &= M^{U.S.} - RE + ED \\
&= M^{U.S.} - (re - 1)\, ED \\
&= M^{U.S.} + (1 - re)\, \alpha + (1 - re)\, \epsilon\, M^\$
\end{aligned}
$$

which, solving for $M^\$$, yields

$$
\begin{aligned}
M^\$ &= \frac{M^{U.S.} + \alpha\,(1 - re)}{1 - \epsilon\,(1 - re)} \\
&= \mu\,[M^{U.S.} + \alpha\,(1 - re)]
\end{aligned}
\tag{A-4}
$$

where $\mu \equiv 1/[1 - \epsilon(1 - re)] > 1$ is the so-called Eurodollar money multiplier. The value of the multiplier increases with the value of ϵ—which is inversely related to Eurodollar leakages—and decreases with the value of re, which is the reserve:deposit ratio. Observe that given the multiplier, μ, equation (A-4) tells us that the world supply of dollars in the hands of the public can increase from two sources: a rising U.S. supply of dollars (i.e., increases in the U.S. money supply, $M^{U.S.}$), or a shift in the preferences of the public toward depositing additional amounts of Eurodollars and reducing domestic deposits (i.e., an increase in the α parameter).

The effect of a given change in the U.S. money supply, $\Delta M^{U.S.}$, on the total world supply of dollars is derived by taking changes in equation (A-4), with the following result:

$$
\Delta M^\$ = \mu\,\Delta M^{U.S.}
$$

Observe that since the Eurodollar multiplier μ is greater than 1, any given increase in the U.S. money supply is magnified into a larger increase in the world supply of dollars. The extent of this multiplier effect is dependent on the value of μ, which, as we saw earlier, depends on the values of the re and ϵ coefficients. The value of re, the reserve:deposit ratio held by Eurobanks, has been estimated[12] to be between 0.01 and 0.05, while the value of ϵ, the fraction redeposited into the Eurodollar market out of any of the additional dollars supplied, is usually regarded as being smaller than 0.20. Assuming that $re = 0.02$ and $\epsilon = 0.20$, and substituting into (A-4), we obtain

$$\Delta M^\$ = \frac{1}{0.804} \, \Delta M^{\text{U.S.}} \cong 1.24 \, \Delta M^{\text{U.S.}}$$

That is, an increase in the domestic supply of dollars increases the total dollar supply (through the Eurodollar market) by 24% more than the domestic increase. This relatively minor expansionary effect suggests that the fears of many authorities as to the explosive deposit expansionary capacity of the Eurodollar market is perhaps mistaken. The present analysis implies that each additional dollar in the U.S. money supply generates only an additional $0.24 in terms of Eurodollars.

The influence of a shift in deposits from domestic to Eurodeposits can be represented by a positive change in the coefficient $\alpha(\Delta\alpha > 0)$, or

$$\Delta M^\$ = \mu(1 - re)\Delta\alpha$$

which is positive, since $\mu > 0$ and $re < 1$. With the approximate actual values of μ and re given earlier ($\mu = 1.24$ and $re = 0.02$), one obtains

$$\frac{\Delta M^\$}{\Delta\alpha} = (1.24)(0.98) = 1.22$$

This means that a shift of $1.00 from the domestic to the Eurodollar banking system generates $1.22 additional dollars. Correspondingly, there is only a marginal expansionary capacity of the Eurodollar market above the creation of dollars arising from the direct shift of the dollar deposit abroad.

[12] For further details, see R. I. McKinnon, *Money in International Exchange* (New York: Oxford University Press, 1979).

Introduction to International Macroeconomics

PART II

CHAPTER 4

A Broad Picture of the Open Economy: The Balance of Payments and Exchange Rate Concepts

In an open economy, domestic residents can engage in a variety of international transactions involving the purchase or sale of goods, services, and assets. For example, U.S. residents buy Japanese TV sets and U.S. airplane manufacturers sell commercial jets to European airlines. Similarly, vineyards in California purchase the services of Mexican temporary workers, while American engineers sell their services to Saudi Arabia. At the same time, U.S. investors are purchasing Swiss bank accounts and U.S. corporations are raising funds by selling stocks to foreign investors. It is these transactions that the balance of payments intends to register. More formally, the *balance of payments* of a given country records all the economic transactions that have taken place during a given period between the country's residents and the rest of the world. This chapter takes a close look at the statistical presentation of the U.S. balance of payments. An examination of these data will acquaint us with the many links existing between the United States and the rest of the world. Before embarking on this task, however, we must make some basic guiding remarks regarding the notion of residency and the mechanics of international transactions accounting.

4–1 U.S. INTERNATIONAL TRANSACTIONS: THE STATISTICAL PRESENTATION

Since U.S. international transactions involve transactions between U.S. residents and the rest of the world, the first thing to clarify is the notion of a U.S. resident. The concept of a resident is intended to encompass individuals, institutions, and the government. So, when we speak of the transactions of U.S. residents, we refer not only to the transactions of U.S. individuals, but also of U.S. firms and the U.S. government at all levels. What designates a U.S. resident is sometimes difficult to determine so that the following—somewhat arbitrary, but necessary—rules of thumb are adopted in U.S. international transactions statistics. Tourists, diplomats, military personnel, and temporary migrant workers are all regarded to be residents of the country from which they come. For example, the expenditures of Japanese tourists in purchasing U.S. goods are regarded as U.S. exports, since they involve U.S. sales to foreign residents (the tourists). Similarly, the expenditures of U.S. tourists abroad are treated as imports in the U.S. balance of payments, since they involve purchases of foreign goods by U.S. residents. The income received by Mexican temporary migrants working in the United States would also be catalogued as an import. It represents a purchase of foreign services by domestic residents and is therefore an international transaction appearing under the service item in the accounts. There are, however, enormous difficulties in accurately measuring such international transactions. For instance, nobody really knows exactly how many foreign temporary workers, legal and illegal, there are in the United States or, for that matter, how much they earn.

Determining the residence of multinational corporations is another tricky problem. How do you assign residence to a firm located in a number of countries? The convention followed in U.S. transactions statistics is to treat foreign affiliates of U.S. (parent) firms as residents of the country where they are located.[1] As a result, transactions between the parent company in the United States and a foreign affiliate are recorded as transactions between a U.S. firm and a foreign resident.

The basic rule of balance of payments accounting is that any transaction giving rise to a receipt from the rest of the world is considered a *credit* and appears as a positive item in the account, while any transaction giving rise to a payment to the rest of the world is a *debit* and appears as a negative item. The way these concepts are used in balance of payments accounting is best visualized through the use of a so-called T account, which records the credit and debit items of a transaction. A stereotype of the use of a T account is shown in Table 4–1, which illustrates a transaction involving $20,000 worth of U.S. exports of automobiles to a British customer who pays with a check drawn on his account at a London bank. For simplicity, we assume the U.S. exporter and the British importer hold Eurodollar accounts at the same London

---

[1] Foreign affiliates of U.S. firms can be broken down into foreign subsidiaries and branches according to their legal status. The foreign subsidiary is legally incorporated in the country where it operates, while the branch is considered an extension of the parent company and is not incorporated abroad. It should be mentioned that, even though for purposes of international transactions accounting, both foreign subsidiaries and branches are considered foreign residents, for tax purposes the subsidiary is considered a foreign resident (a foreign corporation), while the branch is considered a domestic resident (part of a domestic corporation).

TABLE 4–1.   T Account for a Balance-of-Payments Transaction

Credits (+)		Debits (−)	
Exports		*Increase in U.S. Assets Abroad*	
Automobiles	$20,000	Deposits at a London Bank	$20,000

bank and that the transaction is completed by a deposit transfer from the importer to the U.S. exporter.

The T account records credits (positive items) on its left-hand side and debits (negative items) on its right-hand side. Exports of automobiles giving rise to receipts of $20,000 are recorded on the left-hand side of the T account in Table 4–1. The American exporter's purchase of $20,000 worth of foreign assets in the form of a London bank account, on the other hand, is recorded as a debit item on the right side. In general, our international sales, whether in the form of goods, services, or assets, are regarded as credits. Conversely, our international purchases, whether they be in the form of goods, services, or assets, are regarded as debits. In order to avoid confusion, we insist that

TABLE 4–2.   Summary of U.S. International Transactions 1983 (Billions of Dollars)

Transaction	1983
Exports of goods and services	334,233
Merchandise, excluding military	200,203
Other goods and services	134,030
Imports of goods and services	−366,410
Merchandise, excluding military	−260,753
Other goods and services	−105,657
U.S. government grants (excluding military grants of goods and services)	−5,967
Remittances, pensions, and other transfers	−2,632
U.S. assets abroad, net [increase/capital outflow (−)]	−49,297
U.S. official reserve assets, net	−1,196
U.S. government assets, other than official reserve assets, net	−4,897
U.S. private assets, net	−43,204
Foreign assets in the United States, net [increase/capital inflow (+)]	83,018
Foreign official assets, net	6,083
Other foreign assets, net	76,935
Allocations of special drawing rights	0
Statistical discrepancy	7,055

Source: Survey of Current Business (March 1984).

the reader think of the acquisition of the deposit at a London bank above as the purchase of a foreign asset, which is a debit. Finally, Table 4–1 illustrates the basic convention of double-entry bookkeeping by means of which any transaction gives rise to both a credit and a debit of the same value.

Table 4–2 presents the U.S. balance of payments for 1983. It is taken from the March 1984 issue of the *Survey of Current Business* and is based on data collected and published by the U.S. Department of Commerce. Note that the table includes data on U.S. international transactions in goods and services, transfer payments and grants, and assets. Each of these items is discussed in detail below.

Exports of Goods and Services

The first item in the international transactions table[2] is *exports of goods and services,* the value of which is registered as a credit item, since exports represent sales to foreigners and thus give rise to receipts from the rest of the world. As observed, the value of U.S. exports of goods and services in 1983 was $334.2 billion, composed of $200.2 billion worth of merchandise exports and $134.0 billion of service and nonmerchandise exports. The value of merchandise exports is estimated from data received by the Department of Commerce from U.S. customs agents. All exported (and imported) commercial merchandise must be legally registered through customs, which is in charge of assessing tariffs and other levies on the merchandise. As a result, merchandise exports (and imports) are among the most accurate items reported by the balance of payments accounts. They are also the most frequently reported items, available on a monthly basis.

Exports of noncommercial merchandise and services include the following: military transactions such as U.S. sales of military equipment to foreign countries, receipt of income on U.S. assets abroad;[3] and others, such as receipts from transportation services provided to foreigners, receipts from royalties, and license fees obtained from the provision of technical services to foreign residents. Transactions in services are much more difficult to measure than transactions in goods, even though the Department of Commerce keeps tabs on them through surveys and questionnaires. Appropriately enough, these transactions are usually referred to as *invisibles.*

[2] The reader may also find it convenient to refer to Appendix Table 4–A1, which provides a detailed breakdown of the general categories included in Table 4–2. It is located at the end of this chapter. The data for 1983 are preliminary. Revised data can be found in the September 1984 issue of the *Survey of Current Business.*

[3] Income on U.S. assets abroad includes interest payments to U.S. residents, dividend receipts from foreign investments, the share of the retained earnings of foreign subsidiaries of U.S. firms corresponding to U.S. residents, and the earnings of foreign branches of U.S. firms. Earnings of foreign branches and of foreign subsidiaries are considered accruing to the U.S. parent company, even if not actually received. For instance, the undistributed profits of foreign affiliates are included as a U.S. receipt in spite of not being actually remitted to the parent company.

Imports of Goods and Services

The second major item in the U.S. international transactions table regards *imports of goods and services,* the value of which appears as a debit item, since they represent purchases from foreigners and thus give rise to payments to the rest of the world. As observed, the value of U.S. imports of goods and services in 1983 was $366.4 billion, made up of $260.8 billion in merchandise and $105.7 billion in other goods and services. The purchase of foreign goods and services by domestic residents can be broken down into the same categories as the sales of domestic goods and services.

Unilateral Transfers

The next major item in the balance of payments is net *unilateral transfers* and refers to international transactions involving no explicit exchange of goods, assets, or services. Included are U.S. government grants, such as foreign aid provided by U.S. foreign assistance programs and food donations under the PL 480 program. Pension checks received by retired Americans residing abroad are also considered as unilateral transfers, since the retiree does not provide any current services in exchange. A final category includes private unilateral transfers, such as gifts made to foreigners. Unilateral transfers made to foreigners appear as a debit in the balance of payments, since they represent payments to the rest of the world. The United States has traditionally been a net supplier of foreign aid. As a result, the unilateral transfers item in the U.S. balance of payments is generally negative ($8.6 billion in 1983).

U.S. Assets Abroad

A fourth major category in the balance of payments regards *U.S. assets abroad,* which represent the net purchases of foreign assets[4] by domestic residents during the given time period. As Table 4–2 indicates, during 1983 U.S. residents increased their holdings of foreign assets by an amount equal to $49.3 billion. This number appears as a debit in the balance of payments, since the purchase of foreign assets gives rise to a payment to the rest of the world. Purchases of foreign assets consist of the following categories: increases in *U.S. official reserve assets,*[5] which represent increases in the holdings of international reserves by the Central Bank; increases in *U.S. government assets,* which include such trans-

---

[4] The purchase of foreign assets refers to an acquisition of claims on foreigners, that is, a purchase of assets issued abroad. These include, for example, our purchases of stocks and bonds issued by Japanese companies or our purchase of Mexican real estate. Notice that the term *foreign assets* has a different meaning when it is used by U.S. balance of payments statistics in referring to 'foreign assets in the United States.' The meaning of the term *foreign asset* in this latter context refers to domestic assets *owned by foreigners* rather than to *claims on foreigners.*

[5] Such as acquisitions of gold, SDRs, foreign currencies, and increases in the U.S. reserve position at the International Monetary Fund.

actions as new loans made by the U.S. government to foreign countries; and increases in *U.S. private assets abroad,* representing the private sector's net purchases of foreign assets, such as direct private investment abroad, portfolio investment in foreign assets, and private loans to foreigners.[6] Note that, just as any other transaction involving increases in U.S. assets abroad, loans made by U.S. residents to foreigners represent a debit in the balance of payments. This can be realized by visualizing a new loan as involving the acquisition on the part of the lender of an IOU, which is a promissory note by the borrower to repay a certain amount later on. Upon agreement of the IOU, the domestic lender makes a payment to the foreign borrower for the amount of the loan. Since it gives rise to a payment to foreigners, the acquisition of an IOU is then recorded with a negative sign in the balance of payments accounts.[7]

In summary, net increases (or decreases) in U.S. holdings of foreign assets appear as a debit (or credit) in the U.S. balance of payments under the U.S. assets abroad category. Since increases in U.S. assets abroad represent a payment on the part of the United States, they are usually referred to as *capital outflows.* A useful way to remember that capital outflows are a debit in the balance of payments is to visualize the purchase of a foreign asset as an import of assets, just as purchases of foreign goods represent imports of goods. Imports (whether of goods or assets) give rise to payments to foreigners and are thus balance of payments debits.

---

[6] The distinction between direct investment and portfolio investment is sometimes subtle and arbitrary, but the general concept to remember is that direct investment is intended to comprise investments involving a certain degree of control (by the investor) over the use of the funds invested, while portfolio investment lacks such control. Thus, a clear-cut case of direct investment abroad occurs when a domestic resident buys foreign real estate (land, houses), whose ownership is clearly in control of the asset holder. Portfolio investment occurs when a domestic resident buys either foreign short-term securities or bonds, which do not have attached to them any claim on foreign control or ownership of the enterprise. There are more shady cases, however. For instance, what happens when you buy stocks in a foreign enterprise? Is this direct investment or portfolio investment? The stocks give you a nominal claim over the decisions of the enterprise, but to be regarded as direct foreign investment a line has to be drawn as to whether you really have any effective control over the use of your funds at all. The balance of payments conventions here are not completely unambiguous and vary from country to country and from time period to time period. The U.S. Department of Commerce currently considers direct investment a purchase by a U.S. resident of equity in a foreign enterprise in which he or she owns 10% or more of the voting securities. In our example above, had you already owned, say, 20% of the voting securities of the enterprise in which you have purchased stocks, then your purchase of stocks would be considered direct foreign investment.

[7] The subsequent repayment of the amount loaned (the principal) by the foreigner represents a decrease in U.S. assets abroad and a receipt for the United States in the future. At that time, then, it will be recorded as a credit (with a positive sign) in the U.S. assets abroad account. As mentioned earlier, the interest on the loan is recorded as an export of services on the part of the United States.

Foreign Assets in the United States

Returning to Table 4–2, we see that the next item in the balance of payments is *foreign assets in the United States,* which represent the net sales of domestic assets made by U.S. residents to foreign residents during the given time period. U.S. residents sold foreigners a (net) amount of domestic assets worth $83.0 billion in 1983. This amount appears as a credit in the balance of payments, since the sale of domestic assets to foreigners gives rise to receipts from the rest of the world. It also represents an inflow of funds into the country and is thus usually referred to as a *capital inflow.* To remember that capital inflows appear as a credit item in the balance of payments, the sale of a domestic asset to a foreign resident can be thought of as an export of assets, just as sales of domestic goods to foreigners represent exports of goods. Exports (whether of goods or assets) give rise to receipts from foreigners and are thus credits in the balance of payments. Sales of domestic assets to foreigners can be decomposed into two categories: those made to foreign Central Banks, in the form of increases in *foreign official assets in the United States* (such as a purchase of CDs and Treasury bills by the Bank of England), and asset sales to other foreign residents, catalogued as increases in *other foreign assets in the United States* and including direct investment, portfolio investment by foreigners in the United States, and foreign loans to domestic residents. All involve the purchase of domestic assets by foreigners.

It should be stressed that the transactions recorded in the U.S. assets abroad and foreign assets in the U.S. categories of the balance of payments involve *net* asset flows, which register a net change in each entry during a given time period (1 year in the case of Table 4–2). The $49.3-billion figure given above refers then to the amount of U.S. imports of securities and other claims on foreigners, net of U.S. sales of these items during 1983. This as opposed to *gross* flows, which register the total volume of transactions involving purchases of foreign assets and do not subtract the sales of foreign assets during the given time period. Similarly, the $83.0-billion figure given above refers to all foreign purchases of domestic assets, net of the sales of domestic assets by foreigners, during 1983. These are important distinctions because figures on the net flow of assets do not give us any feeling about the actual volume of international transactions involving trade in assets.[8] For example, a single U.S. securities dealer often engages in more than $50 million (and perhaps up to more than $200 million) worth of *daily* international transactions in securities and money market instruments denominated in U.S. and foreign currencies.

---

[8] The reader may visualize the difference between gross transactions and net asset flows by considering a large U.S. corporation that invests abroad (say, in the Eurodollar market) $100 million for 3 months (say, from March to June) but does not roll this over in June. The operation clearly involves a substantial financial transaction but does not appear in the U.S. balance of payments, since it nets out and cancels before the end of the year.

Allocation of SDRs and the Statistical Discrepancy

The last two major items in the balance of payments are the allocation of *special drawing rights* (*SDRs*) and the *statistical discrepancy*. SDRs are a type of international reserve asset created and distributed to member countries by the International Monetary Fund. The allocation of SDRs measures the amount of SDRs allocated to the United States by the IMF over the year. Since this represents some receipts for the United States, it appears as a credit in the balance of payments.

The statistical discrepancy ensures that the items of the balance of payments add up to zero. Consequently, it is a residual item that counteracts the net balance of all the other positive and negative items in the accounts. Why is it that adding all items in the balance of payments must necessarily give us a value of zero? The answer lies in the double-entry bookkeeping nature of balance of payments accounting. Its principle is simple: Any international transaction should be recorded as involving both a credit and a debit of equal size. For example, the transaction involving a sale of Japanese-made automobiles to the United States obviously represents an import of goods, which appears as a debit in the balance of payments. It also gives rise, however, to a payment for the same amount by the American purchaser to the Japanese manufacturer, which involves an export of some kind of U.S. asset or claim on the U.S. and is, thus, a credit. If the auto imports are worth $1 million and the payment occurs, for instance, in the form of a bank transfer, then the foreign assets in the U.S. item in the balance of payments would increase by $1 million. The imports of goods debit should thus be exactly offset by the foreign assets in the U.S. credit, leaving a net balance of zero. A statistical discrepancy arises, however, because of measurement errors and the physical inability of recording instantaneously all international transactions. As a result, a difference will always be observed between the totals of *recorded* credits and debits in the balance of payments accounts. The statistical discrepancy item makes sure all items add up to zero, and it therefore reflects the extent of unrecorded transactions and measurement errors in the balance of payments.

The statistical discrepancy has grown extraordinarily in recent years, soaring from a value of −$1.5 billion in 1969 to $41.4 billion in 1982. It is widely believed that the statistical discrepancy mostly represents unrecorded services—like tourist expenditures—and capital flows. A positive value of the statistical discrepancy, then, represents either unrecorded exports of services or unrecorded capital inflows, that is, unrecorded exports of U.S. assets to foreigners. For instance, in the example above, the U.S. importer may delay payment to its Japanese supplier. As a result, the import of goods is recorded but the export of U.S. assets or claims on the United States (the capital inflow) goes unrecorded. Underreporting of capital inflows also arises from the inherent problems involved in accurately accounting for volatile funds rapidly being transferred among financial centers. This is especially so when some intentional deception is confronted, due perhaps to tax avoidance.

4-2 BALANCE OF PAYMENTS CONCEPTS: SUMMARIZING THE INTERNATIONAL EXPERIENCE

The items in the international transactions table always sum to zero because of the double-entry bookkeeping nature of its accounting. As a consequence, the overall balance of payments is always zero. What is it, then, that economists refer to when they speak of balance of payments surpluses or deficits? Clearly, the numbers quoted must have some meaning since, over the years, they have been blamed for inflation, unemployment, high interest rates, and almost any economic (and sometimes political and social) calamity. They must also provide information of concern to policymakers, as otherwise the late U.S. President John F. Kennedy would not have equated a balance of payments deficit with nuclear war.[9]

The balance of payments can be decomposed into several (sub)balances or accounts. Each of these (sub)balances measures the international trade of the economy in a broad class of transactions. The concepts of surplus and deficit apply to these particular accounts. An account is said to be in *surplus* when credits exceed debits on that account, that is, when receipts outstrip payments. On the other hand, a particular balance shows a deficit when receipts fall short of payments on the items comprised by the account. We now examine some specific balances with the aid of Table 4–3, which provides a summary statement of how balance of payments subaccounts are calculated. Appendix Table 4–A2 extends Table 4–3 in providing additional figures for selected years.

The Trade Balance

Perhaps the most publicized account in the balance of payments is the merchandise trade balance, which summarizes the net trade in (merchandise) goods of the economy with the rest of the world. It is measured by the exports minus the imports of merchandise goods of the economy from the rest of the world. For the United States in 1983 the merchandise trade balance, or just *trade balance,* was equal to −$60.6 billion. The negative sign means that merchandise imports exceeded merchandise exports by the given amount. As a result, there was a so-called trade balance account deficit: The payments from all international transactions involving exchanges of physical (nonmilitary) goods with the rest of the world exceeded the receipts.

[9] Arthur M. Schlesinger, *A Thousand Days* (Boston: Houghton-Mifflin Publishing Co., Inc., 1965), p. 654.

TABLE 4–3. Summary Calculation of Balance of Payments Subaccounts (U.S. 1983, Billions of Dollars)

Current account balance (CAB)		−40.8
Trade Balance	−60.6	
Capital account balance		36.2
Reported capital account	29.1	
Statistical discrepancy	7.1	
Allocation of SDRs		0.0
Official reserve settlements balance (ORS)		−4.6
(Increase in) U.S. official reserve assets		−1.2
(Increase in) foreign official assets in the United States		5.8
Overall balance of payments		0.0

purchase of foreign monetary assets →

Source: Survey of Current Business (March 1984), reproduced as our Table 4-A1. The precise figure for the capital account balance is obtained by adding lines 43, 47, 61, 64, and 75 of Appendix Table 4-A1. The ORS balance can be conveniently calculated as (the negative of) the sum of lines 80 and 81 in Table 4-1A, which register the items below the line—involving official reserve assets. Note that line 81 excludes some foreign official assets in the United States (line 61) which are not regarded as international reserves by foreign monetary authorities. Observe also that the statistical discrepancy has been incorporated into the capital account on the assumption that it represents unrecorded capital flows.

The trade balance provides a summary of the economy's performance and trade patterns as reflected through its trade in goods. Figure 4–1 illustrates how the U.S. trade balance has behaved during the recent past. The pattern is clear: The trade surpluses of the fifties and sixties have given way to increasingly larger deficits during the seventies and early eighties. Note, however, the significant ups and downs that the balance has suffered over the years. Even though the recent trend is toward increasingly large deficits, there have been extended periods of reduced deficits.

What factors account for the overall shifting pattern of U.S. trade? And why does the trade balance fluctuate up and down so much over the short run? These are questions we shall try to answer in the next few chapters. For the moment, let us just state that the trade balance is affected by a whole array of factors, including exchange rate changes, monetary and fiscal growth, income changes abroad, unexpected supply shocks, and the economy's international competitiveness. This last factor has received special attention in the United States in recent years because of the increasing competition that U.S.-manufactured products have suffered at the hands of those produced by Canada, Western Europe, Japan, and the newly industrialized countries (NICs), such as Brazil, Korea, and Taiwan. The early 1970s, for example, saw the emergence

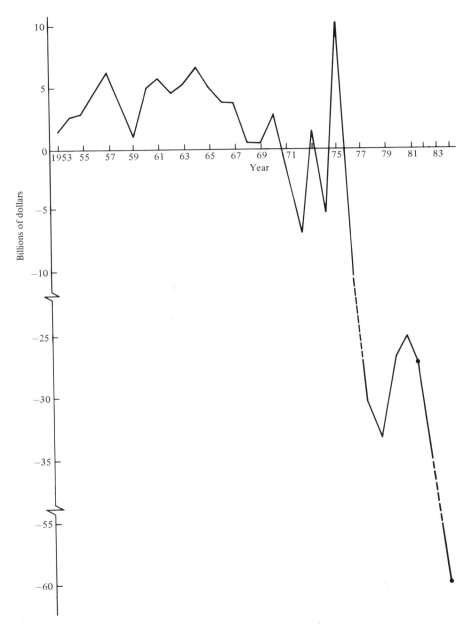

Figure 4–1 The U.S. Trade Balance

of U.S. trade deficits with Japan ($1.4-billion deficit in 1973), West Germany ($2.6-billion 1973 deficit), and Canada ($2.6-billion deficit in 1973). By 1983, the U.S. trade deficit with Japan alone had ballooned to $19.6 billion. The increasing import competition from other NICs in textiles, steel, chemicals, and a variety of other products has also been increasingly felt during the 1980s, not only by the United States, but also by other developed economies. The plight of the declining traded goods industries, which once formed the pillars of the U.S. trade balance surplus, is typified by the U.S. steel industry. During the period of 1959–1969, U.S. exports of steel mill products *increased* at an average pace of 11.2% annually, while during the period 1969–1978, the rate of *decline* of exports was at an average of 8.6% annually. The reasons for the decline and fall of the steel industry have lain in a number of factors, such as relatively high real labor costs (among the top of the industrial wage scale in the United States), the obsolescence of the technology used compared with the Japanese, Brazilian, and other newcomers' more recent technology, and increased raw materials prices and transport costs, among others.[10]

Another factor accounting for the widening of U.S. trade balance deficits has been the increased oil prices of the seventies. A barrel of crude oil was worth (on average) $2.60 in 1972, $13 in 1978, and by 1983 it was $29. The impact has been a burgeoning U.S. oil import bill. In 1973 the value of U.S. crude oil imports was equal to about $8.4 billion. By 1981 it was at a high of $79.4 billion, almost a 10-fold increase in less than 10 years, falling to $61.2 in 1982. We should stress, however, that although the OPEC-induced price shocks of 1973 to 1974 and 1979 to 1980 had an evident impact on the economy, the effects on the trade balance should not be exaggerated. First, oil prices tumbled during 1983. Second, and most important, even though the oil price shock has the effect of increasing oil import bills, its importance in determining the overall trade balance is not so clear. For instance, right after the oil price hikes, the balance of trade of many oil-importing countries turned out to be in surplus.

The Balance on Goods and Services

A second account that can be calculated from the balance of payments is the *balance on goods and services*. This balance measures the net trade in goods and services of domestic residents with the rest of the world. It is calculated by subtracting imports of goods and services from the value of exports of goods and services. In the case of the United States for 1983, the balance on goods and services was equal to −$32.2 billion, determined by subtracting $366.4 billion worth of imports of goods and services from $334.2 billion worth of

---

[10] For a detailed examination of the sources of the problems of the U.S. steel industry, see Robert W. Crandall, *The U.S. Steel Industry in Recurrent Crisis, Policy Options in a Competitive World* (Washington, D.C.: The Brookings Institution, 1981).

exports of goods and services. This meant that, during 1983, there was a deficit in the balance on goods and services; the payments from such transactions exceeded the receipts. Observe that while the 1983 U.S. trade balance deficit was $60.6 billion, the goods and services balance exhibited a deficit of $32.2 billion. The explanation lies in the large amount of income the United States receives from its investments abroad, which partly offsets the merchandise deficit. The income on those investments represents receipts for services rendered by U.S. capital abroad and constitutes a credit in the balance of payments.

The Current Account Balance

A third account that is usually calculated from the international transactions table is the *current account balance* (CAB). The current account balance measures the economy's trade in goods and services with the rest of the world taking into account all unilateral transfers, including private remittances and government transfers. Table 4–3 shows that the CAB for the United States was equal to −$40.8 billion in 1983. This represents a deficit in the CAB; the economy's payments exceeded the receipts from its international trade in goods and services taking into account the payments made by the United States to the rest of the world through unilateral transfers. Note that the only major set of international transactions not included in the CAB involves international trade in assets. This means that, except for statistical discrepancies, a CAB deficit (surplus) must be financed (offset) by a surplus (deficit) in the balance of the economy's international trade in assets. Otherwise, the balance of payments would not add up to zero.

The current account balance corresponds to the net acquisition of foreign assets by the country as a whole. This can be clearly visualized by drawing an analogy between the case of a household and that of an economy or country. A household holds receipts from its sales of goods and services, in the form of salaries, interest earned, yard-sale receipts, and so on, as well as from transfers received from other households, such as gifts from friends. It also makes payments for the purchases of goods and services and for transfers to other people, such as humanitarian donations or charitable contributions. The balance on these purchases and sales of goods and services, plus the net transfers made, is for a household what the current account balance is for a country. The household faces the equivalent of a CAB surplus when its receipts exceed its payments on goods, services, and transfers transactions. It faces the equivalent of a CAB deficit when its payments exceed its receipts from these transactions. Consider the first case in more detail. An excess of receipts over payments in the CAB must give rise to some corresponding (offsetting) transactions involving increases in asset holdings. The household, for example, may lend, buy some stocks and bonds, or increase its holdings of CDs, currency, or bank deposits. All these transactions are analogous to the international transactions of a country under a CAB surplus; the economy may lend abroad, buy some foreign stocks and bonds, or the country's Central Bank may increase its holdings of foreign currencies. The same analogy between a household and a country can also be made for the case of a deficit in the CAB. In this situation, the household would have to borrow from other households or reduce its cash holdings and bank deposits in order to finance the excess of payments over receipts. Similarly, a country facing a CAB deficit has to finance it by borrowing from other countries, selling some of its stocks, bonds, and other financial assets, or reducing its holdings of foreign currencies (its official reserve assets).

In summary, the current account balance measures the net acquisition of foreign assets—the net foreign investment—by the country as a whole. A surplus in the CAB implies that the country is increasing its holdings of foreign assets or lending funds abroad and so it is acquiring net claims on foreigners. A deficit, on the other hand, means that the country is selling assets to foreigners or borrowing funds from abroad.

The U.S. current account balance has undergone major transformations over the years. For long periods of time during the nineteenth century, the United States was a CAB-deficit country, acquiring foreign debt and accepting foreign investment while it developed its industrial base. The CAB deficits were thus associated with the country's economic growth drive—which should warn us against unqualifyingly labeling CAB deficits as a bad thing. The experience of the U.S. CAB during the 1950s and 1960s was, on the other hand, diametrically opposite, with its persistent surpluses financing a boom of U.S. investment abroad. Since then, the CAB has fluctuated, sometimes being in deficit and sometimes in surplus.

The Capital Account Balance

We have grouped all international asset transactions, except the ones made by monetary authorities in those assets that serve as international reserves, in the capital account.[11] The capital account thus registers our purchases of foreign stocks and bonds, U.S. bank lending to foreign corporations and government agencies, and the sales of domestic assets to foreigners such as when a California estate is sold to an Arab sheik. The investments of foreign corporations in U.S. Treasury bills and certificates of deposit are also included in the capital account, but foreign Central Bank investments in those assets are not because they are regarded as official assets in the United States.

[11] Transactions in U.S. official reserve assets—the U.S. monetary gold stock, Federal Reserve and Treasury holdings of foreign currencies, and others—are omitted from the capital account. Also excluded are those transactions involving foreign official assets in the United States. Since the U.S. dollar is an international money widely accepted as a means of international payments, foreign Central Banks hold dollar-denominated assets in the United States, such as U.S. Treasury bills and certificates of deposit issued by New York banks. These foreign official assets in the United States help settle international transactions and are regarded as equivalent to international reserves by foreign Central Banks.

∘∘ Current account deficit.
−financed by selling assets to
foreigners (Capital inflow → borrowing)

A Broad Picture of the Open Economy   **121**

The U.S. capital account was $36.2 billion in 1983, which represents a net acquisition of U.S. assets by foreigners over and above the purchase of foreign assets by Americans. As shown in Table 4–3, the capital account is obtained by adding the statistical discrepancy to the value of the capital account derived from the actual data reported by individual transactors, which we call the reported capital account and amounted to $29.1 billion in 1983. The reason why the reported capital account needs to be supplemented by adding the statistical discrepancy is because a substantial amount of U.S. international capital market transactions are difficult to measure and/or underreported. The statistical discrepancy is widely regarded as reflecting such unreported asset transactions. Consequently, in order to obtain a more accurate measure of the actual capital account, one that includes reported and unreported transactions, the statistical discrepancy is frequently added to the other items in the account. For instance, and as we noted earlier, it is widely believed that the $7.1-billion statistical discrepancy appearing in the 1983 U.S. balance of payments largely represents unrecorded sales of U.S. assets to foreigners (net capital inflows). When this amount is added to the $29.1-billion reported capital account, the capital account becomes equal to a $36.2-billion surplus. The divergence between the capital account as obtained from reported data and that obtained on the assumption the statistical discrepancy represents capital flows is not at all negligible. As Figure 4–2 illustrates, even though the reported U.S. capital account deficit remained undiminished until 1982, the overall (i.e., reported plus unreported) deficit declined drastically after 1978.

This behavior of the overall capital account reflects an increasing tendency for foreign residents to invest in the United States. Most of these increased foreign assets in the United States are in the form of liabilities of U.S. banks (such as CDs), U.S. Treasury securities, and direct foreign investments in the United States. It is interesting to observe that over the period of 1976–1983, foreigners accounted for about 20%—and in some years more than 50%—of the increase in the total public debt privately held. An increasingly important, and perhaps the most visible of capital flows into the United States, however, is direct investment. The general upward pattern of direct foreign investment in the United States can be observed from Figure 4–3, especially its explosion after 1977. In 1981, for the first time during the post–World War II period, direct foreign investment in the United States exceeded U.S. direct investment abroad during the year. This net foreign investment in the United States during 1981 arose from a combination of greatly increased foreign investments in the United States in the face of drastically reduced U.S. investment abroad during that year. Even though foreign direct investment in the United States declined in 1982 and 1983—a sign of worldwide recession—this was accompanied by a crash in U.S. direct foreign investment abroad during the same period.

These new developments have been observed with great concern, as exemplified by the common cries by some journalists and politicians that "foreigners

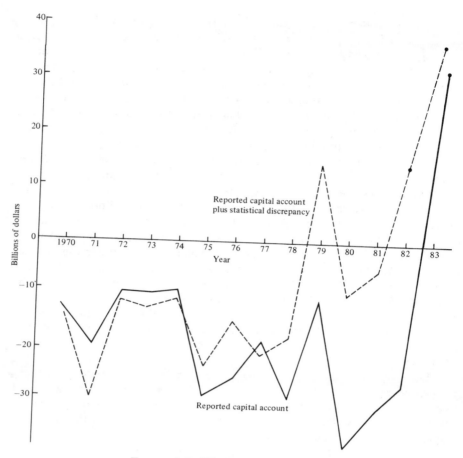

FIGURE 4–2   The U.S. Capital Account

are buying the U.S."[12] Direct foreign investment generally involves some degree of control over the use of the funds invested and creates the image of a Saudi sheik owning and controlling the businesses in which we work, eat, and reside. As a matter of fact, a number of U.S. firms producing goods we consume every day are foreign-owned. Orange Crush, Libby's fruits and vegetables, Keebler cookies, Baskin-Robbins ice cream, Alka Seltzer, Stouffer cakes, the *New York Post*, the *Village Voice*, and many others, are all owned by foreign interests. Lest one lose perspective on the subject, however, it must be stressed that the total book value of foreign investments in the U.S. accumulated over

---

[12] The Iowa legislature in 1980 went so far as to enact a law that absolutely prohibits foreigners from buying farmland in the state. This was in reaction to some real estate investments apparently made by OPEC investors in the state.

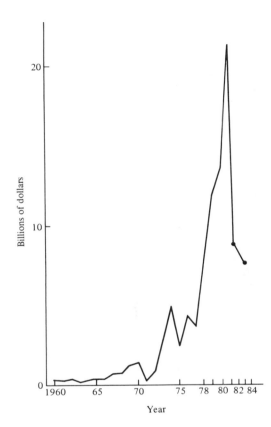

FIGURE 4–3   Direct Foreign Investment in the United States

the years is small relative to the accumulated U.S. direct investments abroad. The latter exceeds the former by a factor of about 2 to 1.

What factors have caused the relative decline of U.S. capital account deficits in the very recent past? What has given rise to the increased capital inflows from abroad observed in recent years? Figure 4–2 shows the substantial ups and downs of the capital account over the years. What causes this short-term volatility? These are questions that shall be answered in the next chapters. Let us just mention here that the capital account is strongly influenced by interest rates, exchange rate expectations, risk perceptions, and a number of other variables determining the movement of funds across borders.

One must realize that the capital account is an aggregate of international transactions involving a wide variety of financial instruments. As a result, one will often observe that the balance of payments statistics of a given country distinguish between different conceptual types of asset transactions such as short-term versus long-term or liquid versus illiquid, and calculate capital account subbalances made on these distinctions. Indeed, the U.S. Department of Commerce used to calculate a variety of payments balances, each of which grouped together a different subset of assets. Since 1976, however, they have stopped presenting these calculations in published statistics.[13] Still, some vestiges remain. For instance, the differentiation between short-term and long-term assets is still present in the detailed presentation of the U.S. international transactions table, shown in Appendix Table 4-A1 at the end of this chapter. What is the basis for this distinction?

Assets whose contractual maturity is less than a year are considered short-term assets while all others are considered long term. According to this definition, 6-month CDs are classified as short-term assets while 3-year notes are considered long-term assets. The basic goal of this distinction is to differentiate capital flows according to their volatility, that is, according to the investors' horizon regarding the period over which they intend to hold an asset. One should be very careful, however, in identifying investments as volatile and nonvolatile. First, some long-term capital flows, such as the transactions of U.S. firms with foreign affiliates, are empirically quite volatile. Second, it is apparent that assets having a short term to maturity are frequently intended to be held as a long-term investment. For instance, a firm investing in 6-month certificates of deposit that are automatically rolled over five times in a row is not making a very different investment than when it purchases an instrument that has a contractual maturity of 3 years. Still, the sequence of 6-month CDs would be catalogued as short-term investments, while the purchase of 3-year instruments would be regarded as long-term investments. The crux of the problem is that whether a capital flow is intended to be short term or long term is not necessarily dependent on the contractual maturity of the instrument used. You can generally sell assets with long-term maturities before they are due and roll over assets with short maturities for long periods of time. A final ambiguity regarding short-term versus long-term capital flows is related to the distinction between the original, or contractual, maturity and the remaining term to maturity of an asset. An asset with a contractual maturity of 10 years issued $9\frac{1}{2}$ years ago is in effect a 6-month short-term security with regard to its remaining term to maturity, which is 6 months. Since the U.S. Department of Commerce has classified short-term versus long-term assets in terms of their original maturity, however, such an asset would be classified as long term.

For all these reasons, the distinction between short-term and long-term capital flows has not been thoroughly pursued recently by the Department of Commerce,

---

[13] For a detailed discussion of the reasons behind the changes in the presentation of U.S. balance of payments statistics, see "Report of the Advisory Committee on the Presentation of Balance of Payments Statistics," *Survey of Current Business* (June 1976). See also *The Presentation of the U.S. Balance of Payments: A Symposium,* Princeton Essays in International Finance, No. 123 (1977). A thorough discussion of some particular balances, such as the liquidity and basic balances, which have fallen into disuse under the present floating exchange rate system, can be found in C. P. Kindleberger, "Measuring Equilibrium in the Balance of Payments," *Journal of Political Economy* (November/December 1969).

although some asset transactions are still catalogued as short term and long term.

The Official Reserve Settlements Balance

The *official reserve settlements balance* (ORS) records, that is, puts above the line, the net balance on all the international transactions of the economy except those engaged by domestic and foreign Central Banks in changing the assets they consider their international reserves. Accordingly, the balance adds the current account, the capital account (including the statistical discrepancy), and the allocation of SDRs. Table 4–3 shows the calculation of the U.S. ORS balance for 1983, which gives a value of −$4.6 billion. As noted earlier, the ORS balance must correspond to the economy's asset transactions left out of the capital account, which must take the form of changes in U.S. official reserve assets and/or foreign official assets in the United States. As Table 4–3 indicates, the U.S. official reserve assets showed an increase of $1.2 billion during 1983. Recall that increases in U.S. official reserve assets represent a purchase by the Federal Reserve of foreign monetary assets, such as foreign currencies, and are catalogued as a debit (with a negative sign) in the balance of payments. Table 4–3 also exhibits a $5.8-billion increase in the U.S. assets that foreign Central Banks consider international reserves. Recall that increases in the holdings of U.S. assets by foreign official institutions (foreign Central Banks) represent a sale, or export, of domestic assets to foreigners and are catalogued as a credit in the balance of payments. Consequently, the 1983 U.S. ORS balance deficit corresponds to an increase of $4.6 billion in foreign official holdings of U.S. assets over and above the increases in U.S. official reserve assets. These net sales, or exports, of official reserve assets by the United States, build up a credit in the balance of payments that offsets the ORS deficit, thereby keeping the overall balance of payments equal to zero.

The official reserve settlements balance can be used to measure the intervention of monetary authorities in foreign exchange markets. How is Central Bank intervention in foreign exchange markets reflected in the ORS balance? Up to now we have not clearly specified which Central Banks do the intervention in foreign exchange markets. Most countries have their own responsibility for supporting their fixed exchange rate, and their Central Banks must correspondingly engage in the intervention. For instance, if there were an excess demand (shortage) for foreign exchange, the domestic Central Bank would supply the needed foreign exchange, at the fixed price in terms of domestic currency the Bank is committed to support. This is reflected in the balance of payments as a decrease in the domestic Central Bank's level of official reserves and corresponds to an ORS deficit. Similarly, the domestic Central Bank would purchase an excess supply of foreign exchange arising from the settling of private transactions, in which case an ORS surplus would occur. In conclusion, when the domestic

Central Bank is in charge of fixing the exchange rate, only changes in domestic official reserves will be affected by intervention in the foreign exchange market. As a result, the ORS balance will correspond most closely to changes in domestic official reserves.

The case of U.S. intervention in foreign exchange markets is more particular, however, because the United States is what is called a *reserve currency country*. A reserve currency is a currency widely held by Central Banks around the world in the form of international reserves. About 70% of the world's official reserves of foreign exchange are in the form of U.S. dollar-denominated assets. Swiss francs and West German marks have been increasingly used over the last few years but not as widely as the dollar. With the dollar being the major world reserve currency, a number of countries fix their currencies against the dollar and then use their dollar holdings to maintain that fixed rate. As a consequence, the United States has not had full responsibility for maintaining its exchange rate fixed against other countries' currencies, leaving most of the action to the countries that fix their rates against the dollar. In this situation, foreign Central Banks intervene in foreign exchange markets by buying and selling their own holdings of dollar-denominated assets. The consequence is that foreign exchange market intervention is carried out through changes in both U.S. official reserve assets and foreign official assets in the United States.[14] This is why the U.S. ORS balance involves both transactions, and not just the official reserve transactions of the U.S. monetary authorities. For instance, if foreign commercial banks hold an excess supply of foreign currencies that they want to exchange for dollars, either the Federal Reserve could buy the foreign currencies, thereby increasing its official reserve assets, or foreign Central Banks could sell the dollars, decreasing their official reserve assets in the United States.

There is one major problem in associating the ORS balance with Central Bank intervention in the foreign exchange market to fix or manipulate the exchange rate. In many cases, Central Banks will autonomously change the level of their international reserves holdings, and not in response or accommodation to the demands and supplies of private actors in the economy. For instance, when a foreign Central Bank decides to reduce its holdings of deutsche mark reserves and to place the proceeds in higher-yielding U.S. Treasury bills, it is increasing its official assets in the United States but is not intervening at all to fix or manipulate the exchange rate in the foreign exchange market. The foreign Central Bank is just responding autonomously to economic incentives. One may speculate that the positive item under changes in foreign official assets in the 1983 U.S. balance of payments may have resulted from relatively high U.S. interest rates and not just from the intervention of foreign Central Banks

---

[14] Often foreign Central Banks will hold dollar-denominated deposits outside the United States. If a Central Bank's intervention occurs by means of reductions in, say, its London-based U.S. dollar deposits, this transaction would not be recorded at all either in the U.S. balance of payments or in the ORS. The ORS balance does not provide a complete measure of foreign Central Bank intervention to stabilize exchange rates against the dollar.

to keep their exchange rates vis-à-vis the dollar from declining. In this situation, the ORS cannot be unequivocally associated with official intervention in foreign exchange markets.

A particularly important case in point is the behavior of the U.S. ORS balance during the 1950s and 1960s. Figure 4–4 shows the values of the U.S. ORS balance during the recent past (solid line). The mostly negative values over the fifties, sixties, and early seventies give the appearance that over this period the United States was losing an inordinate amount of foreign exchange reserves in order to sustain its exchange rate fixed (by selling its holdings of foreign exchange reserves to satisfy the excess of the private sector's payments over receipts). As a matter of fact, during the period 1954 to 1974, the United States lost only $7 billion worth of reserves, out of an initial amount of $23 billion. The minor changes in U.S. official reserves are represented by the dashed line in Figure 4–4. Clearly, the U.S. ORS deficits were financed primarily through the acquisition of dollars and dollar-denominated assets by foreign Central Banks. Their willingness to hoard these dollar assets as international reserves made possible the relatively small loss of U.S. official reserves over

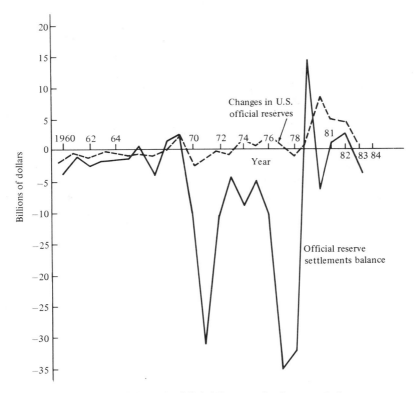

FIGURE 4–4 The U.S. Official Reserve Settlements Balance

the period, (with the loss actually taking the form of reductions in the gold holdings of the Federal Reserve). More specifically, many analysts have argued that the persistent ORS deficits of the sixties furnished the world with needed liquidity by providing foreign Central Banks with holdings of liquid dollars. It is implied that the ORS deficits reflected a strong dollar broadly used and demanded by foreign monetary authorities, as opposed to a weak dollar that had to be supported through Central Bank purchases of dollars. Of course, this situation had changed by the early seventies, when pressures against the dollar developed, resulting in its devaluation and the breakdown of the Bretton Woods system.

4–3   THE INTERNATIONAL INVESTMENT POSITION OF AN ECONOMY

International investments have taken on increasing significance for the United States since World War II. For instance, U.S. assets abroad have expanded enormously, exceeding by far the growth of the gross national product (GNP). Expressed as a proportion of GNP, the external assets of the United States represented 7% in 1952, swelling to 26.8% by 1983. Indeed, these developments have not passed unnoticed. The magnitude and riskiness of U.S. bank assets in the form of loans to developing countries is just one aspect that has attracted much public attention. Not only have U.S. external assets risen dramatically, but foreign assets in the United States have increased as well. As a proportion of GNP, U.S. external liabilities increased from 6% in 1952 to 23.6% in 1983. This largely represents U.S. bank liabilities to foreigners, such as CDs purchased by foreign Central Banks and corporations.

A comprehensive presentation of U.S. assets and liabilities vis-à-vis the rest of the world is given in Table 4–4, which shows the international investment position statement of the United States for selected years. The international investment position is the country's international balance sheet; it shows the composition of the stock of external assets and liabilities accumulated by a country's residents up to a certain date. It is also called, rather appropriately for some countries, the balance of indebtedness. Note that the international investment position measures the stock of foreign claims and liabilities of a country at a certain point in time. In this way it differs from the balance of payments accounts, which record changes or flows in the foreign claims and liabilities of a country during a given time period. As a matter of fact, the flows or changes in asset holdings measured by the balance of payments will be reflected as changes in the stock of assets and liabilities of the country.

Table 4–4 highlights some basic aspects of the international financial condition of the United States. It also illustrates the breadth and diversity of U.S. financial relations with the rest of the world. We shall now explain its items in some detail.

TABLE 4-4. International Investment Position of the United States at Year-End for Selected Years (Billions of Dollars)

Type of Investment	1970	1972	1974	1976	1978	1979	1980	1982	1983[c]
Net international investment position of the United States	58.6	37.1	58.8	83.8	76.2	94.9	120.6	149.5	106.0
U.S. assets abroad	165.5	199.0	255.7	347.2	447.9	510.6	606.7	838.1	887.5
U.S. official reserve assets	14.5	13.2	15.9	18.7	18.7	19.0	26.8	34.0	33.7
Other U.S. government assets	32.1	36.1	38.4	46.0	54.2	58.4	63.5	74.4	79.3
U.S. private assets	118.8	149.7	201.5	282.4	375.0	433.2	516.4	729.8	774.4
Direct investments abroad (book value)	75.5	89.9	110.1	136.8	162.7	187.9	215.4	221.5	226.1
Foreign securities	21.0	27.6	28.2	44.2	53.4	56.8	62.5	75.6	84.8
Claims on foreigners reported by U.S. banks, not included elsewhere	13.8	20.7	46.2	81.1	130.8	157.0	203.9	404.6	430.0
Claims on unaffiliated foreigners reported by U.S. nonbanks	8.5	11.4	17.0	20.3	28.1	31.5	34.7	28.2	26.5
Foreign assets in the United States	106.8	161.8	196.9	263.4	371.6	415.7	486.1	688.6	781.5
Foreign official assets	26.1	63.2	79.8	104.2	173.0	159.7	176.0	189.0	193.9
Other foreign assets	80.7	98.7	117.1	159.1	198.7	256.0	310.1	499.6	587.6
Direct investments in the United States (book value)	13.3	14.9	25.1	30.8	42.5	54.5	68.4	121.9	133.5
Liabilities reported by U.S. banks, not included elsewhere	22.7	21.2	41.8	53.5	77.7	110.3	121.1	231.3	280.3
U.S. Treasury securities	1.2	1.2	1.7	7.0	8.9	14.2	16.1	25.8	33.9
Other U.S. securities[b]	34.7	50.7	34.9	54.9	53.6	58.6	74.1	93.6	114.6
Liabilities to unaffiliated foreigners reported by U.S. nonbanks	8.8	10.7	13.6	13.0	16.0	18.4	30.4	27.1	25.2

Source: Economic Report of the President (1984), and Survey of Current Business, June 1984.
[a] The international investment position is essentially constructed on the basis of reported data. It ignores unrecorded assets and liabilities that correspond to the statistical discrepancy in the balance of payments. The annual balance of payments records year-to-year changes in the items of the international investment position.
[b] Corporate and other bonds and corporate stocks.
[c] Preliminary.

U.S. Assets Abroad

The category of U.S. assets abroad consists of U.S. claims on foreigners and includes U.S. official reserve assets, other assets held by the U.S. government, and foreign assets held by U.S. private residents. As displayed in Table 4–4, the most prominent of these is the latter, whose main constituents are direct foreign investment and claims on foreigners reported by banks.

U.S. direct foreign investment has traditionally been a significant component of U.S. external assets, as well as a source of much controversy abroad. Direct foreign investment provides the investor with a concomitant degree of control over the use of the funds invested. This financial concept involves financial claims on assets located abroad and is not necessarily related to physical investment abroad. For example, when a foreign subsidiary of a U.S. firm acquires equipment that it finances by means of a foreign bank loan, the transaction involves physical investment abroad but does not represent U.S. direct investment, since U.S. residents are not acquiring claims on foreigners that involve a controlling interest; in fact, there is no acquisition of any foreign asset at all. Similarly, when a U.S. firm acquires a controlling interest in a foreign firm by purchasing stocks, this does not involve physical investment abroad at all but is catalogued as direct investment. In a nutshell, avoid regarding direct foreign investment as physical investment abroad; for the present purposes, the two concepts are not equivalent.

The second major current component of U.S. assets abroad involves claims reported by banks. As shown in Table 4–4 these claims represented a relatively minor part of U.S. claims on foreigners until the 1970s, when they skyrocketed. A significant part of these bank claims consists of loans made by U.S. banks to foreign countries. Non-East Bloc developing countries, for example, owed more than $125 billion to U.S. banks as of June 1982. This ballooning external debt of many developing countries has worried many bankers and finance ministers recently, particularly in view of the difficulties these countries confront in repaying their debts. We shall examine the issues behind the external debt of developing countries in Chapter 17. Finally, it should be stressed that the figures on bank claims include only assets and liabilities of banking offices in the United States. Loans made by Eurobanks, that is, external branches and subsidiaries of U.S. banks, are not included as U.S. assets abroad, since Eurobanks are treated as foreign residents. Only the lending by the home office to its affiliated Eurobanks appears as an asset reported by U.S. banks, but not the lending made by the Eurobank itself. The data on the U.S. international investment position essentially neglect the substantial lending made by external branches and subsidiaries of U.S. banks through the Eurodollar market.

The remaining components of U.S. private assets abroad are (1) foreign securities, excluding those that provide some controlling interest, which are catalogued as direct foreign investment, and (2) nonbank claims on unaffiliated foreigners. With respect to this second category, recall that all reported bank claims are already catalogued and that the claims of nonbank residents on affiliated foreigners, such as those relating to the intercompany account of a multinational firm, are also already catalogued under direct foreign investment. Nonbank claims on unaffiliated foreigners consist of items such as loans made, say, by a U.S. firm to a foreign (unaffiliated) importer.

Foreign Assets in the United States

Foreign assets in the United States consist of the liabilities of U.S. residents to foreigners. Included are foreign official assets in the United States and other foreign assets, such as direct foreign investment, in the United States. Foreign official assets in the United States include CDs as well as U.S. Treasury securities owned by foreign Central Banks. As observed in Table 4–4, official assets are a major component of foreign assets in the United States, reflecting the demand for dollar-denominated assets by foreign Central Banks and the role of the U.S. dollar as an international reserve asset. The presentation of other foreign assets in the United States follows basically the same pattern as that of private U.S. assets abroad, but through the liabilities side. Observe how private foreign direct investment in the United States has grown during the 1970s and 1980s but still remains at a substantially lower absolute level than the total stock of U.S. direct investments abroad.

The U.S. international investment position shows the diversity of U.S. international financial relations. Yet it provides an incomplete picture of the financial openness of the economy because it records only assets that are actually traded internationally. The spectrum of assets that are potentially tradable in international markets is far greater than those that are actually traded. Furthermore, the international investment position only records the stocks of assets accumulated by U.S. and foreign residents up to a certain point in time. It does not measure the year-to-year trade in assets, that is, capital flows, recorded by the balance of payments statement. Just as the level of water in a river pond stays more or less fixed in spite of the vast inflow and outflow of water, the stock of assets held, and the international investment position, may stay more or less fixed in the face of massive capital flows in and out of the economy. But the openness of the domestic financial system is also reflected by those capital flows that are critically associated with the integration of the economy to world financial markets.

4–4 EXCHANGE RATE CONCEPTS AND MEASUREMENT

Up to this point, openness of the economy has been examined by observing the wide array of its international trade in goods, services, and assets, as well as the extent of trade in each of these categories, as recorded by the balance of payments. An economy's interactions with the rest of the world, however, are not only directly reflected in the *quantities* of various items traded internationally, but also through the *prices* of these items. The prices of many of the basic items in our daily life are crucially affected, and often determined, by situations in foreign or world markets. The price of oil is an obvious example, but the prices of such a variety of products as automobiles, stereos, refrigerators, grain, sugar, coffee, the clothes you are wearing, and the makeup on your face, are all heavily influenced by events in international markets and by the prices of competitive products available abroad. In order to compare domestic prices with foreign prices, conversion into the same currency has to be made. Exchange rates represent the terms at which currencies can be converted into each other. This section and the next one will examine the basic concepts and problems in the measurement of exchange rates and their interpretation.

Effective Exchange Rates

The exchange rate between any two given currencies, called a *bilateral exchange rate* in the present context, measures the cost of that currency in foreign exchange markets. If the price of a deutsche mark (DM) in foreign exchange markets is equal to 40 cents, the exchange rate between the two currencies is $e_{DM} = \$0.40$ /DM (40 cents per deutsche mark). When the exchange rate increases, the cost in dollars of acquiring foreign currency increases. For instance, if the exchange rate between the dollar and the DM increases to $e_{DM} = \$0.50/DM$, the cost of purchasing a DM increases by 10 cents. This implies that the amount of DMs we can purchase with any given amount of dollars declines. In other words, the value of the dollar declines against the DM, that is, the dollar becomes weaker.[15] A revaluation, or appreciation, of the dollar against the deutsche mark, represents an increase in the value of the dollar, popularly referred to as a stronger dollar relative to the mark in foreign exchange markets.

Making overall statements about whether a currency is weak or strong in foreign exchange markets on the basis of exchange rate changes is a very tricky business. For example, during 1977 and 1978, the U.S. dollar depreciated sharply in terms of the deutsche mark, the Swiss franc, and the Japanese yen. Indeed, it depreciated about 30% with respect to the deutsche mark and the Swiss franc, and more than 40% against the Japanese yen. The so-called sinking dollar became a primary topic of public discussion in financial circles. Besides the fact that this phenomenon turned out to be short lived, with the dollar reemerging strongly against these currencies from 1979 to 1984, a close look at the facts shows that focusing on a few currencies resulted in an exaggerated view of the dollar's decline. For instance, the dollar depreciated only about 15% against the English pound, and it actually appreciated in terms of various other currencies, such as the Canadian dollar, the currency of the main trade

---

[15] The reader should recall that, as the exchange rate has been defined, dollar depreciations are associated with increases in the exchange rate, e_{DM}.

partner of the United States. The overall position of a currency in foreign exchange markets can be distorted by focusing unduly on a small number of currencies.

This example illustrates a general characteristic of exchange rate movements: One does not generally observe a general depreciation or appreciation of a currency vis-à-vis other currencies but, rather, a simultaneous depreciation with respect to some currencies and appreciation with respect to others. It is convenient to develop an index or summary measure of how a currency fares, on average, in foreign exchange markets. Such an index is called an *effective exchange rate,* as differentiated from the usual exchange rates, such as the dollar–yen rate, which, as noted earlier, are called bilateral exchange rates. An effective exchange rate stands in the same relationship to bilateral exchange rates as a price index to the prices of individual commodities: An effective exchange rate is nothing more than an average of bilateral exchange rates.

There are currently more than 100 different national currencies. This means that we can compute more than 100 different bilateral exchange rates, each involving the dollar and a different foreign currency. Of course, it would be burdensome and superfluous to include all these bilateral rates in constructing an effective exchange rate index for the dollar. The first step in constructing an effective exchange rate index involves selecting a representative group of currencies to be included in the index. The group of currencies to be included must be in some way involved in the international trade of the country. For the United States, it makes little sense to include a currency such as the Maltese pound, since there are minimal trade connections between the United States and Malta. The currencies of Canada, the Federal Republic of Germany, and Japan, however, would clearly have to be included in the effective exchange rate index.

Once the currencies to be included in the effective exchange rate are determined, one must decide how to compute the index, that is, how to calculate an average of the various exchange rates. Different weights are assigned to different components of the average, depending on their relative importance. In the case of the U.S. effective exchange rate, the rather obvious weighting scheme is to give more weight to the currencies of those countries with which U.S. international trade is most important. We should give more weight to countries that trade heavily with the United States and less weight to countries with moderate trade. Since Canada is the main trade partner of the United States, the Canadian dollar would then be assigned a larger weight than would the currencies of Germany or Japan. An effective exchange rate index in which a currency's weight is assigned on the basis of the extent of its bilateral trade with the United States is called a *bilateral trade-weighted* index. In practice, there are various variants of bilateral trade-weighted indexes, depending on whether trade is measured on the basis of imports, exports, or total trade (i.e., exports plus imports).

One basic problem with a bilateral trade-weighted effective exchange rate index is that it gives inordinate importance to the currencies of the country's major trading partners. First, the share of a given country in U.S. trade does not necessarily measure its real importance in terms of the influence it has on U.S. external trade. For example, U.S. exports and imports to Germany may be much more sensitive to changes in the dollar–DM exchange rate than Canadian trade would be to a U.S.–Canadian dollar exchange rate change. In this case, an increase in the dollar–DM rate may signify a relatively more important event than an increase in the U.S.–Canadian dollar exchange rate in terms of its effects on the U.S. balance of trade and the overall economy. We would want to assign the deutsche mark a relatively higher weight, even if the share of U.S. trade with Germany is smaller than with Canada. Such an index is calculated by the IMF and is called the *multilateral exchange rate model index* (MERM), attributable to the name of the model of the economy used by the IMF to determine the relative responsiveness of U.S. exports and imports to changes in various exchange rates.[16]

Another reason why bilateral trade-weighted effective exchange rates may overstate the importance of trade partners is that the real significance of a country's currency is often more closely related to the country's participation in *world* trade and not necessarily to participation in U.S. trade. Those countries that trade heavily in world markets, and not necessarily with the United States alone, will be more involved in competing with U.S. products abroad. It is changes in the exchange rates of their currencies that will be of crucial importance to U.S. trade abroad, as well as to its economy. More weight should then be given to these currencies. Under this weighting scheme, the Canadian dollar would receive a smaller weight than the deutsche mark or yen because even though trade of Canada with the United States is indeed very heavy, the Canadian share of world trade is much smaller than is that of Germany or Japan. An effective exchange rate index that assigns weights to a country's currency on the basis of the importance of that country's trade in global or world trade, as opposed to its importance in U.S. trade, is interchangeably called a *multilateral, world,* or *global trade-weighted effective exchange rate index*. An index of this type is published by the Federal Reserve Bulletin.

Effective exchange rates are index numbers, expressed in terms of a base year assigned a value of 100. A value of 200 for the U.S. dollar index means that the average price of foreign exchange has doubled in comparison to the base year; overall, the dollar has depreciated. A value of 50 means that, in general terms, foreign currencies have become cheaper in terms of the dollar; that is, the dollar has appreciated. Column 1 of Table 4–5 exhibits the behavior of the effective exchange rate index for the U.S. dollar from 1976 to 1983 as published by the Morgan Guaranty Trust Co. Actually, the dollar remained

---

[16] Estimating the responsiveness of exports and imports to various exchange rate changes is a difficult task. For this purpose, the International Monetary Fund has developed a statistical model of international trade in many respects similar to the one developed in Parts III and IV.

TABLE 4–5. United States Dollar Effective Exchange Rates 1976 to 1983.[a,b]

Year		Nominal Effective Exchange Rate, e (1)	Ratio of World to U.S. Wholesale Price Indexes, $P*/P$ (2)	Real Effective Exchange Rate, $e_r = eP*/P$ $(3) = (1) \times (2)$ (3)
1976	I	99.5	105.8	105.3
	II	98.7	106.9	105.5
	III	99.9	107.6	107.5
	IV	98.1	106.7	104.7
1977	I	98.3	107.3	105.5
	II	99.0	107.3	106.2
	III	99.1	107.3	106.3
	IV	103.4	105.5	109.1
1978	I	105.6	105.1	111.6
	II	107.0	104.4	111.7
	III	111.7	103.8	115.9
	IV	111.4	102.7	114.4
1979	I	110.7	103.4	114.5
	II	109.2	103.4	112.9
	III	111.1	103.7	115.2
	IV	109.8	102.5	112.5
1980	I	106.5	102.2	108.8
	II	112.9	101.6	114.7
	III	112.7	101.6	114.5
	IV	108.7	100.1	108.8
1981	I	105.6	98.5	104.0
	II	98.1	98.4	96.5
	III	97.1	100.1	97.2
	IV	99.7	98.8	98.5
1982	I	93.7	100.0	93.7
	II	90.0	100.4	90.4
	III	88.3	100.8	89.0
	IV	89.8	99.6	89.4
1983	I	89.3	101.2	90.4
	II	87.5	101.5	88.8
	III	85.7	102.5	87.8
	IV	84.7	102.0	86.4

Source: World Financial Markets, Morgan Guaranty Trust Co. (New York, January 1984). Reproduced by permission.
[a] A bilateral trade-weighted exchange rate index is used with the base period of 1980–1982.
[b] To avoid confusion, the reader may note that effective exchange rates are frequently calculated as the inverse of the way we have computed them.

relatively stable during the 1960s, depreciated about 15% during 1971–73, and has fluctuated around its 1973 level ever since. A pattern that stands out is that the effective exchange rate of the U.S. dollar has fluctuated greatly during the floating exchange rate period, an experience that contrasts with the stability in the sixties under the Bretton Woods regime. The reader should also note that the dollar depreciation of 1977 to 1978 depicted in Table 4–5 is far smaller when compared with the sharp depreciations against specific currencies, such as the more than 40% depreciation against the Japanese yen during that period. Over the 1980s, however, the dollar has generally had a declining effective exchange rate.

In summary, a wide menu of alternative effective exchange rate indexes is published by different organizations, depending on the basket of currencies included in the index, the weight assignment scheme, whether bilateral, global, or MERM, and so forth. However measured, the usefulness of an effective exchange rate index hinges in that it allows us to evaluate a currency's value vis-à-vis other currencies in a multicurrency world. Especially in a system of flexible exchange rates, in which a variety of currencies will be fluctuating up and down, it is often extremely useful to have such a summary measure. It tells us how the currency has fared overall in foreign exchange markets. The information provided can be combined with the data presented by the balance of payments on the quantities of international transactions, including those relating to official reserve assets, to provide us with a clearer view of the economy's interrelationships with the rest of the world.

One aspect that can be illuminated by the effective exchange rate is how the country's competitiveness changes vis-à-vis the rest of the world. To understand this, it must first be realized that, ceteris paribus, a depreciation of the dollar vis-à-vis any given foreign currency tends to make U.S. products more competitive relative to those of the foreign country. For instance, a depreciation of the dollar in terms of the deutsche mark from $0.40 to $0.50 per deutsche mark means that a German Volkswagen priced at DM 20,000 will increase its dollar price from $8,000 to $10,000. If the prices of comparable U.S. automobiles (say, Chevys) remain unchanged, our cars would then become relatively more competitive than German cars. Given that, in general, we shall find the dollar depreciating with respect to some currencies and appreciating vis-à-vis others, the effective exchange rate provides a summary index of how U.S. goods have fared overall relative to foreign goods in terms of price competitiveness. An increase in the effective exchange rate would mean that, overall, the dollar price of foreign currencies has increased, making U.S. products generally more competitive relative to foreign goods. One must be cautious, however, in associating changes in effective exchange rates with changes in the overall price competitiveness of U.S. goods relative to foreign goods. The reason is that the prices of domestic goods will not necessarily stay fixed when the exchange rate changes and could very well increase substantially. In the dollar–DM example above, the prices of Chevys in the United States may go up in response to the switch in demand toward U.S. cars. In addition, foreign prices could also be changing; for example, foreign exporters of Volkswagens may decide to lower the deutsche mark price of their autos. Consequently, in order to illuminate the question of changes in the relative competitiveness of U.S. products, we must adjust exchange rate changes for price changes. The next section will discuss in more detail how this is done.

e = $1.15; coin price of US dollar

Nominal and Real Exchange Rates

A key distinction to bear in mind, now and throughout the rest of this book, is that between nominal and real exchange rates. A *nominal exchange rate* states the home currency price of foreign exchange. The usual bilateral exchange rates, like the U.S. dollar price of sterling, are nominal exchange rates. Similarly, effective exchange rates, being an average of nominal exchange rates, are also nominal rates. *A real exchange rate* is a price-adjusted nominal exchange rate. Specifically, the relationship between a nominal exchange rate, e, and a real exchange rate, e_r, can be expressed algebraically by

$$e_r = e\,\frac{P*}{P}$$

where $P*$ and P represent relevant indexes of foreign and domestic prices, respectively.[17] As observed, the real exchange rate is equal to the nominal exchange rate adjusted by the ratio of foreign to domestic prices.

What can real exchange rates tell us? As noted in the last section, a full measure of the competitiveness of U.S. products relative to foreign products must take into account not only changes in nominal exchange rates, but price changes as well. This is exactly what the real exchange rate does. Consequently, the real exchange rate can be used to illuminate us about how U.S. goods are faring relative to foreign goods in terms of their price competitiveness. To discern this more clearly, consider the real exchange rate between the U.S. dollar and the British pound. As the expression for e_r tells us, the real exchange rate is basically the ratio of the term $eP*$ to the term P. The symbol $P*$ in this example stands for the price level in the United Kingdom, which is the average price of a basket of goods in the United Kingdom expressed in pounds. But since e denotes the exchange rate of the U.S. dollar vis-à-vis the British pound, expressed in dollars per pound, then $eP*$ represents the price of a basket of goods in the United Kingdom expressed in terms of dollars. Of course, P in the present case is the U.S. price level expressed in dollars. As a result, the ratio of $eP*/P$ essentially denotes the ratio of the prices of British and American goods, both expressed in dollars. In other words, the real exchange rate between the dollar and the pound basically shows how the prices of British goods compare

[17] Various alternative indices of prices and costs are commonly used to calculate effective exchange rates, such as consumer prices, wholesale prices, and labor costs. Which index is to be selected depends on the use to which the real exchange rate is going to be put.

depreciation of the dollar

$\frac{ep^*}{P}$

with the prices of U.S. goods when expressed in terms of dollars. An increase in the real exchange rate would imply that U.S. goods become more price competitive relative to British goods, and a reduction of the real exchange rate would imply that British goods have become relatively more competitive. Observe how crucial it is to adjust exchange rate changes for price changes when calculating its effects on the relative competitiveness of U.S. goods relative to foreign goods. For example, if the dollar–pound nominal exchange rate was devalued by 20% (an increase in e), but the U.S. price level increases at the same time by 20%, with the British price level remaining more or less fixed, then the dollar–pound real exchange rate would remain unchanged. In other words, U.S. price competitiveness relative to Britain would not be altered. The devaluation makes British goods absolutely more expensive in terms of dollars but, since U.S. prices have also increased by the same proportion, no net effect would be observed in terms of their *relative* price. If, for example, a dollar devaluation were to increase the prices of U.K. records by $2.00, but at the same time U.S.-made records were to increase in price by $2.00 as well, you would not really observe any change in the relative competitiveness of the two products.

In general, we are interested in obtaining some measure of competitiveness of the United States vis-à-vis its main trading partners, rather than just against a particular country such as the United Kingdom. In other words, we are interested in obtaining a real effective exchange rate index. In order to derive a real from a nominal effective exchange rate, we adjust the latter by means of an appropriate price index for U.S. main trade partners divided by a U.S. price index. In terms of the algebraic expression for e_r above, e would now be the nominal effective exchange rate, P^* would be an index of foreign prices, and P would be an index of U.S. prices.

Column 3 of Table 4–5 displays the behavior of the real effective exchange rate for the U.S. dollar from 1976 to 1984, obtained by adjusting the nominal effective rates in column 1 by means of wholesale price indexes. Two important observations can be made from Table 4–5. First, real effective exchange rates exhibit substantial yearly fluctuations, frequently exceeding 10%. Second, though no clear trend is observed for the period as a whole, two distinct patterns can be identified, the real depreciation of the dollar occurring during 1977 to 1979 and the subsequent sharp real appreciation in the early 1980's.

Although the nominal and the real effective exchange rates of the dollar have roughly moved together during the 1960s and 1970s, this is not a general characteristic. Nominal and real exchange rates frequently move in different directions. A case in point is that of the British pound during 1973 to 1980, a period over which the pound experienced a nominal depreciation and a real appreciation at the same time. This opposite behavior of the two indexes arose because U.K. inflation relative to that of its trade partners exceeded the nominal depreciation of the sterling. As a result, the United Kingdom lost price competitiveness relative to its trade partners, while its currency was depreciating.

4–5 SUMMARY

1. The balance of payments of a country records all the economic transactions that have taken place during a given period between the country's residents and the rest of the world. The basic rule of balance of payments accounting is that any transaction giving rise to a receipt from (payment to) the rest of the world is a credit (debit) and appears as a positive (negative) item in the account.

2. Double-entry bookkeeping conventions mean that the overall balance of payments is always zero. However, the balance of payments can be subdivided into several (sub)balances or accounts, which will be in surplus or deficit, depending on whether each represents an excess or deficiency of receipts over payments on that account.

3. The current account registers the economy's international trade in goods and services as well as its transfers to or from other countries. A surplus in the current account balance means that receipts from sales of goods and services plus transfers received exceed payments in those items to foreigners. The contrary is true for a deficit on current account. The trade balance measures exports minus imports of merchandise.

4. The capital account registers all asset transactions except for those involving the monetary authorities' international reserves. A capital account surplus or deficit arises depending on whether the receipts from the sales of assets registered by the capital account have exceeded or fall short of purchases of those assets.

5. The sum of the current and the capital accounts (plus the allocation of SDRs) is called the official reserve settlements balance. This balance can be used, though imperfectly, to measure the intervention of monetary authorities in foreign exchange markets and is particularly meaningful in an economy under a fixed exchange rate regime. Its calculation loses interest under freely floating regimes when the monetary authorities let the exchange rate fluctuate and follow a hands-off policy with respect to foreign exchange markets. Under a managed floating system, in which the exchange rate is allowed to fluctuate but monetary authorities still intervene in foreign exchange markets in order to smooth out fluctuations in exchange rates, the official reserve settlements balance remains a useful concept to calculate.

6. An effective exchange rate is an average of various bilateral exchange rates. It is used as an index or summary measure of how a currency fares, on average, in foreign exchange markets in a multicurrency world.

7. A real effective exchange rate is a price-adjusted effective exchange rate frequently used as an index of the competitiveness of a country's goods relative to those of other countries.

Problems

1. Using the most recent data available in the *Survey of Current Business,* compute the U.S. trade balance, current account balance, and all the concepts summarized in Table 4–3. (Recalculate Table 4–3.)

2. Indicate which entry in the U.S. balance of payments accounts is to be credited and debited for each of the following transactions, illustrating through the use of T accounts.

   (a) A businessman visiting the United States lures his New York cabdriver into accepting 11,000 yen for a ride in the Big Apple. The cab driver exchanges the yens for $50.00 through his bank.

   (b) A German distributor buys $20 million in high-tech equipment from IBM in the United States. It pays by means of a bank transfer from its Los Angeles bank.

   (c) The U.S. government ships $1 million worth of grain, cheese, and butter as food aid to Bangladesh.

   (d) A U.S. investor purchases $1 million in Japanese securities. He pays by drawing a check on his account in a New York bank.

   (e) A subsidiary of a German multinational firm operating in the U.S. invests part of its retained earnings in American securities.

   (f) A conservative political action committee receives a gift of $100,000 in a check drawn on the Swiss account of a free-enterprise advocate.

   (g) After some negotiation, the U.S. government agrees to lend $200 million to a Latin American country. The payment occurs through an increase in that government's account at the New York Federal Reserve Bank.

   (h) Each author of this book receives $2000 worth in royalties from its foreign edition. Because of a foreign exchange crisis abroad, the money is delivered in foreign currency. They decide to take a vacation and spend all the royalties abroad, bringing back $200 worth in gifts.

   (i) (1) A U.S. automobile manufacturer exports $1 million worth of cars. The foreign importer signs a bill of exchange for the value of the goods.

       (2) The U.S. exporter discounts the bill of exchange with Chase Manhattan Bank, which in turn keeps the bill until maturity. (Assume 10% discount on the bill.)

       (3) On the bill's maturity 90 days later, Chase accepts payment for the bill in dollars in the form of a check drawn on the importer's Citibank account. The interest accrued on the bill is $50,000.

   (j) A consortium of American banks lends $100,000 to a developing country. The country immediately spends one-half the loan in U.S. oil-drilling equipment. The rest is invested in 90-day CDs issued by Chicago banks.

3. Compute the net effect of the transactions reported above on the trade balance, the current account balance, and the official settlements balance of the United States.

4. Indicate how the U.S. balance of payments accounts and the size of the Eurodollar market are affected by the following transactions:

   (a) An American corporation moves $10 million out of certificates of deposit in New York to invest them in Eurodollar CDs issued by Barclays in London.

   (b) Barclays disposes of $10 million through the interbank market. The funds are lent to an American firm abroad, which exchanges the $10 million for deutsche marks to purchase German money market instruments.

5. The growth of the Eurocurrency market, and particularly of Eurodollar deposits, is frequently attributed to U.S. balance of payments deficits and the corresponding accumulation of dollar balances abroad. Evaluate.

6. Would you expect to find a difference in the structure of the balance of payments accounts (e.g., the value of the trade balance, capital account) of countries in different stages of their development? What do the historical data suggest regarding stages of the balance of payments?

APPENDIX: U.S. BALANCE OF PAYMENTS STATISTICS

TABLE 4-A1. U.S. International Transactions

(Credit +; debits −)	Line	1960	1970	1974	1976	1979	1980	1982	1983ᵖ
Exports of goods and services	1	28,861	65,674	146,666	171,630	286,772	342,102	348,324	334,233
Merchandise, adjusted, excluding military	2	19,650	42,469	98,306	114,745	184,473	224,237	211,217	200,203
Transfers under U.S. military agency sales contracts	3	335	1,501	3,379	5,454	6,549	8,306	12,097	12,657
Travel	4	919	2,331	4,032	5,742	8,441	10,058	11,293	11,187
Passenger fares	5	175	544	1,104	1,229	2,156	2,582	2,979	3,153
Other transportation	6	1,607	3,125	5,697	6,747	10,028	11,497	12,437	13,479
Fees and royalties from affiliated foreigners	7	590	1,758	3,070	3,531	4,980	5,780	5,572	5,975
Fees and royalties from unaffiliated foreigners	8	247	573	751	822	1,100	1,185	1,567	1,686
Other private services	9	570	1,294	2,321	3,584	4,396	5,412	6,576	7,282
U.S. government miscellaneous services	10	153	332	419	489	520	362	440	574
Receipts of income on U.S. assets abroad: Direct investment	11	3,621	8,169	19,157	18,999	38,183	37,150	22,888	22,165
Interest, dividends, and earnings of unincorporated affiliates	12	2,355	4,992	11,379	11,303	19,219	20,133	17,565	12,710
Reinvested earnings of incorporated affiliates	13	1,266	3,177	7,777	7,696	18,965	17,017	5,323	9,456
Other private receipts	14	646	2,671	7,356	8,955	23,654	32,987	57,127	50,948
U.S. government receipts	15	349	907	1,074	1,332	2,292	2,549	4,131	4,922

Source: U.S. Department of Commerce, Survey of Current Business (March 1984).
ᵖ: Preliminary estimate.

Line	Item								
16	Transfers of goods and services under U.S. military grant programs, net	209	644	631	465	373	1,818	2,713	1,695
17	Imports of goods and services	−366,410	−351,502	−333,800	−281,677	−162,248	−137,357	−60,050	−23,729
18	Merchandise, adjusted, excluding military	−260,753	−247,606	−249,575	−211,819	−124,051	−103,649	−39,866	−14,758
19	Direct defense expenditures	−12,174	−11,918	−10,777	−8,584	−4,895	−5,032	−4,855	−3,087
20	Travel	−13,944	−12,394	−10,397	−9,413	−6,856	−5,980	−3,980	−1,750
21	Passenger fares	−5,636	−4,772	−3,607	−3,184	−2,568	−2,095	−1,215	−513
22	Other transportation	−12,482	−11,638	−111,073	−10,457	−6,852	−5,942	−2,843	−1,402
23	Fees and royalties to affiliated foreigners	−245	−42	−514	−523	−293	−160	−111	−35
24	Fees and royalties to unaffiliated foreigners	−308	−295	−247	−241	−189	−186	−114	−40
25	Private payments for other services	−4,176	−3,700	−3,065	−2,824	−2,006	−1,262	−827	−593
26	U.S. government payments for miscellaneous services	−2,238	−2,296	−1,769	−1,718	−1,227	−967	−725	−313
27	Payments of income on foreign assets in the United States: Direct investment	−7,161	−4,844	−9,470	−6,357	−3,110	−1,331	−875	−394
28	Interest, dividends, and earnings of unincorporated affiliates	−5,447	−5,008	−3,303	−2,402	−1,451	−266	−441	−220
29	Reinvested earnings of incorporated affiliates	−1,714	164	−6,167	−3,955	−1,659	−1,065	−434	−174
30	Other private payments	−29,579	−33,769	−20,794	−15,481	−5,681	−6,491	−3,617	−511
31	U.S. government payments	−17,714	−18,229	−12,512	−11,076	−4,520	−4,262	−1,024	−332

TABLE 4–A1. U.S. International Transactions (cont.)

(Credit +; debits −)	Line	1960	1970	1974	1976	1979	1980	1982	1983ᵖ
U.S. military grants of goods and services, net	32	-1,695	-2,713	-1,818	-373	-465	-631	-644	-209
Unilateral transfers (excluding military grants of goods and services), net	33	-2,308	-3,294	-7,186	-4,998	-5,561	-6,783	-8,034	-8,599
U.S. government grants (excluding military grants of goods and services)	34	-1,672	-1,736	-5,475	-3,146	-3,550	-4,681	-5,413	-5,967
U.S. government pensions and other transfers	35	-214	-462	-694	-934	-1,180	-1,303	-1,493	-1,577
Private remittances and other transfers	36	-423	-1,096	-1,017	-917	-832	-798	-1,128	-1,055
U.S. assets abroad, net [increase/capital outflow (−)]	37	-4,099	-9,337	-34,745	-51,269	-64,344	-86,026	-118,045	-49,297
U.S. official reserve assets, netᵈ	38	2,145	2,481	-1,467	-2,558	-1,133	-8,155	-4,965	-1,196
Gold	39	1,703	787			-65			
Special drawing rights	40		-851	-172	-78	-1,136	-16	-1,371	-66
Reserve position in the International Monetary Fund	41	442	389	-1,265	-2,212	-189	-1,667	-2,552	-4,434
Foreign currencies	42		2,156	-30	-268	257	-6,472	-1,041	3,304
U.S. government assets, other than official reserve assets, net	43	-1,100	-1,589	366	-4,214	-3,743	-5,126	-5,732	-4,897
U.S. loans and other long-term assets	44	-1,214	-3,293	-5,001	-6,943	-7,676	-9,854	-10,117	-10,197
Repayments on U.S. loans	45	642	1,721	4,826	2,596	3,908	4,459	4,334	5,226
U.S. foreign currency holdings and U.S. short-term assets, net	46	-528	-16	541	133	25	269	51	74

U.S. private assets, net	47	-5,144	-10,229	-33,643	-44,498	-59,469	-72,746	-107,348	-43,204
Direct investment	48	-2,940	-7,590	-9,052	-11,949	-25,222	-19,238	3,008	-7,608
Equity and intercompany accounts	49	-1,674	-4,413	-1,275	-4,253	-6,258	-2,221	8,331	1,848
Reinvested earnings of incorporated affiliates	50	-1,266	-3,177	-7,777	-7,696	-18,965	-17,017	-5,323	-9,456
Foreign securities	51	-663	-1,076	-1,854	-8,885	-4,726	-3,524	-7,986	-7,484
U.S. claims on unaffiliated foreigners reported by U.S. nonbanking concerns:									
Long-term	52	-40	-586	-474	-42	-3,307 }	-3,146 }	6,976 }	n.a. }
Short-term	53	-354	-10	-2,747	-2,254				
U.S. claims reported by U.S. banks, not included elsewhere:									
Long-term	54	-153	155	-1,183	-2,362	-26,213 }	-46,838 }	-109,346 }	-24,966 }
Short-term	55	-995	-1,122	-18,333	-19,006				
Foreign assets in the United States, net [increase/capital inflow (+)]	56	2,294	6,359	34,241	36,518	38,460	54,484	87,866	83,018
Foreign official assets in the United States, net	57	1,473	6,908	10,546	17,693	-13,697	15,442	3,172	6,083
U.S. government securities	58	655	9,439	4,172	9,892	-21,972	11,895	5,089	6,676
U.S. Treasury securities	59	655	9,411	3,270	9,319	-22,435	9,708	5,759	7,140
Other[7]	60	215	28	902	573	463	2,187	-670	-464
Other U.S. government liabilities	61		-456	301	4,627	-73	561	504	318
U.S. liabilities reported by U.S. banks, not included elsewhere	62	603	-2,075	5,818	969	7,213	-159	-2,054	877
Other foreign official assets	63			254	2,205	1,135	3,145	-367	-1,788

TABLE 4–A1. U.S. International Transactions (cont.)

(Credit +; debits −)	Line	1960	1970	1974	1976	1979	1980	1982	1983ᵖ
Other foreign assets in the United States, net	64	821	−550	23,696	18,826	52,157	39,042	84,694	76,935
Direct investment	65	315	1,464	4,760	4,347	11,877	13,666	10,390	9,514
Equity and intercompany accounts	66	141	1,030	3,695	2,687	7,921	7,500	10,554	7,800
Reinvested earnings of incorporated affiliates	67	174	434	1,065	1,659	3,955	6,167	−164	1,714
U.S. Treasury securities	68	−364	81	697	2,783	4,960	2,645	7,004	8,599
U.S. securities other than U.S. Treasury securities	69	282	2,189	378	1,284	1,351	5,457	6,141	8,587
U.S. liabilities to unaffiliated foreigners reported by U.S. nonbanking concerns:									
Long-term	70	1	1,112	−90	−1,000	1,362	6,530 }	−3,104	n.a.
Short-term	71	−91	902	1,934	422				
U.S. liabilities reported by U.S. banks, not included elsewhere:									
Long-term	72	6	23	9	231	1,139	1,152		
Short-term	73	672	−6,321	16,008	10,759	32,607	10,743 }	64,263	51,295
Allocations of special drawing rights	74		867						
Statistical discrepancy (sum of above items with sign reversed)	75	−1,019	−219	−1,620	10,367	25,212	28,870	41,390	7,055
Memoranda									
Balance on merchandise trade (lines 2 and 18)	76	4,892	2,603	−5,343	−9,306	−27,346	−25,338	−36,389	−60,550

Description	Line								
Balance on goods and services (lines 1 and 17)	77	5,132	5,625	9,309	9,382	5,095	8,303	−3,177	−32,177
Balance on goods, services, and remittances (lines 77, 35, and 36)	78	4,496	4,067	7,599	7,531	3,083	6,202	−5,799	−34,809
Balance on current account (lines 77 and 33)	79	2,824	2,331	2,124	4,384	−466	1,520	−11,211	−40,776
Transactions in U.S. official reserve assets and in foreign official assets in the United States:									
Increase (−) in U.S. official reserve assets, net (line 38)	80	2,145	2,481	−1,467	−2,558	−1,133	−8,155	−4,965	−1,196
Increase (+) in foreign official assets in the United States (line 57 less line 61)	81	1,258	7,364	10,244	13,066	−13,624	14,881	2,668	5,765

TABLE 4–A2. **Balance of Payments Subaccounts: Selected Years (billions of dollars)**

	1970	1972	1974	1976	1978	1979	1980	1982	1983
Current account balance	2.3	−5.8	2.1	4.4	−14.8	−.5	1.5	−11.2	−40.8
Capital account balance	−13.1	−11.3	−10.8	−14.9	−17.1	14.1	−9.4	13.5	36.2
Allocation of SDRs[a]	0.9	0.7	—	—	—	1.1	1.2	—	—
Official reserve settlements balance	−9.9	−10.3	−8.7	−10.5	−31.9	14.7	−6.7	2.3	−4.6

Source: U.S. Department of Commerce, *Survey of Current Business* (March 1983).

[a] For completeness, we include the allocation of SDRs. Special drawing rights are a form of international reserve asset distributed by the International Monetary Fund. Its allocations are considered an international transaction, thus appearing in the balance of payments accounts.

Income, Trade, and Capital Flows Under Fixed and Flexible Exchange Rates

PART III

CHAPTER 5

Determination of Output, Employment, and the Trade Balance

This is the first of five chapters that provide an introduction to the macroeconomics of an open economy under fixed and flexible exchange rate regimes. Our main goal is to analyze the determinants of output, trade, and capital flows. We are particularly interested in the role of the balance of payments in bringing about macroeconomic adjustment under fixed exchange rates and the corresponding role of exchange rate changes under floating exchange rates. For instance, how does the general, drastic appreciation of the U.S. dollar vis-à-vis most other major currencies during the 1981 to 1984 period affected domestic competitiveness in international markets? What would be the effects of such changes on domestic trade and output? These are questions to which we shall provide an introductory answer in the next five chapters. In addition, we shall examine and compare the effects of specific government policies, such as fiscal, monetary, and commercial policies, under fixed and flexible exchange rates. It is often argued, for instance, that the U.S. recession of late 1981 and 1982 resulted from the contractionary monetary policies of the U.S. government at the time. The strong dollar during that period is also frequently attached to the administration's policies. Is there any basis for these statements? Chapters 5 through 9 provide an introductory framework of analysis within which such questions can be examined. Finally, we shall follow the basic contributions and controversies that have historically arisen in the field of open economy macroeconomics, looking at those of the past with the benefits of hindsight and those of the present in the light of their most recent state of development.

In this chapter we shall look at the primary considerations involved in the macroeconomic analysis of the open economy, stressing the differences from a closed economy. We begin by relating balance of payments concepts to those of national income accounting. This approach provides us with an overview of how the external sector is linked to the national economy. We then proceed to analyze the effects of international trade in goods on the determination of

153

the level of output and employment under fixed exchange rates using a simple Keynesian model of the open economy. The effects and possible combination of government policies, say exchange rate and fiscal policies, required to attain the goals of full employment and balanced trade are examined within this context.

5–1 NATIONAL INCOME ACCOUNTING AND THE OPEN ECONOMY

The basic national income accounting concept is the national income or gross national product (GNP) identity. It breaks down GNP—the value of all the goods and services produced by a country's residents during a given period—into various spending categories. In an open economy, the goods produced by a country's residents can be purchased by foreign and domestic residents. This is in sharp contrast to a closed economy, that is, one that has no trade connections with the rest of the world. The expenditures of foreign residents on domestic goods and services are our exports, symbolized by X_N.[1] What categories make up the purchases of domestic goods on the part of domestic residents?

The expenditure of our residents on domestic products is given by the total aggregate amount they spend minus their spending on foreign goods and services, that is, our imports, symbolized by M_N. The total expenditures of domestic residents include a variety of items that can be catalogued as private consumption expenditures, C_N, investment expenditures, I_N, and government expenditures, G_N. In other words, domestic expenditures include not only our purchases of vegetables, Coca Cola, and meat, and the expenditures of firms and investors on new machines, new buildings, and the accumulation of inventories, but also government outlays on B1 bombers, paper, and stamps. The total spending of domestic residents is thus given by

$$A_N \equiv C_N + I_N + G_N$$

referred to by the special name of *domestic absorption.* If one nets imports out of domestic absorption, the residual then represents that part of the total spending by local residents that falls exclusively on domestic goods. Symbolically, this component is given by

$$A_N - M_N \equiv C_N + I_N + G_N - M_N$$

The value of national output (GNP), symbolized by Y_N, is accounted for by the sum of domestic and foreign expenditures on domestic goods. Symbolically,

---

[1] The subscript N below a variable is used in this book to indicate that the variable is expressed in nominal terms. A nominal variable is measured in terms of currency, such as dollars in the United States, as opposed to real variables, which refer to physical quantities of goods, such as bushels of wheat.

$$Y_N \equiv C_N + I_N + G_N - M_N + X_N$$

$$\equiv A_N + X_N - M_N \quad CAB = T \tag{1}$$

where $X_N - M_N$ is the net value of exports minus imports. Equation (1) shows the basic accounting identity in an open economy. If the various categories— production, consumption, investment, and so forth—were defined and measured appropriately, equation (1) would always hold exactly. This is so because the equation represents an accounting definition: The spending items are defined such that they can account for all the domestic output measured on the left-hand side. Sometimes, broad definitions are necessary to cover all possible uses of national output. For instance, unsold goods are classified as an investment expenditure made by firms in the form of inventory accumulation; they are thus catalogued under the investment category in the national accounts. Adequate accounting and measurement ensure the identical equality of production and spending.

The identity stated in equation (1) can be used to show how the spending categories accounting for domestic output in the open economy compare with their closed economy counterparts. In a closed economy, the basic national income identity states that the value of domestic output must equal absorption, that is, $Y_N \equiv A_N$. The reason is that, in the absence of foreign trade, aggregate spending on domestic goods and services must be identical to the aggregate spending of domestic residents (i.e., absorption). In an open economy this does not have to be so. Foreign trade implies that some spending on domestic goods comes from foreign sources (e.g., Japanese buying American refrigerators), and a part of domestic spending falls on foreign goods (e.g., Americans buying imported automobiles). In order to derive aggregate spending on *domestic goods and services* from the aggregate spending of *domestic residents* (absorption), one has to add to absorption the foreign spending on domestic goods and services (exports) and then substract the spending of domestic residents on foreign goods and services (imports). That is exactly what the expression on the right-hand side of equation (1) shows.

The GNP or national income identity can be rearranged to yield

$$X_N - M_N \equiv Y_N - A_N \tag{2}$$

which expresses the balance on goods and services as the gap between national income and domestic absorption.[2] Note that, in the absence of unilateral transfers,

---

[2] The present discussion disregards the distinctions between GNP and national income arising from the need to adjust for investment depreciation and indirect taxes. In a more detailed presentation, one would have to subtract both of these from GNP to obtain national income. Note also that if one subtracts net factor income from abroad from both sides of equation (2), one finds that the balance on goods and services other than factor payments equals the gap between gross domestic product (GDP) and absorption.

the balance on goods and services corresponds to the current account balance, CAB. Thus, equation (2) leads to

$$T = \text{CAB} \equiv Y_N - A_N \tag{3}$$

which tells us that the current account balance is identically equal to the difference between national income and domestic absorption. A current account balance deficit (CAB < 0) implies an excess of the spending of domestic residents over their income, while a surplus (CAB > 0) means an excess of income over spending. The insights of this formulation of the current account in terms of aggregate categories in national income accounts rather than as a relationship between the country's credits and debits in its international transactions accounts were coherently formulated by Sidney Alexander in 1952 and received the label of the *absorption approach* to the current account (or the balance of payments).[3] The absorption approach analyzes the CAB by examining the economic factors determining the gap between income and absorption. Its influence on the thinking of both international monetary economists and policymakers during the post–World War II period has been immense, as we shall see.

The Current Account and Asset Accumulation

How does the income minus absorption view of the current account balance fit into that derived from the balance of payments accounts, which identifies a CAB surplus with a net accumulation of foreign assets by domestic residents? Just as we as individuals use an excess of income over spending to acquire assets, whether in the form of bank deposits or as stocks and bonds, a country uses an overall excess of income over spending to accumulate foreign assets, such as foreign currencies or foreign stocks and bonds. Accordingly, the interpretation of a CAB surplus as the excess of income over spending of domestic residents is clearly the same as that of net accumulation of foreign assets (net foreign investment). Similarly, an excess of spending over income is associated with a net decumulation of foreign assets, or, alternatively, with increased liabilities to foreigners; whether by selling stocks and bonds or by borrowing, the excess of spending over income has to be financed. Consequently, the view of a CAB deficit as an excess of spending by domestic residents over their income is equivalent to viewing it as a net decumulation of foreign assets or, alternatively, as an accumulation of liabilities to foreigners.

If we consider that the current account balance represents the net acquisition of foreign assets, can we validly identify the CAB with changes in domestic wealth so that a CAB surplus would be associated with increasing domestic

---

[3] Sidney Alexander coined the terminology of absorption. A key contributor to the macroeconomic approach to the open economy was Nobel prize winner James Meade in his book *The Balance of Payments* (London: Oxford University Press, 1951).

wealth and a CAB deficit with decreasing wealth? The answer is no—we generally cannot identify the CAB with changes in wealth. To clarify the issue, consider a situation of current account deficit. Since this situation represents a net decumulation of *foreign* assets by the country as a whole, it tends to reduce domestic residents' asset holdings. Nevertheless, domestic residents can also increase their total wealth through accumulation of *domestic* assets.

A CAB deficit does not necessarily connote shrinking wealth if domestic assets are being accumulated at the same time, as would be the case in a growing economy that invests in both physical and human capital. Within this context, a CAB deficit suggests that the country is selling or mortgaging part of the newly created assets. It cannot be deduced that the country's total wealth is decreasing. As a matter of fact, a CAB deficit might imply that the country is borrowing abroad to complement its own resources in order to invest and import the machines and equipment necessary for economic growth. In this situation, the CAB deficit is associated with a growth of domestic wealth in the form of domestic capital accumulation and increased claims on it. There is clearly no necessary connection between changes in domestic wealth and CAB deficits.

The representation of the current account as the difference between income and expenditure as depicted by equation (3) can provide us with additional insights when we disaggregate it into its constituents. We can easily do this through a slight modification of the right-hand side of equation (3), by subtracting and adding taxes, TX_N, implying

$$\rightarrow Y_N - TX_N - C_N$$

$$T = CAB \equiv (Y_N - TX_N - C_N - I_N) + (TX_N - G_N)$$
$$\equiv (S_N) - I_N) + (TX_N - G_N) \tag{4}$$

Budget Surplus

where $S_N \equiv Y_N - TX_N - C_N$ represents private savings, which are the excess of disposable income, $Y_N - TX_N$, over consumption, C_N. Note that the term $(TX_N - G_N)$ represents the excess of the government's receipts in the form of taxes over its expenditures, generally referred to as the government budget surplus.

Equation (4) tells us that the current account balance can be associated with the gap between savings and investment and the gap between domestic taxes and government spending. What is the connection between this concept of the current account balance and the notion of net accumulation or decumulation of foreign assets? Consider first the savings–investment gap, and let us assume for the moment that the government budget is balanced ($TX_N = G_N$). If the economy faces a current account surplus, this means that the savings of domestic residents exceed domestic investments by the amount of the current account surplus. This excess of domestic savings over investment is invested abroad and represents a net accumulation of foreign assets. Therefore, equation (4) is just another way of visualizing the association between the accumulation of net foreign assets and the current account balance. Similarly, a CAB deficit associated with a shortfall of domestic savings relative to investment corresponds to a net decumulation of foreign assets, or, equivalently, with increased liabilities to foreigners in the form of net external borrowing.

The second component of equation (4) is the government budget surplus expressed in terms of the excess of taxes over government spending. If the economy's savings are equal to investment, then a current account deficit will be associated with a budget deficit. The interpretation is that the government sector is borrowing abroad to finance an excess of its expenditures over its income (i.e., taxes). This foreign borrowing is the counterpart of the current account deficit. Similarly, a budget surplus would correspond to a current account surplus.

5–2   THE SIMPLE KEYNESIAN GOODS MARKET EQUILIBRIUM AND INTERNATIONAL TRADE

Up to this point, we have been explicitly concerned with accounting relationships and their interpretation. We now turn to an examination of the factors determining the national income accounting categories examined earlier and how they interact to determine equilibrium output in the open economy. In approaching this task, we shall focus on the trade balance and ignore trade in services, capital flows, and monetary considerations. Our purpose in this chapter is to introduce the reader to the simple analytics of the open economy, within the context of a simple Keynesian model. More complex and sophisticated analyses will be gradually developed over the next few chapters.

The simple Keynesian framework used in the present discussion assumes that the prices of domestic goods are fixed and that firms producing these goods can supply all the output that is demanded of them at the given prices. That is, the aggregate supply curve of domestic goods is perfectly horizontal. Since sales are constrained only by the level of demand, it is the level of aggregate demand for domestic goods, that is, desired spending on domestic goods, that determines the output of the economy. This framework could be applicable to economies suffering from severe unemployment and recession, at least within a short-run context. One must always remember Keynes's concern with short-run phenomena, as dramatically expressed in his famous dictum: "In the long run, we are all dead." The study of situations in which unemployment and underutilization of the economy's productive capacity are prevalent was one of the main motivations behind Keynes's theoretical masterpiece, *The General Theory of Employment, Interest and Money,* published in 1936, just when the impact of the Great Depression was being felt all over the world.

Within a simple Keynesian context, domestic output is determined by the aggregate demand for domestic goods. It thus becomes apparent from our earlier specification of different categories of spending on domestic goods in equation

(1), that domestic output will be influenced by the determinants of domestic absorption and the balance on goods and services (which corresponds to the trade balance if services are ignored).

Nominal and Real Variables

Up to this point, most variables have been expressed in *nominal* terms, that is, in terms of their currency (i.e., dollar, for the United States) values. It will be convenient, from this point on, to express them in real terms, that is, in terms of physical units of domestic output. Since a nominal variable involves a quantity multiplied by a price, if we wish to transform it into a real variable (which involves only a quantity), we have to deflate it, that is, divide by an appropriate price. The real values of absorption, A, and the trade balance, T, can be obtained from their nominal values, A_N and T_N, by dividing by the price of domestic goods.[4]

To clarify the steps involved in transforming nominal variables into real variables in the open economy, consider the definition of the trade balance in nominal terms:

$$T_N = X_N - M_N$$
$$= PM^* - eP^*M \tag{5}$$

Note that M^* denotes the physical quantity of domestic goods (say, U.S.-produced Hotpoint appliances) exported, which, when multiplied by the price of domestic goods, P, becomes the value of exports, PM^*. The variable M depicts the physical amount of foreign goods (say, Japanese-produced Toyotas) imported. When M is multiplied by the price of foreign goods in foreign currency, P^*, and then converted into domestic currency using the prevailing exchange rate, e (say, dollars per Japanese yen), it becomes the value of imports expressed in domestic currency (in dollars, for the case of the United States). The equality in (5) therefore involves export and import categories expressed in domestic currency.

To express the trade balance in real terms, we divide both sides of equation (5) by the domestic price level, P. The result is

$$T = \frac{T_N}{P} = M^* - \frac{eP^*}{P} M$$
$$= M^* - qM \tag{6}$$

---

[4] We follow the standard simplifying assumption of open economy Keynesian analysis, which is that the country be specialized in producing exportables, part of which it consumes and part of which it exports. The price of domestic goods will then be the price of these goods, that is, the price of exports. If the country produces both exportables and importables, then the price of domestic goods is an index of the prices of both of these categories of goods; that is, it includes the prices of both exports and imports.

where $q \equiv eP^*/P$ represents the relative price of imports in terms of domestic goods, which allows us to convert quantities of foreign goods (M) into their equivalent in domestic goods (qM). The variable q, that is, the price of goods produced abroad (i.e., the price of imports) relative to that of domestic goods (i.e., the price of exports), is a central variable in our analysis of an open economy and is a particular version of the concept of price level-adjusted or real exchange rate defined in Chapter 4. Note that q is defined as the ratio of the price of imports to the price of domestic goods, both measured in *domestic* currency. Since P^* is the price of goods produced abroad measured in foreign currency (pounds sterling per unit of British imports), and e is the exchange rate (measured in dollars per pound sterling), eP^* represents the price of imports in domestic currency (dollars per unit of British imports). By dividing this foreign price, eP^*, by the price of domestic goods, P (which is always measured in domestic currency), we obtain q. An increase in q means that imports become more expensive relative to domestic goods, improving domestic competitiveness in international goods markets. A reduction of q, on the other hand, means that domestic goods become relatively expensive as compared with foreign goods, worsening the competitiveness of domestic goods in international markets. In a nutshell, q measures the relative price of foreign goods in terms of domestic goods. Its use in equation (6) is required in order to avoid adding apples and oranges—or Hotpoint appliances and Toyotas—when domestic exports and imports involve different commodities. By multiplying the physical volume of imports, M, by their relative price in terms of domestic goods, q, we express them in terms of domestic output. The term qM can then be substracted from the exports of domestic goods, M^*, in determining the economy's trade balance, T, expressed in real terms. Similar adjustments would have to be made in transforming nominal absorption, expressed in domestic currency, A_N, into real absorption, A.

Exports, Imports, and the Determinants of International Trade

What are the determinants of the trade balance? The trade balance represents the difference between domestic exports and the value of imports. Exports correspond to the foreign demand for domestic goods and, as with any demand relationship, depend on relative prices and foreign income. Symbolically, domestic exports, M^*, can be represented by

$$M^* = M^* (q, Y^*)$$

(7)

where q is the relative price of foreign goods in terms of domestic goods and Y^* is foreign real income. Note that as the relative price of foreign goods increases, as q goes up, foreign residents will switch their spending out of foreign and into domestic goods, with a consequent positive effect on domestic exports.

Similarly, as foreign income increases (as Y^* rises), some of that income would be spent on domestic goods and domestic exports, M^*, would expand.

Domestic imports, M, correspond to the quantity demanded of foreign goods by domestic residents, and are influenced by the relative price of foreign goods, q, and domestic real income, Y, or

$$M = M(q, Y) \atop - \quad +$$
(8)

where an increase in the relative price of foreign goods (i.e., a rise in q) results in a switch of domestic demand away from the relatively more expensive foreign goods and toward domestic goods. This reduces domestic imports (M declines). A rise in domestic income (i.e., an increase in Y), on the other hand, is associated with higher imports (i.e., a higher M), since some of the additional income will be spent on foreign goods.

Substitution of the expressions for the demand for exports and imports shown by equations (7) and (8), respectively, into the trade balance equation in (6) yields

$$T = M^*(q, Y^*) - qM(q, Y)$$
$$= T(q, Y^*, Y)$$
$$= \overline{T} - mY$$
(9)

where the second row summarizes the three basic determinants of the trade balance: the price of foreign goods relative to that of domestic goods, foreign income and domestic income. The third row of (9) breaks down the trade balance into two parts: The first term is the *autonomous trade balance*, $\overline{T}$, which represents that portion of the balance of trade that does not depend on domestic income. The second term depicts the influence of domestic income on the trade balance and is equal to mY, where m is the marginal propensity to import, defined as that fraction of the value of additional income spent on imports. The autonomous trade balance depends on foreign income, Y^*, which is assumed to be exogenously determined, an assumption to be relaxed later on in the chapter, and on the relative price of foreign goods in terms of domestic goods, q. Given the simple Keynesian assumption that the prices of domestic and foreign goods are fixed, the presence of a fixed exchange rate implies that the relative price of foreign goods in terms of domestic goods, $q \equiv eP^*/P$, is exogenously determined. It can only be altered by exchange rate changes, as when there is a revaluation or a devaluation of the domestic currency. Changes in q are therefore in the hands of policymakers.

The balance of trade expression in (9) is graphically portrayed by locus $\overline{T}T$ in Figure 5–1. Note that the slope of the $\overline{T}T$ locus is negative; that is, as income increases, with all else constant, imports increase and the trade balance

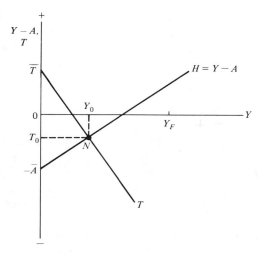

FIGURE 5–1. Hoarding, Trade Balance, and Goods Market Equilibrium

worsens. Its vertical intercept is given by $\overline{T}$, since the trade balance becomes the autonomous trade balance $(T = \overline{T})$ when the level of domestic income is zero $(Y = 0)$.

Domestic Absorption, Income, and Hoarding

What are the determinants of domestic absorption? Absorption is the aggregate spending of domestic residents and includes consumption, investment, and government spending components. Each component is influenced by a whole range of variables, both economic and noneconomic. We start here by emphasizing the role of income in domestic absorption, leaving the analysis of the impact of other variables, such as the relative price of foreign goods in terms of domestic goods and interest rates, for later discussion. Investment spending, which is heavily influenced by interest rates, is assumed to be exogenous. Government expenditures are also considered to be exogenously determined, as given perhaps by the preferences of policymakers or by the influence of the public on the political process.

In order to simplify the following diagrams and their algebraic representations, most of the relationships we shall be dealing with are in linear form. The linear representation of absorption as a function of income,

$$A = A(\overline{G}, Y) = \overline{A} + aY \tag{10}$$

states explicitly that absorption is a function of the exogenously given government expenditures, $\overline{G}$, and domestic income, Y. The term $\overline{A}$ refers to *autonomous absorption,* that amount of domestic demand that does not depend on domestic income. Note that $\overline{A}$ is a function of the exogenously given government expenditures, $\overline{G}$ (and of any variables other than income affecting domestic absorption), with an increase in the level of government spending raising autonomous absorption. The positive parameter a is equal to the marginal propensity to spend, which is that fraction of additional income spent by domestic residents. The parameter a is positive on the assumption that, as domestic income increases, domestic residents consume more, thereby increasing their aggregate spending. It is also less than 1, meaning that out of any additional dollar of income, only a fraction is spent.

What happens to the fraction of domestic income that is not spent? It is hoarded, that is, it represents the acquisitions of monetary assets on the part of the country as a whole. Hoarding is the excess of income over the spending of domestic residents, algebraically shown by[5]

$$H = Y - A$$

Using (10), we can restate the excess of income over spending (hoarding) as

$$H = Y - A = Y - (\overline{A} + aY) = -\overline{A} + (1 - a)Y = -\overline{A} + sY \qquad (11)$$

where s is the marginal propensity to save, that fraction of additional income that is saved. It is easy to visualize why $s = 1 - a$. The simplified framework presented in this section assumes that investment and government expenditures are determined exogenously, that is, they do not vary with income. This implies that additional income is spent exclusively on consumption; hence the marginal propensity to spend is equal to the marginal propensity to consume. This means that additional income must be either spent on consumption or saved. As a consequence, the marginal propensities to spend (consume) and save must add up to 1, that is, $s + a = 1$.

The last expression in (11) represents the equation of a straight line with vertical intercept equal to $-\overline{A}$ and slope equal to s. We represent it graphically in Figure 5–1 by means of the $H = Y - A$ locus. This locus has the following interpretation. At zero level of income, domestic residents spend an amount equal to their autonomous spending, $\overline{A}$. As a consequence, hoarding would be equal to $-\overline{A}$, that is, it would be negative, representing an excess of spending over zero income, which is called *dishoarding*. The reader may think of dishoarding as entailing the decumulation of monetary assets or international reserves. As domestic income increases, however, domestic resident spending does not increase by the same amount, since a fraction is set aside as savings. As a

---

[5] There is a basic distinction between saving and hoarding. Abstracting from the government sector, saving is the difference between income and consumption, $S = Y - C$. Hoarding is the difference between income and absorption (expenditure by domestic residents), $H = Y - A$. Remember, absorption (A) includes not only consumption (C) but investment (I) as well.

consequence, the excess of spending over income is reduced, that is, dishoarding decreases. If domestic income continues to increase, at a certain point the excess of spending over income must disappear, and further increases of income would induce an excess of income over spending. That is, hoarding would become positive and would keep rising with income. This is what the upward-sloping $H = Y - A$ curve represents in Figure 5–1.

5–3 EQUILIBRIUM INCOME AND THE OPEN ECONOMY INCOME MULTIPLIER

The Keynesian goods market equilibrium condition expressed in real terms states that domestic output, Y, is determined by the aggregate demand for domestic goods, which is equal in turn to absorption, A, plus the trade balance, T. Therefore, in equilibrium

$$Y = A + T \tag{12}$$

Rearranging, we obtain

$$Y - A = T \tag{12a}$$

which states that an excess of equilibrium income over absorption is associated with a trade balance surplus.[6] This is what we hinted at in equation (2). It constitutes the basic insight of the absorption approach to the balance of payments, where, in the present context, the service account is being ignored.

Equation (12a) means that the economy is in equilibrium when hoarding, $H = Y - A$, is equal to the trade balance, T. This equality is represented geometrically by the intersection of the two loci described by $\overline{T}T$ and $H = Y - A$ in Figure 5–1. Equilibrium output in the economy is then equal to Y_o,

---

[6] It should be noted that the equality in (12) [and 12a)] represents a goods market equilibrium relationship and it is *not* an identity (as it would be in a national income accounting framework). The reason is that the aggregate demand variables used in (12), such as consumption, and investment, involve specific behavioral relationships of economic agents and all represent *planned* spending levels. This means that $A + T$ depicts the aggregate demand for domestic goods that households, firms, government authorities and foreigners *plan* to spend. Usually, one does not expect to see a substantial gap between actual and planned government and consumer spending. In the case of firms, however, planned spending differs from actual spending whenever they find themselves carrying out unplanned investment in the form of unsold goods, which occurs quite frequently. If they do, the equality in (12) would not be satisfied, since there would be an excess of production over planned spending (firms would be accumulating unwanted inventories), and the economy would be out of equilibrium. The equality stated in (12), then, does not always necessarily hold, as an identity must. It holds only when equilibrium is attained. When planned aggregate spending on domestic goods equals the aggregate supply of domestic goods, households and firms find themselves buying and selling the amount of goods they planned, and there is equilibrium in the goods market.

and there is a balance of trade deficit equal to T_0. Observe that equilibrium in the Keynesian model does not necessarily imply full employment, represented by Y_F in Figure 5–1, nor does it imply balanced external payments. Point N depicts a situation of both external payments deficit and unemployment.

The precise value of the equilibrium level of income in the economy is obtained by substituting the expressions in (9) and (11) into (12a), obtaining

$$H = -\bar{A} + sY = \bar{T} - mY = T$$

Solving for Y, we obtain

$$Y_o = \frac{1}{s + m} (\bar{A} + \bar{T}) = \alpha (\bar{A} + \bar{T}) \tag{13}$$

where $\alpha = 1/(s + m)$ is the so-called *open economy Keynesian income multiplier.* This multiplier can be easily calculated if one knows the specific values of the marginal propensities to save and import in the economy. Suppose, for example, that the marginal propensity to save is equal to 0.2 and that the marginal propensity to import is equal to 0.3. In this case

$$\alpha = \frac{1}{s + m} = \frac{1}{0.2 + 0.3} = 2.0$$

which is the value of the multiplier for an economy with $s = 0.2$ and $m = 0.3$. The implication is that any change in autonomous absorption, $\bar{A}$, or in the autonomous trade balance, $\bar{T}$, will tend to have a magnified effect on domestic income. The precise amount of this magnified effect depends on the precise value of the open economy multiplier. Expressing (13) in terms of changes yields

$$\Delta Y = \alpha (\Delta \bar{A} + \Delta \bar{T}) \tag{13a}$$

where ΔY represents the change in domestic income resulting from changes in autonomous absorption, $\Delta \bar{A}$, and/or changes in autonomous trade, $\Delta \bar{T}$. As observed, ΔY depends directly on the multiplier, α, as well as on the amount of the changes given by $\Delta \bar{A}$ and $\Delta \bar{T}$. How different policies are subsumed into $\Delta \bar{A}$ and $\Delta \bar{T}$ is the topic of the next sections. We can note here, however, that in an open economy, any given autonomous expansion will tend to have a smaller impact on income than in a closed economy. The reason lies in the fact that the open economy multiplier is smaller than the closed economy multiplier. If the economy is a closed one, it does not engage in international trade. As a result, $m = 0$, and the Keynesian multiplier becomes $1/s$, which is larger than $1/(s + m)$. In the example above, $1/s = 1/0.2 = 5.0$, which exceeds the

2.0 value for the open economy multiplier. The explanation is that, in an open economy, some of the expansionary effects of increased spending leak out of the domestic economy as increased demand for foreign goods. If the economy were a closed economy, additional spending would have to fall on domestic goods; other things being equal, it would then be more expansionary.

5–4   THE ANATOMY OF GOVERNMENT INTERVENTION IN AN OPEN ECONOMY

Is there any rationale in the present framework for government intervention in the economy? This is a highly controversial subject to which we shall return in later chapters. The first issue that must be addressed concerns what possible goals the government or policymakers in an open economy could have. At this point, two objectives come to mind: the objectives of *internal balance* and *external balance.*

The goal of internal balance is the attainment of full employment. Unemployment implies that the economy produces below its potential capacity; in that sense, it is wasteful. Unemployment also carries a concomitant net welfare loss suffered by those individuals who are involuntarily unemployed. As a consequence, most governments consider internal balance a priority goal.

External balance means that there is no surplus or deficit in the balance of payments; in the absence of capital mobility and trade in services, it corresponds to balanced trade. But why should there be any concern for external balance? First, a country under fixed exchange rates cannot continuously finance a balance of payments deficit without eventually running out of foreign exchange reserves. The depletion of these reserves would then imply an inability of the government to intervene in foreign exchange markets and to maintain its commitment to fixed exchange rates. This would possibly force a devaluation and/or a foreign exchange crisis, leading perhaps to a severe dislocation of the foreign trade and financial sectors of the economy. As a consequence, persistent balance of payments deficits are usually seen as a state of affairs to be avoided. If the country faces a persistent balance of payment surplus, on the other hand, it will systematically be acquiring foreign exchange reserves. If held in the form of non-interest-bearing assets, increasing reserves will imply an increasing cost for the government in the form of foregone interest. Foreign exchange reserves, however, are frequently held in the form of interest-bearing assets. In this case, increasing holdings of foreign exchange reserves do not involve a loss in the form of foregone income. Nevertheless, governments are still reluctant to accumulate funds that could otherwise be used to buy and consume goods currently. It would appear to be a legitimate policy objective to eliminate a persistent balance of payments surplus.

In equating the balance of payments with the trade balance, we have ignored international capital flows and focused exclusively on analyzing trade in goods. But if international trade in both goods and financial assets were considered, a trade deficit could be financed by external borrowing and would not therefore necessarily imply a payments deficit. No major payment difficulties would then be associated with balance of trade disequilibria. Still, countries often do not desire to borrow or lend abroad excessively. Large indebtedness, for example, places a heavy debt service burden on the economy as the principal to be repaid and the interest payments accumulate. As a result, even if the funds acquired through external borrowing are used to finance productive domestic capital accumulation and can be successfully repaid, many countries still want to avoid growing indebtedness. This is evident in the current plight of those developing countries that, during the seventies, financed huge current account balance deficits without major losses of international reserves, largely through the easy availability of external financing. Their current debt service problems serve well to illustrate the dangers of excessive external indebtedness—Mexico's and Brazil's annual interest payments on their external public debt alone hover each above the $5-billion figure. Hence the balance of trade (or, more accurately, the current account balance) is often considered an external balance goal.

What policies can the government undertake to achieve external balance? Within the present Keynesian context, the formulation of the balance of trade represented by equation (12a) is particularly illuminating in dissecting the problems involved in correcting trade balance disequilibria. It shows that a balance of trade deficit ($T < 0$) means that domestic spending is in excess of domestic income ($A > Y$). This suggests that policies for correcting a deficit can be classified into two types: those that tend to reduce spending, at any given level of income, and those that tend to increase domestic income, at any given level of spending by domestic residents.[7] Policies that tend to decrease total spending (absorption) at any given level of income, are called *expenditure-reducing* policies. A typical example of an expenditure-reducing policy is contractionary fiscal policy. We shall examine the effects of fiscal policy in Section 5–5. Policies that tend to increase domestic income, given total spending by domestic residents, are called *expenditure-switching* policies. They are called expenditure-switching policies because, in a Keynesian framework, domestic income is determined by aggregate demand for domestic goods, which (given total spending by domestic residents) can only be increased by inducing a switch in the *composition* of spending (from foreign to domestic goods). Typical examples of expenditure-switching policies are commercial and exchange rate policies. Later on in the chapter, we will analyze how these policies switch expenditures.

5–5 THE EFFECTS OF FISCAL POLICY

This section examines the macroeconomic impact of fiscal policy. Suppose the government increases its purchases of domestic goods and services.[8] The effects of this fiscal expansion on income and the trade balance are illustrated by Figure 5–2. First, the balance of trade locus, $\overline{TT}$, is not affected, since the government's increased expenditures fall on domestic goods and services and do not directly change exports or imports. By contrast, the hoarding locus, $H = Y - A$ shifts, as an increase in government spending, $\Delta \overline{G} > 0$, raises autonomous absorption. As determined by equation (8), when autonomous spending $\overline{A}$ increases, the vertical intercept of the $Y - A$ locus shifts downward, moving from $-\overline{A}$ to $-\overline{A}'$ in Figure 5–2. Since the slope of the locus stays the same, its shift is a parallel one, as depicted by $H' = Y - A'$.

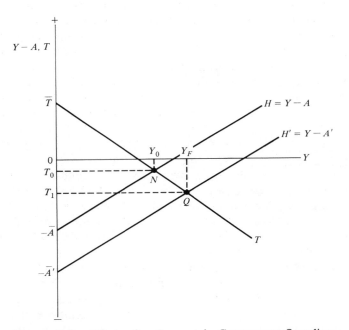

FIGURE 5–2.   Effects of an Increase in Government Spending

[8] Of course, the changes in government spending examined in the text have to be financed. There are three possible sources of government financing: taxation, government borrowing, and money creation (i.e., printing money to pay for expenses). Since we have not yet examined explicitly the monetary and financial sectors of the economy, it does not make sense at this point to compare these alternative means of government financing. In evaluating the spending changes examined in the text, you should be aware that some financing scheme is being used, such as borrowing from the public or printing money. The effects of fiscal policy also depend on the substitutability between government and private spending. For instance, a school lunch program may result in reduced private spending on food, offsetting the aggregate demand effects of the program.

The economy's equilibrium moves from point N to point Q, showing an increase in income, from Y_o to Y_F, but a further deterioration of the trade balance, from T_o to T_1. The increase in income is a result of the Keynesian assumption that aggregate demand determines output. Increased government spending raises aggregate demand and, therefore, output. The deterioration of the trade balance is a result of the fact that part of the increase in income is spent on additional imports.

The effects of changes in government spending on output and the trade balance can be easily derived algebraically. First, the change in the equilibrium level of domestic income, ΔY, can be derived from equation (13a) by noting that the only autonomous change under consideration is the change in government spending. Given that the government spends only on domestic goods, the autonomous trade balance does not change at all, implying $\Delta \bar{T} = 0$. Consequently, from (13a), we obtain

$$\Delta Y = \alpha \Delta \bar{A} = \alpha \Delta \bar{G} \tag{14}$$

The increase in government spending, $\Delta \bar{G}$, has a positive multiplier effect on domestic income. Second, we can obtain the change in the equilibrium level of the balance of trade from

$$\Delta T = \Delta \bar{T} - m \Delta Y \tag{15}$$

which is simply equation (9) expressed in terms of changes. Since $\Delta \bar{T} = 0$, changes in the trade balance can arise only from changes in domestic income, ΔY, which have just been computed. Consequently, substituting (14) into (15), one obtains

$$\Delta T = -m \Delta Y = -m \alpha \Delta \bar{G}$$

That is, the trade balance deteriorates.

5–6 INTRODUCTION TO THE ANALYTICS OF A DEVALUATION

We can now move to the Keynesian analysis of devaluation. A domestic currency devaluation, an increase in e, changes domestic economic variables by affecting the relative price of imports in terms of exports. If the exchange rate increases, the relative price of imports in terms of exports rises ($q = eP^*/P$ increases), a result of the assumption that P and P^* are fixed. For example, a devaluation of the dollar increases the dollar price of imports (i.e., given the yen price of Toyotas, a devaluation of the dollar will increase the dollar price of Toyotas) so that more units of exports will have to be given up in order to buy 1 unit of imports (e.g., a Toyota).[9]

The effects of a domestic currency devaluation on the balance of trade and the equilibrium level of income are represented graphically in Figure 5–3. First, from equation (11) we can observe that the hoarding locus ($H = Y - A$) is not affected by the devaluation. This is because we neglect any possible direct effects of q on absorption (a topic to be discussed in Section 5–7). Devaluation, on the other hand, affects the trade balance locus, $\overline{TT}$, as depicted by its shift in Figure 5–3. This upward shift of the $\overline{TT}$ curve reflects the positive direct impact of devaluation on the trade balance, that is, its effect on the trade balance at any given level of income. What is the nature of this particular effect of devaluation?

$$\rightarrow T = T(q, Y^*, Y)$$
$$= \overline{T} - mY$$

Devaluation and the Trade Balance: The Marshall–Lerner Condition

As can be recalled from equation (9), the trade balance is

$$T = M^* (q, Y^*) - qM (q, \overline{Y}) \tag{9}$$
$$+ \quad + \qquad - \quad +$$

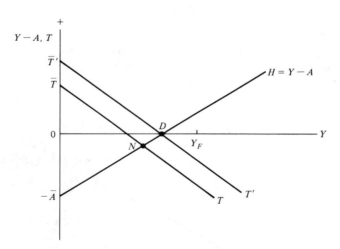

FIGURE 5–3.   Effects of Currency Devaluation

[9] In a more general setting, a devaluation would also induce changes in the prices of foreign and domestic goods, making the analysis more complicated. Our discussion in Part IV examines this important issue in detail.

where the bar over the variable Y means that we are keeping it fixed for the moment. A devaluation increases the relative price of imports in terms of exports, q, which tends to raise exports (i.e., M^* increases) and decrease autonomous imports (i.e., M declines). The reason is that as q increases, domestic goods become cheaper relative to foreign goods, so both foreign and domestic residents tend to buy more domestic goods. This tends to improve the trade balance. The net effect of the devaluation on the trade balance is not clear, however, because an increase in q raises the amount that has to be paid per unit of imports. As a result, and as can be more easily visualized from (9), even though physical imports, M, decline, the total cost of imports in terms of the amount of domestic goods that have to be paid for them (qM) may increase, and this may more than offset the increase in the volume of exports, M^*. Nevertheless, the more responsive the physical amounts of exports and imports are to the devaluation, the more likely it is that there will be a direct improvement in the trade balance. In this situation, the increase in exports, M^*, and the decline in imports, M, dominate the rise in q, with a net improvement in the trade balance.

The responsiveness of the demand for domestic exports and imports to a devaluation is measured by so-called price elasticities of demand for domestic exports and imports. The price elasticity of demand for domestic exports, η^*, measures the percentage change in exports due to a 1% change in the relative price of foreign goods in terms of domestic goods. That is,

$$\eta^* = \frac{\Delta M^*/M^*}{\Delta q/q} = \frac{\Delta M}{\Delta q} \cdot \frac{q}{M}$$

The higher η^* is, the more responsive exports are to a change in q. The price elasticity of demand for domestic imports, η, on the other hand, measures the (negative of the) percentage change in imports due to a 1% change in the price of foreign goods relative to domestic goods. Symbolically,

$$\eta = -\frac{\Delta M/M}{\Delta q/q} = -\frac{\Delta M}{\Delta q} \cdot \frac{q}{M}$$

Note that since $\Delta M/\Delta q < 0$, that is, a rise in the relative price of foreign goods reduces imports, the elasticity η is positive. It is standard to express elasticities as a positive number. The higher η is, the more responsive imports are to a change in q.

As explained before, the higher the price elasticities of demand for domestic exports and imports, η^* and η, respectively, the more likely it is that a devaluation will have positive direct effects on the trade balance. The exact expression for the direct effect of a devaluation on the trade balance (with fixed income) is given by[10]

$$\Delta T_{Y=\bar{Y}} = M^* (\eta^* + \eta - 1)\, \hat{e} \qquad (16)$$

with ΔT denoting the change in the trade balance, the subscript $Y = \bar{Y}$ is a reminder that we are keeping income fixed for the moment, and $\hat{e} = \Delta e / e$ is the devaluation expressed in proportional terms (a devaluation of 10% means $\hat{e} = 0.10$). The term $M^*(\eta^* + \eta - 1)\,\hat{e}$ measures the direct responsiveness of the trade balance to devaluation; therefore, whether a devaluation directly improves the trade balance depends on the sign of the expression inside the parentheses in this term. For a devaluation to have a positive (direct) effect on the trade balance, the sign of $(\eta^* + \eta - 1)$ must be positive, or equivalently,

$$\eta^* + \eta > 1 \qquad (17)$$

The inequality in (17) is the so-called *Marshall–Lerner condition* stating that the direct effect of a devaluation on the trade balance will be positive when the sum of the price elasticities of demand for domestic exports and imports exceeds 1.

Devaluation, Income, and the Trade Balance

If we assume that the Marshall–Lerner condition holds, a devaluation will improve the trade balance at any given level of income and shift the $\bar{T}T$ locus

---

[10] The direct effects of a devaluation on the trade balance can be found by expressing equation (9) in terms of changes:

$$\Delta T_{Y=\bar{Y}} = \Delta M^* - q\Delta M - M\Delta q$$

where ΔM^* represents the change in exports resulting from the devaluation, $q\Delta M$ shows the change in imports (expressed in terms of domestic goods) and $M\Delta q$ denotes the change in the cost of imports connected to a change in the relative price of foreign goods, q. Expressing ΔT explicitly as the change in the trade balance arising from a change in q, and assuming, for simplicity, that the economy devalues from a starting point of external balance ($M^* = qM$), then

$$\frac{\Delta T}{\Delta q} = \frac{\Delta M^*}{\Delta q} - q\frac{\Delta M}{\Delta q} - M\frac{\Delta q}{\Delta q}$$

$$= \frac{M^*}{q}\left(\frac{\Delta M^*}{\Delta q} \cdot \frac{q}{M^*} - \frac{\Delta M}{\Delta q} \cdot \frac{q}{M} - 1\right)$$

$$= \frac{M^*}{q}(\eta^* + \eta - 1)$$

or, more conveniently:

$$\Delta T_{Y=\bar{Y}} = M^* (\eta^* + \eta - 1)\frac{\Delta q}{q} = M^* (\eta^* + \eta - 1)\,\hat{e}$$

where $\hat{e} = \Delta e / e = \Delta q / q$ is easily derived by recalling that since $q = eP^*/P$, with p and p^* exogenous, then $\Delta q = (p^*/p)\Delta e$, and dividing both sides by q: $\Delta q / q = \Delta e / e$.

in Figure 5–3 upward. The equilibrium of the economy thus moves from point N to point D, inducing an increase in the equilibrium level of income. We can derive this change in income algebraically, through the use of equation (13a):

$$\Delta Y = \alpha(\Delta \bar{A} + \Delta \bar{T}) = \alpha(\Delta \bar{T}) \tag{13a}$$

where, as mentioned earlier, we neglect any possible effects of a devaluation on autonomous absorption, so that $\Delta \bar{A} = 0$. What is the impact of a devaluation on the autonomous trade balance, $\bar{T}$? Since $T = \bar{T} - mY$, note that a change in the autonomous trade balance is equal to the change in the trade balance keeping the level of income fixed, that is, $\Delta \bar{T} = \Delta T_{Y=\bar{Y}}$. Substituting the expression derived earlier for $\Delta T_{Y=\bar{Y}}$, we obtain[11]

$$\Delta \bar{T} = M^* (\eta^* + \eta - 1) \, \hat{e} \tag{16a}$$

Finally, substituting (16a) into (13a) yields

$$\Delta Y = \alpha (\Delta \bar{T}) = \alpha M^* (\eta^* + \eta - 1) \, \hat{e} \tag{18}$$

That is, a devaluation has a positive multiplier effect on domestic income. Note, however, that in contrast to fiscal policy, the effects of the devaluation depend not only on the multiplier (α), but also on the demand elasticities for domestic exports and imports (η and η^*). The reason is that a devaluation works its effect on income by means of an expenditure-switching effect, shifting the expenditures of foreign and local residents toward domestic goods. As a consequence, the larger the demand elasticities for imports and exports, the stronger the impact of the devaluation on income.

The next task is to determine the effects of a devaluation on the trade balance, taking into account the impact of the devaluation on income as just derived. We found earlier that a devaluation has a positive effect on the autonomous trade balance. As shown by (18), however, a devaluation also results in an increase of domestic income, which raises imports. Could not this income-induced increase in imports worsen the trade balance by an amount sufficiently large to offset the direct improvement of the autonomous trade balance associated with the devaluation?

Substituting the expressions for $\Delta \bar{T}$ and ΔY in (16a) and (18) into (15), one obtains:[12]

---

[11] In deriving equation (16a), we assume that the economy devalues from a starting point of external balance. As a result, the effects of the devaluation shown in Figure 5–3, which is undertaken from a situation of trade deficit, will not correspond exactly to those based on equation (16a). We leave for an exercise the complications introduced when a country devalues from a position of trade deficit (see Problem 6 at the end of the chapter).

[12] In deriving (19), we have used the relationship: $1 - m\alpha = 1 - m/(s + m) = s/(s + m) = s\alpha$.

$$\Delta T = \Delta \bar{T} - m \Delta Y$$

$$= M^* (\eta^* + \eta - 1) \hat{e} - m\alpha M^* (\eta^* + \eta - 1) \hat{e}$$

$$= s\alpha M^* (\eta^* + \eta - 1) \hat{e} \tag{19}$$

which is positive, since all the parameters s, α, M^*, $(\eta^* + \eta - 1)$ and $\hat{e}$ are positive. That is, a devaluation unambiguously improves the trade balance, even after considering the negative effects of increased income on the trade balance. The reason can be obtained through the use of our now familiar equation, $Y - A = T$. An increase in q (a devaluation) has no impact effect on absorption but tends to induce an increase in income, which in turn raises absorption. The increase in absorption, however, is smaller than the increase in income because the marginal propensity to spend is less than 1. This means that $Y - A$ must increase in response to the devaluation. In order to maintain equilibrium, $Y - A = T$; thus, the trade balance, T, must improve, even after we consider the induced income effects. This result is observed graphically in Figure 5–3 by the fact that the movement from point N to point D reduces, and, in fact, eliminates, the trade balance deficit of the economy.

The direct effect of a devaluation on a trade balance, which we refer to as the impact on the *autonomous* trade balance, involving as an integral part the Marshall–Lerner condition, was at the crux of the so-called *elasticities approach* to the balance of payments, developed independently by C. F. Bickerdike, L. Metzler, and J. Robinson. At first, when Sidney Alexander (among others) developed the so-called *absorption approach* to the balance of payments, through the use of equation (12a), it was thought that the two approaches were at odds with each other. As realized later by S. C. Tsiang, Harry Johnson, and other economists, both approaches can be integrated quite nicely. This integration is implicit in our discussion above, as reflected by equations (18) and (19).

Policies to Achieve Internal and External Balance

Our analysis can illustrate the policy conflicts faced by an economy plagued by unemployment and a balance of payments deficit. First, fiscal policy can move the economy to full employment[13] but worsens the balance of payments deficit, as illustrated by the movement from point N to point Q in Figure 5–2. Devaluation, on the other hand, can eliminate a trade deficit but it cannot simultaneously attain full employment, as shown by the movement from point N to point D in Figure 5–3. It is obvious that no single policy will suffice to

[13] The reader has probably wondered whether domestic output could actually exceed the full employment level. This problem will be dealt with in Part IV (it involves the question of changes in prices, which is ignored in this and the next few chapters). For the moment, let us simply state that output can be increased above its full-employment level over short periods of time.

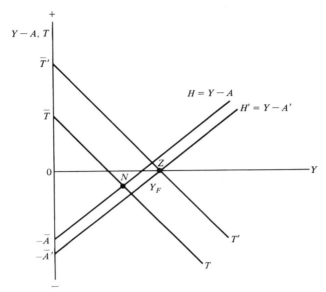

FIGURE 5–4. The Economic Policy Mix to Attain Internal and External Balance

attain the two goals of internal and external balance. The corrective is to administer both policies jointly, that is, to use a policy mix. In order for an economy suffering from a trade deficit and underemployment to attain full employment and balanced trade, both devaluation and fiscal policy would have to be employed. For instance, if the economy's equilibrium is at point N in Figure 5–4, a devaluation could shift the $\bar{T}T$ curve in Figure 5–4 upward to $\bar{T}'T'$ and an expansionary fiscal policy could move the $Y - A$ curve until it intersects $\bar{T}'T'$ at point Z, with full employment and external balance.

5–7 DEVALUATION, ABSORPTION, AND THE LAURSEN–METZLER EFFECT

Up to this point, we have examined the effects of devaluation on the assumption that domestic absorption, A, is not affected by changes in the relative price of foreign goods in terms of domestic goods, q. As shown by equation (10), domestic absorption is assumed to depend on government expenditures and domestic income but not on relative prices. In our analysis of devaluation this meant that the autonomous trade balance responded to the rising q but not the autonomous absorption component, $\bar{A}$. This might be a reasonable assumption, but it does not generally hold. A devaluation makes imports more expensive in terms of domestic goods. Therefore, the purchasing power of domestic residents declines: Any given amount of domestic output is now able to purchase a smaller amount of foreign goods. This effect is usually referred to as a domestic terms of trade deterioration. The *terms of trade* are defined as the ratio of the price of exports in domestic currency, *p*, to the price of imports in domestic currency, *ep**, and is just the reciprocal of *q*.

A decrease in the purchasing power of domestic goods, with our assumption that spending *in terms of domestic goods* remain unchanged, must then imply that there is a reduction in the real spending of domestic residents, that is, a decline in their standard of living. As the unwillingness of oil-importing countries to allow their standard of living to decrease in the face of oil price increases during the 1970s tended to indicate, at least over short periods of time, one could very well expect that domestic residents will try to maintain their standard of living (i.e., real spending) relatively constant, even in the face of increased import prices. A completely legitimate alternative to our earlier assumption, then, is that domestic residents keep their real expenditure constant whenever they face a reduction in purchasing power. In this case, a devaluation leads to an increase in absorption (i.e., an increase in expenditure measured in terms of domestic goods) in order to offset the decrease in purchasing power of domestic output. This positive effect of devaluation on absorption has been called the *Laursen–Metzler effect*.[14] We have seen that the effect arises whenever domestic residents try to maintain their standard of living in the face of changes in the purchasing power of their income.

The fact that devaluation tends to reduce the domestic standard of living should alert us to the fact that the adjustments brought about by devaluation are not without cost and might be quite painful. Even when the economy's competitiveness is improved and a surge of exports and production occurs, these results cannot be obtained without the sacrifices generally implied by worsening terms of trade. This is one of the reasons why, in spite of its frequent use, devaluation is a decision that has to be very carefully considered before it is implemented.

5–8   EVIDENCE ON THE IMPACT OF DEVALUATION: THE *J*-CURVE EFFECT

The chief means through which a devaluation works in increasing domestic production is by improving the trade balance. What has experience shown us about the effects of devaluation on the trade balance?

[14] This effect is named in honor of S. Laursen and L. Metzler, who analyzed it in their paper: "Flexible Exchange Rates and the Theory of Employment," *Review of Economics and Statistics* (November 1950). For a particularly illuminating (but advanced) exposition of the effect, see R. Dornbusch, *Open Economy Macroeconomics* (New York: Basic Books, Inc., 1980) 78–81.

Evidence on Devaluation and the Trade Balance

In spite of the popular belief that devaluation improves the trade balance, in practice there appears to be a rather intricate relationship between them. First, a worsening of the trade balance is commonly observed over the period of time immediately following a devaluation. Eventually, however, an improvement in the trade balance does come about. This type of pattern is referred to as the *J-curve effect,* depicted by the curve in Figure 5–5, which shows the change in the trade balance induced by a given devaluation plotted against time. This curve illustrates the initial worsening of the trade balance in response to a devaluation, and the subsequent swing toward a positive effect over time. Since the shape of the curve is that of a *J,* the rationale for the terminology is clear.

The time lag involved in the improvement of the trade balance to a devaluation varies significantly from country to country. For example, Jacques Artus found that the 1967 devaluation of the pound had an adverse effect on the trade balance of the United Kingdom only during the first half of 1968, eventually turning into an improvement of about £940 million ($2501 million) by 1971.[15] A variety of possible time profiles of the effects of devaluation in different countries has been studied by Erich Spitaller, who has examined what would happen to the trade balances of several countries if their exchange rates were devalued by 10%. According to his calculations, a temporary deterioration of the trade balance would arise and last about 3 months in Japan, 7 months in Belgium,

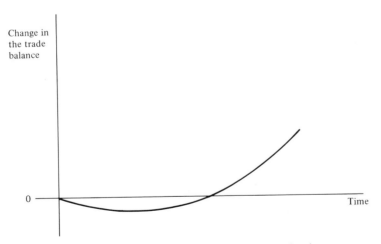

FIGURE 5–5.   The *J*-Curve Effect of a Devaluation

[15] See Jacques Artus, "The 1967 Devaluation of the Pound Sterling," *IMF Staff Papers,* 595–640 (November 1975). Others characterized the initial deterioration of the trade balance as having persisted throughout 1968.

9 months in the United States, 10 months in Sweden, 11 months in France, and 1 year (or longer) in Germany and the United Kingdom.[16] Subsequently, the trade balance appears to respond positively to the devaluation, a result also found by studies of actual devaluations.

In conclusion, even though most studies suggest that devaluation has a positive effect on the trade balance at some point, it appears that the impact is only a modest, or negative, one during the immediate time period following the devaluation. What determines this behavior of the trade balance in response to devaluation? That is, what explains the *J*-curve effect?

Explaining the J-Curve Effect

Whether a devaluation improves or worsens the trade balance is closely connected to the question of whether the Marshall–Lerner condition is satisfied. The condition states that an increase in the relative price of imports will improve the trade balance only if the sum of the price elasticities of imports and exports is larger than 1. It appears, however, that over the short run, the value of these elasticities is rather small. In other words, the evidence tends to indicate that, over short periods of time, both exports and imports are quite unresponsive to changes in relative prices. This is because consumers and producers generally adjust slowly to the devaluation. There are various reasons for this. First, there is a *consumer-response lag:* It takes time for buyers to recognize a changed competitive situation, and this delay can be expected to be longer in international than in domestic trade because of language differences and distance obstacles. In addition, preexisting contracts might not permit adjustments in quantities purchased over the immediate short run. Second, there is a *production-response lag:* It takes time for new business connections to be formed and new orders to be placed; even if buyers can be rapidly found, the contracting of new equipment, raw materials, building capacity, and so on, to increase production could require a substantial amount of time.

That the adjustment of exports and imports to devaluation occurs only slowly over time has been found in many studies. For example, in their sample of 13 industrial countries, Junz and Rhomberg found the responses of exports of manufactured goods to a change in relative prices to spread over a period of about 5 years, with only 50% of the full effect occurring during the first 3 years. Others have found similar results for both imports and exports, although the time span involved is frequently found to be shorter.[17] This evidence provides

---

[16] Erich Spitaller, "Short-Run Effects of Exchange Rate Changes on Terms of Trade and Trade Balance," *IMF Staff Papers* (June 1980).

[17] Helen B. Junz and Rudolf R. Rhomberg, "Price Competitiveness in Export Trade Among Industrial Countries," *American Economic Review* (May 1973); and T. Gylfason, "The Effects of Exchange Rate Changes on the Balance of Trade in Ten Industrial Countries," *IMF Staff Papers* (October 1978).

much of the explanation for why the trade balance fails to respond positively (and often worsens) during the time period immediately following devaluation. With quantities of exports and imports relatively unchanged, the devaluation would have little positive effect on the trade balance and may worsen it by increasing the value of imports (through increases in import prices). Of course, over longer periods of time, the amounts of exports and imports would respond to relative price changes and the effects on the trade balance would tend to be positive.[18]

5–9 Interdependence and the International Transmission of Aggregate Demand Disturbances

Up to this point, our emphasis has been on determining a given economy's macroeconomic equilibrium and how it is affected by domestic disturbances, assuming that foreign variables (foreign income, foreign prices) remain unchanged. Here we extend the discussion to determine how changes in foreign income alter domestic equilibrium.

Spillover Effects and Interdependence

In an interdependent world, disturbances affecting income in one country can have significant effects on other countries. As a result, an economy can be subject to major dislocations associated with economic events abroad. For instance, by reducing foreign demand for domestic goods, hence our exports, a recession and unemployment abroad can *spill over* or be transmitted into recession and unemployment in the domestic economy. How is our earlier framework extended to take into its breadth the analysis of these foreign income disturbances on domestic output?[19]

Our earlier discussion assumed foreign income, Y^*, to be fixed, submerging its influence on domestic exports into the autonomous trade balance, $\bar{T}$. The effects of foreign income on domestic exports can then be taken into account

[18] The fact that devaluation might worsen the trade balance over the period immediately following the currency devaluation suggests the actual impact of exchange rate increases over the short run might be contractionary rather than expansionary. Indeed, a range of studies have found devaluation to have short-run contractionary effects. For instance, R. N. Cooper finds this experience common in developing countries, sometimes lasting only a few months, not infrequently longer than a year. See his "Devaluation and Aggregate Demand in Aid-Receiving Countries," in J. N. Bhagwati et al, eds., *Trade, Balance of Payments and Growth* (Amsterdam: North-Holland Publishing Company, 1971).

[19] For the detailed mechanics of interdependence within a Keynesian framework of the open economy, see R. Dornbusch and A. K. Swoboda, "Adjustment, Policy, and Monetary Equilibrium in a Two-Country Model," in M. Connolly and A. K. Swoboda, *International Trade and Money* (Toronto: University of Toronto Press, 1973), and R. Dornbusch, *Open Economy Macroeconomics*, (New York: Basic Books, Inc., 1980), Chapter 3, pp. 43–56.

by breaking down the autonomous trade balance, $\overline{T}$, into two components: One component, T_o, representing that part of the trade balance that is not influenced by foreign (or domestic) income, and another component, m^*Y^*, accounting for the influence of foreign income on domestic exports. Symbolically, this effect is represented by[20]

$$\overline{T} = T_o + m^*Y^* \tag{20}$$

where m^* is the marginal propensity to import domestic goods by foreign residents. The term m^*Y^* can tell us what part of their additional income foreigners spend on domestic goods, which represents domestic exports. If we assume that everything else is constant, a change in foreign income, ΔY^*, will influence the autonomous trade balance by $\Delta \overline{T} = m^* \Delta Y^*$. This expression can be substituted into equation (13a) to determine the influence of changes in foreign income on domestic income:

$$\Delta Y = \alpha m^* \Delta Y^* \tag{21}$$

where $\Delta \overline{A} = 0$ in the absence of domestic disturbances. Equation (21) is usually expressed in proportional terms by dividing both sides by domestic income, yielding

$$\hat{Y} \equiv \frac{\Delta Y}{Y} = \alpha m^* \frac{Y^*}{Y} \frac{\Delta Y^*}{Y^*} = \alpha m^* \frac{Y^*}{Y} \hat{Y}^* \tag{22}$$

where $\hat{Y} \equiv \Delta Y / Y$ and $\hat{Y}^* = \Delta Y^*/Y^*$ represent the proportional rates of change of domestic and foreign income.

Equation (22) highlights the major factors determining the influence of a foreign income disturbance on domestic income. The first factor is the foreign marginal propensity to import, m^*, which is associated with the degree of openness of the economy. If the economy is a relatively closed economy so that foreign residents do not spend on domestic goods to any significant extent, then m^* becomes close to zero, and foreign income growth will have minimal influence on domestic growth. If foreign residents spend a large fraction of their income on domestic goods, on the other hand, any given reduction in foreign growth will bring about a substantial drop in demand for domestic goods, and therefore a sharp domestic recession.

A second factor influencing the magnitude of spillover effects is the economic size of the foreign trading partners relative to the size of the domestic economy. This is measured by the ratio of foreign to domestic income, Y^*/Y, in equation (22). If foreign income and, therefore, the foreign demand for domestic goods,

---

[20] It is assumed foreign income, Y^*, is measured in terms of domestic goods, to ensure consistency of units.

represents a negligible fraction of domestic income, a foreign recession will have a minor effect on domestic growth. The larger the relative size of the foreign economy, on the other hand, the greater the impact of foreign disturbances on domestic growth.

Finally, the size of the domestic income multiplier, α, will influence the effects of foreign disturbances on domestic growth. The larger (or smaller) the multiplier, the stronger (or weaker) the transmission of a foreign recession into the domestic economy.

Repercussion Effects and the Income Multiplier

Spillover effects point to the global nature of income determination in an interdependent world. Suppose a fiscal expansion results in a U.S. boom. As income grows, U.S. imports will swell because some of the additonal spending falls into purchases of foreign goods and services. Since higher domestic imports correspond to an increase in foreign, say European, exports to the United States, the U.S. income expansion generates an export-led production and income expansion abroad. In other words, the U.S. boom is transmitted to Europe as Americans spend more on European goods.

The matter does not end there, though. The induced expansion of European income can be expected to increase European spending on U.S. goods, feeding back into the U.S. economy in the form of increased exports to Europe and therefore increased U.S. production and income. The process involves a *repercussion effect* of the initial U.S. autonomous spending expansion on the U.S. economy. This repercussion effect is positive in the sense that it serves to further expand U.S. income. Our discussion of economic policy in previous sections ignored repercussion effects by assuming an exogenously given foreign income. It is apparent, however, that in interdependent economies, foreign income can be affected by domestic disturbances. Since the repercussion effects amplify the expansionary impact of a rise in domestic autonomous spending (or enhance the contractionary effects of a spending reduction), the income multiplier taking into account repercussion effects is generally larger than the one derived earlier, which ignored repercussions. The precise algebraic expression for the multiplier in this context is derived in the Appendix to this chapter.

Table 5–1 shows the results of a recent Organization for Economic Cooperation and Development (OECD) study estimating the effects of a 1% increase in the autonomous spending of each of several industrial countries (listed in the left-hand column) on their own and other countries' income and current account balance. The results reported in Table 5–1 show how increased autonomous spending would raise domestic and foreign income while deteriorating the country's current account balance and improving that of its trading partners. There are, however, wide differences in the precise, quantitative effects of each country's disturbance on the others. These divergences are connected to the differences in the magnitude of spillover and repercussion effects for each particu-

TABLE 5–1.   Spillover Effects and the International Transmission of Aggregate Demand Disturbances

Economy Originating a 1% Increase in Autonomous Spending	Economy Affected by International Transmission of Disturbance[a,b]							
	United States		Germany		Japan		Canada	
	Income (%)	CAB ($)	Income (%)	CAB ($)	Income (%)	CAB ($)	Income (%)	CAB ($)
United States	1.47	−3.4	0.23	0.4	0.25	0.9	0.68	0.4
Germany	0.05	0.5	1.25	−2.4	0.10	0.3	0.10	0.2
Japan	0.04	0.4	0.05	0.1	1.26	−1.2	0.06	0.0
Canada	0.06	0.6	0.03	0.1	0.03	0.1	1.27	−1.0
OECD	1.81	−1.1	2.38	−0.1	1.84	0.7	2.32	0.0

Source: Organization for Economic Cooperation and Development, *Economic Outlook* (Occasional Studies, Paris, 1979).

[a] Income change is measured in percentages.

[b] Current account balance (CAB) change is measured in billions of U.S. dollars.

lar country. For instance, an increase in U.S. autonomous spending of one percentage point would raise U.S. income by approximately 1.5% while also substantially raising Canadian income by 0.68% and Japan's income by 0.25%. A similar increase of autonomous spending in Canada, on the other hand, would induce a 1.3% rise in that country's income but would have a relatively minor impact on other economies. The explanation partly lies in the larger relative economic size of the United States as compared with Canada (U.S. GDP is about 10 times that of Canada) and the generally greater relative impact of U.S. income changes on its major foreign trading partners. Similarly, the lack of influence of a 1% increase in Japanese autonomous spending on other countries' income growth, as shown in Table 5–1, is related to the relatively small marginal propensity to import assigned in the OECD study to Japan as compared with the United States.

5–10   POLICY COORDINATION AND CONFLICT IN THE WORLD ECONOMY

A major conclusion of the analysis in Section 5–9 is that, within a context of Keynesian recession and unemployment, raising domestic autonomous spending is not only associated with domestic recovery but it also tends to spur foreign income growth. As a matter of fact, if all countries involved were to raise their own autonomous expenditures, the result would be a stronger income expansion than if each country alone were to pursue its expansionary objectives. This is indeed what the results reported in the last row of Table 5–1 indicate. These numbers show what the effect of a concerted, simultaneous 1% expansion of autonomous spending in all OECD countries would be. The U.S. level of income, for instance, would rise by 1.8%, Germany's by 2.4%, and so on. It is therefore apparent that expansionary autonomous spending policies do not result in policy conflict and a joint expansion of autonomous spending would heighten each country's expansionary efforts rather than hinder them.

One curious aspect of a simultaneous global expansion of income, bringing to the fore the nature of interdependence, regards its effects on the trade balance. An increase in domestic income raises imports and thereby worsens the trade balance. What happens when all countries concerned expand their income? Would the trade balance of all these countries deteriorate? Emphatically not. Since one country's imports are another country's exports, the sum of the trade balances of all countries trading with each other must add up to zero. That is, the global trade balance deficit is equal to zero. When there is joint economic expansion of all countries concerned, those countries growing above the average tend to have trade deficits, while those whose income grows at a rate below the average will have trade balance surpluses. The deficits of the faster-growing countries then balance the surpluses of the slower-growing countries, producing a zero global trade balance.

Competitive Devaluations and Policy Conflict

In examining the effects of devaluation on the domestic economy, we have thus far assumed that foreign countries behave passively, accepting without protest the effects that the associated revaluation of their currencies vis à vis domestic currency have on their economies. But a currency revaluation has effects exactly opposite those of a devaluation. By switching expenditure toward domestic goods, a foreign currency revaluation reduces demand for foreign goods, worsening the foreign trade balance and reducing foreign output. Devaluation is therefore often referred to as a *beggar-thy-neighbor policy:* When it increases domestic output, it does it at the expense of the output of the country's trading partners. Foreign authorities might then react by devaluing their own currencies vis à vis the currency of the country originally following devaluation. Such a change would offset the original policy action; if large enough, it could turn things around by switching demand toward foreign goods and away from domestic goods. Domestic authorities might then retaliate by devaluing their currency even further, and so on.

These *competitive devaluations* followed by countries seeking domestic expansion at the expense of their trading partners point to a basic weakness of a system in which currency devaluation is a policy that is easy to execute. In situations of global recession and unemployment, domestic policymakers in each country might have an incentive to export the problems to foreign countries, thereby engaging in competitive devaluations. As a matter of fact, the experience of the thirties during the Great Depression years was permeated by competitive devaluations. The general disruption of international trade created by the policy conflicts implied by competitive devaluations during the 1930s gave impetus to the more rigorous restrictions imposed by the International Monetary Fund (IMF) on the use of devaluation as a macroeconomic adjustment policy under the Bretton Woods regime.

5–11 SUMMARY

1. In an open economy, domestic resident spending (absorption) diverges from domestic income. This gap between income and absorption corresponds to the trade balance, that is, the net foreign demand for domestic goods.

2. The simple Keynesian framework assumes that the prices of domestic goods are fixed and that firms producing these goods can supply all the output demanded of them at the given prices. In this case, the equilibrium level of domestic output is determined by the level of aggregate demand for domestic goods.

3. The objectives of policymakers in an open economy can be expected to include external balance in addition to internal balance (i.e., full employment). External balance is generally associated with balanced payments, corresponding to a balanced trade account in the absence of international capital movements. Even under capital mobility, with trade imbalances financed by capital flows, external balance is often associated with long-term trade balance (or current account balance) targets. Countries might wish to avoid the debt service problems that may arise from the growing external indebtedness required to finance persistent trade balance deficits.

4. Within the Keynesian context examined in this chapter, the economy's equilibrium does not ensure either full employment or balanced trade. As a result, government intervention with the intention of attaining internal and external balance might be expected. One alternative is fiscal policy. Increases in autonomous government spending in the present framework raise aggregate demand and spur an equilibrium output expansion. The multiplier effects of changes in autonomous spending on domestic income are generally smaller the more open the economy, in the sense of a higher marginal propensity to import. In an open economy, part of the spending expansion leaks out of the economy through increased spending on foreign goods. Increases in domestic autonomous spending therefore increase income but raise imports and deteriorate the trade balance.

5. Exchange rate (devaluation) and commercial policies can be used to alter equilibrium output. By switching demand away from foreign and toward domestic goods, a domestic currency devaluation would increase domestic output while simultaneously improving the trade balance. This result requires that the sum of the price elasticities of the demand for domestic imports and exports be greater than 1, a condition referred to as the Marshall–Lerner condition.

Experience has demonstrated that, over the short run, these elasticities might be quite small and that devaluation might worsen the trade balance and have a contractionary effect on output. The so-called *J*-curve effect alludes to the initial deterioration but eventual improvement of the trade balance in response to a devaluation.

    6. In an interdependent world, domestic disturbances will spill over into foreign economies. Changes in one country's income and employment will therefore be transmitted abroad. The degree of influence of a foreign income disturbance on domestic income depends on the foreign marginal propensity to import, the economic size of the foreign relative to the domestic economy, and the magnitude of the Keynesian income multiplier.

    7. With interdependence, an increase in domestic autonomous spending will spill over into foreign income expansion. Since some of the increased foreign spending will fall on domestic goods, spillovers result in further expansionary repercussions on domestic income.

    8. In contrast to expansionary autonomous spending policies, which have positive repercussions abroad, a devaluation raises domestic production by improving the domestic trade balance, thereby worsening the trade balance of the rest of the world and contracting foreign production. Devaluation is therefore often categorized as a beggar-thy-neighbor policy.

PROBLEMS

1. Suppose that you are given the following absorption and trade balance relationships for a certain fixed exchange rate economy:

$$A = \bar{A} + aY$$
$$= 390 + 0.75\,Y$$
$$T = \bar{T} - mY$$
$$= 50 - 0.25\,Y$$

with all symbols as defined in the text and all variables measured in real terms (in terms of billions of domestic output):

(a) What is the equilibrium level of income in the economy (in numerical terms)? What is the value of the Keynesian multiplier? What is the balance of trade? Is this a surplus or a deficit?

(b) Suppose that there is an exogenous increase in the foreign demand for domestic exports reflected in an autonomous trade balance increase of 50 billion. What is the effect on

    (1) The equilibrium level of income in the economy?

    (2) The balance of trade?

(c) Consider the impact of an exogenous reduction in government spending of 50 billion. What would be the effect on
(1) The equilibrium level of income in the economy?
(2) The value of exports, imports and the trade balance?
Explain the economic reasoning behind these results. Do you think the effects of government spending cuts, as you have analyzed them here, would apply to the particular case of cuts in school lunch programs? What additional considerations have to be taken into account?

2. You are advising Banania, a large, tropical country that currently has a balance of trade equal to zero but is facing a high rate of unemployment. You are told that the economy is under a system of fixed exchange rates, and you are given the following information:
(1) The marginal propensity to import is 0.1.
(2) The marginal propensity to save is 0.2.
(3) The price elasticity of demand for imports is equal to 2.1.
(4) The price elasticity of demand for Banania's exports is 1.8.
(5) Domestic exports (which equal the value of imports) are 50 million.
   (a) Suppose that the government decides to devalue the bananian (Banania's currency) by 10%. What would be the impact on the balance of trade and on equilibrium income? Give a numerical answer and explain.
   (b) Now suppose that the government's intentions in devaluing the bananian are to cut unemployment. At the same time, the policymakers do not want external balance to be disturbed. Given your results in part (a), what would you recommend the government do (if anything) to sustain external balance in response to the devaluation?

3. Consider two interdependent economies, the domestic one being the same as that described in question 1. You are also provided with the following information regarding the foreign economy:
(1) The foreign marginal propensity to save is 0.04.
(2) The foreign marginal propensity to import is 0.04.
   (a) What is the value of the domestic open economy Keynesian multiplier in this case, that is, with repercussion effects? How does it compare with the multiplier determined in Problem 1?
   (b) Suppose that there is an exogenous reduction in government spending on domestic goods of 50 billion. What would be the effect on
   (1) The equilibrium level of domestic income?
   (2) The value of domestic exports, imports and the trade balance?
   Compare your results with those obtained in Problem 1(c).

4. Suppose that you are given the following behavioral relationships:

$$C = 90 + 0.8 Y_D \qquad T = 0.2 Y$$

$$\bar{I} = 100 \qquad M = 0.1 Y_D$$

$$\overline{G} = 200 \qquad\qquad Y_D = Y - T$$

$$\overline{X} = 50$$

where C refers to the value of consumption spending in the economy (in billions of dollars) Y_D is disposable income, $\overline{I}$ is investment, $\overline{G}$ is government spending, $\overline{X}$ is the value of exports, M refers to the value of imports, Y is domestic income, and T refers to the value of taxes gathered by the government. All variables are measured in billions of dollars.

(a) What is the equilibrium level of income in the economy? What is the balance of trade? Is this a surplus or a deficit? What is the value of the Keynesian multiplier in this economy? Is the government budget in surplus, deficit, or balance? (HINT: The equilibrium equality of income and aggregate spending on domestic goods is given by

$$Y = A + T = C + \overline{I} + \overline{G} + \overline{X} - M)$$

(b) Suppose that government spending goes down by $44 billion. What is the impact on
 (1) The equilibrium level of income in the economy?
 (2) The value of exports, imports, and the trade balance?
 (3) The government budget?

(c) Suppose that exports go up by $44 million. What is the impact on
 (1) The equilibrium level of income in the economy?
 (2) The balance of trade?
 (3) The government budget?
 All your answers should be numerical, and you should explain how they are obtained.

5. Domestic absorption can be disaggregated in alternative ways. One way is to emphasize its consumption, investment and government components, as in the text. Another is to decompose it into

$$A_N = D_N + G_N + M_N$$

where D_N denotes the value of private domestic resident spending on domestic goods, G_N is government spending, and M_N is the value of imports. Interpret this expression for domestic absorption, assuming that government expenditures fall only on domestic goods. Then express absorption in real terms, that is, in terms of domestic goods. Does the relative price of foreign goods in terms of domestic goods, q, enter into the resulting expression showing real absorption?

6. Show the direct effect of a devaluation on the trade balance (at a fixed level of income), assuming that the economy is initially in a trade deficit. (HINT: derive the counterpart to equation (16) assuming that domestic exports, M^*, are only a fraction of domestic imports, qM, that is, $M^* = \theta q M$, where

$0 < \theta < 1$). Does the Marshall–Lerner condition still hold? Explain your answer.

7. A government facing external payments deficits, unemployment, and budget deficits adopts the advice of a committee recommending the imposition of a tariff on imports. The experts report that this policy represents the best of all worlds, since it improves the trade balance, stimulates the economy, and provides revenues to the government. Analyze the macroeconomic effects of a tariff on imports within the Keynesian framework described in this chapter. What are the effects on the domestic economy? How are foreign countries affected? What are the global effects of many countries following such a protectionist route?

APPENDIX: THE OPEN ECONOMY MULTIPLIER WITH REPERCUSSIONS

This appendix discusses the interactions between the domestic economy and the rest of the world. Substituting equation (20) into (9) in the text yields

$$T = T_o + m^*Y^* - mY \tag{A-1}$$

Note that the domestic trade balance deficit (surplus) must be equal (but in opposite sign) to the trade balance surplus (deficit) of the rest of the world, that is $T = -T^*$, where T^* is the foreign trade balance.

Equilibrium in the domestic goods market is

$$Y = A + T = \bar{A} + aY + T_o + m^*Y^* - mY \tag{A-2}$$

where we have made use of (A-1). Equilibrium in the foreign goods market is

$$Y^* = A^* + T^* = \bar{A}^* + a^*Y^* - T_o - m^*Y^* + mY \tag{A-3}$$

where A^* is foreign absorption, $\bar{A}^*$ is autonomous foreign absorption, and a^* is the foreign marginal propensity to spend. By solving (A-3), we can determine the equilibrium level of income abroad

$$Y^* = \alpha^*\bar{A}^* - \alpha^*T_o + \alpha^*mY \tag{A-4}$$

where $\alpha^* = 1/(s^* + m^*)$ is the foreign income multiplier ($s^* \equiv 1 - a^*$). Substituting the value of Y^* in (A-4) into (A-2) and simplifying, we now obtain

$$Y = \hat{\alpha}(\bar{A} + m^*\alpha^*\bar{A}^* + s^*\alpha^*T_o) \tag{A-5}$$

where $\hat{\alpha} \equiv 1/(s + m - \alpha^*m^*m)$ is the Keynesian income multiplier with repercussion effects. This multiplier measures the impact of a change in autonomous spending on domestic income taking into account repercussions.

CHAPTER 6

Money, Output, and Trade Balance Adjustment

In Chapter 5 we took a first look at the analysis of macroeconomic problems in the open economy under fixed exchange rates. We used a simple Keynesian model without explicitly considering asset holdings in the economy. As a consequence, we talked mostly about production and trade in goods. It is now time to introduce assets explicitly into the discussion. The purpose of introducing money and other assets into the analysis is threefold. First, it shows the role of asset portfolios and interest rates as central variables in the behavior of the economy and on the possible effects of various government policies. Second, only by having money explicitly can one analyze the effects of monetary policy, which is, of course, a primary aspect of government policymaking. Finally, as we shall see, balance of payments disequilibria involve essential monetary phenomena. Accordingly, the dissection of an external payments surplus (or deficit) and the nature of corrective policy measures demands a framework that includes assets markets. Some of the conclusions reached in Chapter 5 will then have to be qualified in the present, more sophisticated framework.

The assets markets are the markets in which money, bonds, stocks, real estate, and other forms of wealth or stores of value are exchanged. Asset claims can be traded within borders, as in the case when a New Yorker purchases Treasury bills from Merrill Lynch, or they can be traded across borders, such as when an Italian movie star buys some real estate in California. The volume and variety of assets being traded within and across borders are enormous. To simplify matters, we shall consider the presence of only two types of assets: domestic bonds and domestic money. We assume that domestic residents hold only domestic bonds and domestic money, which foreign residents do not hold. These assumptions mean that, for the moment, we shall ignore two important aspects of any analysis of an open economy. The first one regards *international capital movements,* which would occur if domestic residents were to hold foreign assets and foreign residents to buy domestic assets. The implication is that we are neglecting the analysis of the capital account of the balance of payments. The second aspect we ignore here is *currency substitution,* which would occur

189

if (private) domestic residents were to hold foreign money (foreign currencies) and/or if foreign residents demanded domestic money (dollars). Both aspects will be dealt with later on, in Chapters 7 and 15.

Under a regime of fixed exchange rates, the Central Bank holds reserves in the form of foreign currencies and/or international assets (such as gold) in order to be able to determine and maintain fixed the exchange rate. It may prove useful at this point to leaf through Chapter 1 again to refresh your understanding of the institutional aspects of Central Bank intervention in the determination of the exchange rate.

6–1 INTRODUCTION TO THE ASSETS MARKETS

This section develops a concise presentation of the basic analytics of assets market equilibrium.[1] In our simplified framework, two types of assets are held by domestic residents: domestic bonds and domestic money. Domestic money does not yield any interest but it serves as a store of value and as a means of transaction. At any given moment in time, the nominal money supply is fixed, although it may change over time. We represent this fixed money supply existing at any given moment in time by M^S. This implies that the real money supply would be M^S/P, where P is the price of domestic goods (exports), as defined earlier. If P is rigid, as in the Keynesian model used in this chapter, a fixed nominal supply of money implies a fixed real supply of money.[2] The (real) supply of bonds, which are interest-yielding assets, is also assumed to be fixed. Expressed in terms of domestic goods, the stock of bonds in the economy is represented by V^S. Total (real) wealth in the economy is then given by

$$\frac{W}{P} = \frac{M^S}{P} + V^S \tag{1}$$

where W is the nominal wealth in the economy (i.e., wealth measured in dollars).

Domestic residents face a wealth constraint, in the sense that the aggregate value of bonds and money that they decide to hold (the amount they demand of money and bonds) cannot exceed their wealth. Since no one will throw away wealth, the demand for money and bonds will equal the supply of wealth in the economy, that is

---

[1] For a detailed discussion of the material in this section, see R. Dornbusch and S. Fischer, *Macroeconomics,* 3rd ed. (New York: McGraw-Hill Book Company, 1984), Chapter 4; and R. Gordon, *Macroeconomics,* 3rd ed. (Boston: Little, Brown and Company, 1984), Chapter 4. These books should serve as a good background for the discussion carried out in the following chapters.

[2] Note that, following the literature, we express real variables in terms of export goods, even though strictly speaking a variable such as the money supply should be deflated by a price index that includes imports.

$$\frac{W}{P} = L^D + V^D \tag{2}$$

where L^D is the real demand for money (in terms of domestic goods) and V^D is the real demand for bonds.

Equating the expressions in (1) and (2), we obtain

$$\frac{M^S}{P} + V^S = L^D + V^D$$

or

$$\left(L^D - \frac{M^S}{P}\right) + (V^D - V^S) = 0 \tag{3}$$

This implies that, as long as the money market is in equilibrium (i.e., as long as $L^D = M^S/P$), the bond market will also be in equilibrium ($V^D = V^S$). This result, usually referred to as *Walras's law,* justifies that we concentrate our attention on analyzing equilibrium in only one of the markets (either the bond or the money market). Following the literature, we choose the money market, the equilibrium of which will now be analyzed in detail.

The money market equilibrium would occur when

$$L^D = \frac{M^S}{P} \tag{4}$$

that is, when the demand for money is equal to its supply. On what variables does the demand for money depend? The real demand for money is given by

$$L^D = L(i, Y) \tag{5}$$

That is, real money demand, L^D, is a decreasing function of the interest rate, i, and an increasing function of real income in the economy, Y. Note that, as the interest rate goes up, the opportunity cost of holding money increases, and domestic residents increase the proportion of their wealth invested in bonds relative to the proportion of their wealth invested in money (i.e., they shift funds out of money and into bonds). The positive effect of income on money demand is attributable to the fact that people hold money to finance their spending transactions; as income increases, the demand for money created by these transactions rises.

The demand-for-money function in (5) can be linearized to

$$L^D = kY - hi \tag{6}$$

where k is a positive parameter representing the positive response of money demand to income, and h is a positive parameter that represents the responsiveness of money demand to the interest rate. Other variables affect the demand for money—domestic wealth and the development of the financial system, among others—but are held constant for purposes of this analysis.

6–2   THE MONEY SUPPLY PROCESS IN AN OPEN ECONOMY

This section develops a simple, yet essential, approach to the determination of the money supply in an open economy. The discussion is brief in institutional detail, emphasizing instead the open economy aspects of the money supply process. This approach presents a more comprehensive and encompassing view of the money supply process than is usually carried out within the context of a closed economy. It will explain many of the divergences of our results from those traditionally derived in introductory (closed economy) macroeconomics textbooks. It is, thus, important that the reader grasp the main points of this section.

A wide range of measures are used by monetary authorities and economists regarding the definition of the money supply. We assume that the nominal money supply is composed of currency in the hands of the nonbank public and demand deposits. Symbolically,

$$M^S = C^P + DD \tag{7}$$

where M^S is, as before, the nominal money supply, C^P refers to currency (coin, dollar notes) in the hands of the public, and DD is demand deposits (checkable deposits). This definition of the money supply corresponds to what is called in U.S. banking jargon M1, as defined by the Federal Reserve Board. In March 1984, the amount of currency in public hands in the United States was $150 billion and the amount of demand (checking) deposits was roughly $378 billion so that the U.S. money supply, in terms of our definition, was equal to $528 billion. There are, of course, other measures of the money supply, depending on how much liquidity the concept of money used is chosen to have.[3]

In a closed economy, the Central Bank could completely determine the money supply, given stability in the preferences and desired behavior of banks and individuals. This is not so for an open economy under fixed exchange rates. In the latter case, the money supply is not only influenced by the Central Bank but also by the *balance of payments of the country*, that is, by the actions

---

[3] For example, short-term liquid assets, such as savings accounts and short-term time deposits, are sometimes considered money. They are included in the definition of the so-called M2 by the Federal Reserve Board. Note also that C^P includes only cash in the hands of the nonbank public and excludes cash in bank vaults.

of domestic and foreign residents in trading with the rest of the world. This is perhaps the most crucial point of this chapter and we proceed to explain it in detail.

The Monetary Base and the Money Supply Multiplier

What is the role of the economy's Central Bank—the Federal Reserve in the United States—in the money supply process? The Central Bank affects the domestic money supply by influencing high-powered money or, as it is often called, the monetary base. The monetary base, H, is defined as

$$H = C^P + RE \tag{8}$$

where C^P refers to the value of currency in the hands of the public and RE refers to the reserves held by commercial banks (which are held in the form of deposits at the Central Bank and in the form of cash in the banks' vaults). In March 1984, the monetary base was equal to \$186 billion, broken down into \$150 billion in currency held by the public and \$36 billion as bank reserves.

The monetary base is closely linked to the money supply, and it is through this link that the Central Bank and the balance of payments influence the money supply. We shall now proceed to analyze how the monetary base and the money supply are related. It will be shown that, in the simple framework used, the monetary base is proportional to the money supply, symbolically represented as

$$M = \mu H$$

where μ is a constant; thus, changes in the monetary base will affect the money supply proportionally. We then specify how the Central Bank and the balance of payments situation of the country affect the monetary base.

The first step in discovering the link between the monetary base and the money supply is to discuss two key parameters involved in the determination of the money supply: the reserve:deposit ratio and the currency:deposit ratio. The currency:deposit ratio, cu, is defined as

$$cu = \frac{C^P}{DD}$$

where C^P represents currency and DD demand deposits. This parameter reflects the public's preferences in allocating its money holdings between currency and demand deposits. The larger cu is, the larger the amount of currency that the public decides to hold relative to holdings of demand deposits in commercial banks. Using our earlier figures for March 1984, we find that the currency:deposit ratio at that time was $cu = 0.40$ (\$150 billion divided by \$378 billion).

The reserve:deposit ratio, re, is defined as

$$re = \frac{RE}{DD}$$

where RE represents bank reserves and DD demand deposits. This ratio is chosen by commercial banks so that they can maintain enough reserves to finance withdrawals by their customers and to satisfy reserve requirements set by the Central Bank. Commercial banks hold these reserves as cash-in-vault and as deposits at the Central Bank. An increase in re means that banks would decide to hold more reserves for each dollar of deposits they receive from their customers; a decrease in re, on the other hand, denotes a reduced reserve:deposit ratio. In March 1984, the reserve:deposit ratio was approximately $re = 0.10$, since banks were holding \$36 billion as reserves out of a volume of demand deposits equal to \$378 billion.

We can now easily derive an expression showing the relationship between the money supply and the monetary base. For this purpose, we shall take cu and re as constants.[4] Dividing (7) by (8), we obtain

$$\frac{M^S}{H} = \frac{C^P + DD}{C^P + RE}$$

To make this equation more illuminating, we divide both the numerator and the denominator of the right-hand side by DD. The result is

$$\frac{M^S}{H} = \frac{(C^P/DD) + (DD/DD)}{(C^P/DD) + (RE/DD)} = \frac{cu + 1}{cu + re}$$

where we have substituted for the definitions of cu and re described above. A simple rearrangement then yields

$$M^S = \left[\frac{cu + 1}{cu + re} \right] H = \mu H \tag{9}$$

where $\mu = (cu + 1)/(cu + re)$ is the so-called *money supply multiplier*, which tells us by how much the money supply would increase if the monetary base

---

[4] In general, however, cu and re will not be fixed constants but stable functions of some parameters. For example, cu depends on how confident depositors are in the banking system, and re is affected by interest rates, the so-called discount rate, and reserve requirements. The discussion here is just intended to illustrate the role of openness of the economy in the determination of the money supply. The general case, with full discussion of these and other institutional details is given by K. Brunner, "Money Supply Process and Monetary Policy in an Open Economy," in M. Connolly and A. Swoboda, eds., *International Trade and Money* (Toronto: University of Toronto Press, 1973).

were to increase by \$1. Note that $\mu > 1$, since the reserve:deposit ratio, *re*, is less than 1. As a consequence, any given change in the monetary base will lead to a multiple increase in the money supply. This explains why μ is called a multiplier, and why H is called high-powered money. For the case of the United States, around March 1984, one can obtain a rough estimate of the money supply multiplier using the previously calculated values of 0.10 for *re* and 0.40 for *cu*. Substituting these into the definition of the multiplier implies that

$$\mu = 2.80 = \frac{0.40 + 1.00}{0.40 + 0.10}$$

For any dollar increment in the monetary base, the U.S. money supply (M1) would increase by \$2.80. What is the economic mechanism behind this multiple expansion of money arising from a given change in the monetary base?

When commercial banks accept deposits, their reserves increase by a corresponding amount. Since, as mentioned earlier, banks hold only a fraction of their deposits as reserves (in the form of precautionary cash-in-vault and deposits at the Central Bank), they will proceed to lend their excess reserves. Those funds that are lent by any given bank are then spent by the borrowers. The recipients of these funds in turn will deposit some of them back into the banking system, depending on how much currency vis à vis demand deposits they want to hold. The funds that are actually deposited lead to an increase in the volume of deposits for the banking system as a whole, since the initial deposits (on the basis of which loans were made) are still outstanding. The implication is that a dollar deposited in a given bank can lead to a multiplier expansion of deposits in the overall banking system.

The size of this multiplier effect clearly depends on the size of μ and therefore on the parameters *re* and *cu*. Note from equation (9) that an increase in the reserve:deposit ratio, *re*, tends to decrease the money supply multiplier, μ. A larger reserve:deposit ratio implies that, for each dollar of deposits, banks hold a larger fraction as reserves and thus lend a smaller fraction. As a consequence, for any given value of the monetary base and the currency:deposit ratio, bank deposit creation would be smaller. Similarly, an increase in the currency:deposit ratio *cu*, will result in a decrease in the multiplier. The explanation, which is not really obvious by just looking at (9), is as follows. A larger *cu* means that a larger amount of currency leaks out of the banking system as currency held by the public. Out of any given amount of high-powered money, banks are left with less reserves. This reduction in reserves implies that the deposits created by the banking system will decline by an even larger amount. The latter is so since $re = RE/DD < 1$ so that each dollar of reserves supports more than 1 dollar of deposits. Thus, even though an increase in *cu* induces an increase in the currency component of the money supply, the demand deposits component will decline even more, and the net effect on the money supply is negative. That is, at given levels of the monetary base and the reserve:deposit ratio, increases in the currency:deposit ratio will tend to reduce the money multiplier. To summarize, note that increases in cu and re tend to decrease the multiplier, since both imply that a higher proportion of funds in the economy will leak out of the credit-creating portion of the banking system's portfolio.

Given the value of the money multiplier, equation (9) shows the proportional relationship between the monetary base, H, and the money supply, M^s. Note that the monetary base represents the total amount of money potentially available to commercial banks as reserves and, thus, it serves as a basis for the creation of bank deposits. The larger the monetary base, given cu and re, the larger the volume of deposits in the banking system of the country. Having determined how the monetary base affects the money supply, we can now proceed to analyze the factors influencing the base.

Central Banks, the Balance of Payments, and the Money Supply

Even though in a closed economy the monetary base is determined by the actions of the Central Bank, in an open economy it is determined by the actions of the Central Bank *and* by the balance of payments. To clarify these issues, we now take a closer look at the monetary base and its relationship to the Central Bank's financial statement (i.e., balance sheet). The simplified balance sheet of a hypothetical Central Bank is shown in Table 6–1.

High-powered money is created when the Central Bank acquires assets in the form of *international reserves* (foreign exchange and gold) and *Central Bank credit* (loans, discounts, and government bonds). The Central Bank pays for these assets by issuing checks on itself. These checks are deposited in commercial banks and end up in the form of currency and commercial (member) bank deposits at the Central Bank. Algebraically,

TABLE 6–1. Simplified Central Bank Balance Sheet[a] (in Billions of Dollars)

Assets		Liabilities	
International reserves	100	Currency	240
		Cash in vaults 20	
		Currency in the hands of the public 220	
Central Bank credit	200	Commercial bank deposits at the Central Bank	60
Monetary base	300	Monetary base	300

[a] In general, one should examine the consolidated monetary account of the government, which includes other institutions (such as the Treasury) in addition to the Central Bank. Furthermore, a complete Central Bank balance sheet would include an item adding up all other assets (such as building and equipment) on the assets side, and a net worth item as a residual on the liabilities side. One would also have to differentiate between international reserves and net foreign assets, which are equal to international reserves net of the Central Bank's liabilities to foreign Central Banks. The latter are in the form of foreign official deposits held at the domestic Central Bank and generally compose a relatively minor item in the Central Bank's balance sheet.

$$IR + CBC = C^P + RE \equiv H \tag{10}$$

where IR represents international reserves, CBC is Central Bank credit, and C^P and RE refer to currency and commercial bank reserves, as before. The implication is that the monetary base, H, can be looked at from both the assets side (as $IR + CBC$) and the liabilities side (as $C^P + RE$) of the Central Bank balance sheet.

The next step is to analyze how changes in the different components of this balance sheet occur. We start with the Central Bank credit component and how it can change, that is, how Central Bank credit is created. Central Bank credit refers to the securities held by the Central Bank (such as Treasury bills), loans and discounts made by the Central Bank (such as an overnight loan made to Morgan Guaranty), and various other credit assets of the Central Bank. Credit creation occurs if the Central Bank increases its holdings of any of these assets. Let us take the example of a Central Bank purchase of securities in the open market (an *open market operation*). What is the exact process and impact of Central Bank credit creation on the Bank's balance sheet? The first step occurs when the Central Bank pays for the securities by issuing a check on itself. The seller of the securities bought by the Central Bank then deposits this check in his private bank. The bank may do one of two things. First, the bank may decide to convert the check into cash. In this case, the increase in the securities held by the Central Bank (on the assets side of the balance sheet) has as a counterpart an increase in currency (on the liabilities side). We illustrate this operation through the use of the T account represented in Table 6–2, showing the changes in the Central Bank's balance sheet on the assumption that the Bank buys $20 million in bonds.

Table 6–2 is based on the assumption that the bank in question converts its check into cash. Alternatively, the commercial bank may deposit the check in its account at the Central Bank. This will increase commercial bank deposits at the Central Bank. In terms of a T account, see Table 6–3 for the changes in the balance sheet.

Observe that in both cases (Tables 6–2 and 6–3), the monetary base, H, increases by the same amount ($20 million). All else being constant, changes

TABLE 6–2. Effects of an Open Market Purchase on the Central Bank Balance Sheet

Change in Assets (in millions)		Change in Liabilities (in millions)	
International reserves	0	Currency in vaults	+20
Central Bank credit	+20	Commercial bank deposits	0
Monetary base	+20	Monetary base	+20

TABLE 6–3.   **Effects of an Open Market Purchase on the Central Bank Balance Sheet**

Change in Assets (in millions)		Change in Liabilities (in millions)	
International reserves	0	Currency	0
Central Bank credit	+20	Commercial bank deposits	+20
Monetary base	+20	Monetary base	+20

in Central Bank credit will tend to alter the monetary base and therefore the money supply, as reflected by (9).

The balance of payments situation of the economy can also affect the monetary base. The nature of this connection will be examined shortly. First we must clarify which balance of payments concept is to be used in our analysis. This is a vital question since, as discussed in Chapter 4, there are various possible concepts of the balance of payments depending on which items are placed above and below the line. The balance of payments concept that best captures the net effect of international transactions on the money supply, and that is thus the most useful in the discussion of the money supply process in economies under fixed exchange rates, is called *the money account of the balance of payments.* It is defined as the changes in the international reserves of the domestic Central Bank (or, more generally, as the changes in the Central Bank's net foreign assets). A money account balance of payments surplus then corresponds to an accumulation of international reserves on the part of the Central Bank. A deficit involves a reduction in international reserves.

Note that the money account does not exactly correspond to any of the balance of payments concepts discussed in Chapter 4. It does not, for example, correspond exactly to the official reserve settlements (ORS) balance. An ORS balance of payments deficit associated with increased foreign official deposits at a New York commercial bank does not affect the international reserves held by the domestic Central Bank and would thus be associated with a zero money account deficit. It does not affect the monetary base either. Intuitively, the ORS deficit results in a transfer of commercial bank deposits from U.S. residents to foreign Central Banks. Although this changes the ownership of the deposits, it does not affect the monetary base or total demand deposits.

For a reserve currency country like the United States, which accepts a substantial amount of foreign official deposits in its commercial banking system, this distinction between the money account and the ORS balance is not negligible and should not be taken lightly. For other countries, however, the difference between the money account and the ORS does not amount to much and can be safely ignored. We now proceed to examine the connections between the money supply process and the balance of payments, as defined.

Suppose that the economy is in a situation of balance of payments deficit. As previously explained in Chapter 1, under a system of fixed exchange rates, the deficit represents an excess demand for foreign exchange on the part of the private sector. The Central Bank satisfies this excess demand by providing (selling) the appropriate amount of foreign exchange to the private sector. Exactly how does this Central Bank foreign exchange market intervention occur? Usually, the Central Bank will sell foreign exchange to commercial banks (which then sell it to importers). In this case, the (domestic) Central Bank debits member bank accounts in payment for the foreign exchange sold. Therefore, the external payments deficit appears in the Central Bank's balance sheet as a reduction in commercial bank deposits at the Central Bank (through the liabilities side) and as a reduction in the international reserve holdings of the Bank (through the assets side). Table 6–4 displays a T account illustrating how the Central Bank balance sheet is affected by a balance of payments deficit of $20 million; the deficit surfaces as a $20 million decrease in the monetary base. This implies that the payments deficit reduces the money supply in the economy, by means of the link established in equation (9).

TABLE 6–4. **Effects of a Drain of International Reserves on the Central Bank Balance Sheet**

Change in Assets (in millions)		Change in Liabilities (in millions)	
International reserves	−$20	Currency	0
Central Bank credit	0	Commercial bank deposits	−$20
Monetary base	−$20	Monetary base	−$20

In the case of a balance of payments surplus, the private sector will face an excess supply of foreign exchange. Under fixed exchange rates, the Central Bank will then buy this excess supply and will pay the private sector—for their sales of foreign exchange—by drawing a check on itself. This type of operation is very similar to an open market purchase of bonds by the Central Bank. The Central Bank thus acquires international reserves (as reflected on the assets side of the balance sheet) at the same time that currency and/or commercial bank deposits increase (as reflected on the liabilities side). The implication is that a payments surplus increases the monetary base and, therefore, tends to increase the money supply in the economy.

Fixed Exchange Rates and the Control of the Money Supply

We have been covering a lot of material at a relatively fast pace. It may be wise to stop for a moment to review the preceding discussion, as well as its implications. We have shown that the money supply in the economy is basically determined by the monetary base (high-powered money), given the preferences of banks and individuals (as represented by the reserve:deposit and currency:deposit ratios). This relationship between the monetary base and the money supply is represented by the money market multiplier, assumed to be fixed in our simplified framework. Clearly, those factors affecting the monetary base will essentially determine the money supply. In an open economy under fixed exchange rates, the two basic factors tending to influence the monetary base are Central Bank actions, which affect credit creation in the economy, and the balance of payments situation of the economy, which alters the international reserve holdings of the Central Bank. The impact effect of increases (or decreases) in credit creation is to raise (or reduce) the monetary base and thus the money supply, *ceteris paribus*. Balance of payments deficits (or surpluses), on the other hand, tend to reduce (or increase) the Central Bank's international reserve holdings, and to decrease (or increase) the monetary base and the money supply.

The most important conclusion so far regards the difference that exists between an analysis of the money supply process geared toward a closed economy compared with one that is oriented toward an open economy. In the closed economy case one could plausibly assume that high-powered money, or some version of it in more sophisticated analyses, can be directly manipulated by the Central Bank. This means that monetary policy (e.g., an open market operation) is well defined in terms of how it affects the monetary base (and the money supply). An expansionary (or contractionary) open market operation can be defined as being associated directly with an increase (or decrease) in the monetary base and thus the money supply. In an open economy, however, this direct association between monetary policy in the form of credit creation by the Central Bank and changes in the monetary base (and the money supply) cannot be made. The reason is that, in this case, control of the monetary base is not completely in the hands of the Central Bank. Let us explain.

High-powered money, H, looked at from the assets side of the Central Bank's balance sheet, is composed of international reserves, IR, and Central Bank credit, CBC, or

$$H = IR + CBC \qquad (10)$$

Expressing (10) in terms of changes,

$$\Delta H = \Delta IR + \Delta CBC \qquad (11)$$

which expresses algebraically what we have verbally discussed above: Changes in the monetary base, ΔH, can arise from changes in Central Bank credit, ΔCBC, *and* changes in the international reserves of the Central Bank, ΔIR. The implication is that the Central Bank can manipulate or control directly only one component of high-powered money: Central Bank credit. The second component (international reserves) cannot be directly controlled by the Central

Bank since, in an economy under fixed exchange rates, it depends essentially on the balance of payments situation of the economy. The balance of payments is endogenous to the economy; that is, it is determined by the decisions of the private sector in buying domestic and foreign goods and securities, which depend on basic economic variables such as income, and export and import prices. As a consequence, the influence of the Central Bank on the monetary base is very difficult, or impossible, to isolate. What the monetary authorities clearly affect in the economy is credit creation, through their purchases or sales of bonds in the open market. The effects of changes in Central Bank credit on the monetary base, and therefore on the money supply, however, are not clear and depend on how credit creation affects the balance of payments. This can be seen by expressing equation (9) in terms of changes and then substituting equation (11), yielding

$$\Delta M^S = \mu \Delta H = \mu(\Delta IR + \Delta CBC) \tag{12}$$

which represents a general equation specifying changes in the money supply in an open economy. In order to determine how the Central Bank affects the money supply, then, it is necessary to determine how credit creation affects international reserves. The link between these two will be examined in depth in the following sections. Since the balance of payments is endogenous to the economy, however, a complete and integrated analysis of the assets and goods markets is necessary. That is the topic to which we now turn.

6–3   ASSETS MARKET (MONEY MARKET) EQUILIBRIA: THE *LM* CURVE

According to Walras's law, we can concentrate our analysis of assets market equilibria by looking explicitly only at the money market. Equilibrium in the money market occurs when money supply equals money demand. Algebraically, using equations (4) and (6), we obtain

$$\frac{M^S}{P} = L^D(i, Y) = kY - hi \tag{13}$$

Since the price of domestic goods, P, is rigid, there are only three variables in (13): M^S, i, and Y; k and h are exogenous parameters.

As discussed in Section 6–2, the domestic money supply, M^S, is a variable that changes over time in response to the monetary policy actions of the country's Central Bank and in response to the balance of payments situation of the economy. At this point, however, our analysis will reflect a snapshot of the economy *at any given moment in time,* holding the current level of the money supply fixed. The equilibrium condition in (13) represents a so-called short-run stock equilibrium of the money market, in the sense that it shows that the money stock in the economy, at any given point in time, is willingly held by domestic residents.

By solving (13) for the interest rate, it is transformed into

$$i = \frac{1}{h}\left(kY - \frac{M^S}{P}\right) \tag{14}$$

Equation (14) expresses the relationship between income and the interest rate that keeps the money market in equilibrium, given the money supply. Note that the implied relationship between income and interest rates is positive. An increase in domestic income raises the demand for money; given the money supply, the interest rate (the opportunity cost of money) must increase to clear the market.

Representing the interest rate on the vertical axis and domestic real income on the horizontal axis, Figure 6–1 plots money market equilibrium as a positively sloped locus, which is called the *LM* curve. The *LM* curve shows the alternative combinations of the interest rate and real income that keep the money market in equilibrium and is drawn for a given level of the money supply, M_o. In algebraic terms,

$$i = \frac{1}{h}\left(kY - \frac{M_o}{P}\right) \tag{15}$$

In Section 6–2, we saw how the money supply can change in response to the actions of the Central Bank and the balance of payments. The impact of changes in the money supply can be visualized from (15). For instance, an increase in the money supply, say from M_o to M_1, gives rise to an excess supply of money, requiring a market-clearing reduction in the interest rate at any given level of income. This is shown in Figure 6–1 by means of the shift of the *LM* curve to *LM'*. The reader should not confuse *shifts* of the *LM* curve and *movements* along the *LM* curve itself. Shifts of the *LM* curve occur when a change in

shift to the right ↗

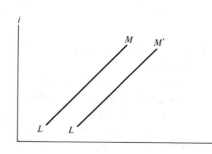

FIGURE 6–1. The *LM* Curve: Assets Market Equilibrium

some variable affecting the money market (e.g., the money supply) alters the interest rate consistent with money market equilibrium, *at a given level of income*. Movements along the *LM* curve reflect the fact that alternative levels of income require different interest rates for money market equilibrium to occur, *ceteris paribus*, that is, keeping all other variables affecting the money market constant.

In summary, points along the *LM* curve represent different alternative or possible pairs of income and interest rates consistent with money market equilibrium. To be able to select one of these pairs as the economy's equilibrium, one has to consider the goods market, to which we now turn.

6–4 DOMESTIC GOODS MARKET EQUILIBRIUM

This section modifies the introductory analysis of the goods market in Chapter 5 to incorporate the influence of the interest rate. Goods market equilibrium occurs when the aggregate supply of domestic goods, *Y*, equals aggregate demand for domestic goods, which is equal to the sum of absorption and the trade balance:

$$Y = A + T \tag{16}$$

where *A* denotes absorption and *T* is the trade balance. Absorption, the aggregate spending of domestic residents, includes consumption, investment, and government expenditures and depends on some exogenous parameters and on domestic real income. [See equation (12) in Chapter 5 for further details.] In addition, domestic aggregate spending is responsive to domestic interest rates because of the influence of interest rates on investment spending. Investment spending is intended to increase (or maintain) the domestic capital stock. To finance the acquisition of capital, however, the firm (or household) has to borrow (or tie up) a certain amount of funds. The cost of these funds is the interest rate that has to be paid (or given up) for their use. Therefore, if the interest rate increases, the cost of purchasing new capital will rise and investment spending can be expected to decline. This effect is particularly important with respect to residential investment.

On the basis of these considerations, the investment spending function, *I*, is explicitly made a function of domestic interest rates:

$$I = I(i)$$
$$= I_0 - bi$$

where I_0 represents autonomous investment (that part of investment that is exogenous, or independent of both domestic income and the interest rate), and *b* is a positive parameter representing the responsiveness of investment with respect to the domestic interest rate, i. Note that $\Delta I/\Delta i = -b$, which is negative; in other words, the higher the rate of interest, the more firms (and households) have to pay to finance their investments, with the result that investment spending decreases.[5]

Given the dependence of absorption on the interest rate, the goods market equilibrium condition (16) can be restated in the following functional form:

$$Y = A(\overline{G}, i, Y) + T(q, Y) \tag{17}$$

where $A(\overline{G}, i, Y)$ represents the influence of government spending, $\overline{G}$, the interest rate and the level of domestic income on domestic absorption, and $T(q, Y)$ the influence of the relative price of foreign goods in terms of domestic goods, q, and domestic income, Y, on the trade balance. Linearizing the expression for absorption, we obtain

$$A(\overline{G}, i, Y) = \overline{A} + aY - bi \tag{18}$$

where a is the marginal propensity to spend out of income, $\overline{A}$ represents autonomous absorption (which now represents that part of absorption that does not depend on domestic income or on interest rates), and b measures the responsiveness of absorption with respect to the interest rate. Note that $\overline{A}$ depends on the level of government expenditures, autonomous investment, and autonomous consumption, all of which are assumed to be independent of domestic income and the interest rate. In addition, since the only component of absorption that is assumed to depend on the interest rate is investment, the responsiveness of absorption to the interest rate corresponds to the responsiveness of investment to the interest rate, b.

Carrying out a similar linearization with respect to the trade balance, we find that

$$T = T(q, Y) = \overline{T} - mY \tag{19}$$

where $\overline{T}$ and m are the autonomous trade balance and the marginal propensity to import, respectively. [Note that equation (19) is identical to (9) in Chapter 5.]

Equations (18) and (19) can be substituted into the goods market equilibrium condition to yield

$$Y = A + T = \overline{A} + aY - bi + \overline{T} - mY \tag{20}$$

---

[5] The interest rate relevant for the investment decision is the *real* interest rate, which is equal to the nominal interest rate adjusted for the rate of inflation. In the present framework, however, the real interest rate coincides with the nominal interest rate, since prices are assumed to be rigid. (See Chapter 12.)

Simplifying, we obtain

$$Y(1 - a + m) = \bar{A} - bi + \bar{T}$$

or

$$Y = \alpha(\bar{A} - bi + \bar{T}) \qquad (21)$$

where

$$\alpha \equiv \frac{1}{1 - a + m} = \frac{1}{s + m}$$

is the open economy Keynesian multiplier derived in Chapter 5.

Equation (21) expresses the relationship between the level of domestic income, Y, and the interest rate, i, that keeps the domestic goods market in equilibrium, given a certain value of the Keynesian multiplier, autonomous absorption, and the autonomous trade balance. Note that an increase in the interest rate reduces domestic investment; as a consequence, it decreases aggregate demand, requiring a reduction in domestic output (and real income) to maintain goods market equilibrium. This negative relationship between domestic income and the interest rate is reflected in the negative slope of the so-called *IS* curve. The *IS* curve depicts the combinations of the interest rate and income that keep the domestic goods market in equilibrium. This graphic representation of equation (21) is shown in Figure 6–2.

Two main variables are assumed constant in deriving the *IS* curve: the relative price of foreign goods in terms of domestic goods, q, and the level of government spending, $\bar{G}$. An increase in government spending, at a given level of the interest rate, will tend to raise aggregate demand (by increasing $\bar{A}$) and, therefore, domestic income by means of a multiplier effect. An increase in q, such as that brought about by a domestic currency devaluation, will shift demand away from foreign and toward domestic goods. By increasing $\bar{T}$, this raises the aggregate demand for domestic goods and tends to increase domestic income.

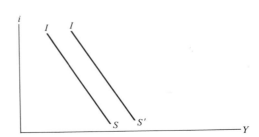

FIGURE 6–2. The *IS* Curve: Goods
Market Equilibrium

↗Shift to the right.

Both changes, an increase in $\bar{G}$ and an increase in q, shift the *IS* curve upward, as represented in Figure 6–2 by the rightward shift of the *IS* curve to *IS'*.

In analyzing shifts of the *IS* curve, it is important to remember the following rules: (1) Any factor that increases aggregate demand shifts the *IS* curve to the right because of its positive income multiplier effect, and (2) any factor that reduces aggregate demand shifts the *IS* curve to the left, by means of a negative multiplier effect.

The *IS* curve represents the pairs of income and interest rates which would maintain the goods market in equilibrium. Which of these pairs represents the equilibrium of the economy must be determined by considering both the goods and the money markets simultaneously. To that we proceed.

6–5 SHORT-RUN EQUILIBRIUM IN THE GOODS AND ASSETS MARKETS

Up to this point, we have independently derived a set of pairs of income and interest rates that keep the money market in equilibrium (given the money supply and other parameters) and a set of pairs of interest rates and income that keep the goods market in equilibrium (given the level of government spending, the exchange rate, and other parameters). Short-run equilibrium in the goods and assets markets is obtained when both the money and the goods markets are in simultaneous or general equilibrium, given the various parameters assumed constant during the period of analysis. This implies that the short-run equilibrium levels of the interest rate and income in the economy must be such that both the goods and money markets are in equilibrium simultaneously.

The short-run equilibrium of the economy occurs on the basis of a given level of the money supply, which is assumed to be fixed during the time period of concern. Clearly, the domestic stock of money will be changing over time in response to the balance of payments situation of the country. If the country is in deficit, the Central Bank will be losing international reserves. As a result, the monetary base and, consequently, the money supply, will be decreasing. Similarly, if the country has a surplus in the balance of payments, then the domestic money supply will be rising. Only if the economy is in balance of payments equilibrium (i.e., the balance of payments is equal to zero) will there be no change in the money supply (assuming, as we do throughout this section, that the Central Bank does not alter domestic credit). In that case, and if there are no other changes in government policy parameters (such as government spending or the exchange rate), the economy will also be in *full equilibrium*. Full equilibrium exists, then, when there is external balance and money holders are neither adding to nor subtracting from their money balances.[6]

---

[6] The concept of full equilibrium is seldom used in introductory macroeconomics textbooks, since endogeneity of the money supply through the influence of the balance of payments is rarely

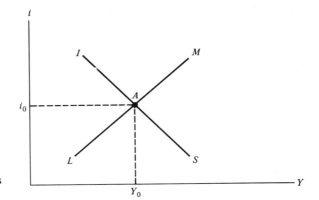

FIGURE 6–3. Short-Run
Equilibrium in the Goods
and Assets Markets

We shall now proceed to characterize the short-run equilibrium of the economy (assuming a fixed money supply). In the following section we analyze the adjustment process toward full equilibrium, by examining how the balance of payments affects the domestic money supply and output over time.

Short-run equilibrium in the economy is depicted graphically by point A in Figure 6–3, which represents the intersection of the IS and LM loci. Point A shows that pair of the interest rate and income, i_0 and Y_0 respectively, at which the goods and money markets are in simultaneous equilibrium in the short run. At those levels, the demand for domestic goods is equal to its supply, as specified by the fact that point A lies along the IS curve. The given supply of money in the short run is also equal to the demand for money, so that the money market is also in equilibrium, as represented by the fact that point A lies along the LM curve. Note that since the money market is in short-run equilibrium, the bond market will also be in short-run equilibrium; thus, the assets market, in general, is in short-run equilibrium at point A in Figure 6–3.

---

taken into account. It is a concept widely used in open economy macroeconomics, however. It should be noticed that full equilibrium in an economy in the environment discussed in this section (fixed exchange rates and no capital mobility) can be attained only over time. This makes the distinction between short-run equilibrium (which occurs on the basis of a given money supply at any moment in time) and full equilibrium (which occurs when the money supply is not changing in response to the balance of payments) important. For a discussion of the various problems of defining equilibrium in an open economy, see Alexander Swoboda, "Monetary Approaches to Balance of Payments Theory," in E. Claasen and P. Salin, eds., *Recent Issues in International Monetary Economics* (Amsterdam: North-Holland Publishing Co., 1976), especially pp. 9–16. As a final note, we should mention that our concept of full equilibrium is often referred to as long-run equilibrium. We prefer to use the terminology of full equilibrium in order to associate the concept of long-run equilibrium to longer-run economic adjustments that are ignored in the present simplified Keynesian framework. These involve changes in prices, the gradual recovery of the economy toward full employment, wealth adjustments, and so on. These aspects will be treated in later chapters.

6–6   SHORT-RUN EQUILIBRIUM: AN ALGEBRAIC TREATMENT

The short-run equilibrium of the economy, depicted by the intersection of the *IS* and *LM* curves, can also be described algebraically. The procedure is to solve the equations representing the goods and money market equilibrium conditions simultaneously for the equilibrium interest rate and income, expressing these as functions of exogenous variables. Restating equations (15) and (20) above, we find that the money and goods market equilibrium conditions are

$$i = \frac{1}{h}\left(kY - \frac{M_o}{P}\right) \tag{15}$$

$$Y = \bar{A} + \bar{T} + aY - mY - bi \tag{20}$$

To solve these two equations simultaneously, we proceed by substituting the value of the interest rate given by (15) into equation (20), obtaining

$$Y = \bar{A} + \bar{T} + aY - mY - b\left[\frac{1}{h}\left(kY - \frac{M_o}{P}\right)\right]$$

And, simplifying, by moving all terms involving domestic income to the left-hand side:

$$Y\left(1 - a + m + \frac{bk}{h}\right) = \bar{A} + \bar{T} + \frac{b}{h}\frac{M_o}{P} \tag{22}$$

By defining $\gamma = b/h$, and simplifying (22) a bit further, we obtain

$$Y_o = \frac{1}{s + m + \gamma k}\left(\bar{A} + \bar{T} + \gamma\frac{M_o}{P}\right)$$

$$= \tilde{\alpha}\left(\bar{A} + \bar{T} + \gamma\frac{M_o}{P}\right)$$

$$= \tilde{\alpha}(\bar{A} + \bar{T}) + \tilde{\alpha}\gamma\frac{M_o}{P} \tag{23}$$

where $\tilde{\alpha} = 1/(s + m + \gamma k)$. The solution, Y_o, depicts the level of income that clears both the money and goods markets in the short run as a function of the exogenous variables in the system. The latter are the money supply (which affects M_o/P), the level of government spending (which affects $\bar{A}$), the exchange rate (which affects $\bar{T}$), the price of domestic goods (which affects M_o/P and also $\bar{T}$, through its effects on the relative price of foreign to domestic goods), and the behavioral parameters of the economy, such as the marginal propensity to import, *m*, and the interest sensitivity of the demand for money, *h*. Changes in any of these exogenous variables can alter the equilibrium level of domestic income, Y_o, at least in the short-run context we are concerned with in this section. Such changes will also tend to alter the equilibrium level of the interest rate. Even though we have derived only the algebraic value of the short run, equilibrium level of domestic income, the value of the equilibrium interest rate can also be easily derived by substituting the expression for income in (23) into (15).

As mentioned at the beginning of this section, short-run equilibrium is defined as the equilibrium of the economy given a level of the money supply. Clearly, if there is an imbalance, or disequilibrium, in the balance of payments, the domestic money supply will change, and the short-run equilibrium must change as well. Thus, there will be an adjustment process of the economy toward a full equilibrium in which external payments are balanced, with the money stock remaining in a state of rest or equilibrium.

How do changes in the money supply affect short-run equilibrium (e.g., as portrayed in Figure 6–3)? How does the adjustment from a short run to a full equilibrium occur? The answers to these questions are discussed in the next section.

6–7 FULL EQUILIBRIUM IN THE GOODS AND ASSETS MARKETS

Suppose that we observe a given economy in short-run equilibrium, such as that described by point A in Figure 6–3. If the economy has a balance of payments deficit at that point, then there will be an excess demand for foreign exchange on the part of the private sector at the given, fixed exchange rate. This excess demand for foreign exchange is supplied by the Central Bank, which sells some of its holdings of international reserves to the private sector. As a result, the balance of payments deficit induces a reduction in the monetary base and a consequent decrease in the money supply. If the economy has a balance of payments surplus, there is an excess supply of foreign exchange held by the private sector that must be purchased by the Central Bank. The gain in international reserves implies a rise of the monetary base, which leads to a consequent increase in the money supply. Symbolically, from equation (12) it is easily seen that

$$\Delta M^s = \mu \Delta H = \mu \Delta IR \tag{24}$$

where ΔM^s represents the change in the money supply, μ is the money market multiplier, ΔH is the change in the economy's monetary base, and ΔIR represents the change in international reserves over time. On the assumption that the Central Bank does not alter domestic credit (a crucial assumption, as we shall see later), the change in the monetary base must equal the change in the international reserve holdings of the Central Bank; that is, from equation (11),

$\Delta H = \Delta IR$. This means that a short-run equilibrium sustaining a balance of payments deficit and losses of international reserves leads to a decline in the money supply and a leftward shift of the LM curve, parallel as in Figure 6–1. A balance of payments surplus, on the other hand, must shift the LM curve rightward. In order to examine the adjustment of an economy from short run to full equilibrium, it must be known whether the economy is experiencing a balance of payments deficit or surplus. Diagrammatically, we must be able to determine whether a point such as A, showing a certain short-run equilibrium in Figure 6–3, represents a point of balance of payments deficit or surplus. To visualize this, we must determine a locus showing the balance of payments equilibrium ($B = 0$) of the economy in diagrammatic form.

From the behavioral expression for the trade balance [see equation (19)], we know that balance of payments (trade) equilibrium must be achieved at that point where

$$B = T = \overline{T} - mY = 0$$

Alternatively, the balance of payments will be in equilibrium at that level of domestic income, referred to as Y_T, where

$$Y_T = \frac{\overline{T}}{m} \tag{25}$$

Only at a level of income equal to Y_T will there be equilibrium in the trade balance. At a lower level of income, $Y < Y_T$, there is a smaller amount of imports, and the trade balance moves into surplus; if $Y > Y_T$, imports increase above the level necessary to maintain trade balance, moving the balance of trade into a deficit. Consequently, balance of payments equilibrium can be represented by a vertical line at Y_T, as shown in Figure 6–4. Balance of payments

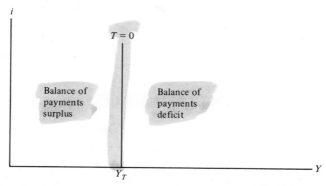

FIGURE 6–4.   Trade Balance and Balance of Payments Equilibrium in the Absence of Capital Mobility

equilibrium is independent of the interest rate, since we are ignoring capital flows.

In Figure 6–5 we have transferred the short-run equilibrium of the economy shown in Figure 6–3 to Figure 6–4. The purpose is to show whether the short-run equilibrium at point A represents a balance of payments deficit or surplus. In this particular case, the short-run equilibrium is to the right of the balanced payments locus, representing a balance of payments deficit.[7] That is,

$$B = T = \overline{T} - mY < 0$$

The reason for the deficit lies in the fact that the short-run equilibrium level of income Y_0 implies an amount of imports too large to support balanced external payments. Accordingly, the question we wish to answer is how the short-run equilibrium represented by point A changes over time. → loss of IR.

A payments deficit leads to a reduction of the domestic money supply over time, as long as the Central Bank does not alter domestic credit over that period. The money supply will stop shrinking when the balance of payments disequilibrium is eliminated, which occurs only when the external payments deficit is zero. At that point, the Central Bank no longer loses international reserves and, therefore, the monetary base (and the money supply) stops changing. Symbolically, if balance of payments equilibrium is attained,

$$\Delta M^S = \mu \Delta H = \mu \Delta IR = 0 \tag{26}$$

Equation (26) represents the full equilibrium condition for the economy. How can we illustrate this condition graphically? In terms of Figure 6–5, the

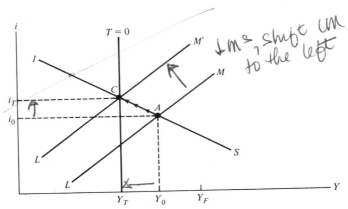

↓ ms, shift LM to the left

FIGURE 6–5. The Short-Run and Full Equilibria of the Economy

[7] Diagrammatically, the balance of payments of the economy can be represented by the horizontal distance of the short-run equilibrium point from the $T = 0$ locus. In Figure 6–5, the payments deficit is directly related to the horizontal distance between point A and the $T = 0$ line.

short-run equilibrium at point A will move in the northwest direction, as the LM curve shifts to the left in response to the external payments deficit. Full equilibrium is at that point at which the deficit is eliminated. This would occur at point C, where the IS and LM curves intersect just precisely at that level of domestic income which would maintain balance of payments equilibrium. At that point, the domestic money supply would stop changing and the economy would attain full equilibrium at a level of income equal to Y_T and an interest rate equal to i_T. The monetary contraction entailed by the process of adjustment toward full equilibrium involves rising interest rates and a reduction in income and imports, which is what eliminates the trade deficit.

Our analysis suggests that there is an automatic adjustment process in the economy that tends to eliminate the balance of payments deficit. The private sector, through its own laissez-faire actions, would eradicate it over time. A similar type of adjustment can be shown to exist if the economy is at a balance of payments surplus. The surplus tends to raise the domestic money supply (as the Central Bank gains international reserves), increasing domestic income and leading to a consequent rise in imports. The latter then tends to reduce the payments surplus. This adjustment process ends only when the external payments disequilibrium is completely eliminated.

6–8   STERILIZATION OPERATIONS

We can now easily visualize that a balance of payments deficit or surplus can only be temporary, as long as the Central Bank does not intervene to maintain the payments disequilibrium. The Central Bank has an incentive to intervene, though, in order to prevent the adjustment toward external balance from occurring. The reason? External balance is realized only through a process involving a protracted recession. This is a cruel choice, in the sense that external balance is attained only at the cost of a reduction in domestic output and employment. Naturally, certain governments would have an incentive to interfere with the market mechanism in order to prevent this balance of payments adjustment through recession from occurring. Historically, the result of this recognition of high employment as a primary goal of economic policy (with priority over the goal of external balance, whenever they are in conflict) has resulted in government intervention geared toward preventing the automatic adjustment process of the balance of payments from occurring. This government-induced general breakdown of the automatic mechanism of balance of payments adjustment in the world economy has been labeled the international disequilibrium system by Robert Mundell (in his article, "The International Disequilibrium System," reprinted as Chapter 15 of his book, *International Economics*). The question that arises is: How might a Central Bank intervene to keep the economy from adjusting to an external payments disequilibrium? It can intervene by means of what are called *sterilization operations.*

Sterilization operations refer to operations carried out by the Central Bank in order to neutralize (sterilize) the effects that its intervention in foreign exchange markets has on the monetary base. Under a regime of fixed exchange rates, the Central Bank's actions in the foreign exchange market are linked to the balance of payments surplus or deficit of the country. For example, in the case of a deficit, the Central Bank has to sell its foreign exchange reserves to the public. As a consequence, the monetary base would tend to decline. In this situation, if the Central Bank wants to sterilize the effects of the deficit on the monetary base it would have to increase domestic credit creation by exactly the same amount. A typical sterilization operation in this case would then be a purchase of bonds by the Central Bank in the open market, a purchase that would have to be of an amount equal to the loss of international reserves induced by the balance of payments deficit. Symbolically, a constant monetary base means

$$\Delta H = \Delta IR + \Delta CBC = 0 \qquad (12)$$

or, alternatively:

$$\Delta CBC = -\Delta IR$$

In other words, the increase in Central Bank credit, ΔCBC, must be equal in value but opposite in sign to the loss in international reserves, ΔIR, generated by the deficit in the balance of payments account. If there were a balance of payments surplus in the economy, on the other hand, a typical sterilization operation would be an open market sale of bonds by the Central Bank. Can you explain why?

The effects of sterilization operations can be illustrated graphically. Looking back at Figure 6–5, what sterilization operations would do is to keep the economy at its short-run equilibrium at point A and prevent it from moving to its full equilibrium at point C. That is, the Central Bank would prevent the operation of the automatic adjustment mechanism of the balance of payments. By sterilizing the effects of the deficit on the monetary base, it effectively prevents any changes in the domestic money supply. Symbolically,

$$\Delta M^s = \mu \Delta H = \mu(\Delta IR + \Delta CBC) = 0 \qquad (27)$$

where the reduction in international reserves over any given period of time is exactly offset by an equal increase in the credit creation of the Central Bank ($\Delta IR = -\Delta CBC$). With a fixed money supply, the LM curve remains unchanged and unresponsive to the payments deficit. The economy then remains at point

A with the balance of payments in deficit, artificially sustained by the Central Bank and its sterilization operations.[8]

The only way in which sterilization operations can be carried out over an extended period of time, in the presence of a persistent external payments disequilibrium, is if the Central Bank's holdings of international reserves and bonds are large enough. Suppose, for example, that the economy faces a persistent payments deficit. If the Central Bank chooses to sterilize, it will have to sell foreign exchange reserves continually, since the payments deficit is kept alive by the sterilization. Experiencing dwindling reserves, the Central Bank would have to stop sterilizing or else abandon foreign exchange intervention in support of the fixed exchange rate. In the case of countries with persistent balance of payment surpluses, on the other hand, the monetary authorities would have to maintain a continuous sale of bonds in the open market to keep the monetary base fixed. Only countries with substantial Central Bank bond holdings would be able to maintain such intervention.

A final point to recognize with respect to sterilization is that these operations are used by monetary authorities in order to prevent the external payments situation of the country from affecting internal monetary and credit conditions. They are therefore employed whenever the effects of the balance of payments on these conditions weaken the impact of the government's policies. But what is the effect of balance of payments adjustments on the effectiveness of government policies in the absence of sterilization? The following sections determine the various effects of monetary and fiscal policies, stressing the role of the monetary adjustments implied by balance of payments disequilibria.

6–9   THE EFFECTS OF MONETARY POLICY IN THE OPEN ECONOMY

The Central Bank can affect the money supply by altering the monetary base through deliberate changes in Central Bank credit, such as those involved in open market operations.[9] The effects of monetary policy can be subdivided into its effects on the short-run equilibrium of the economy (its short-run or impact effects), and its effects on the full equilibrium of the economy (its longer-run or full-term effects). We first describe the short-run impact of monetary policy and then analyze how the adjustment of the economy to full equilibrium modifies these results.

---

[8] This situation, where a short-run equilibrium is maintained by government intervention over the automatic adjustment mechanism of the economy has been called quasi-equilibrium by Swoboda is his well-known article, "Equilibrium, Quasi-Equilibrium and Macroeconomic Policy Under Fixed Exchange Rates," *The Quarterly Journal of Economics* (February 1972).

[9] The Central Bank could also influence the money supply by affecting the money supply multiplier through the use of policy instruments such as reserve requirements on member banks and the discount rate. In assuming a fixed money supply multiplier, we ignore such policies although the analysis could be easily altered to incorporate them.

↗ ↑CBℓ

Suppose, for example, that the monetary authorities engage in an open market purchase of bonds. Its impact effect will be to increase the monetary base, hence the money supply. This in turn reduces the interest rate because of the increased availability of credit in the economy. As a result, investment spending is stimulated, raising aggregate demand and, hence, domestic income. The rise in income, in turn, raises imports, with a consequent deterioration of the balance of payments. In Figure 6–6, point A shows an economy with balanced payments but suffering from unemployment. The latter is reflected in that the initial equilibrium level of domestic income, Y_0, is lower than full employment income, which is represented by Y_F. Let us now suppose that the increase in the money supply associated with the Central Bank's open market purchase of bonds is represented by the shift of the *LM* curve to *LM'*. The economy then moves to a new, short-run equilibrium at point B. This leads to full employment, through lower interest rates, but to a deterioration in the balance of payments brought about by increased imports. The latter is reflected graphically by the fact that point B is to the right of the $T = 0$ balance of payments equilibrium line, representing a point of deficit. In conclusion, an expansionary monetary policy increases short-run equilibrium income in the economy but tends to worsen the balance of payments.

We have just considered the short-run, or impact, effects of monetary policy. The next step is to consider its longer-run effects, that is, its effects on the full-equilibrium of the economy. The balance of payments deficit reflected by the short-run equilibrium at point B must imply that the Central Bank loses reserves over time. In the absence of sterilization operations, the money supply would then decline. Interest rates would begin to rise, reducing investment spending and, hence, domestic output. Diagrammatically, the *LM'* curve shown in Figure 6–6 would start shifting back toward its original position. This process will not stop until full equilibrium is attained, at which point balanced external payments are reached. This occurs back at point A in Figure 6–6, where the intersection of the *IS* and *LM* curves coincides with the balanced payments

↓ ↓ ↓R,
↓ H ↓
↓ mˢ

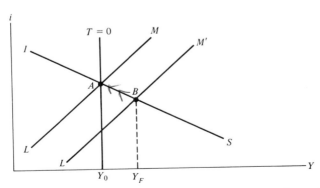

FIGURE 6–6. Effects of Monetary Policy Under Fixed Exchange Rates

locus, $T = 0$. Point A is the only point consistent with full equilibrium, *ceteris paribus,* and the economy returns to it in spite of the Central Bank's creation of credit. The effects of the monetary expansion are exactly offset over time by a loss of international reserves that moves back the domestic money supply to its original level.

In summary, a once-and-for-all increase in Central Bank credit has absolutely no effect on the full-equilibrium level of the money supply, output, and interest rates, though it affects these variables in the short run. In full equilibrium, the only effect of monetary policy is to change the portfolio composition of the Central Bank between international reserves and Central Bank credit but not the overall size of the portfolio.

6–10   FISCAL POLICY, CROWDING OUT AND THE TRADE BALANCE

This section examines the impact of fiscal policy in the open economy by looking at the effects of an increase in the government's expenditures on domestic goods and services. Such an increase raises aggregate demand for domestic goods, which is reflected graphically by the shift of the IS curve to IS' in Figure 6–7.[10] The short-run impact of the fiscal expansion shown by the movement from point A to point B, is then to raise income to full employment (from Y_0 to Y_F). This increases the transaction's demand for money and raises interest rates. At the same time, the income spurt leads to a surge of imports that switches the balance of payments into deficit. Diagrammatically, point B lies to the right of the balanced payments locus, $T = 0$. To reiterate, over the short run, an increase in government spending raises domestic income, but causes a deterioration in the balance of payments. $(\downarrow IR, \downarrow H, \downarrow M^s)$

The full equilibrium effect of an increase in government spending is illustrated in Figure 6–7. Over the short run, the increased spending raises imports, which deteriorates the balance of payments. As a consequence, the money supply de-

---

[10] It is assumed that the increase in government spending affects only the IS curve. This is more likely to be so if the increased spending is financed by an emission of government bonds. The emission of bonds does not affect the domestic money supply, since the money obtained by the government in selling the bonds returns to the public as the government spends it. From this source, then, the LM curve is not directly affected by the changes in government spending. Other forms of financing government spending are by printing money and by means of tax increases. The analysis of government spending with these types of financing is more complicated because the LM and the $B = 0$ loci would be directly affected in addition to the IS curve. If the government spending is financed by money creation, then both the IS and the LM curves would be affected. If the spending is financed by taxation, the $B = 0$ locus will be affected, in addition to the IS curve. For a detailed analysis of the effects of fiscal policy under alternative financing strategies, see the classic paper by Alan S. Blinder and Robert Solow, "Analytical Foundations of Fiscal Policy," in A. S. Blinder, et al., *The Economics of Public Finance* (Washington, D.C.: The Brookings Institution, 1974). The open economy extension is examined by M. Fratianni, "On the Effectiveness of Monetary Policy Under Fixed Rates of Exchange," *Journal of Monetary Economics* (January 1976).

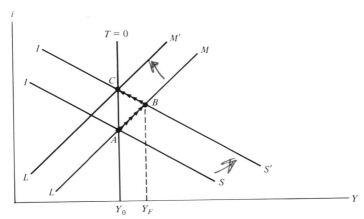

FIGURE 6–7. Short-Run and Full-Equilibrium Effects of a Fiscal Expansion

clines over time, shifting the *LM* curve to the northwest. The full equilibrium would then occur at point *C,* where balance of payments equilibrium is attained. There is therefore no impact of an increase in government spending on the level of income and employment in full equilibrium. The increased income associated with the fiscal expansion in the short run is only short lived and temporary. Note that because domestic output returns to its initial level over the long term, domestic aggregate demand stays fixed over this time horizon. But given that government spending has increased, the movement from point *A* to point *C* must be associated with a reduction of some other component of domestic spending by domestic residents. Indeed, the increase in interest rates implied by the movement from point *A* to point *C* is associated with a reduction in private investment spending. As a consequence, the fiscal expansion does not raise overall domestic spending but only shifts its composition from the private sector (private investment) to the government sector. Increased government spending crowds out private investment spending, leaving domestic income intact.

We can conclude that under fixed exchange rates and no capital mobility, both monetary and fiscal policy are entirely ineffective in influencing full-equilibrium income and employment although exhibiting short-run impact. What is at the crux of the long-run ineffectiveness of these policies in affecting domestic output? Under the present environment, involving no international capital movements, the balance of payments is equivalent to the balance of trade, which is assumed to depend on income but not on the interest rate. Graphically, this has been represented by the vertical balanced external payments locus, $T = 0$. The insensitivity of the balance of payments to the interest rate means that there is a unique level of income which is consistent with balance of payments equilibrium, irrespective of the interest rate. This level of income, Y_T, the full equilibrium level of income, can be affected only by factors that shift the balanced payments, $T = 0$, locus, which does not include monetary and fiscal policy among them.

In other words, monetary and/or fiscal policies alone cannot achieve the two goals of internal balance (i.e., full employment) and external balance (i.e., balanced payments). This conclusion confirms our results in Chapter 5 to the effect that the attainment of internal and external balance requires the use of an expenditure-switching policy to supplement expenditure-changing policies. The main additional consideration introduced in this chapter on this point is that there are now two different expenditure-changing policies—fiscal and monetary policy—whereas the analysis of Chapter 5 considered only fiscal policy. Exchange rate policy is an expenditure-switching policy and could then be combined with monetary and/or fiscal policies to achieve internal and external balance. A devaluation, for instance, will tend to shift the $T = 0$ locus to the right (by improving the autonomous trade balance, $\bar{T}$, a devaluation will raise the level of domestic income consistent with balanced trade, $Y_T = \bar{T}/m$), permitting domestic output to increase while improving the trade balance. By combining devaluation with appropriate monetary and/or fiscal policies, both internal and external balance could then be reached in the short-run.

If we were to relax the assumption of no capital mobility, the present results as to the inability of fiscal and/or monetary policies alone (without the joint use of an expenditure-changing policy) to achieve both internal and external balance would generally change. This will be demonstrated in Chapter 7. But insofar as the economy under consideration is not well integrated into world capital markets and cannot borrow or lend to finance external payments deficits or surpluses, the results in this section are more relevant.

6–11   QUANTITATIVE EFFECTS OF GOVERNMENT POLICIES

Having analyzed the effects of various government policies through the use of verbal and geometric arguments, the quantitatively oriented student might be interested in translating them into algebraic form. With this in mind, we shall focus on the impact of policies on the short-run equilibrium levels of income and the trade balance.

A general expression showing the effect of various government policies on the short-run level of domestic income can be derived by expressing (23) in terms of changes. The result is

$$\Delta Y = \tilde{\alpha}\,(\Delta \bar{A} + \Delta \bar{T}) + \tilde{\alpha}\gamma\,\frac{\Delta M_o}{P} \qquad (28)$$

where ΔY represents a given change in the short-run equilibrium level of income, which can result from changes in autonomous absorption, $\Delta \bar{A}$, changes in the autonomous trade balance, $\Delta \bar{T}$, and changes in the money supply, ΔM_o. Note that, as before

$$\tilde{\alpha} = \frac{1}{s + m + \gamma k} \quad \text{and} \quad \gamma = \frac{b}{h}$$

where s denotes the marginal propensity to save, m is the marginal propensity to import, k represents the income sensitivity of the demand for money, h represents the interest sensitivity of money demand, and b shows the responsiveness of investment spending with respect to the interest rate.

To derive the effects of various policies on the trade balance, we can use the following general expression, derived by taking changes in equation (19), and then substituting the value of ΔY obtained in (28)

$$\Delta T = \Delta \bar{T} - m \Delta Y$$

$$= \Delta \bar{T} - m \left[\tilde{\alpha} (\Delta \bar{A} + \Delta \bar{T}) + \tilde{\alpha} \gamma \frac{\Delta M_o}{P} \right]$$

$$= (1 - m\tilde{\alpha}) \Delta \bar{T} - m\tilde{\alpha}\Delta \bar{A} - m\tilde{\alpha}\gamma \frac{\Delta M_o}{P} \quad (29)$$

With equations (28) and (29) in the bag, we can gracefully leap into an examination of the short-run impact of government policies.

The first policy to consider is monetary policy. Assuming that the only disturbance in the economy is a change in domestic credit, as determined by the Central Bank, we obtain from (28)

$$\Delta Y = \tilde{\alpha} \gamma \frac{\Delta M_o}{P} \quad (30)$$

which shows the precise effect produced by a change in the money supply on domestic income. Notice that an increase in the money supply raises domestic income, depending on the values of $\tilde{\alpha}$ and γ. The latter depend, in turn, on such parameters as the interest sensitivity of the demand for money and the interest responsiveness of investment spending. Graphically, the values of these parameters determine the slopes of the IS and LM curves and specify by how much income responds to changes in the money supply. For example, we can derive from equation (30) that as the responsiveness of investment to the interest rate, b, increases, the effects of a given change in the money supply on domestic income will tend to increase. A large value of b tends to make the IS curve relatively less steep, making the impact of any given shift of the LM curve on income relatively greater. This is because of the larger responsiveness of investment, and therefore aggregate demand and output, to the interest rate reduction caused by the monetary expansion. The impact of a change in the money supply on the trade balance is given by

$$\Delta T = -m\tilde{a}\gamma \frac{\Delta M_o}{P}$$

That is, a monetary expansion leads to a worsening of the trade balance, while a contraction improves it. By increasing income, a monetary expansion raises imports and worsens the trade balance, while a monetary contraction decreases imports and improves the trade balance. $(\downarrow Y)$

A second government policy for which we can analyze the short-run impact algebraically is fiscal policy. From equation (28), a change in government spending will alter domestic income by affecting autonomous absorption:

$$\Delta Y = \tilde{a}\, \Delta \bar{A} = \tilde{a}\, \Delta G \tag{31}$$

where ΔG is equal to the given change in government expenditures. As observed, an increase (or a decrease) in government spending increases (or reduces) domestic income. The impact effect of government spending on the trade balance is

$$\Delta T = -m\tilde{a}\, \Delta \bar{A} = -m\tilde{a}\, \Delta G$$

which is negative if fiscal policy is expansionary (increasing income and thus imports) and positive if fiscal policy is contractionary (which decreases income and imports).

6–12 SUMMARY

1. The open economy *IS–LM* framework takes into account the interaction of the goods and money markets in determining equilibrium levels of income and interest rates in the economy. It also stresses the crucial impact of the external payments situation of the economy, reflected by the trade balance in the absence of capital mobility, on equilibrium output, employment, and interest rates.

2. The money supply process in an open economy is generally distinct from that in a closed economy. The reason is that the monetary base is composed not only of Central Bank credit creation, but of the Central Bank's holdings of international reserves as well. Under fixed exchange rates, balance of payments deficits (or surpluses) tend to decrease (increase) the domestic money supply by decreasing (or increasing) foreign exchange reserves and thus the monetary base. In this case, the Central Bank can influence Central Bank credit in the economy but not necessarily the monetary base or the money supply.

3. Short-run equilibrium in the goods and assets markets is obtained when both the goods and money markets are in equilibrium, on the basis of a given level of the money supply. The balance of payments situation of the economy affects short-run equilibrium by changing the money supply. The economy will attain full equilibrium, in the sense that the money supply will be fully adjusted and will stop changing, when external payments are balanced. Graphically, short run equilibrium corresponds to the intersection of the *IS* curve (depicting goods market equilibrium), and the *LM* curve (representing money market equilibrium) drawn for a given level of the money supply. Full equilibrium corresponds to the intersection of the *IS*, *LM*, and $T = 0$ (external balance) curves.

4. An economy under fixed exchange rates faces an automatic adjustment mechanism that tends to move the economy toward balanced payments (external balance). This adjustment process is a monetary one in the sense that it moves the economy toward full equilibrium by adjusting the domestic money supply through the balance of payments. Sometimes, however, this adjustment toward balanced payments involves a protracted recession, which some government authorities find untenable. As a consequence, they intervene to prevent the operation of the automatic adjustment mechanism. They do this by sterilizing the influence of the balance of payments on the monetary base through the use of offsetting open market operations. These sterilization operations, however, keep the economy at a payments disequilibrium and may be impossible to sustain over extended periods of time if the Central Bank does not have enough holdings of securities or foreign exchange reserves.

5. Even though one can expect the economy, left to its own devices and without government intervention, to move toward external balance automatically, within the Keynesian context of this chapter there is no automatic adjustment mechanism moving the economy toward full employment. Thus there is room for policy intervention with the purpose of moving the economy toward both external and internal balance.

6. A basic distinction exists between the effects of policies in the short run (at a given level of the money supply) and over the longer run (when the economy has fully adjusted to any external payments disequilibria). Monetary and fiscal policies, for instance, have effects on equilibrium income but only in the short run. Over the longer-run context characteristic of full equilibrium, monetary and fiscal policy in economies under fixed exchange rates facing international capital immobility has no effects on output. This means they have to be combined with expenditure-switching policies, such as exchange rate changes, to attain both internal and external balance.

PROBLEMS

1. Spell out in detail the precise mechanics involved in the process by means of which a balance of payments surplus surfaces as a money supply increase in an economy under fixed exchange rates. Using T accounts describe how the Central Bank's balance sheet is affected.

2. You are given the following data regarding a Latin American country with

a banking system similar to that of the United States (all figures in pesos, the currency of the country concerned)

Currency = 50 billion

Demand deposits = 160 billion

Bank reserves = 20 billion

(a) Define and calculate the following:
  1. the monetary base
  2. the money supply
  3. the money multiplier

(b) Suppose that during the month of April the country's Central Bank gains international reserves by an amount equal to 10 billion pesos. Assuming Central Bank credit remains unchanged, what will be the impact of the gain in reserves on: the monetary base, the money supply?

(c) The government wants to keep the money supply unchanged in spite of the gain of reserves. What offsetting operation could it engage in? For all of these questions, provide numerical answers and explain how they are obtained.

3. Examine the likely effects of a decline in the demand for domestic exports on output, interest rates and the trade balance. Illustrate by means of an *IS–LM* diagram and distinguish the short-run and full-equilibrium effects. What alternative policy packages could be pursued to remedy the situation? Evaluate them.

4. In the face of a persistent trade deficit, government authorities impose a surcharge on imports and restrict tourist expenditures abroad. How would those measures affect domestic output and the trade balance? How would they alter government finances?

5. Consider a country whose Central Bank holds international reserves in the form of U.S. dollars and gold, and suppose that the price of gold doubles. How does this affect the level of the country's international reserves? How would the doubling in the price of gold affect the country's money supply?

6. Using the linear expressions for the goods and money market equilibrium conditions presented in the text, solve for the value of the economy's short-run equilibrium interest rate. [HINT: Substitute the value of Y_0 given by equation (23) into the money market equation (15).] Then derive an algebraic expression for the effects of a change in the domestic money supply on domestic interest rates. What parameters are relevant for the determination of the short-run effects of a money supply increase on domestic interest rates? Explain the economic rationale supporting your results.

7. Consider an economy under fixed exchange rates that is at full equilibrium. Using the linear equations in the text, derive the precise algebraic expressions for the effects of a reduction in government spending on the *full equilibrium* levels of

(a) Income and the trade balance.

(b) The monetary base and the money supply (assuming the Central Bank does not engage in any credit creation).

(c) Interest rates and domestic investment.

Interpret the economic meaning of your results.

8. Examine the effects of a domestic currency devaluation, using diagrammatic and algebraic analysis. What will be the economic impact on the following:

(a) Short-run equilibrium levels of output, trade balance, and interest rates.

(b) Full equilibrium output, trade balance, and interest rates.

Could devaluation be used by itself to attain the goals of internal and external balance? Explain why or why not. Do your results differ from those derived in Chapter 5? Again, explain why or why not.

9. Suppose that, in the previous question, the country's Central Bank decides to monetize the capital gains on its international reserves accruing from the devaluation. Examine the effects of this action on the short-run and full equilibria of the economy. Does the devaluation in the present situation necessarily improve the trade balance in the short run? Illustrate by means of an *IS–LM* diagram.

10. Examine the economic effects and differences among the following examples of government fiscal policy:

(a) A temporary (only 1 year in effect) increase in government spending.

(b) A permanent increase in government expenditures financed by money creation (printing money).

(c) A permanent increase in government spending financed by an increase in tax rates. (H I N T : Use Problem 4 in Chapter 5.)

CHAPTER 7

Balance of Payments Adjustments and International Capital Movements

In Chapters 5 and 6 it was assumed that the economy under consideration did not trade in financial assets with the rest of the world, perhaps because of a lack of access, or lack of integration, to international capital markets. Most economies, however, are in fact integrated to international capital markets and do engage in international trade in financial assets. For example, American residents buy British and French stocks and bonds, while U.S. corporations and individuals raise funds by selling securities to British and French investors or real estate to wealthy OPEC sheiks. These transactions involve international trade in financial assets; as such, they are recorded in the capital account of the balance of payments. A *capital account surplus* means that a net capital inflow is occurring in the economy. That is, domestic residents are selling more financial assets than they are buying abroad, implying that the economy as a whole is borrowing from abroad. This capital inflow—at any given level of the current account—brings about an inflow of international reserves and tends to improve the balance of payments. A *capital account deficit,* on the other hand, means that there is a net capital outflow; that is, the country as a whole is buying foreign financial assets, or lending abroad, which tends to generate an outflow of international reserves and a worsening of the balance of payments.

The access to international financial capital represented by an economy's capital account suggests that current account balance deficits do not necessarily have to be associated with losses of international reserves but can be financed by net capital inflows, that is, by net borrowing from abroad. Table 7–1 shows the balance of payments accounts of the non-oil-developing countries during recent years. The figures depict how the huge current account deficits of the developing countries during the 1970s were financed by net financial capital inflows, with their overall holdings of international reserves increasing, rather than declining. The problems faced by some developing countries in obtaining additional external financing during 1982—a topic to be discussed in Chapter

224

TABLE 7-1. Financing Current Account Deficits: The Non-Oil-Developing Countries (*In Billions of U.S. Dollars*)[a]

	1973	1974	1975	1976	1977	1978	1979	1980	1981	1982	1983
Current account balance	−11.3	−37.0	−46.3	−32.6	−28.9	−41.3	−61.0	−89.0	−107.7	−86.8	−67.8
Capital account balance[b] (Net capital inflows)	21.7	39.7	44.6	45.6	41.4	58.7	73.6	93.5	109.8	79.7	75.0
Changes in official reserves	10.4	2.7	−1.7	13.0	12.5	17.4	12.6	4.5	2.1	−7.1	7.2

Source: International Monetary Fund, *World Economic Outlook* (1983), p. 197.
[a] The non-oil-developing countries include all developing countries members of the International Monetary Fund, excluding the following oil-exporting countries: Algeria, Indonesia, Iran, Iraq, Kuwait, Lybia, Nigeria, Qatar, Saudi Arabia, United Arab Emirates, and Venezuela.
[b] Includes net use of IMF credit and errors and omissions.

17—also surfaces in the data: The current account deficit of $86.8 billion was associated with a $7.1-billion loss of official international reserves. In conclusion, in the presence of international capital mobility there is no necessary connection between losses (or gains) of international reserves and current account deficits (or surpluses).

Access to international financial markets offers some clear-cut benefits by providing additional sources of financing and investments to the domestic economy. On the other hand, openness to international financial capital movements can impose some severe constraints on the behavior of the economy and on the effectiveness of domestic economic policies. Many a Central Bank has found its foreign exchange reserves rapidly depleted in the face of sudden, massive capital outflows. Also, monetary authorities often find it extremely difficult to control basic economic variables in the presence of international capital mobility, even over short periods of time. It is therefore of the utmost importance to examine international capital movements, their determinants and their influence on the economy.

7–1   THE BALANCE OF PAYMENTS AND INTERNATIONAL CAPITAL MOVEMENTS

With international trade in assets, the balance of payments, B, is given by

$$B = T(q, Y) + K(i) \tag{1}$$

where the service account is ignored for the sake of expositional simplicity. Note that the trade balance, T, is assumed to depend (as in previous chapters) on the relative price of foreign goods in terms of domestic goods, q, and on domestic income, Y. The capital account is represented by K, with a capital account surplus—a positive value of K—associated with net capital inflows (a net sale of domestic bonds) and a deficit—a negative value of K—with net capital outflows (a net purchase of foreign bonds). For the present, we shall assume that domestic and foreign bonds share the same characteristics in terms of liquidity, maturity, default risk, political risk, exchange risk, and so on. In addition, the exchange rate is assumed to be, and expected to remain, fixed; there are no anticipated exchange rate changes. These assumptions are relaxed in later chapters.

Equation (1) relates the capital account to the level of the domestic interest rate, i. How exactly does the domestic interest rate[1] influence the capital account?

---

[1] In general, the world interest rate, i^*, will also affect the capital account (as i^* increases, the capital account deteriorates, since investors shift out of domestic and into foreign assets, while the opposite occurs if i^* declines). In this chapter, however, we shall assume that the economy is a small one in the international capital markets in the sense that it can not affect the world interest rate. In this situation, the world interest rate will be an exogenous variable that is left out of the capital account expression for simplicity of notation.

One extreme case is one where there is *perfect capital mobility,* which refers to an environment of highly integrated capital markets, with investors rapidly obtaining information about interest rates in different countries and engaging in portfolio adjustments among national assets instantaneously and with minimal transaction costs. In this situation, the domestic economy can, at any time, borrow all it wants (sell all the bonds it wants) and lend all it wants (buy all the bonds it desires) at the prevailing world interest rate, i^*. Accordingly, the capital account is perfectly elastic (responsive) with respect to changes in the domestic interest rate: Capital inflows and outflows emerge without requiring changes in domestic interest rates (or involving instead only negligible changes in interest rates). Any rise of the domestic interest rate above the world rate would tend to induce a massive capital inflow immediately into the economy, as investors shift out of foreign bonds and into the more profitable domestic bonds. A decrease of the domestic interest rate below the world rate, on the other hand, would tend to induce an immediate massive capital outflow, as investors shift out of domestic and into more profitable foreign bonds.

A less extreme case than perfect capital mobility involves *imperfect capital mobility.* Imperfect capital mobility arises when the domestic economy has to raise the domestic interest rate in order to attract foreign funds or lower it in order to make domestic funds more attractive to borrowers. In this situation, if the country wants to increase its borrowing (lending) it has to increase (decrease) its interest rate, i, above (below) the given world level, i^*. In addition, and in contrast to the case of perfect capital mobility, deviations of the domestic interest rate from the world interest rate will not generate massive capital flows but will rather induce only a certain definite flow, which will unfold gradually over time. Imperfect capital mobility can arise when domestic capital markets are not well integrated with world capital markets or when investors can adjust their portfolios only slowly, over time. In these cases, changes in the domestic interest rate above or below the interest rate abroad produce sluggish changes in portfolio composition and capital flows therefore take place gradually over time. The instantaneous adjustments possible under perfect capital mobility are impossible here.

In summary, changes in interest rates give rise to changes in the desired amounts and/or location of stocks of various types of assets. These then give rise to capital movements geared toward eliminating the gaps between the desired and actual stocks of assets. How long it takes to complete stock adjustments depends on the speed at which actual and desired stocks of assets can be brought into equality. Under perfect capital mobility, the speed of adjustment is infinite: You can adjust your portfolio instantaneously just by engaging in telephone calls. Under imperfect capital mobility, the capital account responds to changes in interest rates but to a lesser extent than in the case of perfect capital mobility. Given the world interest rate, an increase (or decrease) in the domestic interest rate will attract a certain inflow (or outflow) of funds over time, but it will not create a massive flood (or exodus) of funds as in the case of perfect capital mobility. The capital account will be positively, but not infinitely, elastic with respect to the domestic interest rate.

7–2   BALANCE OF PAYMENTS EQUILIBRIUM AND THE DEGREE OF CAPITAL MOBILITY

We now proceed to discuss the implications for the balance of payments of the presence of alternative degrees of capital mobility and interest elasticity of the capital account in the economy.

From equation (1), balance of payments equilibrium (zero surpluses or deficits) is achieved when

$$B = T(q, Y) + K(i) = 0 \tag{2}$$

This balance of payments equilibrium condition is illustrated in Figure 7–1, for varying degrees of capital mobility. For an economy facing no capital mobility (no international trade in financial assets), the capital account is always identically equal to zero so that $B = T(q, Y)$, which does not depend on the interest rate. As in the previous chapter, then, the balance of payments equilibrium locus is represented by the vertical line $T = 0$. For an economy under imperfect capital mobility, on the other hand, the balance of payments equilibrium locus is represented by the upward-sloping $B = 0$ locus in Figure 7–1.

The reason the $B = 0$ locus is upward-sloping is the following. Consider, for the sake of the argument, a situation in which the economy is in balanced payments and balanced trade initially. Suppose, now, that domestic income increases. At any given level of the interest rate, as income increases, imports surge and the trade balance deteriorates. As a consequence, the economy moves into a payments and trade account deficit. In order to correct the payments deficit (assuming a fixed exchange rate), the domestic interest rate would then have to rise. As the domestic interest rate increases, domestic bonds become more attractive relative to foreign bonds and a capital inflow occurs. This capital inflow moves the capital account into a surplus ($K > 0$) and tends to improve the balance of payments. For any given degree of capital mobility, there will then be an increase in the domestic interest rate sufficiently large to induce the capital inflows required to finance the trade deficit (eliminate the balance of payments deficit) created by the increase in income. Hence, as domestic income increases, balanced payments can be maintained through an appropriate rise of the domestic interest rate. In other words, the balance of payments equilibrium locus in the case of imperfect capital mobility must be upward sloping. This is precisely what the $B = 0$ locus in Figure 7–1 illustrates. Note that, moving along the points in that curve, any trade balance deficit ($T < 0$)

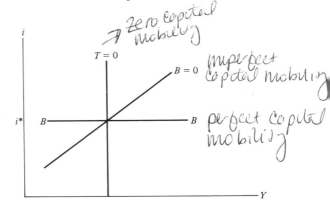

FIGURE 7–1. Capital Flows and
Balance of Payments Equilibrium

is financed by external borrowing or by foreign financial investments in the domestic economy, that is, by purchases of domestic assets by foreigners ($K > 0$). Therefore, no external payments or money account deficit develops. Similarly, any trade surplus ($T > 0$) is offset by external lending or domestic purchases of foreign assets ($K < 0$) so that no net inflow of money or international reserves results ($B = 0$).

A final case to consider is perfect capital mobility. In an economy facing perfect capital mobility, balance of payments equilibrium can occur only if the economy is on the perfectly horizontal *BB* locus shown in Figure 7–1, for the following reason. Consider an economy with balanced external payments. Suppose now that domestic income increases. As a result, imports increase and the trade balance worsens, which deteriorates the balance of payments. In the case of imperfect capital mobility, a given increase in the domestic interest rate would be required to raise the capital inflows necessary to "finance" the trade deficit, that is, to move the economy back into a payments balance. In the case of perfect capital mobility, however, the domestic interest rate does not have to increase—or has to increase by a very small or infinitesimal amount—because any amount of funds necessary to finance the trade deficit is available in the world capital markets at the world interest rate, i^*. If the domestic interest rate had to increase at all (to attract a capital inflow), it would only be by a small, negligible amount. Geometrically, then, the *BB* locus must be perfectly horizontal, placed at a vertical distance given by i^*, the world interest rate, which is the interest rate that the economy under perfect capital mobility has to take as given. Note also that, moving rightward along the *BB* locus, the economy's trade balance deteriorates: As income increases, imports tend to rise, ceteris paribus. The worsening trade deficit is, of course, financed by a capital account surplus.

How is our analysis of Chapter 6 modified when the assumption of no trade in financial assets with the rest of the world is relaxed? The case of perfect capital mobility is considered first.

7–3 EQUILIBRIUM OF THE ECONOMY UNDER PERFECT CAPITAL MOBILITY

This section discusses the determination of equilibrium in the goods and assets markets under conditions of perfect capital mobility. First, the goods market equilibrium condition is stated by the equality of the output of domestic goods, Y, with the aggregate demand for domestic goods, as given by

$$Y = \alpha (\bar{A} + \bar{T} - bi) \quad \text{IS Curve} \tag{3}$$

where $\bar{T}$ represents that part of the trade balance which is autonomous of domestic income, $\alpha = 1/(s + m)$ is the open economy Keynesian multiplier, $\bar{A}$ is autonomous absorption, and b is a parameter representing the sensitivity of investment spending with respect to the interest rate. The goods market equilibrium condition, algebraically stated in equation (3), can be represented geometrically by the now familiar *IS* curve shown in Figure 7–2.[2]

Assets market equilibrium can be represented by money market equilibrium, which obtains when the demand for money equals the money supply given at any specified moment in time. Algebraically,

$$\frac{M^s}{P} = L^D (i, Y) \tag{4}$$

with M^s equal to the money supply, P is the fixed price of domestic goods, and $L^D(i, Y)$ represents the money demand function. (For more details, see our analysis surrounding equation (13) in Chapter 6, which remains unchanged in the present context.) The money market equilibrium condition in (4) is depicted by the upward-sloping *LM* curve in Figure 7–2.

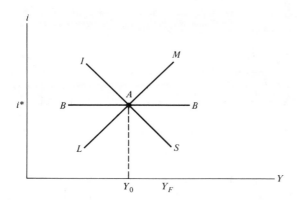

FIGURE 7–2. Equilibrium Under Perfect Capital Mobility

[2] For more details, see the discussion relating to equation (21) in Chapter 6.

In a situation in which the domestic economy faces perfect capital mobility, the following condition must be satisfied

$$i = i^* \qquad (5)$$

stating the equality of domestic and world interest rates. The balance of payments equilibrium condition is then given by equation (2) above, subject to the constraint given by (5). Geometrically, balance of payments equilibrium occurs when the economy is along the horizontal *BB* locus illustrated in Figure 7–2, the vertical height of which is given by the world interest rate, i^*. This is precisely the payments equilibrium locus drawn in Figure 7–1 for the case of perfect capital mobility, which we have just transposed to the present diagram. Points above the *BB* locus represent balance of payments surpluses. This can be realized by noting that if the domestic interest rate were to be above its world level, there would be a massive capital inflow into the economy. This would induce a huge increase in the capital account and move the economy into a payments surplus. A similar argument can be used to show that points below the *BB* locus represent balance of payments deficits.

The equilibrium of an economy under fixed exchange rates and perfect capital mobility occurs at the point at which there is goods and money market equilibrium as well as balance of payments equilibrium (point *A* in Figure 7–2). This equilibrium point corresponds to both short-run and full equilibrium as defined in the previous chapter. The explanation is the following. In Chapter 6, we analyzed an economy that did not engage in any international trade in financial assets. In that case, the economy's short-run equilibrium was consistent with payments disequilibrium. In the absence of sterilization and depending on the loss or gain in international reserves, the short-run equilibrium shifted over time in response to the implied changes in the money supply. This adjustment process stopped when full equilibrium was attained, at balanced trade. The speed of adjustment depended mainly on the size of the trade deficit in the short run. The larger the trade deficit, the larger the effect on the domestic money supply and, therefore, the faster the adjustments in the economy.

Under perfect capital mobility, the adjustment process of an economy in short-run equilibrium but payments disequilibrium is very fast, perhaps instantaneous, because international capital flows allow the economy's money supply to adjust immediately to its full equilibrium level. Consider, for example, a hypothetical case in which the economy's short-run equilibrium interest rate is above its full-equilibrium level. In that event, the domestic interest rate would be out of line with the world interest rate and a balance of payments disequilibrium would exist. Massive inflows of funds would occur in response to the differential between the domestic interest rate and the world rate. Such massive capital inflows would generate huge payments surpluses, changing the domestic money supply precipitously. The adjustments in the domestic economy can therefore be quite large and occur over a very short period of time. As a consequence, within the context of perfect capital mobility, the short-run and full-equilibrium distinctions are not necessary. With negligible adjustment and information costs, investors adjust their portfolios quite quickly, and any purchase or sale of bonds in the world market would finance any payments surplus or deficit, moving the money supply to its full-equilibrium level instantaneously. In this situation, full equilibrium can be attained in the short run.

It should be stressed that the fact the economy can attain balanced payments (full-equilibrium) quickly by means of changes in portfolio composition (by buying or selling bonds) does not preclude other changes from occurring. The Keynesian framework employed here ignores some long-run aspects of the adjustment process in the economy. First, one can expect wages and prices to adjust over time in response to deviations of employment from its full-employment level. These long-run changes in wages and prices will be discussed in Chapter 10. In addition, there is a second set of adjustments that take place over the long run. These involve changes in the level of domestic wealth by means of capital accumulation (decumulation) and/or through the accumulation (decumulation) of monetary and financial assets by domestic residents. These wealth adjustments are set aside in the present discussion but will be examined in Chapter 14.

The equilibrium of an open economy under fixed exchange rates and perfect capital mobility is graphically portrayed by point A in Figure 7-2, where the *IS, LM,* and *BB* loci intersect. At that point, the economy is in equilibrium in the goods and assets markets as well as in the balance of payments. Note that the equilibrium domestic interest rate, i, coincides with the world interest rate, i^*; otherwise, massive capital flows will emerge, inducing the domestic interest rate to return immediately to the world level.

As was stressed earlier, with perfect capital mobility the domestic economy can always finance a trade deficit (or surplus) by means of capital inflows (or outflows) at the given world interest rate. Simple interchanges of bonds and money can alter the domestic money supply and adjust it to full equilibrium, with the economy moving instantaneously to balanced payments. Given that external balance can be immediately attained through the private international capital markets, is there any reason for government intervention in the economy? As discussed in previous chapters, in an open economy, the government can be expected to have two main goals: external balance and internal balance. Within the Keynesian framework followed in this chapter, the private sector would tend to move the economy to external balance but not to internal balance. Point A in Figure 7-2, for instance, shows an equilibrium level of domestic income, Y_o, below the full-employment level, Y_F, with no inherent tendency for the economy to move toward internal balance. Accordingly, there is scope for government intervention in achieving internal balance jointly with external balance. The next sections examine the various effects of government policies. Let us begin with monetary policy.

7–4   THE INEFFECTIVENESS OF MONETARY POLICY UNDER PERFECT CAPITAL MOBILITY

↗ ↑CBC , ↑H , ↑MS

In this section we analyze the effects of monetary policy on the equilibrium of the economy. Suppose, for example, that there is a once-and-for-all increase in the Central Bank's holdings of bonds. Potentially, this would increase the money supply, reduce domestic interest rates and spur investment and output. In terms of Figure 7–3, the *LM* curve would shift to *LM'* and a new equilibrium would arise at point *C,* with increased output and lower domestic interest rates. The problem, however, is that point *C* is not an equilibrium point. If the domestic interest rate were to decrease below *i**, a massive capital outflow would occur, moving the capital account and the balance of payments into deficit. Further-more, as domestic income increases (from point *A* to point *C*), imports increase and the trade balance deteriorates, which also tends to worsen the balance of payments.

↗ Want foreign securities

The balance of payments deficit at point *C* implies an excess of the private demand for foreign exchange over its supply, as investors now try to acquire foreign exchange with which to buy the more profitable foreign financial assets. The Central Bank satisfies this excess private demand for foreign exchange by selling some of its holdings of foreign exchange reserves. The money supply will then decrease in response to the loss in international reserves. Diagrammati-cally, the *LM'* curve would have to shift back toward the initial *LM* curve. Clearly, the outflow of capital would continue as long as the domestic interest rate tends to be below the world level. As a consequence, the adjustment process of the economy, which occurs instantaneously under perfect capital mobility, stops only when there are no pressures on domestic interest rates to decrease below the world interest rate.[3] But, at that point, the payments deficit is elimi-

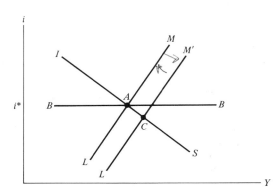

FIGURE 7–3.   Effects of Monetary Expansion Under Perfect Capital Mobility

[3] As an expository device, we have made our arguments as if the domestic interest rate could differ from the world rate for a split second, after which it moves back to the world level. An alternative way of viewing the effects of monetary policy (or lack of them) is to observe what

nated. The domestic money supply thus returns to the level existing before the government engaged in the open-market purchase of bonds. In other words, in an economy under fixed exchange rates and perfect capital mobility, *monetary policy is completely ineffective* in influencing the economy's equilibrium. This result, in contrast to the one arrived at in the previous chapter, holds even in the short run, making it a quite powerful conclusion.

What Central Bank credit creation can be observed to do is just to change the composition of the asset structure of the Central Bank portfolio, by increasing its holdings of bonds and decreasing foreign exchange reserves. The overall change in the monetary base, ΔH, is, however, equal to zero. Since changes in the monetary base can be decomposed into changes in Central Bank credit and changes in international reserves [see equation (11) in Chapter 6], then:

$$\Delta H = \Delta CBC + \Delta IR = 0$$

An increase in Central Bank credit, $\Delta CBC > 0$, would lead to offsetting capital flows, reducing international reserves, $\Delta IR < 0$, by the same amount as the initial increase in Central Bank credit ($\Delta CBC = -\Delta IR$). This inability of monetary policy to affect the economy's equilibrium can be better understood if we realize that the effectiveness of monetary policy depends basically on how it alters domestic interest rates. Under a regime of fixed exchange rates with perfect capital mobility, domestic monetary authorities would not be able to affect the domestic interest rate, which has to align with the interest rate given by world capital markets. What happens, then, is that the increase in Central Bank credit generates an excess supply of money—at the given world interest rate—which tends to push down the domestic interest rate. This downward pressure on the domestic interest rate induces capital outflows, reducing the domestic money supply and eliminating the excess supply of money created initially. On the assumption of perfect capital mobility, all of these adjustments take place instantaneously.

In conclusion, in the case of perfect capital mobility, monetary policy is not able to influence the domestic money supply, even over the short run. It is therefore improper to define monetary policy in terms of changes in the domestic money supply. Monetary policy is correctly defined in this case in terms of credit creation by the Central Bank. We cannot overemphasize that

---

domestic residents do when the money supply increases, assuming that they face a given world interest rate. If we suppose that investors are initially at portfolio equilibrium, when the Central Bank raises domestic credit, domestic investors will find themselves holding excess money balances. Therefore, in order to move their portfolio composition back to an optimum, they will then invest the excess money balances. They do this by buying foreign bonds, at the given world interest rate, which requires the acquisition of foreign exchange from the Central Bank. In the process, the Central Bank loses international reserves and the domestic money supply decreases back to its original level. Credit creation by the Central Bank just gives rise to an offsetting operation by the private sector, in the form of a purchase of foreign bonds.

the availability of some instruments of monetary policy does not imply that the Central Bank has control of the domestic money supply or that monetary policy is effective in achieving some government goal, such as stabilizing income.

7–5 FISCAL POLICY AND ITS FULL EFFECTIVENESS UNDER PERFECT CAPITAL MOBILITY

The next government policy to analyze is fiscal policy. Consider, as an illustration, the effects of an increase in the level of government spending on domestic goods (financed by, say, an issuance of government bonds). First of all, by increasing government spending, aggregate demand for domestic goods rises; this tends to increase domestic income. As a result, money demand increases, credit becomes tighter, and upward pressure on interest rates builds up. This is reflected in Figure 7–4 by the upward shift of the *IS* curve to *IS'*, which would give rise to a domestic interest rate above the world interest rate, as shown by point *C*. This situation, however, is not an equilibrium for the economy, since it represents a balance of payments surplus. If the domestic interest rate were to increase above the world level, *i**, massive capital inflows would result, moving the capital account and the balance of payments into a huge surplus. This payments surplus occurs in spite of the fact that at point *C* the trade balance has worsened. Even though the movement from point *A* to point *C* is associated with increased income and imports and, therefore, a worsened trade deficit, it also implies an increase in the interest rate and a massive surplus in the capital account. The capital account surplus would always dominate the trade balance deficit under perfect capital mobility, leaving a surplus in the overall balance of payments.

The external payments surplus at point *C* means that, at that point, there would be an excess of the private supply of foreign exchange over its demand, as investors sell foreign exchange to acquire domestic currency and buy domestic financial assets. The Central Bank acquires this foreign exchange as reserves and, hence, the domestic money supply rises. This increase would be represented in Figure 7–4 by a rightward shift of the *LM* curve, such as that from *LM* to *LM'*. Notice that, insofar as domestic interest rates exceed their world counterparts, capital inflows would persist and the *LM* curve would continue to shift to the right. This process continues until the full equilibrium following the increase in government spending is reached at point *E*. Note that point *E* is attained in the short run, since the speed of the adjustment process under perfect capital mobility is very fast.

The new equilibrium at point *E* represents an increase in domestic output and a worsened trade deficit—since income and imports have increased—financed by an improved capital account. The domestic interest rate would remain at the level it was before the fiscal expansion (at *i**). It can be concluded, then, that expansionary fiscal policy is quite effective in increasing the real

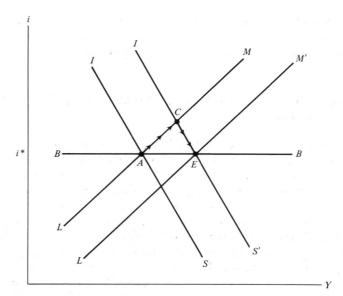

FIGURE 7–4.   Effectiveness of Fiscal Policy Under Perfect Capital Mobility

income of an economy under fixed exchange rates and perfect capital mobility. The economic reasoning behind this result lies in the tendency of the initial spurt of income associated with the increased government spending to create a credit tightness—which, under perfect capital mobility, instead of raising domestic interest rates, induces capital inflows, increasing the domestic money supply and generating further increases in income. In contrast to the traditional crowding-out effect of government spending on private investment, in this situation interest rates do not increase but rather remain at their world level and there is thus no negative impact on domestic investment. This makes fiscal policy especially effective in moving the economy toward internal balance.

7–6   STERILIZATION OPERATIONS ONCE AGAIN

Sterilization operations refer to operations carried out by the economy's Central Bank to neutralize (sterilize) the effect that its intervention on foreign exchange markets has on the monetary base (see Section 6–8). The basic conclusion of this section is that sterilization operations are not viable under fixed exchange rates and perfect capital mobility.

Consider the following example, which assumes that the economy is initially at balanced payments and that the Central Bank is committed to sterilization policies in the face of any payments disequilibria. Suppose, then, that government spending suddenly declines, entailing a negative multiplier effect on income.

As a result, transactions demand for money would decrease, generating an excess money supply that places downward pressure on domestic interest rates. There would then be a massive capital outflow as investors tend to shift out of the now relatively unattractive domestic bonds. A balance of payments deficit would arise. The deficit, of course, implies a loss in the Central Bank's holdings of international reserves. If the Central Bank does not sterilize, this reduction in reserves would tend to reduce the domestic money supply until the excess money supply is eliminated and the downward pressure on domestic interest rates ends. Suppose, however, that the authorities, through sterilization operations, buy an amount of bonds in the open market equal to the loss of international reserves. In this case, the downward pressure on domestic interest rates would be sustained, since the domestic money supply is not allowed to adjust in response to the payments deficit. In other words, the excess money supply would still exist. Given the downward pressure on domestic interest rates, massive capital outflows would continue to occur. To maintain its sterilization operations, and as long as it remains committed to maintaining a fixed exchange rate, the Central Bank would have to sell continuously a massive amount of foreign exchange reserves. No matter how large the holdings of these reserves are, however, the Central Bank would not be able to support its sterilization operations to any significant extent in the face of the massive capital outflows that would occur under perfect capital mobility. International reserves would be quickly depleted. At that point, a devaluation becomes necessary. Something must give, and it must either be the sterilization operations or the Central Bank's pegging of the exchange rate. Sterilization policies and fixed exchange rates are, in this context, inconsistent.

7–7 THE ECONOMY UNDER PERFECT CAPITAL MOBILITY: A SUMMARY

We have now analyzed in detail the economy under fixed exchange rates and perfect capital mobility, including the effects of various government policies in this environment. To summarize, in an economy under fixed exchange rates and perfect capital mobility, the following generally hold:

1. The economy will adjust instantaneously toward external balance (balanced payments), since trade deficits or surpluses can always be immediately financed by borrowing or lending at fixed interest rates in the world capital markets and since portfolio adjustments occur immediately, implying the full-equilibrium level of the money supply can be attained rapidly.

2. Monetary policy has no effects at all on the equilibrium levels of income, interest rates, the balance of payments or the trade balance. The only effect of an open market operation is to change the composition of the Central Bank's portfolio because a purchase (sale) of bonds will imply an equal loss (gain) of international reserves.

3. Fiscal policy is highly effective in altering equilibrium income and employment since it does not crowd out investment.

4. Sterilization operations cannot be sustained and would be inconsistent with the Central Bank's commitment to support a fixed exchange rate.

Up to this point, we have concentrated our attention on the economic plight of an economy under perfect capital mobility. It is time to relax this assumption. The major alternative yet to be analyzed is the case of imperfect capital mobility, to which we turn.

7–8   IMPERFECT CAPITAL MOBILITY AND MONETARY POLICY

The equilibrium of an economy facing imperfect capital mobility is represented by means of our standard *IS–LM* diagram, with the only caveat that the balance of payments equilibrium locus is now the upward-sloping $B = 0$ locus. We illustrate an initial equilibrium of the economy by means of point A in Figure 7–5. At point A, the economy is in balanced payments as well as in goods and money market equilibrium. What are the effects of monetary and fiscal policies in this context?

An expansionary monetary policy, say a Central Bank open market purchase of bonds, tends to shift the *LM* curve to the right, as represented in Figure 7–5 by the shift to *LM'*. The equilibrium of the economy would then move to point C, with an increase in income and a decline in domestic interest rates, both of which tend to worsen the balance of payments. This means that point C represents only a short-run equilibrium of the economy. The balance of payments deficit would lead, over time, to a decrease in the domestic money supply, which would shift the *LM'* curve upward, back toward its initial position. Over longer periods of time, then, monetary policy would be ineffective and the full equilibrium of the economy would be back at point A in Figure 7–5. Only if the Central Bank engages in sterilization operations will a point like C be maintained over time. With imperfect capital mobility, sterilization is a feasible policy in the short run, although over the longer run the Central Bank runs the risk of running out of foreign exchange reserves.

That monetary policy tends to be ineffective under fixed exchange rates after all the monetary adjustments induced by the balance of payments have taken place is a result that can be obtained no matter what the degree of capital mobility. This can be visualized by noticing that whatever the degree of capital mobility is, that is, no matter what the shape of the $B = 0$ curve is, the *LM* curve will always move back to the point determined by the intersection of the *IS* and $B = 0$ curves, as illustrated by point A in Figure 7–5. It is apparent, then, that monetary authorities under fixed exchange rates might face great difficulty in controlling the money supply and that the role of monetary policy in affecting output in this regime might be quite limited, especially over the long run. What is the evidence on these issues?

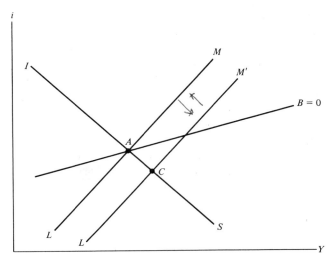

FIGURE 7–5.   Monetary Policy Under Imperfect Capital Mobility

7–9   CAN WE CONTROL THE MONEY SUPPLY? OFFSETTING CAPITAL FLOWS AND MONETARY POLICY

International capital mobility places stringent boundaries on how much domestic interest rates can diverge from those that prevail in world markets and makes very difficult the task of controlling the money supply of an economy under fixed exchange rates. Expansionary monetary policy in the form of an open market purchase of Treasury bills, for example, increases the Central Bank credit component of the monetary base but (ceteris paribus) places downward pressures on domestic interest rates and induces capital outflows that reduce the monetary base's international reserves component. Capital outflows can thus offset the effects of an open market operation on the money supply. In its most extreme form, capital outflows would be of the same amount as the initial increase in Central Bank credit. This is the case in which Central Bank credit expansion is *fully offset*. The only net effect of the operation is then to alter the Central Bank's portfolio composition (increased credit but reduced international reserves) and domestic residents' portfolios (reduced holdings of domestic Treasury bills but increased holdings of foreign securities). There would be no change in the domestic money supply and, ceteris paribus, no change in domestic interest rates away from their world levels.

A critical question concerns how fast the offset can be completed. If portfolio adjustments can be made very rapidly, no constraints exist on the extent to which capital movements can flow in and out of an economy and, consequently, offsetting capital flows can occur freely and quickly, perhaps instantaneously. When transactions costs, information lags, and government controls—such as capital controls—prevent these rapid adjustments from happening, the full offset of open market operations would then take longer to complete, as described in Section 7–8.

What evidence exists regarding offsetting capital flows? Or, rephrasing the question, what do the data say on the effectiveness of open market operations in affecting the monetary base in actual economies under fixed exchange rates? In Figure 7–6 we have plotted how the two components of the monetary base (domestic credit and international reserves) in Mexico changed during the seventies. A general negative correlation can be noticed between changes in Central Bank credit and changes in international reserves, but they clearly do not appear to offset each other completely. The question thus arises as to by how much exactly are changes in Central Bank credit offset by capital flows in this, and other, cases.

Most empirical studies start by postulating the following equation:

$$K_N = K_0 - b \; \Delta CBC \qquad\qquad (6)$$

where K_N is defined as total capital flows ($K_N > 0$ if a capital inflow); K_0 represents those capital flows which are not directly related to domestic credit creation; ΔCBC is Central Bank credit creation, and b is a parameter called the *offset coefficient*. The offset coefficient measures how much of a given change in domestic credit is offset by capital flows over a given period of time (holding everything else constant). When $b = 1$, there is a full offset of open market operations by capital flows during the time period analyzed. When $b = 0$, there is no offset, and changes in Central Bank credit are not found to be offset at all by capital flows.

The evidence regarding the offset coefficient gives a wide range of results, depending on the country considered, the time period examined, and the empirical procedures used. The best-known results are those provided by P. Kouri and M. Porter on Germany, Australia, Italy, and the Netherlands during the sixties. They find the quarterly offset coefficients to vary from $b = 0.43$ for Italy to $b = 0.77$ for Germany.[4] In other words, it appears that 43 to 77% of changes in Central Bank credit are offset by international capital flows during a quarter. A similar range of estimates is provided by a multitude of other studies done for the same, and other, countries.[5] Thus the conclusion from these studies is that changes in Central Bank credit do not tend to be associated

[4] See P. K. Kouri and M. G. Porter, "International Capital Flows and Portfolio Equilibrium," *Journal of Political Economy* (May 1974).

[5] Such as M. J. M. Neumann, "Offsetting Capital Flows: A Reexamination of the German Case," *Journal of Monetary Economics* (January 1978); and L. Girton and D. Roper, "A Monetary Model of Exchange Market Pressure Applied to the Postwar Canadian Experience," *American Economic Review* (September 1977).

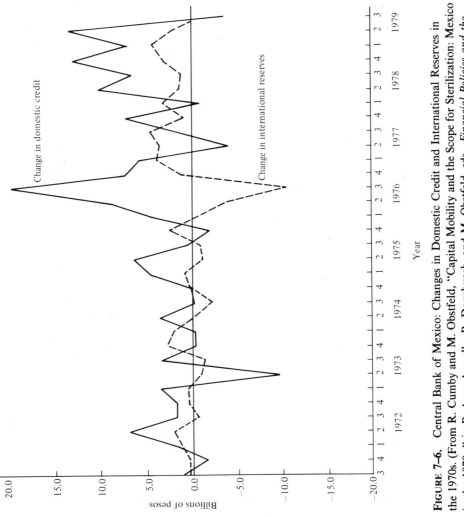

FIGURE 7-6. Central Bank of Mexico: Changes in Domestic Credit and International Reserves in the 1970s. (From R. Cumby and M. Obstfeld, "Capital Mobility and the Scope for Sterilization: Mexico in the 1970s," in P. Aspe Armella, R. Dornbusch, and M. Obstfeld, eds., *Financial Policies and the World Capital Market: The Problem of Latin American Countries*, Chicago: The University of Chicago Press, 1983, p. 249.)

241

with completely offsetting capital flows—at least over short periods of time—but that for some countries the offset coefficient may indeed be relatively close to $b = 1$.

One of the main problems with these studies, however, is that they ignore the role of sterilization policies in controlling the effects of balance of payments deficits on the domestic money supply. For countries that engage in sterilization, changes in Central Bank credit are not exogenously given, but respond to the balance of payments situation of the economy—its losses or gains in reserves. For example, the Central Bank may pursue the following behavior with regard to its open market operations:

$$\Delta CBC = (\Delta CBC)_0 + \gamma K_N \qquad (7)$$

where $(\Delta CBC)_0$ refers to factors influencing the Central Bank's credit creation decisions other than observed capital flows, K_N is the capital account ($K_N > 0$ if capital inflows), and γ is a negative parameter called the *sterilization coefficient*. The sterilization coefficient measures how much of a given capital inflow is sterilized by the Central Bank through countervailing open market operations. If $\gamma = -1$, the Central Bank tries to sterilize completely the effects of capital inflows on the monetary base; if $\gamma = 0$, no sterilization occurs and the actions of the Central Bank follow other goals, as represented by $(\Delta CBC)_0$. When γ is between 0 and -1, some sterilization operations occur but do not completely neutralize capital flows.

When the Central Bank engages in sterilization operations, as represented by equation (7)—called a *reaction function*—the estimates of offset coefficients must be interpreted very carefully. Estimates of offset coefficients may not just be measuring the offsetting capital flows arising from changes in Central Bank credit—through equation (6)—but also the correlation between (spontaneous) capital flows and changes in Central Bank credit arising from sterilization—as given by equation (7). For example, suppose that, all of a sudden, capital outflows spontaneously occur, say because U.S. investors abruptly decide to buy more French bonds. This induces the Central Bank to engage in expansionary open market operations—in order to sterilize the outflows. In this situation, capital outflows and increases in Central Bank credit will be associated but, of course, one does not want to attribute these capital flows to the credit creation, since in fact the opposite is true. One must thus use the adequate statistical procedures[6] to isolate the offsetting capital flows generated by a given change in Central Bank credit from those (spontaneous) capital flows giving rise to sterilization.

[6] These are called simultaneous equation methods. In the present context, the problem arises because of the simultaneity between equations (6) and (7): Changes in Central Bank credit generate offsetting capital flows—through equation (6)—but capital flows induce the Central Bank to change Central Bank credit through sterilization, from equation (7).

In general, these studies have found offset coefficients much smaller than those obtained by the earlier studies. Obstfeld, for example, finds the German quarterly offset coefficient during the 1960s to be around 10%, much smaller than the 0.77 found by Kouri and Porter.[7] Similarly, in a study of Mexico, Obstfeld has found the offset coefficient to be in the range of $b = 0.31$ to 0.37 on a quarterly basis.[8] These results tend to indicate that, for the countries considered, national monetary authorities do appear to have widespread ability to control their money supplies over short periods of time (i.e., on a quarterly basis).

The next natural question refers to the longer-run effects of changes in Central Bank credit. Even if there is very little offset of open market operations by means of capital flows over the short run, the value of the offset coefficient over the long run may still be equal to 1. The evidence available on this topic is scarce and is an area of current research. In his paper on Mexico in the 1970s, Obstfeld finds that, including all portfolio adjustments made over time in response to an open market operation, the long-run offset coefficient is equal to 0.50. This is larger than the short-run coefficient of 0.31 noted earlier, but it still leaves open an influential role for monetary policy, even over the long run.

Another conclusion that can be derived from these studies is that sterilization operations can be successfully engaged in over short periods of time, since capital flows do not generally appear to move massively in or out of the economy in response to changes in domestic interest rates.[9] It also seems that most industrial countries are permitted some leeway over control of domestic interest rates. The main constraining force on monetary policy then lies in the fact that capital flows do occur; over time, wide divergences of domestic interest rates from world levels lead to persistent losses (or gains) in international reserves. Given that foreign exchange inventories are depletable, there are some clear long-run constraints on the influence of domestic monetary authorities on the money supply and domestic interest rates.

---

[7] M. Obstfeld, "Sterilization and Offsetting Capital Movements: Evidence from West Germany, 1960–70," Working Paper No. 494, National Bureau of Economic Research, Cambridge, Mass. (1980). See also R. Herring and R. Marson, *National Monetary Policies and International Financial Markets* (Amsterdam: North-Holland Publishing Co., 1977).

[8] M. Obstfeld, "Capital Mobility and the Scope for Sterilization: Mexico in the 1970s." In P. Aspe Armella, R. Dornbusch, and M. Obstfeld, eds., *Financial Policies and the World Capital Market: The Problem of Latin American Countries* (Chicago: University of Chicago Press, 1983).

[9] A clear exception arises when expectations regarding a potential currency devaluation generate a sudden run on the currency. In these cases, to be examined in Chapter 12, the Central Bank may not be able to cope with the growing capital outflows, resulting in an eventual balance of payments crisis or a retreat from support of a fixed exchange rate. Such was the case preceding the Mexican devaluation of the peso in 1976. The data in Figure 7–6 show the substantial loss of reserves sustained during that period, which eventually resulted in a financial crisis and the effective devaluation of the peso.

7–10   FISCAL POLICY AND THE DEGREE OF CAPITAL MOBILITY

We now show that, under imperfect capital mobility, expansionary fiscal policy can stimulate output and employment but raises interest rates and inhibits investment. An increase in government spending, say financed by government borrowing, raises the demand for domestic goods, shifting the *IS* curve upward to *IS'* in Figure 7–7. The economy's equilibrium then switches from point *A* to point *B*, resulting in higher income and interest rates. Is point *B* a point of balance of payments deficit or surplus? Note that, since income increases, this tends to worsen the balance of payments by deteriorating the trade balance. But there is also an increase in interest rates, which tends to improve the balance of payments by improving the capital account. Which of these effects dominates? Clearly, it will depend on the relative strength of each effect, which is influenced by the degree of capital mobility (determining how much the capital account improves in response to a given increase in domestic interest rates) as well as by the marginal propensity to import (which determines by how much imports increase and trade balance deteriorates in response to an increase in income). If the latter is high relative to the former, then the trade balance deterioration will dominate the capital account improvement and the balance of payments will deteriorate overall. The opposite holds when if the marginal propensity to import is small relative to the degree of capital mobility.

These cases are illustrated in Figure 7–7 by noting that if the balance of payments equilibrium locus is represented by the steeply sloped *B* = 0 curve

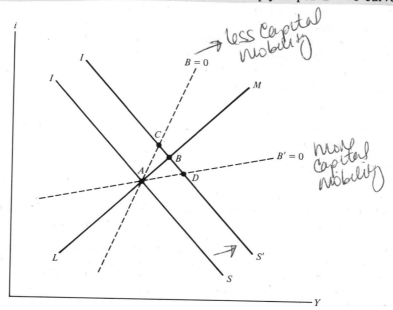

FIGURE 7–7.   Fiscal Policy Under Imperfect Capital Mobility

(depicting a relatively low degree of capital mobility compared with the marginal propensity to import), then the short-run equilibrium point B lies below the $B = 0$ curve and there is a balance of payments deficit. If the balance of payments equilibrium locus is the gently sloped $B' = 0$ curve (representing a relatively high degree of capital mobility compared with the marginal propensity to import), then point B would be a point of balance of payments surplus.

The full equilibrium effects of expansionary fiscal policy vary according to whether short-term equilibrium entails a balance of payments deficit or surplus.

When a balance of payments deficit arises (corresponding to the steeply sloped $B = 0$ line) the money supply will decrease over time, inducing income to decrease (until a point such as C in Figure 7–7 is attained) and partially offsetting the initial boom. In the case in which a balance of payments surplus arises (corresponding to the gently sloped $B' = 0$ locus) the money supply will increase, generating an additional income expansion over time (until a point such as point D in Figure 7–7 is attained). Note that the positive connection between the degree of capital mobility and the effectiveness of fiscal policy in affecting domestic output is consistent with our earlier results. For instance, in the case of capital immobility discussed in Chapter 6, we found that fiscal policy had no full-equilibrium effects on domestic income. This would occur, in terms of Figure 7–7, when the $B = 0$ locus becomes perfectly vertical. In the case of perfect capital mobility discussed earlier in this chapter, on the other hand, we found that fiscal policy had its full effectiveness. This would arise if the $B' = 0$ curve in Figure 7–7 were perfectly horizontal.

We have now analyzed the effects of monetary and fiscal policies under imperfect capital mobility in both the short run and in full equilibrium. In the forthcoming sections we restrict ourselves to the short-run horizon within which most policymakers act and set aside the modifications entailed by the longer-run monetary adjustments of the economy (it might thus be assumed that the policymakers systematically sterilize the effects of the balance of payments on the money supply).

7–11 THE MONETARY–FISCAL POLICY MIX

It is the purpose of this section to show that, within the context of imperfect capital mobility, the government can attain the goals of internal balance (full employment) and external balance (balanced payments) through the exclusive use of monetary and fiscal policies. There is no need to use additional policies, such as exchange rate changes or tariffs. This result is quite different from the one derived under capital immobility (see Section 6–10 in Chapter 6). Within that context, both expenditure-switching and expenditure-changing policies are required to move an economy with, say, unemployment and payments deficit, toward internal and external balance. Since, with capital immobility, monetary and fiscal policies are both expenditure-changing policies, there is a need for an additional policy, such as exchange rate policy, which could act as an expenditure-switching policy. We proceed to examine how this result is modified by capital mobility.

Figure 7–8 shows the upward-sloping balance of payments equilibrium locus B=0 under imperfect capital mobility. Notice that if the equilibrium of the economy lies along the $B = 0$ curve there would be external balance. If the equilibrium is to the right of $B = 0$ instead, a balance of payments deficit prevails, and if it lies to the left, the economy is in surplus. Figure 7–8 also shows the level of domestic output associated with full employment, which corresponds to the vertical line at output Y_F. If the equilibrium of the economy lies on this curve, there would be internal balance; if it lies to the right, the economy would be in a situation of overemployment, and if to the left, it would face unemployment.

Through the use of Figure 7–8, one can catalog how a given equilibrium of the economy fares with respect to the government's goals. If the economy is in region I, at a point like A, for example, it would suffer a payments deficit and unemployment. If the equilibrium were to take place in region II, at a point like B, it would imply overemployment and deficit, and correspondingly for regions III and IV. Clearly, the desired point in terms of the government's goals is point E, where both internal and external balance are obtained. The exact combination of policies required to attain that point depends on the initial position of the economy.

Suppose that the economy's IS and LM curves intersect at point A, with a consequent balance of payments deficit and unemployment. Observe that, in

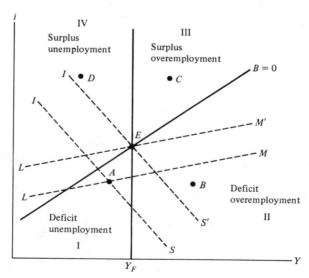

FIGURE 7–8. The Fiscal-Monetary Policy Mix

this case, expansionary fiscal policy (such as that shifting the *IS* curve to *IS'*) and contractionary monetary policy (such as that shifting the *LM* curve to *LM'*) would move the economy to balanced payments and full employment at point *E*. An appropriate combination of fiscal and monetary policies is therefore sufficient to attain internal and external balance. The same conclusion can be derived for economies whose equilibrium lies in quadrants II, III, and IV.

The sufficiency of monetary and fiscal policies to attain internal and external balance diverges from our previous results under capital immobility. What explains this divergence? With no international trade in assets, the balance of payments coincides with the trade balance, in which case there is indeed a need for both expenditure-switching and expenditure-changing policies: Trade balance equilibrium requires an expenditure-switching policy to twist spending away from foreign and toward domestic goods. In the presence of international capital movements, however, balanced payments do not coincide with balanced trade because of the presence of the capital account. As a consequence, any policy that serves to switch demand away from foreign and toward domestic assets can be employed to improve the balance of payments by affecting the capital account. By changing interest rates, monetary or fiscal policy can influence the capital account and consequently the balance of payments without the need for an expenditure-switching policy. In terms of the *IS–LM* paradigm, instead of there being only one single level of income at which balanced payments could be attained (Y_T in Chapter 6), there is now a set of combinations of interest rates and income consistent with balanced payments. Accordingly, one of these combinations involves the full-employment level of income, Y_F. The two instruments of monetary and fiscal policy can then be used to attain this exact combination of interest rates and income at which both balanced payments and full employment would be obtained (point *E* in Figure 7–8).[10]

7–12   Shortcomings of the Monetary Fiscal Policy Mix

This section states the various shortcomings of a policy mix consisting of only monetary and fiscal policies. First, up to this point the discussion has been carried out on the assumption that the government desires to attain external balance, defined as zero balance of payments. The implication is that the country is indifferent with respect to the composition of the balance of payments as long as it is balanced. Balanced payments with a capital account deficit (and a trade balance surplus) is assumed to be valued by the policymakers in the economy in equal terms as balanced payments with a capital account surplus (and a trade deficit). In general, however, a country is not indifferent with

---

[10] The policy mix approach to the attainment of internal and external balance was developed by Robert Mundell in an influential series of articles that have been gathered in his book *International Economics* (New York: Macmillan Publishing Company, 1968).

respect to the composition of its balance of payments. Even if balanced payments are sustained, persistent capital account surpluses are often considered to be a negative burden on the economy. The reason is that a persistent capital account surplus implies persistent capital inflows into the economy. In other words, the surplus implies that there is a persistent net external borrowing on the part of the economy as a whole; that is, the country's debts to the rest of the world would be increasing. If the economy is borrowing in order to accumulate capital, the economy's productive capacity would increase over time, raising, in turn, its ability to repay the debt. If the borrowing is for current consumption purposes, however, the capital account surplus just implies that the economy is substituting future consumption for present consumption. Future consumption would thus have to decline in order for the debt to be repaid. Furthermore, the accumulation of debt through persistent capital account surpluses would imply a huge interest payments burden. Over time, this burden could absorb a substantial amount of the productive activities of the economy. Because of these factors, a major policy objective in some economies is not balanced payments as such but balanced trade.

When the goals of policymakers are *balanced trade* and full employment, the policy mix of monetary and fiscal policies breaks apart. In an economy facing a trade deficit, for example, it is necessary now to use an expenditure-switching policy, which could swing demand away from foreign goods and improve the trade balance. Neither monetary nor fiscal policies are expenditure-switching policies, since they only change the level of spending on domestic and foreign goods; that is, they are expenditure-changing policies. The implication is that the analysis carried out in previous chapters, as to the need to use both expenditure-switching and expenditure-changing policies to attain internal and trade balance simultaneously, also applies here. The policy mix for an economy with unemployment and a trade balance deficit would regress to our earlier prescription to use devaluation as an expenditure-switching mechanism, combined with monetary and/or fiscal policies as an expenditure-changing mechanism. These policies could then move the economy toward both internal and trade balance.

In addition, a goal of balanced payments implicitly assumes that the Central Bank desires its holdings of international reserves to remain unchanged. It should be recognized, however, that this is an ad hoc assumption and that the preferences and requirements of the Central Bank in determining an optimal level (or rate of change) of international reserves have not been yet considered adequately. Given the commitment of the Central Bank to pegging exchange rates, it may then be an important goal of the Central Bank to attain or maintain a target level of international reserves. Balance of payments equilibrium at a low level of reserves (below the target level), for example, may generate speculative financial transactions and may not be consistent with a stable exchange rate regime. Furthermore, an increasing level of international reserves may be the adequate policy for a growing economy with ever-increasing transactions with the rest of the world. This implies that, before stating the goals of the policymakers, one must analyze in detail Central Bank preferences and the determination of its desired level of international reserves.

The monetary–fiscal policy mix also neglects the effects of the mix on the composition of aggregate demand in the economy. It assumes, first, that domestic residents are indifferent as to the size of the private sector relative to the government sector and, second, that the authorities are indifferent as to the size of the investment component in aggregate demand relative to the consumption component. In general, however, domestic government authorities will have specific goals as to the relative size of the investment component of aggregate demand, depending on their preferences toward economic growth. Furthermore, domestic residents will usually also have some preferences toward the relative size of the government sector vis à vis the private sector. It is not clear, then, that a policy of contractionary monetary policy and expansionary fiscal policy oriented toward eliminating a payments deficit and unemployment would be attractive to both domestic residents and policymakers. This policy mix generally induces an increase in domestic interest rates, which reduces investment and increases the size of the government sector vis à vis the private sector. Both of these may be unattractive side effects of the mix.

A fourth problem with the monetary–fiscal policy mix is that it neglects the lags involved in policy formulation and implementation. It usually takes a longer period of time for fiscal legislation to pass through the legal–legislative process than it takes monetary policy to pass through the decision-making process of the Central Bank authorities. If this is so, the policy mix concept breaks apart again (at least in the context of short-run policy making), since fiscal policy would not be available as a functional policy. The problems do not end here, however. There also exist lags in terms of the impact of both fiscal and monetary policies. The policymaker lacks knowledge not only about the magnitude of the impact of its policies, but also about the lag with which these policies act on the economy. Consequently, in a continually changing environment, the policy mix may destabilize the economy and move it away from, rather than toward, internal and external balance. One can easily visualize a situation in which a policy takes so long to operate that, when it does, it is no longer necessary and is perhaps counterproductive.

A fifth problem of the policy mix is that it assumes monetary and fiscal policies are independent of each other. In many countries, however, fiscal policy is financed in large part through monetary expansion, that is, by printing money. In this situation the two policy instruments are dependent, so that a given level of public spending implies a particular change in the domestic money supply. If fiscal policy is used, say, to attain the goal of internal balance, then monetary policy is not free to change in accord with the requirements of the goal of external balance. For any operational purposes, the two policy instruments, monetary and fiscal policy, have collapsed into one, and the economy remains one instrument short.[11]

7–13 SUMMARY

1. Under imperfect capital mobility, domestic interest rates will diverge from world interest rates, inducing capital inflows or outflows depending on whether they are higher or lower than the world rates.

2. An expansionary monetary policy generates a rise in income and a decrease in interest rates over the short run. Both lead to a payments deficit, which, if the Central Bank does not sterilize, induces in turn a gradual reduction of the money supply back toward its original level, diluting its initial effects on the economy.

3. Fiscal policy, in the form of increased government expenditure, affects positively both the short-run level of income and the interest rate. As these have opposite effects on the balance of payments, either a surplus or a deficit may develop over the short run, depending on how large the degree of capital mobility is relative to the marginal propensity to import. Over the longer run, monetary adjustments tend to move the economy toward balanced payments.

4. A mix of monetary and fiscal policies can succeed in attaining the goals of internal balance and balanced payments in the short run. An expenditure-switching policy is required, however, to attain the goals of balanced trade and full employment.

PROBLEMS

1. Determine algebraically what would be the equilibrium level of income in an economy under perfect capital mobility as a function of exogenous variables. Then provide algebraic expressions for the effects of the following on domestic income:

(a) A decrease of autonomous government expenditures.
(b) An exogenous increase in domestic exports.
(c) An increase in the world interest rate.

2. Suppose that you are given the following numerical expressions for absorption, A, the trade balance, T, and the world interest rate, i^*:

$$A = \bar{A} + aY - bi = 480 + 0.75Y - 900i$$
$$T = \bar{T} - mY = 50 - 0.25Y$$
$$i^* = 0.10 \ (10\%)$$

[11] The present analysis draws upon Marina V. N. Whitman, Policies for Internal and External Balance," *Special Papers in International Economics*, No. 9 (Princeton, N.J.: Princeton University, 1970), pp. 7–8.

with variables measured in billions of domestic output. The economy is perfectly integrated into world capital markets.

(a) What is the equilibrium level of output in the economy (in numerical terms)? Is the balance of trade in surplus or deficit? What about the balance of payments?

(b) Suppose that there is an exogenous increase in the foreign demand for domestic exports, which is reflected in an autonomous trade balance increase of 50 billion. What is the effect on:
  (1) The equilibrium level of output in the economy?
  (2) The balance of trade, the capital account, and the balance of payments?

(c) Consider the impact of an exogenous reduction in government spending of 50 billion. What would be the effect on:
  (1) The equilibrium level of output in the economy?
  (2) The value of exports, imports, the trade balance, and the capital account?

Explain the economic reasoning behind your answers. Then compare your results for parts (a) and (b) with those obtained in Problem 1, Chapter 5. Do they differ? How can this happen?

3. In the previous question, assume that the domestic real money demand function has been estimated to be

$$L^D = 0.20\,Y - 3000i$$

Each unit of domestic output has a domestic currency price of $P = \$1.00$.

(a) What is the economy's equilibrium money supply (in billions of dollars?)

(b) Consider the impact of a reduction in government spending of $50 billion. What would be the effect of this reduction on the domestic money supply? Provide numerical answers. Explain your results.

4. Examine the effects of a domestic currency devaluation on output, the trade balance and the capital account under perfect capital mobility. Use the *IS–LM* framework developed in the text. Then, assuming that the economy is initially in balanced trade, specify what condition determines whether the devaluation moves the trade balance into surplus or not. Provide an algebraic answer [H I N T : From previous chapters, determine how a devaluation affects the autonomous trade balance, then use the goods market equilibrium condition (3) to determine how changes in the autonomous trade balance affect domestic output.]

5. Suppose that you can depict the short-run relationship between the capital account and domestic interest rates by $K = \beta i$, where β is a positive parameter representing the degree of international capital mobility facing the economy. (Note that as β becomes smaller—as it goes to zero—the domestic interest rate has less impact on the capital account, that is, the degree of capital mobility declines; a higher value of β implies a higher degree of capital

mobility.) Using this expression for the capital account, determine the equation defining the balance of payments equilibrium locus, $B = 0$, and show how its slope is affected by the marginal propensity to import, m, and the degree of capital mobility as represented by β. [H I N T : Substitute our earlier expression for the trade balance: $T = \bar{T} - mY$ and the capital account equation, $K = \beta i$, into the balance of payments equilibrium condition in equation (2) of the text.]

6. Determine the exact combination of monetary and fiscal policies necessary to reach external and internal balance if the economy is in a situation of:

   (a) Balance of payments deficit and overemployment.

   (b) Payments surplus and overemployment.

   (c) Payments surplus and unemployment.

   Describe your results geometrically.

7. In his article, "The Appropriate Use of Monetary and Fiscal Policy Under Fixed Exchange Rates," Robert Mundell argues that, in the monetary–fiscal policy mix framework, a policymaker acting under incomplete information on the value of basic economic parameters (without knowledge of the exact slopes of the *IS, LM,* and $B = 0$ curves) should assign monetary policy to the attainment of external balance and fiscal policy to reaching internal balance. Show diagrammatically how such an assignment rule would assure that the goals of internal and external balance are eventually attained. What would happen if the opposite policy assignment rule is followed, using fiscal policy to the attainment of external balance and monetary policy to reach internal balance? Explain diagrammatically.

CHAPTER 8

Equilibrium Output and Exchange Rate Determination

The seventies and eighties have seen a general increase in the flexibility of exchange rates as compared with previous decades. Before 1973, few countries could be found that had allowed their currencies to float over extended periods of time. Among the industrial countries, the only one having an extended experience with flexible exchange rates was Canada, which let its exchange rate float during the period of 1950 to 1962 and then again after 1970. Since 1973, most industrial countries have faced an environment of considerable exchange rate flexibility. This is clearly visualized in Figure 8–1, which shows the value of the exchange rate of the dollar against the British pound, the Japanese yen, and the deutsche mark after 1973. What factors affect the level of the exchange rate in a flexible exchange rates regime? And why is it that exchange rates have been so turbulent—that is, so variable—over the time span covered by Figure 8–1? These are the kind of questions that we try to answer in the following chapters. Specifically, Chapters 8 and 9 examine the macroeconomics of flexible exchange rates and the experience of actual economies under such a regime.

The present chapter is concerned with the determination of output, interest rates, and the level of the exchange rate in an economy operating under flexible exchange rates. We shall be particularly interested in the problems of countries suffering from recession and unemployment. To do so, the analysis follows the Keynesian point of view developed in Chapters 5 through 7. Within this context, Sections 8.2 through 8.8 examine first the effects of government policies and the behavior of the exchange rate under conditions of perfect capital mobility. Sections 8.9 and 8.10 extend the discussion to examine the role the degree of capital mobility plays in the analysis and to discern the influence of current and capital account imbalances on the determination of the economy's equilibrium output and exchange rate. Chapter 9 examines exchange rate turbulence, the role of exchange rate expectations and the so-called overshooting hypothesis, and the relationships between spot and forward rates.

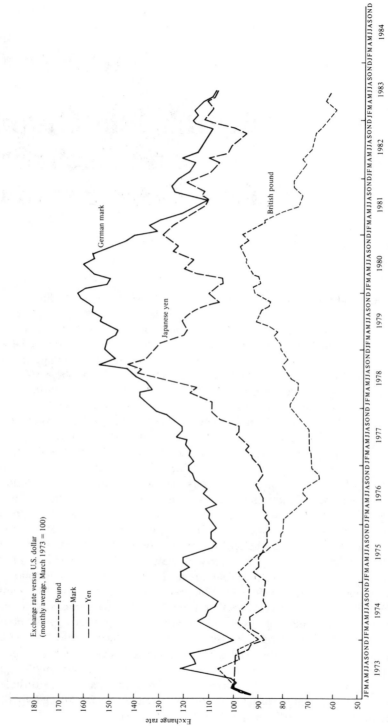

FIGURE 8–1. Behavior of Selected Foreign Exchange Rates Versus the Dollar, 1975 to 1983. (From *Federal Reserve Bulletin*, various issues.)

254

8–1   FLEXIBLE EXCHANGE RATES AND THE BALANCE OF PAYMENTS

Under flexible exchange rates, monetary authorities do not face a "balance of payments problem," in the sense that they are not obliged to intervene in foreign exchange markets and thus do not have to worry about losing or gaining international reserves. As a matter of fact, in a world of *freely floating* exchange rates, in which Central Banks completely refrain from intervening in foreign exchange markets, there would be no changes at all in the international reserve holdings of Central Banks. In this situation, the balance of payments of the economy—whether defined by the official reserve settlements balance or the money account—will be equal to zero. With Central Banks keeping their hands off foreign exchange markets, any excess demand or supply in the private sector would have to clear by itself. Therefore, the balance of payments deficits or surpluses that emerge under fixed exchange rates would no longer be a natural outcome; under freely floating exchange rates the exchange rate would adjust to guarantee external payments balance. In other words, the economy's international transactions carried out and recorded by the current account, T, and capital account, K, will balance to zero. Symbolically,

$$B = T + K = 0 \qquad (1)$$

stating that balance of payments deficits or surpluses disappear under flexible exchange rates.

Suppose, for the sake of the argument, that the U.S. economy is initially at balanced payments and that there is a sudden surge of capital outflows as investors—perhaps due to an increase in interest rates abroad or because of reduced domestic interest rates—seek to sell dollars to purchase more attractive foreign assets. Under fixed exchange rates, these increased capital outflows (net purchases of foreign assets) would—other things being equal—generate a balance of payments deficit. But suppose that, as is the case under a freely fluctuating exchange rate regime, Central Banks do not intervene in foreign exchange markets. Then, how is the balance of payments deficit that would arise under fixed exchange rates eliminated? Everything else being constant, the excess supply of dollars associated with the capital outflows indicates that some investors trying to dispose of dollars would not be able to do so at the original exchange rate. In order to attract buyers, they have to accept a lower price for their dollars in terms of foreign currencies. That is, the dollar depreciates in foreign exchange markets. The increased exchange rate of the dollar vis à vis foreign currencies (in terms of dollars per foreign currency) will then tend to eliminate the excess supply of dollars arising from the sudden capital outflow. In other words, the exchange rate would adjust—all else being constant—to eliminate the balance of payments deficit that would otherwise arise at a given exchange rate. The precise mechanisms involved in the interaction of exchange rate changes with balance of payments adjustments will be discussed in more detail in later sections. Suffice it to say that an increase in the exchange rate generally tends to shift demand toward domestic goods and away from foreign goods, thus improving the current account balance. This acts to eliminate the payments deficit that would arise if the exchange rate were fixed. Similarly, factors that tend to generate a balance of payments surplus under fixed exchange rates— such as a sudden surge of capital inflows or an increased demand for domestic exports—tend to induce a currency appreciation under flexible exchange rates, ensuring that the surplus is eliminated.

8–2   EXCHANGE RATE FLEXIBILITY AND THE MONEY SUPPLY PROCESS

The absence of Central Bank intervention in foreign exchange markets has important implications for the money supply process and for the ability of the Central Bank to control the money supply in an open economy under flexible exchange rates. The main way through which the Central Bank can influence the domestic money supply is by affecting the monetary base. The relationship between the monetary base and the money supply is given by

$$M^S = \mu H = \mu(\text{CBC} + \text{IR}) \tag{2}$$

with M^S denoting the domestic money supply and μ the money multiplier.[1] Notice that, by changing its credit, CBC, the Central Bank can indeed determine the money supply but only if international reserves, IR, stay unchanged. Under fixed exchange rates, the Central Bank is committed to buying or selling foreign currencies on demand in order to prevent the exchange rate from moving away from its peg. This means that the Central Bank's holdings of international reserves are influenced by the international transactions of domestic and foreign residents. Therefore, unless direct restrictions are imposed on the foreign trade and finance activities of domestic residents, the variable that the Central Bank can control under fixed exchange rates is Central Bank credit, not the overall monetary base. This constraint on the ability of the Central Bank to control the money supply does not extend to a flexible exchange rate regime. Since the Central Bank has no obligation to buy or sell foreign exchange reserves, it will have complete control of the monetary base. Indeed, in the absence of Central Bank intervention in foreign exchange markets, changes in Central Bank credit will directly correspond to changes in the monetary base. Symbolically, taking changes in both sides of equation (2), one obtains

---

[1] This relationship was derived, and a general description of the monetary process in open economies provided, in Section 6–2.

$$\Delta M^S = \mu(\Delta \text{CBC} + \Delta \text{IR})$$

$$= \mu(\Delta \text{CBC}) \tag{3}$$

where the absence of Central Bank intervention in foreign exchange markets implies that $\Delta \text{IR} = 0$. In a flexible exchange rate regime, then, the Central Bank can control the money supply, as compared with the situation under fixed exchange rates.[2] This autonomy of the domestic money supply from the vagaries of international transactions and the balance of payments is one of the basic characteristics of a flexible exchange rate regime, differentiating it from fixed exchange rates.

But just as it provides monetary authorities in open economies with relatively more control over the money supply, a floating exchange rate regime limits, on the other hand, the Central Bank's direct control over exchange rates. The latter fluctuate in response to market forces and are heavily influenced by international transactions and events. The next sections examine some of the factors that generate changes in the exchange rate in a floating exchange rate regime. The role of capital account transactions is discussed at the outset.

8–3 PERFECT CAPITAL MOBILITY, OUTPUT, AND THE EXCHANGE RATE

The modern industrial economy is subject to a relatively high degree of interaction with other countries as far as it regards capital account transactions. We live in a world where information about foreign interest rates and stock market prices, exchange rates, and so on, is widely available at a low cost by reaching a phone or a computer console. We thus initiate our discussion of flexible exchange rates under the context of perfect capital mobility.

The Goods Market Equilibrium Condition

The first building block in the analysis is the domestic goods market equilibrium condition, derived from the equality of the supply (output) of domestic goods, Y, with the demand for domestic goods. It is stated by

$$Y = A + T$$

$$= \bar{A} + aY + \bar{T}\left(\frac{eP^*}{P}\right) - mY - bi$$

---

[2] Note, however, that the money supply is determined not only by the monetary base, but also by the money multiplier. Since the monetary authorities do not directly control the money multiplier, even when the monetary base can be directly monitored, the money supply will still not be completely under their control.

which yields

$$Y = \alpha\left[\bar{A} + \bar{T}\left(\frac{eP^*}{P}\right) - bi\right] \tag{4}$$

where

$$\alpha = \frac{1}{1 - a + m} = \frac{1}{s + m}$$

is the simple open economy Keynesian multiplier, $\bar{A}$ is autonomous absorption, b measures the responsiveness of investment to changes in the domestic interest rate, and $\bar{T}\,(eP^*/P)$ is the autonomous trade balance, representing that part of the trade balance which is independent of domestic income and which, in the present discussion, will be assumed to depend explicitly on the relative price of foreign goods in terms of domestic goods, $q \equiv eP^*/P$. Note that, within the present Keynesian context, foreign and domestic prices are assumed to be rigid so that P^*/P is fixed as well. As a consequence, the autonomous trade balance, $\bar{T}\,(eP^*/P)$ will change only in response to exchange rate changes.

At a given level of the exchange rate, and in the absence of any disturbances affecting autonomous spending, equation (4) provides us with the combinations of domestic interest rates and income that clear the goods market. This is, of course, the familiar *IS* curve, drawn in the top diagram of Figure 8–2. Note that a domestic currency depreciation—an increase in the exchange rate, e—raises the relative price of foreign goods in terms of domestic goods, switching demand away from foreign and toward domestic goods and improving the autonomous trade balance. This raises output at any given level of the interest rate, shifting the *IS* curve to the right. Similarly, a domestic currency appreciation would—everything else constant—shift the *IS* curve to the left by inducing a switch in spending away from domestic and toward foreign goods, reducing the demand for domestic goods at a given level of the interest rate.

Assets Market Equilibrium

The second building block in the analysis is the assets market equilibrium, which is represented here by the money market. The money market is in equilibrium when the domestic demand and supply of money are equal,

$$M^S = L^D\,(i,\ Y)$$
$$= kY - hi \tag{5}$$

where M^S/P is the real money supply and $L^D(i,\ Y)$ represents the real demand for money, which depends on domestic interest rates, i, and income, Y. Note

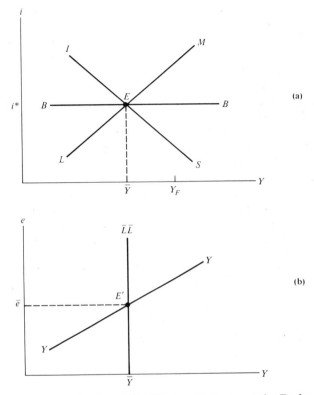

FIGURE 8–2. Determination of Equilibrium Output and the Exchange Rate

that the nominal money supply under flexible exchange rates is exogenously given, being determined by the monetary authorities. As seen before, this is not so under fixed exchange rates; the money supply in that case is also affected by the balance of payments situation of the country. With a fixed money supply, equation (5) states the combinations of income and interest rates that clear the money market. This yields, of course, the familiar *LM* curve, which is depicted by the upward-sloping curve in the top diagram of Figure 8–2.

Perfect Capital Mobility and Balance of Payments Equilibrium

Perfect capital mobility means domestic investors can borrow or lend freely and instantaneously at the world interest rate, *i**, and foreigners can similarly lend and borrow in domestic capital markets at the domestic interest rate, *i*. Arbitrage between domestic and world capital markets then guarantees an alignment of domestic and world interest rates.[3] This is represented symbolically by the condition that, in equilibrium: $i = i^*$.

In terms of Figure 8–2(a) perfect capital mobility imposes the constraint that balanced payments occur along the *BB* curve, which is drawn at a vertical distance equal to the world interest rate, i^*. The underlying reason for this constraint lies in the fact that under perfect capital mobility the capital account is extremely sensitive to deviations of the domestic interest rate from the world interest rate. When the domestic interest rate increases above the world level (when $i > i^*$), there is a huge inflow of foreign funds into the economy, generating a massive capital account surplus that would swamp any existing current account deficit and move the balance of payments into surplus at a given exchange rate. Domestic currency would then have to appreciate in order for the current account to worsen and eliminate the payments surplus. The exchange rate will stop adjusting and equilibrium in the balance of payments will be reached when the domestic and world interest rates are equal. Similarly, if the domestic interest rate were to fall below the world interest rate, the capital account and the balance of payments would move into deficit and the domestic currency would persistently depreciate to restore balance of payments equilibrium. Again, in terms of Figure 8–2(a), balanced payments are obtained only when the economy lies along the *BB* curve.

The Determination of Equilibrium Output Under Flexible Exchange Rates

The equilibrium of the economy under perfect capital mobility occurs when there is simultaneous equilibrium in the goods and assets markets at the given world interest rate i^*. According to Figure 8–2(a), the equilibrium of the economy occurs at point *E*, which shows the intersection of the *IS* and *LM* curves along the *BB* curve and an equilibrium level of output equal to $\overline{Y}$. One of the key properties of output determination under flexible exchange rates and perfect capital mobility is that domestic output is completely specified by the money market equilibrium condition, as represented by the *LM* curve. To visualize this important result, let us set $i = i^*$, as established by perfect capital mobility, in the money market equilibrium condition (5), yielding

---

[3] In general, under perfect capital mobility, the domestic interest rate will be associated not only with the world interest rate, but also will reflect the expected rate of depreciation of the domestic currency. With static expectations, however, the expected rate of depreciation is equal to zero, leading to the direct link between domestic and foreign interest rates stated in the text. The topic of exchange rate expectations and their influence on the economy will be examined in detail in the next chapter. Note also that we assume domestic and foreign bonds are perfect substitutes; that is, they have identical characteristics in terms of maturity, liquidity, political risk, exchange risk, and so forth, making them freely interchangeable in investors' portfolios. This assumption is relaxed in Chapter 15.

$$\frac{M^S}{P} = L^D (i^*, Y)$$
$$= kY - hi^* \tag{5a}$$

With the money supply fixed by the monetary authorities, domestic prices rigid over the present short-run context, and with i^* the given world interest rate, equation (5a) completely determines the equilibrium level of income in the economy. Solving for that equilibrium level of income, we obtain

$$\overline{Y} = \frac{M^S}{kP} + \frac{h}{k} i^* \tag{5b}$$

Equation (5b) shows the striking result that the equilibrium level of income, $\overline{Y}$, can be completely determined by the knowledge of three variables, M^S, P, and i^*. Combined with the world interest rate, i^*, M^S and P fully specify the equilibrium at point E. Still, note that neither Equation (5b) nor Figure 8–2(a) tells us what is the equilibrium level of the exchange rate.

Determination of the Exchange Rate

Figure 8–2(b) shows the determination of the exchange rate under perfect capital mobility. The vertical $\overline{LL}$ curve represents all combinations of the exchange rate and income that keep the money market in equilibrium. From equation (5b), it can be seen that the money market equilibrium specifies a level of income, $\overline{Y}$, which is not directly affected at all by the exchange rate, e. Money market equilibrium is consequently represented by the vertical line $\overline{LL}$, resting at a level of income $\overline{Y}$ in Figure 8–2(b).

The YY line, on the other hand, depicts all combinations of the exchange rate and income keeping the goods market in equilibrium. It is derived by observing that, with $i = i^*$, equation (4) becomes

$$Y = \alpha \left(\bar{A} + \overline{T} \left(\frac{eP^*}{P} \right) - bi^* \right) \tag{4a}$$

→devaluation

which denotes a positive relationship between the exchange rate and income. An increase in the exchange rate switches demand from foreign to domestic goods, requiring an increased output to maintain goods market equilibrium. A domestic currency appreciation, on the other hand, switches demand out of domestic goods and requires a reduction of domestic output. This positive connection between exchange rates and income in sustaining goods market equilibrium is what curve YY depicts. The equilibrium exchange rate is specified by the condition that the goods market clear at a level of income ($\overline{Y}$) consistent

$e\downarrow$

with equilibrium in the money market. In terms of Figure 8–2(b), this occurs at the intersection of the YY and $\bar{L}\bar{L}$ loci at point E', with a corresponding exchange rate equal to $\bar{e}$.

Having established the factors determining equilibrium output and the exchange rate, in the following sections we shall examine the effects of various economic disturbances and investigate how the economy behaves in its adjustment toward a new equilibrium. We start with the effects of a fiscal policy disturbance.

8–4   INEFFECTIVENESS OF FISCAL POLICY UNDER FLEXIBLE EXCHANGE RATES

One of the main ideas of Keynesian economics is that the economy's short-run equilibrium level of output can settle below full employment; unemployment and recession can remain a stubborn and ugly feature of a laissez-faire economy. Government policy intervention is then believed to be instrumental in moving the economy out of recession, with increased government spending having a leading role in that recovery. The purpose of this section is to examine the effects of an increase in government spending on the economy's equilibrium and to determine whether, under flexible exchange rates, such an increase can indeed stimulate output growth. The answer, as we shall see, is in the negative.[4]

Figure 8–3 analyzes the impact of increased autonomous expenditures on the economy. Initial equilibrium is shown by points E and E', with output and the exchange rate equal to $\bar{Y}$ and e_0, respectively. An expansion of government spending raises aggregate demand for domestic goods and tends to shift the IS curve upward, from IS_0 to IS' in Figure 8–3(a). This results in upward pressures on domestic interest rates, generating incipient capital inflows as investors shift their portfolios toward the relatively more attractive domestic assets. These capital inflows surface as an excess supply of foreign exchange, as foreigners attempt to dispose of their foreign money to acquire domestic assets. The result is a reduction in the price of foreign currencies, or, in other words, a domestic currency *appreciation*. This appreciation, however, induces a switch of aggregate demand out of domestic goods, deteriorating the current account balance and shifting the IS curve back to its original position at IS_0 in Figure 8–3(a).

As long as there is any pressure on the domestic interest rate to remain above the world rate, capital inflows will continue to appreciate domestic currency and reduce aggregate demand. The IS curve will therefore stop shifting

---

[4] This strong result was derived by Robert Mundell and Marcus Fleming during the early 1960s; see Robert Mundell, "Capital Mobility and Stabilization Policy Under Fixed and Flexible Exchange Rates," *International Economics* (New York: Macmillan Publishing Company, 1968), Chapter 18 (originally published in 1963), and Marcus Fleming, "Domestic Financial Policies Under Fixed and Floating Exchange Rates," *IMF Staff Papers* (November 1962).

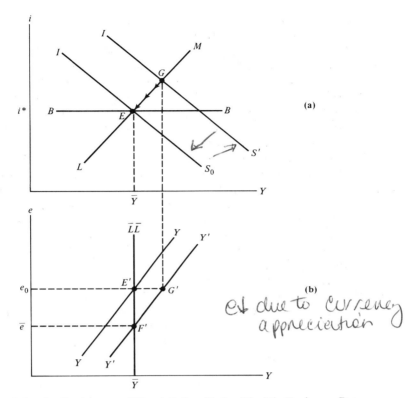

FIGURE 8–3.   Ineffectiveness of Fiscal Policy Under Flexible Exchange Rates

back only when it reaches the original equilibrium at point E, where it intersects the LM curve precisely at the world interest rate, i^*. In other words, a fiscal expansion in the present context has no effects on the equilibrium level of output of the economy, which remains at $\overline{Y}$. The increased aggregate demand brought about by the rise in government spending is exactly compensated by the reduction in aggregate demand associated with the domestic currency appreciation, the deterioration of the price competitiveness of domestic goods in world markets and the consequent reduction of net domestic exports. In effect, the increase in government expenditures *crowds out* the private sector of the economy producing goods for export. Only the composition, but not the total level of output, is altered by the fiscal intervention.

A better understanding of these results is obtained by examining the effects of a fiscal disturbance on the exchange rate determination diagram in Figure 8–3(b). The increased government expenditures raise aggregate demand, at any given level of the exchange rate, shifting the YY locus to $Y'Y'$. The effects of this change at the original exchange rate would be to increase income, as represented by point G'. The higher income raises money demand and, at a given level of the money supply, requires a market clearing rise in the interest rate. The upward pressure on domestic interest rates induces domestic currency to appreciate, as depicted by the movement from point G' to F' in Figure 8–3(b). The equilibrium of the economy thus moves to point F', with a reduction of the exchange rate from e_0 to $\bar{e}$ but no change in output, which remains at $\bar{Y}$. Geometrically, as long as the $\bar{L}\bar{L}$ curve in Figure 8–3(b) remains unaltered, output will also remain unchanged. Fiscal intervention cannot then be called upon to bring about an economic recovery.

The same conclusions apply to the effects of other real disturbances. A real disturbance refers to any policy measure or exogenous disturbance that does not alter money demand or money supply, as opposed to nominal disturbances, which originate in the money market. For instance, commercial policy in the form of protection against imports is a real disturbance and, following the analysis above, would have no lasting effects on output and would only be associated with an exchange rate appreciation.[5] Another real disturbance in the economy would be a sudden, exogenous increase in domestic exports, such as may arise from an income boom abroad that spreads into an increase in demand for domestic goods. This boom has no lasting effect on the domestic trade balance or on domestic output. The implications of this analysis for the operation of actual economies under flexible exchange rates is examined in the following section, in which the effects of North Sea oil exports on the U.K. economy are discussed.

8–5 · The Exchange Rate and International Competitiveness: Oil and Deindustrialization in the United Kingdom

The massive increase of oil production in the United Kingdom during the late seventies associated with the exploitation of North Sea reserves represented a significant real disturbance to the British economy. Its effects serve well to illustrate the issues involved in the impact of real disturbances on open economies under flexible exchange rates. The case of Britain is particularly interesting, since the United Kingdom represents the situation of a country that discovered it is richly endowed with energy resources, proceeds to a drastic exploitation of those resources and, at the same time, undergoes widespread decline in economic activity. The analysis in this section will try to provide an answer—not necessarily the only one—to this paradox, emphasizing its open economy ramifications.

---

[5] For details on the issue of the impotence of commercial policy under flexible exchange rates, see Robert Mundell, "Flexible Exchange Rates and Employment Policy," *International Economics* (New York: Macmillan Publishing Company, 1968), Chapter 17. Note that if account is taken of the distortionary effects tariffs have in increasing the relative cost of imports, protective commercial policy may in effect reduce domestic real income.

If one takes a casual look, it seems perfectly reasonable to assert that the effects of increased oil production on domestic income would be positive and the impact of an increase in oil exports (or a reduction in oil imports) would be to improve the trade balance. But not everything that glitters is gold (or, in the present case, black gold), and looking casually at the issue may be immensely misleading. Our discussion in the last section, showing that an exogenous increase in domestic exports may not have any significant positive effects on either income or the trade balance, should make us realize that, in a complex modern industrial economy, the effects of economic disturbances may diverge substantially from what they appear to be. For this reason, one must look carefully at the overall impact of increased oil production on the economy, and not just at its clear direct expansionary effects; but such a closer look shows that a sudden expansion of oil production and exports may not be as good a blessing as it appears.

The increased domestic income initially associated with the hike in oil production would raise money demand and, with a fixed money supply, would place upward pressures on domestic interest rates. Foreign financial capital would then flow into the economy, reducing the exchange rate; but the appreciation hurts the international competitiveness of domestic goods by making them relatively expensive vis à vis foreign goods. The production of exports and import competing manufactured goods will then decline, offsetting the positive impact of the increased oil exports. In other words, increased oil production crowds out the production of manufactured export and import competing products, not necessarily causing a net increase in domestic output. This phenomenon, in which an energy-sector boom leads to deindustrialization in the form of a decline in the production of the economy's traditional export and import-competing goods has been referred to by economists as the *Dutch disease,* named after the squeeze placed on the traditional export sectors of the Dutch economy by the rapid development of the natural gas industry in that country.[6]

In the case of the United Kingdom, the association between increased production of North Sea oil and gas in the late seventies and the decline of the manufacturing sector is striking, as reflected by the data shown in Figure 8-4. This figure plots the behavior of the share of North Sea oil and gas in the gross domestic product of the United Kingdom and the share of manufacturing in U.K. GDP over time. Even though major discoveries of oil and gas reserves in the North Sea date back to the sixties and early seventies, the first year in which substantial quantities of North Sea oil were forthcoming was in 1976. The following years saw rapidly rising production and widespread expectations

---

[6] For an economic analysis of the issues relating to the Dutch disease, see W. M. Corden and J. P. Neary, "Booming Sector and De-Industrialization in a Small Open Economy," *Institute for International Economic Studies Discussion Paper No. 195* (February 1982). The application to the U.K. case has been made by W. M. Corden, "The Exchange Rate, Monetary Policy, and North Sea Oil: The Economic Theory of the Squeeze on Tradeables," in W. A. Eltis and P. N. Sinclair, *The Money Supply and the Exchange Rate* (New York: Oxford University Press, 1981).

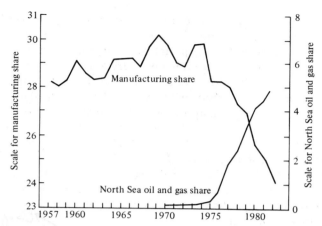

FIGURE 8–4. Oil and Deindustrialization in the United Kingdom. The figures are for the shares of manufacturing and North Sea oil and gas in U.K. gross domestic product at 1975 factor cost. (Sources: Central Statistical Office, United Kingdom, Annual Abstract of Statistics, 1983; and U.K. Department of Energy, Digest of U.K. Energy Statistics, 1980).

that exploitation of reserves would continue to increase rapidly.[7] The growth of North Sea oil and gas production and the decline of manufacturing over this period is clearly discerned from Figure 8–4.

Our analysis emphasizes an appreciation of the exchange rate as the major link in the deindustrialization effects of an oil boom. Figure 8–5 shows the sharp appreciation of the pound vis à vis the currencies of U.K.'s main trading partners in the late seventies. This can be closely associated with a sharp deterioration of the international competitiveness of British manufactured exports over this time period and the dismal performance of this sector reflected in Figure 8–4.

The consequence of these developments was the absence of any realized boom in U.K. GDP as a result of the expansion of North Sea oil production. The British economy moved into sharp recession in the late seventies and remained so during the early eighties. We must stress, however, that even though the North Sea oil-induced deindustrialization certainly had its effect, the recession of the British economy during the late seventies and early eighties was brought about by a combination of factors, including a reduction in money supply (M1) growth at the time. The effective appreciation of the pound sterling and the deterioration of the manufacturing sector can also be linked to the monetary

[7] For details on the development of North Sea oil production, see Great Britain, Department of Energy, "Development of the Oil and Gas Resources of the U.K." (1977); and H. S. Houthakker, "The Use and Management of North Sea Oil," in R. E. Caves and L. B. Krause, *Britain's Economic Performance* (Washington, D.C.: The Brookings Institution, 1980).

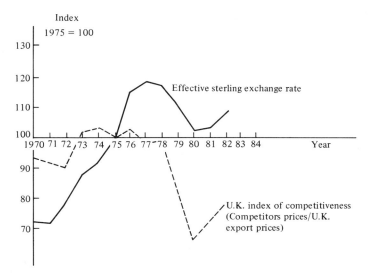

FIGURE 8–5.   Sterling Exchange Rate and U.K. Export Competitiveness, 1970–1982. The U.K. index of competitiveness records relative export unit values; it is an index of relative costs and prices vis-à-vis 14 other countries. (From International Monetary Fund, *International Financial Statistics*, 1984.)

restrictionist regime.[8] Why this is so will be discussed in Section 8–7, which is concerned with the effects of monetary policy in economies under flexible exchange rates.

8–6   INSULATION AND INTERDEPENDENCE UNDER FLOATING EXCHANGE RATES

The inability of an exogenous increase in domestic exports to lead to economic expansion under flexible exchange rates and perfect capital mobility suggests a basic ineffectiveness of export-led recoveries in such economies. Expansion

---

[8] The particulars of economic policy and change in the United Kingdom over this period can be obtained from the various articles in the collection *Britain's Economic Performance*, edited by R. E. Caves and L. B. Krause (Washington, D.C.: The Brookings Institution, 1980). The argument that monetary policy was too tight in the early years of the Thatcher administration is made by W. Buiter and M. Miller, "The Thatcher Experiment: The First Two Years," *Brookings Papers on Economic Activity* (1981). On the other hand, if one uses a broad measure of the money supply, M3, one does not find clear-cut evidence supporting tighter monetary policy during the period. See K. Alec Chrystal, "Dutch Disease or Monetarist Medicine? The British Economy Under Mrs. Thatcher," *Review,* Federal Reserve Bank of St. Louis (May 1984); and Thomas J. Sargent, "Stopping Moderate Inflations: The Methods of Poincaré and Thatcher," in R. Dornbusch and M. H. Simonsen, *Inflation, Debt and Indexation* (Cambridge, Mass.: The M.I.T. Press, 1983).

in one country, spilling over into increased imports from other countries does not increase the overall exports or income of these other countries but rather appreciates their currencies, offsetting the initial boom in demand for their products. In other words, an income expansion in one country is not transmitted into higher income in other countries under exchange rate flexibility. Domestic authorities should not count on foreign recovery as a sure way out of recession and unemployment.

The underlying analytical explanation of this result is the earlier-noted connection between the determination of domestic income and the money market equilibrium condition [equation 5(b)]. Any country's real income is determined by the country's real money supply, interest rates and other money demand parameters. If these are fixed, an exogenous increase in the foreign demand for a country's goods cannot have any impact on that country's output and must be associated with offsetting effects on aggregate demand, as described in Section 8–5.

Note that the knife here cuts both ways: Just as an income boom abroad is not transmitted locally, a recession would not be transmitted either. A reduction of foreign income would indeed spill over into reduced demand for domestic exports, at given exchange rates. This reduced aggregate demand, however, places downward pressures on domestic interest rates. As a consequence, capital flows out, generating a currency depreciation that switches demand back toward domestic goods. Only when the initial (foreign-income related) reduction in exports is offset by an (exchange rate depreciation-induced) improvement of the trade balance will adjustments stop. A country's recession is therefore not transmitted internationally. In this sense, an economy under flexible exchange rates and perfect capital mobility has macroeconomic independence from business cycles in the rest of the world. This insulation from external disturbances makes countries operating under a flexible exchange rate regime diametrically different from the way they would behave under fixed exchange rates. In the latter case, business cycles are transmitted internationally, giving rise to the saying that "When one country sneezes, the others catch cold" (for more details, see Section 5–10).

Coordinated Aggregate Demand Disturbances and Interdependence Under Flexible Exchange Rates

The insulation provided by floating exchange rates from foreign autonomous spending disturbances hinges on the critical assumption that the disturbance originates in a single country abroad and does not have a global connotation. A coordinated expansion by a group of foreign countries or disturbances in large, major foreign countries would be able to impinge on domestic output and employment. For instance, if all countries except the Netherlands pursue expansionary aggregate demand policies—through, say, increased government expenditures—this will tend to raise each expanding country's interest rate, inducing the world interest rate to rise. Under perfect capital mobility, however, a rise in the world interest rate above its Dutch counterpart would generate massive capital flight out of the Netherlands, a sharp depreciation of the Dutch guilder and output expansion in that country. It is consequently, quite possible to have international transmission of disturbances under fluctuating exchange rates.[9] A foreign income disturbance associated with changes in world interest rates will generally be transmitted domestically. A coordinated fiscal expansion in Europe might thus aid in pulling the U.S. economy out of recession, and vice versa. Note that the channel of transmission of the foreign aggregate demand disturbance originates in changes of the world interest rate and involves exchange rate changes as a key link.

In conclusion, floating exchange rates provide insulation of an economy from foreign spending disturbances when these involve single, uncoordinated actions with no impact on world interest rates. If the foreign disturbance, however, is simultaneously engaged by major foreign countries, it will be transmitted domestically through its effects on world interest rates. In contrast to fixed exchange rates, then, under floating rates the international transmission of fiscal policy disturbances requires the disturbances to influence world interest rates. Without such an effect, fiscal policy in one country has no effect on the income of either the country imposing it or on any other foreign country.

8–7 MONETARY POLICY UNDER FLEXIBLE EXCHANGE RATES

The central role of money market equilibrium in determining output in an economy under flexible exchange rates and perfect capital mobility suggests that monetary policy in such an environment may be particularly effective. This indeed is what is shown in this section.

Monetary policy under flexible exchange rates is well defined as an increase in the economy's stock of money. In contrast to the case under fixed exchange rates, changes in central bank credit under floating rates are directly associated with changes in the money stock. Suppose, then, that the Central Bank expands the money supply through, say, an open market purchase of bonds. What are the effects of this disturbance? The analysis is carried out in Figure 8–6, where the initial equilibrium is assumed to occur at points E and E', with corresponding levels of income and the exchange rate equal to Y_o and e_o, respectively.

An expansion of the money supply affects directly the money market by generating an excess supply of money at the original income and exchange rate. This puts downward pressure on the domestic interest rate. Geometrically, the increased money supply would shift the LM curve to the right: At any given level of income, the domestic interest rate would have to be lower to

---

[9] For further details, see R. Dornbusch and P. Krugman, "Flexible Exchange Rates in the Short Run," *Brookings Papers on Economic Activity* (1976), particularly pp. 543–548.

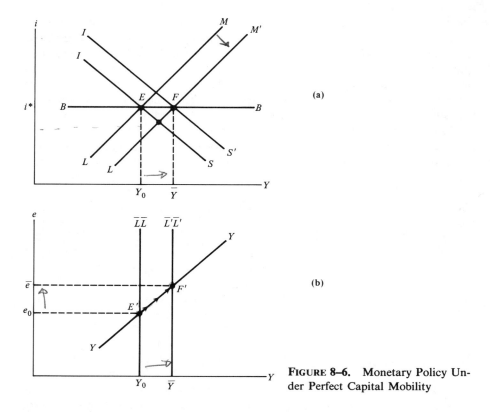

FIGURE 8–6. Monetary Policy Under Perfect Capital Mobility

absorb the excess supply of money. This shift of the *LM* curve is represented in Figure 8–6(a) by its move toward *L'M'*. As a result of the downward pressure on domestic interest rates, however, the economy would face massive capital outflows as investors switch toward the relatively more attractive foreign assets. At a fixed exchange rate, these incipient outflows would result in an excess supply of domestic currency in foreign exchange markets as domestic investors dispose of their domestic money to acquire foreign assets. The result is a reduction in the price of domestic currency or, in other words, an increase in the exchange rate.

This depreciation, in turn, shifts aggregate demand toward domestic goods by increasing the relative price of foreign goods in terms of domestic goods. This is shown in Figure 8–6(a) by the rightward shift of the *IS* curve. The outcome is a rise of domestic income, which induces the demand for money to increase and partially releases the downward pressure on the domestic interest rate. As long as there is any pressure on the domestic interest rate to remain below the world rate, capital outflows will induce domestic currency to depreciate and income to increase. Therefore, the *IS* curve will stop shifting rightward only when it reaches point *F*, where it intersects the *L'M'* curve at the world interest rate, i^*. Point F is thus the new equilibrium of the economy. The result of the monetary expansion is to increase output by inducing a domestic currency depreciation. Notice that the expansionary effects of an increased money stock on the economy are spearheaded here, not by reductions in interest rates, such as in a closed economy—interest rates here remain fixed at i^*—but by an expansion of the domestic exports sector, connected to a domestic currency depreciation.

In conclusion, monetary policy under flexible exchange rates can constitute a highly effective policy in influencing output over the short run, particularly if the environment is one of perfect capital mobility. Within this context, *expansionary* monetary policy can be an instrumental policy in leading recovery in an economy suffering from severe recession. Contractionary monetary policy, on the other hand, would have the opposite effects: It would effectively worsen the recession. The next section provides an example of the operation of these principles in the unfortunate case of monetary authorities that used contractionary monetary policy in the midst of a bitter recession.

8–8 Employment, the Exchange Rate, and Capital Flows: the Canadian Float of 1950 to 1962

In early October 1950, the Canadian government decided to abandon the system of fixed exchange rates it had adopted since World War II and to allow the value of the Canadian dollar to float in response to market forces, with only limited official intervention from the Central Bank. The Canadian experience with floating exchange rates during the period of 1950 to 1962 offers a splendid opportunity to apply our analysis so far, especially as regards the behavior of the economy over the crisis period of 1958 to 1961. By that time, there was a relatively high degree of capital mobility between the United States and Canada, making the situation one close to perfect capital mobility.[10] In addition, even though the economy had operated at relatively high employment over the period of 1950 to 1956, the years 1957 and 1958 saw a sharp rise in the unemployment rate, moving from close to 3% in 1956 to above 6% in 1958 and hovering above that level in the remaining years of the float.

Furthermore, in spite of the fact that the early years under flexible exchange rates saw a sharply appreciating exchange rate accompanied by a rise in Canadian prices, the period of 1956 to 1961 was one of remarkable price stability. It thus seems apparent that the environment of the Canadian economy during the last year of the float closely approximated the one described by our earlier discussion in this chapter. In terms of economic policy, then, the clearly reces-

[10] Our discussion will assume that perfect capital mobility did exist, although in reality the case was one of relatively high, but not perfect, capital mobility. See Richard E. Caves and Grant L. Reuber, *Canadian Economic Policy and the Impact of International Capital Flows* (Toronto, Canada: University of Toronto Press, 1969).

sionary state of the economy in the period 1958 to 1960 would have required expansionary monetary action on the part of the monetary authorities. In contrast, the Bank of Canada, following the fixation of its governor with a "sound" tight monetary policy, adopted contractionary monetary measures. The contractionary period lasted from 1958 to 1961, as exemplified in its extreme form by the $200-million decrease in the money supply that occurred between July and December 1959.

In terms of the *IS–LM* framework, tight monetary policy causes the *LM* curve to shift leftward, placing upward pressure on domestic interest rates and inducing capital to flow into the economy. This leads to an appreciation of the currency, which has a recessionary impact on the demand for domestic goods and shifts the *IS* curve to the left. Both the *LM* and *IS* shifts imply that the economy's recession will deepen; the tight monetary policy has negative output and employment effects by causing the domestic export and import-competing industries to suffer a loss of competitiveness in international markets.

As a matter of fact, the picture that emerged during the 1958 to 1960 period in Canada followed closely what would be expected from this analysis. Upward pressures on Canadian interest rates were associated with substantial capital inflows, an appreciation of the Canadian dollar—from a value of around 1.02 U.S. dollars in early 1958 to 1.06 U.S. dollars by the autumn of 1959, a peak value for the 1950s—and a deteriorated current account balance. All these factors probably contributed to the fact that, in spite of an expansionary fiscal policy and increased demand for Canadian exports connected to the behavior of GNP in the United States over this period, the unemployment rate remained high during 1958 and increased during 1959 and 1960. All these events, of course, did not go unnoticed by the public and the economics profession at large in Canada, generating bitter controversy. In 1960, a group of Canadian academic economists called for the dismissal of the governor of the Bank of Canada and, finally, in July 1961, the minister of finance discharged the governor in a move surrounded by political confrontation.[11]

The system of floating exchange rates received a substantial amount of negative publicity from these events, especially since the Canadian experiment with floating exchange rates was very much unparalleled in the world. It should thus be emphasized that the 1958 to 1960 events by themselves do not show any inherent difficulties of a floating exchange rate regime in correcting recessionary pressures in the economy. More accurately, the events illustrate the immense disruptions that inappropriate policies may cause—something that unfortunately can happen under both fixed and flexible exchange rates.

[11] For more details, see Paul Wonnacott, *The Canadian Dollar, 1948–1962* (Toronto Canada: University of Toronto Press, 1965), and H. Scott Gordon, *The Economists Versus the Bank of Canada* (Toronto, Canada: The Ryerson Press, 1961). The appreciation of the Canadian dollar seems insignificant when compared to exchange rate fluctuations since 1973, but it was not perceived to be so within the context of the remarkable stability of the Canadian dollar—U.S. dollar exchange rate at the time.

8–9   THE ECONOMY'S EQUILIBRIUM AND IMPERFECT CAPITAL MOBILITY

This section considers the behavior of an economy in which the degree of capital mobility is less than perfect. In this type of setting, collectively referred to as *imperfect capital mobility*, a rise in the domestic interest rate attracts capital inflows but to a lesser degree than under perfect capital mobility. This means that domestic investors cannot borrow or lend all the amount they wish at the world interest rate. A rise in the domestic interest rate above the world rate is required to attract a higher amount of foreign funds and a lower rate to lead domestic residents to lend abroad. The resulting positive relationship between the capital account and domestic interest rates is algebraically depicted by

$$K(i) = \beta i \tag{6}$$

where β is a positive parameter representing the sensitivity of the capital account to changes in the domestic interest rate relative to the world interest rate.[12]

The analytics of imperfect capital mobility entail some basic modification of our earlier framework. In particular, the domestic interest rate will no longer be constrained to equal the world interest rate, as in the case of perfect capital mobility discussed in previous sections. A rise in domestic interest rates above world rates generates capital flows but not in such massive amounts as to require a return to the world rate. Similarly, a reduction of domestic interest rates below world rates will result in capital outflows but not to such an extent as to require the domestic interest rate to return to the world level. Intercountry interest rate differentials arise naturally under imperfect capital mobility.

Consider first the goods market equilibrium condition, $Y = A + T$. As noted before, under freely flexible exchange rates the balance of payments will equal zero. As a result, the capital and trade balance accounts must offset each other in adding up to zero. Symbolically, $T = -K$. Substituting this relationship into the goods market equilibrium condition yields

$$Y = A + T \quad \rightarrow -K$$
$$= A(Y, i, G) - K(i)$$
$$= \bar{A} + aY - bi - \beta i \tag{7}$$

---

[12] As a matter of fact, the capital account expression in equation (6) should be a function of the interest rate differential between domestic and foreign bonds, $i - i^*$. For simplicity, we are assuming that i^* is fixed and have thus deleted it from (6). In addition, the reader should observe that capital flows arising from portfolio adjustments tend to disappear over time, as desired changes in portfolio composition are realized. The capital flows represented by equation (6) should then be interpreted as occurring over the short run.

Where use has been made of the linearized absorption expression,

$$A = \bar{A} + aY - bi$$

equation (7) can be simplified to yield

$$Y = \bar{a}[\bar{A} - (b + \beta) i] \tag{8}$$

where the parameter $\bar{a} = 1/(1 - a) = 1/s$ is the reciprocal of the marginal propensity to save. Equation (8) shows the combinations of domestic interest rates and income that keep the goods market and the balance of payments in equilibrium, given some fixed parameters. It represents a modified IS curve that takes into account the adjustments of the exchange rate required to move the balance of payments to equal zero. Algebraically, equation (8) represents not only the goods market equilibrium condition, $Y = A + T$, but also the balanced payments condition, $T = -K$. The diagrammatic representation of this joint goods market–balance of payments equilibrium condition is given by the downward-sloping XX curve in Figure 8–7.

To visualize the negative relationship between domestic interest rates and output depicted by the curve XX, suppose that there is a reduction in the domestic interest rate below the world rate. This stimulates investment and raises the equilibrium level of output. In addition, the reduction in domestic interest rates causes capital outflows and a consequent deterioration of the capital account. Domestic currency then depreciates, improving the trade balance and equilibrating the balance of payments. This exchange rate depreciation also tends to raise domestic output. The implication is that changes in domestic interest rates will be associated with opposite changes in output to maintain goods market and balance of payments equilibrium. Observe that the slope of the XX curve will depend, among other factors, on the degree of capital mobility

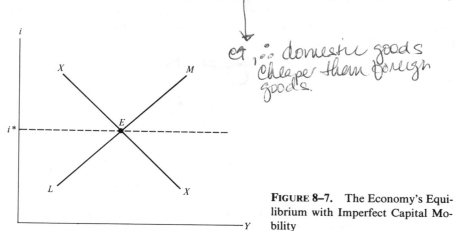

e.g. :: domestic goods cheaper than foreign goods.

FIGURE 8–7. The Economy's Equilibrium with Imperfect Capital Mobility

facing the economy. The higher the degree of capital mobility (the larger the β coefficient), the flatter the XX curve will be. This occurs because the higher the degree of capital mobility, the larger the capital outflows that result from a given reduction in domestic interest rates, thus requiring a larger depreciation of the exchange rate to maintain balanced payments. Hence, the increase in output is larger. If the degree of capital mobility is low, however, the XX curve will be steeper; in this case, a reduction of domestic interest rates will induce minor capital outflows with negligible effects on the exchange rate and output.

The money market equilibrium condition remains as represented by equation (5), shown diagrammatically by the LM curve in Figure 8–7. Goods, money, and balance of payments equilibrium then occur at point E in Figure 8–7, where the XX and LM curves intersect. This is the combination of domestic output and interest rates consistent with the general equilibrium of goods, assets, and foreign exchange markets. For expository reasons, the equilibrium domestic interest rate in Figure 8–7 is shown to coincide with the world interest rate. In general, however, under imperfect capital mobility, domestic and world interest rates do not have to equalize.

Figure 8–8 illustrates the effects of an expansionary monetary policy. Such an expansion shifts the LM curve to the right. In contrast to the case of perfect capital mobility, the economy's equilibrium after the shock occurs with higher output as well as with a lower interest rate, as shown by point F in Figure 8–8. Under perfect capital mobility, the new equilibrium would occur at point H, with the domestic interest rate perfectly aligned with the world interest rate, and with an increment in output larger than the one obtained in the case of imperfect capital mobility. The reason for the dampened effect of monetary policy under imperfect capital mobility lies in the fact that the currency depreciation required to eliminate balance of payments disequilibria under imperfect

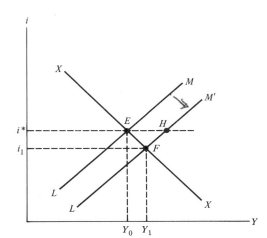

FIGURE 8–8.   Effects of Monetary Policy Under Imperfect Capital Mobility

capital mobility will be smaller than in the case of perfect capital mobility, increasing output by a smaller proportion.

The effects of fiscal policy within the present framework are left to the reader as an exercise. Suffice it to say that, under imperfect capital mobility, fiscal policy is effective in raising output but tends to increase domestic interest rates and to appreciate domestic currency, crowding out to some extent both the investment and export sectors of the economy. Still, the net expansionary effect of fiscal policy under imperfect capital mobility is positive and becomes stronger as the degree of capital mobility declines.

Capital inflows, ∴
appreciate dollar
∴ *et ; switch to*
foreign goods

8-10   ANATOMY OF EXCHANGE RATE ADJUSTMENT AND CAPITAL MOBILITY

This chapter has provided an introduction to the economics of flexible exchange rates, emphasizing the determination of output and the exchange rate and the role played by the degree of capital mobility. To round out the discussion, it may be useful to summarize the basic principles that have been—and have not been—established regarding the determination and behavior of the exchange rate.

In an economy under flexible exchange rates, the exchange rate adjusts to ensure the elimination of balance of payments disequilibria. Symbolically, exchange rate changes would ultimately guarantee that

$$B = T(q, Y) + K(i)$$

$$= \overline{T}\left(\frac{eP^*}{P}\right) - mY + \beta i = 0 \tag{1a}$$

derived by substituting equation (6) into equation (1). It is clear from (1a) that the nature of balance of payments disequilibrium depends on the degree of capital mobility in the economy. In the absence of capital mobility, for instance, balance of payments surpluses or deficits will coincide with trade balance surpluses or deficits. This case can be symbolized in equation (1a) by setting $\beta = 0$, in which case $K(i) = \beta i = 0$, and the balance of payments accounts become a record of international transactions in goods.

The case in which the exchange rate adjusts to ensure the immediate elimination of trade balance disequilibria, with capital flows having no role in exchange rate adjustment, formed the basis for much of the economic analysis of flexible exchange rates up to the late fifties. Although indeed a special case by present standards, the development of economic analysis along those lines should not be surprising. The world of high capital market integration and rapid portfolio adjustment one observes in most industrial countries today is a relatively recent event. At least up to the fifties, most short-term capital flows between countries were heavily regulated by governments and, as a result, turned out to be relatively minor as compared with the value of international trade in goods and services. The theory of flexible exchange rates developed over these years thus understandably emphasized the role of the trade balance in exchange rate adjustment. The focus of concern was on whether (and how) exchange rate changes would guarantee the elimination of balance of trade disequilibria. The fear was that a flexible exchange rate regime could be inherently unstable if Marshall–Lerner elasticities conditions[13] were not satisfied and exchange rate depreciation did not improve, but rather worsen, the trade balance. The finding that, in some instances, the values of the elasticities of demand for exports and imports were lower than those required for the fulfillment of the Marshall–Lerner condition, led to the influential school of "elasticity pessimism" after World War II, which was frequently associated with "flexibility pessimism," the belief that a flexible exchange rate regime was inherently unstable and, thus, infeasible.[14]

During the 1960s and 1970s, however, increasing financial liberalization, the growth of multinational business and international portfolio finance, and to topple it all, the massive recycling of OPEC oil revenues and the expansion of Eurocurrency banking, all combined to generate an environment of high mobility of financial capital. As a result, international economic analysis—spearheaded by the contributions of Mundell and Fleming discussed earlier in this chapter—proceeded to incorporate the assumption of perfect capital mobility into its breadth. The consequence was a shift in emphasis toward the effects of short-term capital movements on the adjustment of the exchange rate. In terms of equation (5a), the capital mobility parameter (measuring the responsiveness of capital flows to changes in the domestic interest rate relative to foreign rates) was assumed to be very large. In this situation, slight pressures on domestic interest rates generate massive (actual or threatened) capital flows that induce the exchange rate to adjust. The capital account became a predominant factor in explaining exchange rate changes.

It is within this historical and analytical context that our discussion should be viewed. The important conclusion to be remembered is that the behavior of the exchange rate is closely linked to the degree of capital mobility in the economy. The higher that degree, the more one should look at capital account behavior and to short-run capital movements to explain exchange rate adjustments, particularly within the short-run milieu the present chapter has been concerned with.[15]

[13] For a detailed discussion of the so-called Marshall–Lerner condition within the context of fixed exchange rates, see Chapter 5.

[14] See Egon Sohmen, *Flexible Exchange Rates* (Chicago: University of Chicago Press, 1969), Chapter 1, for a discussion of the issues surrounding this controversy at the time.

[15] Over the long run, the trade balance may have an important role in exchange rate adjustment, even if there is perfect capital mobility. This basic point, associated with the wealth-adjustment role of trade imbalances, will be discussed in detail in Chapter 15 within the context of the assets market approach to exchange rate determination.

The inescapable reality of high capital mobility facing most industrial economies today has generated fears and pessimism regarding the operation of a
flexible exchange rate regime different from those of the flexibility pessimists
of earlier vintage. The boogey-man of flexible exchange rates in the 1970s and
1980s regards destabilizing short-term speculative capital movements and widespread exchange rate turbulence, rather than trade elasticities. These fears have
not been at all abated by the performance of the current regime of floating
exchange rates under which most industrial economies operate. Considerable
exchange rate variability has indeed characterized the international scene since
the breakdown of the Bretton Woods system in the early seventies. What factors
are associated with this variability? Our analysis in this chapter provides a
basis for an eventual answer to this question. The main problem still remains
that, to focus on the introductory analytics of flexible exchange rates with a
minimum of complexity, we have had to make the assumption of a tranquil
economic environment in which individuals do not anticipate disturbances to
the economy. The continuous changes surfacing not only in exchange rate behavior, but also in economic policies and a range of other economic and noneconomic
variables, should make us aware of the need to take into account that flux
and its influence on the behavior of agents in the economy. It is the purpose
of the next chapter to begin this effort by analyzing exchange rate dynamics
and the role of expectations formation—and particularly of exchange rate expectations—on the operation of economies under flexible exchange rates.

8–11 SUMMARY

1. Under a system of floating exchange rates, there is no "balance of payments
problem." Exchange rate changes guarantee the disappearance of the balance
of payments deficits or surpluses that would arise under a regime of fixed exchange rates.

2. With the Central Bank not intervening in foreign exchange markets to
fix exchange rates, the money supply is in principle under the control of the
monetary authorities. This nominal monetary autonomy is obtained, however,
at the loss of direct control over the exchange rate.

3. Under perfect capital mobility, fiscal policy measures adopted by a single,
small country are not effective in changing output. An increase in government
expenditures, for example, would raise aggregate demand for domestic goods
and place upward pressures on domestic interest rates. This induces financial
capital to flow into the economy, leading to an appreciation of the exchange
rate and switching demand away from domestic goods. This aggregate demand
reduction would offset the direct expansionary effects of increased government
spending.

4. Monetary policy is highly effective in influencing output under perfect
capital mobility. An increase in the money supply, for example, places downward

pressure on domestic interest rates, inducing incipient capital outflows and depreciating domestic currency. This depreciation switches demand toward domestic goods and is expansionary. At the same time, since the domestic currency depreciation amounts to a foreign currency appreciation, higher domestic money growth might adversely affect output abroad. In this sense, monetary policy can be a beggar-thy-neighbor policy under flexible exchange rates.

5. The relative effectiveness of government policies under flexible exchange rates is opposite to that obtained in our analysis of fixed exchange rates. With fixed exchange rates, monetary policy under perfect capital mobility is ineffective in influencing domestic output, while fiscal policy is highly effective. The basic reason for the divergence in results lies in the differences of the money supply process under the two regimes.

6. Under imperfect capital mobility, both monetary and fiscal policies will influence domestic output, with the effectiveness of fiscal policy oppositely related to the degree of capital mobility in the economy.

7. Flexible exchange rates insulate the economy from isolated foreign autonomous spending disturbances but not from a general coordinated disturbance by a group of foreign countries. A coordinated fiscal policy initiative by a group of major countries abroad affects world interest rates and is transmitted worldwide. Within this context, expansionary fiscal policy simultaneously engaged in by major countries will stimulate income growth in the world economy.

PROBLEMS

1. Flexivia is a small industrial country operating under flexible exchange rates and perfect capital mobility (with a world interest rate equal to $i^* = 0.10$). The economy's money supply is 400 billion flexivians (Flexivia's currency, which freely floats in value against other currencies), and the price of Flexivia's products is $P = 1$ flexivian. Assume that the real money demand in Flexivia, L^D, has been estimated to be

$$L^D = 0.25\,Y - 4000i$$

which is measured in terms of Flexivian goods. Find the equilibrium level of output of the economy. What would be the impact on output of an increase in the money supply of 50 billion flexivians? Provide numerical answers.

2. The government of a country facing perfect capital mobility imposes a tariff on imports, distributing the tariff revenues back to the public in the form of tax rebates. Find the effects of the tariff on the level of income and the exchange rate using *IS–LM* curves. Explain the economics behind your results.

3. This problem is concerned with the determination of the exchange rate under perfect capital mobility.

(a) Using the aggregate demand equation (4a) solve for the exchange rate as a function of the level of income; that is, find a formula for the curve *YY* under perfect capital mobility. [HINT: Assume $\bar{T} = T_0 + \phi q$ with $q = (eP^*/P)$ and ϕ a positive parameter.]

(b) Determine the equilibrium exchange rate as a function of exogenous variables. [HINT: Substitute the equilibrium level of income in equation (5b) into the exchange rate expression obtained in part (a).]

(c) What is the effect on the equilibrium level of income and the exchange rate of an exogenous increase in the world interest rate, i^*? Illustrate graphically and algebraically which factors determine the magnitude of the impact of this disturbance on output and the exchange rate.

4. Consider the imperfect capital mobility setup described in the text.

(a) Solve for the level of income as a function of exogenous variables. [HINT: Use the expression for the interest rate obtained from equation (5) to substitute into (8).]

(b) Determine and illustrate by means of *IS–LM* curves the impact of a change in government spending on income. What happens to this impact when the degree of capital mobility increases? When it decreases? Why?

5. Consider a country with no capital mobility and flexible exchange rates.

(a) Solve for the exchange rate that clears the trade balance as a function of the level of income, *Y*. (Assume that the trade balance is of the form $T = T_0 + \phi q - my$, where ϕ is a positive constant and $q = (eP^*/P)$.)

(b) Solve for the level of income as a function of all exogenous variables. [HINT: Substitute the value of *e* determined in part (a) into the aggregate demand equation (4).] In what way does the multiplier differ from all other open economy multipliers computed in the previous three chapters?

(c) Suppose that there is an exogenous increase in the demand for the country's exports. Determine algebraically the effect on the exchange rate and on income. Illustrate geometrically by means of the open economy *IS–LM* diagram. [HINT: Assume that T_0 increases.]

(d) Suppose that government spending on domestic goods increases. Determine algebraically and illustrate graphically the effects on output and the exchange rate.

(e) Compare the results from parts (c) and (d) above. Why do they differ qualitatively even if both disturbances initially increase desired spending on domestic goods? What principle does this exercise illustrate regarding the impact of internal and external real disturbances under flexible exchange rates and capital immobility?

6. Short-run import and export elasticities are smaller than their longer-run counterparts. This gives rise to the possibility that a domestic currency depreciation may deteriorate the trade balance in the short run. What does this suggest regarding the short-run effectiveness of monetary policy on output and employment under flexible exchange rates?

7. Within a framework of perfect capital mobility and flexible exchange rates, what effects does a domestic monetary expansion have on the country's foreign trade partners? Could the effects of the domestic policy, if any, be undone by foreign authorities? How?

CHAPTER 9

Expectations, Exchange Rate Dynamics, and Economic Policy

This chapter is concerned with the role of exchange rate expectations in the behavior of open economies under flexible exchange rates. In a world of fluctuating exchange rates, future currency values become essential in determining the costs of and benefits from international investments. The capital account records these movements and it is, consequently, highly sensitive to expected exchange rate changes. Rumors that a currency will depreciate in the future may ignite massive capital outflows, drastically worsening the capital account. Under a regime of fixed exchange rates, such changes would tend to generate balance of payments deficits, massive losses of international reserves and—if persistent—may eventually lead to a balance of payments crisis. Under flexible exchange rates, no balance of payments crises arise, since exchange rate adjustments ensure the elimination of any balance of payments deficits. Still, exchange rate expectations can feed massive short-term capital flows and generate a relentless speculative attack on a currency's value. This chapter examines the role of exchange rate expectations in determining the level and turbulence of exchange rates, interest rate differentials among countries, and the response of the economy to macroeconomic disturbances.

9–1 EXCHANGE RATE EXPECTATIONS AND INTEREST RATES

The introduction of exchange rate expectations forces into the open the fact that interest rates do not always equalize internationally; that is, it demonstrates that the equality $i = i^*$ is not an ever-holding condition even under perfect capital mobility. If domestic currency is expected to depreciate, the domestic interest rate, i, rises above the world interest rate i^*, to compensate investors in domestic assets for the anticipated capital gains they forego by holding assets denominated in domestic rather than foreign currency. An expected appreciation of the domestic currency, on the other hand, will be associated with lower domestic interest rates in order to offset the anticipated capital gains from holding domestic currency instead of foreign currency. In a nutshell, equalization of net expected rates of return among comparable domestic and foreign assets implies[1]

$$i = i^* + x \tag{1}$$

where i is the domestic interest rate, i^* is the world interest rate, and x is the expected rate of depreciation of the domestic currency, all over a given time period. If, for instance, the world interest rate is equal to 5% and the expected rate of depreciation of domestic currency is equal to 2%, then equation (1) implies a domestic interest rate equal to 7%. The higher domestic interest rate compared with the world rate serves to compensate holders of domestic assets for the expected (currency) loss arising from the expected depreciation.

What factors give rise to expected exchange rate changes? To answer this question, one must know how individuals form expectations about the future value of economic variables. The following discussion assumes so-called *rational expectations* formation. This means that individuals gather and process all relevant information about economic variables and their interrelationships, and use these facts efficiently in predicting the effects of economic disturbances.[2] For instance, when the government formulates a reversal in economic policy, investors will immediately calculate the effects of such policies on the exchange rate, interest rates, and other relevant economic variables. On this account, they form rational expectations about the future behavior of the economy. Clearly, to determine how economic disturbances, such as policy changes, affect the economy over time requires knowledge of how the economy reacts to such disturbances. In forming expectations, then, investors need to understand such dynamic adjustments. Rational expectations formation appears to be an adequate description of situations in which individuals actively search for and process information regarding the future of the economy. Such is certainly the case of corporate treasurers, bankers, and international investors regarding exchange rates. The day-to-day life of the foreign exchange trader or the international financial manager is a constant search for leads and hints that may provide relevant information about the future levels of various exchange rates. Failure to gather and interpret adequately important news on the matter can be disastrous.

---

[1] Equation (1) is referred to as the uncovered interest parity condition. As examined in Chapter 2, in order for (1) to hold risk considerations must be set aside. The discussion in this chapter will disregard the influence of risk and exchange risk premia on exchange rate determination, a topic to be discussed in Chapter 15.

[2] A thorough discussion of rational expectations will be presented in Chapter 12.

9–2   ECONOMIC DYNAMICS AND THE GOODS AND ASSETS MARKETS

There are two basic concepts required to understand the dynamic adjustment of an economy in the present context. First, organized assets markets tend to clear relatively fast as compared to goods markets, and, second, a sudden excess demand for (or supply of) domestic goods tends to give rise to increases (or reductions) in domestic output but only gradually over time. The first concept regards the relative speed at which assets and goods markets clear. Transactions in assets markets, such as portfolio adjustments between money and bonds and between domestic and foreign assets, can be made rapidly and with ease by means of modern communications and through the close integration of national capital markets with the world financial community. Interest rates and exchange rates also tend to adjust rapidly, changing with a disheartening speed in response to new information on economic and noneconomic events. These rapid adjustments insure that assets market equilibrium, in terms of the equality of demand and supply of given stocks of assets, is attained very rapidly, often instantaneously. It is thus appropriate to assume that the money market continuously, or almost continuously, clears. The same cannot generally be said, however, of goods markets.

Output response to changes in economic variables occurs sluggishly over time. For instance, available evidence tends to suggest that export growth in response to a currency depreciation takes place slowly because of lags in the recognition of relative price changes, production lags, and so forth. As Dornbusch and Krugman conclude:

> "the evidence [provided] makes clear that a sustained depreciation will improve a country's competitive position and that such an improvement will raise exports over time. In the short-run, though, elasticities [of exports with respect to relative price changes] are small; for example, the U.S. elasticity for the first four quarters is only 0.33, or less than 20 percent of the full adjustment elasticity.[3]

The response of investment spending to changes in interest rates also shows a lagged behavior: Investment adjusts at a slow pace, and the timing here is in terms of months or years, not hours, days, or weeks.[4] Furthermore, goods market prices in the short run tend to adjust sluggishly, especially in the downward direction and under recessionary conditions, a situation that has been stylized

---

[3] Rudiger Dornbusch and Paul Krugman, "Flexible Exchange Rates in the Short-Run," *Brookings Papers on Economic Activity,* 564 (1976). The full-adjustment elasticity is equal to 1.72, over a period of 3 years. See also the evidence provided by M. C. Deppler and D. M. Ripley, "The World Trade Model: Merchandise Trade," *IMF Staff Papers* (March 1978), and our discussion of the *J*-curve effect in Chapter 5.

[4] See Dale W. Jorgenson, "Econometric Studies of Investment Behavior: A Survey," *Journal of Economic Literature* (December 1971); and Peter B. Clark, "Investment in the 70's: Theory, Performance, and Prediction," *Brookings Papers on Economic Activity* (1979).

in the present Keynesian analysis by assuming that goods market prices are indeed fixed.

The conclusion is that assets markets can be assumed to clear continuously while goods markets may be presumed to adjust slowly and to possibly remain out of equilibrium, in disequilibrium, for extended periods of time. The output response to an excess demand or supply of domestic goods thus extends over a period of time, resulting in a sluggish movement of the economy toward equilibrium. The details of these adjustments will be examined in the following sections.

9–3 EXCHANGE RATE EXPECTATIONS, DISEQUILIBRIUM DYNAMICS, AND ADJUSTMENT TOWARD FULL EQUILIBRIUM

This section focuses on the dynamic adjustment toward equilibrium in economies under flexible exchange rates, perfect capital mobility, and sluggish output response. The equilibrium established by the Mundell–Fleming framework developed in Chapter 8 will be labeled *full equilibrium* to convey the notion that it is the equilibrium toward which the economy moves *after all the disequilibrium adjustments* arising from sluggish output response are over.[5] When full equilibrium is attained, no further changes in economic variables are expected to occur, in the absence of disturbances. In particular, the exchange rate would not be expected to change, implying that $x = 0$ and suggesting that domestic and world interest rates will equalize, that is, $i = i^*$.

Figure 9–1, which corresponds to Figure 8–2(b) in Chapter 8, depicts the full equilibrium of the economy at point E. The upward-sloping YY curve represents the positive connection existing between the exchange rate and domestic output in maintaining goods market equilibrium. An increase in the exchange rate, e, by increasing the relative price of foreign goods, raises the demand for domestic goods and requires an increase in domestic output, Y, in order to clear the goods market. The $\bar{L}\bar{L}$ curve, on the other hand, represents the equality of money demand and supply at full equilibrium. The reason for the perfectly vertical nature of the $\bar{L}\bar{L}$ curve is visualized from the money market condition at full equilibrium (at $i = i^*$),

e depreciates.

$$\frac{M^s}{P} = L^D(i^*, Y) \tag{2}$$

---

[5] Our concept of full equilibrium is referred to as long-run Mundell-Fleming equilibrium by Rudiger Dornbusch in his paper, "Exchange Rate Expectations and Monetary Policy," *Journal of International Economics* (August 1976). We prefer to use the terminology of full equilibrium in order to associate long-run adjustments strictly with price adjustments. The Mundell–Fleming framework assumes that prices are fixed within the time context considered.

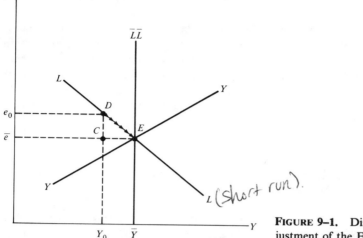

FIGURE 9–1. Disequilibrium Adjustment of the Economy

which is independent of the exchange rate, and, given the money supply, the price level, and the world interest rate, determines a level of output, $\overline{Y}$, consistent with assets market clearing at full equilibrium. Assuming no disturbances, point E is that point at which both goods and assets markets are in equilibrium. It thus represents the economy's full equilibrium and determines accordingly a *full equilibrium exchange rate* equal to $\bar{e}$ and a full equilibrium income equal to $\overline{Y}$. The exchange rate $\bar{e}$ prevails when goods market disequilibria in the economy are eliminated. Accordingly, it is the exchange rate toward which individuals believe the economy would move over time if left undisturbed. But how is full equilibrium attained? In other words, what is the dynamic behavior of the economy in disequilibrium?

Disequilibrium Dynamics in the Open Economy

Consider a reduction in income from its full equilibrium level, $\overline{Y}$, to Y_o. Algebraically, from the money market equilibrium condition

$$\frac{M^s}{P} = L^D(i, Y) \tag{3}$$

we see that a reduction in income, Y, decreases money demand relative to the given real money supply, M^s/P, which places downward pressure on domestic interest rates to maintain equilibrium in the money market. The downward pressure on domestic interest rates would then generate incipient capital outflows and depreciate domestic currency.

In short, a reduction of domestic income below its full-equilibrium level is associated with a jump in the exchange rate above its full-equilibrium value. This is represented by point D in Figure 9–1, where the reduction of income from $\overline{Y}$ to Y_0 is associated with an increase in the exchange rate from $\bar{e}$ to e_0. Note that as long as the current spot exchange rate is above the full equilibrium rate, $\bar{e}$, and as long as individuals recognize the structure of the economy is such that the exchange rate will eventually return to its full-equilibrium value, an expected appreciation of the domestic currency emerges at point D. Symbolically, at that point, $x < 0$. Even though the reduction in income from $\overline{Y}$ to Y_0 immediately *increases* the exchange rate up to e_0, individuals still expect the exchange rate to decline over time to its longer-term, full-equilibrium value $\bar{e}$. Just how much the currency is anticipated to appreciate is examined next.

As mentioned earlier, we assume that individuals form rational expectations of future variables in the economy. Accordingly, x represents the rational expectation of the rate of depreciation of domestic currency, which can be expressed as[6]

$$x = \theta \left(\frac{\bar{e} - e}{e} \right) \tag{4}$$

where e is the current spot exchange rate, $\bar{e}$ is the long-run equilibrium exchange rate, and θ is a positive number representing that fraction of the gap between the current and full-equilibrium exchange rate that is expected to be eliminated in any given time period. Note that as long as the full-equilibrium exchange rate is below the current exchange rate (if $\bar{e} < e$), there will be an expected appreciation of the domestic currency ($x < 0$), as agents in the economy realize that the exchange rate will eventually decline toward its full-equilibrium value. Such is the case at point D, where the expected rate of appreciation of the domestic currency over the next time period is given by

$$x = \theta \left(\frac{\bar{e} - e_0}{e_0} \right) < 0$$

If, on the other hand, the full-equilibrium exchange rate were to be above the current value of the exchange rate (if $\bar{e} > e$), individuals would then expect the exchange rate to rise—the currency to depreciate over time ($x > 0$). Only when the current spot exchange rate is equal to the full-equilibrium exchange rate (when $\bar{e} = e$) will there be no further expected exchange rate changes, in the absence of economic disturbances.

Substituting the expression for the expected rate of depreciation of domestic

[6] Even though equation (4) appears ad hoc, it can be rigorously shown to hold in the type of setting we are considering. The proof is not of particular interest here and can be obtained from R. Dornbusch. "Expectations and Exchange Rate Dynamics," *Journal of Political Economy* (December 1976).

currency in equation (4) into equation (3) yields the following expression for the *money market equilibrium condition in the short run*

$$\frac{M^S}{P} = L^D(i, \; Y)$$
$$= L^D(i^* + x, \; Y)$$
$$= L^D \left[i^* + \theta \left(\frac{\bar{e} - e}{e} \right), \; Y \right] \tag{3a}$$

Equation (3a) shows a connection between domestic income and the exchange rate, given the level of the money supply, the domestic price level, the world interest rate, and the equilibrium exchange rate. Equation (3a), therefore, provides the combinations of domestic income and the exchange rate that keep the money market in short-run equilibrium. This is the algebraic counterpart of the curve LL in Figure 9–1. The LL curve is downward sloping, indicating the fact that equation (3a) represents a *negative* relationship between domestic income and the exchange rate. Note that point D lies along LL, since it is a point of short-run assets market equilibrium, with equation (3a) at this point equal to

$$\frac{M^s}{P} = L \left[i^* + \theta \left(\frac{\bar{e} - e_o}{e_o} \right), \; Y_o \right]$$

The reduction in income from $\bar{Y}$ to Y_o is associated with an increase in the exchange rate from $\bar{e}$ to e_o in maintaining short-run money market equilibrium.

Points along the LL curve represent points of short-run assets market equilibrium, but not generally of goods market equilibrium. Point D is clearly not a goods market equilibrium point, since, although it satisfies *assets* market equilibrium, it is off the YY curve; accordingly, it is not one of the combinations of income and the exchange rate that maintains goods market equilibrium. At point D there is an *excess demand* for domestic goods, since the increased exchange rate shifts demand toward domestic goods by increasing the price of foreign goods relative to domestic goods. This excess demand generates an increase in output, but only after the domestic exports sector has had enough time to expand its production level. Over time, the economy would move away from point D (which represents only a *short-run* equilibrium point in the asset markets) and toward the longer-run equilibrium at point E. This adjustment from the goods market disequilibrium existing at point D to full equilibrium at point E always occurs with the assets market clearing, that is, with money demand equal to money supply, as given by equation (3a). Consequently, it is shown in Figure 9–1 by the pointed arrows lying along the short-run assets market equilibrium locus, LL.

This section has examined how the economy adjusts over time in response to a movement out of full equilibrium, that is, the disequilibrium dynamics of the economy. The next step is to determine which particular factors may disturb full equilibrium and exactly how the economy adjusts to such disturbances. The following section examines the impact of monetary shocks—in the form of an unanticipated increase in the domestic money supply—on the economy, and the resulting exchange rate dynamics.

9–4   UNANTICIPATED SHOCKS AND EXCHANGE RATE OVERSHOOTING

One of the most remarkable features of the world experience with flexible exchange rates during the seventies and eighties has been the relatively large and abrupt exchange rate movements suffered by the currencies of major industrial countries. These exchange rate fluctuations have perplexed many of the proponents of flexible exchange rates, which expected a more tranquil—and less turbulent—exchange rate behavior. What factors can explain the volatility of exchange rates over the recent past? It is the purpose of the following sections to present a first view of the analytics of exchange rate dynamics over the short run. In particular, an attempt is made to provide an explanation for the observed association between exogenous economic disturbances—such as monetary shocks—and rapid and drastic movements in the exchange rate. This section begins by analyzing the effects of an unanticipated monetary shock, in the form of an unexpected increase in the money supply.

Figure 9–2 shows the initial full equilibrium of the economy at point E, with a level of output equal to Y_0 and an exchange rate of e_0. Point E is the

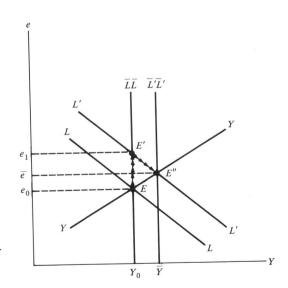

FIGURE 9–2.   Unanticipated Monetary Shocks and Exchange Rate Dynamics

→ shift $\bar{L}\bar{L}$ to the right

↑ re

point at which the initial goods and money market loci, YY and $\bar{L}\bar{L}$, intersect. Suppose, however, that there is a sudden, unanticipated increase in the domestic money supply, say because of a Central Bank purchase of bonds in the open market. First of all, the disturbance generates changes in the full-equilibrium values of income and the exchange rate. This is so because the increased money supply places downward pressures on domestic interest rates, depreciating domestic currency and shifting demand toward domestic goods, which requires domestic output to increase. The full response of the economy to the money supply expansion is represented by the shift of the full-equilibrium money market locus from $\bar{L}\bar{L}$ to $\bar{L}'\bar{L}'$, implying a switch of the full equilibrium point from E to E''. The new equilibrium levels of output and the exchange rate would then be $\bar{Y}$ and $\bar{e}$, respectively.

Even though point E'' represents the new equilibrium toward which the economy will move over time, this full equilibrium cannot be expected to be reached immediately, because of the sluggishness with which domestic output will expand. Accordingly, the short-run behavior of the economy has to be specified. Over the time period immediately after the unanticipated monetary expansion, output may be expected to remain more or less at its initial level, Y_0. The monetary disturbance, however, generates immediate exchange rate and domestic interest rate changes that combine to eliminate the excess supply of money existing at the initial point E. In diagrammatic terms, the immediate adjustment of the economy would be from point E to point E'. Point E' lies along the $L'L'$ curve, which is the short-run money market equilibrium locus, as derived in the previous section. The result of the money supply expansion would thus be an immediate increase in the exchange rate from e_0 to e_1. This represents the exchange rate change required to clear the money market in response to the monetary disturbance, given the initial level of output, Y_0. Note that the exchange rate depreciation will induce a switch of demand toward domestic goods and, at the initial level of output, will result in an excess demand for domestic goods. Point E' represents a point of short-run assets market equilibrium but of goods market *disequilibrium*. This is reflected in the fact that point E' lies along the $L'L'$ curve, the short-run money market equilibrium locus, but is above the YY curve, the goods market equilibrium curve. Of course, over time, the domestic export sector will expand in response to the domestic currency depreciation and the output of domestic goods will gradually adjust to match the increased demand. The economy will accordingly move along the $L'L'$ curve toward point E''. This full equilibrium point differs from the short-run equilibrium at point E' in that it represents the equilibrium of the economy in *both* the goods and assets markets. Graphically, point E'' lies along both the $L'L'$ and YY curves. Since the goods market adjusts toward equilibrium sluggishly, full equilibrium at E'' is attained only after an extended period, with the economy immediately moving to point E' instead.

The behavior of the exchange rate in response to the money supply expansion is illustrated in Figure 9–3. At time t_0, the exchange rate is equal to e_0; in

← excess demand for domestic goods

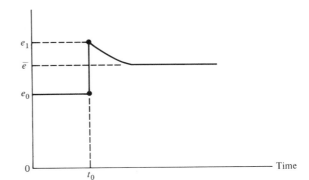

FIGURE 9–3. Overshooting of the Exchange Rate in Response to an Unanticipated Monetary Expansion

response to the monetary shock, it adjusts immediately to e_1 and then gradually moves to its new, long-run equilibrium value, $\bar{e}$. This pattern, in which the short-run response of the exchange rate to a given disturbance exceeds the change that would occur if the economy's full equilibrium were attained immediately is referred to as *overshooting* of the exchange rate.[7] As depicted in Figure 9–3, it represents an exchange rate adjustment that is rather choppy and abrupt, first increasing above its full-equilibrium level and then gradually decreasing toward that level. It is thus suggestive of the exchange rate movements that have been frequently observed during the recent experience of industrial countries with floating exchange rates.

As long as economic agents recognize the overshooting response of the exchange rate to an unanticipated money supply disturbance, they will anticipate domestic currency appreciation. In other words, even though domestic currency immediately depreciates in value in response to the money supply expansion, individuals expect it to appreciate over time. This is apparent in Figure 9–3. An individual watching the behavior of the exchange rate immediately after the disturbance at time t_0 would see a drastic exchange rate increase. At the same time, what goes up comes down and, if the exchange rate follows the behavior depicted in Figure 9–3, the investor knows that the exchange rate will be declining in the future toward its lower, full-equilibrium value, $\bar{e}$. That is, over the adjustment period toward full equilibrium, there is an expected currency appreciation, $x < 0$.

Given the apparent consistency of the present framework with the recent experience of industrial countries with floating rates, one is led to inquire about which specific factors contribute to generate the exchange rate overshooting. First, note that if the economy were to move to its long-run equilibrium immediately; that is, if domestic output could be increased without any time lags, the

[7] The concept of exchange rate overshooting was formally developed by Rudiger Dornbusch in his article, "Expectations and Exchange Rate Dynamics," *Journal of Political Economy* (December 1976). For further extensions of Dornbusch's framework, see J. S. Bhandari, *Exchange Rate Determination and Adjustment* (New York: Praeger Publishers, Inc., 1982).

behavior of the exchange rate would exhibit no overshooting. The increased money supply would immediately induce capital outflows, depreciate domestic currency, and increase output. In terms of Figure 9–2, the economy would move immediately from point E to E''. This is the same type of adjustment implied by the Mundell–Fleming framework discussed in Chapter 8. The unanticipated monetary shock generates immediate adjustments, leaving no room for exchange rate overshooting or any other type of sophisticated exchange rate dynamics. In the present framework, overshooting in the exchange rate is closely related to the assumption that assets markets clear fast relative to goods markets, as embodied by the fixity of output over the immediate short run versus the full flexibility of the exchange rate and domestic interest rates. With output fixed, the unanticipated money supply increase requires a reduction of the domestic interest rate to maintain money market equilibrium. Given world interest rates, domestic interest rates can decline only if an expected domestic currency appreciation develops. From the uncovered interest parity condition, $i = i^* + x$, domestic interest rates decline if x becomes negative. This implies that, to maintain money market equilibrium over the short run, the exchange rate will have to move above its full-equilibrium level, giving rise to an expected domestic currency appreciation, a reduction in domestic interest rates, and an increase in money demand that matches the money supply expansion. This is the nature of the overshooting of the exchange rate in the present framework: It is required in order for assets market equilibrium (money market equilibrium) to be sustained in the short run.

The role of exchange rate expectations on macroeconomic adjustment and exchange rate behavior is evident from our discussion so far. But, as we examined in Chapters 1 and 2, exchange rate expectations are also connected to the behavior of the forward foreign exchange market. It is the purpose of the following sections to analyze the dynamic behavior of exchange rate expectations and the forward exchange rate.

9–5   THE FORWARD FOREIGN EXCHANGE MARKET UNDER FLOATING EXCHANGE RATES

Forward exchange rates, and hence the forward premium, are closely linked to the expectations that participants in the foreign exchange market hold about future exchange rates. Presently, it will be assumed that the forward premium is equal to the expected rate of depreciation of the domestic currency.[8] In this case, the forward premium becomes an accurate indicator of expected currency depreciation over the life of the forward contract considered. Algebraically,

---

[8] A divergence of the forward premium from the expected rate of domestic currency depreciation can arise within the context of an uncertain world. Essential in explaining these deviations is the presence of risk aversion on the part of investors and of a risk premium in the determination of the forward premium. These issues were examined in Chapter 1 and will reappear in Chapter 15.

the equality of the forward premium for a given maturity, f, with the expected rate of depreciation of the domestic currency for that maturity, x, is given by

$$f = x$$

A 30-day forward premium on the pound, for example, means that the pound is expected to increase in value relative to the dollar, or, in other words, there is an expected depreciation of the dollar. If, for instance, the 30-day forward premium on the pound is $f = 0.10$, this suggests that participants in the foreign exchange market expect the dollar to depreciate in value by 10% over the 1 month of the forward contract, that is, $x = f = 0.10$. By the same token, a forward discount on the pound (a negative value of f) would imply that there is an expected appreciation of the value of the dollar.

Merely knowing that the forward premium is equal to the expected rate of depreciation of domestic currency does not provide us with an answer to the question of how the forward premium is determined: We have yet to specify the factors affecting the expected rate of domestic currency depreciation. In Section 9–3, we discussed how expected exchange rate changes are determined, relating them to deviations of the full-equilibrium exchange rate, $\bar{e}$, from the current spot exchange rate, e. This expectation-formation relationship was stylized by equation (4), which shows how, when the full-equilibrium exchange rate exceeds (or is exceeded by) the spot exchange rate, an expected domestic currency depreciation (or appreciation) arises, a natural consequence of anticipating an eventual adjustment of the economy to full equilibrium.

Equating the expression for the expected rate of domestic currency depreciation in (4) with the forward premium yields

$$f = x = \theta \left(\frac{\bar{e} - e}{e} \right) \tag{5}$$

where θ is a positive parameter that shows by how much participants in the foreign exchange market expect the exchange rate to increase (or decrease) over the term of the forward contract. For instance, if the full-equilibrium exchange rate is $\bar{e} = 3.00$, the current spot exchange rate is $e = 2.00$, and individuals expect the difference between the full-equilibrium and the current exchange rate to diminish by 20% during next month (implying $\theta = 0.20$), then the (1-month) forward premium is equal to

$$f = 0.20 \left(\frac{3.00 - 2.00}{2.00} \right)$$
$$= (0.20)(0.5) = 0.10$$

The pound will thus be at a 10% forward premium, meaning that the 1-month forward exchange rate exceeds the spot exchange rate by 10%. Since individuals expect a 10% increase of the exchange rate during the 1-month life of the forward contract, arbitrage will ensure the equality of this expected rate of domestic currency depreciation with the forward premium, as described in Chapter 1.

The relationship between the forward premium and the current and full-equilibrium exchange rates indicated by equation (5) can be easily transformed to provide a clearer picture of the factors influencing the forward exchange rate in the present framework. Using the definition of the forward premium and combining it with equation (5), we obtain

$$f = \frac{F - e}{e} = \theta \left(\frac{\bar{e} - e}{e} \right) \tag{5a}$$

with F equal to the forward exchange rate. Since the exchange rate in the denominator of each side of equation (5a) cancels out, a simple modification of (5a) provides us with the following expression for the forward exchange rate:

$$F = \theta \bar{e} + (1 - \theta)e \tag{6}$$

Equation (6) expresses the forward rate as a weighted average of the full-equilibrium exchange rate, $\bar{e}$, and the current spot exchange rate, e, with the weights equal to the parameter θ and the related fraction $(1 - \theta)$. For instance, if $\theta = 0.20$, the current exchange rate between the dollar and the pound is $e = \$2.00/£$, and the full-equilibrium exchange rate is $\bar{e} = \$3.00/£$, then the 1-month forward exchange rate will equal $F = \$2.20/£$, obtained from

$$F = (0.2)\,(\$3.00/£) + (0.8)\,(\$2.00/£)$$
$$= \$2.20/£$$

Notice that the greater the extent individuals expect the exchange rate to adjust toward its long-run level during the term of the forward contract (the closer θ is to 1), the closer F will be to the full equilibrium exchange rate. As a matter of fact, if individuals expect the exchange rate to adjust fully toward $\bar{e}$ during the 30 days covered by the forward contract, then $\theta = 1$ and, from equation (6), $F = \bar{e}$, (the forward exchange rate equals the long-run exchange rate). More generally, since the presence of rigidities prevents the immediate attainment of full equilibrium, it can be assumed that individuals expect only part of the exchange rate adjustment to occur over the term of the forward contract. Actually, if the economy adjusts very slowly, individuals may expect no perceptible change toward equilibrium to occur within the next 30 days. In this case, the parameter θ is close to zero and, from (6), the forward exchange rate will approximate the current spot exchange rate, e. That is, since individuals expect no significant change in the economy over the next 30 days, they will expect the exchange rate to remain unchanged. This expectation is reflected in the forward exchange rate. Again, this is an extreme case and one can assume that, in general, θ will be larger than zero. The forward exchange rate is, therefore, related to both the current exchange rate and the full-equilibrium exchange rate, with the relative importance of each of these in influencing the forward rate determined by how fast individuals expect the economy to adjust over time. The faster the expected adjustment toward full equilibrium, the larger the weight carried by the full-equilibrium exchange rate in determining the forward rate. The slower the adjustment toward full equilibrium, the larger the influence of the current exchange rate on the forward rate.

The interaction between the forward, spot, and full-equilibrium exchange rates is best illustrated by examining how they are affected by economic disturbances. This is discussed in Section 9–6.

9–6 THE DYNAMICS OF THE FORWARD EXCHANGE RATE

Figure 9–4 shows the behavior of the 90-day forward exchange rate between the dollar and the pound sterling from 1978 to 1983 and compares it with the path of the contemporaneous dollar–pound spot exchange rate during that period. Two striking observations can be discerned from the data. First, the forward exchange rate appears to be subject to substantial volatility during the period and, second, spot and forward exchange rates generally tend to move together, in the same direction. What explains these two patterns of behavior of forward rates during the recent experience with floating exchange rates? This section investigates forward exchange rate dynamics, examining the role of unanticipated disturbances on those dynamics. We illustrate by taking the case of an unexpected money supply expansion.

Let us return to the analytics of an unanticipated money supply disturbance, as described previously through the use of Figure 9–2. Prior to the monetary expansion, the economy rests at point E and agents expect the exchange rate to remain at its prevailing level, e_o. The spot and full-equilibrium exchange rates coincide and the forward exchange rate is consequently equal to both. Symbolically, at point E,

$$F_o = e_o = \bar{e}_o$$

with F_o representing the forward exchange rate prevailing before the unanticipated monetary disturbance and $\bar{e}_o$ the initial full-equilibrium exchange rate. Now, an unanticipated money supply expansion leads to a sudden upward movement of the spot exchange rate, as represented by the switch of equilibrium in the economy from point E to point E'. As explained previously, the spot exchange rate overshoots its full-equilibrium level, $\bar{e}$, moving upward to e_1.

What happens to the forward exchange rate? The increased money supply

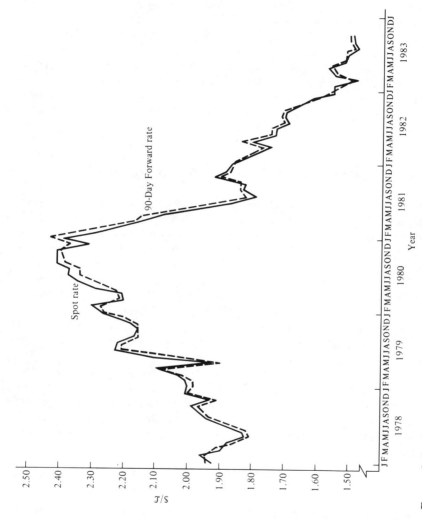

FIGURE 9–4. 90-Day Forward Exchange Rate and Contemporaneous Spot Rate for the Pound Sterling, 1978 to 1983. (Monthly data, from *The Wall Street Journal*, Dow Jones & Company, Inc., end-of month issues.)

raises the exchange rate individuals in the economy expect to prevail in future periods, compared with the initial exchange rate, e_o. Since the expected exchange rate is reflected in the forward exchange rate, the latter increases in response to the monetary disturbance. From equation (6), immediately after the monetary shock (with the economy at point E'), the forward exchange rate rises to

$$F_1 = \theta \bar{e} + (1 - \theta) e_1 \tag{6a'}$$

Since both $\bar{e}$ and e_1 are higher than the initial exchange rate, the forward exchange rate will jump above its initial value ($F_1 > F_o$). Note, however, that the forward rate does not increase by the same amount as the long-run equilibrium exchange rate. Instead, following the spot exchange rate, the forward exchange rate overshoots its full-equilibrium value. The full-equilibrium forward exchange rate is determined by the full equilibrium at point E''. At that point, the economy's output would have fully expanded to match the increased demand for domestic goods arising from the monetary expansion. When the economy reaches point E'', the spot exchange rate will equal the full-equilibrium exchange rate and, consequently, both will equal the forward exchange rate. Full equilibrium, however, is attained only after an extended period of time. Meanwhile, the forward exchange rate will remain *above* its full-equilibrium value.

The reason for the overshooting of the forward exchange rate lies in the overshooting of the spot exchange rate. Since the current spot exchange rate overshoots its full-equilibrium value, and given that the economy attains full equilibrium only after an extended period of time—presumably longer than the, say, 1-month term of the forward contracts—individuals will expect the exchange rate to remain above its full equilibrium for some time to come. With the forward exchange rate reflecting the foreign exchange market's expected exchange rate at the time of expiration of the forward contract (say, 1 month in the future), its value immediately after the monetary disturbance will then exceed the full-equilibrium exchange rate.

In a framework where asset markets clear relatively fast compared with goods markets, the immediate response of the forward exchange rate to an unanticipated monetary disturbance is to increase suddenly and drastically, overshooting its longer-run value. This choppy and abrupt forward exchange rate adjustment is consistent with the behavior of forward rates during the recent floating exchange rate regime. In addition, we have found the movement of the forward exchange rate follows closely that of the spot exchange rate, rapidly depreciating at first and then appreciating toward its long-run equilibrium value. The joint movements of spot and forward rates are again suggestive of the recent behavior of the exchange rates of major currencies, as typified by Figure 9–4. In conclusion, it is apparent that the present framework explains well the most striking regularities observed during the recent experience with floating exchange rates. This feature has made it a very popular framework of analysis of economic events in an environment of flexible exchange rates.

9–7 ECONOMIC POLICY, INTEREST RATES, AND EXCHANGE RATE ADJUSTMENT: THE U.S. DOLLAR IN THE EARLY EIGHTIES

This section provides an overview of the main issues we have discussed within a real-world context. The case taken to illustrate them is that of the U.S. dollar in the eighties. Figure 9–5 shows the behavior of the *value* of the dollar (the reciprocal of the U.S. dollar effective exchange rate) in the early eighties. The trend is clearly one of general appreciation of the dollar. As a matter of fact, during 1982 the value of the dollar against other major currencies exceeded its highest levels since the beginning of the floating exchange rate regime in 1973. What are the reasons for this general appreciation of the dollar? This section emphasizes the role of U.S. economic policies and, in particular, the monetary policies followed by the Federal Reserve after 1979—under the aegis of the Volcker chairmanship—even though other explanations can be postulated and will be discussed in Chapter 15.

One of the most visible policies followed by the United States during the early eighties involved a general tightening of monetary policy in the hopes

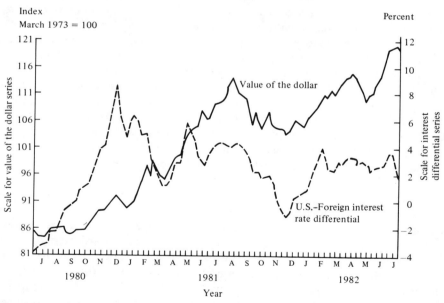

FIGURE 9–5. Foreign Exchange Value of the Dollar and the U.S.-Foreign Interest Rate Differential. The value of the dollar is a trade-weighted average of the foreign currency value of the dollar. The interest rate differential is the U.S. three-month commercial paper rate minus a trade-weighted average of corresponding foreign rates. (From D. S. Batten and J. E. Kamphaefner, "The Strong U.S. Dollar: A Dilemma for Foreign Monetary Authorities," *Review of the Federal Reserve Bank of St. Louis,* August/September, 1982, p. 4).

of, and with a commitment to, reducing inflation. The results of the monetary tightening follow closely those we predicted earlier would arise from an unanticipated contractionary monetary policy. The effects were a sharp rise in U.S. interest rates, growing capital inflows, and an immediate appreciation of the dollar. The economy also gradually moved into a sharp recession, with unemployment climbing from an average of 5.9% in 1978 and 1979 to 7.4% in 1980, 8.3% in 1981, and 10.7% in 1982. Given the gradual adjustment of output to the monetary policy disturbance, and following our analysis of exchange rate dynamics in Section 8–4, it may be postulated that the sharp appreciation of the dollar over this period represented a case of exchange rate overshooting.[9] That is, it could be argued that the monetary contraction induced a downward move of the dollar exchange rate below its long-run equilibrium value. With the economy adjusting sluggishly toward its new equilibrium, the exchange rate remained below its longer-term value over the short run.

One question is raised, however, when using the exchange rate overshooting hypothesis as an explanation for the behavior of the dollar in the early eighties. With the adjustment of the economy to the monetary disturbance effectively taking the form of growing recession and receding inflation, why didn't the dollar depreciate to any significant extent but continued to appreciate? One clue can be found in the behavior of the differential between the U.S. and foreign short-run interest rates ($i - i^*$, in terms of our terminology), shown by Figure 9–5. A generally positive interest rate differential over the time period under consideration is clearly discerned. Now, if we associate this interest rate differential with the expected rate of depreciation of the dollar,[10] its positive tendency would imply a sustained expected depreciation of the dollar. But, as Figure 9–5 shows, the dollar did not depreciate over this time period; it actually tended to appreciate, leaving a discrepancy between the expected depreciation of the dollar and its actual behavior. In other words, it seems plausible that an unanticipated appreciation of the dollar recurred over and over during the early eighties. Most likely, this behavior might be connected to an unexpectedly staunch commitment to monetary tightness on the part of the Federal Reserve. An unanticipated monetary contraction tends to maintain U.S. interest rates high and gives rise to appreciation of the dollar. The recurrence of these monetary shocks over time and the stubborn expectation that the monetary tightness would be reversed sustained the appreciation of the dollar.

There are alternative views on the failure of the dollar to depreciate to any significant extent over the 1980 to 1983 period. One regards the possibility

[9] Such an association has been made by C. Fred Bergsten, R. Dornbusch, and others; see "From Rambouillet to Versailles, a Symposium," *Princeton Essays in International Finance*, No. 149 (Princeton, N.J.: Princeton University, December 1982).

[10] For the pitfalls of such an association, see Chapter 1. For the present purposes, the general, directional, coincidence of the two variables is sufficient to establish the argument; it does not rely on a strict equality of the differential with the expected depreciation.

of speculative effects embodied in so-called exchange rate bubbles, to be discussed in the next section.

9–8 THE DOLLAR OVERVALUATION AND EXCHANGE RATE BUBBLES

A situation in which a given economic variable progressively or cumulatively deviates from the path consistent with its fundamental, long-run value is called a *bubble*. In the foreign exchange market, a bubble may cause the currency to remain *overvalued* or *undervalued,* that is, to remain above or below its fundamental long-run value for extended periods of time. What gives rise to exchange rate bubbles? The most frequent explanation is provided by the existence of extraneous beliefs or misperceptions about the future exchange rate that gradually become prevalent or progressively catch up with investors in the foreign exchange market. For example, unfounded rumors may generate a belief that the dollar will soon change drastically in value. As these extraneous beliefs catch up with investors in the foreign exchange market, in much the same way that fads and fashions spread, they will strongly influence exchange rate expectations and, as a result, the behavior of the exchange rate. Note that, in the same way as fashions change and misperceptions are found to be incorrect, eventually the bubble will recede or burst and the exchange rate will return to its fundamental value—but it might take an extended period of time for the speculative effects to be eliminated.

A second explanation of bubbles does not rely on individuals holding false beliefs or making consistently incorrect future evaluations. Instead, it assumes that individuals form rational expectations about the future, basing their anticipations on all the information currently available about the fundamental determinants of future exchange rates and about the structure of the foreign exchange market. The bubble is explained in the following terms. Once a specific economic disturbance, such as a contractionary monetary policy, generates changes in the exchange rate in a given direction, say, a currency appreciation, and if individuals are not certain about the exact magnitude of the movement in that direction, they will expect, with some probability, that the movement will continue. As long as the probability is high, and with no other forces or disturbances occurring, the result will be a continuing appreciation. As new investors enter the market with an expectation that the original exchange rate movement will continue, the movement will become self-sustained, originating a persistent exchange rate deviation from its long-run, fundamental value. For example, if increasing numbers of investors and speculators get into the bandwagon of an expected dollar appreciation, the consequent sustained capital inflows will maintain the exchange rate appreciation. Note that the bubble here is a rational bubble: Participants in the market are not relying on any extraneous beliefs in predicting that the original disturbance will give rise to an exchange rate movement. They just do not know exactly by how much the movement will be and, consequently, assign a probability that the bubble will continue and also a probability that the bubble will collapse or crash toward the long-run fundamental exchange rate. This type of behavior may then be applied to the recent appreciation of the dollar.[11]

The presence of bubbles underlies the fact that the exchange rate does not always necessarily adjust toward its long-run value but often deviates and remains persistently away from it. The implications of this result are best summarized by Rudiger Dornbusch:[12]

> Why should we be concerned about such deviations? The obvious reason is that given the path of policy variables an exchange rate bubble will have real effects on competitiveness, inflation and employment. It represents a macro-shock that, if possible, we would want to offset. The possibility of rational bubbles is important to recognize because it represents a fundamental departure from the view that markets do things right, all the time.

We should conclude this section by stressing that, for expositional reasons, the description and explanation of exchange rate movements in this chapter, and their application to the case of the dollar in the early eighties, have not considered the effects of changes in prices. It is the purpose of the next chapter to initiate the discussion of the problem of inflation in open economies.

9–9 ANTICIPATED ECONOMIC DISTURBANCES AND EXCHANGE RATE DYNAMICS

This section is concerned with the effects of anticipated economic disturbances on the economy's equilibrium. In particular, we study the channels by which a monetary expansion anticipated to occur in the future impinges on the economy even before it actually takes place.

Suppose that the Federal Reserve Board announces today that it will increase the money supply by a certain amount 2 weeks from today. What would be

---

[11] Although it is apparent that this phenomenon explains the persistent appreciation of the dollar, it is not exactly obvious how it explains the also persistent interest rate differential in favor of U.S. assets. Note, however, that the fact that a rational speculator will always accurately anticipate the possibility of a crash means that he or she knows it is playing a risky business and will require a compensation for that risk taking. A positive interest rate differential in favor of the United States during the early 1980s may then just represent this compensation for risk bearing. From Chapter 1, it may be recalled that the domestic interest rate is influenced by the world interest rate, the expected rate of depreciation of the domestic currency, and an exchange risk premium. The bubble and the associated risk of its bursting at any moment give rise to a positive exchange risk premium on the dollar, thus possibly explaining the interest differential in favor of the United States.

[12] R. Dornbusch, "Equilibrium and Disequilibrium Exchange Rates," National Bureau of Economic Research, Working Paper No. 983 (September 1982) p. 16.

↓i, capital outflow, currency depreciation, et

the response of the exchange rate to such an announcement? With the money supply scheduled to increase in 2 weeks, individuals will immediately anticipate an exchange rate increase. The forthcoming domestic currency depreciation tends to reduce expected returns on domestic assets, at any given level of the domestic interest rate, generating capital outflows that would immediately depreciate the spot exchange rate. In other words, even though the money supply has not yet actually increased, the expectation of the money supply hike immediately increases the exchange rate. Of course, this currency depreciation would tend to raise the demand for domestic goods and would have an expansionary effect on domestic output. Some of the increased output may then be forthcoming even before the monetary expansion actually takes place. One can thus conclude that anticipated monetary policy will usually generate immediate changes in the economy; economic adjustment to the disturbance starts even before the expected or announced change actually takes place.[13]

The economic effects generated by anticipated disturbances are not necessarily positive and may, in effect, be very distressing. Suppose, for instance, that there is a sudden expectation among foreign exchange market participants that the dollar will appreciate vis-à-vis the pound in the future. This will immediately lead to speculative capital flows into the United States, reducing the spot exchange rate between the dollar and the sterling. This dollar appreciation will then result in a loss of competitiveness of U.S. goods in international markets, a switch in demand away from U.S. goods, and a reduction in domestic output and employment.

Reiterating, we note that exchange rate expectations have, in general, important short-run macroeconomic consequences, some of which are not necessarily a blessing. The next section provides a particular example of this proposition.

9–10 EXCHANGE RATE EXPECTATIONS AND THE ECONOMY: THE DISCOVERY OF NORTH SEA OIL IN THE UNITED KINGDOM

This section examines the short-run effects of an anticipated real disturbance in the economy in the form of a discovery of oil deposits. This was the case involved in the U.K. North Sea oil deposit discoveries of the seventies. The realization in 1976 that massive exploitation of these reserves would be undertaken in the near future fueled anticipations that the net oil exports of the United Kingdom would increase in the years ahead, leading in turn to immediate effects on the value of the pound and on the economy in general.

The effects of an oil discovery on exchange rates and the economy overall depend on how the future increases in oil exports are anticipated to affect the

---

[13] For an advanced and more detailed exposition of the effects of anticipated monetary policy on the economy, see C. Wilson, "Anticipated Shocks and Exchange Rate Dynamics," *Journal of Political Economy* (June 1979).

economy at that time. In Section 8–5 of Chapter 8, we examined the possible effects of an exogenous increase in the net exports of an economy and applied it to the specific case of U.K. North Sea oil exports. As shown, the increased oil exports could be expected to lead to an appreciation of the pound sterling. But an expected currency appreciation would lead to sudden capital inflows into the United Kingdom and would cause an immediate appreciation of the pound. Even though the extraction and exportation of the discovered oil would not occur until after an extended period of time, the anticipation of such exports immediately appreciates domestic currency, with consequent deleterious effects on output and employment. Therefore, even though, superficially, one would think the oil discoveries would have a positive effect on the economy by sparking hopes of economic expansion in the future, they actually might become counter-productive in the short run, having instead a recessionary impact. The behavior of the U.K. economy during the period in which it became evident massive exploitation of North Sea oil discoveries would occur is consistent with these conclusions, being associated with a sharp appreciation of the pound and a growing economic recession.

9–1   SUMMARY

1. The introduction of exchange rate expectations into the analysis implies that interest rates do not always equalize internationally and that the equalization of net expected rates of return among domestic and foreign assets only means that domestic interest rates have to equal foreign interest rates plus the expected rate of depreciation of domestic currency.

2. Dynamic adjustments in the open economy are shaped by two basic conditions: (a) Organized asset markets clear relatively fast compared with the goods markets. (b) Any sudden excess demand for (or supply of) domestic goods tends to give rise to increases (or reductions) of domestic output but only gradually over time. The implication is that the economy can remain out of equilibrium, that is, in disequilibrium, over extended periods of time as long as the goods market adjusts sluggishly.

3. The full equilibrium of the economy is that equilibrium toward which the economy moves after all the disequilibrium adjustments connected to sluggish output response are over. It corresponds to the equilibrium established within the Mundell–Fleming framework studied in Chapter 8. In the absence of disturbances, full equilibrium does not entail anticipated changes in exchange rates and other economic variables.

4. The recent experience of most industrial countries with flexible exchange rates has been characterized by frequent and drastic exchange rate movements. These movements can be explained within the framework developed in this chapter. For instance, an unanticipated shock to the economy in the form of an unanticipated money supply increase will be associated with an overshooting of the exchange rate, meaning that the short-run response of the exchange rate exceeds the change that would occur if the economy's full equilibrium were attained immediately. This choppy short-run adjustment is caused by the fact that, with output and income fixed in the short run, a money supply increase must be associated with a reduction of domestic interest rates so as to maintain money market equilibrium. Given world interest rates, however, the only means by which domestic interest rates can decline under perfect capital mobility is if an expected appreciation of the domestic currency arises. Such an expectation implies that the exchange rate must immediately rise above its anticipated longer-run value.

5. The case of the sharp appreciation of the U.S. dollar in the early eighties serves well to illustrate some of the basic issues relating to exchange rate dynamics. One explanation for the appreciation relies on the contractionary monetary policies of the Federal Reserve, which might have generated a short-run over-shooting in the value of the dollar above its longer-term value. The persistence of the dollar appreciation may then be explained by the unanticipatedly staunch pursuit of monetary tightness on the part of the Federal Reserve.

6. Since the forward exchange rate is a weighted average of the full-equilibrium exchange rate and the current spot exchange rate, its movements tend to follow those of spot rates. The turbulence of the forward exchange rate under the current regime of floating exchange rates can then be associated with the turbulence of the contemporaneous spot exchange rate.

7. Anticipated economic changes have immediate repercussions in the economy even before they are actually realized. The prospect of a money supply expansion, for instance, will generate an expected domestic currency depreciation, which reduces the expected return on domestic assets at a given interest rate. This induces capital outflows, depreciating the currency immediately, even before the monetary expansion is actually engaged in by the monetary authorities.

PROBLEMS

1. You are examining a country whose economic relations are confined to trading with the United States exclusively. The country's currency is the peso, which freely floats against the U.S. dollar. Suppose that the country's real money demand has been estimated to be

$$L = 0.20\,Y - 3000\,i$$

where Y is income and i is the interest rate prevailing on 3-month CDs in the economy's financial markets. The country faces perfect capital mobility and is initially in equilibrium, with its interest rate equal to the fixed 10% U.S. interest rate ($i^* = 0.10$). The money supply is equal to 300 billion pesos and the price of the country's products is, on average, $P = 1$ peso. Suppose that the country's Central Bank unexpectedly reduces the money supply by 20 billion pesos. Assuming that the country's income is fixed over the short run and that investors form rational expectations, would the monetary contraction increase or decrease the peso's exchange rate against the dollar. What would be the change in the country's interest rate? Would investors anticipate further changes in the value of the peso? If the answer is positive, determine the numerical value of the anticipated rate of change of the currency over the next 3 months.

2. In the text we saw how the exchange rate overshoots its long-run equilibrium value in response to an unanticipated money supply expansion. This result was derived, however, under the assumption of perfect capital mobility. Assume instead that the economy does not trade in assets with the rest of the world so that it faces zero capital mobility. Will overshooting still occur? What happens as the economy's degree of capital mobility increases?

3. Describe diagrammatically the effects of an unanticipated fiscal policy expansion within the dynamic framework developed in the text. Would there be any effects of this disturbance on output? Explain how and why your results differ from, or are similar to, those derived in Chapter 8.

4. Assume that the expectations investors form about the exchange rate are described by

$$x = 0.50 \left(\frac{\bar{e} - e}{e} \right)$$

with all symbols as described in the text. The U.S. 3-month interest rate is 15%, while the comparable U.K. interest rate is 10%. If the current exchange rate between the dollar and the pound is $2.00 per pound, what would be the implied full-equilibrium exchange rate, on the assumption that there are no anticipated economic disturbances in the foreseeable future? What would be the 90-day dollar–pound forward exchange rate? Assuming perfect foresight, what would be the exchange rate 3 months from now and what would be the numerical value of the forward rate at that time? (You can assume that uncovered interest parity holds in this question.)

5. In his book *Debt Shock, The Full Story of the World Debt Crisis* (New York: Doubleday & Company, Inc., 1984) p. 39, D. Delamaide states: "Japan may indeed have the world's most efficient steel plants, but its commercial success is due partly at least to keeping its currency, the yen, undervalued." What does this mean? Do you agree with it? How do you go about measuring whether the yen is undervalued against the dollar?

6. Country X is a West European country operating under flexible exchange rates. During the administration of the current laissez-faire party, the government has followed strong austerity measures and restraint in monetary matters. All this seems to be over, however, as the returns from the country's

current election shows the antiausterity, pro state intervention party winning by a landslide. What effects would the election have on the country's exchange rates? Even though, due to traditional practice, the day of the inauguration of the new administration is 5 months in the future, would there be any significant current impact on the economy?

Inflation, Unemployment, and Economic Policy in the Open Economy

PART **IV**

CHAPTER 10

Production, Prices, and Unemployment in the Open Economy

Throughout Part III, we examined how domestic output, interest rates, the money supply, and other important economic variables are determined in open economies. The determination of domestic prices, however, has not been on our agenda up to this point. It is the purpose of Chapters 10 and 11 to study how the domestic price level is determined in an open economy and to inquire about how various economic policies affect it. Our everyday experience reminds us, in an often uncomfortable way, that the general price level is indeed rising over time. Figure 10–1 illustrates this tendency by plotting the behavior of the U.S. consumer price index (CPI). The generally rising trend of the price level can be detected, as well as the significant price deflation during the 1930s. What causes prices to change, and how is output altered by such changes? In order to answer these questions, we have to modify in a significant way the analytical framework developed in earlier chapters.

We have so far carried out the analysis on the basis of the simple Keynesian assumptions that the prices of domestic goods are fixed and that the firms producing those goods supply all the output that is demanded of them at the given prices. In general, however, prices do change over time (i.e., inflation and deflation occur), and firms often find that they cannot supply all the output demanded of them without running into full-employment and capacity constraints. To take account of these situations, one has to modify the simple Keynesian framework, in which changes in output are brought about solely by changes in aggregate demand without any consequent effects on prices. The following chapters show how both prices and output are determined by the interaction of aggregate demand for and aggregate supply of domestic goods in much the same way as the price and output of a given commodity are determined by its demand and supply. The present chapter focuses on output and price determination under fixed exchange rates, while Chapter 11 extends the discussion to flexible exchange rate regimes.

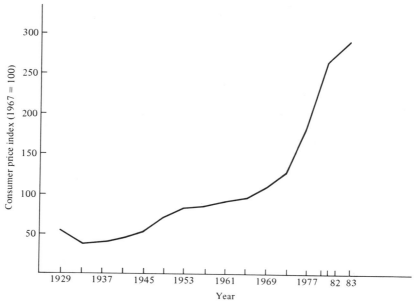

FIGURE 10–1.   Prices in the United States in the Twentieth Century. (From Economic Report of the President, Washington, D.C., February 1984.)

We shall first derive in detail the concepts of aggregate demand and aggregate supply within the context of an open economy and then show how their interaction determines the dynamic behavior of output and prices. This will involve analyzing the short-run and long-run equilibria of the economy as well as the process of adjustment of prices and output over time. The effects of fiscal, monetary, and exchange rate policies are reexamined, including their short-range and long-range impacts. We start by considering an economy that faces no international capital movements and then move on to discuss capital mobility.

10–1   AGGREGATE DEMAND IN AN OPEN ECONOMY UNDER FIXED EXCHANGE RATES

The *aggregate demand* curve depicted in Figure 10–2(b) represents the economy's desired spending as a function of the price level. That is, it represents a relationship between the *aggregate quantity demanded* of domestic goods and the *price level* of domestic goods, at given levels of the domestic money supply, the exchange rate, and fiscal parameters such as the level of government spending and tax rates. It must be stressed that, in contrast to our analysis in previous chapters, in the present framework aggregate demand does not completely determine the level of output of domestic goods. The equilibrium level of output is

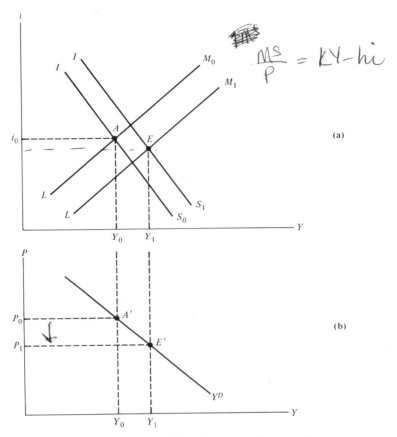

$$\frac{MS}{P} = kY - hi$$

FIGURE 10–2. Derivation of the Aggregate Demand Curve

established by the interaction of the aggregate demand and aggregate supply functions and not solely by aggregate demand. Aggregate demand just establishes a relationship specifying the quantity demanded of domestic goods at different prices. Which of these combinations of price and quantity demanded is actually chosen as the price and equilibrium output of the economy will depend on the aggregate supply function, which shows the relationship between price and quantity supplied of domestic goods. As discussed below, the equilibrium level of output and price of domestic goods will be determined by the equality of quantity demanded and quantity supplied of domestic goods, that is, by the point at which the aggregate demand and aggregate supply curves intersect in Figure 10–5. In this section we shall be concerned exclusively with deriving the aggregate demand curve; in later sections we derive aggregate supply and then join the two together to determine equilibrium prices and output in the economy.

In Chapter 6, we addressed the problem of determining the equilibrium level of aggregate demand in the economy on the assumption that the prices of domestic goods were fixed. We proceed now to examine how this equilibrium level of aggregate demand changes when the prices of domestic goods are varied. This will provide us with a relationship between the quantity demanded of domestic goods and their prices, which is what the aggregate demand function represents.

To summarize our earlier work on the determination of the equilibrium level of aggregate demand, let us restate our two basic equilibrium relationships. First, the money market equilibrium condition equates real money supply with real money demand. Algebraically,

$$\frac{M_o}{P_o} = kY - hi \qquad \text{LM curve} \tag{1}$$

where real money demand is positively related to income, Y, and negatively related to the interest rate, i; and the real money supply is M_o/P_o, with P_o the price of domestic goods and M_o the level of the money supply at any given moment. The level of the money supply can change over time if the Central Bank engages in monetary policy and/or depending on the balance of payments situation of the economy. For the purposes of deriving the aggregate demand function, however, the level of the money supply is assumed fixed, a context referred to as the short run. We will examine later how changes in the money supply affect aggregate demand.

The money market equilibrium condition determines the LM curve, that is, the combinations of the interest rate and income that keep the money market in equilibrium, given the money supply, M_o, and given the price level, P_o. A particular case is represented by the LM_o curve in Figure 10–2(a).

Desired spending on domestic goods, Y, can be represented by

$$Y = A + T = \bar{A} + \bar{T}\left(\frac{eP^*}{P_o}\right) + (a - m)Y - bi \tag{2}$$

Simplifying, we obtain

$$Y = \alpha\left[\bar{A} - bi + \bar{T}\left(\frac{eP^*}{P_o}\right)\right] \qquad \text{IS curve} \tag{2a}$$

where $\alpha = 1/(s + m)$ and all symbols remain as defined in earlier chapters. [For further details, see equations (20) and (21) in Chapter 6.] If the price of domestic goods is fixed at P_o, equation (2a) yields a negative relationship between desired spending and interest rates, given fixed fiscal policy parameters, the exchange rate, e, and the price of foreign goods in world markets, P^*. This is the basis of the IS curve represented in Figure 10–2(a) by IS_o.

The short-run level of aggregate demand (desired real spending) in the economy is Y_o, determined by the intersection of the IS_o and LM_o curves in Figure 10–2(a). This equilibrium point is established on the basis of a given level of the money supply, M_o (so that it represents a given short-run equilibrium), a fixed level of government spending, and a *given price of domestic goods, P_o.*

What happens when we vary the price of domestic goods, P? Suppose that we decrease P from P_o to P_1, where $P_1 < P_o$. What are the effects on aggregate demand? Two effects exist. First, there is a real money balances effect: As the price of domestic goods decreases, real money balances increase (from M_o/P_o to M_o/P_1). As a consequence, domestic interest rates decline and investment and aggregate demand increase. This effect is analogous to the effect of an exogenous increase in the *nominal* money supply (an increase in M), since both tend to increase *real* money balances. In geometric terms, a decrease in the price of domestic goods would be represented by a rightward shift of the LM curve: At any given level of the interest rate, aggregate real income and spending would have to increase to eliminate the excess supply of real balances arising from the decline in P. In terms of Figure 10–2(a), the LM curve would shift from LM_o to LM_1, tending to raise desired spending.

The second effect of a reduction in the price of domestic goods, P, is the *foreign trade effect:* A decrease in the price of domestic goods tends to switch demand out of foreign and toward domestic goods, raising aggregate desired spending on domestic goods.[1] This effect is analogous to that of a devaluation on aggregate demand in the sense that it operates by affecting the relative price of foreign goods in terms of domestic goods, $q \equiv eP^*/P$. A devaluation, at fixed prices of foreign and domestic goods, would tend to raise q. A decrease in the price of domestic goods, at a fixed exchange rate and fixed prices of foreign goods, would raise q, tending to improve the autonomous trade balance, $\bar{T}$. Geometrically, the positive effect of a reduction in P on the aggregate demand for domestic goods is reflected by an upward shift of the IS curve: At a given level of the interest rate, the decrease in P shifts demand toward domestic goods and tends to raise desired spending and real income. In Figure 10–3(a), this is depicted by the upward shift of the IS curve from IS_o to IS_1.

Both the real money balances and the foreign trade effects imply that decreases in the price of domestic goods generate increases in the short-run quantity demanded of domestic goods, suggesting that the aggregate demand function has a negative slope: As the price of domestic goods decreases, desired spending increases. This is shown in Figure 10–2. At the initial price level, P_o, the IS_o

---

[1] This assumes that the Marshall–Lerner condition is satisfied. Just as devaluation could worsen the trade balance and reduce the aggregate demand for domestic goods, a decrease in the price of domestic goods could also have the same consequences. The reader should remember the economic intuition of this result derived in Chapter 5.

and LM_0 curves determine the initial level of quantity demanded of domestic goods at Y_0. When the price level decreases to P_1, *ceteris paribus* (given the money supply and given fixed fiscal parameters), the *IS* curve shifts upward from IS_0 to IS_1 and the *LM* curve shifts rightward from LM_0 to LM_1. The new short-run quantity demanded would then be determined by the intersection of the IS_1 and LM_1 curves—point E—at an income level of Y_1, which is larger than Y_0. This relationship is illustrated in Figure 10–2(b) by the curve Y^D, which simply plots the pairs of price and aggregate quantity demanded of domestic goods corresponding to points A and E in Figure 10–2(a). The curve Y^D is the aggregate demand curve for domestic goods.

The aggregate demand curve is derived on the basis of a given level of the money supply, the exchange rate and fiscal policy parameters. Changes in any of these will tend to shift the aggregate demand curve. First, suppose that the domestic nominal money supply increases (with fiscal parameters still fixed). This increase can arise mainly from two sources: through an open market purchase of bonds by the Central Bank or through a balance of payments surplus of the economy. The rise in the nominal money supply, say from M_0 to M_1, increases real money balances, at a given level of the price of domestic goods. As domestic interest rates decline, investment and aggregate demand for domestic goods increase, at a given price level, P_0. This is represented in Figure 10–3 by the movement from point A to point B. The implication is that the aggregate demand curve, Y^D, would shift to the right, from Y_0^D to Y_1^D. If the money supply decreases, exactly the opposite occurs. When real balances decline, the aggregate demand for domestic goods decreases, at any given price level. In other words, the aggregate demand curve shifts to the left.

Changes in the exchange rate also tend to shift the aggregate demand sched-

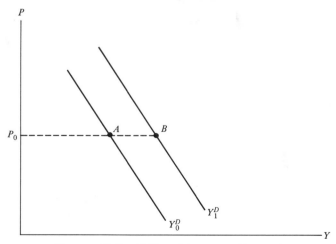

FIGURE 10–3. Shifts of Aggregate Demand

ule. A devaluation switches demand toward domestic goods, at any given level of domestic prices, thus shifting the aggregate demand curve to the right. Similarly, a revaluation, a decrease in the exchange rate, shifts the Y^D curve to the left. Finally, expansionary fiscal policy (say an increase in government spending) has a positive multiplier effect on the aggregate demand for domestic goods, at any given level of prices, shifting the aggregate demand curve to the right.

The effects of fiscal, monetary, and exchange rate changes on aggregate demand can be visualized more clearly by determining the algebraic expression for the aggregate demand curve. Solving for the interest rate in equation (1) and substituting the result into equation (2) yields

$$Y_o = \tilde{\alpha}\left[\bar{A} + \bar{T}\left(\frac{eP^*}{P_o}\right)\right] + \tilde{\alpha}\gamma\frac{M_o}{P_o} \tag{3}$$

where

$$\tilde{\alpha} = \frac{1}{s + m + \gamma k}$$

is the Keynesian fiscal multiplier, and $\gamma = b/h$ depends on investment and money demand parameters determining the effects of the real money supply on aggregate demand. For given levels of autonomous spending and the nominal money supply, equation (3) shows that a reduction of domestic prices from P_o to P_1 raises desired spending on domestic goods, Y, by raising real balances, M_o/P, and improving the autonomous trade balance, $\bar{T}$. This is precisely what the aggregate demand curve, Y_o^D shows. In addition, by changing $\bar{A}$, M_o, and e in equation (3) we can determine the effects of fiscal policy, money supply changes and exchange rate changes on the aggregate demand curve in Figure 10–3. The rule to remember is that any exogenous factor increasing (or decreasing) the demand for domestic goods will cause the demand curve to shift rightward (or leftward) at any given level of prices.

10–2 EMPLOYMENT, CONTRACTS, AND THE THEORY OF AGGREGATE SUPPLY

The aggregate demand curve derived in Section 10–1 specifies combinations of desired spending and prices of domestic goods. Which of these combinations actually prevails in the economy depends on aggregate supply. The aggregate supply function represents a relationship between the aggregate quantity supplied of domestic goods and the price of domestic goods. The interaction of aggregate supply and aggregate demand then determines the equilibrium level of output (real income) and prices in the economy.

Our analysis of aggregate supply in previous chapters was limited to stating the assumption that domestic firms be capable of supplying the output demanded of them at fixed prices. In that situation, domestic output is determined by aggregate demand. For that reason, our emphasis was on the determinants of aggregate demand and on the possible effects of government policies on output and employment. This framework, a simple version of Keynes's paradigm, was widely used by macroeconomists during the post–World War II era but has been widely criticized in recent years. First, the assumption of fixed prices does not seem to hold in any modern industrial nation. In the case of the United States, the behavior of the price level during the 19th and early 20th centuries exhibited both extended periods of generally falling prices and sustained inflation. Recent experience, on the other hand, has been one of sustained—although variable—rises in prices. These price changes have been sometimes quite drastic, as during the 1973 to 1975 period, when the consumer price index increased by more than 36%, or almost 10% per year. Second, it is clear that firms cannot supply unlimited amounts of output; they will run into full-capacity constraints at some point. But when such constraints are faced, increases in aggregate demand will not necessarily raise output but may rather generate shortages and, as a consequence, rising prices. Any economy operating at close to its potential level of output cannot be expected to adjust supply without having some effect on prices.

In conclusion, the main problem with the analysis in previous chapters is that it can fully apply only to an economic environment in which price stability and conditions of high unemployment prevail, a situation that has existed only for small periods of time in the recent experience of most industrial economies. In the case of the United States, for example, high unemployment and relatively stable prices have coexisted only during the periods 1938 to 1940 and 1970 to 1971. Periods of high unemployment have usually been associated with declining prices (deflation), as was the case during most of the Great Depression (when prices fell drastically) or with reduced inflation, as in the case of the 1982 recession when U.S. inflation (as measured by the CPI) tumbled to about 6.1%, down from 13.5% and 10.4% during 1980 and 1981, respectively. Periods of moderate (or rising) unemployment and stagnation, however, have sometimes been associated with rising prices, a phenomenon that has been called *stagflation*.

This section initiates the study of the factors affecting the supply of goods in an open economy. Production in any economy requires the employment of some factors of production (e.g., capital and labor) that are combined by means of a certain technology, such as an assembly line. Often, however, the blueprints of technology tend to be given over extended periods of time and the capital available to firms is more or less fixed. As a result, the economy can alter its output supply mostly through changes in labor employment.[2] Our task, then,

---

[2] In general, firms can also alter production through a more intensive use of capital. In order to concentrate on unemployment changes, this factor will be bypassed.

is to show how employment (and thus output) changes when the price of domestic goods varies.

Employment Contracts and the Labor Market

Employment in a market economy is determined by the interaction of firms demanding the services of workers, and households supplying those services through participation in the labor force. Figure 10–4(a) illustrates the aggregate labor market equilibrium of an economy. The vertical axis represents real wage rates, W/P, where W denotes nominal wage rates, and the horizonal axis represents employment, N. The downward-sloping WW locus depicts the demand for labor by firms in the economy. It represents the fact that a decrease in real wage rates reduces unit costs of production, increases profitability and, therefore, induces firms to increase employment. Firms can raise employment along WW by hiring additional workers or by using their labor force more intensively through increased hours of work (overtime). All points along WW represent possible points of employment in the economy. Which of these points is actually prevalent at a given time period depends on what real wage rate employers face. The latter depends on the conditions or terms at which individuals are willing to supply their labor. Employment contracts explicitly or implicitly specify the conditions at which individuals are hired. These stipulate the nominal wage rates to be paid and the duration of the contract (2 or 3 years). The hours of work the individual will be required to engage in, however, are not

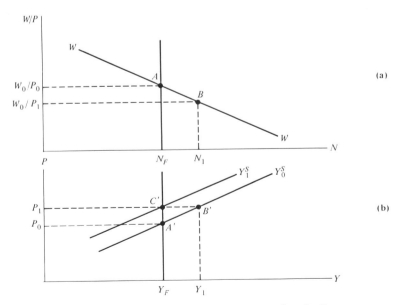

FIGURE 10–4. Derivation of the Aggregate Supply Curve

usually rigidly specified. These are frequently changed by firms on the basis of the fluctuations in demand they face, requiring extra hours under periods of high production and laying off workers when production is slack.[3]

The determination of the nominal wage rate at which contracts are settled is affected by a wide array of factors, including employer–employee bargaining and the search of employers and employees for alternative candidates and job opportunities, respectively. Suppose that all firms and individuals are bargaining over new employment contracts in an unregulated market in which no side enjoys monopoly power. The resulting equilibrium real wage rate would be determined at W_o/P_o in Figure 10–4(a). This is the rate clearing the labor market, representing equality of the existing labor demand and supply. Consequently, at the wage rate W_o/P_o, employment would be equal to N_F, denoting full employment. That the labor market's equilibrium would be at full employment is easily visualized by noting that, if contracts were settled at wage rates above W_o/P_o, labor demand would be lower and as a result some workers would not find employment. In other words, there would be an excess supply of labor. The unemployed workers would then bid down wages by offering to accept contracts with lower wage rates than those being offered to other workers. This labor market competition, involving thorough search and negotiation, would then move the labor market toward N_F and W_o/P_o. Similarly, low-wage contracts for which employment is above N_F imply some workers would have to labor more than the amount they desire to at those lower wages. Since they would not voluntarily accept such contracts, firms would have to bid up their wage offers. Again, the labor market would move to equilibrium at point A, which represents a fully employed economy.[4]

---

[3] The study of labor contracts in this context was pioneered by Costas Azariadis in his article, "Implicit Contracts and Underemployment Equilibria," *Journal of Political Economy* (December 1975) and has also been associated with the names of Martin N. Baily, Herschel Grossman, and Edmund S. Phelps, among many others. Labor contracts often specify extra compensation for overtime. This, however, does not basically alter the text's argument, since the employee will still be required to work extra hours at the predetermined overtime rate in periods of high demand. We should finally stress that the type of employment contract considered in this chapter—involving nominal wage rigidity in the short run—is part of an array of possible employment arrangements. Chapter 11 will undertake a fuller discussion of this topic.

[4] It should be stressed that full employment as defined here may be associated with some workers reported unemployed. Even if the aggregate labor market in the economy clears, with overall labor demand equal to supply, some unemployed workers can still exist. There are clearly some firms and sectors in the economy that are at any given time contracting while others expand. The labor released by the declining industries may take time to be absorbed by the expanding ones; thus, even though aggregate demand and supply for labor are equal, some unemployment would still arise. Because of its nature, this type of unemployment has been called *frictional* or *structural unemployment*. Given our present interest in analyzing how changes in the *aggregate* quantity demanded of labor generate unemployment (referred to as *cyclical unemployment*), we shall ignore structural unemployment. For informative purposes, some economists have calculated the frictional or structural component of unemployment (often referred to as the *natural* rate of unemployment) to have been between 4 and 5% during the sixties and higher since the seventies.

Prices, Employment, and the Aggregate Supply Curve

What happens to employment when the domestic price level increases? Suppose, for example, that the economy is initially at point A and that there is a sudden increase in the domestic price level. On the assumption that an important part of the economy's labor force is covered by existing contracts that prefix nominal wage rates, real wages would decline. Symbolically, if the price level increases from P_0 to P_1, and the nominal wage rate is fixed at W_0 because of previously engaged labor contracts, then real wages would decline from W_0/P_0 to W_0/P_1.[5] In this situation, employers will find it profitable to overemploy workers, that is, to employ workers above their full employment (by requiring extra hours of work or by delaying planned layoffs). In terms of Figure 10–4(a), employment, N_1, would move above full employment, N_F. Consequently, over the short run, increases in domestic prices will be associated with increases in employment. Over time, however, labor contracts will come up for renegotiation, and workers will try to regain their lost real wages by raising their nominal wage quotes and requesting upward adjustment of their wage rates. This means that, over the long run, labor market equilibrium would be restored back to point A in Figure 10–4(a).

The rise of employment induced by an increase in the price of domestic goods is the consequence of the nominal wage rigidities in the economy over the short run. If nominal wage rates were fully flexible, the labor market would clear at its full-employment level. Given the labor market rigidities existing in most economies, however, this full-employment equilibrium of the labor market may not be attainable within a short-run time horizon.

In summary, as the price of domestic goods increases, employment will also tend to rise over the short run. The result is an increase in output. This positive relationship between changes in prices and quantity supplied of domestic goods in the short run is the *short-run aggregate supply curve of domestic goods*. It is represented in Figure 10–4(b) by means of the upward-sloping Y_0^S curve. As prices rise from P_0 to P_1, employment increases from N_F to N_1 in Figure 10–4(a) corresponding to an increase in output from Y_F to Y_1. From the initial price–quantity supplied combination at point A', the economy thus moves to point B'. This movement corresponds to the switch from point A to point B in the labor market diagram in Figure 10–4(a).

The increase in output above full employment implied by the rise in prices, however, cannot persist. As noted earlier, the overemployment associated with the output expansion is the result of a reduction in real wages. Diagrammatically,

---

[5] This assumes that workers do not expect the increase in prices from P_0 to P_1. Otherwise, they would make sure to bargain for cost-of-living increases. In the latter case, the price hike would be matched by an indexed increase in wage rates and the labor market equilibrium would not be disturbed away from full employment. The present chapter will omit situations in which price increases are anticipated, a topic that requires a separate, more detailed treatment. Chapter 12 examines the role of inflationary expectations.

at point B in Figure 10–4(a) workers face a lower real wage than at full employment at point A. As a consequence, when their employment contracts expire, they will demand higher nominal wage rates. As nominal wage rates increase, the real wage moves upward from W_0/P_1 back toward its original level. As this happens, firms will reduce employment and production back toward the initial (full-employment) level. This is represented in Figure 10–4(b) by the leftward shift of the short-run aggregate supply curve from Y_0^S to Y_1^S. That is, at the price level P_1, the rise in wages forces firms to reduce their aggregate quantity supplied. This brings about a leftward shift of the short-run aggregate supply curve.

Over the long run, production must return to its full-employment level, since employment must return to N_F, the point at which the labor market is at long-run equilibrium. This suggests that the *long-run aggregate supply curve* is a vertical line lying, as drawn in Figure 10–4(b), at the full-employment level of output, Y_F. The long-run quantity supplied of domestic goods is, thus, unresponsive to changes in the price of domestic goods. Only over the short run will price changes have an effect on the aggregate quantity supplied in the economy, with the output constraints imposed by the economy's limited labor force and other resources surfacing over the long run.[6] Notice that, just as a rise in prices can generate short-run increases in output, a decrease in prices of domestic goods will result in a short-run decline in employment and output that is eliminated over the long run.

The aggregate supply curve, whether in the short or long run, specifies some combinations of aggregate quantity supplied and price of domestic goods. Which of these combinations is actually chosen as the equilibrium level of output and price in the economy is determined by the interaction of aggregate supply with aggregate demand, as will be shown in the next section.

10–3   THE SHORT-RUN EQUILIBRIUM OF THE ECONOMY

We now proceed to integrate our analyses of aggregate demand and aggregate supply into an analysis of overall equilibrium in the open economy. We start by circumscribing our attention first to a short time horizon. Over this *short run,* monetary parameters (mainly the domestic money supply), fiscal parameters (mainly government spending and taxation) and the exchange rate are all assumed to be given. This determines a particular aggregate demand curve, represented in Figure 10–5 by the $Y_0^D Y_0^D$ curve. In addition, over the short run, nominal wage rates are rigid because of binding employment contracts previously

---

[6] See the appendix to this chapter for the derivation of an explicit, algebraic expression of the aggregate supply curve. For a sophisticated exposition of aggregate supply within the aggregate supply–demand framework developed in this chapter, see M. Schmid, "Devaluation: Keynesian Trade Models and the Monetary Approach," *European Economic Review* (January 1982).

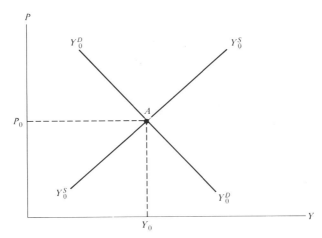

FIGURE 10–5. The Economy's Short-Run Equilibrium

engaged in. This nominal wage rigidity determines a given short-run aggregate supply curve, shown by means of $Y_o^S Y_o^S$ in Figure 10–5.

The economy will be in *short-run equilibrium* when the quantity demanded of domestic goods equals the quantity supplied of domestic goods in the short run. This occurs at that point at which the aggregate demand curve intersects the short-run aggregate supply curve. There is then a simultaneous short-run equilibrium in the goods, money, and labor markets. The goods and money markets are in short-run equilibrium in the sense that they clear, given the money supply and other fiscal and exchange rate parameters. The labor market is also in short-run (or quasi) equilibrium in the sense that the quantity of workers employed is determined by the demand for labor, at the *given rigid nominal* wage rate in the short run.

Short-run equilibrium in the economy occurs at point A in Figure 10–5, where aggregate supply and aggregate demand intersect. The short-run equilibrium output of domestic goods is therefore Y_0 and the equilibrium level of the price of domestic goods P_0. Policy disturbances, such as fiscal, monetary, and exchange rate changes will alter the short-run equilibrium of the economy by affecting the aggregate demand curve.

10–4 THE BALANCE OF PAYMENTS AND LONG-RUN EQUILIBRIUM

The short-run equilibrium of the economy represented by point A in Figure 10–5 is based on a given level of the money supply and a fixed nominal wage rate. It is clear, however, that the domestic stock of money will change over time in response to the balance of payments situation of the country. In addition, nominal wages will be adjusting in response to the deviations of employment from its full-employment level and the consequent revision of employment contracts over time. Only when the economy is in balance of payments equilibrium will there be no change in the money supply, assuming that the Central Bank does not alter domestic credit, and only at full employment will nominal wage rates stop adjusting. When the economy attains balance of payments equilibrium and full employment, given fixed policy parameters, it will be in *long-run equilibrium*. Long-run equilibrium exists, then, when the money market is in long-run equilibrium (when the money supply is not changing in response to the balance of payments) and when the labor market is at full-employment equilibrium (at which point nominal wages stop changing in response to deviations from full employment). We shall now proceed to characterize the long-run equilibrium of the economy and then describe the adjustment process involved in the movement from short-run to long-run equilibrium. To carry out this analysis, however, we need to characterize the balance of payments of the economy.

The balance of payments, B, is given by

$$B = T(q, Y) + K(i) \qquad (4)$$

where T represents the trade balance (which is a function of the relative price of domestic goods, q, and domestic real income, Y) and K the capital account (which depends on the domestic interest rate on the assumption that the foreign interest rate is fixed). For the sake of expository simplicity, we shall momentarily assume that the country faces no international capital movements. In that case, $K = 0$, and the balance of payments becomes the trade balance. Graphically, we illustrate the balance of payments by means of the trade balance equilibrium locus of the economy. This locus shows the combinations of real income, Y, and the price of domestic goods, P, which maintain a zero trade balance. Suppose that there is a reduction in the price of domestic goods. This will tend to improve the trade balance, as demand shifts from foreign to domestic goods. In order to maintain balanced trade, domestic real income would have to increase to raise imports and offset the improvement in the trade balance. This means that income and price are inversely related along the trade balance equilibrium locus. This is portrayed by the downward-sloping TT curve in Figure 10–6. Note that points above the TT curve depict points of trade deficit and points below it represent points of trade surplus. This is easy to visualize: Suppose that we are along TT. At any given level of P, if we increase real income, Y, this will raise imports causing the trade balance to go into deficit. Similarly, at a given P, a reduction in Y would decrease imports and create a trade surplus.

Figure 10–6 illustrates the long-run equilibrium of an open economy under capital immobility at point E, which corresponds to the intersection of the long-run aggregate supply curve (the vertical line at the full-employment level of output, Y_F), and the trade balance equilibrium curve TT. At point E, the

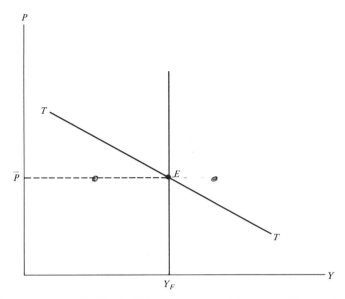

FIGURE 10–6.   The Trade Balance Locus and Long-Run Equilibrium

economy is at full employment and balanced trade. The money, goods, and labor markets are all in long-run equilibrium.

10–5   THE MONETARY-PRICE ADJUSTMENT MECHANISM

How does the adjustment from the economy's current, or short-run, equilibrium to its long-run equilibrium occur? That is, suppose that we have an economy facing a certain amount of unemployment and suffering from trade deficits. Starting from this point of short-run equilibrium, would there be any tendencies in the economy to move toward its long-run equilibrium (with full employment and external balance), without any need for policy intervention? The answer is yes. We represent the problem in Figure 10–7.

Point H in Figure 10–7 shows the short-run equilibrium of a given economy, as determined by the intersection of the short-run aggregate supply curve, $Y_o^S Y_o^S$, and the aggregate demand curve, $Y_o^D Y_o^D$. Short-run output is equal to Y_o, and the price of domestic goods is equal to P_o. Given that $Y_o < Y_F$, the economy faces unemployment. Since point H lies above the TT curve, there is a trade balance deficit. What happens to the economy over time? Given that there is unemployment, nominal wages will decline, shifting the short-run aggregate supply curve to the right. In addition, the trade deficit implies that the Central Bank loses foreign exchange reserves and, in the absence of sterilization, the money supply would shrink, shifting down the aggregate demand curve. As

$\rightarrow \downarrow w, \uparrow N, \uparrow Y$

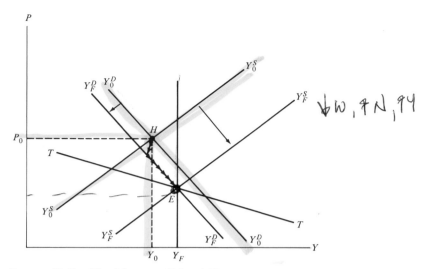

FIGURE 10–7.   The Monetary-Price Adjustment Mechanism

shown in Figure 10–7, even though these *price and monetary adjustments* may leave employment more or less unchanged (and may even increase unemployment) over short periods of time, both tend to reduce the price of domestic goods. This decrease in P tends to make domestic goods cheaper relative to foreign goods, stimulating net domestic exports and improving the trade balance. In addition, in spite of the reduction in the price of domestic goods, real wages are generally declining (why?), raising the profitability of production and eventually moving the economy toward full employment.

Over the long run (and if given enough time), the economy will move to point E. This is the result of monetary contractions associated with the balance of payments deficit at point H, which move the aggregate demand curve down from $Y_o^D Y_o^D$ to $Y_F^D Y_F^D$. It is also the result of reductions in nominal wages triggered by the unemployment associated with point H, which move the aggregate supply curve rightward from $Y_o^S Y_o^S$ to $Y_F^S Y_F^S$. At point E, there is full employment; the labor market is in long-run equilibrium with no incentive for nominal wages (and prices) to change. In addition, balanced trade has been achieved, with the money market in long-run equilibrium and no further changes in the domestic money supply. In conclusion, the unhampered functioning of the market economy leads to both internal and external balance over the long run. The big question, however, is how long it takes for the economy to adjust toward its long-run equilibrium. Given that the adjustment process just discussed involves a rather protracted recession, the problem arises as to whether the policymakers could speed it up by engaging in monetary, fiscal, and/or exchange rate policies. The answer to this question is explored in the next section.

10–6   MACROECONOMIC ADJUSTMENT PROGRAMS AND THEIR CONSEQUENCES

A broad array of situations can destabilize an economy, leading it to either balance of payments difficulties, recession, accelerated price increases (inflation), or to all of them combined. This section examines the issue of macroeconomic adjustment to destabilization and of the various alternative policy actions possible. We shall pay special attention to the adjustment policy alternatives open to developing countries and, in particular, those policy packages propounded by the International Monetary Fund (IMF), whose aim is "the restoration and maintenance of viability to the balance of payments in an environment of price stability and sustainable rates of economic growth."[7] These are generally accepted goals of policy intervention in this context, and there is very little quarrel with them. The means by which they are to be attained, however, and the success of specific programs have bred deep disagreements. The IMF-supported adjustment programs followed by many developing countries in recent years, for example, are often perceived to rely heavily on the use of tools intended to correct balance of payments and inflation difficulties, with relatively little attention paid to their effects on output and employment. Also, it is clear that a wide array of policy strategies are possible, each with a different approach regarding the adjustment path the economy should follow. This section starts our examination of alternative adjustment programs and their effects.

Consider an economy whose initial condition is one of unemployment and balance of payments deficit, such as that represented by point H in Figure 10–8. A number of disturbances can bring an economy to that particular situation. An external shock in the form of increased raw material prices would raise the costs of imported inputs, inducing the aggregate supply curve to shift to the left, causing domestic prices to rise and output to fall. Internal events in the economy may also contribute to destabilization. Populist governments in Latin American countries, for example, are conspicuous in supporting (and maintaining) massive across-the-board wage hikes right after their takeovers.[8] These hikes shift the economy's aggregate supply leftward, increasing domestic prices, deteriorating the economy's international competitiveness, and worsening its trade balance. Whatever the background that leads the economy to a point like H in Figure 10–8, one can ask what adjustment policy alternatives can eliminate (or at least reduce) the economy's unemployment and balance of pay-

[7] Manuel Guitian, "Economic Management and International Monetary Fund Conditionality," in T. Killick, ed., *Adjustment and Financing in the Developing World: The Role of the International Monetary Fund* (Washington, D.C.: International Monetary Fund, 1982), p. 93.

[8] For detailed description and analysis of populist economic policies in Latin America, and of many of these countries' macroeconomic adjustment programs, see Carlos Diaz Alejandro, "Southern Cone Stabilization Plans," in W. R. Cline and S. Weintraub, eds., *Economic Stabilization in Developing Countries* (Washington, D.C.: The Brookings Institution, 1981).

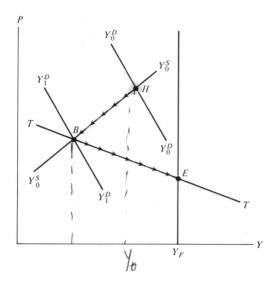

FIGURE 10–8. Simple Analytics of Macroeconomic Adjustment Programs

ments deficit, and simultaneously offset upward pressures on domestic prices, reversing the economy's deteriorated competitiveness in world markets.

The laissez-faire adjustment process discussed in the last section is the most obvious alternative. Under this option, government authorities would dismantle any expansionary fiscal and monetary policies previously followed and would adopt a hands-off approach to the economy. The behavior of prices, output, and the balance of payments would then follow the time path we analyzed in Figure 10–7. With the Central Bank allowing its international reserves to decrease, the domestic money supply would contract and aggregate demand would shift down. With wages and prices free to vary, the aggregate supply curve would shift to the right over time. Eventually, equilibrium would be attained at point E, with balanced payments and full employment. Of course, when countries start off at point H, facing dwindling foreign exchange reserves, the protracted payments deficit implied by this adjustment mechanism may be untenable. In these cases, a complementary government policy aimed at eliminating the balance of payments disequilibrium may lie in active contractionary monetary and fiscal policies. This shock-treatment approach to the economy's problems is represented in Figure 10–8 by the shift of the aggregate demand curve from $Y_0^D Y_0^D$ to $Y_1^D Y_1^D$. The aggregate demand contraction serves to attain the goal of external balance but leads to a short-run worsening of the recession. Only over time do recession and unemployment reduce real wages, stimulating the private sector and moving the economy toward full employment. A possible adjustment path is shown by the move from point H to point B and then to point E in Figure 10–8, highlighted by pointed arrows.

The shock-treatment type of macroeconomic program thus appears to be favorable in rapidly eliminating balance of payments deficits and in controlling inflation, but does not seem to have any positive short-run effects on output and employment and may actually intensify the economy's recession. Its social consequences are thus highly questionable and may not be acceptable to some governments. Of course, the whole question relies on how much unemployment may be created by the program over the short run, and by how much and how fast real wage rate reductions can drive a private sector's output expansion. The evidence available suggests that, over the short run, programs relying on sharp contractions of aggregate demand tend to increase unemployment and reduce output quite drastically. Using data from 29 developing countries, Mohsin S. Khan and Malcolm D. Knight have found that a program of contractionary monetary-fiscal policies intended to increase a country's level of foreign exchange reserves by 50% within a period of 1 year would lead to an average of 5% increase in unemployment during that period, an increase which is, however, sharply reversed in the ensuing years. Less drastic plans, instituting contractionary policies to improve the balance of payments more moderately, over several years, were also found to be recessionary, although less so than in the drastic program. They conclude, "Programs designed to achieve quick results on the balance of payments via sharp deflation are likely to have significant and undesirable effects on output, employment, and factor incomes, particularly in the short run."[9]

Is there an alternative adjustment program that would at least minimize the short-run output and employment effects on the economy? Our analysis in earlier chapters suggests that exchange rate changes can constitute an important part of a policy package intended to attain internal and external balance. What would be the effects of a devaluation in the present context?

Consider an economy that is originally at point H in Figure 10-9, at the intersection of the $Y_0^D Y_0^D$ and $Y_0^S Y_0^S$ curves. The trade balance locus is given initially by $T_0 T_0$, implying that point H is a point of short-run balance of payments deficit. The impact effect of a devaluation is to switch demand toward domestic goods, shifting the aggregate demand curve upward and to the right. This would immediately tend to ignite increases in prices. In order to avoid such price hikes—in order to control inflation—the economy would have to follow contractionary policies to maintain the aggregate demand curve more or less unchanged. We assume that these policies are combined with the devaluation so that, in terms of Figure 10-9, the aggregate demand curve remains unchanged at $Y_0^D Y_0^D$. Note that if contractionary policies were not adopted, the devaluation could in principle move the economy to a high-employment point such as point F, but it would clearly generate rampant inflation. We assume that authorities in the economy avoid the inflation by means of contractionary demand policies, such as fiscal and monetary contractions, which maintain the short-run equilibrium of the economy at point H.

---

[9] Mohsin S. Khan and Malcolm D. Knight, "Stabilization Programs in Developing Countries: A Formal Framework," *IMF Staff Papers* (January 1982), p. 43. This article provides a summary of the evidence on the issue and estimates the probable effects of various hypothetical policy measures.

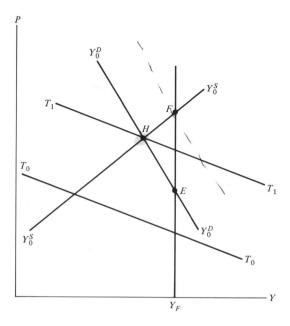

FIGURE 10–9. The Role of Devaluation in Macroeconomic Adjustment Programs

The devaluation also tends to shift the trade balance locus to the right since, at any given domestic price level, it would improve the trade balance (assuming that the Marshall–Lerner condition is satisfied). This shift of the trade balance curve is represented in Figure 10–9 by the shift from T_oT_o to T_1T_1. We thus assume, for illustrative purposes, that the devaluation undertaken is large enough to completely wipe out the economy's balance of payments deficit. In terms of Figure 10–9, the new trade balance locus T_1T_1 passes through point H. As a consequence, short-run equilibrium now occurs at balanced external payments. In conclusion, an adequate devaluation-cum-contractionary demand policy could move the economy to balanced payments without sharp deflationary (or inflationary) effects. Therefore, exchange rate policy may serve an important role in macroeconomic adjustment programs not willing to tolerate widespread social costs, although it is apparent that it must be combined with other policy measures as a package.

The specific example we have discussed in this section illustrates the inherent difficulties of attaining multiple objectives in an open economy. Contractionary monetary and fiscal policies oriented toward a rapid improvement in the balance of payments will generate a sharp recession and increased unemployment. Alternatively, if a devaluation is used to attain balanced payments and to raise output, prices will rapidly increase, fueling inflation. Finally, if contractionary demand policies are attached to devaluation as a package, price stability and balanced payments can in principle be attained, but unemployment will not be completely eliminated. The main reason for these conflicts of objectives lies in that, with an unchanged aggregate supply curve, the range of possible equilibria of the economy will lie along that curve, implying a short-run tradeoff between output and price increases. This suggests that policies oriented toward increasing aggregate supply (shifting the aggregate supply curve to the right) may have an important role in macroeconomic adjustment programs. This type of approach has been popularized recently by so-called *supply-side economics,* whose emphasis is on the use of tax cuts, labor market incentive policies, and other policies intended to manipulate aggregate supply.[10]

10–7 DEVALUATION IN THE SHORT AND LONG RUN

We have seen how devaluation combined with adequate contractionary aggregate demand policies can aid an economy with balance of payments deficits to adjust faster toward external balance. The use of devaluation as an economic policy, however, has been tarnished by long-standing controversies over its effects. In this section, we discuss some of the issues related to its short-run and long-run effects.

Consider an economy blessed with external and internal balance. In terms of Figure 10–10, the economy is initially at the long-run equilibrium corresponding to point *A*. Suppose that a devaluation of the domestic currency is undertaken. As was seen in Section 10–6, both the aggregate demand and the trade

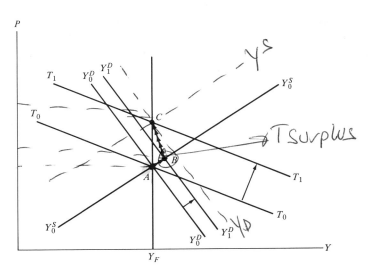

FIGURE 10–10. Short-Run and Long-Run Effects of Devaluation

[10] See V. Canto, D. Joines, and A. Laffer, *Foundations of Supply-Side Economics* (New York: Academic Press, Inc., 1983), for an advanced exposition of this approach.

balance curves would shift upward and to the right. These changes are shown in Figure 10–10, where the aggregate demand curve shifts upward from $Y_o^D Y_o^D$ to $Y_1^D Y_1^D$ and the trade balance curve from $T_o T_o$ to $T_1 T_1$. The short-run equilibrium of the economy then moves from point A to point B, with a higher level of the output and price of domestic goods and an improvement of the trade balance, reflected by the fact that point B lies below the $T_1 T_1$ locus.[11] But, as long as the trade balance moves into surplus, the domestic money supply will increase over time. As a result, over the long run, the aggregate demand curve for domestic goods will shift upward and to the right. In addition, since the economy has moved above full employment, nominal wages will rise and the short-run aggregate supply curve will shift to the left. Figure 10–10 does not show exactly how the aggregate demand and aggregate supply curves shift over time, but it does show one particular path of points reflecting one possible path of their intersections over time. This path is represented by the pointed arrows.

Full-employment equilibrium and balanced trade after the devaluation occur at point C, where the new trade balance curve, $T_1 T_1$, and the long-run aggregate supply curve, at Y_F, intersect. Point C, then, represents the new long-run equilibrium. No matter how the adjustment of the economy occurs from point B to point C, the latter must be the destination point. What has happened, compared with the initial equilibrium at point A? There has been no permanent increase in employment, since output is back at its full-employment level. In addition, there has been no permanent effect on the trade balance, since monetary adjustments in the economy have moved the trade balance back to its zero level. These monetary adjustments, however, imply that the Central Bank's foreign exchange reserves have increased and that, as a result, the domestic nominal money supply has risen as well. Finally, the price of domestic goods has increased from P_o to P_1. As a matter of fact, the price of domestic goods increases by exactly the same proportion as the exchange rate. Let us see why.

From the trade balance definition, we know that

$$B = T(q, Y) = T\left(\frac{eP^*}{P}\right) - mY \tag{5}$$

that is, the trade balance is composed of a component that depends on domestic real income, Y, and a part that is autonomous of income and that depends on the relative price of foreign goods in terms of domestic goods, q. Note, however, that in the long run the devaluation has no effect on real income so

---

[11] This assumes that the Marshall–Lerner condition holds. In addition, even though the exchange rate increase has a positive direct effect on the autonomous trade balance, the movement from point A to point B is connected also to increases in domestic income and prices, both of which tend to worsen the trade balance. One thus wonders whether a devaluation in the present case always improves the trade balance in the short-run. As it turns out, it always does. The derivation is left to the reader as Problem 3 at the end of the chapter.

that Y in equation (5) remains unchanged. In addition, the economy must return to balanced trade through the monetary adjustment mechanism so that a devaluation has no long-run effects on the overall trade balance, $T(q, Y)$, either. This implies that the autonomous trade balance, $\overline{T}(eP^*/P)$, cannot be permanently affected by a devaluation, meaning that eP^*/P cannot be permanently altered either. In other words, over the long run, the price of domestic goods increases in the same proportion as the increase in the exchange rate. It should be intuitively clear why this should be so. The devaluation tends to make the economy relatively more competitive in the short run, operating through a reduction in real wages and a decline in the relative price of domestic goods vis à vis foreign goods. As time transpires, however, labor contracts are revised and domestic real wages increase to their level before the devaluation. As a consequence, the competitiveness and productivity of domestic production must return to its previous level, as will the relative price of domestic goods, q. In other words, the price of domestic goods must rise in the same proportion as the devaluation so as to keep relative prices, $q = eP^*/P$, unchanged.

The hypothesis that a devaluation does not have any effects on the relative price of domestic goods is associated with the long-standing doctrine of *purchasing power parity*. The present analysis suggests that this hypothesis should tend to hold only over the long run, and not over short periods of time. In addition, the discussion has been carried out on the assumption that the economy starts from a position of long-run equilibrium, with an external and internal balance that is only temporarily disturbed by the devaluation. If the economy were out of long-run equilibrium instead, suffering perhaps from unemployment and balance of payments deficits, devaluation could very well induce changes in the relative price of domestic goods toward equilibrium. In this situation, the economy's employment and external payments difficulties hinge heavily on a lack of international competitiveness, represented by high prices of domestic goods relative to those of foreign goods. A devaluation can then aid the economy in regaining its competitiveness by helping adjust the relative price of domestic goods down toward its long-run equilibrium level.

10–8   DEVALUATION AND RELATIVE PRICES: THE EVIDENCE

What are the data regarding the effects of devaluation on relative prices? Available evidence suggests that devaluation generally has significant short-run effects on relative prices but that these disappear over the long run, and that the short-run increase in domestic competitiveness due to devaluation takes different amounts of time to disappear, depending on the country. The time span is shorter for such countries as Belgium, Canada, Italy, and Japan, for which most of the increase in competitiveness of exports may be expected to disappear in less than 1 year, and longer for such countries as France, Sweden, the United Kingdom, and the United States, where significant increases in competitiveness

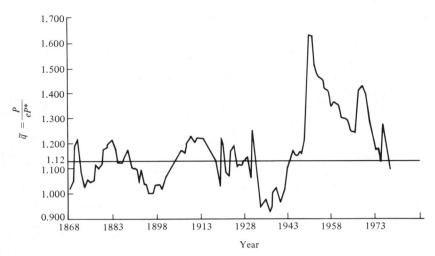

FIGURE 10–11. Behavior of the Ratio of the U.S. Price Index to the Dollar-Converted U.K. Price Index, 1868 to 1978. (From Milton Friedman, "Prices of Money and Goods Across Frontiers: The £ and $ over a Century," *World Economy,* January 1979.)

can still be observed after 1 year.[12] The same lack of influence of devaluation on relative prices over the long run is detected in many instances of devaluations in developing countries.[13]

These results are also illustrated in the U.S.–U.K. data plotted in Figure 10–11, showing the behavior of an index of the U.S. price level relative to an index of U.K. prices (converted to dollars). Symbolically, we are just plotting

$$\tilde{q} = \frac{P}{eP^*}$$

where P is the U.S. price level, e is the exchange rate ($/£), and P^* is the U.K. price level, so that $\tilde{q}$ is the reciprocal of q. As observed, $\tilde{q}$ varies significantly from period to period, even though over the long-run it tends to return toward a level somewhere around 1.12. This is more evident for the period before 1932, when the fluctuations around $\tilde{q} = 1.12$ were only within a band of plus and minus 10%. After 1932, however, there appear to be persistent deviations from that level, associated quite closely with two quite major jumps (peaks) in 1949 and 1967. It may not be a coincidence that these 2 years corresponded

---

[12] For more details on these results, see Erich Spitaller, "Short-Run Effects of Exchange Rate Changes on Terms of Trade and Trade Balance," *IMF Staff Papers* (June 1980), and W. Robinson, T. R. Webb, and M. A. Townsend, "The Influence of Exchange Rate Changes on Prices: A Study of 18 Industrial Countries," *Economica,* 27–50 (February 1979).

[13] R. N. Cooper, "Currency Devaluation in Developing Countries," *Essays in International Finance* (Princeton, N.J.: Princeton University, June 1971), p. 23.

to major devaluations of the pound. The picture suggested is one in which the government exchange rate policies appear to generate significant changes in $\bar{q}$, giving rise to deviations from purchasing power parity. As Friedman remarks, the ratio of relative prices, $\bar{q}$, changes because

> "every now and then, for whatever reason, the British government has stepped in and either devalued the currency deliberately or permitted it to depreciate. . . . Then market forces set in to correct it. The highest peak is for 1949–50 and that corresponds to the immediate post-World War II devaluation of the pound in 1949. The market then gradually starts to bring the ratio back down towards about 1.2. Before it gets there, another devaluation occurs and the ratio shoots up again. The market again brings it down, the United States devaluation in 1971 speeding up the process.[14]

In summary, the evidence tends to indicate that devaluation has effects on relative prices, but only over the short run. This ineffectiveness of devaluation in affecting relative prices may explain some recent findings showing a lack of any lasting effect of devaluation on the trade balance.[15]

10–9 FISCAL AND MONETARY POLICIES UNDER PERFECT CAPITAL MOBILITY

Up to this point, we have assumed that the economy faces no international capital mobility. It is clear, however, that this is not a realistic assumption for most industrial economies. It is time to relax it.

With perfect capital mobility, the aggregate demand function can be represented by

$$Y = \alpha\left[\bar{A} + \bar{T}\left(\frac{eP^*}{P}\right) - bi^*\right] \tag{6}$$

where $\alpha = 1/(s + m)$ is the open economy Keynesian multiplier, b is the interest elasticity of investment spending, and i^* is the world interest rate. Note that equations (2a) and (6) are equivalent expressions except that now the interest rate is exogenously given by i^*,[16] as the environment of perfect capital mobility requires.

[14] Milton Friedman, "Prices of Money and Goods Across Frontiers: The £ and $ Over a Century," *World Economy* (January 1979), pp. 509–510.

[15] See Marc Miles, *Devaluation, the Trade Balance and the Balance of Payments* (New York: Marcel Dekker, Inc., 1978).

[16] The expression for aggregate demand represented in equation (6) shows the combinations of aggregate quantity demanded and price of domestic goods consistent with full money market equilibrium, given fiscal policy and behavioral parameters and given the exchange rate. Equation

(continued)

The conclusions reached in our earlier analysis of economic policy under perfect capital mobility (see Chapter 7) were that, for an economy under fixed exchange rates, fiscal policy would be highly effective in increasing domestic output while monetary policy would be ineffective. Even though the latter conclusion remains unscathed in the present context, the former is fundamentally altered. That monetary policy in the form of changes in Central Bank credit has no effect on output, whether in the short run or in the long run, is evident from equation (6), which is independent of the domestic money supply. With no effect on aggregate demand, changes in Central Bank credit have no impact on the economy's equilibrium.

Changes in government spending, on the assumption the economy is at full employment, have short-run effects on output but none over the long run. An increase in government spending, for instance, raises aggregate demand for domestic goods, increasing domestic output in the short run. With output above full employment, however, nominal wages start climbing, reducing employment and output back to their original full-employment levels. The chief impact of fiscal policy in this context is to raise domestic prices. Note that since domestic output remains unchanged over the long run, the increased aggregate spending associated with the fiscal expansion must be offset by a decline in another component of aggregate demand. It is spending on domestic exports and import-competing industries that worsens. Domestic price increases worsen domestic competitiveness in international markets, hurting domestic export and import-competing industries. In terms of equation (6), as $\bar{A}$ rises in response to increased government spending, $\bar{T}$ declines in response to the reduction in $q \equiv eP^*/P$ associated with hikes in domestic prices. Note finally that increased government spending could have a permanent positive effect on output if the economy starts from a point of unemployment, but, at the same time, it will be inflationary if not combined with measures such as tax cuts, that shift aggregate supply.

10–10 SUMMARY

1. The equilibrium level of prices and output of domestic goods is established by the equality of aggregate demand and aggregate supply. Geometrically, this equilibrium corresponds to the intersection of the aggregate demand and aggregate supply curves.

2. The aggregate demand curve represents a relationship between the aggre-

---

(6) already embodies the instantaneous adjustments of the domestic money supply that occur in response to payments disequilibria under perfect capital mobility. Note that this differs from the aggregate demand expression in (3) above, which represents the combination of quantity demanded and price of domestic goods that clears the money market, given fiscal and exchange rate parameters, and given a level of the domestic money supply.

gate quantity demanded of domestic goods and the price level of domestic goods, given a certain level of the domestic money supply, the exchange rate, and some fiscal parameters such as tax rates and government expenditures.

3. The aggregate supply curve shows the relationship between price and quantity supplied of domestic goods. The short-run aggregate supply curve represents how quantity supplied responds to price changes over short periods of time, in the presence of nominal wage rigidities. The long-run aggregate supply curve is vertical at the full-employment level and represents how, in the absence of long-term rigidities, wage rates would adjust to clear the labor market.

4. The long-run equilibrium of an economy occurs at that point where there is full employment and balanced payments.

5. In the absence of disturbances generated by government intervention, an automatic adjustment mechanism tends to move the free-market economy over time toward its long-run equilibrium with full employment, balanced payments, and price stability.

6. Macroeconomic adjustment programs are intended to speed up the adjustment of an economy toward long-run equilibrium. Programs that rely on strong deflationary measures intended to obtain rapid improvement in the balance of payments will tend to generate sharp decreases in employment and output.

7. Devaluation used as a package with other policies can serve as an important tool in macroeconomic adjustment programs by generating improvements in the balance of payments without increasing unemployment in any significant way.

8. Policies oriented toward affecting aggregate supply can form a central part of macroeconomic programs oriented toward moving an economy to full employment and balanced payments without simultaneously igniting inflation in the short run.

9. For an economy close to or at full employment and balanced payments, devaluation will only generate a temporary improvement in the balance of trade. The long-run effects of a devaluation in this context are to increase domestic prices by the same proportion as the devaluation.

PROBLEMS

1. Consider the zero capital mobility framework developed in the text. Assume that the autonomous trade balance is given by $\overline{T}\,(eP^*/P) = \phi\,eP^*/P$, with ϕ a positive parameter. If the economy is in long-run equilibrium, determine the equilibrium price of domestic goods as a function of the exchange rate, foreign prices, and full-employment income. Determine also the economy's equilibrium interest rate. [HINT: Note that in long-run equilibrium $Y = Y_F$ and $T = 0$ and use equation (2) as well as the trade balance equation

$$T = \overline{T}\left(\frac{eP^*}{P}\right) - mY$$

2. Examine diagrammatically the short-run and long-run effects of the following disturbances in an economy under fixed exchange rates with no international trade in assets. Assume that the economy is initially in long-run equilibrium:
   (a) An increase in autonomous government expenditures.
   (b) A reduction of Central Bank credit.
   (c) An increase in the foreign price level, P^*.
3. Consider the effects of a domestic currency devaluation under international capital immobility. Show that the devaluation would necessarily improve the trade balance in the short run. [HINT: First show that a devaluation will tend to raise $q = eP/P^*$ over the short run; then substitute the expression for Y in equation (3) into the trade balance expression: $T = \bar{T}(eP^*/P) - mY$. Assume that the Marshall–Lerner condition is satisfied.]
4. Draw the aggregate demand curve described by equation (6) in the text jointly with an aggregate supply curve. Then answer the following:
   (a) Determine the short-run and long-run equilibria of an economy under perfect capital mobility and fixed exchange rates. Does long-run equilibrium require balanced trade?
   (b) Show diagrammatically the short-run and long-run effects of a reduction in domestic Central Bank credit, assuming that the economy is initially in long-run equilibrium.
   (c) Describe the short-run and long-run impact of a domestic currency depreciation.
   (d) Diagrammatically show the effects of an increase in autonomous government expenditures.
   Compare your results with those obtained under the assumption of zero capital mobility. Are there any differences? Explain.
5. Banania is a small tropical country whose only item of production is bananas. The country only trades with the United States and has fixed exchange rate equal to $\bar{e} = 2$ bananians per dollar (where a bananian is Banania's currency). The economy operates under perfect capital mobility and the following numerical expressions for absorption, A, the trade balance, T, and the world interest rate, i^*, have been determined:

$$A = 480 + 0.78\,Y - 900\,i^*$$
$$T = 100\,\frac{ep^*}{P} - 0.22\,Y$$
$$i^* = 0.10\ (10\%)$$

with absorption and the trade balance measured in terms of millions of Banania's output. Assume that Banania imports goods from the United States at an average price of 1 U.S. dollar per unit ($P^* = \$1.00$), and that the economy is producing at the full-employment level of output (440 million bananas).

(a) Determine the price of a unit of Banania's output (the price of a banana in bananians). How much would a banana cost in U.S. dollars?
(b) Suppose that Banania decides to devalue the bananian by 10%. What would be the long-run effect on the price of a banana in bananians?
(c) Assume that the world interest rate faced by Banania rises to $i^* = 0.20$ (20%). What would be the effect on Banania's long-run equilibrium price level? Explain your results.
(d) Suppose that Banania's government increases its autonomous expenditures on bananas by 20 million. What would be the impact on domestic prices, on the autonomous trade balance?

Questions (a) to (d) are independent of each other. Give numerical answers for each.

APPENDIX: AGGREGATE SUPPLY: AN ALGEBRAIC TREATMENT

This appendix derives an analytical expression for the aggregate supply curve. This requires establishing relationships (1) between changes in prices and changes in employment, and (2) between employment and output.

The behavior of employment in response to changes in prices [described in the text in relation to Figure 10–4(a)], can be algebraically depicted by

$$\frac{N - N_F}{N_F} = \theta \left(\frac{P - P_{-1}}{P_{-1}} \right) \tag{A-1}$$

where N is current employment, which can be above or below its long-run, full-employment level, N_F; P is the current price level, which can be above or below its previous level, P_{-1}; and θ is a positive parameter to be interpreted in a moment. Equation (A-1) suggests that if domestic prices rise above their previous level (as they did in our earlier example, from P_o to P_1), employment will increase above its full-employment level (as it did in Figure 10–4, from N_F to N_1). Symbolically, if $(P - P_{-1})$ is positive, then $(N - N_F)$ is positive as well. Observe also that if the domestic price level were to stop increasing, at that point $P = P_{-1}$ and employment would return to full employment (N would again equal N_F).

The parameter θ represents how much a given percentage increase in domestic prices would tend to increase employment. The smaller (or larger) θ is, the smaller (or larger) the influence of an increase in the price of domestic goods on employment. The value of θ in any economy depends on the degree to which employment contracts pervade the economy. The less important these are, and the less rigid nominal wages are, the faster they will adjust to changes in prices. In this case θ will be relatively small: Increases in price will have relatively little impact on real wages and thus on employment. The opposite occurs if labor contracts are important in the economy.

Equation (A-1) can be interpreted in a different way if it is transformed into

$$U = \frac{N_F - N}{N_F} = -\theta \left(\frac{P - P_{-1}}{P_{-1}} \right) \qquad \text{(A-2)}$$

a so-called *Phillips curve*. It relates the rate of unemployment, $U = (N_F - N)/N_F$, to the rate of inflation, $(P - P_{-1})/P_{-1}$, suggesting a negative relationship between the two. A negative value of U in the present context means that employment is above full-employment, and it thus represents overemployment. The analysis in this chapter suggests the presence of a downward-sloping Phillips curve in the short run.

The next link in determining an analytical expression for aggregate supply is to specify how output is affected when employment changes. It is assumed that output behaves in the following way in relation to employment:

$$Y = Y_F + \beta \left(\frac{N - N_F}{N_F} \right) \qquad \text{(A-3)}$$

where β is a positive parameter that measures how the output of domestic goods increases above its full-employment level when employment increases above full employment. The larger the parameter β is, the stronger the response of output to any given change in employment. When β is very small, changes in the use of labor will affect domestic output in a minor way.

The aggregate supply function of the economy can be derived by substituting equation (A-1) into (A-3), obtaining

$$Y = Y_F + \theta\beta \left(\frac{P - P_{-1}}{P_{-1}} \right) \qquad \text{(A-4)}$$

Equation (A-4) reflects algebraically the short-run upward-sloping Y_o^S curve in Figure 10–4(b). Since θ and β are positive, if the current price level, P, increases above its previous level, P_{-1}, the supply of domestic goods, Y, increases above Y_F. Equation A-4 also reflects the behavior of aggregate supply over the long run. Once the labor market fully adjusts to a once-and-for-all disturbance, prices will stop increasing so that P would equal P_{-1}, in which case $Y = Y_F$; output returns to its full-employment level.

CHAPTER 11

Prices, Output, and Stagflation Under Flexible Exchange Rates

The seventies saw a major shift in international monetary relations toward increased flexibility in the exchange rates of major industrial countries. They also saw a general increase in both the level and diversity of inflation rates among these countries. The inflation rates before and after the start of the recent period of floating exchange rates are compared in Table 11–1. In the United States, for example, the average annual inflation rate for the fixed exchange rate period 1963 to 1972 was 3.5%; the corresponding inflation rate for the floating exchange rate period 1973 to 1982 was 7.6%. Table 11–1 also displays the increased variability of inflation rates among industrial countries. What explains this experience under the recent floating exchange rate regime? It is clear that the answer to this question must be related to the particular inflationary effects of economic policies under floating exchange rates, as well as to the massive oil price hikes of 1973 and 1979 and the role of floating exchange rates on the adjustment of industrial economies to these shocks.

In this chapter we use the concepts of aggregate demand and aggregate supply to analyze the determination of the price level and unemployment in open economies under flexible exchange rates, and to examine the effects of policy changes and external disturbances. The initial discussion sets aside the problem of the formation of expectations about the future, which is given careful study in Chapter 12. The overall emphasis of the present chapter is on the longer-run effects of economic disturbances under flexible exchange rates, rather than the details of short-run exchange rate dynamics.

TABLE 11–1. The Industrial Countries and Stagflation in the Seventies and Early Eighties

	1963–1972	1973	1974	1975	1976	1977	1978	1979	1980	1981	1982
Real GNP (percentage change from previous year)											
United States	4.0	5.8	-0.6	-1.2	5.4	5.5	5.0	2.8	-0.4	1.9	-1.7
European countries	4.4	5.8	2.0	-1.2	4.6	2.6	3.0	3.4	-1.5	-0.2	0.2
United Kingdom	2.8	7.2	-1.8	-1.1	3.4	1.6	3.9	2.0	-2.1	-2.2	0.7
Germany, FDR	4.5	4.6	0.5	-1.6	5.6	2.8	3.5	4.0	1.8	-0.2	-1.1
France	5.5	5.4	3.2	0.2	5.2	3.0	3.7	3.4	1.1	0.4	1.6
Japan	10.5	8.8	-1.2	2.4	5.3	5.3	5.1	5.2	4.8	3.8	3.0
Inflation (percentage change in GNP price deflator)											
United States	3.5	5.7	8.8	9.3	5.2	5.8	7.4	8.6	9.3	9.4	6.0
European countries	5.0	8.2	11.7	13.8	9.8	9.6	8.8	9.0	10.7	9.9	9.5
United Kingdom	5.2	7.0	14.9	26.9	14.6	14.1	10.9	15.0	19.2	12.2	8.0
Germany, FDR	4.1	6.5	6.8	6.1	3.4	3.7	4.2	4.0	4.4	4.2	4.8
France	4.8	7.8	11.2	13.3	9.9	9.0	9.5	10.3	11.8	12.0	12.1
Japan	4.7	11.7	20.6	8.1	6.4	5.7	4.6	2.6	2.8	2.6	2.0
Unemployment rates											
United States	4.7	4.9	5.6	8.5	7.7	7.1	6.1	5.8	7.2	7.6	11.0
United Kingdom	2.4	2.6	2.6	3.9	4.0	5.7	5.7	5.4	6.5	10.1	11.9
Germany, FDR	0.9	1.1	2.3	4.1	4.0	3.9	3.8	3.3	3.4	4.9	6.8
France	1.9	2.6	2.8	4.1	4.4	4.7	5.2	5.9	6.3	7.3	8.6
Japan	1.2	1.2	1.4	1.9	2.0	2.0	2.2	2.1	2.0	2.2	2.4

Source: *World Economic Outlook*, International Monetary Fund, Washington, D.C., 1983.

11–1 AGGREGATE DEMAND AND PRICES UNDER FLEXIBLE EXCHANGE RATES

This section discusses the concept of aggregate demand within the context of flexible exchange rate regimes. The aggregate demand function specifies how spending on domestic goods responds to the price of domestic goods. It is represented graphically in Figure 11–2 as the aggregate demand curve, $Y^D Y^D$. We now examine the role of exchange rate flexibility on the aggregate demand curve.

Figure 11–1(b) shows our now standard diagram depicting the determination of aggregate spending on domestic goods by the intersection of the IS_0 and LM_0 curves. To simplify the exposition, our analysis assumes perfect capital mobility, in which case (ignoring exchange rate expectations and exchange risk) the domestic interest rate will be constrained to equal the world interest rate,

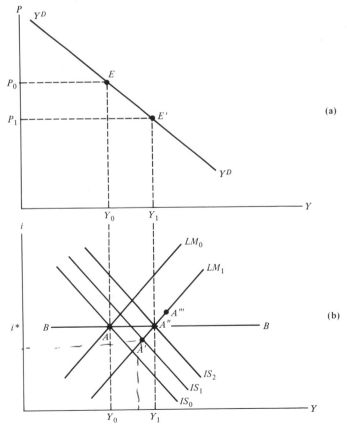

FIGURE 11–1. Derivation of the Aggregate Demand Curve

that is, $i = i^*$. This constraint on domestic equilibrium is depicted by the horizontal BB curve in Figure 11–1(b).

The intersection of the IS_0, LM_0, and BB curves at point A in Figure 11–1(b) determines aggregate desired spending on domestic goods, given the money supply, the level of autonomous spending, and the domestic price level. At that point, the spending decisions of domestic residents are consistent with assets market equilibrium and balanced payments.

Suppose now that we vary the price of domestic goods, P, say by a shift from P_0 to P_1, where P_1 is smaller than P_0. What are the effects on desired aggregate spending? First, a reduction in the price of domestic goods increases real money balances—from M_0/P_0 to M_0/P_1—which, at a given interest rate, i^*, would require an increase in domestic spending to increase money demand and maintain money market equilibrium. This is represented by the rightward shift of the LM curve from LM_0 to LM_1 in Figure 11–1(b).

In addition, the reduction in domestic prices shifts the IS curve to the right. At a given level of the exchange rate, a reduction in domestic prices would raise the relative price of foreign goods in terms of domestic goods, $q = eP^*/P$, enhancing the price competitiveness of domestic goods relative to foreign goods in international markets and switching demand toward domestic goods. The stimulated spending on domestic goods then shifts the IS curve rightward, from IS_0 to IS_1 in Figure 11–1(b). This effect is called the *real exchange rate* effect, to stress that in the present context the relative price of foreign goods in terms of domestic goods, q, corresponds to the concept of real exchange rate. A real exchange rate is a price-adjusted nominal exchange rate, generally computed by multiplying the nominal exchange rate by the ratio of an index of the foreign and domestic price levels. Since we define the domestic price level in terms of domestically produced export goods, and the foreign price level in terms of import goods produced abroad, the real exchange rate would correspond to our concept of q. (For more details on the computation of real exchange rates, see Chapter 4.)

As depicted by point A', the net impact of the shifts in the IS and LM curves associated with a reduction in domestic prices—at a given level of the exchange rate—would be to increase spending and to lower domestic interest rates. Point A', however, cannot be a full-fledged equilibrium of the economy. Before the economy ever reaches that point, other changes will occur. The reason is that a reduction in domestic interest rates below world interest rates would immediately generate massive incipient capital outflows, inducing a domestic currency depreciation. The exchange rate increase then shifts the IS curve upward until a point like A'' is reached. At that point, the domestic interest rate equals the world interest rate, and there is consequently no further capital flight and no subsequent changes in the exchange rate. The equilibrium increase in aggregate spending in response to a reduction of the domestic price level is thus from Y_0 to Y_1. This adjustment in desired spending takes into account both the direct effects of the decrease in the price of domestic goods on domestic spending as well as those of the associated depreciation of the domestic currency.[1]

Our analysis has shown the negative connection existing between prices and spending on domestic goods, thereby establishing the downward-sloping nature of the aggregate demand curve, as shown by the $Y^D Y^D$ curve in Figure 11–1(a).

Points E and E' in that diagram lie along aggregate demand and correspond to points A and A'' in Figure 11–1(b): A decrease in the price of domestic goods from P_0 to P_1 is associated with an increase in desired aggregate spending from Y_0 to Y_1. We should stress that the exchange rate is not constant along the aggregate demand curve; the latter incorporates those exchange rate adjustments that equilibrate the goods market and maintain balanced payments under flexible exchange rates.

What are the effects of monetary disturbances and changes in autonomous spending on the aggregate demand curve? First, changes in the nominal money supply induce shifts of the aggregate demand curve. For instance, an open market purchase of bonds by the Central Bank will clearly increase the money supply, and, at a given price level, the resulting increase in real money balances would then place downward pressure on domestic interest rates, inducing capital to flow out of the economy and depreciating domestic currency. The consequence would be an expenditure switch out of foreign and into domestic goods, with a resulting increase in spending on domestic goods. In other words, at a given price level, desired aggregate spending on domestic goods would increase. This corresponds graphically to a shift of the aggregate demand curve to the right. When the money supply decreases, exactly the opposite occurs: If real balances decline, aggregate demand for domestic goods will contract at any given price of domestic goods. Geometrically, the aggregate demand curve shifts to the left.

---

[1] A decrease in the price of domestic goods will not necessarily be associated—everything else constant—with a currency depreciation. It all depends on how the initial shift of the IS curve and the shift of the LM curve compare. In the case we have described in the text, the initial shift of the IS curve is relatively small compared with the shift of the LM curve. As a consequence, the resulting intersection of the curves occurs at a domestic interest rate below the world level. If the IS curve were to shift by a higher proportion, as if it intersected the LM_1 curve at point A''' instead of at point A', there would be an *increase* in the domestic interest rate above its world level. Incipient capital inflows and an appreciating domestic currency would result. The full equilibrium of the economy would remain, however, at point A'': The appreciation of domestic currency would immediately shift the IS curve back from its hypothetical intersection with the LM_1 curve at point A''' to intersection at point A''. Finally, since the domestic interest rate has to return to its world level, the increase in domestic spending from Y_0 to Y_1 must be associated with a net increment of the real exchange rate: The decline of the exchange rate from point A''' to A'' is more than offset by the initial decline in the price of domestic goods, leaving $q = eP^*/P$ at a higher level.

In contrast to monetary disturbances, changes in autonomous spending—such as may arise from fiscal policy changes or an exogenous change in the demand for domestic exports—will *not* induce any shifts in the aggregate demand curve in the present framework. The explanation is that the increased spending would at the same time raise money demand and place upward pressures on domestic interest rates. This would then be associated with incipient capital inflows and an immediate appreciation of domestic currency, which shifts aggregate spending back down toward its original level. Since, under perfect capital mobility, these changes occur instantaneously, the increased autonomous spending would not generate any perceptible shifts of aggregate demand; it would only change its composition among autonomous expenditures (that increase) and net exports (that decrease in response to the domestic currency appreciation).

The reader can visualize more clearly the striking contrast between the effects of changes in the money supply and in autonomous expenditures on aggregate demand by transforming the money market equilibrium condition

$$\frac{M^S}{P} = kY - hi$$

making use of the interest rate constraint $i = i^*$ and interchanging the dependent variable to show aggregate spending on domestic goods:

$$Y = \frac{M^S}{P}\frac{1}{k} + \frac{h}{k}i^* \qquad AD \qquad (1)$$

This equation establishes a connection between aggregate spending, Y, and the price of domestic goods, P, at a given level of the world interest rate, i^*, and the money supply, M^S. Equation (1) can be interpreted as an equation of aggregate demand where—in the background—the exchange rate is being allowed to adjust in order to equilibrate the goods market. Increases in the money supply can be clearly seen to raise spending on domestic goods, at any given level of domestic prices. Changes in autonomous spending, on the other hand, do not affect in any perceptible way the relationship between price and spending shown by equation (1) and would have no effect on aggregate demand; the presence of exchange rate changes in the background offsets the direct effects of changes in autonomous spending leaving aggregate demand unchanged.

The lack of influence of changes in autonomous spending on overall spending in the economy can be better visualized by showing the components of aggregate desired spending. At a given price of domestic goods, P_o, and with the domestic interest rate constrained to equal world interest rates, desired spending on domestic goods is given by

$$Y = \alpha \left[\bar{A} + \bar{T}\left(\frac{eP^*}{P_o}\right) - bi^* \right] \qquad (2)$$

Now, as we have seen, a rise in autonomous domestic spending—an increase in $\bar{A}$—will reduce the exchange rate, e. This lowers the real exchange rate, $q = eP^*/P_o$, deteriorating the international competitiveness of domestic products and worsening the autonomous trade balance, $\bar{T}$. The declining net exports then offset the increased autonomous expenditures, leaving desired aggregate spending on domestic goods, Y, unchanged.

11–2   DETERMINATION OF PRICES AND OUTPUT IN THE SHORT RUN

The last section summarized the nature of demand behavior in the economy as portrayed by the aggregate demand curve. In order to determine the equilibrium levels of price and output of domestic goods, however, we have to join aggregate demand with aggregate supply; that is, we have to examine the interaction of the aggregate supply *and* aggregate demand curves.

Following our discussion in Chapter 10, it is assumed that nominal wage rates are relatively rigid over the short run, as specified by binding employment contracts previously engaged in. This determines a certain short-run aggregate supply curve, shown by $Y_o^S\,Y_o^S$ in Figure 11–2(a), indicating how the quantity supplied of domestic goods changes over the short run when prices change. In addition, with fixed fiscal and monetary policy parameters, a certain aggregate demand curve will be given, showing how the quantity demanded of domestic goods changes when prices change. The curve $Y_o^D\,Y_o^D$ depicts this aggregate demand relationship in Figure 11–2(a).

The economy is in short-run equilibrium when the quantity demanded of domestic goods is equal to the short-run quantity supplied. This occurs at the point where the domestic aggregate demand curve intersects the given short-run aggregate supply curve. There is then a simultaneous short-run equilibrium of the goods and money markets in the sense that they all clear, given the rigid nominal wage existing in the short run and given fixed fiscal and monetary parameters. This short-run equilibrium of the economy is illustrated graphically by means of point A in Figure 11–2(a), which is the point of intersection of the aggregate demand curve, $Y_o^D\,Y_o^D$, with the short-run aggregate supply curve, $Y_o^S\,Y_o^S$. The resulting short-run equilibrium output of domestic goods is Y_o and the short-run equilibrium price of domestic goods is P_o.

The economy's short-run equilibrium level of output can generally differ from its full-employment level. Such is the case depicted by point A in Figure 11–2(a), where short-run output, Y_o, is below its full-employment level, Y_F. This means that the economy suffers from unemployment. Is this a short-run phenomenon or does it remain permanently as a characteristic of the economy in the absence of economic policy or other disturbances? This question will be answered in the next section.

11-3   THE ADJUSTMENT PROCESS, REAL WAGES, AND THE REAL EXCHANGE RATE

We shall now focus on the role played by the real wage rate and the real exchange rate in the adjustment of the economy toward long-run equilibrium.[2]

In Figure 11-2 we illustrate an economy's long-run process of recovery from a short-run position of unemployment, depicted by point A. In the presence of unemployment, nominal wage rates tend to decline over time. As labor contracts come up for revision, the availability of unemployed workers and their effective competition with the employed bids down wage rates. At the initial prices, the nominal wage cuts reduce real wages. The resulting lower real unit labor costs induce producers to raise output and to pass on some of the cuts in real labor costs to consumers in the form of price reductions. Geometrically, a reduction in nominal wages at a given level of prices—a reduction in real wages—will shift the aggregate supply curve to the right. In terms of Figure 11-2(a), the economy would move along the pointed arrows, representing the intersection points of the shifting short-run aggregate supply curve with the unchanged aggregate demand curve. (Note that the latter remains fixed, as determined by monetary and fiscal policy parameters.) This *wage–price automatic adjustment mechanism* of a laissez-faire economy ends when full-employment output is reached, at which point (cyclical) unemployment has been eliminated and nominal—and real—wage rates stop declining. This is the long-run equilibrium of the economy, obtained when goods and money markets are in equilibrium *and* the labor market is at full-employment. It is depicted by point E in Figure 11-2(a), which shows the intersection of the long-run aggregate supply curve with the aggregate demand curve. The implication is that the economy's initial state of unemployment is eliminated over time. The declining nominal—and real—wage rates shift the aggregate supply curve all the way from its initial position at $Y_0^S Y_0^S$ to the one consistent with full employment at $Y_1^S Y_1^S$.

What is the behavior of the exchange rate over the adjustment process? In the present case, the path of the exchange rate cannot be exactly pinned down unless knowledge of the specific structure of the economy is available. This is because the net effect on the exchange rate of the changes in income and prices involved is not completely determinate. Declining domestic prices, at a given level of income, would raise the real money supply, place downward

[2] A third basic variable is involved—the *real interest rate*. Domestic investment spending depends on nominal interest rates adjusted for anticipated inflation, that is, real interest rates. Changes in the latter over time will influence the aggregate demand curve and, consequently, the long-run behavior of the economy. For the moment, however, we are ignoring expectational considerations and assuming that the anticipated rate of inflation is zero. In this case, the domestic real interest rate becomes identical to the nominal interest rate, which, under perfect capital mobility, is constrained to equal the world interest rate. With the latter assumed fixed, no changes in real interest rates would arise. The effect of expectations and changes in the real interest rate on the behavior of the economy will be examined in Chapters 12 and 13.

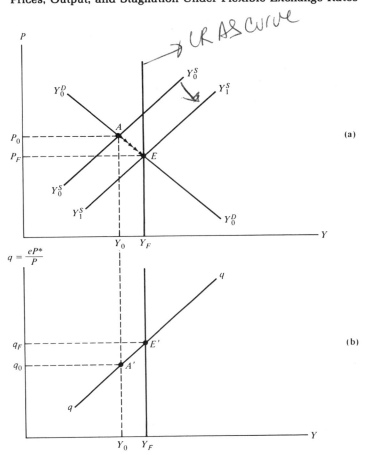

handwritten: → CR AS curve

FIGURE 11–2. Short-Run Equilibrium and the Adjustment Toward Long-Run Equilibrium

handwritten: → depreciate currency e↑, $q = \frac{eP*}{P \cdot \downarrow}$

pressure on interest rates and induce incipient capital outflows tending to raise *handwritten: ↑ m^d* the exchange rate. On the other hand, at a fixed price level, rises in domestic income would have the opposite effect. They would raise money demand, place upward pressures on domestic interest rates, and induce capital inflows that *handwritten: shift curve left* tend to lower the exchange rate. The net balance of these two effects is not determinate and depends on such parameters as the income elasticity of money demand and the effects of exchange rate changes on the trade balance. *handwritten: ↓U*

The variable that is indeed determinate in the adjustment process is the real exchange rate, which corresponds in our analysis to the relative price of foreign goods in terms of domestic goods, $q = eP*/P$. The real exchange rate rises over the process of adjustment toward full employment. In other words, the increase in output from Y_0 to Y_F in Figure 11–2(a) is directly associated with an increase in the real exchange rate, say from q_0 to q_F. This connection between output of domestic goods and the real exchange rate is due to the fact that, with domestic interest rates fixed at world levels and with aggregate autonomous spending fixed, changes in the demand for domestic goods can only be associated with changes in the autonomous trade balance, which are a direct function of the real exchange rate. This is best seen from the aggregate demand function,

$$Y = \alpha[\bar{A} + \bar{T}(q) - bi^*]$$ (2)

With autonomous expenditures fixed at $\bar{A}$ and the domestic interest rate equal to the—fixed—world rate, i^*, the quantity demanded of domestic goods, Y, will be altered only when the real exchange rate, q, changes. An increase in the real exchange rate—an increase in q—is associated with an increase in domestic competitiveness in world markets, inducing a switch in expenditure toward domestic goods and increasing its quantity demanded. Reductions of the real exchange rate—decreases in q—on the other hand, would deteriorate competitiveness, worsen the autonomous trade balance, and reduce the aggregate quantity demanded of domestic goods. This positive connection between the real exchange rate and domestic output is represented by means of the upward-sloping qq curve in Figure 11–2(b). The vertical axis in Figure 11–2(b) shows the values of the real exchange rate, while the horizontal axis is the same as in Figure 11–2(a), displaying the level of domestic output.

The basic problem behind the unemployment existing at the short-run equilibrium of the economy at point A is the fact that real wages are too high for full employment to be attained. In other words, the short-run aggregate supply curve, $Y_o^S Y_o^S$, lies above the curve required to attain full employment, $Y_1^S Y_1^S$. The effect of the high real wage rates is to make domestic real labor costs high, compared with foreign firms, thereby generating domestic production at prices that are not competitive in world markets. In other words, the real exchange rate at point A'—q_o in Figure 11–2(b)—is below the level necessary to gain the access to international markets needed to attain the full-employment level of output (the required real exchange rate is denoted by q_F). The resulting slack demand for domestic goods is then associated with the shortfall of domestic output and employment below their full-employment levels at point E'.

As nominal and real wages decline over time, real labor costs also decline. This surfaces as an increase in the international competitiveness of domestic goods—an increase in q—eventually moving the economy to full employment. The output boom is spearheaded by rising net exports, reflected in an improvement of the autonomous trade balance. The increased real exchange rate is thus instrumental in transmitting the changes in real wages into changes in aggregate quantity demanded of domestic goods and increased output. In terms of Figure 11–2(b), the increase in output from Y_o to Y_F is associated with an increase in the real exchange rate from q_o to q_F. Note that this gain in international competitiveness is directly connected to the reduction of domestic prices

$$\eta \mathcal{B} = \frac{e p^*}{P \downarrow} \mathcal{B} \uparrow$$

from P_o to P_F. It may also be associated, although not necessarily, with a rising nominal exchange rate, e.[3]

In summary, within the present framework there appears to be an automatic wage–price adjustment mechanism, which tends to move the laissez-faire flexible-rates economy toward full employment over time. This mechanism, which operates by influencing real wages and the real exchange rate, works when domestic output is above full employment just as well as it does when it is below. With overemployment, a rising wage–price spiral would raise real wages, reduce real exchange rates, and move the economy back to full employment. This suggests that, unless the full-employment level of output can be increased, the full utilization of the economy's limited resources will prevent permanent increases in output over the current level of full employment. The policy implications of this important point are examined in the next section. Note finally that the adjustment process under floating exchange rates does not rely on the nominal money supply changes that take place under fixed exchange rates. Under freely floating exchange rates, the economy's exchange rate will adjust to ensure balance of payments equilibrium, and there will be no changes in the economy's monetary base except those initiated by the Central Bank in altering its credit.

11–4 AGGREGATE DEMAND POLICIES, EMPLOYMENT, AND INFLATION UNDER FLEXIBLE EXCHANGE RATES

This section examines the output and inflationary effects of government policies under floating exchange rates. In order for an aggregate demand policy disturbance to have perceptible effects on domestic output—whether in the short run or over time—it must be able to influence aggregate demand positively. As we concluded earlier, however, real disturbances in the form of changes in autonomous spending—such as fiscal policy disturbances—do not tend to be effective in altering aggregate demand under flexible exchange rates and perfect capital mobility. Any positive effects of the increased autonomous spending on aggregate demand are seriously hampered by the negative impact of the spending increase on the real exchange rate, and, hence, on domestic exports. With no net effect on domestic spending, real disturbances would be powerless to shift aggregate demand, and, consequently, to increase domestic output, whether in the short run or in the long run.

Monetary disturbances, on the other hand, tend to be more successful in altering the aggregate demand curve under flexible exchange rates. Consider

---

[3] To understand that the increase in output from point A to point E is not necessarily associated with an increase in the nominal exchange rate, the reader may want to return to Figure 11–1 and, in particular, the related discussion in footnote 2 regarding the movement from point E to point E' along the aggregate demand curve $Y^D Y^D$. The exchange rate behavior behind this movement is similar to that relating to the movement from point A to point E along $Y_o^D Y_o^D$ in Figure 11–2(a).

the case of an expansionary monetary policy in the form of an open market purchase of bonds by the Central Bank. The sudden injection of money into the banking system places downward pressure on domestic interest rates, causing incipient capital outflows and a depreciation of domestic currency. The consequence is a switch in expenditures toward domestic goods, shown by the shift of the aggregate demand curve from $Y_o^D Y_o^D$ to $Y_1^D Y_1^D$ in Figure 11–3(a). The economy thus moves from its initial equilibrium at point A to the short-run equilibrium depicted by point E, at the intersection of the aggregate demand curve $Y_1^D Y_1^D$ with the short-run aggregate supply curve $Y_o^S Y_o^S$. Domestic output rises above full employment—from Y_F to Y_1—but at the cost of domestic inflation—domestic prices rise from P_o to P_1.

The short-run output boom induced by the increase in the money supply is closely linked to the decline in real labor costs associated with this disturbance. With nominal wage rates rigid over the short run, the inflationary spur associated with the monetary expansion will reduce real wage rates. These reduced real labor costs and the consequent stimulus to domestic production have, as a counterpart, a greater competitiveness of domestic goods in international markets, which is reflected in an increased real exchange rate. In terms of Figure 11–3(b), the equilibrium increase in output above full employment—from Y_F to Y_1—is associated with an increase in the real exchange rate from q_F to q_1. This occurs in spite of the rising prices of domestic goods, which, by themselves, tend to cause a deterioration in the international competitiveness of domestic products. The nominal exchange rate depreciation associated with the monetary expansion more than offsets the effects of the domestic price hike, leaving a net positive impact on the real exchange rate. Symbolically, even though domestic prices, P, increase, the rise of the nominal exchange rate, e, more than compensates for it, leaving the real exchange rate, $q = eP^*/P$ at a higher level. The real depreciation of domestic currency improves the autonomous trade balance by switching demand away from foreign and toward domestic goods. In conclusion, the short-run expansionary impact of the monetary disturbance is closely linked to the decline of real wages, which spearheads an increase in net exports.

The reduction in real wages associated with output above full employment is reversed over the long run. As employment contracts come up for renewal, workers seeking to regain their lost real income will revise nominal—and real—wage rates upward. The outcome is an increase in real labor costs, partly passed on to consumers in the form of higher prices of domestic goods. This deteriorates domestic competitiveness in world goods markets, causing a loss of net exports, and reducing domestic output back toward its full-employment level. Diagrammatically, over the long run, inflationary pressures result in a real appreciation of domestic currency from q_1 back to q_F, and a leftward shift of aggregate supply from $Y_o^S Y_o^S$ to $Y_1^S Y_1^S$. The resulting long-run equilibrium is at point C, with output back at Y_F and domestic prices at a level equal to P_1. At this equilibrium point, domestic real wages will have returned to their original level

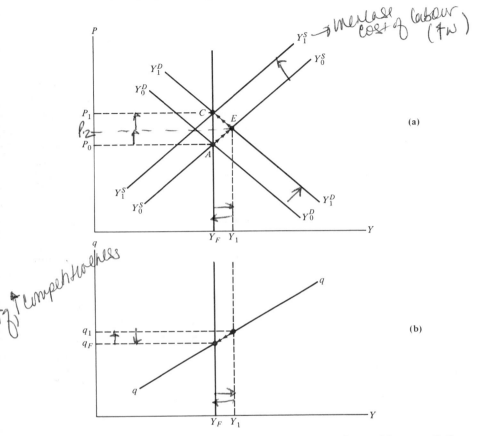

FIGURE 11-3.   Short-Run and Long-Run Effects of Expansionary Monetary Policy

with the labor market at full employment and no further wage adjustments required.[4] It appears that the long-run effect of expansionary monetary policy is only inflation. The constraints imposed on the economy by full employment of limited resources cannot be permanently avoided and are directly associated with the lack of effectiveness of expansionary aggregate demand policies on output.

[4] Even though point C is the long-run equilibrium to which the economy would eventually move, the adjustment process toward that point may not be as direct and smooth as we have described. For instance, there may be an overshooting of the shifting aggregate supply curve above point C, leading to a momentary shortfall of output below full employment. Over time, of course, the supply curve would shift precisely to $Y_1^S Y_1^S$ in response to the resulting unemployment. Similarly, real exchange rates generally will not approach long-run equilibrium in a smooth and direct way, as shown by Figure 11-3(b).

Monetary Policy, Prices and Currency Depreciation

An implication of the analysis is that, in a fully employed economy, monetary disturbances do not have permanent effects on the real exchange rate. At points A and C, domestic output, interest rates, and autonomous spending are all the same. Consequently, from equation (2), the autonomous trade balance and the corresponding real exchange rate will also have to be the same. But note that the monetary expansion increases domestic prices. In order for the real exchange rate to remain unchanged an exchange rate depreciation of the same proportion as the rise in prices has to occur. Symbolically, since the real exchange rate is $q = eP^*/P$, taking proportional changes on both sides implies that, over the long run,

$$\hat{q} = \hat{e} + \hat{P}^* - \hat{P} = 0 \tag{3}$$

where $\hat{q}$, $\hat{e}$, $\hat{P}^*$, and $\hat{P}$ are the proportional changes in the long-run equilibrium values of the real exchange rate, the nominal exchange rate, foreign prices, and domestic prices, respectively. Equation (3) states that, if the real exchange rate is to remain constant, the proportional changes in the nominal exchange rate and in foreign and domestic prices must add up to zero; that is, they must offset each other. Given that, for simplicity, we are assuming foreign inflation ($\hat{P}^*$) to be zero, the implication is that $\hat{e} = \hat{P}$: The proportional depreciation of the nominal exchange rate must equal the proportional increase in prices to leave the real exchange rate, q, unchanged.

The hypothesis that monetary disturbances do not affect the real exchange rate is associated with the doctrine of *purchasing power parity* (discussed in Chapter 10 in relation to an economy under fixed exchange rates and examined in greater detail within the context of flexible exchange rates in Chapter 15). Our present analysis suggests that, in the face of monetary disturbances, the hypothesis, in its version expressed by equation (3), should tend to hold only over the long run and not necessarily over short periods of time. Over the short run, sudden monetary disturbances can generate all kinds of changes in the real exchange rate, thereby causing deviations from purchasing power parity. In addition, the long-run real exchange rate may be altered by real disturbances, such as fiscal policy changes and changes in full-employment output, in which case equation (3) may fail to hold even over the long run.

This section has examined the effects of aggregate demand policies within the context of an economy that operates initially at full employment and whose starting background is one of price stability. In this case, the full-employment constraint prevents expansionary aggregate demand policies from having any long-run effects on domestic output and leads them instead to fuel domestic inflation. Often, however, policies must be enacted in situations in which the economy is not characterized by full employment and price stability but is instead suffering initially from unemployment, chronic inflation, or both. What would be the effects of policy intervention within this context? For example, must expansionary monetary policy be associated only with price inflation over the long run? The following sections attempt to answer these questions.

11–5   SUPPLY SHOCKS IN THE OPEN ECONOMY: OIL PRICES AND STAGFLATION DURING THE SEVENTIES

A wide range of disturbances can destabilize an economy, leading it to stagnation, unemployment, inflation, or to all these problems combined. This section is concerned with the effects of a supply disturbance in the form of a sudden increase in the price of raw materials imported by the economy. This was the case facing most industrial economies during the seventies, when oil prices spiraled, particularly during the periods of late 1973 to early 1974, and 1979. From 1972 to 1974, for instance, the price of oil, according to Saudi Arabian quotes, increased from $1.90 per barrel to $9.76, as spearheaded by the Arab oil embargo and the start of OPEC price hikes during the last quarter of 1973. In the United States, the price increase was rapidly translated into rising gasoline and motor oil prices, which soared by 39% during the period September 1973 to May 1974 alone. The second massive oil price shock occurred during 1979, associated with political events in Iran and Iraq, and resulted in an increase in the price of oil, from $12.70 to $28.67 per barrel during the period 1978 to 1980. Both of these sharp price hikes made big dents in the economies of most of the oil-importing industrial countries, significantly destabilizing them. It is the purpose of this section to discuss these effects.

Table 11–1 shows the behavior of real gross national product, inflation, and unemployment in the United States, western Europe, and Japan during the seventies and early eighties. The immediate impact of the 1973 to 1974 and 1979 oil price shocks on these countries was clearly recessionary, associated with falling real GNP and rising unemployment. In the case of the United States, for example, real GNP declined by 0.6% and 1.2% during the years 1974 and 1975 and by 0.4% during 1980, while unemployment rose from a rate of 4.9% in 1973 to 8.5% in 1975 and from 5.8% in 1979 to 7.4% and then 7.6% in 1980 and 1981, respectively. Both episodes were also associated with rising inflation rates, although not in all countries. In the United States, inflation jumped from 5.7% in 1973 to 9.3% by 1975 and from 8.6% in 1979 to 9.4% in 1981. The term *stagflation,* a combination of recession (stagnation) and inflation, has been coined to characterize the general features of the industrial world following the oil shocks of the 1970s.

Relatively large differences in the behavior of the various industrial economies in the aftermath of the oil shocks can be extrapolated from Table 11–1. For instance, economic recovery in the United States during the post-oil shock period of 1976 to 1978 was stronger than the European recovery, with only the United States able to achieve real GNP growth rates comparable to pre-oil shock levels.

Even among the western European countries, a wide variation of experience can be found. The recessionary period 1974 to 1975, for instance, appeared to be milder for France than for the other European countries, particularly the United Kingdom and West Germany. The experience in controlling inflation after the oil shock, on the other hand, seemed to be better for West Germany. The case of Japan stands out because of its steadily falling inflation rates from 1974 to 1982. What factors could give rise to these observed divergencies in the response of the industrial economies to the supply shocks of the seventies? Differences in the policy actions of each country combined with basic differences in the institutional wage-setting processes among them clearly had an important role. The following sections describe these differences and their links to the relative economic performance of the industrial countries in the aftermath of the oil shocks.

11–6   STAGFLATION, MONETARY ACCOMMODATION, AND NOMINAL WAGE RIGIDITY

What are the economic mechanisms through which a supply shock gives rise to stagflation? This section examines in detail the various mechanisms through which an increase in the price of imported raw materials, say oil, affects the economy. We begin by analyzing the effects of such a disturbance using the standard aggregate demand–aggregate supply framework described earlier in this chapter. We then specify the policy options open, discussing in some detail the particular case of the United States and its experience during the 1973 to 1978 period.

Figure 11–4 shows the initial equilibrium of the economy at point E, corresponding to the intersection of the short-run aggregate demand and aggregate supply curves, $Y_o^D Y_o^D$ and $Y_o^S Y_o^S$, at the full-employment level of output, Y_F. Suppose there is a sudden increase in the price (real cost) of raw materials, everything else remaining constant, and that the economy considered is, for simplicity, wholly dependent on foreign supplies of these inputs. This disturbance will, first of all, increase the costs of production and raise the prices at which domestic producers are willing to supply any given quantity of domestic goods. This means that the short-run aggregate supply curve will shift in the northwest direction, as depicted by the shift from $Y_o^S Y_o^S$ to $Y_1^S Y_1^S$ in Figure 11–4. The impact effect of the rise in the price of imported raw materials is thus an increase in the prices of domestic goods and a reduction of domestic output, as represented diagrammatically by the move of the economy from point E to point G. In other words, the supply shock is stagflationary, as it produces both recession and inflation.

Note that the leftward shift of the aggregate supply curve is exclusively associated with the rise in price of the imported raw materials and is drawn

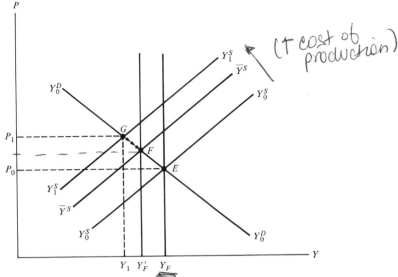

FIGURE 11–4. The Stagflationary Effects of a Supply Shock

for a given level of the nominal wage rate. The assumption is that current nominal wage rates are stipulated and fixed by existing labor contracts and cannot therefore change over the short run. This is referred to, quite logically, as short-run *nominal wage rigidity* and constitutes a significant attribute of the economy as long as long-term labor contracts—whether explicit or implicit—are an important feature of the domestic labor market. In the presence of nominal wage rigidity, the inflationary effects of a supply shock will reduce real wages in the short run. For instance, if the nominal wage rate was initially at W_0, the rise in prices from P_0 to P_1 lowers real wages from W_0/P_0 to W_0/P_1.

In the absence of government intervention, the short-run equilibrium of the economy at point G will not be sustained over time. Given the presence of a pool of unemployed workers, when labor contracts come up for renewal, nominal wages will be bid down, inducing the short-run aggregate supply curve to shift in the southeastern direction and moving the economy toward full employment in the labor market. Note, however, that the supply shock reduces the full-employment level of output and, as a result, the economy will not return to its initial level of income, Y_F, moving instead to full employment at Y'_F. The reason for the decline in the level of domestic output at full employment lies in the fact that the rise in the real cost of oil implies a transfer of real income from oil-importing nations to the oil-producing countries. The implied reduction of real income in industrial oil-importing countries is reflected in a decrease in the output any of these economies can produce with its available labor force *net of the real cost of the imported oil input.* This is what the decrease in (net) full-employment output from Y_F to Y_F' in Figure 11–4 depicts.[5] Therefore, when the economy adjusts to full employment in the labor market, a lower amount of net output will be produced. Note that the counterpart of this decline of domestic real income in oil-importing countries is an increase in the standard of living of the oil exporters. Similarly, note that over the long run, the price level does not return to its original level. The reason for this long-run increase in domestic prices in the present context lies in the shortage effect induced by a permanently reduced full-employment income. We should stress, however, that the effect of a supply shock on world inflation must be examined in order to specify its full implications for domestic inflation. The topic of world inflation will be covered in Chapter 13.

Monetary Accommodation

Up to this point, we have ruled out active government intervention in the form of monetary and/or fiscal policies, showing how full employment can be reestablished after a supply shock, but only in response to a protracted recession that reduces real wages over time. The alternative to laissez-faire is for the authorities to engage in activist policies intended to counteract the unemployment effects of the supply shock in the short run and to ameliorate its consequent social disruption. Given the general impotence of autonomous fiscal policy actions followed independently by any single country[6] under flexible exchange rates and in the presence of a high degree of capital mobility, one possibility is to engage in an expansionary monetary policy.

An expansion of the money supply will tend to shift the aggregate demand curve upward; from $Y_0^D Y_0^D$ to $\overline{Y}^D \overline{Y}^D$ in Figure 11–5, which reproduces Figure 11–4 with less detail and depicts the short-run equilibrium of the economy after the supply shock by means of point G. By increasing the money supply, policymakers could, in principle, move the economy to full employment, as depicted by point H. This, of course, does not prevent the loss of real income represented by the decline in the potential level of output from Y_F to Y_F', but it serves to speed up the adjustment of the economy toward full employment in the labor market. It speeds it up by igniting inflation and therefore reducing real wages in the short run. In its absence, real wages would adjust, but only gradually over time, as the discipline imposed by unemployment is felt in the labor market and wage contracts embody lower nominal wages in response.

The effects of expansionary monetary policy in driving the economy to full

---

[5] For estimates of the reduction in the potential full-employment level of output in the United States, see R. H. Rasche and J. A. Tatom, "Energy Resources and Potential GNP," *Review, Federal Reserve Bank of St. Louis* (June 1977). See also P. H. Clark, "Potential GNP in the United States, 1949–80," *Review of Income and Wealth* (1979).

[6] As opposed to a coordinated fiscal expansion by the major industrial countries (which, as discussed in Chapter 8, may result in a worldwide economic recovery).

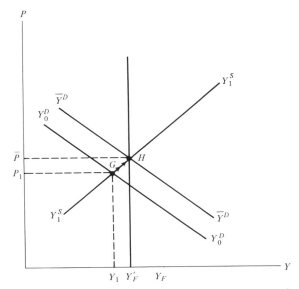

FIGURE 11–5. Supply Shocks and Monetary Accommodation

employment operate by offsetting the negative effects of the supply shock on the aggregate quantity demanded of domestic goods. The inflation associated with the shock shrinks real money balances, reducing economic activity. By increasing the nominal money supply, expansionary monetary policy acts to offset this recessionary effect, raising the quantity demanded of domestic goods, and moving the economy to full employment. This type of policy is referred to as *monetary accommodation.*

It must be realized that the expansionary monetary policy characterized by monetary accommodation will ignite domestic inflation. For those policymakers who are committed to controlling inflation, such an effect would be undesirable and anticlimactic. They would rather follow restrictive or contractionary monetary policy, if necessary, to maintain or reduce the rate of domestic inflation. Clearly, depending on the specific policies followed by specific countries, different inflation rates will surface in the aftermath of a supply shock. Situations may consequently arise where inflation declines after the shock. Such appears to be the situation of Japan and Germany in the aftermath of the 1973 to 1974 oil price shock. In the case of Japan, the quantity of money grew at higher and higher rates during the period of 1971 up to early 1973. At that point, monetary policy was sharply reversed, with the growth of the money supply[7] declining from more than 25% per year during the spring of 1973 to around 10% by mid-1974. Inflation in Japan, even though increasing during 1974, de-

[7] Figures for the money supply in this section refer to currency and demand deposits plus large certificates of deposit.

clined drastically in 1975, as recorded in Table 11–1. In the second oil price shock of 1979, monetary growth was curtailed from 12.3% in the first quarter of 1979 to 8.4% by the third quarter of 1980. Japanese inflation declined from 4.6% to 2.8% during the period of 1978 to 1980 and continued its downward movement in 1981 and 1982. In the case of Germany, the rate of growth of the money supply was approximately halved between the first quarter of 1973 and mid-1974. The German inflation rate slightly increased from 6.5% in 1973 to 6.8% in 1974, but then declined to 6.1% and 3.4% during 1975 and 1976, respectively. Contractionary monetary policy during the 1979 to 1980 period was also drastic and was associated with controlled, or declining, German inflation in the aftermath of the oil shock.

Oil Shocks, the Current Account and the Exchange Rate

One final aspect of supply shocks that has given rise to much confusion and misunderstanding is its effects on the current account balance and the exchange rate. For instance, it is popularly believed that the increased U.S. oil imports resulting from the 1973 to 1974 oil shock were the *cause* of current account balance deficits and of the fall in the value of the dollar in its aftermath. Indeed, an exogenous increase in the bill paid on oil imports that would, *everything else being constant,* tend to deteriorate the current account and—at the original exchange rate—generate a balance of payments deficit, would induce a currency depreciation. The problem, however, is that the everything-else-constant assumption does not generally hold. As Figure 11–4 illustrates, in addition to the increase in the price of oil there will be changes in a number of other variables. In particular, the supply shock will tend to be recessionary. Therefore, as domestic income declines, imports of final goods will be reduced, tending to improve— rather than worsen—the current account. This appears to be part of the reason behind the very substantial *surplus* in the U.S. current account in 1975.[8] In any case, even if the situation were one in which the current account balance does deteriorate significantly as a result of the oil shock, this does not imply any definitive connection with short-run currency depreciation. Over the short run, the exchange rate adjusts to eliminate balance of payments disequilibria, not trade balance or current account balance disequilibria. Since in a world of high capital mobility, the capital account dominates the short-run behavior of the exchange rate, one must consider how the capital account reacts to a supply shock. There is no clear-cut answer as to how the capital account of any single country will indeed behave in the aftermath of the shock. It is clear that a key variable affecting the behavior of the capital account of any specific (oil-importing) country will be how the oil exporters (OPEC) invest their trade

[8] No statistically significant connection has been found either between oil import bills and current account deficits in other OECD countries. See J. Sachs, "Aspects of the Current Account Behavior of OECD Economies," National Bureau of Economic Research, Working Paper No. 859 (February 1982).

surpluses, which depends on their asset preferences.[9] If OPEC investments in dollars are large enough, the consequent U.S. capital account improvement would tend to induce an exchange rate appreciation of the dollar—rather than a depreciation. With the portfolio of OPEC investors determined by a number of variables, such as interest rates and political risk, no a priori generalization can be made as to the effects of a supply shock on either the current account or the exchange rate of any single country.

This conclusion appears to be supported by the wide variety of exchange rate behavior in the aftermath of the 1973 to 1974 oil shock. Even though the U.S. dollar did depreciate in effective terms from 1974 to 1975—the currencies of both Germany and Japan appreciated in effective terms during this time period, in spite of the fact that both countries imported more oil as a percentage of GNP than the United States. Consequently, there is no simple causal connection between a supply shock and a domestic currency depreciation.

11-7 THE 1973 TO 1974 OIL PRICE SHOCK AND THE U.S. ECONOMY

The general framework developed in this chapter and used up to this point to analyze the effects of supply shocks serves well to illustrate the impact of the 1973 to 1974 oil price hike on the U.S. economy. This is so because the basic assumptions that the economy be initially at full employment and that nominal wage rigidity characterize labor market behavior in the short run seem to be applicable to the case of the United States at the time. By any measure, the U.S. economy was relatively close to, if not exactly at, its potential level of output during the period immediately preceding the oil shock. Furthermore, labor market practices in the United States, as embodied in the widespread presence of nonsynchronized, 3-year labor contracts, do tend to generate a relatively high degree of nominal wage stickiness.

The strong recession suffered by the U.S. economy during 1974 and 1975— evident in the figures shown in Table 11-1—clearly reflected the recessionary impact of the sharp rise in the real cost of oil, as was described in the previous section. It also reflected, however, the unfortunate restrictive monetary and fiscal policies followed by the government during 1973 and the lack of any reversal of these policies during 1974. As Blinder remarks,[10]

---

[9] For a formal framework specifying the influence of current account and capital account behavior on the dollar exchange rate, see Paul Krugman, "Oil and the Dollar," in J. S. Bhandari and B. H. Putnam, eds., *Economic Interdependence and Flexible Exchange Rates* (Cambridge, Mass.: The M.I.T. Press, 1983). For a less technical description of the connections (and lack of them) between oil shocks and the behavior of exchange rates, see D. R. Mudd and G. E. Wood, "Oil Imports and the Fall of the Dollar," *Federal Reserve Bank of St. Louis Review* (August 1978).

[10] A. S. Blinder, *Economic Policy and the Great Stagflation* (New York: Academic Press, Inc., 1979), p. 205.

both monetary and fiscal policy turned brusquely from stimulus to restraint in 1973. Anyone who has ever been in an automobile that was brought to an abrupt halt knows that, at best, this violent wrenching gives you an uneasy feeling in your stomach and, at worst, it puts you through the windshield. The economy got indigestion in 1973.

In terms of Figure 11–4, the leftward shift of the aggregate supply curve was combined with a leftward shift of aggregate demand, thereby heightening the negative effects of the oil shock on U.S. output and employment.

The rising prices associated with the supply shock—documented in Table 11–1—were also connected to a reduction of U.S. real wages, as predicted by our framework. This is the picture obtained from Table 11–2, the last column of which shows U.S. real wages declining an average of 0.3% during the period 1973 to 1975. When combined with the gradual movement toward more expansionary policies during the 1976 to 1978 period, this reduction of real wages laid the basis for a strong recovery in these later years. Still, it must be stressed that the restrictive aggregate demand policies sustained over the 1973 to 1974 period clearly contributed to delaying the recovery. As a matter of fact, many economists have argued that the opposite policies should have been followed and that the oil shock should have been accommodated by means of expansionary monetary policy.[11] In the light of the present framework—and especially in the environment of relative nominal wage rigidity implicit in U.S. labor market institutions—such a conclusion can be easily understood.

11–8   EFFECTS OF STABILIZATION POLICY WITH REAL WAGE RIGIDITY

The onset of widespread recession and unemployment combined with inflation in the aftermath of the oil shock of 1973 to 1974 led to major debates in European circles regarding the adequate policies to follow in such a situation. Just as the United States relaxed its unfortunate monetary and fiscal restraints of 1973 to 1974 with a more expansionary policy regime during 1976 to 1978, other OECD economies refused to follow the same path, in spite of strong encouragement on the part of the United States. The arguments of European policymakers were that a rapid expansion of the money supply in their economies would only increase inflation without affecting output to any significant extent. Is there any rationale for such a position? In this section we examine this question and the available evidence on the matter.

The discussion in the previous sections makes clear that in a situation of nominal wage rigidity, expansionary aggregate demand policies can, in principle,

---

[11] See the book by A. S. Blinder quoted in the previous footnote and also P. Kouri and J. Braga de Macedo, "Perspectives on the Stagflation of the 1970's," in H. Giersch, ed., *Macroeconomic Policies for Growth and Stability: A European Perspective* (Tubingen: J. C. Mohr, 1979).

TABLE 11–2. Rates of Growth of Real Hourly Compensation for the Aggregate Economy, 1962 to 1978

| Period | Real Compensation (annual average, in percent) | | | | | | |
	Canada	France	Germany	Italy	Japan	United Kingdom	United States
1962–1969	3.7	5.7	5.4	8.3	8.0	2.9	3.4
1969–1973	3.0	5.9	8.2	9.8	11.6	4.6	2.7
1973–1975	4.8	5.9	5.7	7.0	5.3	6.3	−0.3
1975–1978	1.6	5.2	3.3	1.8	2.2	−1.3	1.9

Source: J. Sachs, "Wages, Profits and Macroeconomic Adjustment: A Comparative Study," *Brookings Papers on Economic Activity* 273 (1979).

have an effective impact on output in the short run by fueling domestic inflation and reducing real wage rates as a result. Faced with relatively lower real labor costs, employers will increase employment and output, spearheading a rapid recovery of the economy; but it was precisely the connection between expansionary aggregate demand policies and declining real wages that European policymakers questioned. Jeffrey Sachs[12] notes that

> there was widespread doubt, voiced by economists in West Germany in particular, that expansionary policies could moderate real wages and they rejected the Keynesian view that the stickiness of nominal wages made it possible for policy-induced price inflation to reduce real wages.

The alternative view propounded in European circles was that, because of the presence of automatic wage indexation or the existence of short-term labor contracts allowing workers to bargain in order to maintain undiminished their real earnings, the adjustment of nominal wages to changes in prices was consequently rapid and automatic in Europe, leading to the alleged lack of responsiveness of real wages to expansionary aggregate demand. This real wage rigidity made it impossible for expansionary monetary policy to move the economy to full employment.[13]

The problems of economic policy in the presence of real wage rigidity are examined through the use of Figure 11–6, which shows an economy operating initially at the short-run equilibrium point E, with a level of output Y_0—below full employment—and an initial price level P_0. Given this situation, the policy

[12] J. D. Sachs, "Wages, Profits and Macroeconomic Adjustment: A Comparative Study," *Brookings Papers on Economic Activity,* 271 (1979). A comparative analysis of economic policies in the major industrial countries is carried out by S. Black, *Floating Exchange Rates and National Economic Policy* (New Haven: Yale University Press, 1977).

[13] For details on the differences in labor market institutions among the United States, western Europe, and Japan, as well as the implications, see the article by Sachs, op cit. Details on west European indexation schemes can be found in M. Emerson, "A View of Current European Indexation Experience," in R. Dornbusch and M. H. Simonsen, eds. *Inflation, Debt and Indexation* (Cambridge, Mass.: The M.I.T. Press, 1983).

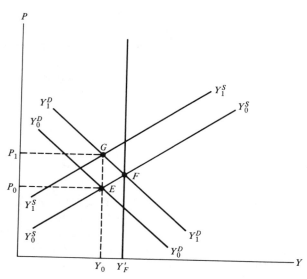

FIGURE 11–6.   Economic Policy in the Presence of Real Wage Rigidity

debate regarded the effectiveness of aggregate demand policies in increasing output in the presence of real wage rigidity.

Suppose that the Central Bank engages in expansionary monetary policy. This would shift the aggregate demand curve upward and, if large enough *and with rigid nominal wages,* it could move the economy to point F at full employment. This was exactly the argument made earlier in reference to Figure 11–5. To derive this result, however, the assumption is made that long-term contracts fix the nominal wage rate so as to prevent it from rising during the short-run period of analysis. If, instead, we assume it is real wages that are rigid, in the sense that labor market institutions react immediately to the policy by raising nominal wages in response to the implied price inflation (from P_0 to P_1 in Figure 11–6), both aggregate demand and aggregate supply shift. In terms of Figure 11–6, if at the original output, Y_0, the aggregate demand shift implies an increase in prices from P_0 to P_1, real wage rigidity in the short run means that nominal wages would immediately rise to match the price hike. This is reflected by the leftward shift of the aggregate supply curve from $Y_0^S\ Y_0^S$ to $Y_1^S\ Y_1^S$. The resulting equilibrium occurs at point G, with an increase in prices from P_0 to P_1 but no increase in output. With real wage rates fixed in the short run, domestic producers do not have any incentive to increase employment and thus output. Therefore, the expansionary policy would not be able to move the economy toward full employment. Eventually, of course, real wages would decline in response to unemployment. But given real wage rigidity in the short run, expansionary monetary policy will not be able to speed up this process.

In conclusion, expansionary monetary policy in the presence of real wage rigidity appears to lack significant effects on output and to lead only to price inflation in the short run. Consequently, there is some basis for the European and Japanese lack of confidence vis à vis the United States in the use of expansionary aggregate demand policies to move their economies toward recovery in the aftermath of the oil shock of 1973 to 1974. This is due to the presence of wide differences in the labor market institutions setting wage rates in the United States, on the one hand, and western European countries on the other. The presence of overlapping long-term wage contracts that are only partially indexed in the United States versus the more indexed and synchronized system of wage setting in Europe, generates significant differences in the effectiveness of macroeconomic policies in these countries.

The differences in the behavior of real wages in the aftermath of the oil shock of 1973 to 1974 among the industrial countries is shown by Table 11–2, which provides evidence supporting the hypothesis of the relative real wage rigidity faced by labor market institutions in western Europe as compared with the United States.[14] In the United States, real wage rate growth declined drastically after the 1973 oil shock, while in western Europe (and Japan) real wage rate growth continued throughout the period. These data also serve to partially explain the relative difficulty of western Europe to recover from the oil shock, at least when compared with the United States. The decline of real labor costs in the United States served as a boost to production, leading the American economy to a stronger recovery relative to western Europe.

Just as short-run real wage rigidity makes it more difficult for expansionary monetary policy to stimulate output and employment within short time contexts, it also makes it relatively easier for contractionary monetary policy to control inflation over short periods of time. When nominal wages respond immediately to offset changes in prices, a monetary contraction that reduces prices at any given level of output would immediately be associated with lower nominal wages. The reduced real labor costs would then serve as an incentive for domestic producers to increase aggregate supply. Both the aggregate demand contraction arising from the monetary shock and the associated aggregate supply expansion implied by the declining nominal wages tend to place downward pressure on domestic prices. Hence there is some basis for expecting real wage rigidity to serve as an aid in controlling inflation. At the same time, the direct negative effects of restrictive aggregate demand policy on domestic output will be minimized by the positive impact of declining nominal wages on aggregate supply. In other words, with real wage rigidity, declining inflation will have a lesser impact on output than in the comparable situation with nominal wage rigidity, where a monetary contraction lowers prices, raises real wages and induces domestic production to decline in the short run. As Sachs summarizes the issues: "with sluggish nominal wages, monetary policy can affect output; with rigid

---

[14] For more evidence regarding the behavior of nominal and real wages in OECD countries in the aftermath of the oil shock, see William H. Branson and Julio J. Rotemberg, "International Adjustment with Wage Rigidity," *European Economic Review* (May 1980).

real wages, monetary policy works on prices. Thus, in the latter case, monetary contraction is a powerful tool for controlling inflation."[15]

11–9 SUMMARY

1. The equilibrium level of prices, output, and the exchange rate are established by the intersection of the economy's aggregate demand and aggregate supply curves.

2. Under a regime of flexible exchange rates, the aggregate demand curve depicts the relationship between the aggregate quantity demanded and price of domestic goods, given the money supply and fiscal parameters, and incorporating exchange rate adjustments.

3. The long-run equilibrium of the economy occurs at that point at which there is full employment. Exchange rate flexibility then guarantees balanced payments.

4. An automatic wage–price adjustment mechanism exists, which operates by influencing real wages and real exchange rates and tends to move the laissez-faire economy toward full employment over time.

5. Supply shocks tend to destabilize the economy, shifting the short-run aggregate supply curve to the left and leading to short-run recession and to a reduction of the full-employment level of income.

6. Stagflation refers to episodes of stagnation and inflation like those generally occurring in the industrial world during the aftermath of the massive oil price hikes of 1973 to 1974 and 1979.

7. Stabilization policies are intended to speed up the adjustment of a destabilized economy toward its long-run equilibrium. However, fiscal policies pursued by a single country under flexible exchange rates will be ineffective in affecting the economy's output and employment both in the short run and in the long run. The expansionary effects of fiscal policy on aggregate demand, for instance, would be offset by a current account balance deterioration arising from induced real exchange rate reductions.

8. A monetary accommodation policy can prevent the recessionary effects of reduced real liquidity resulting from sudden price hikes in the economy. In the presence of nominal wage rigidity, the monetary expansion allows rising prices to speed up the adjustment of the economy by reducing real wages and encouraging output expansion.

9. Real wage rigidity exists in economies where labor market institutions guarantee the automatic indexing of nominal wages to cost of living increases over the short run. Under real wage rigidity, expansionary monetary policy is not significant in speeding up the adjustment of the economy toward full employment and will only result in inflation over the short run.

[15] J. Sachs, "Wages, Profits, and Macroeconomic Adjustment: A Comparative Study," *Brookings Papers on Economic Activity,* 301 (1979).

PROBLEMS

1. Consider an economy in long-run equilibrium with price stability and full employment. Suppose that, owing to increasing labor solidarity and militancy, unions are able to obtain a sudden 30% increase in nominal wage rates.
   (a) Describe verbally and diagrammatically the effects of this disturbance on domestic prices, output, trade balance, and nominal and real exchange rates. Distinguish between short-run and long-run effects.
   (b) What would be the impact of the union-led wage hikes if the government decides to increase the money supply simultaneously? Would this ameliorate the impact of the wage disturbance on the economy? If so, in what sense?

2. The discussion in the text considered exclusively the case of perfect capital mobility. Consider the opposite extreme of an economy that does not trade in financial assets with the rest of the world. Would the results derived above as to the ineffectiveness of policies on long-run output and the real exchange rate still hold? Would any conclusions be altered at all? Explain.

3. It is the year 2001 and the moon and planets are populated by aliens who trade in goods, services, and assets with the countries of the Earth. The small lunar country of Selenia trades only with the United States and its exchange rate, the selenian, freely fluctuates against the U.S. dollar. Selenia faces perfect capital mobility with a fixed interest rate $i* = 0.10$. In addition, the lunar colony is at full employment, with a real level of output equal to 2000 units (in millions of Selenian goods). If we assume that the following real money demand function has been calculated for Selenia's residents,

$$L^D = 0.20\,Y - 2000\,i*$$

(measured in millions of Selenian goods), and that Selenia's (nominal) money supply is currently equal to 600 million selenians.
   (a) What would be the current equilibrium price of Selenian goods?
   (b) Assume that you are provided with the following additional information regarding Selenia's absorption and trade balance relationships:

$$A = 480 + 0.78\,Y - 900\,i*$$

$$T = 490\,\frac{eP*}{P} - 0.22\,Y$$

where $\overline{T} = 490\,eP*/P$ represents the autonomous trade balance, with e equal to the selenian-dollar exchange rate (in selenians per dollar), $P*$ is the average price of U.S. goods imported by Selenia (in dollars), and P is the price of Selenian goods. Calculate the current value of the exchange rate on the assumption that $P* = 6.00$.
   (c) Suppose that Selenia's Central Bank doubles the money supply from 600 to 1200 million selenians, what would be the long-run equilibrium

impact on prices? How would the selenian exchange rate vis-à-vis the dollar be affected?

(d) Regarding the previous question, assume that, simultaneously with the doubling of Selenia's money supply, the United States decides to double its money supply. Assuming that the U.S. economy adjusts rapidly to long-run equilibrium, how would the U.S. monetary expansion affect Selenia? Would the U.S. policy alter in any way the effects of Selenia's policy? What does this suggest about interdependence in economies under flexible exchange rates?

(e) Consider the effects of a rise in the Universe's interest rate from 10% to 15%. What would be the impact on lunar output, prices, and exchange rate?

(f) The Selenian government decides to reduce its expenditures on Selenian goods by 40 million units. Assuming the government expenditures form part of the 480 million autonomous absorption component in the absorption function A, what would be the inflationary, output, exchange rate, and trade balance effects of the reduced government spending over the long run? Would you expect the short-run effects of the policy to be any different?

4. In a controlled floating exchange rate regime, the Central Bank intervenes in foreign exchange markets at its discretion. Analyze, within the framework of this chapter, the impact of a Federal Reserve purchase of foreign exchange. What would be the effects of this operation on the U.S. money supply and on the dollar exchange rate? Explain.

5. Consider an economy in long-run equilibrium under flexible exchange rates and perfect capital mobility. Assume that because of disputes with a neighboring country, a war erupts with unfortunate long-term destruction of domestic industrial capacity. What would be the effects of these events on the output, prices, and nominal and real exchange rates of the country? Would there be inflation or deflation, and by how much? Illustrate diagrammatically and distinguish between the short run and the long run.

CHAPTER 12

Expectations, Inflation, and Business Cycles

The often painful effects of the general ups and downs of aggregate economic activity usually referred to as business cycles, and the particularly traumatic experience of the Great Depression years of the 1930s, led to Keynesian economics and its emphasis on active government intervention intended to counteract or control these cycles. These so-called stabilization policies (also referred to as countercyclical policies), which include both monetary and fiscal policies, act as a package intended to restore the economy toward its longer-run trend path, away from which business cycles have moved it. Actual experience, however, has shown the difficulties involved in fine-tuning the economy. The relative stability of the U.S. economy during the 1950s and early 1960s, for instance, has given way to periods of rampant inflation and/or unemployment during the 1970s and 1980s. These events have raised serious questions about the effectiveness of stabilization policy, generating renewed study and controversy on the topic. Chapters 12 and 13 will study the effectiveness of stabilization policies in open economies. The possibilities and problems of stabilization policies are closely related to how individuals react to those policies, both ex-ante (as when they try to anticipate policy changes), and ex-post (such as when they respond to unanticipated policy changes). It is therefore of utmost importance to be able to assess the role of expectations, particularly inflationary expectations, in the effectiveness of stabilization policies.

The global inflationary experience after 1970 has led to increased awareness and anticipation of inflation. Inflation today seems to be viewed with serious concern by both the public and government. Such is the result obtained by public opinion polls asking individuals what they consider to be the most pressing economic problems. Inflation is usually among the top concerns, often outranking unemployment—although there is a marked difference among the responses of different groups in the population (high-income, educated, white Republicans tend to worry the most about inflation). In cross-country studies, it appears that it is *unanticipated* inflation which worries most of the public. In countries where inflation has occurred for some extended period of time, and is viewed as a normal phenomenon, individuals and firms devise instruments, such as cost-of-living provisions or other indexation schemes, to deal with it and do not appear to worry so much about inflation. The public's concern with inflation is also suggested by the observed negative association between the inflation rate in the year preceding elections and the likelihood of reelection of a government administration. Inflation seems to be an effective way through which an administration can get toppled. It is thus not surprising that most governments assign a high priority to reducing, or at least controlling, the rate of inflation in the economy.

We now proceed to introduce inflationary expectations into the aggregate demand and supply framework developed in Chapters 10 and 11. We begin with the simple analytics of fixed exchange rate regimes; later sections broaden the discussion to encompass exchange rate expectations and economies under flexible exchange rate regimes.

12–1   THE EXPECTATIONS-AUGMENTED AGGREGATE SUPPLY CURVE

The role of inflationary expectations in the economy can best be introduced by determining their influence on aggregate supply, which depicts the relationship between prices and quantity supplied of domestic goods.

Suppose, for the sake of the argument, that the economy is initially at full employment and that there is an increase in the domestic price level. What effect would this have on the output domestic firms wish to supply? The answer to this question hinges crucially on whether the price level hike is anticipated by agents in the economy or whether it comes as a complete surprise to them. In an environment where price changes occur frequently and where workers and employers expect inflation to occur in the future, labor contracts stipulating future wage rates will in general include escalating nominal wage rate clauses, such as cost-of-living adjustments (COLAs). In their attempt to maintain desired standards of living in an inflationary environment, workers bargain with employers nominal wage rate raises in parity with inflationary expectations during the duration of the contracts. As a consequence, anticipated price increases will have no effect on real wages: They are exactly matched by the nominal wage rate hikes stipulated in labor contracts. But with real labor costs unchanged, employers would have no incentive to change employment and, thus, output. In other words, if the increase in domestic prices is fully anticipated by agents in the economy it will have no impact on either employment or output.

If the price rise is unanticipated, on the other hand, it would not be embodied in the nominal wage rate adjustments stipulated by labor contracts and would result in reduced real wages. The implied reduction of real labor costs would then induce domestic producers to increase employment and output of domestic goods. The suggestion is that only unanticipated increases in price, that is, price surprises, have a positive effect on the aggregate quantity supplied of domestic goods. Similarly, unanticipated reductions in the price of domestic goods would be associated with a decrease in the output producers wish to supply.

The theoretical connection between changes in output and unanticipated (vs. anticipated) price changes are summarized by the so-called expectations-augmented aggregate supply curve given by

$$Y = Y_F + \bar{\beta}\left(\frac{P - P^e}{P^e}\right) \qquad AS \qquad (1)$$

where Y denotes domestic output, Y_F is the full-employment level of output, and $(P - P^e)$ represents unanticipated price changes, equal to the difference between the current price level, P, and the price level agents in the economy anticipated would arise, P^e. Unanticipated price changes (price surprises) are expressed in proportional terms by dividing by the expected price level, P^e. Finally, $\bar{\beta}$ is a positive parameter representing the quantitative influence that unanticipated price changes have on domestic output. For instance, if output is measured in millions and $\bar{\beta} = 20$, then an unanticipated price increase equal to 5%—$(P - P^e)/P^e = 0.05$—would increase domestic output above full employment by 1 million, obtained by multiplying (20)(0.05), which equals one.

Equation (1) states that only unanticipated changes in domestic prices will generate deviations of domestic output from its potential level. For a given anticipated price of domestic goods—as determined by the information available to individuals in a previous time period—equation (1) describes a positive relationship between domestic prices and output of domestic goods. This relationship is depicted by the upward—sloping expectations—augmented aggregate supply curve, AS, in Figure 12–1. If the domestic price level, P, is equal to its anticipated value, P_0^e, then output remains at full employment (when $P = P_0^e$, $Y = Y_F$). On the other hand, when the domestic price level rises above anticipated levels (such as in the case of $P_1 > P_0^e$), domestic output rises above full employment ($Y_1 > Y_F$ as depicted). Finally, when domestic prices are below their anticipated value (such as if $P' < P_0^e$), domestic output declines below full employment ($Y' < Y_F$).[1]

---

[1] Note that the aggregate supply relationship established in Chapters 10 and 11 is just a special case of equation (1). In our analysis at that point we assumed agents in the economy exhibited static expectations in the sense that they behaved on the presumption that prices would not change. The price level expected to prevail today, P^e, was therefore equal to the price level in the previous time period, P_{-1}. In this case, equation (1) becomes

$$Y = Y_F + \bar{\beta}\left(\frac{P - P_{-1}}{P_{-1}}\right)$$

which is precisely the aggregate supply function we used in Chapters 10 and 11 (see the Appendix to Chapter 10 and set $\bar{\beta} = \theta\beta$).

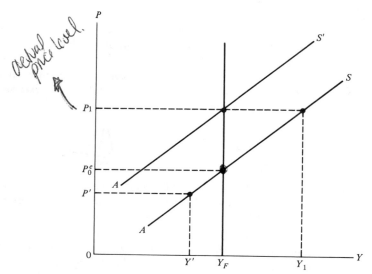

actual price level.

FIGURE 12–1.   Expectations-Augmented Aggregate Supply Curve

As described above, the existence of labor contracts can explain the positive connection between unanticipated price changes and output of domestic goods. It is essential for the argument, however, to get the timing correct. Inflation that is anticipated *at the start of* a given contract should have no impact on output, since it is embodied into the nominal wage rate adjustments stipulated in advance. On the other hand, inflation that is perceived or anticipated *after the start of* a contract, so that it is unanticipated at the moment the contract is signed or agreed upon, could very well have an impact on domestic output, since it is not embodied into the wage contracts previously signed.

Note, though, that what is unanticipated today becomes known tomorrow and, as a result, any unanticipated price changes that occur over the duration of a preexisting labor contract will be embodied into new contracts when the existing ones expire. This suggests that, in the absence of additional disturbances, nominal wage rate raises matching unanticipated price hikes will eventually be incorporated into revised contracts. Real wage rates will thus be pressured upward, toward their original levels, and output will consequently return to its full-employment level. Algebraically, even though a rise in prices above previously anticipated levels ($P_1 > P_0^e$) may induce an expansion of output above full employment ($Y > Y_F$), when individuals revise their price expectations to conform with the realized increase in prices ($P_1 = P_1^e$), output must return to full employment ($Y = Y_F$). Geometrically, the revision in expectations embodied in new labor contracts tends to shift the aggregate supply curve to the left by raising real labor costs, thereby reducing employment and output at any given price level. In terms of Figure 12–1, the original aggregate supply curve *AS* would shift to the left toward AS', suggesting that when the anticipated price level has been revised to equal the actual price level, P_1, and has correspondingly been embodied into negotiated wage contract raises, the domestic level of output would be at full employment ($Y = Y_F$). In other words, over the long run, the aggregate supply curve will become vertical. Exactly how much time is required for this to occur depends on the length of labor contracts and the particular labor market institutions existing in the economy, among other factors.

12–2   INFLATIONARY EXPECTATIONS AND THE ADJUSTMENT MECHANISM IN THE OPEN ECONOMY

Having described how inflationary expectations enter into the determination of aggregate supply, we now combine this analysis with that of aggregate demand and the balance of payments in specifying the economy's short-run equilibrium under fixed exchange rates and its adjustment over time.

The aggregate demand curve shows the relationship between changes in prices and quantity demanded of domestic goods, given the money supply and fiscal parameters. It is graphically depicted by the AD curve in Figure 12–2. The intersection of the aggregate demand curve AD with the short-run aggregate supply curve AS at point E in Figure 12–2 determines the short-run equilibrium

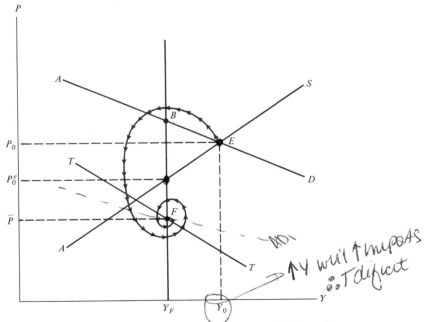

FIGURE 12–2.   Output and Prices in the Short Run and the Long Run

of the economy. At that point, quantity demanded of domestic goods is equal to quantity supplied. The balance of payments situation of the economy corresponding to this short-run equilibrium is determined in reference to the now familiar relationship:

$$B = T(q, Y) + K(i) \tag{2}$$

where B is the money account of the balance of payments, T represents the trade balance, and K the capital account. For the sake of expositional simplicity—and following earlier strategy—we concentrate our attention first on the case of no international capital movements. This implies that $K = 0$ and the balance of payments can thus be identified with the trade balance. The trade balance equilibrium locus TT in Figure 12–2 shows the combinations of price and output of domestic goods that sustain external balance. As real income increases, imports also increase, requiring a reduction in domestic prices to promote the expansion of net exports necessary to restore balanced trade. Observe that, since points above TT represent balance of payments deficits, the economy's short-run equilibrium at point E is associated with one such deficit. The domestic price level, P_0, is above the level required for the international competitiveness of domestic goods to sustain that (higher) level of net exports necessary to attain external balance. The level of domestic income, Y_0 on the other hand, is above that required to generate the (lower) level of domestic imports necessary for external balance.

Two observations can be made about the economy's short-run equilibrium at point E in Figure 12–2. First of all, the domestic price level that agents in the economy anticipated would currently prevail has not actually been realized. This is visualized by recalling that the expected price level is determined by the intersection of the aggregate supply curve with the full-employment line. In Figure 12–2, this occurs at an expected price level equal to P_0^e, which is below the actual price level, P_0. As a matter of fact, the unanticipated inflation implied by the equilibrium at point E—algebraically given by $(P_0 - P_0^e)/P_0^e > 0$—is directly associated with the presence of an equilibrium level of output above full employment. Note, however, that individuals will, whether slowly or rapidly, adjust their expected domestic price level to take into account the unanticipated inflation. To do otherwise would imply that agents in the economy stubbornly persist in forecasting domestic prices below those that are observed to prevail in the economy. If individuals do revise their price expectations, they would stop their adjustments only when their anticipated price level exactly matches actual domestic prices. In this situation, the agents' expectations are fulfilled and, given no other disturbances in the economy, they would have no reason to alter them. But with prices perfectly anticipated, the unanticipated rate of inflation would be zero. Consequently, the eventual equilibrium toward which the economy would move if undisturbed would be with output at full employment.

The second observation regarding the short-run equilibrium at point E is that the associated balance of payments deficit will result in losses of international reserves and, other things being equal, in monetary contractions. The consequent decline of the domestic money supply tends to shift downward the aggregate demand curve, AD, toward an equilibrium consistent with the balance of payments locus, TT.

What would be the final destination point of the economy? Long-run equilibrium occurs when the economy's income is at full employment ($Y = Y_F$) and when external payments are balanced ($T = 0$). At that equilibrium, depicted by point F in Figure 12–2, and in the absence of other disturbances, expectations formed by individuals about the future price level would be realized and unanticipated inflation would not arise. In addition, no gaps between income and expenditure would emerge, and the Central Bank would therefore face a stable level of international reserves. How exactly does the economy adjust from its short-run equilibrium to its long-run equilibrium? The answer to this question depends on how individuals adjust their inflationary expectations and on the speed with which they make the monetary adjustments intended to correct income–expenditure imbalances reflected by the balance of payments. In Chapter 14 we shall discuss the details behind the monetary process of adjustment. The next section emphasizes our present concern: how expectations about economic variables are formed and revised.

12–3 THE FORMATION OF EXPECTATIONS

Up to this point, we have seen the key role inflationary expectations have in the economy's equilibrium. We have not yet discussed how agents in the economy form expectations about relevant economic variables. This section examines the alternative ways economists have developed to analyze the formation of expectations.

The problem of expectations formation arises in almost any human activity, whether it is when planning to purchase a car or buying stocks, or when deciding whether or not to go to Mexico next summer. No matter if you are evaluating the price of a car or a stock, or the value of the Mexican peso, or whatever, you have to base your actions on expectations about how these variables will change in the future. The study of the formation of expectations examines how individuals determine their forecasts of the behavior of relevant economic variables in the future.

Two basic types of expectations behavior have been widely examined in macroeconomics. The first regards the *adaptive expectations* mechanism, first emphasized by Phillip Cagan, of Columbia University, and Marc Nerlove, of Northwestern University, in the 1950s. The second is the *rational expectations* approach, associated with the names of John Muth, Robert Lucas, Thomas Sargent, Neil Wallace, Robert Barro, and many others. In order to illustrate the differences involved in these mechanisms, let us consider the problem of how individuals revise their expectations when the actual price level turns out to exceed people's forecasts.

The basic concept behind the adaptive expectations mechanism is that individuals use information relating to past forecasting errors to revise expectations. For instance, if the expected domestic price level in a previous time period is denoted by, P^e_{-1}, and the actual price level turns out to be P, then, the expected level of domestic prices in the next period, P^e, will be revised according to

$$P^e - P^e_{-1} = \xi (P - P^e_{-1}) \tag{3}$$

where ξ is a positive coefficient between zero and one to be interpreted momentarily. Equation (3) states that if the actual price level observed in a given time period turns out to be above the expected price level for that period (if $P - P^e_{-1}$ is positive), the expected prices for the subsequent period are revised upward ($P^e - P^e_{-1}$ is positive). The parameter ξ indicates by how much the expected price level is adjusted in response to past mistakes. For example, if ξ is very small (close to zero), expectations are not adjusted in any significant way and P^e remains approximately equal to P^e_{-1}.

Adaptive expectations represent actual behavior in instances in which information is difficult or expensive to acquire. In these situations, it becomes easier to make predictions on the basis of rules concerning present and past values of the variables at stake. Such is the case of the person who looks out the window and assumes that the afternoon weather will be more or less like that of the morning. At the same time, however, one should recognize that adaptive expectational behavior can be consistently out of target. Its historical, or backward-looking, nature makes for slow reaction to sudden changes. Consider the following example:

> Suppose that OPEC is meeting next week but that the outcome of their deliberations is a formality; everyone knows that they will announce a doubling of oil prices. Surely economists will be predicting higher inflation from the moment at which news of the prospective oil price increase first becomes available. Yet the hypothesis of Adaptive Expectations asserts that individuals raise inflation expectations only after higher inflation has gradually fed into the past data from which they extrapolate. Adjustment of expectations is very sluggish. Using such a rule, individuals would make systematic mistakes, underpredicting the actual inflation rate for many periods after the oil price rise. It is not plausible that individuals would take no action to amend the basis of their forecasting rule under such circumstances.[2]

It is because of this problem that in recent years adaptive expectations has been increasingly discarded as forming the basis of expectations behavior in economic analysis. The alternative has become rational expectations.

[2] From David K. H. Begg, *The Rational Expectations Revolution in Macroeconomics: Theories and Evidence* (Baltimore: The Johns Hopkins University Press, 1982), p. 26.

In contrast to the person who relies on more or less arbitrary rules or hunches in deciding about the future, the person following rational expectations looks around for information and makes decisions on this basis. In contrast to someone who makes adaptive expectations adjustments, the person who forms rational expectations immediately embodies new information into his or her decisions. This is the person who calls the weather bureau for a forecast of climate conditions tomorrow and relies on all available current information to determine the expected weather. The starting point of rational expectations behavior is that people incorporate all the relevant systematic information available in forming their expectations of a given variable. As a result, expectational errors are unsystematic; they arise from unanticipated, random disturbances about which the person did not have any information available or could not have predicted beforehand. The rational expectation of a given variable X^e is thus equal to

$$X^e = E[X|I_t]$$

where $E[X|I_t]$ symbolizes[3] the fact that X^e is defined as the expected value of the variable X, given all the information available at time t, which is denoted by I_t. For instance, the rational expectation of the inflation rate—given the available information at time t—is

$$\Pi \equiv \hat{P}^e = E[\hat{P}|I_t]$$

where $\hat{}$'s represent proportional changes, $\hat{P}^e$ denotes anticipated inflation, $\hat{P}$ actual inflation, and so on.

In the case of predicting the weather, individuals rely heavily on information provided by weather bureau forecasts, which offers them the likely future weather as determined by the best meteorological models of climatic behavior. In the case of expectations regarding economic variables, what information can we assume that individuals have? The analogy to the weather case is to assume that individuals form expectations *as if* they knew the structure of the economic models under consideration. Thus, in our aggregate demand-aggregate supply framework, the rational expectations approach would assume that individuals behave as if they knew the equations and parameters involved in the model (e.g., output, prices, the exchange rate, and money demand elasticities), and form expectations on the basis of that model and on the information they have about the likelihood of various possible disturbances to the economy in the future. Obviously, no pedestrian goes around every day calculating marginal propensities to consume or income elasticities of demand for money. Nevertheless, investors—and unions and firms, for that matter—do rely on the best information they have available about the future of the economy in making

---

[3] The reader who has had statistics will realize that E represents the (conditional) mathematical expectation operator, which is taken over all the possible values of X, conditional on the given value of the variable I_t.

predictions, and thus implicitly or explicitly they do have to make use of economic models when making these predictions. Of course, they may not have the same model of the economy that we are using in this analysis. But the arguments for using rational expectations to model expectations formation in an economic model do not rely on whether or not individuals do know or actually believe in the economic framework under consideration.

Every single economic model is a simplification of reality and clearly has to ignore factors occurring in the real world which, hopefully, do not distort the model's conclusion or the problem considered in a significant way. Although no economic model can be expected to consider all aspects of human behavior and one cannot therefore assume that agents in the economy believe or act on its basis, the model must still be consistent with the way in which agents behave and process information. If individuals form rational expectations using their own models of the economic world, in our simplified economic model we must assume that individuals make rational expectations on the basis of their knowledge of that simplified economic world. Hence, the main question regarding rational expectations must be whether individuals actually do acquire information as postulated by the approach. The answer to this question is that in general they do, unless information costs are so high that rules of thumb and hunches become a more profitable (or least costly) way of making forecasts. Given the wide availability of economic statistics and the interest in acquiring information on the part of vital economic agents—unions, investors, firms, consumers—it has seemed more and more reasonable for economists to assume that rational expectations do actually mold expectations formation in their economic models.

The following discussion, for the most part, assumes that rational expectations characterize the formation of expectations by agents in the economy. Before proceeding, however, it may be useful to illustrate how the adjustment path of the economy toward its steady state differs with adaptive and rational expectations. Returning to Figure 12–2, the initial position is at point E, which is the short-run equilibrium of the economy. Now, assume first that adaptive expectations are followed. Since at point E actual prices turn out to be above the level anticipated by individuals, they will adjust their expected price level upward. With adaptive expectations behavior, the expected price would be adjusted upward but only by a fraction of the difference between actual prices and the previous price level. As a result, the aggregate supply curve would gradually shift leftward. In addition, trade deficits would cause gradual losses of international reserves and shift the aggregate demand curve downward and to the left. One possible path of the economy is shown by the pointed arrows in Figure 12–2. Observe that the adaptive expectations path to point E involves a protracted recession and deflation, with significant and persistent deviations of output from full employment. In general, the sluggishness of adaptive expectations generates a seesaw adjustment toward full employment and balanced trade compared with the rational expectations path.

With rational expectations, the path followed by the economy would be different: There would be immediate return to full employment. The reason is that, in the absence of further unanticipated disturbances, rational expectations implies that past mistakes are completely redressed by adjusting expected prices to equal actual prices. The equilibrium of the economy would therefore immediately move to a point along the full-employment vertical line, such as point *B*. There would subsequently be a gradual movement of equilibrium downward along the full-employment line in response to balance of payments disequilibria until point *F* is reached.

We must mention that in practice the economy will not move immediately to its trend level of output even under rational expectations. There are various reasons for this. The most obvious is that it takes all of us time to recognize the nature of the disturbances affecting prices and output. As a result, expectational adjustments will not be instantaneous, giving rise to sustained deviations from full employment, in spite of rational expectations. In addition, even if all individuals recognize completely the structure of the current and future price changes, only those with labor contracts up for renewal will be able to embody their revised expectations into immediate nominal wage adjustments or cost-of-living clauses. Those whose labor contracts do not expire in the near future will be unable to revise their nominal wages, being stuck with (now obsolete) adjustments made when their contracts were negotiated in the past.[4] The presence of overlapping labor contracts thus makes the adjustment toward full employment less than instantaneous, even under rational expectations.

12–4 RATIONAL EXPECTATIONS AND MONETARY POLICY IN THE OPEN ECONOMY

The presence of rational expectations causes important, controversial, and often baffling effects on the analysis of economic policymaking. Two considerations clearly surface as being critical. First, policy effectiveness will depend on whether the policy change under consideration is anticipated by individuals in the economy or whether it is completely unanticipated by them. Second, policy effectiveness will depend on whether the policy is a permanent policy change—a change in the policy rule followed by the authorities—or whether it is a temporary shock, after which the authorities return to their previous behavior. This section examines the role of these considerations in the effects of monetary policies.

The issues involved are best examined through the use of Figure 12–3. The economy is originally at its long-run equilibrium with balanced payments and full employment at point *F*. In the absence of disturbances, the anticipated level of domestic prices would equal the actual price level. Consider the effects

---

[4] For an advanced exposition of this point, see Stanley Fischer, "Long-Term Contracts, Rational Expectations and the Optimal Money Supply Rule," *Journal of Political Economy* (February 1977), and John Taylor, "Staggered Wage Setting in a Macro Model," *American Economic Review* (May 1979).

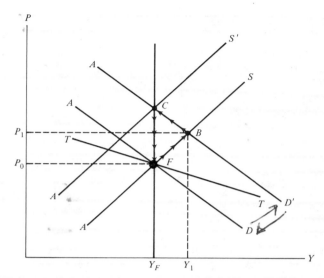

FIGURE 12–3.   Effects of Anticipated and Unanticipated Monetary Policy

now of a policy disturbance in the form of Central Bank credit creation. It is assumed that this is the only disturbance to the economy and that individuals form expectations following the rational expectations hypothesis. The latter implies that we can proceed as if agents in the economy determine their anticipated inflation rate by observing what inflation rate is predicted by the structural model of the economy described above, given, for example, their expectations about money supply changes. This is, as noted earlier, the weatherman's approach to forming expectations: Given some expected changes in atmospheric pressure, wind directions, and so on, the weatherman plugs all these variables into his meteorological model of weather determination, obtaining some forecasts of how climate conditions will be tomorrow. Individuals here are assumed to do so with regard to the aggregate supply–demand model of the economy utilized.

The Effects of Unanticipated Monetary Policy

We examine first the impact of an unanticipated once-and-for-all increase in Central Bank credit. With the Central Bank's policy change unanticipated, and assuming that no other disturbances are expected to arise, individuals presume the economy will remain at its long-run equilibrium, as given by the intersection of AD and AS. They thus expect domestic prices to remain at P_0. With monetary authorities expanding domestic credit, however, the aggregate demand curve will shift to the right, shown in Figure 12–3 by means of the upward shift of the aggregate demand curve from AD to AD'. Given that the aggregate supply curve remains unaltered—the expected price level remains at P_0—the new short-run equilibrium at the moment the Central Bank increases its credit would occur at point B, with higher prices, P_1, and higher output, Y_1. Domestic output rises because the inflation associated with the increased Central Bank credit is unanticipated. As a result, it tends to reduce the real wages rates effectively offered by labor contracts not embodying cost of living adjustment clauses. The lower real labor costs stimulate production.

Point B in Figure 12–3 is only a point of short-run equilibrium and will respond to changes in expected prices and international reserves. For expositional convenience, we consider first the impact of changes in the expected domestic price level and then return to analyze the effects of changes in international reserves.

Once Central Bank credit increases, individuals will not only observe the increased money supply, but also the consequent inflation. They will adjust their expectations accordingly. This may occur slowly or rapidly, depending on the accuracy of monetary and price statistics, the degree of information diffusion, and, most important, on the similarity of the present shock with previous shocks. Whatever the case, once the increased prices are recognized, revised labor contracts will embody the higher cost of living in the form of higher nominal wage rates. Employers will then find it optimal to reduce employment and output back toward their original level at full employment. In terms of Figure 12–3, the upward revision in price expectations would shift the aggregate supply curve from AS to AS', with the economy adjusting from point B to point C. The short-run equilibrium would thereby move back toward full employment, with the actual domestic price level correctly anticipated by agents in the economy.

A second adjustment of the economy would occur in response to the fact that rising domestic prices, in the absence of foreign price changes and under fixed exchange rates, result in a domestic loss of competitiveness in world goods markets and generate a balance of payments deficit. The consequent decline in international reserves is then associated with a reduction of the domestic money supply back toward its initial level. The AD' curve will shift back toward AD. Only when point F is attained will enough domestic competitiveness be restored to sustain a level of exports consistent with external balance. The Central Bank stops losing reserves and long-run equilibrium is attained.

To reiterate, an unanticipated once-and-for-all increase in Central Bank credit leads to a temporary rise in output but at the cost of a temporary surge in domestic inflation. Note the two key assumptions in deriving this result: (1) The change in Central Bank credit occurs within an environment of imperfect (zero) capital mobility, and (2) the policy change is unanticipated by agents in the economy. In previous chapters we have seen how changes in Central Bank credit under perfect capital mobility cannot alter the domestic money supply, in which case there would be no effects of the policy on either prices or output (the aggregate demand curve would not shift). We have not previously examined, on the other hand, the effects of monetary policy when individuals in the economy accurately anticipate such a policy move.

The Ineffectiveness of Anticipated Monetary Policy

In contrast to the case of unanticipated monetary policy, an anticipated increase in the money supply has no effects on domestic output, not even momentarily. The explanation is that as long as individuals form rational expectations, they will realize that the increased money supply will generate short-run inflation and will therefore embody the expected increased prices in the cost-of-living adjustments of their employment contracts. When the money supply increases and inflation ignites, employment contracts will call for scheduled nominal wage increases matching the rising prices. Real wages would thus remain unaltered, in spite of the inflation, and production changes would not be made. In terms of Figure 12–3, the anticipated Central Bank credit creation shifts both the AD and AS curves simultaneously. The aggregate demand curve shifts from AD to AD' in response to the increased money supply associated with the credit creation. The aggregate supply curve also shifts—from AS to AS'—in response to the rising nominal wage adjustments previously negotiated by workers in anticipation of the current inflation. As a result, the anticipated monetary expansion moves the economy's short-run equilibrium from point F to point C. The subsequent adjustments of the economy follow those of an unanticipated monetary expansion once the latter is fully recognized as such, and they involve the gradual decline of the domestic money supply (and aggregate demand) back to its original level in response to the trade deficits associated with equilibrium above the TT locus. Note that these adjustments take place at full employment: If the inflationary effects of monetary policy are anticipated, the policy has no impact on output.

The conclusions of the present analysis suggest that anticipated money growth should not have systematic effects on output, while unanticipated money growth may have effects over the short run, but none over the long run. What do the data say in this respect? Empirical evidence has yielded mixed results, with some early work supporting the above conclusions and other studies unable to confirm it.[5] A major stumbling block on the empirical work in this area

[5] For evidence confirming that it is unanticipated money growth that matters for policy effectiveness, see R. J. Barro, "Unanticipated Money Growth and Unemployment in the United States," *American Economic Review* (1977), which uses annual data for the 1941 to 1973 period, covering mostly the fixed exchange rates Bretton Woods system; and R. J. Barro and M. Rush, "Unanticipated Money and Economic Activity," in S. Fischer, ed., *Rational Expectations and Economic Policy*, (Chicago: University of Chicago Press, 1980), which includes data up to 1977. For a critical reexamination of Barro's results, see F. Mishkin, "Does Anticipated Monetary Policy Matter? An Econometric Investigation," *Journal of Political Economy* (February 1982), and R. J. Gordon, "Price Inertia and Policy Ineffectiveness in the United States, 1890–1980," *Journal of Political Economy* (December

lies in the problems associated with decomposing money growth into its antici- pated and unanticipated components. Since these are not observed variables, they have to be estimated. This turns out to be a difficult statistical problem, as assumptions have to be made regarding the information individuals have available in forming their expectations, the government's behavior, and so forth.

12–5 MONETARY GROWTH AND DOMESTIC AND WORLD INFLATION

Up to this point, we have examined the effects of once-and-for-all changes in Central Bank credit creation. Suppose, on the other hand, that the Central Bank engages in repeated credit expansions, so as to give rise to a sustained growth of the domestic money supply. What effects would such a persistent Central Bank credit creation have on the economy? It is assumed, for expository purposes, that this is the only economic disturbance and that agents in the economy form expectations following the rational expectations hypothesis.

Once the Central Bank steps on the monetary machine, individuals will not only observe the credit growth, but also the consequent inflation. They will thus adjust their price expectations upward. In terms of Figure 12–4, the upward shifts of the aggregate demand curve implied by a sustained increase of the domestic money supply will be associated with equal leftward shifts of the aggregate supply. As long as individuals recognize the commitment of the Central Bank to maintain credit growing at a certain rate, they will embody the resulting, anticipated, inflation into the nominal wage adjustments stipulated in their labor contracts. Real labor costs will remain unchanged and production will be maintained at full employment.

Domestic prices, however, will be rising continuously. Wouldn't this hurt domestic competitiveness in world goods markets? Not if the domestic inflation is matched by an equal rate of increase of foreign prices. In that case, world inflation and domestic inflation offset each other, leaving the relative price of foreign goods in terms of domestic goods unchanged. Algebraically, at a fixed exchange rate, e, the relative price of foreign goods in terms of domestic goods, $q = eP^*/P$ would be fixed if foreign and domestic prices (P^* and P, respectively) rise at the same rate. Hence there would be no deleterious effects on the domestic trade balance. Diagrammatically, the exogenously rising foreign prices would shift the trade balance equilibrium locus, TT, upward in the same proportion as the aggregate demand and aggregate supply curves, leaving the economy in external balance.

1982). Barro himself, in his article "Money and Output in Mexico, Colombia, and Brazil," published in J. Behrman and J. Hanson, eds., *Short-Term Macroeconomic Policy in Latin America,* (New York: Ballinger, 1979), finds that anticipated money growth has systematic effects on output in Mexico, contradicting his results for the United States.

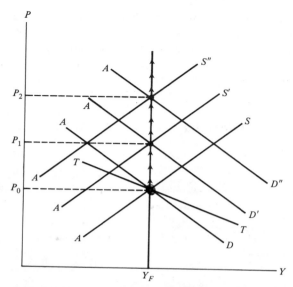

FIGURE 12-4. Monetary Growth and Domestic Inflation

If the rate at which the Central Bank increases its credit is, however, high enough to induce a domestic rate of inflation above world inflation, the resulting deterioration in the relative competitiveness of domestic products relative to foreign goods would result in acute trade balance deficits. Clearly, such a situation cannot be sustained permanently. The massive loss of international reserves implied by such deficits would eventually lead the Central Bank either to abandon its "excessive" credit growth or to devalue the currency. A devaluation alleviates the loss of reserves but, with domestic inflation exceeding world inflation, the balance of payments deficits will eventually grow again, requiring further devaluations.

The bottom line here is that openness of the economy under fixed exchange rates and the requirement that domestic products do not persistently become less price-competitive relative to foreign products—which would wipe out the exports sector—impose a strict constraint on what the rate of domestic inflation can be over the long run. Still, it is apparent that Central Bank credit growth can induce rates of domestic inflation well above the world rate for extended periods of time. As a matter of fact, when governments realize the need for domestic inflation to realign with world inflation and alter their monetary policy toward a contractionary one, they often find that domestic inflation does not simmer down over the short run. Chapter 13 examines in detail the problems involved in reducing inflation (i.e., disinflation) in economies under fixed exchange rates.

12–6   EXPECTED DEVALUATION, SPECULATIVE CAPITAL FLOWS, AND BALANCE OF PAYMENTS CRISES

The present concern with the role of expectations in the behavior of inflation and business cycles in the open economy makes clear that international capital movements must form a crucial part of that analysis. Short-term capital flows are highly sensitive to expectational forces, such as expected exchange rate changes. An expected currency devaluation, for instance, may trigger massive capital outflows that can completely wipe out the foreign exchange reserves of a Central Bank in a matter of weeks, days, or even hours. In most of such cases, a financial and external payments crisis is precipitated by the outflow of funds caused by the speculative run on the currency. The case of Mexico in 1982 is one case in point. Under massive dollar outflows encouraged by an expected peso devaluation, the government was forced to let the currency float (and effectively depreciate) and to impose restrictions on dollar outflows.

It is not only speculative capital *outflows* that may precipitate a foreign exchange crisis: Speculative capital *inflows* may also lead to intolerable consequences. The classic case is the German expected revaluation of the mark in early 1973. In the face of the continued trade surplus of Germany with the United States in previous years, there was widespread speculation that the deutsche mark would have to be revalued vis-à-vis the dollar. The expected revaluation led to dramatic increases in the expected rate of return on deutsche mark-denominated assets relative to U.S. dollar assets. As a result, a massive shift of funds from dollars into marks occurred. Under the pegged exchange rate system at the time, the West German Central Bank was committed to purchase dollars and exchange them for marks. The result was a huge accumulation of foreign exchange (dollar) reserves on the part of the Bundesbank, which led to a tremendous money supply expansion. In little more than 1 month during January to February 1973, the Bundesbank of Germany acquired $10 billion of international reserves, which amounted to about 20% of the German money supply at the moment. With the inability to sterilize such massive capital inflows—and without the intention to let the economy's money supply explode with its obvious inflationary and destabilizing impact—the Bundesbank abandoned its intervention in foreign exchange markets, letting the mark float freely. It is apparent then that expectations concerning the exchange rate and the associated capital flows may have an immense effect on the economy. It is time to introduce these factors explicitly into the analysis.

Expected Exchange Rate Changes, Interest Rates, and Foreign Exchange Crises

Exchange rate expectations are a major determinant of nominal interest rates. Under perfect capital mobility, the uncovered interest parity condition establishes the connection between domestic and world (nominal) interest rates, i and i^*, respectively, and exchange rate expectations. Algebraically (as derived in Chapter 2, with adequate caveats), we obtain

$$i = i^* + x \qquad (5)$$

where x is the expected rate of devaluation of domestic currency.

Recognizing the role of expected exchange rate changes in interest rate determination, as depicted by equation (5), is essential for the understanding of foreign exchange crises.[6] Suppose, for example, that we have an economy where the Central Bank increases its credit at such a high rate as to induce domestic inflation above the world inflation rate. In this situation, as was shown earlier in relation to Figure 12–4, the Central Bank would lose reserves year in and year out. The Bank's stock of international reserves would eventually dry out. At that point, a devaluation, or a series of currency depreciations, would be required.

Suppose, then, that investors in the economy predict that the Central Bank will devalue the currency within a few days. What happens? Initially, before the devaluation is expected, the domestic interest rate would equal the world rate, that is, $i_o = i^*$. At that transitional moment when the devaluation is expected to occur but has not yet taken place, however, there would be a rise in the domestic (nominal) interest rate above the world rate. From equation (5), the domestic interest rate would increase to $i_1 = i^* + x$, to reflect the expected devaluation. In other words, the information about the expected depreciation of the exchange rate is immediately embodied into the domestic interest rate. The rise in the interest rate compensates for the expected capital loss in holding domestic currency vis-à-vis foreign currency. What is the consequence of the increase in domestic interest rates?

The economy's money market equilibrium can be depicted by

$$\left(\downarrow\right) \frac{M}{P} = kY_F - hi \left(\uparrow\right)$$

with Y_F equal to the economy's potential output, at which production will remain in the absence of unanticipated disturbances, i is the domestic nominal interest rate, and k and h are positive parameters measuring income and interest rate responsiveness of the demand for money. Originally, $i = i^*$, but after the expected devaluation the interest rate becomes $i_1 = i^* + x$. As a result, the

---

[6] For advanced expositions of the analytical aspects of external financial crises, see Paul Krugman, "A Model of Balance of Payments Crises," *Journal of Money, Credit, and Banking* (1979); R. Dornbusch, "Comment on Paul Coulbois, "Central Banks and Foreign Exchange Crises Today," in C. P. Kindleberger and J. P. Laffargue, *Financial Crises; Theory, History, and Policy* (New York: Cambridge University Press, 1982); and M. Obstfeld, "Balance of Payments Crises and Devaluation," *National Bureau of Economic Research, Working Paper No. 1103* (April 1983).

demand for money declines, making necessary a decrease in the real money supply, M/P. With the devaluation anticipated, but not yet undertaken, domestic inflation remains unchanged at its current world inflation level. If the Central Bank obnoxiously continues to create credit, in order for the domestic money supply to decline, a sudden run on the Central Bank's international reserves would be required. With declining money demand and the Central Bank pumping out more money, a massive capital outflow would emerge, resulting in a critical loss of international reserves. A balance of payments crisis develops.

Another way of visualizing the crisis is to note that the immediate impact of an expected devaluation is to make domestic assets relatively unattractive at their initial interest rates. Hence, investors shift to other currencies *en masse*, leading to huge capital outflows and a corresponding loss of international reserves. The outflows stop only when domestic interest rates rise by an amount sufficient to compensate investors for their anticipated loss from holding domestic currency.

Balance of payments crises are a pain in the neck for bankers and finance ministers. Not only do they seem to arise quite frequently, but also recur. In order to deal with such crises and avoid future ones, it is important to recognize that speculative capital flows generally arise from the decisions of rational investors making forecasts on the basis of the real conditions and information they have available at the time. In order to reverse a draining run on a currency, the conditions that give rise to the speculative flow must be reversed. In the example above, stepping on the monetary brakes would be a possible solution, although only a committed policy would change the investors' expectations. A casual, temporary, once-and-for-all decline in the money supply would have no effect on agents' expectations and would not prevent the crisis. Long-term commitments to policy changes would be required.

12–7 REAL INTEREST RATES, EXPECTATIONS, AND AGGREGATE DEMAND

We now proceed to determine how the links between domestic and foreign interest rates under perfect capital mobility affect the analysis of inflation and business cycles. One of the basic points to be discerned is the distinction that exists between nominal and real interest rates in an inflationary environment.

When you buy an asset you are interested in how much it will earn you as a rate of return. The (domestic) *nominal interest rate* is the rate of return on any given asset in terms of domestic currency. For example, if you invest $100.00 in a U.S. asset and earn $5.00 after a period of 1 year, the nominal interest rate is equal to 5%, since that is the amount of U.S. dollars you net out at the end of the year as a proportion of the original investment. The (domestic) *real interest rate*, on the other hand, is the rate of return on any given asset *in terms of its purchasing power in domestic goods*. For instance, if *nominal int rate = 5%*

during the year that you invest the above-mentioned $100.00, the prices of goods in the economy increase by 5%, then the real interest rate would be equal to zero. The nominal gain in interest of 5% just exactly keeps pace with the 5% loss of purchasing power during the year. As a result, the $105.00 you have at the end of the year are just worth, in terms of domestic goods, as much as the $100.00 were worth 1 year before. The real rate of return on the asset has been reduced to zero by inflation.

The real interest rate is equal to the nominal interest rate adjusted for inflation. In general, however, when evaluating an investment opportunity, you do not know what the rate of inflation will be in the future and can not therefore calculate the exact real rate of interest beforehand. You have to make an estimate of what the inflation rate will be. Consequently, the domestic anticipated (ex-ante) real interest rate, r, can be defined as

$$r = i - \Pi \tag{6}$$

where i is the (domestic) nominal interest rate and Π is the expected rate of inflation in the economy.

By substituting equation (5) into (6), we obtain the following expression for the (ex-ante) domestic real interest rate:

$$r = i - \Pi$$

i = i* + x

$$r = (i^* + x) - \Pi \tag{6a}$$

Assuming that the world interest rate is fixed and cannot be significantly influenced by domestic forces, the domestic real interest rate will vary in response to expected exchange rate changes and anticipated inflation. The larger the expected devaluation of the domestic currency, the higher the domestic real interest rate will have to be to equalize domestic and foreign expected rates of return. The higher the anticipated domestic inflation rate, on the other hand, the lower the real interest rate, since the value of the return on domestic assets in terms of their purchasing power declines.

Aggregate Demand and the Real Interest Rate

The real interest rate is the relevant interest rate for investment decisions. When a firm, say a construction company, borrows to acquire capital or equipment, it calculates not only the nominal interest rate cost of the funds acquired, but also the real cost of borrowing, which is equal to the nominal interest rate adjusted for changes in the real value of the debt arising from increases in the general price level of the economy. Suppose, for example, that a firm borrows $100.00 at a 5% nominal rate of interest to finance the purchase of some equipment. The annual nominal interest cost of the investment is thus 5%. If the general price level is expected to increase by 5%, however, the real interest rate and, therefore, the real cost of borrowing is zero. The reason is that, although there is a 5% nominal interest cost, there is also a 5% gain arising from the decrease in the real value of the debt undertaken 1 year earlier. The increase in prices implies the $100.00 the firm pays back 1 year later is worth 5% less in terms of its purchasing power. Consequently, this gain to the borrower would exactly compensate the 5% nominal interest cost, leaving no net real interest cost on the borrowing.[7] Therefore, when firms undertake investments, they take into account the real cost of borrowing, which is the real rate of interest. Even though nominal rates may be very high, if the expected rate of inflation is also very high, the real cost of borrowing may be much smaller and investments more profitable. The higher the real interest rate, the more costly investing is, while the lower the real rate the less costly investment becomes.

By affecting investment, real interest rates are pivotal in the determination of aggregate demand.[8] Aggregate demand[9] can be represented by

$$Y^D = \alpha[\bar{A} + \bar{T}(q) - br] \tag{7}$$

where $\alpha = 1/(s + m)$ is the Keynesian open-economy multiplier, $\bar{A}$ is autonomous domestic spending, $\bar{T}$ is the autonomous trade balance, and r is the real interest rate. Observe that b is a positive parameter representing the sensitivity of investment spending to the real interest rate: The higher the real interest rate, the higher the real cost of capital is. As a result, investment spending declines, shifting down aggregate demand. A declining real interest rate, on the other hand, would stimulate aggregate demand.

Substituting the expression for the real interest rate in equation (6a) into the aggregate demand function in (7), we obtain

[7] We are ignoring capital depreciation and taxes. In reality, the costs to the company of using the equipment purchased would have to include depreciation costs in addition to the interest costs and be adjusted for tax considerations.

[8] Real interest rates also affect capital accumulation by channeling investment toward real assets. They thus affect aggregate supply too. In the presence of gestation lags in the actual process of capital accumulation, however, this would be a longer-term effect. Given our present concern with how actual output deviates from its potential, we shall not consider this effect explicitly. It is clear, however, that when anticipated inflation reduces real interest rates, capital accumulation occurs and thus output increases. This is an often neglected positive effect of (anticipated) monetary policy on the economy. For a detailed dicussion, see Stanley Fischer, "Anticipations and the Non-Neutrality of Money," *Journal of Political Economy* (April 1979).

[9] Equation (7) was derived in previous chapters. Note that the only difference between equation (7) and an equation such as (3) in Chapter 7 is that the domestic interest rate, r, is now equal to the *real* interest rate. In Chapter 7 we were not explicitly concerned with the problems of inflation and the role of expectations and they were thus ignored. The nominal interest rate was equated with the real rate.

$$Y^D = \alpha\left[\bar{A} + \bar{T}\left(\frac{eP^*}{P}\right) - b(i^* + x - \Pi)\right] \tag{7a}$$

This aggregate demand relationship,[10] illustrated in Figure 12–5 by means of the downward-sloping $Y_0^D Y_0^D$ curve, shows how changes in the price of domestic goods affect the quantity demanded of domestic goods given autonomous spending, the exchange rate, foreign prices, and the real interest rate. It is downward sloping, since an increase in domestic prices induces consumers to switch demand from domestic and toward foreign goods. Increases in government spending and in the exchange rate, and reductions of the real interest rate, all tend to shift the aggregate demand upward.

Aggregate supply in the economy is as given by equation (1) and is represented in Figure 12–5 by means of the upward-sloping AS_0 curve. The long-run equilibrium of the economy is then illustrated by point E, where aggregate demand and aggregate supply intersect and where full employment and price stability exist. Any point of short-run equilibrium away from full employment would imply that the domestic price level differs from its expected value, from equation

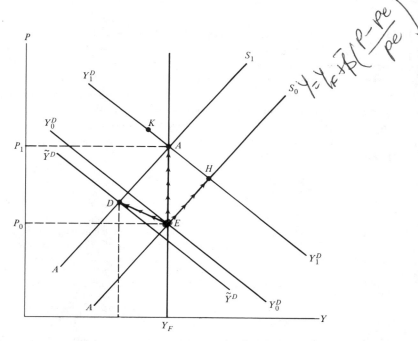

FIGURE 12–5. Effects of Devaluation Under Rational Expectations

[10] Observe that, in deriving (7a), perfect capital mobility is assumed. The aggregate demand curve $Y_0^D Y_0^D$ thus differs from the aggregate demand curve AD of previous diagrams, which was drawn on the assumption of zero capital mobility.

(1). As a result, individuals would keep adjusting their expected price level until it equates the actual one. At that point no subsequent adjustments would arise and full employment would occur. Symbolically, at point E, $P_o = P^e$, and therefore $Y = Y_F$.

Observe that the long-run equilibrium at point E is not necessarily a point of balanced trade. With perfect capital mobility, trade deficits can be financed immediately through capital accounts deficits. Monetary equilibrium at point E must entail balanced payments and, hence, no further monetary adjustments, but not necessarily balanced trade. We shall assume, for the sake of simplicity, that the Central Bank does not engage in any active monetary policy that would generate continuous losses of international reserves. The present is not a context of balance of payments crises as discussed in the previous section. Finally, we also assume the absence of world inflation so that the long-run equilibrium at point E implies domestic price stability and the equality of nominal and real interest rates.

With the analytical framework set up, the first disturbance we consider is a currency devaluation.

12–8   EFFECTS OF DEVALUATION UNDER RATIONAL EXPECTATIONS

Under rational expectations, individuals will form forecasts about variables in the economy on the basis of available information, including the structure of the economy. With regard to devaluation, a number of variables can be used to assess its likelihood, such as the stock of international reserves at the Central Bank—the lower the level of reserves, the more likely the devaluation—the rate of change of those reserves, and others.[11] Whatever the variable or set of variables utilized to assess the likelihood of devaluation, it is clear that certain assumptions about the behavior of the government will have to be made. For instance, even though a Central Bank may be running out of reserves, there is always the possibility that, instead of devaluing, the government will seek loans or swap agreements with which to stock up foreign exchange reserves instead. It is accordingly not possible to predict with perfect foresight whether or when a devaluation will arise, even if individuals are rational and use all the information available. Uncertainty about government behavior would prevent such foresight. Consequently, although still under the assumption of rational expectations, there are three possible cases to consider. The first one is when a devaluation is correctly anticipated before it actually occurs. The most obvious example of this case is when a devaluation is preannounced and it is consequently

---

[11] One variable frequently used to assess the likelihood of devaluation is the deviation of the actual exchange rate from its purchasing power parity value. The concept of purchasing power parity exchange rate is examined in Chapter 15. For a model investigating expected devaluation, see Alex Cukierman and Edi Karni, "Economic Policy in an Open Economy Under Fixed Exchange Rates and Rational Expectations for Exchange Rate Changes," mimeo. (June 1976).

anticipated with perfect foresight, and expectations fulfilled. We must stress, though, that devaluations do not have to be preannounced in order to be correctly anticipated. Often, the proximity of a devaluation is quite obvious even if the government does not announce it. The second alternative is when devaluation is anticipated, but the government stubbornly decides not to devalue, with the result that expectations go unfulfilled. The third case is when the devaluation is completely unanticipated.

(1) Preannounced Devaluations

The case of an announced devaluation is the easiest to examine. Suppose, for instance, that the government suddenly announces it will devalue the currency in a period of 1 month. What happens immediately, that is, over the transition period? Let us assume that individuals form rational expectations so that they know the structure of the economy and the possible effects of the devaluation. Once the exchange rate change is announced, individuals will expect the demand for domestic goods to rise and thus inflation to increase. Since over the long run, the devaluation would lead to an equiproportional rate of inflation of domestic prices, individuals will expect domestic prices to rise by the same proportion as the devaluation after the latter occurs. Algebraically, $\Pi = x$, the rational expectation of inflation after the devaluation, Π, is equal to x, the announced rate of devaluation (assuming foreign prices stay fixed at P^* in terms of foreign currency). The domestic real interest rate would then remain unaltered. The explanation is that the expected devaluation induces an increase in the domestic nominal interest rate to compensate investors in domestic assets for their expected losses from the announced devaluation, as can be realized from equation (5). Consequently, the rate of inflation and the increased nominal interest rate exactly compensate each other in leaving the real interest rate unchanged, as seen from equation (6a).

With real interest rates unchanged, aggregate demand would also remain unaffected as far as it regards investment. Since domestic prices and the exchange rate have not yet changed, however, the relative price of foreign vis-à-vis domestic goods is also unchanged, with no consequent effect on aggregate demand from the trade balance side either. To reiterate, in the absence of other disturbances, the announced devaluation will have no effect on the aggregate demand curve ($Y_o^D Y_o^D$ in Figure 12–5) during the transition period, that is, before the devaluation actually occurs. As a result, with the devaluation not yet in effect, domestic prices will remain at their original level and will be expected to remain so during the predevaluation period. With actual and expected prices equal, the aggregate supply curve also remains unaffected and the economy's equilibrium would continue to be at point E in Figure 12–5. Within this framework, the most visible immediate effect of the devaluation announcement is to lead to some capital outflows and losses of international reserves, and to an increase of domestic nominal interest rates. In the background, however, workers and firms are bargaining over the nominal wage adjustments to be in effect after the devaluation. With inflation expected to jump at that time, employment contracts will embody corresponding cost-of-living adjustments.

After the devaluation is undertaken, domestic prices would increase in proportion. The devaluation shifts aggregate demand upward, from $Y_0^D Y_0^D$ to $Y_1^D Y_1^D$ in Figure 12–5, and it also shifts the aggregate supply curve from AS_0 to AS_1, since the bargained wage increases obtained by workers during the transition period would be in effect. Consequently, there is no effect on output, employment, real interest rates, or real wages. The bottom line here is that a preannounced devaluation does not have any real effects under rational expectations and appears to have adverse effects by inducing losses of international reserves and fueling domestic inflation.

The Stagflationary Effects of Unrealized Devaluations

What would be the effects of a devaluation that is anticipated but not actually effected, in other words, a devaluation that individuals rationally expect but that—because of the uncertainty of government behavior—does not materialize, at least during the period of concern. During the period preceding the point in time at which a devaluation is expected to occur, the economy behaves very much like it would under an announced devaluation: Workers rationally expect prices to increase proportionally to the devaluation and bargain for cost-of-living increases to be in effect after the moment the devaluation is expected to arise; in addition, nominal interest rates rise and the government loses international reserves. (due to expected devaluation)

What happens at that moment when the government is expected to devalue, but no action is actually undertaken by the Central Bank?[12] Since labor contracts are already drawn with corresponding cost-of-living clauses embodied in them, real wage rates will increase, causing labor costs to rise and shifting the aggregate supply curve leftward, from AS_0 to AS_1, in Figure 12–5. As a result, inflationary pressures will ensue in spite of the fact that an actual devaluation has not materialized. Now, if individuals retain their expectations that devaluation is imminent, they will continue to believe that inflation will be fueled by the expected devaluation; but given that prices are already increasing, they will rationally expect the devaluation to generate a less than proportionate increase in prices when it occurs. In other words, the expected rate of devaluation will exceed the expected rate of inflation, causing an increase in real interest rates that reduces investment and aggregate demand (shown by the shift from $Y_0^D Y_0^D$ to $\tilde{Y}^D \tilde{Y}^D$ in Figure 12–5). The economy's path during this time period would be along the pointed arrows between points E and D. The unfulfilled expected

---

[12] For a detailed, but advanced, examination of the issues involved in this type of situation, see Stephen J. Turnovsky, "The Effects of Devaluation and Foreign Price Disturbances Under Rational Expectations," *Journal of International Economics* (February 1981).

devaluation will then be highly contractionary and mildly inflationary. In modern terminology, the expected but unfulfilled devaluation is stagflationary.

Of course, the short-run equilibrium at point D would not be the end of the story. If investors and agents in the economy remain firm in their expectations and the government keeps finding increasingly innovative ways of avoiding devaluation, the stalemate would remain and the equilibrium would be sustained at point D. But, clearly, something must give: Either the government will run out of means to support the exchange rate or individuals will reverse their expectations. At that moment, the economy would return to full-employment equilibrium. We conclude this discussion by noting that some of the empirical evidence on the effects of devaluation shows that stagflation is often associated with devaluation. It is quite possible that these contractionary effects of devaluation may arise from long delayed, but obviously imminent and widely anticipated, devaluation.

(3) The Expansionary Effects of Unanticipated Devaluation

The third possible devaluation alternative involves an unanticipated devaluation. Suppose, for instance, that all of a sudden and by surprise the government announces that it is devaluing domestic currency. As a result, there will be an upward shift of the aggregate demand curve, which increases output and employment above its trend, and which generates domestic inflation as well. In terms of Figure 12–5, the $Y_0^D Y_0^D$ curve would shift upward to $Y_1^D Y_1^D$, with the new short-run equilibrium occurring at point H. Initially, the rise in domestic prices is less than proportional to the devaluation. Over the long run, however, inflationary expectations arise, which shift the aggregate supply curve up and to the left, increasing prices further and inducing a long-run equilibrium at point A. Note that the source of the short-run output increase is the unanticipated price increase resulting from the unanticipated devaluation. Being unexpected, the price hike is not embodied in labor contracts and results in reductions of real wages, making increased production profitable. As contracts are revised, however, the expected increase in prices is embodied in them and no long-run output expansion would be sustained.

Observe finally that if expectations were to be formed adaptively, instead of following the rational expectations hypothesis that we have adopted, the expected rate of inflation would adjust only sluggishly, and, hence, the aggregate supply curve might overshoot the final equilibrium at point A, shifting to an intersection with the aggregate demand curve at a point such as K before settling back to its long-run equilibrium at point A. The reason for this is that, under adaptive expectations, the inflationary episode involved in the movement from point H to point A builds up an expectation that prices would continue to rise. The result would be further increases in negotiated wages, prices, and a consequent decline in output below full employment. Of course, with unemployment arising, individuals will eventually realize that the long-run equilibrium price level is below the one that exists at points like K. Nominal wages would then decline until point A is reached. The adjustment to devaluation will thus be quite different depending on the expectational assumptions made.[13]

In summary, comparing the overall performance of preannounced, anticipated-but-delayed, and unanticipated devaluation, the third case appears to be the most positive in terms of generating short-run increases in output, whereas the second one is the most negative, being stagflationary. In all three cases, however, the long-run consequences of devaluation are to increase domestic prices proportionally to the devaluation.

12–9   FLEXIBLE EXCHANGE RATES, ANTICIPATED REAL EXCHANGE RATE CHANGES, AND AGGREGATE DEMAND

This section extends our discussion of the role of expectations formation on the economy to a regime of floating exchange rates. The incessant exchange rate changes arising under exchange rate flexibility add an important dimension to the analysis: They make the formation of exchange rate expectations a bread and butter aspect of that regime. In examining the behavior of the economy and government policy effectiveness, one must then incorporate as an integral part not only the role of inflationary expectations, but also that of exchange rate expectations. Since, in general, price and exchange rate changes are not independent of each other and may have common origins, one must closely examine their interrelationships. Therefore, we shall analyze how price and exchange rate changes determine fluctuations in *real* exchange rates. By showing the ratio of the domestic currency prices of foreign goods relative to the prices of domestic goods, real exchange rates are a basic measure of the relative competitiveness of domestic goods in foreign markets. Real exchange rates thus influence heavily the equilibrium and adjustment of the open economy. Figure 12–6 shows the considerable short-term variability of the U.S. real exchange rate during the period of increased exchange rate flexibility after 1973. What explains this real exchange rate variability? It is one of the purposes of the next sections to answer this question. We fuel the discussion by examining the connections between anticipated real exchange rate changes, real interest rates, and aggregate demand under floating exchange rates.

Anticipated Real Exchange Rate Changes and Real Interest Rate Differentials

The domestic (ex-ante) real interest rate expression in equation (6a) above can be slightly modified by decomposing the nominal interest rate on foreign assets,

---

[13] For an advanced analysis of the path of output, prices, and international reserves in response to a devaluation, on the assumption that individuals adjust inflationary expectations adaptively, see J. F. O. Bilson, "A Dynamic Model of Devaluation," *Canadian Journal of Economics* (May 1978).

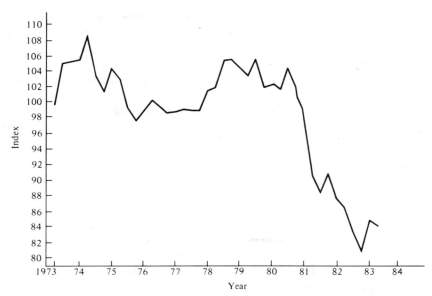

FIGURE 12–6. The U.S. Dollar Real Exchange Rate, 1973 to 1983. The data are for the U.S. dollar's nominal effective exchange rate multiplied by the ratio of an index of foreign to U.S. wholesale prices. Reproduced from Table 11, *World Financial Markets*, by permission of Morgan Guaranty Trust Co., New York, January 1984, pp. 14–15 (1980–82 = 100).

i^*, into its components. We assume that $i^* = r^* + \Pi^*$. That is, the foreign nominal interest rate equals the foreign (ex ante) real interest rate, r^*, plus the anticipated rate of foreign inflation, Π^*. Substitution into equation (6a) yields:

$$r = i^* + x - \Pi$$
$$= r^* + x + \Pi^* - \Pi$$
$$= r^* + \hat{q}^e \tag{8}$$

where $\hat{q}^e$ represents the anticipated proportional rate of change of the *real* exchange rate over a given time period and is equal to:

$$\hat{q}^e = x + \Pi^* - \Pi \tag{9}$$

anticipated changes in the real exchange rate

Observe that since the real exchange rate, $q = eP^*/P$, depends on the exchange rate, e, and the ratio of foreign to domestic prices, P^*/P, anticipated changes in the real exchange rate will be determined by how these three variables are anticipated to change. With everything else constant, an anticipated domestic currency depreciation will increase the expected real exchange rate. This is what the first term on the right-hand side of equation (9) shows, where the symbol x represents the anticipated domestic currency depreciation. Similarly, with domestic prices and the nominal exchange rate fixed, an anticipated foreign inflation equal to Π^* will also be anticipated to raise the real exchange rate. Finally, anticipated domestic inflation will—everything else being constant—be associated with an anticipated decline of the real exchange rate. How the real exchange rate is anticipated to change overall depends then on how each of these factors—anticipated nominal exchange rate changes and domestic and foreign inflation—fare against one another. If, for instance, the annual anticipated rate of depreciation of the domestic currency is equal to $x = 10\%$, the foreign rate of inflation is anticipated to be $\Pi^* = 5\%$ and domestic inflationary expectations equal $\Pi = 8\%$, the real exchange rate will be anticipated to increase by 7% over a year, or

$$\hat{q}^e = 10\% + 5\% - 8\% = 7\%$$

$r = r^* + \hat{q}^e$ *Anticipated real domestic currency depreciation.*

Equation (8) suggests that a key factor generating deviations between domestic and foreign (ex ante) real interest rates involves anticipated real exchange rate changes.[14] To understand the economic reasoning behind this, recall that the domestic real interest rate is the rate of return on holding domestic assets in terms of its purchasing power over domestic goods while the foreign real interest rate is the rate of return on holding foreign assets in terms of its purchasing power over foreign goods. An anticipated increase in the real exchange rate means that there is an expected increase in the relative price of foreign goods in terms of domestic goods, suggesting that a certain amount of purchasing power in foreign goods would have a higher value in terms of domestic goods. In order to competitively compensate asset holders for this expected increase in the foreign rate of return in terms of domestic goods, the domestic real interest rate would have to rise relative to its foreign counterpart. In other words, the anticipated increase of the real exchange rate would be associated with a positive differential between domestic and foreign (ex ante) real interest rates. Similarly, an anticipated real domestic currency appreciation would be associated with a reduction of domestic real interest rates relative to foreign real interest rates.

$\hat{q}^e$

Aggregate Demand Under Floating Exchange Rates

Substitution of the expression for the real interest rate shown by equation (8) into equation (7) yields

[14] Our present discussion ignores risk considerations. The presence of an exchange risk premium, however, would also generate real interest rate differentials. A discussion of the macroeconomic role of exchange risk is provided in Chapter 15.

$$Y^D = \alpha[\bar{A} + \bar{T}(q) - b(r^* + \hat{q}^e)] \tag{10}$$

where equation (10) shows desired aggregate spending on domestic goods as a general function of autonomous expenditures, $\bar{A}$, the current value of the real exchange rate, q, the foreign real interest rate, r^*, and the anticipated proportional change of the real exchange rate, $\hat{q}^e$. This last factor illustrates that, by influencing domestic real interest rates, anticipated real exchange rate changes will tend to affect domestic investment and therefore aggregate desired spending on domestic goods. (will influence domestic real int. rates)

Equation (10) is the algebraic counterpart of our now standard aggregate demand curve. Under floating exchange rates and perfect capital mobility, the curve shows the relationship between domestic prices and desired aggregate spending on domestic goods, given exchange rate flexibility and holding everything else constant. The aggregate demand curve in the present context is thus precisely the same as that derived in the last chapter, as shown in Figures 11–1 and 11–2. The only caveat is that, now, the factors held constant along the demand curve include the anticipated change of the real exchange rate, $\hat{q}^e$. Changes in the latter will then generate shifts of the aggregate demand curve. Suppose, for instance, that $\hat{q}^e = 0$ initially and that suddenly agents in the economy anticipate the real exchange rate to decline ($\hat{q}^e < 0$). Other things being equal, we find that such an expectational disturbance will result in lower domestic real interest rates: Since there is an anticipated increase in the value that any given amount of purchasing power in domestic goods has in terms of foreign goods, domestic asset holders will have to face a reduction in real interest rates to offset their relative gain of purchasing power in terms of foreign goods. Lower real interest rates, however, induce higher investment expenditures and, therefore, increase aggregate domestic spending, shifting the aggregate demand curve to the right.

↓ currency appreciation

12–10 UNANTICIPATED DISTURBANCES AND REAL EXCHANGE RATE OVERSHOOTING

Expectational considerations force into the open the fact that the effectiveness of government policy intervention on the economy depends on whether the policy disturbance under consideration is anticipated by agents in the economy or whether it is unanticipated. Let us consider the effects of monetary policy. The issues are examined through the use of Figure 12–7, which shows the economy initially in long-run equilibrium at point A, depicting the intersection of the aggregate demand AD_0 and aggregate supply AS_0 curves. With no anticipated disturbances, the economy would have price stability and full employment; no real exchange rate changes would be anticipated either ($\hat{q}^e = 0$). Figure 12–7(b) illustrates the determination of the real exchange rate. The curve qq depicts the positive connection between domestic output and the real exchange

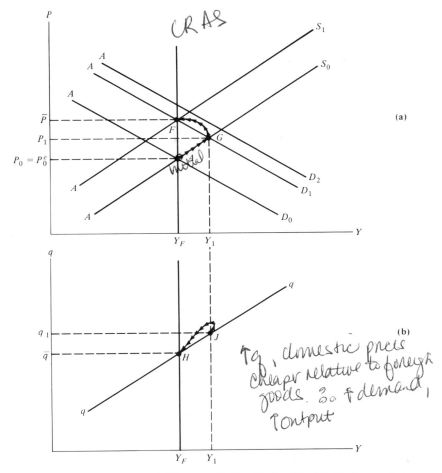

FIGURE 12-7. Unanticipated Monetary Policy Under Flexible Exchange Rates

rate given no anticipated real exchange rate changes. The economy's full employment output, Y_F, corresponds to a real exchange rate equal to $\overline{q}$.

The Impact of Unanticipated Monetary Policy Under Floating Exchange Rates

We examine first the impact of an unanticipated money supply increase. An unanticipated monetary expansion has no effects on the long-run aggregate supply curve, anticipated real exchange rate changes, and the (ex ante) real interest rate. Since the disturbance is unexpected, individuals presume the economy will remain at its initial, long-run equilibrium, as given by the intersection of the AD_o and AS_o curves. The domestic price level is expected to remain at $P_o^e = P_o$. This fixes the aggregate supply curve at its initial position. In addition, the real exchange rate is not anticipated to change over the period of analysis so that $\hat{q}^e = 0$, implying domestic (expected) real interest rates would remain unchanged at $r = r^*$ [from Equation (8)]. $r = r^* + \hat{q}e$

What the money supply growth does is to place downward pressure on domestic nominal interest rates, inducing capital outflows and an increase of the nominal exchange rate. As a consequence, at the original price of domestic goods, the real exchange rate would increase, boosting domestic net exports and increasing aggregate spending on domestic goods: The aggregate demand curve shifts to the right from AD_o to AD_1. The resulting short-run equilibrium of the economy in response to the unanticipated monetary expansion will occur at point G in Figure 12–7(a), where the aggregate demand curve AD_1 intersects the unchanged aggregate supply curve AS_o. The equilibrium level of output thus increases above full employment from Y_F to Y_1 and the domestic price level also rises, from P_o to P_1. The explanation behind the short-run increase in domestic output lies in that the money supply growth is unanticipated. Its effects on domestic prices are consequently not embodied into the cost of living adjustments stipulated by previously bargained labor contracts and reduce real wages. With lower real labor costs, employers are induced to raise employment and thus output.

Point G is only a point of short-run equilibrium and will change as agents revise their expectations in response to new information about the economy. Consider the formation of inflationary expectations first. Once the Central Bank increases its credit, agents in the economy will observe the resulting domestic inflation (equal to $(P_1 - P_o)/P_o$ in Figure 12–7) and will thus adjust upward their expectations regarding the price level. By how much? In the presence of rational expectations, it will be recognized that, over the long run, and in the absence of other anticipated disturbances, the economy will return to full employment. The implied long-run equilibrium of the economy would then occur at the intersection of the aggregate demand curve, AD_1, with the vertical long-run aggregate supply curve lying at the full-employment level of output, Y_F. This is represented by point F in Figure 12–7(a). The long-run equilibrium price of domestic goods will then be given by $\bar{P}$, and individuals will consequently revise price expectations upward toward that level. As these inflationary expectations are embodied in labor contracts, real labor costs will rise, inducing producers to cut production. The short-run aggregate supply curve thus shifts leftward stopping when it reaches the level consistent with long-run equilibrium.

In addition to inflationary expectations, the monetary disturbance influences real exchange rate expectations and ex-ante real interest rates. The short-run movement of the economy from point F to point G generates a rise of the domestic real exchange rate. Individuals will recognize such a change and adjust their expectations regarding the future behavior of real exchange rates accordingly. In the presence of rational expectations, individuals would realize that

[margin notes: Pe (devalue), less demand for $ $q = \frac{e \cdot px}{P}$, $q = \frac{eP^*}{P}$]

over the long run, and with no other anticipated disturbances, output will return to full employment and the real exchange rate must thus decline toward its original level at $\bar{q}$, which is the real exchange rate anticipated to prevail over the long run. Since the short-run real exchange rate is given by q_1, which exceeds its long-run level, individuals will anticipate a real exchange rate reduction over time. Symbolically, $\hat{q}^e$ becomes negative. But with agents in the economy anticipating their current purchasing power in domestic goods to increase in terms of foreign goods over the near future, the expected real return on domestic assets would tend to rise over its foreign counterpart and the domestic real interest rate would have to decline to offset this. The decline of the domestic real interest rate, r, will then raise investment spending and will immediately shift the aggregate demand curve to the right. This is depicted by the shift from AD_1 to AD_2 in Figure 12–7(a) and potentially increases the short-run expansionary impact of the monetary disturbance. Note, however, that as the real exchange rate declines over time back toward its initial level, the anticipated real currency appreciation disappears, raising the real interest rate back toward its original level. Graphically, the aggregate demand curve shifts leftward, back to AD_1, over the long run.

The combination of the leftward shift of the aggregate supply curve with the described shifts of aggregate demand over time induces an adjustment path of the economy toward long-run equilibrium such as that depicted by the pointed arrows in Figure 12–7(a).

Even though over the short run, the unanticipated monetary policy has effects on output, over the long run the only effects are on domestic prices. In spite of the fact that rising real exchange rates and declining real interest rates push short-run output above full employment, both real exchange rates and real interest rates move back to their original levels. Figure 12–8 shows this result with regard to the behavior of the domestic real exchange rate. With the horizontal axis measuring time elapsed after the unanticipated disturbance, the short-run rise of the real exchange rate from $\bar{q}$ to q_1 is assumed to take an amount of time equal to t_0. As time continues to elapse, that is, as we move from t_0 to t_1 in Figure 12–8, the real exchange rate adjusts back to its long-run value, $\bar{q}$. The fact that, in response to the unanticipated disturbance, the real exchange rate has temporarily jumped above its long-run equilibrium value is referred to as the *overshooting of the real exchange rate*.[15] In the present framework, real exchange rate overshooting is associated with the failure of the economy, and the labor market in particular, to completely and immediately adjust to unanticipated disturbances.

Note that, just as an unanticipated monetary increase moves the real exchange rate above its long-run value, an unanticipated *decline* of the money

[15] The term *real exchange rate overshooting* has been coined by W. H. Buiter and M. Miller in "Real Exchange Rate Overshooting and the Output Cost of Bringing Down Inflation," *European Economic Review* (May/June 1982).

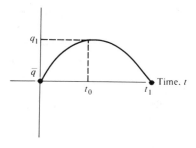

FIGURE 12–8.   Overshooting of the Real Exchange
Rates

supply would induce the real exchange rate to move below its long-run value. This seems to represent the experience of the United States in the early eighties. In response to monetary contraction real exchange rates tumbled sharply, deteriorating U.S. competitiveness in international markets and throwing the economy into recession. Insofar as this movement was perceived as an overshooting of the real exchange rate below its long-run equilibrium level, an expected real exchange rate increase resulted, pushing up real interest rates and sinking the economy deeper into recession.

To summarize, instability in monetary policy, alternating between expansions and contractions of money supply growth, leads to instability in real exchange rate behavior and provides an explanation for the real exchange rate turbulence shown in Figure 12–6.

What about the behavior of the nominal exchange rate? As we saw earlier in Chapter 9, in a disequilibrium framework, nominal exchange rate overshooting would be a natural outcome of unanticipated disturbances. Does this apply in the present framework? Not necessarily. In the case of an unanticipated increase of the money supply, the nominal exchange rate will increase, as in the analysis of Chapter 9, but its short-run response will not necessarily be large enough to overshoot the new long-run value. There might be a relatively smooth rise of the exchange rate over time, unlike the abrupt exchange rate behavior obtained in Chapter 9. Whether overshooting of the nominal exchange rate occurs depends on, among other factors, how the exchange rate adjusts relative to domestic prices and domestic income in the short run and on the income elasticity of demand for money.[16] Note that, if the overshooting of nominal exchange rates does occur, its nature in the present framework does not relate to disequilibria in the goods market of the economy but to the informational imperfections and labor market rigidities present in any economy.

Insofar as the response of the nominal exchange rate to unanticipated monetary policy can be to either overshoot or undershoot its long-run equilibrium

[16] For an analysis of the exact conditions required for nominal exchange rate overshooting in a framework similar to the one developed in this chapter, see Kent P. Kimbrough, "Price, Output and Exchange Rate Movements in the Open Economy," *Journal of Monetary Economics* (February 1983).

value, the monetary expansion can give rise to either an anticipated appreciation or depreciation of domestic currency. Since domestic nominal interest rates are equal to the world interest rate (assumed fixed) plus the anticipated rate of change of the exchange rate, the implication is that unanticipated money growth can be associated with either a rise or a fall in domestic nominal interest rates. It then becomes apparent that, in contrast to usual practice, the level of domestic nominal interest rates cannot be effectively and unequivocally utilized as a measure of the government's monetary policy. An expansionary monetary policy might possibly be associated with rising rather than declining nominal interest rates.

We conclude by stressing that, in contrast to the effectiveness of unanticipated monetary policy in affecting the output of economies under flexible exchange rates in the short run, anticipated monetary policy has no output effects even in the short run. The reason lies in that, as long as individuals form rational expectations, they will recognize that the money supply growth will be inflationary and will embody the expected inflation in the cost-of-living clauses of their labor contracts. When the money supply expansion occurs and inflation arises, nominal wage rate hikes of the same proportion match the anticipated price increases, leaving real wages, employment, and output unaltered.

12–11   SUMMARY

1. This chapter has examined the role of expectations formation, particularly inflationary expectations, on the effectiveness of stabilization policies under fixed and flexible exchange rates.

2. The aggregate demand–aggregate supply framework developed in Chapters 10 and 11 is easily extended to take into account the influence of expectations on the economy. The aggregate supply curve, in particular, can be modified to become an expectations-augmented aggregate supply curve.

3. The expectations-augmented aggregate supply curve shows how the quantity supplied of domestic goods is related to the unanticipated rate of domestic inflation. Unanticipated inflation induces domestic output to increase above its potential level. Anticipated inflation, on the other hand, has no effects on output. This is explained by the fact that, in an inflationary environment, employment contracts will embody nominal wage adjustments based on the anticipated inflation at the time the contract is drawn. As a result, inflation that is unanticipated when contracts are drawn (even if recognized or anticipated after the fact) will affect real wages and employment, hence output. Inflation that is anticipated at the time labor contracts are drawn, on the other hand, will be taken into account in cost-of-living adjustments, generating no change in real wages, employment, and output.

4. The rational expectations hypothesis states that individuals incorporate all the relevant information available in forming their expectations regarding the future value of a given variable. Expectations errors are thus unsystematic, arising from unanticipated disturbances. This contrasts with adaptive expectations formation, in which individuals adopt rigid rules in revising their expectations and can therefore incur systematic forecasting errors.

5. Under rational expectations, an anticipated increase in Central Bank credit leaves output unaltered even in the short run, since whatever price changes are induced by the monetary disturbance are matched by cost-of-living adjustments, leaving real wages unchanged. Only unanticipated disturbances might affect output and then only temporarily until workers revise their labor contracts in response to the new economic scenario.

6. A key mechanism through which expectations formation influences the open economy is through its influence on international capital flows. An expected devaluation of a currency may trigger massive capital outflows that can completely wipe out the foreign exchange reserves of a Central Bank in a matter of weeks, days or even hours, precipitating a balance of payments crisis.

7. Expectations form an integral part of the determination of both nominal and real interest rates. The ex ante (expected) real interest rate is equal to the nominal interest rate adjusted for expected inflation. Investment and, therefore, aggregate demand are negatively associated with the real interest rate, which represents the real cost of borrowing. Money demand is negatively associated with the nominal interest rate, which represents the opportunity cost of holding money.

8. The announcement of a devaluation, or the anticipation on the part of the public that a devaluation will be carried out, has no effects on output but drives up interest rates reducing money demand and inducing a loss of international reserves. Once the exchange rate increase occurs, domestic inflation is fueled, although there are still no output effects. If the devaluation does not occur, inflation will still be fueled because of prearranged cost-of-living raises, which shift the aggregate supply curve to the left. With labor costs rising, employment and output also decline. In addition, expected inflation will be revised downward, resulting in a rise of real interest rates and a deepening of the output contraction. The unfulfilled devaluation is therefore stagflationary. Unanticipated devaluations have an expansionary effect on output, but only temporarily, generating inflation over the long run.

9. An essential factor associated with real interest rate differentials among countries under perfect capital mobility is anticipated real exchange rate changes. To compensate for the associated loss in relative purchasing power, an anticipated real exchange rate increase (or decrease) is connected with a real interest rate differential in favor of (or against) domestic assets.

10. Under flexible exchange rates, an unanticipated Central Bank credit expansion will result in increased output and prices over the short run but only in inflation over the long run. During the adjustment process, real exchange rates increase but gradually return to their initial value, a behavior referred to as real exchange rate overshooting. Even though associated with lower (ex ante) real interest rates, the unanticipated monetary expansion is not necessarily connected to a reduction (or increase, for that matter) of nominal interest rates. Nominal interest rates cannot therefore be used to reflect unequivocally the state of the economy's monetary policy.

PROBLEMS

1. Consider the short-run and long-run output and inflationary effects of an unanticipated increase in government spending in an economy under fixed exchange rates. Then determine the impact of an anticipated increase of government expenditures and compare with your results on the unanticipated disturbance. Does it matter whether you assume that individuals follow rational expectations or adaptive expectations? How do the present results differ from those derived in earlier chapters? Illustrate all your conclusions diagrammatically.

2. The government of a small Latin American country announces it will devalue its currency by 5% in 20 days. The interest rate on the economy's 1-month Treasury bills, i, is initially equal to the world interest rate $i* = 10$ (10%). The money supply of the country is currently equal to 600 million pesos, with the monetary base composed of 400 million pesos worth of Central Bank credit and 200 million pesos worth of international reserves (and a money supply multiplier equal to $\mu = 1$). You are told that real money demand in the economy is given by:

$$L = 0.25\,Y - 2000i$$

and the country's output is $Y = 2000$ million units with the price of each unit of output equal to $P = 2$ pesos. Assuming that there is no change in Central Bank credit, what would be the effect of the peso devaluation announcement on the country's level of international reserves? Provide a numerical answer and speculate on what the government might be forced to do before the 20 days pass. (HINT: Assume uncovered interest parity holds, with $x = 0.05$ and substitute into the real money demand equation.)

3. Evaluate the statement: "Expansionary monetary policy is inflationary" for the cases of fixed and flexible exchange rates. See any differences? Consider the cases of perfect and zero capital mobility and differentiate between the short run and the long run.

4. During the early 1980s, the Federal Reserve of the United States followed contractionary monetary policies. Using the framework developed in the latter part of this chapter, determine the effects of U.S. monetary tightness on:
   (a) U.S. real and nominal interest rates.
   (b) The dollar real (effective) exchange rate.
   (c) The dollar nominal (effective) exchange rate.

(d) Real income.

(e) Inflation.

Check out the data regarding the behavior of these variables during 1980 to 1984. Do your answers fit the data?

5. Consider an economy in long-run equilibrium under floating exchange rates and suppose that a massive military buildup has caused government expenditures to rise drastically, generating huge budget deficits. To finance these deficits, the government starts printing money (by drawing checks on itself). What would be the effects of this type of increased government spending on the following?

(a) Domestic real interest rates.

(b) The country's currency value, in nominal and real terms.

(c) Domestic inflation.

CHAPTER **13**

The Anatomy of Inflation in the Open Economy

How do you make a compulsive eater lose weight? Although in a completely different realm, the answer to this question is similar to the one required in solving the problem of how to control inflation. As in the case of the compulsive eater, it is apparent that the problem is not easy to resolve, and, in some cases, it looks as if there was no desire for it to be solved: Some prefer the short-run pleasures of overeating to its longer-run heart disease consequences. It is also clear that drastic measures are required. Just as short-term crash diets do not appear to work over extended periods of time (at least not for the authors), the patch-up treatment approach to controlling inflation does not appear to help much for long. This chapter surveys the problems of controlling inflation in the open economy. We start by examining the issues for economies under fixed exchange rates, moving in later sections to the analysis of floating exchange rates.

13–1 THE ANATOMY OF INFLATION IN OPEN ECONOMIES UNDER FIXED EXCHANGE RATES

In order to find the cure, you must find the causes of the disease. What causes inflation in open economies operating under fixed exchange rates? Over the long run, the domestic rate of inflation is predominantly determined by the world rate of inflation. There is no way around the fact that long-term deviations of domestic from world inflation would, ceteris paribus, generate significant downward or upward trends in the international competitiveness of a country, eventually wiping out or overextending the production of traded goods. Before that happens, however, the forces of adjustment we have discussed many times before (such as wage–price deflation, the monetary mechanism of payments adjustments and international goods arbitrage) would tend to realign domestic and foreign inflation. As Arnold Harberger remarks,

405

"if a country initially does not fully share in an ongoing world inflation, it is only a matter of time before it will, so long as it maintains its fixed exchange rate, . . . in much the same way that water finds its own level in the different parts of an interconnected hydraulic system."[1]

This view of domestic inflation as closely linked to world inflation is supported by the experience of industrial countries during the Bretton Woods period, as shown in Table 13–1. It appears that 80% of the countries listed had inflation rates within a range of 1.7 and 3.7% during the period 1952 to 1967, and within a range of 3.9 to 6.1% in the period 1967 to 1972. Hence there is a remarkably similar inflation experience in these countries, all of them clustering around the median rates of inflation of 3.0% and 4.6% for each period.

Even though over the long-run, and when countries abstain from regulating international trade, domestic inflation is predominantly determined by world inflation, it is clear that over the short run and when countries impose exchange

TABLE 13–1. Industrial Countries, Average Annual
Inflation Rates (Percent per Annum)

	1952–1967	*1967–1972*
United States	1.5	4.6
Canada	1.7	3.9
Japan	4.3	5.9
Australia	2.5	4.3
New Zealand	3.2	6.6
Austria	3.1	4.3
Belgium	1.9	4.0
Denmark	3.9	6.1
France	3.7	4.7
Germany	1.9	3.5
Italy	3.1	3.9
Netherlands	3.0	6.0
Norway	3.3	6.1
Sweden	3.5	5.1
Switzerland	2.1	4.3
United Kingdom	2.8	6.6
Median	3.0	4.6
Range encompassing 80% of observations	1.7–3.7	3.9–6.1

Reprinted, with permission, from Arnold C. Harberger, "A Primer on Inflation," *Journal of Money, Credit, and Banking,* 10 (November 1978), p. 508. Copyright © 1978 by the Ohio State University Press.

[1] Arnold Harberger, "A Primer on Inflation," *Journal of Money, Credit, and Banking* (November 1978), p. 516.

TABLE 13–2.   **Examples of Acute Inflation**

| | | Average Annual Percentage Increase | |
Country	Period	In prices[a]	In money supply[b]
Argentina	1974–1976	293	262
Bolivia	1952–1959	117	100
Chile	1971–1976	273	231
Indonesia	1965–1968	306	223
Paraguay	1951–1953	81	54
South Korea	1950–1955	102	101
Uruguay	1965–1968	95	66
	1971–1974	83	63

Reprinted, with permission, from Arnold C. Harberger, "A Primer on Inflation," *Journal of Money, Credit and Banking,* 10 (November 1978), p. 507. Copyright © 1978 by the Ohio State University Press.
   [a] Basic data were yearly averages of monthly price levels.
   [b] Basic data were end-of-year money supply figures.

controls and other means of interfering with international transactions, substantial deviations may arise. Table 13–2 shows a selected group of countries exhibiting chronically high inflation rates during the post–World War II period. For these countries, domestic inflation dramatically exceeded world inflation, in some cases for quite sustained periods of time. What factors can cause domestic inflation to exceed world inflation? A number of factors have been postulated along the path of our discussion in earlier chapters. These include money supply growth, devaluation of the currency, budget deficits and their monetization, and aggregate supply shocks (such as bad weather or climate), to name a few. Obviously, each specific country would have to be closely examined to discern the details of inflation in each situation. The conclusion is clear, however, that domestic inflation can get quite out of line with world inflation. Assuming that policymakers become fully committed to reducing the chronic inflation, what possibilities are open? What programs are available to disinflate the economy? The following sections examine various alternatives and their limitations.

13–2   STICKY INFLATIONARY EXPECTATIONS AND THE PROBLEM OF STABILIZATION

Most stabilization programs of the type sponsored by the IMF in developing countries have been heavily oriented toward eliminating balance of payments deficits and correcting inflation, with the emphasis on the speedy adjustment of the balance of payments. The standard prescription frequently involves some sort of aggregate demand contractionary package (like reduced budget deficits, or decreased monetization of the debt, or both), and setting the exchange rate right, which usually requires continued devaluations of the currency. The available evidence[2] seems to indicate that this type of stabilization program, though apparently inducing significant balance of payments improvements, does not appear to help appreciably in reducing inflation and tends to be associated with sharp recessions. Why these difficulties?

One of the basic problems faced by stabilization programs in reducing inflation is the inelasticity, or stickiness, of inflationary expectations to changes that are visualized by agents in the economy to be only temporary. We illustrate the issues involved through the use of Figure 13–1, which shows the economy's initial equilibrium at point E, at the intersection of the now standard aggregate demand and supply curves AD and AS, respectively (for more details, see Sections 12–1 through 12–5). It is assumed that the Central Bank has been injecting credit into the economy for an extended period of time and that individuals expect prices to increase from P_0 to P^e during the following time period. The anticipation of agents in the economy is thus that equilibrium will be achieved at point E', where the shift in aggregate demand from AD to AD' is what individuals expect based on the past and present behavior of the economy's Central Bank, and the shift in aggregate supply from AS to AS' is a result of

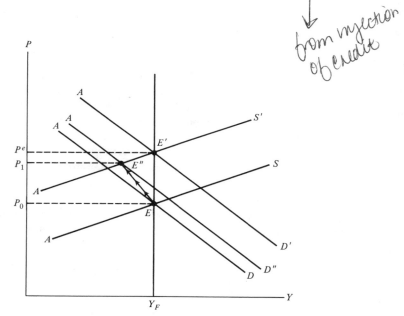

from injection of credit

FIGURE 13–1.   The Problem of Disinflation in the Open Economy

[2] See Donal J. Donovan, "Macroeconomic Performance and Adjustment Under Fund-Supported Programs: The Experience of the Seventies," *IMF Staff Papers* (March 1982); Carlos Diaz Alejandro, "Southern Core Stabilization Plans," in W. R. Cline and S. Weintraub, eds., *Economic Stabilization in Developing Countries* (Washington, D.C.: The Brookings Institution, 1981). See also the references in our earlier discussion of stabilization programs in developing countries in Chapter 10, Section 6.

the inflationary expectations associated with the anticipated monetary growth.

Suppose now that the government engages in a sudden, unanticipatedly restrictive aggregate demand policy (through reduced government spending and/or reduced credit creation), meaning the aggregate demand curve actually shifts to AD'', instead of shifting to AD' as anticipated by individuals in the economy. Does this unanticipated policy shift reduce domestic inflation? As observed in Figure 13–1, the equilibrium of the economy would occur at point E'', determined by the intersection of the aggregate demand curve prevailing under the restrictionist government policy regime, AD'', with the aggregate supply curve associated with the inflationary anticipations of agents in the economy, AS'. The economy, therefore, still faces unyielding inflation (equal to $\hat{P} = (P_1 - P_0)/P_0$), but there is in addition a decline in production, throwing the economy into recession. What are the basic factors behind this result? First of all, given the unexpected nature of the policy shock, individuals mistakenly anticipated that inflation would remain at the level $\Pi = (P^e - P_0)/P_0$ and, as a result, nominal wage rate hikes of the same proportion were embodied in labor contracts. These adjustments keep fueling inflation in spite of the relative contraction of monetary growth. Diagrammatically, even though the aggregate demand shifts only from AD to AD'', aggregate supply, as determined by inflationary expectations, shifts upward more than proportionally, from AS to AS'. The restrictive aggregate demand policy shift combined with the real wage growth sustained through preestablished cost-of-living adjustments then throws the economy into recession while keeping inflation going. Note that the decline of output relative to price increases depends on the steepness of the aggregate supply curve, AS'. The flatness of AS' shown in Figure 13–1 means that output is highly influenced by the expectational errors of agents in the economy, while inflation deviates relatively little from its anticipated rate. This may be attributable to a large share of labor contracts being indexed in previous periods and thus to a relative insensitivity of current labor contracts to the unemployment arising from negative deviations of output from its potential level.

What happens to inflationary expectations over time in the present situation? Depending on whether individuals believe the restrictive aggregate demand policy is permanent or not, they may or may not adjust their inflationary expectations downward. If the government sticks to its stabilization program, it may eventually become credible; at that moment, inflation expectations would decline, causing the aggregate supply curve to shift leftward. On the other hand, it is highly likely that agents in the economy will lack confidence in the government's willingness to maintain a restrictive aggregate demand policy. In this situation, inflationary expectations would not diminish. Wage settlements would continue to embody high nominal wage adjustments, which are then passed on to consumers as price increases. Inflation would therefore continue unabatedly, with a stalemate between the stubborn sticky-downward inflationary expectations of agents in the economy and the government's continued policy of restrictive aggregate demand.

In conclusion, a major element in the success or failure of any stabilization program in reducing inflation is how agents in the economy revise their expectations in response to the program. We examine next some of the issues and evidence regarding how inflationary expectations can be affected by policy and how differences in institutions among countries may influence the effectiveness of stabilization policies.

13–3 DISINFLATION POLICY, OUTPUT, AND UNANTICIPATED INFLATION

The problem with disinflation policies that lack credibility is that agents in the economy will maintain expectations that such policies will be reversed, in spite of the continuous attempts of the government to sustain them. As a consequence, inflation will repeatedly turn out to be lower than anticipated, causing real wages to be unexpectedly high and sustaining a recession without containing inflation. How strong the recessionary effect of these policies is depends on institutional, informational, and technological aspects of the specific economy under consideration (as embodied into the slope of the aggregate supply curve). For Latin American or Southern Cone economies, labor market rigidities and inflexibilities, and lack of confidence in government ability to keep its promises, may cause industrial output to be highly sensitive to unforeseen disturbances.[3] In other economies with relatively more flexible labor market structures, however, unanticipated inflation may not have significant output effects.[4] In economies where such is the case, disinflation policies that are expected to be temporary would have minor contractionary effects. Consequently, the authorities could support their policies longer without major catastrophes, until they are finally accepted as permanent by the public.

What are the policy alternatives in situations where labor market rigidities and sticky inflationary expectations prevent domestic inflation from being significantly affected by stabilization programs in the short-run, while at the same time spreading recession? One possibility is to impose temporary wage and

---

[3] A good example of a labor market inflexibility that causes industrial output to be highly sensitive to fluctuations in inflation regards wage indexing with wage increases related to past inflation. Under this scheme, a sudden decrease in the rate of inflation following an inflationary episode will result in increased real wages, since nominal wages are indexed to increase on the basis of past inflation. This, in turn, will have a negative effect on output.

[4] The evidence suggests that there are wide variations in the behavior of output in response to unanticipated inflation across countries. The studies of Robert Barro and others for the United States, mentioned earlier in Chapter 12, suggest a strong such relationship. Studies by L. Leiderman also indicate that unanticipated domestic inflation has positive effects on output in the United States, Canada and Italy, but none in France, Germany, the United Kingdom, and Japan [see his "Expectations and Output-Inflation Trade-Offs in a Fixed Exchange Rate Economy," *Journal of Political Economy* (December 1979) and "Output Supply in the Open Economy: Some International Evidence," *Review of Economics and Statistics* (May 1980)].

price controls that would constrain short-run inflation during the time period necessary to deflate inflationary expectations.[5] Another possibility is to engage in such drastic and convincing policy reforms that the agents' expectations of the government's prospective policies become one of continued restraint. Individuals would then be convinced a policy reversal in the future would be unlikely due to the abrupt change of policy. Such an approach may still be highly recessionary due to its mere force in restricting aggregate demand, but it may induce a faster downward shift of the aggregate supply curve through its deflation of inflationary expectations. As Thomas Sargent remarks,

> it would not be easy to eradicate inflation. On the contrary, it would require far more than a few temporary restrictive fiscal and monetary actions. It would require a change in the policy regime: there must be an abrupt change in the continuing government policy, or strategy, for setting deficits now and in the future that is sufficiently binding as to be widely believed.[6]

In his own analysis of successful historical attempts to stop Austrian, Hungarian, Polish, and German hyperinflations, Sargent finds such drastic and resolute government behavioral changes essential.

Finally, it should be mentioned that stabilization programs involving disinflation do not always entail a high cost in terms of unemployment and recession. Sometimes, recovery in income and employment sets in with the implementation of a disinflation program. These cases tend to be associated with situations in which past government policy has been completely out of control, creating widespread disorder and inefficiency in addition to inflation and recession. A credible package of measures intended to 'get the house in order' will simultaneously improve the government's economic management and wind-down inflationary expectations, resulting in balanced growth.

13–4   THE INTERNATIONAL TRANSMISSION OF INFLATION UNDER FIXED EXCHANGE RATES

Up to this point, we have examined the nature and possible cures of inflation on the assumption that foreign prices stay fixed. One key aspect of domestic inflation in economies under fixed exchange rates is, however, that it can be imported from abroad. This section examines the nature of *imported inflation* and ways to control it in interdependent economies. To concentrate on analyzing

---

[5] This type of approach is recommended by R. Dornbusch, "Stabilization Policies in Developing Countries: What Have We Learned?" *World Development* (May 1980). Of course, the controls would have to be complemented with reforms, such as fiscal reform and long-term exchange rate policies, that guarantee price stability after the freeze.

[6] Thomas Sargent, "The Ends of Four Big Inflations," in Robert E. Hall, *Inflation: Causes and Effects* (Chicago: University of Chicago Press, 1982), p. 42.

inflation, the framework utilized is simplified by assuming that domestic and foreign output stay fixed during the time period concerned. In addition, only two (interdependent) economies are considered, the domestic and the foreign (or rest of the world) economies. Asterisks are used to denote variables associated with the foreign country.

Domestic and foreign real money demand functions are assumed to be given by *To get nominal multiply by P.*

$$L = kY \quad \text{and} \quad L^* = k^* Y^*$$

where k and k^* are assumed constant. In other words, real money demands depend exclusively on income, with the effect of interest rates assumed to be negligible. Note that nominal money demands can be easily obtained by multiplying real money demands by the corresponding price levels. The equality of world money supply and demand is then given by

$$M + M^* = kPY + k^* P^* Y^* \tag{1}$$

$(\uparrow)$ $\quad$ $(\downarrow) \to$ to maintain equil.

with M and M^* equal to the domestic and foreign nominal money supplies, respectively, and where the exchange rate is, for simplicity, normalized to equal $e = 1$. Observe that, given nominal money supplies in each country, if the price of domestic goods rises, there is an increase in nominal money demand, requiring a decrease in the price of foreign goods to eliminate the excess world demand for money. This negative relationship between domestic and foreign prices in maintaining world money market equilibrium is shown by the downward-sloping *MM* curve in Figure 13–2.

If we assume capital immobility, balanced payments will occur when the trade balance is equal to zero, that is,

$$T = \bar{T}\left(\frac{eP^*}{P}\right) - mY = 0 \tag{2}$$

With domestic and foreign income fixed, equation (2) expresses an implicit relationship between domestic and foreign price levels: An increase in domestic prices, P, requires an offsetting rise of foreign prices, P^*, to sustain domestic competitiveness in international markets and, therefore, balanced trade. This positive connection between domestic and foreign prices in maintaining external balance is depicted by the *TT* curve in Figure 13–2. Observe that domestic trade balance deficits or surpluses correspond to rest-of-the-world trade surpluses or deficits ($T = -T^*$). Points to the right of the *TT* curve depict domestic trade surpluses (foreign deficits), easily visualized by realizing that a movement to the right of *TT* implies a rise in the price of foreign goods at any given price of domestic goods. The gain in domestic price competitiveness improves

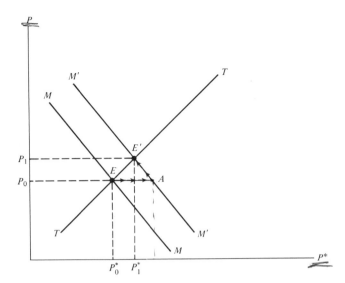

FIGURE 13–2.   International Transmission of Inflation

the domestic trade balance. Similarly, points to the left of TT represent domestic trade balance deficits (foreign surpluses).

Long-run equilibrium is achieved when equations (1) and (2) are simultaneously satisfied, as illustrated by point E in Figure 13–2. We assume the economies considered are initially at that point.

Consider now the effects of a foreign Central Bank credit expansion. At a given level of domestic prices, the foreign price level would have to rise in proportion to the monetary expansion in order to sustain world money market equilibrium. This is illustrated by the move from point E to point A in Figure 13–2, a result of the shift of the MM curve to $M'M'$ following the expansion of the world money supply implied by the foreign credit creation. At point A, however, there is a domestic trade balance surplus (and a deficit abroad). Consequently, the domestic money supply will rise while the foreign money supply shrinks. This redistribution of the world money supply fuels domestic inflation while diminishing foreign inflation. Diagrammatically, this is shown by the move from point A to point E' along the $M'M'$ locus. Only when balanced trade occurs—at point E'—will the money supply redistribution stop. At that point, a new world long-run equilibrium has been reached. Note, however, that the foreign credit creation and inflation spill over into the domestic economy, causing domestic inflation of $\hat{P} = (P_1 - P_o)/P_o$; this represents imported inflation. At the same time, since the foreign price level at point A exceeds that at point E, the repercussion effects of the foreign monetary expansion act to ameliorate the inflationary impact in the foreign economy. In a sense, foreign monetary authorities export part of their inflationary problem.

Assuming that domestic policymakers do not wish to tolerate imported inflation, what action, if any, could they take? One possibility is sterilization. The domestic Central Bank can engage in open market operations (selling bonds in the open market) in order to offset the effects of trade surpluses in raising the domestic money supply. In doing this, the domestic nominal money supply is kept at its initial level and the foreign disturbance cannot therefore influence domestic prices. Note, however, that the reduction in the international reserves of the foreign Central Bank in response to the foreign payments deficit decreases the world money supply, shifting the $M'M'$ curve back to its original level at MM. The domestic sterilization operations thus offset the foreign Central Bank credit expansion, leaving the long-run world money supply unchanged, and eliminating upward pressures on foreign, as well as domestic, prices. Thus, under fixed exchange rates, the United States could insulate itself from European monetary policy by sterilization. At the same time, this type of action robbed European monetary policy from having effects on European inflation or other variables. This point serves well to illustrate the drastic, but sometime subtle, interdependence to which open economies under fixed exchange rates are subject.[7]

World Inflation and Global Monetarism

The purpose of this section has been to describe the potentially close relationship between domestic and world inflation in open economies. This link is one of the benchmarks of so-called *global monetarism,* which argues that in a fixed exchange rate regime, it is the *world* rate of growth of the money supply (an aggregate of all countries' money supply growth) that determines the world rate of inflation and is thus closely related to domestic inflation.[8] This is opposed to *local (domestic) monetarism,* which argues that it is the *domestic* rate of growth of the money supply that determines domestic inflation. The present discussion should help us understand the pros and cons of a fixed exchange

---

[7] For more details, see A. K. Swoboda and R. Dornbusch, "Adjustment, Policy, and Monetary Equilibrium in a Two-Country Model," in M. Connolly and A. K. Swoboda, eds., *International Trade and Money* (Toronto, Canada: University of Toronto Press, 1973). See also M. Mussa, "Macroeconomic Interdependence and the Exchange Rate Regime," in J. Frenkel and R. Dornbusch, eds., *International Economic Policy,* (Baltimore: Johns Hopkins University Press, 1979); and L. B. Krause and W. S. Salant, eds., *Worldwide Inflation, Theory and Recent Experience* (Washington, D.C.: Brookings Institution, 1977).

[8] Studies developing and evaluating the global monetarism doctrine include Marina V. N. Whitman, "Global Monetarism and the Monetary Approach to the Balance of Payments," *Brookings Papers on Economic Activity* (1975); David I. Meiselman, "Worldwide Inflation: A Monetarist View, in D. A. Meiselman and A. B. Laffer, eds., *The Phenomenon of Worldwide Inflation* (Washington D.C.: American Enterprise Institute, 1975); Michael Parkin, "A 'Monetarist' Analysis of the Generation and Transmission of World Inflation: 1958–71," *American Economic Review* (February 1977); and W. H. Branson, "Monetarist and Keynesian Models of the Transmission of Inflation," *American Economic Review* (May 1975).

rate regime with respect to the goal of controlling inflation. On the one hand, fixed exchange rates tend to constrain the inflationary impact of government policies, limiting domestic inflation from going above the world inflation rate. On the other hand, countries that desire inflation rates below the world level may not be able to attain that goal, particularly if they are small economies with relatively little power over prices set in world markets.

13–5   ACCOUNTING FOR INFLATION UNDER EXCHANGE RATE FLEXIBILITY

One of the essential differences between fixed and flexible exchange rate regimes lies in the greater degree of monetary control facilitated by exchange rate flexibility. It is often asserted, however, that such control might not be a blessing but a curse. The fear is that expansionary monetary policy will be used indiscriminately, leading to skyrocketing inflation. What is the connection between monetary growth and inflation? We start by examining how inflation and once-and-for-all changes in the money supply are related.

The initial step is to recall the money market equilibrium condition given by

$$\frac{M^S}{P} = L^D(i, Y) \tag{3}$$

stating the equality of the domestic real money supply, M^S/P, with the real demand for money, $L^D(i, Y)$, which is itself a function of the domestic nominal interest rate, i, and domestic income, Y. For an economy initially at full employment, with a given money supply $M^S = M_0$ and price level $P = P_0$, and facing perfect capital mobility so that the domestic nominal interest rate aligns itself with the foreign interest rate, i^*, equation (3) becomes

$$\frac{M_0}{P_0} = L^D(i^*, Y_F) \tag{3a}$$

Within this context, a once-and-for-all increase in the domestic money supply will generally tend to change output, interest rates, and/or prices over the short run but will be associated only with an increase in prices over the long run. This is so since, in the absence of other disturbances—anticipated and unanticipated—the economy would return over time to full employment and the domestic interest rate would align itself back with the world interest rate. If the money supply expansion is not linked to any long-run effects on output and nominal interest rates, however, money demand would remain unchanged at $L^D(i^*, Y_F)$. Therefore, the real money supply would also remain unaltered.

If we denote the economy's long-run price level after the monetary expansion by P_1, then M_1/P_1 must be equal to M_o/P_o. That is, the domestic price increase must exactly match the money supply increase. This is indeed a remarkable result, suggesting that a close quantitative connection may exist between changes in the money supply and changes in the domestic price level. Notice, however, that this does not mean that inflation is determined by money supply changes.

First of all, the strict one-to-one relationship between changes in the money supply and price level changes is really relevant within a long-run time context. During the short run, changes in the money supply will generally be associated with changes in output and interest rates in addition to inflation. An output expansion in response to a given unanticipated jump in the money supply, for example, will tend to boost real money demand, requiring a short-run increase in the real money supply in order to sustain money market equilibrium. As a consequence, in this short-run context, domestic prices will rise by a smaller proportion than the money supply. How much inflation actually occurs vis-à-vis output expansion in the short run is then a matter that relates to the short-run aggregate demand–aggregate supply structure establishing short-run changes in prices and output in the economy. The particular type of labor market institutions present, the nature of the transmission and acquisition of information by agents in the economy, the responsiveness of real interest rates and real exchange rates to the unanticipated monetary disturbance, and a whole range of other factors will all influence the determination of short-run changes in prices.

Moving away from the analysis of once-and-for-all changes in the money supply and toward a more dynamic analysis, what is the relationship between money growth and inflation? Even if domestic output does not change in response to the monetary expansion, divergencies will arise between the rate of monetary growth and the associated short-run inflation. The explanation lies in that increased monetary growth will in general be associated not only with spiralling prices, but also, in order to sustain domestic competitiveness, with domestic currency depreciation. This will give rise to a given anticipated rate of increase of the exchange rate that, following the uncovered parity condition, will raise domestic nominal interest rates and reduce money demand. In order to sustain money market equilibrium, the real money supply would have to decline. In other words, money supply growth would have to fall short of the short-run inflation rate.

This process is illustrated in Figure 13–3, which shows the paths of the real money supply [Figure 13–3(a)] and nominal money growth and inflation [Figure 13–3(b)] before and after an increase in money supply growth from $\hat{M}_o$ to $\hat{M}_1$ at time t_0. Notice that since nominal interest rate rises reduce money demand, the real money supply has to decline from $(M/P)_o$ to $(M/P)_1$. In order for this to occur, domestic prices will have to rise at a higher pace than the nominal money supply over a certain period of time. This is represented in Figure 13–3(b) by the faster rate of growth of prices, depicted by the PP curve, as compared to the money supply growth of $\hat{M}_1$. Over the time period

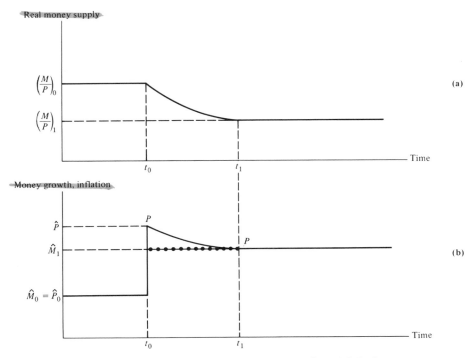

FIGURE 13-3. Changes in Money Growth and Inflation

from t_0 to t_1, the real money supply then adjusts downward to its new, equilibrium level. Note, however, the lack of coincidence of monetary growth and domestic inflation over this time period in Figure 13–3(b). Once again, the one-to-one relation between money growth and inflation breaks down in the short run.

This is especially so if the economy is being subject not only to money supply changes but to other disturbances as well. The economy's adjustment to real disturbances, such as oil price shocks, will generally give rise to short-run price level changes, even if the domestic money supply is being held fixed. The reduction in the level of potential output associated with a sudden rise in the price of imported materials, for instance, could in principle generate substantial short-run domestic inflation in the absence of domestic money supply changes, as explained in Chapter 11. Capital accumulation and increased growth of potential output, on the other hand, will tend to make possible a lower short-run rate of inflation consistent with any given rate of monetary growth.

The lack of association between money supply growth and short-run inflation is graphically depicted by Figure 13–4, which shows U.S. money supply growth and contemporaneous inflation. As a matter of fact, the two statistics even move opposite to each other in several instances. This, however, may not be surprising since the money supply growth–inflation connection is really a long-

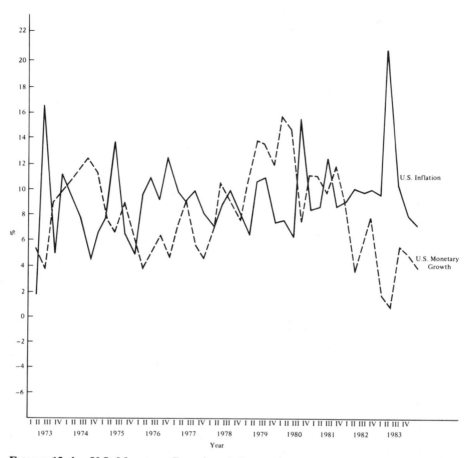

FIGURE 13–4.   U.S. Monetary Growth and Contemporaneous Inflation, 1973 to 1983. The U.S. inflation rate is the annual rate of change of the consumer price index; from International Monetary Fund, International Financial Statistics. U.S. monetary growth is the annual growth rate of what is currently called M1; from Federal Reserve Bulletin.

run one, establishing a close link between current monetary growth changes and inflation *sometime in the future.* In other words, since the association between money supply growth and inflation occurs only over time, a period must be allowed for inflation to adjust to changes in money supply growth. Estimates of the lag in the adjustment of inflation to money growth changes vary widely and depend on the specific country considered. For the case of the United States in the seventies the lag has been estimated to be between 1 and 2 years. Figure 13–5 shows the relationship between current money supply growth and inflation 2 years later in the United States. The fit is much closer than that

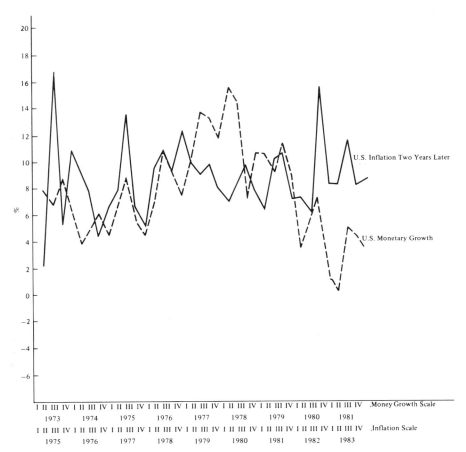

FIGURE 13–5. U.S. Money Supply Growth and Inflation 2 Years Later. Source is the same as in Figure 13–4.

between contemporaneous money supply growth and inflation. Still, significant deviations can be observed (as during the 1980 to 1981 period), a result of the presence of factors other than past monetary disturbances that influence current inflation.

In conclusion, there appear to be strong reasons for expecting changes in the rate of inflation of a country under flexible exchange rates to be highly correlated with changes in money supply growth over the long run. The connection is more tenuous in the short run, leaving domestic inflation subject to the wide array of real and monetary factors that affect aggregate supply and demand in the short run.

13–6   FLOATING EXCHANGE RATES AND THE DIVERGENCE OF NATIONAL INFLATION RATES

The relatively close connection between changes in domestic inflation and changes in money supply growth over the long-run points to the key role of national monetary authorities in influencing national inflation rates under flexible exchange rates. By stepping on the monetary accelerator, Central Banks can, over the long run, impose a skyrocketing inflation rate on the economy. In the same way, they can also reduce the rate of inflation by tightening money supply growth, although this reduction will take place with a lag. Given the relative ability of Central Banks to influence domestic inflation under flexible exchange rates, one would expect to observe a wide variability of inflation rates among countries under such a system, with each country facing an inflation rate basically dictated by the particular policies of its Central Bank. Such is the picture shown by Table 13–3, where the average inflation rates of major industrial countries before and after the Bretton Woods era of fixed exchange rates (demarcated by the year 1973) are depicted. The increased variability of inflation rates in the post-1973 period is reflected in the increased range of inflation rates. The latter remained between 2.7% and 5.3% before 1973 but have fluctuated within the range of 4.3% and 16.4% after 1973.[9]

This variability of inflation rates in the seventies and eighties has been closely associated with the greater degree of domestic control over the money supply possible under flexible exchange rates. This stands in sharp contrast to a system of fixed exchange rates, with its implied lack of Central Bank control over the money supply and its forced alignment of domestic inflation with world inflation in the long run. With fixed exchange rates, rates of domestic inflation persistently above or below world inflation would generate systematic and growing shifts in the relative price of domestic goods relative to those of foreign goods, either wiping out or overextending the economy's traded goods sector. Since such persistent changes in international competitiveness cannot be sustained, eventually domestic inflation moves closer to world inflation or otherwise exchange rate changes have to be undertaken.

The factor that makes possible persistent divergences of national inflation rates under flexible exchange rates is precisely its exchange rate flexibility. Inflation differentials can be sustained because exchange rate changes can offset the changes in international competiveness implied by such differentials. For example, if domestic inflation exceeds world inflation, a depreciation of domestic currency would restore domestic competitiveness in international markets by

---

[9] The increased variability of inflation rates in the industrial countries is more accurately represented by their standard deviation, which increased by more than five times (from 0.9 to 4.6) when one compares the pre- and post-1973 periods.

TABLE 13–3   Variability of Inflation Rates and Exchange Rate Flexibility

Country	Average Annual Rate of Inflation, Compounded		Average Rate of Depreciation(−) or Appreciation(+), Compounded	
	1958–1972	*1973–1983*	*Dollar Rate*	*Effective Rate*
Switzerland	3.4	4.3	4.2	5.6
West Germany	2.8	4.7	0.4	3.1
Japan	5.3	7.7	1.3	3.0
France	4.4	11.2	−5.5	−3.3
United States	2.7	8.4	—	2.4
United Kingdom	4.1	13.6	−4.9	−3.3
Italy	3.7	16.4	−10.1	−8.5
Average	3.8	9.5		

Source: International Monetary Fund, International Financial Statistics. The inflation data are for the consumer price index; the rate of depreciation is that of each currency vis-à-vis the dollar; the effective rates are measured by the IMF's MERM effective exchange rate index. For an analysis of these data, see A. K. Swoboda, "Exchange Rate Flexibility in Practice: A Survey of Experience from 1973 to 1979," in H. Giersch, ed., *Macro Policies for Growth and Stability: A European Perspective* (Tübingen, West Germany: J. C. Mohr, 1979).

reducing the foreign currency price of domestic goods. The inflation differential would then be matched by a persistently rising nominal exchange rate, leaving the real exchange rate unchanged. Similarly, if domestic inflation is below world inflation, domestic currency appreciation could offset the relative gain in domestic competitiveness such a differential implies, avoiding a long-run systematic deterioration of foreign competitiveness.

The implication is that, on the average, in a regime of floating exchange rates there will be a tendency for the currencies of countries with relatively high inflation to depreciate and for the currencies of low-inflation countries to appreciate. This notion is supported by the recent experience of industrial countries with flexible exchange rates, as shown by the general positive connection between higher inflation rates in column 2 and currency depreciation in columns 3 and 4 of Table 13–3.

We conclude by stressing that exchange rate changes do not exactly compensate for the relative price changes implied by inflation differentials over the short run. In other words, there are substantial deviations from purchasing power parity (PPP) in the short run. This observation was made in previous chapters in relation to the conclusion that unanticipated monetary disturbances generally give rise to short-run deviations from PPP and to real exchange rate variability. In Chapter 15 we shall investigate more closely the mechanics of short-run exchange rate behavior and the breakdown of purchasing power parities under flexible exchange rates.

13–7 VICIOUS CIRCLES AND EXCHANGE RATE FLEXIBILITY

The relative autonomy of monetary policy under flexible exchange rates has given rise to the frequent argument that flexible exchange rates is a regime that lacks monetary discipline and will consequently be more inflationary than a fixed exchange rate regime. Consider the case, for instance, when a sudden pressure for higher nominal wages in the labor market—linked perhaps to expectations of future inflation or to an increased relative bargaining power of unions vis-à-vis employers—serves to raise real labor costs and places upward pressures on prices and downward pressures on employment. If the Central Bank follows a completely accommodating monetary policy, it will increase the money supply to offset any negative effects of rising prices on real money balances, hence on output. The monetary expansion validates the price increase, however, and is correspondingly associated with an exchange rate depreciation that sustains domestic competitiveness in international markets and, thus, employment and output. Note, however, that the rising prices may in turn induce workers to bargain for further nominal wage increases in order to sustain their newly gained raise in standard of living. This is especially so if labor contracts are subject to indexation schemes automatically adjusting nominal wages upward in response to cost-of-living increases. A wage–price–currency depreciation spiral will then arise, as workers continue to demand nominal wage hikes and monetary authorities validating them through money supply increases that further fuel inflation, renewing nominal wage hikes, and so on. This *vicious circle hypothesis,* [10] as it is usually referred to, is based upon the relative control over the money supply that domestic monetary authorities have under exchange rate flexibility and on the fact that currency depreciation prevents rising prices from deteriorating domestic competitiveness in international markets. The notion of a vicious circle has often been used as an argument by opponents of flexible exchange rate regimes.

The key point to bear in mind is that the vicious circle can be sustained only if the monetary authorities create the additional money to finance the initial increase in nominal wages and prices. [11] In other words, it requires a Central Bank that lacks discipline in this respect. Consequently, vicious circles are not an inherent aspect of a regime of flexible exchange rates but the result of the particular policies of Central Banks in such a regime. In addition, even though the data provided by Table 13–3 suggest that increased exchange rate flexibility has been associated with increased inflation in the industrial countries—increasing the average rate of inflation from 3.8% to 9.5%—it must be recalled that the 1970s were a period in which massive real disturbances struck

---

[10] For a detailed presentation of the vicious circle phenomenon, see John F. O. Bilson, "The Vicious Circle Hypothesis," *International Monetary Fund Staff Papers* (March 1979).

[11] This point has been made forcefully by Milton Friedman, "The Case for Flexible Exchange Rates," in his *Essays in Positive Economics* (Chicago: University of Chicago Press, 1953), p. 181.

in the form of oil price hikes, and that inflation in these countries might have been required to absorb these disturbances with a minimum effect on unemployment. Furthermore, it is well known that Central Banks operating under fixed exchange rates do have their money-printing mania and can also generate high inflation within the context of that regime. The use of exchange controls, trade barriers, and a whole range of other instruments, the existence of black markets operating at the margin of legality, and reliance upon repeated devaluations make possible domestic rates of inflation above world inflation for extended periods of time under a regime of fixed (but adjustable) exchange rates. The high rates of inflation of many Latin American countries in the recent past substantiate this point.

It must be concluded, then, that even though higher inflation rates may be associated with exchange rate flexibility and, in particular, depreciating currencies, there is no necessary causal influence of exchange rate flexibility on inflation. Rather, both the inflation and the depreciating currency may be due to other factors, key among which is increased monetary growth.

13–8   INTERDEPENDENCE AND INTERNATIONAL POLICY CONFLICT UNDER FLEXIBLE EXCHANGE RATES

A domestic currency depreciation vis–à–vis a foreign currency represents an appreciation of that foreign currency. Therefore, whatever the impact of domestic currency depreciation on the domestic economy, the foreign currency appreciation might be expected to have the opposite effect on the foreign country concerned. For instance, a domestic monetary expansion leading to increases in nominal and real exchange rates raises aggregate demand by improving the trade balance. At the same time, this policy implies that the foreign countries whose currencies appreciate both in nominal and real terms will face deteriorating net exports and a contraction of aggregate demand. There is a sense, therefore, in which expansionary domestic monetary policy is a beggar-thy-neighbor policy: It raises domestic real income—albeit, if temporarily—at the expense of a reduction in real income abroad. International policy conflicts arise from currency-depreciating policies under flexible exchange rates just as they emerge from the use of devaluation under fixed exchange rates.

In a world of unemployment and recession, for instance, one might observe countries undertaking competitive money supply expansions intended to raise domestic output by exporting the unemployment abroad. Similarly, in a world of inflationary pressures, countries tightening their money supplies might be able to reduce their inflation rate by transmitting it to other countries. A domestic monetary contraction, for example, would lower domestic prices but, at the same time, would tend to appreciate domestic currency, implying foreign currency depreciation. Even though such depreciation might be associated with a short-run improvement in net exports and output abroad it might also raise foreign prices, which is not a welcomed event in economies close to full employment, whose main worry is inflation. (import π)

The drastic appreciation of the dollar vis-à-vis major European currencies in the early 1980s shows the acute interdependence of countries under floating exchange rates. Even though the dollar appreciation has led to increased U.S. imports from Europe, its impact on European inflation seems to have been significant, igniting the rage of European policymakers. French finance ministry officials, for example, have estimated that the appreciation of the dollar added approximately 1% to French retail prices during 1983. Similar results are obtained by P. Hooper from his simulations[12] regarding the effects of a 20% dollar appreciation on U.S. and German output and inflation: He finds that the appreciation would lower U.S. inflation by 0.4% during the first year, 0.5% during the second year and 0.1% in the third year, while raising German inflation by 1.6%, 1.4%, and 0.7% during the 3 years following the disturbance. Output effects would be positive for Germany, though, with a cumulative 3-year incremental output growth of 4.8 percentage points. The net detrimental effects on U.S. output would be minor over the 3 years.

In situations where countries share unemployment and recession, or under worldwide inflationary pressures, monetary policy with floating rates may engender in international policy conflicts. On the other hand, when business cycles in different countries are out of phase, such policies may in effect have positive repercussion effects abroad. For instance, suppose that the United States is in a recessionary situation while Europe suffers from overemployment and rampant inflation. In this context, U.S. expansionary monetary policy could potentially stimulate the economy by inducing a U.S. dollar nominal and real depreciation. The impact of the policy abroad, on the other hand, might be deflationary, resulting in lower inflation and output. Given the stage of the business cycle abroad, however, such effects would be like manna from heaven. It can thus be concluded that international policy conflicts will not always erupt from the use of monetary policy under floating exchange rates.[13]

13-9   SUMMARY

1. Under fixed exchange rates, if the rate of increase of domestic prices is in excess of world inflation, the resulting deterioration of domestic competitive-

[12] See P. Hooper, "Impact of the Recent Dollar Appreciation on GNP and Prices in Major Industrialized Countries: Simulations with the MCM," unpublished manuscript, Federal Reserve Board, 1982. See also R. Fair, "On Modelling the Economic Linkages Among Countries," in R. Dornbusch and J. Frenkel, eds., *International Economic Policy: Theory and Evidence* (Baltimore: Johns Hopkins University Press, 1979); and M. R. Darby, et al., *The International Transmission of Inflation,* National Bureau of Economic Research (Chicago: University of Chicago Press, 1983).

[13] For more details on the issue of interdependence under floating exchange rates, see R. Dornbusch, "Equilibrium and Disequilibrium Exchange Rates," *Zeitschrift für Wirtschafts-und Sozialwissenshaften* (1982); and his "Flexible Exchange Rates and Interdependence," *IMF Staff Papers* (1983).

ness in world markets would lead to growing balance of payments deficits. The continuous loss of international reserves then either results in eventual devaluation of domestic currency or in a foreign exchange crisis. Consequently, there are strong forces in fixed exchange rate economies tending to align domestic inflation with world inflation.

2. Evidence suggests that stabilization programs in developing countries, though inducing significant short-run balance of payments improvements, are not frequently successful in reducing domestic inflation. One of the basic problems faced by some stabilization programs in reducing inflation is the inelasticity or stickiness of inflationary expectations to government policies that lack credibility and are visualized by agents in the economy to be only temporary. Wage and price controls validated by consistent disinflation measures and convincingly drastic policy reforms are two alternative possibilities that have been proposed as to how disinflation can be successfully undertaken in countries where sticky inflationary expectations prevail.

3. In a world of fixed exchange rates, world inflation is determined by the world money supply, a major proposition of global monetarism. In the absence of government intervention, world inflation will be transmitted among the countries in the system, tending to push single-country rates toward world levels.

4. There is a close connection between changes in monetary growth and changes in domestic inflation in economies under flexible exchange rates, though this connection is a long-run one and arises only in the absence of real disturbances in the economy.

5. Under exchange rate flexibility, the monetary authorities have tight control over the money supply and can generate deviations of domestic inflation from world rates. In order to prevent systematic changes in international competitiveness, however, countries with relatively high inflation will have depreciating currencies, while countries with relatively low inflation will have appreciating currencies.

6. Increased exchange rate flexibility might lead to higher inflation rates if Central Banks adopt a purely accommodating monetary policy posture, automatically raising the money supply in response to deflationary disturbances, and tending to increase domestic prices.

7. Floating exchange rates can generate as much—if not more—interdependence as fixed exchange rates. A money supply expansion linked to a domestic nominal and real exchange rate increase will be associated with foreign nominal and real exchange rate reductions, having contractionary effects abroad.

PROBLEMS

1. The analysis in this chapter has shown how sterilization can potentially offset the effects of a foreign monetary disturbance on domestic inflation in large economies under fixed exchange rates. Assume that you have a world of

recession and unemployment, with price stability. In the case of a foreign monetary expansion, would sterilization prevent the export of unemployment from that country to the domestic economy? (Refer to Chapters 6 and 7 for more details.)

2. Determine the spillover effects of a fiscal expansion in a large country on foreign inflation under fixed exchange rates.

3. Consider two interdependent economies A and B operating in a world of fixed exchange rates and capital immobility. If country A devalues its currency vis-à-vis country B, what would be the short-run and long-run impact on each country's inflation?

4. Evaluate the following statement: "Exchange rate flexibility accelerates the inflationary response to aggregate demand policies." Do you agree or disagree?

5. Consider the following quote from Harry G. Johnson, "The Case for Flexible Exchange Rates, 1969," reprinted in his *Further Essays in Monetary Economics* (London: George Allen & Unwin, 1972):

> The fundamental argument for flexible exchange rates is that they would allow countries autonomy with respect to their monetary, fiscal and other policy instruments. . . . The argument for flexible rates can be put more strongly still: Flexible exchange rates are essential to the preservation of the national autonomy and independence consistent with efficient organization and development of the world economy.

With your knowledge so far, would you agree or disagree with this statement? Explain.

6. Under flexible exchange rates, monetary contraction in one country may raise inflation in its trading partners, as described in Section 13–8. If you suppose that foreign countries do not wish higher inflation rates, what policies could they undertake to retaliate against the domestic policy move? Examine, in particular, the effects of foreign exchange market intervention. What is the effect of a simultaneous monetary contraction by a major group of countries?

Asset Markets, the Balance of Payments, and the Exchange Rate

PART V

CHAPTER 14

The Monetary Approach to the Balance of Payments

The development of the monetary approach to the balance of payments during the early seventies has set afire the discussions of open economy macroeconomics for years to come. Academic journals, the financial press, and professional conferences have all addressed the issues for and against. Influential international organizations, such as the International Monetary Fund (IMF), have evaluated and repeatedly used the monetary approach to derive policy prescriptions considered highly questionable by economists unfriendly to the approach. If there is anything on which everyone can agree, it is the controversial nature of the approach and the heat it has generated. Notwithstanding the intensity of the debate (and sometimes because of it), much confusion remains as to the nature of the monetary approach and about what it does and does not assert. The discussion in this chapter presents a detailed view of the monetary approach and some of the empirical issues surrounding it.

The intellectual origins of the approach can be traced back to David Hume's writings on money, but its modern form evolved during the 1950s and 1960s out of the work of economists associated mostly with the IMF, the University of Chicago, and the London School of Economics. The list includes the original writings of Robert Mundell, the late Harry Johnson, and J. J. Polak, followed by those of a younger generation, which includes Rudiger Dornbusch, Jacob Frenkel, Arthur B. Laffer, and Michael Mussa, among many others. The strength of their writings[1] and the solidity of their analysis can account for much of the widespread diffusion and influence of the approach during the last decade.

What is the essence of the monetary approach to the balance of payments? The monetary approach stresses that the balance of payments involves essential monetary phenomena. We shall explain in detail what this statement says in

[1] The classic collection of papers on the subject, most of them written by the above-mentioned economists, is *The Monetary Approach to the Balance of Payments,* edited by Frenkel and Johnson and published by the University of Toronto Press and George Allen & Unwin Ltd. in 1976. The important research conducted under the auspices of the IMF is gathered in *The Monetary Approach to the Balance of Payments* (Washington, D.C.: International Monetary Fund, 1977).

the next sections, but we should discuss now what it does not say. First, it does not say that the balance of payments is only a monetary phenomenon; rather it says that money plays a vital role (is essential) in understanding the balance of payments. The approach, as such, does not deny the importance of nonmonetary factors (such as productivity changes, tariffs, government spending, and taxation) on the balance of payments. If anything, it would stress the links between these aspects and the money market (the demand and supply of money), but it would certainly not reject them as unimportant.

A second misinterpretation of the above statement is that it implies a *monetarist* point of view on the economy. The confusion probably arises from the fact that most of the developers of the approach have been closely associated with monetarist centers, such as the University of Chicago, and/or strongly influenced by monetarist thought. This has resulted in their identification with monetarism, an identification that is misleading and, strictly speaking, incorrect. As stated, the monetary approach emphasizes monetary considerations in the study of open economies and the balance of payments. It also pays special attention to the behavior of the open economy over time, particularly the monetary adjustment mechanisms involved. Both in principle and in practice, these concerns can be incorporated into diverse theories of the economy: monetarist, Keynesian, supply-side, or otherwise.[2] The monetary approach, then, is *not* a theory but, as its name clearly indicates, a general approach to (a way of looking at) the balance of payments. It is consistent with a variety of economic environments, including inflation and recession, unemployment and full employment, stagflation, and so on. It is also as relevant to the problems faced by a small country as it is to those of a country that is large in the world markets.

One particular confusion about the monetary approach, regarding its policy implications, is that its proponents think that "only money matters when it comes to balance of payments policy." This is, again, a misinterpretation. As Frenkel and Johnson state,[3]

> The monetary approach to the balance of payments asserts neither that monetary mismanagement is the only cause nor that monetary policy change is the only possible cure, for balance of payments problems; it does suggest, however, that monetary processes will bring about a cure of some kind—not necessarily very attractive— unless frustrated by deliberate monetary policy action, and that policies that neglect or aggravate the monetary implications of deficits and surpluses will not be successful in their declared objectives.

[2] In fact, the original works of Robert Mundell on the monetary approach followed the Keynesian framework prevalent at the time. See his *International Economics* (New York: Macmillan Publishing Company, 1968). Arthur Laffer and Marc Miles, on the other hand, have combined a version of supply-side economics and the monetary approach in their *International Economics in an Integrated World* (Goodyear, 1981).

[3] Jacob Frenkel and Harry Johnson, "The Monetary Approach to the Balance of Payments: Essential Concepts and Historical Origins," in Frenkel and Johnson, eds., op. cit., p. 24.

The approach does stress the important role that overall government policies have in the economy, especially in the balance of payments. Careful examination of the government sector is thus standard, including both its Central Bank and budgetary functions.

Having clarified from the outset some common misconceptions about the monetary approach, we shall now proceed to examine its basic features in detail. The following section reviews some balance of payments and monetary concepts of relevance in understanding the approach. Later sections analyze its implications to a variety of different economic situations. We shall give special attention in this chapter to the study of the open economy macroeconomics and the policy problems of a small economy under fixed exchange rates, an aspect frequently neglected by conventional writers on the subject.

14–1 THE BALANCE OF PAYMENTS AND THE MONETARY SECTOR OF THE ECONOMY

The environment characterizing any modern economy is one of flux. Interest rates, prices, income, Central Bank credit, and many other economic variables change with a frequency that is sometimes astonishing, sometimes horrifying. Goods and assets markets reflect all these changes and have to respond accordingly. In the market for money, for example, changes in income, prices, Central Bank credit, and so on, all tend to affect the demand and/or supply of money. As a result, equilibrium in the market is often disturbed, and adjustments have to take place to maintain or restore market equilibrium. The monetary approach stresses these adjustments and how they are related to the balance of payments.

The market for money will be maintained in equilibrium when the changes in money demand occurring over any given time period are equal to the changes in the money supply forthcoming in the economy. Symbolically, we obtain

$$\Delta M^D = \Delta M^S \qquad (1)$$

where ΔM^D represents changes in the demand for nominal money balances (demand for dollars, in terms of the United States), and ΔM^S represents changes in the domestic money supply.

What induces individuals to change their demand for money, that is, what factors give rise to ΔM^D? As the reader should know by now, changes in income and interest rates (among others) tend to generate changes in the amount of money individuals desire to hold. If individuals get richer, for instance, their bank accounts tend to swell, reflecting a desired increase in monetary assets. Similarly, increases in interest rates induce people to shift toward holding interest-earning assets, reducing their desired money balances and, therefore, their demand for money.

The factors determining money supply changes in an open economy were discerned in Section 6–2. As discussed at that point, changes in the money supply, ΔM^S, are proportional to changes in high-powered money, ΔH, that, in turn, can be represented as the sum of changes in the international reserves of the Central Bank, ΔIR, plus changes in Central Bank credit, ΔCBC. Algebraically, we find that

$$\Delta M^S = \mu \, \Delta H = \mu(\Delta IR + \Delta CBC) = \Delta IR + \Delta CBC \tag{2}$$

which is equation (12) in Chapter 6, but where, for expositional convenience, we have assumed that the money market multiplier is a fixed constant equal to 1 ($\mu = 1$). As before, the concept of the balance of payments we utilize, and the relevant one for the money supply process, is the money account of the balance of payments, B_N, which, in our simplified framework, is equal to ΔIR.[4] It follows that

$$\Delta M^S = B_N + \Delta CBC \tag{2a}$$

The money account surplus or deficit in conjunction with Central Bank credit creation emerge as the sources of change in the domestic money supply. Substituting equation (2a) into equation (1), we obtain the following relationship between monetary variables and the balance of payments:

$$\Delta M^D = B_N + \Delta CBC \tag{1a}$$

suggesting the following representation of the balance of payments:

$$B_N = \Delta M^D - \Delta CBC \tag{3}$$

Equation (3) states that the balance of payments corresponds to those additions to (or subtractions from) money balances that domestic residents demand but are not provided by the Central Bank in the form of changes in credit. For example, a balance of payments surplus ($B_N > 0$) represents a situation in which domestic residents increase their demand for money balances by more than the Central Bank increases its supply ($\Delta M^D > \Delta CBC$). A balance of payments deficit ($B_N < 0$), on the other hand, represents a situation in which credit creation by the Central Bank outpaces the growth of money demand ($\Delta CBC > \Delta M^D$). What is the meaning of this in terms of the actions of agents in the economy? Suppose that there is a balance of payments deficit ($B_N < 0$). Equation (3) suggests that part of the money supply created by the Central

---

[4] The balance of payments expression B_N is in nominal terms (in dollars, from the point of view of the United States), and is not in real terms (in terms of domestic goods). In earlier chapters, we denoted the balance of payments in real terms as simply B. Recall that a real variable is always obtained by dividing the nominal variable by a corresponding price.

Bank in the period of concern is not being demanded by domestic residents, who thus find themselves holding excess money balances. How does this come to be reflected in a balance of payments deficit?

An analogy here with the case of an individual person may be illuminating. What would you do, for example, if you find yourself holding excess cash? Spend it, of course! You may buy some interest-earning assets (like some bonds) or some goods you want (like an open-economy macroeconomics textbook). What is the counterpart of your actions in terms of an overall economy? In other words, what do domestic residents do when they as a whole have excess balances of domestic money? They spend it on *foreign* goods and/or assets. But these purchases require the use of foreign exchange. As domestic residents sell their money (local currency) in exchange for these foreign currencies, the Central Bank loses international reserves and the money account moves into a deficit. The balance of payments deficit thus measures the amount of money domestic residents want to "get rid of," or spend, which they do through net purchases of foreign goods and/or assets. Note that the deficit may continue over an extended period of time. Individuals do not generally adjust their money holdings instantaneously but rather make the corrections gradually over time. Observe also that the excess money can be used to purchase either foreign goods or foreign financial assets. Since the trade balance measures the economy's overall net purchases of foreign goods, and the capital account measures its net purchases of foreign financial assets, then

$$(X - M) \qquad B_N = \Delta M^D - \Delta CBC = T_N + K_N \tag{4}$$

where T_N represents the trade balance (expressed in nominal terms, i.e., in dollars for the case of the United States) and K_N the capital account.[5]

In summary, equation (3) is the basis for the emphasis of the monetary approach on the fact that the balance of payments involves essential monetary phenomena. As represented, the balance of payments corresponds to an excess of changes in money demand over the credit created by the Central Bank in the economy. It should be clear, though, that to look at the balance of payments in terms of money demand and supply (even if particularly illuminating, as we shall see), does not exclude other ways of looking at (other approaches to) the balance of payments. We shall expand this idea in Sections 14–8 and 14–9.

Equation (3), simple as it is, already suggests some policy implications difficult to visualize otherwise. Since a balance of payments deficit represents an excess of Central Bank credit creation over the increases in money demanded by domes-

---

[5] Recall that variables with subscript N always represent nominal variables. In earlier chapters, we utilized more often the trade balance and the capital account as expressed in terms of domestic goods (or the *real* trade and capital accounts, T and K). At this point, it is more convenient to utilize these concepts by means of their nominal representations.

tic residents, one obvious way of eliminating it—and the corresponding loss of international reserves—is to limit the amount of Central Bank credit creation, that is, through some sort of *domestic credit ceiling*. Such a policy may also be combined with *financial programming* of government activities, which involves forecasting money demand changes and gearing Central Bank credit creation to fulfill those demands. Actually, this type of policy recommendation has frequently been advocated by the IMF.

The reader may find it disconcerting, at first, to think about the balance of payments in terms of money demand and supply. The next section presents a simple exposition highlighting the basic mechanism relating the balance of payments and the monetary sector.

14–2   A MONETARY MECHANISM OF BALANCE OF PAYMENTS ADJUSTMENT

One of the main features of the monetary approach is its concern with the long-run effects of disturbances on the economy and the influence of monetary factors on the response of the balance of payments to such disturbances. It therefore tries to answer the question: Suppose that equilibrium in an open economy is lost, are there any tendencies for equilibrium to be restored, and how is that long-run equilibrium reached? This concern of the monetary approach with how adjustments are made over time is a dynamic concern and contrasts with its apparent neglect in most conventional analyses of the balance of payments at the time the approach sprouted in the 1950s and 1960s.

Basic Setup

The dynamic processes involved in any modern economy are disturbingly complicated, involving changes in prices, interest rates, employment, output, and a wide array of interrelated factors. The reader can recall the increasing complexity with which we proceeded from Chapters 5 through 13. To simplify the present exposition, we shall concentrate our attention on the case of a small open economy perfectly integrated to world markets and producing at its potential level of output. The small country assumption implies that the prices of goods bought and/or sold in international markets are completely determined by prevailing prices in those markets and cannot be affected by any changes in domestic production or consumption. This means that the country is a price taker in international goods markets. As a consequence, the domestic prices of these goods must be equal to the domestic currency equivalent of world prices (that are usually denominated in foreign currencies). In addition, the small country assumption implies that the rate of interest at which the country borrows or lends is externally determined and cannot be affected by domestic economic conditions. In other words, the country is a price taker in international capital markets. Finally, in assuming that the economy produces at its potential level of output, the implication is that domestic output, and real income, are not affected by changes in aggregate demand but depend on long-run factors, such as population growth, changes in labor force participation, and technical change, whose determination is outside the purview of the present discussion. In contrast to the analysis in previous chapters, output is thus assumed not to deviate from its potential level, not even in the short run.

We start by restating our earlier expression for absorption, A (equal to the expenditures of domestic residents on both domestic and foreign goods) but emphasizing something overlooked before, which is the influence of asset holdings (wealth) on expenditure:

$$A = \bar{A} + aY - bi + \rho\, \frac{W}{P} \tag{5}$$

where $\bar{A}$ refers to autonomous absorption, P is the domestic price level, W represents the value of the nominal wealth holdings of domestic residents (and W/P represents their *real* wealth), and a, ρ, and b are all positive parameters, suggesting that higher levels of income and wealth, and lower interest rates, lead to higher levels of domestic spending. For purposes of comparison: equation (5) is exactly the same as equation (18) in Chapter 6, except that the wealth effect on domestic absorption has been added.

The hypothesis that wealth is a determinant of expenditure was stressed by the economist A. C. Pigou and is sometimes referred to as the Pigou effect. It relies on the influence of wealth on consumption, derived from the fact that a part of consumer spending is financed out of wealth holdings. The consumption expenditures of retired citizens, for example, are financed essentially out of assets they have accumulated over their lifetime. Hence a rise in the level of wealth will support higher levels of spending. This type of effect is what the variable W/P in equation (5) intends to represent.

Monetary Assets and Absorption

In order to simplify the present exposition, we shall ignore nonmonetary assets for the moment and assume that domestic residents hold only domestic money as wealth. Symbolically, $W/P = M/P$. In this case, since international trade in nonmonetary assets is ignored, the capital account disappears and the balance of payments equals the trade balance. As a result, the present discussion can be visualized as examining the role of the trade balance in balance of payments adjustments. Balance of payments adjustments, however, may involve capital flows in addition to the trade balance adjustments stressed in this section and in the following sections. The role of portfolio choice and capital movements in the balance of payments will be examined later in this chapter.

With no assets other than money, the interest rate loses importance (since there is no possible substitution between money and bonds) and, for our purposes, it can be ignored. Equation (5) then becomes

$$A = \bar{A} + aY + \rho \frac{M}{P}$$

$$= \bar{A} + aY_F + \rho \frac{M}{P} \tag{5a}$$

where we have made use of the assumption that the economy produces at its potential level of output, Y_F (implying $Y = Y_F$), and the small-country assumption, indicating that the domestic price level, P, is determined by world markets at a level denoted by $\bar{P}$.[6]

Equation (5a) is represented graphically by means of the AA curve in Figure 14–1. Note that AA is upward sloping because of the positive association of wealth and expenditure: An increase in the real money balances held by domestic residents will increase their expenditures, holding everything else constant. The horizontal line $Y_F Y_F$ shows the level of absorption corresponding to the full-employment level of income.

The trade balance deficit or surplus of the economy at any given point in time is represented by the vertical distance between the AA curve and the $Y_F Y_F$ line in Figure 14–1. Suppose, for example, that the quantity of money in the

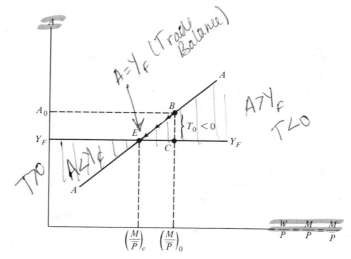

FIGURE 14–1. The Purely Monetary Adjustment Mechanism

[6] We are ignoring goods that are not traded internationally, so-called nontraded goods. The prices of nontraded goods are determined in local markets and are not, therefore, exogenously given by world market conditions. The appendix to this chapter examines the implications of incorporating nontraded goods into the analysis.

economy is $(M/\bar{P})_0$. At that level of monetary wealth, the expenditures of domestic residents would be given by equation (5a) as $A_o \equiv \bar{A} + aY_F + \rho \left(\dfrac{M}{\bar{P}} \right)_o$, which, as shown in Figure 14–1, exceeds the full-employment level of income, Y_F. Domestic residents would be spending more than their income. Since the trade balance is equal to the excess of income over absorption ($T = Y - A$), in this case it would be in deficit ($T_o = Y_F - A_o < 0$). Indeed, any level of monetary wealth above that of $(M/\bar{P})_e$ would give rise to an excess of domestic expenditure over income, inducing trade deficits. Similarly, any level of monetary wealth *below* that of $(M/\bar{P})_e$ would give rise to an excess of income over expenditure and a trade balance surplus. Only at a level of monetary wealth equal to $(M/\bar{P})_e$ will income and expenditure be the same, at which point there would be balanced trade and payments. This external balance point is shown by point E in Figure 14–1. It can be represented algebraically by the equality of full-employment income and absorption:

$$Y_F = A^e \equiv \bar{A} + aY_F + \rho \left(\frac{M}{\bar{P}} \right)_e \tag{6}$$

where A^e is the level of domestic absorption associated with monetary holdings of $(M/\bar{P})_e$. By solving this equation for $(M/\bar{P})_e$, we can find the exact level of the monetary stock consistent with external balance:

$$\left(\frac{M}{\bar{P}} \right)_e = \frac{1}{\rho} [(1 - a)Y_F - \bar{A}] \tag{7}$$

which is a function of full-employment income and various parameters. The expression in equation (7) can also be visualized as specifying the long-run demand for money or the target amount of money toward which individuals strive.

Having specified the external balance equilibrium of the economy, the question still remains of whether (and how) that balance can be reached. The monetary approach suggests that there are tendencies in a laissez-faire open economy inducing it to move toward balanced payments, toward point E in Figure 14–1. These tendencies arise from the changes in monetary holdings implied by payments (trade) deficits and surpluses. Consider the case of a deficit, represented by the gap between points B and C in Figure 14–1. The deficit implies that domestic residents are spending more than their income ($A_o > Y_F$). In order to finance these "excess" expenditures, they have to draw upon their asset holdings, that in the present simplified context are in the form of monetary balances. If we assume the Central Bank acts passively (does not inject new money into the economy), there would then be a reduction in the money supply. In other words, domestic residents would be disposing of, or "getting rid of," some of their money balances by buying a net amount of foreign goods.

What happens over time? As domestic residents reduce their money holdings, domestic absorption starts to decline and, given the full-employment level of income, the trade deficit also tends to decrease ($T \equiv Y_F - A$ goes down). This is represented in Figure 14–1 by the pointed arrows, which show the economy's leftward move along the AA line. Only when the trade and payments deficit is eliminated will the monetary adjustments stop occurring. At that point, point E in Figure 14–1, domestic income will equal absorption and, consequently, monetary wealth stops changing. The adjustment process has generated a reduction in money holdings, from their original level at $(M/\bar{P})_o$, to their long-run level at $(M/\bar{P})_e$. Domestic residents reach their desired (target) amount of money and have no need to adjust their money balances any further.

Observe that the trade and payments deficits have been eliminated without any changes in prices, income, and interest rates occurring. This is a *purely monetary automatic adjustment mechanism,* moving the economy toward balanced trade on the basis of changes in monetary wealth holdings. It is one of the key suggestions of the monetary approach, indeed, that external balance can be reached without any need for prices, income, or interest rates to change in the process. In particular, attaining external balance *does not have to* involve the painful deflationary adjustments in the economy discussed in previous chapters. This does not mean, of course, that such adjustments cannot occur. The presence of short-run rigidities in the economy, for example, may make impossible the monetary adjustments just mentioned without concurrent increases in unemployment. This was the point made in Chapter 10, Section 5. In any case, whether alone or combined with changes in other basic economic variables, the monetary mechanism of adjustment represents one force tending to move the economy toward external balance.

One important aspect that has to be discussed is the time factor. How long does it take monetary wealth adjustments to move the economy toward external balance? The answer to this question depends on how quickly domestic residents adjust their money balances. If the Central Bank acts passively, domestic monetary holdings will change only through the trade balance; but the trade balance is the excess of income, Y_F in the present case, over absorption, A, as given by equation (5a), or

$$T = Y_F - A$$

$$= (1 - a)Y_F - \bar{A} - \rho \frac{M}{\bar{P}} \qquad (8)$$

Since equation (7) tells us that

$$(1 - a)Y_F - \bar{A} = \rho \left(\frac{M}{\bar{P}}\right)_e$$

we can substitute this expression into equation (8) and obtain

$$T = \rho \left[\left(\frac{M}{\bar{P}} \right)_e - \left(\frac{M}{\bar{P}} \right) \right] \tag{8a}$$

Equation (8a) states that adjustments in monetary wealth (represented in the present case by the trade balance) are made in proportion to the gap existing between the long-run equilibrium stock of money holdings, $(M/\bar{P})_e$, and the actual stock of money at any given point in time, $(M/\bar{P})$. This formulation of monetary wealth adjustments over time represents a so-called *stock adjustment mechanism* and, in our case, it describes how domestic residents respond to temporary disequilibria in the monetary sector. Equation (8a) shows that two factors determine the speed at which changes in monetary wealth occur:

1. The gap between the existing stock of money, $(M/\bar{P})$, and its desired level, $(M/\bar{P})_e$. The larger this gap, the farther away the economy is from its long-run, desired state and, everything else being constant, the larger the changes in money balances over any given time period. As a result, the economy moves faster toward long-run equilibrium.
2. The value of the parameter ρ. From equation (8a), ρ represents the fraction of the gap between desired and actual money holdings that is eliminated in any given time period. The larger ρ is, the larger the proportion of excess money balances that is spent and, consequently, the faster the adjustment toward long-run equilibrium.

The empirical evidence yields a low value of ρ, indicating a slow monetary adjustment. Studies by Clements, Craig, and Jonson, among others,[7] tend to show that the time required to dispose of excess money balances through trade balance deficits may be at the level of years, perhaps as long as 7 years. In general, consumers dislike sharply fluctuating patterns of spending and try to smooth out any desired changes so that they occur gradually. As a consequence, monetary adjustments that require changes in wealth usually take long periods of time. This, however, should not be taken to imply that monetary adjustments are always slow. As we shall see later on, rapid changes in money holdings can take place by means of capital flows.

We have shown how monetary adjustments tend to eliminate external payments imbalances automatically. One important qualification is necessary. The monetary mechanism of adjustment can be interrupted by sterilization opera-

[7] For more details, see P. D. Jonson, "Money and Economic Activity in the Open Economy: The United Kingdom, 1880–1970," *Journal of Political Economy*, 979–1012 (October 1976); G. Craig, *A Monetary Approach to the Balance of Trade*, Ph.D. thesis (Department of Economics, University of Chicago, 1979); and Kenneth W. Clements, *The Trade Balance in Monetary General Equilibrium*, Ph.D. thesis (Department of Economics, University of Chicago, 1977).

tions. Sterilization operations refer to operations carried out by the Central Bank to neutralize the effects of the balance of payments on the monetary base. For instance, the Central Bank may prevent a payments deficit from decreasing the domestic money supply by injecting money into the economy at the same time. The monetary approach asserts that sterilization operations can indeed interrupt the automatic monetary mechanism (which has given rise to the statement that sterilization causes "monetary interruptus"). At the same time, it stresses that by injecting money into the economy, the Central Bank may be really perpetuating the monetary disequilibrium the deficit was trying to correct. Individuals find themselves trying to get rid of money while the Central Bank keeps pumping it into the economy, accentuating the disequilibrium and perhaps causing larger deficits later on.

In the absence of sterilization, monetary wealth adjustments tend to move an economy with payments imbalances back toward external balance. What factors may disturb that balance in the first place? Equation (8) shows that factors affecting potential output, Y_F, autonomous absorption, $\bar{A}$, and/or the real money supply, $M/\bar{P}$, will disturb the balance of trade and payments of the economy. The next sections examine the role of government policies, beginning with the effects of exchange rate changes. Other factors are considered in exercises at the end of this chapter.

14–3 DEVALUATION: A MONETARY APPROACH

To study the effects of a devaluation, we shall first analyze what are the determinants of the price level in the case of a small open economy that is closely integrated to world markets.

The domestic price level represents the cost of a given basket of goods purchased by a representative domestic consumer. If we consider only the consumer's purchases of traded goods (exportables and importables), the domestic price level, $\bar{P}$, can be expressed as an index of the prices of these goods:[8]

$$\bar{P} = \theta P_x + (1 - \theta)P_M \tag{9}$$

where P_x is the domestic price of exportable commodities, P_M is the domestic price of importable commodities, and θ is the share of exportables in the consumption bundle of a domestic consumer (so that $1 - \theta$ is the importables' share).

For a small economy, the domestic prices of traded goods are determined by their prices in world markets (the economy is a price taker). Hence, to calculate domestic prices, one converts world prices into their domestic currency

---

[8] It would be useful to refer now to the brief introduction to exchange rate and price indices in Chapter 4, Section 4.

values. If, for example, the price of importables in world markets is P_M^* (in foreign currency), then the domestic price, faced by local consumers, would be

$$P_M = eP_M^* \tag{10}$$

where e is the exchange rate converting the foreign currency price into domestic currency. Similarly, the domestic price of an exportable commodity would be

$$P_x = eP_x^* \tag{11}$$

given the foreign-currency price, P_x^*, available in world markets.

Substituting the expressions for P_M and P_x in (10) and (11) into equation (9), one easily finds that the domestic price level is equal to

$$\bar{P} = \theta e P_x^* + (1 - \theta) e P_M^*$$
$$= e(\theta P_x^* + (1 - \theta) P_M^*)$$
$$= e\bar{P}^* \tag{9a}$$

where $\bar{P}^* \equiv \theta P_X^* + (1 - \theta) P_M^*$ is the world price (foreign-currency price) of the typical consumption basket of a domestic resident.

Having cleared up what the determinants of the domestic price level are, we can easily see how a devaluation affects domestic residents. As equation (9a) shows, an increase in the exchange rate, e, will raise the domestic price level, $\bar{P}$, since it immediately increases the prices of traded goods purchased locally. As a consequence, the real value of the money balances held in the economy declines below their initial equilibrium level. This is illustrated in Figure 14–2 by the reduction in real monetary wealth from its initial (long-run) level at $(M/P)_e$ to the lower level at $(M/P)_1$. The monetary process of adjustment is then triggered: Domestic residents will reduce spending below income so as to accumulate money balances with which to replenish their reduced real money stock. As a consequence, the immediate effect of the devaluation is to create a trade surplus, which is shown in Figure 14–2 by $T = Y_F - A_1$, the gap between the AA curve and the $Y_F Y_F$ line. This impact effect of a devaluation can be better visualized by looking back at equation (8). A devaluation, by increasing the price level, $\bar{P}$, induces a reduction in real money balances, $M/\bar{P}$, which reduces absorption and improves the trade balance.

But the payments surplus will generate additions to the economy's money supply over time. The equilibrium of the economy should then move along the pointed arrows in Figure 14–2 all the way until the desired, long-run level of monetary wealth, $(M/P)_e$, is reached. At that point, absorption will again equal income, and the trade imbalances will disappear. The devaluation improves the trade balance only temporarily. Its long-run effects are to increase the domes-

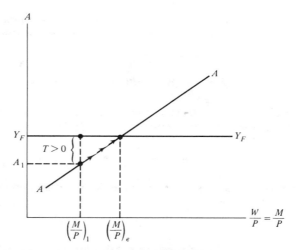

FIGURE 14–2.   The Monetary Approach to Devaluation

tic price level and the *nominal* money supply by the same proportion, leaving *real* money balances unchanged. The level of international reserves at the Central Bank also increases, a result of the temporary trade surpluses arising during the adjustment process.

Observe that, even though the *absolute* price level of the economy, $\bar{P}$, has increased, the *relative* price of imports in terms of exports, P_M/P_x, is not affected. The reason for this is that, in a small open economy, devaluation increases P_M and P_x by the same proportion. From equations (10) and (11)

$$\frac{P_M}{P_x} = \frac{eP_M^*}{eP_x^*} = \frac{P_M^*}{P_x^*}$$

Since world prices, P_x^* and P_M^*, are unaffected by the devaluation (the country is too small to affect world prices in any noticeable way), P_M/P_x remains unchanged over the whole process. It is one of the outcomes of the monetary approach that devaluation can affect the trade balance (at least temporarily) without changing relative prices. This does not mean that such changes cannot occur. In previous chapters we saw how a country that faces rigidities in the prices of the goods it produces and exports can affect the relative price of those goods relative to the prices of imports. In this context, an increase in the exchange rate raises the domestic prices of imports but not those of domestically produced export goods (or at least not immediately). As a result, the relative price of imports in terms of exports increases, inducing a shift in spending away from foreign and toward domestic goods, and improving the trade balance. To analyze devaluation in such an environment was the purpose of Chapters 5 through 7; Chapter 10 did acknowledge the effects of a devaluation on the prices of domestic exports and viewed changes in relative prices only as a tempo-rary phenomenon that is eliminated over the long run. The point made by the monetary approach is that, whether or not relative price changes occur, devaluation has a positive effect on the trade (and payments) balance by reducing real money balances and therefore domestic spending.

Finally, observe that devaluation is not the only factor impinging on the domestic price level in a small open economy. Increases in the world price level, $\bar{P}*$, for example, will tend to raise domestic prices and have effects similar to a devaluation. In addition, commercial policies, such as tariffs and quotas, will also affect prices. A tariff on imports will increase the prices of import goods faced by domestic residents and reduce real money balances. As we have seen, these monetary effects generate temporary trade imbalances.

14–4   MONEY, BUDGET DEFICITS, AND THE BALANCE OF PAYMENTS

Monetary policy in the form of open market operations, where the Central Bank buys or sells securities in the open market, is an essential tool of monetary policy in modern industrial economies. As such, previous chapters have empha-sized its workings and possible effects. A second way by which monetary policy often occurs, however, is by "printing money." In this situation, the government in effect prints money and distributes it to the public. Economists refer to this operation as a "helicopter operation," which suggests the picture of a government (or politician) throwing money from a helicopter in the sky. Of course, even though some kings and dictators have been known to run through the streets throwing money into the hands of their subjects, helicopter operations do not appear to occur in reality. If you look closely, however, the same type of operation is involved when a government makes expenditures that it pays for by simply printing money. Budget deficits, the excess of government spending over its revenues, are often financed by printing money. Politicians sometimes find it distressing to raise taxes (especially during election years) and may also prefer, or find it easier, to print money than to engage in government borrowings to finance the deficit. Accordingly, government fiscal and monetary policies are often interconnected, with deficits linked to corresponding increases in the money supply.

Suppose that there is an increase of the domestic money supply due to an issuance of money. As a consequence, domestic residents will find themselves holding excess money balances that they will try to get rid of through trade deficits. This can be visualized from equation (8): An increase in monetary wealth (an increase in $M/\bar{P}$) induces an increase in absorption relative to income, worsening the trade balance (bringing down T). Graphically, if the economy starts from a point of external balance at point E in Figure 14–1, an increased money supply [from, say $(M/P)_e$ to $(M/P)_o$] would result in a trade deficit equal to $T_o < 0$.

The economy will adjust to the monetary disturbance over time. The monetary process of adjustment described in Section 14–2 operates to eliminate the excess money balances that the money printing spree has generated. Only when the economy has moved back to external balance will the mechanism stop. This is illustrated in Figure 14–1 by the pointed arrows, indicating the motion of the economy after the monetary injection.

The implication here is that government deficits financed by printing money will tend to generate balance of payments deficits, everything else being constant. If the budget deficit is only temporary (say, a 1-year event), then the Central Bank just pumps a fixed amount of money into the economy. As a consequence, the external deficit will be temporary, as domestic residents get rid of the fixed amount of money printed by the government. Since the money supply returns again to its initial level, the increased Central Bank credit is exactly matched by a loss of international reserves. In other words, the government, which initially tries to finance its deficit by creating more money, finds out that the deficit is really being financed out of foreign exchange reserves.

If budget deficits are sustained over time, and everything else is constant, the economy's balance of payments deficits brought about by deficit finance through printing money would also tend to be persistent. The Central Bank would face continuous losses of international reserves. This process, of course, cannot continue forever, since foreign exchange reserves are limited in amount. Observing its international reserves dwindle, what could the Central Bank do? Clearly it could devalue its currency. As we saw earlier in Section 14–3, devaluation tends to improve the balance of payments by increasing domestic prices and reducing the real value of the money balances that the government keeps pumping into the economy. This will ameliorate, if not eliminate, the loss of reserves. It is, however, a temporary palliative. As we have seen before, the effects of a devaluation on the balance of payments are only temporary. As domestic prices settle at their new (higher) levels, the sustained money creation will again move the balance of payments into deficit, renewing the loss of international reserves. Eventually, another devaluation is required. This spiral in which balance of payments deficits and relative price stability are followed by devaluation and soaring inflation to be followed by periods of payments deficit and renewed price stability, and so on, has been called the "devaluation–inflation spiral."[9] It points out that the ultimate source of rising prices (inflation) in developing countries with deficit government spending may not be devaluation per se—in cases where the country frequently devalues—but rather the government deficits and their monetization, which give rise to payments deficits and the need for devaluation. Actually, some evidence does exist associating devaluation with the presence of relatively large, monetized budget deficits.[10]

[9] For an advanced exposition of this phenomenon, see Carlos Rodriguez, "A Stylized Model of the Devaluation-Inflation Spiral." *International Monetary Fund Staff Papers* (March 1978).

[10] See A. C. Harberger, "In Step and Out of Step with the World Inflation," in A. Razin and J. Flanders, eds., *Development in an Inflationary World* (New York: Academic Press, Inc., 1981).

In this section, we have focused on analyzing the effects of an increase in the money supply through printing money and particularly on the long-run monetary adjustments it fosters. In the next section we shall analyze the role of nonmonetary financial assets in balance of payments adjustments.

14–5   PORTFOLIO CHOICE IN THE OPEN ECONOMY

Real-world investors diversify their portfolios among a variety of assets that include not only monetary, but also domestic and foreign nonmonetary assets.[11] This is recognized here by observing that domestic residents can hold their wealth in the form of financial assets, represented by bonds,[12] V, in addition to money, M/P:

$$\frac{W}{P} = \frac{M}{P} + V \tag{12}$$

This means that two main decisions have to be made: what the *size* of the portfolio is going to be (how much wealth is going to be held), and what its *composition* will look like (what type of assets are going to be held).

Determining Portfolio Size and Composition

Figure 14–3(a) shows our familiar absorption and full employment loci, where it must be remembered that wealth now includes nonmonetary as well as monetary holdings. The desired portfolio size of domestic residents is represented by $(W/P)_e$. At that level of wealth, income equals absorption, as shown by point E, and thus there is balanced trade. Figure 14–3(b) describes, on the other hand, the portfolio composition decision. If the total wealth to be invested is given by $(W/P)_e$, the possible combinations of bonds and money that can be held is represented by the downward-sloping line in Figure 14–3(b) called the *wealth constraint line*. The equation for this line is determined by noting that $(W/P)_e = (M/P) + V$, or

$$V = \left(\frac{W}{P}\right)_e - \frac{M}{P} \tag{13}$$

---

[11] For a full (but advanced) treatment of the portfolio models discussed here, see R. Dornbusch, *Open Economy Macroeconomics* (New York: Basic Books, 1980). Part 5; and J. Frenkel and C. Rodriguez, "Portfolio Equilibrium and the Balance of Payments," *American Economic Review* (September 1975).

[12] We are assuming that domestic and foreign bonds are perfect substitutes, in which case they can be aggregated into the general category of V. For a general discussion of cases in which they are not perfect substitutes, see Chapter 15.

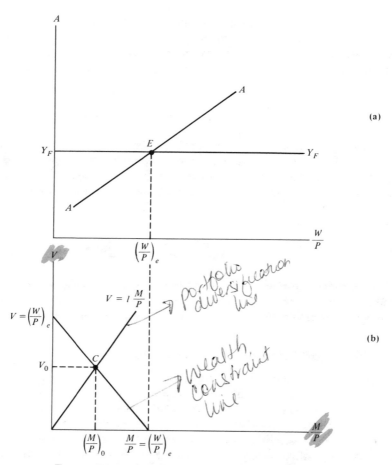

FIGURE 14–3. Portfolio Choice in the Open Economy

indicating that, given a certain amount of wealth, additional bonds can be acquired only by sacrificing some money holdings. If the whole portfolio is held as money [if $(W/P)_e = M/P$], then no bonds will be held ($V = 0$); we obtain the horizontal intercept of the wealth constraint line. If, on the other hand, all of the portfolio is invested in bonds [if $V = (W/P)_e$], no money can be held and the vertical intercept shown in Figure 14–3(b) results. Other intermediate combinations, with both bonds and money held, are depicted by the wealth constraint line. Which of these combinations is actually chosen in the economy? In other words: How do individuals prefer to divide or distribute a given amount of wealth between money and bonds?

The theory of portfolio choice briefly discussed in Chapter 2 shows how investors diversify their asset holdings on the basis of risks, returns, and other characteristics. Given these characteristics, investors decide which proportion of their portfolio to hold in bonds versus money. We denote the ratio of bonds to money individuals wish to hold by the parameter l so that

$$V = l\frac{M}{P} \tag{14}$$

For example, if $l = 2$, for every dollar held in monetary assets, two dollars' worth of bonds would be held ($V = 2M/P$). Even though we shall assume that l is fixed, its value is not an absolute constant and will be affected by various factors, the most obvious of which is interest rates. The higher the interest rate, the larger the value of l, as investors shift toward holding more bonds and less money. Equation (14) is the equation of a straight line, with slope l, and is represented in Figure 14–3(b) by an upward-sloping line called *portfolio-diversification line*.

Desired portfolio composition is obtained at point C, at the intersection of the wealth-constraint and portfolio-diversification lines. At that point, the relative amounts of bonds and money desired by domestic residents will be satisfied (the point lies along the portfolio-diversification line), given the boundary imposed by the amount of wealth to be invested (represented by the wealth constraint line).

In general, domestic residents will hold both money and bonds. Bonds, of course, can be domestic or foreign since in open economies domestic residents can certainly purchase foreign assets. In this section we thus return to our conception of the balance of payments as

$$B_N = \Delta M^D - \Delta CBC = T_N + K_N \tag{4}$$

whereas in the last few sections we ignored the capital account, K_N. What main differences arise now in terms of our analysis?

Money, Capital Flows, and Balance of Payments Adjustment

Consider the effects of a sudden increase in the money supply through the "printing of money." This gives rise to an excess supply of money, which domestic residents will try to get rid of. They have two possible mechanisms to change their money holdings. First, as discussed in detail in the previous sections, they can spend it by buying foreign goods. This mechanism operates through a trade balance deficit and, by itself, is associated with a reduction in the total size of the portfolio. That is, the decline of money balances by means of a trade deficit causes a reduction of total domestic assets, constituting a *portfolio-size* adjustment mechanism. The second mechanism to dispose of excess money is to spend it on the purchase of foreign assets, which is recorded as a capital account deficit. This exchange of money to acquire foreign assets involves no change in the size of the total portfolio, only a change in its composition (less money and more bonds) and is called a *portfolio-composition* adjustment mechanism. Both mechanisms can be used to eliminate excess money balances. There is, however, a general difference between them.

Portfolio-composition adjustments are usually carried out instantaneously, or over short periods of time. Portfolio-size adjustments generally take longer because they can occur only through changes in spending relative to income. Given that individuals do not in general like sudden changes in spending or standard of living, they will adjust only gradually in response to desired changes in asset holdings. To illustrate this basic difference between portfolio-size and portfolio-changing mechanisms, we shall carry out explicitly all the effects of our printing money example. See the graphic representation in Figure 14–4.

Figure 14–4(a) shows the initial full equilibrium of the economy at point E, with a portfolio size equal to $(W/P)_e$. With that amount of wealth, the desired amounts of bonds and money are V_e and $(M/P)_e$, respectively, shown by point C in Figure 14–4(b). When the government prints money, implying a rise in real balances from $(M/P)_e$ to $(M/P)_1$, the stock of financial assets increases, as shown by the movement from $(W/P)_e$ to $(W/P)_1$ in Figure 14–4(a). In terms of portfolio composition, the effect of printing money is to create excess money holdings, represented by the movement from point C to point D in Figure 14–4(b). Point D is a point of portfolio disequilibrium, since it lies away from the portfolio diversification line.

In order to attain their desired portfolio composition, domestic residents will exchange money for bonds, generating a capital account deficit. This is shown in Figure 14–4(b) by the adjustment from point D to point F. The balance of payments will instantaneously move into deficit. This adjustment of money balances through the capital account, although moving the composition of domestic portfolios back to their desired level, along the portfolio diversification line, does not move the economy to its desired total holdings of financial assets, that is, to its desired portfolio size. The excess money that has been disposed of has been supplanted by acquisitions of foreign bonds and, so, total asset holdings are still higher than they were at their initial level. This is represented in Figure 14–4 by the fact that the portfolio composition adjustment leaves the economy at a level of wealth equal to $(W/P)_1$, above its long-run level, $(W/P)_e$.

The adjustment of total portfolio size toward its original level—toward points E and C in Figure 14–4—must occur over time, by means of net purchases of foreign goods, which get rid of (deplete) asset holdings overall. This slower adjustment is reflected by trade balance deficits. It is shown by the pointed arrows in Figure 14–4(a) and by the movement from point F to point C in Figure 14–4(b).

Once the economy moves back to its desired portfolio size—once asset holdings overall, both monetary and nonmonetary, have been adjusted to long-run equilibrium levels—absorption will equal income and the trade balance deficit

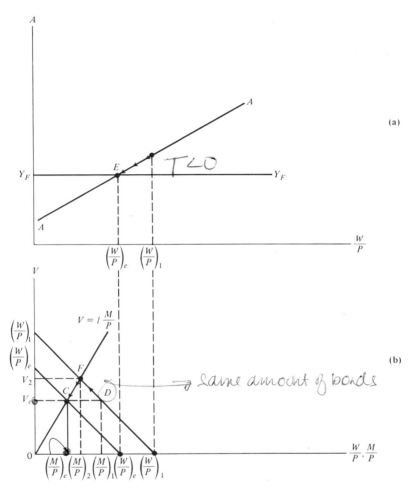

FIGURE 14–4. Printing Money and the Adjustment of the Economy

is eliminated. At that point, the balance of payments deficit will also have been eliminated: All excess money balances will have been spent away. In conclusion, an increase in the money supply through printing money will induce both the balance of trade and the balance of payments to worsen over the short run. If no other disturbances occur, however, these payments and trade deficits will be eliminated over time. The monetary injection then only reduces international reserves, without any other major real consequence. We must stress that the initial adjustment of the balance of payments represents mostly a portfolio-composition move, operating through the capital account, while the subsequent adjustment represents mostly a move to reduce portfolio size, operating through the trade balance.

14-6.   GROWTH, INFLATION, AND THE MONEY ACCOUNT

Persistent and continuous changes in economic variables are a fact of life in any modern economy. Output grows, prices rise (or fall) for extended periods of time—even the monetary policy of the Central Bank acquires a dynamic flavor, indicating target levels for the *rate of growth* of the money supply, instead of just stating increases in the *level* of the money supply. In this environment, economic changes occur in the form of disturbances in the rate of growth of some variable, such as an increase in the rate of growth of output, or a reduction in the rate of growth of Central Bank credit. This differs from the analysis of a stationary (nongrowing) economy, focusing on the impact of once-and-for-all changes in the level of several variables, such as, for example, an increase in Central Bank credit or an increase in the exchange rate.

This section shows how the monetary approach links growth in basic economic variables to the behavior of the money account of the balance of payments. Our attention is thus focused on the overall external payments situation of the economy and not on specific accounts, like the trade or capital accounts.

The growth of various economic variables (such as income and Central Bank credit) gives rise to changes in money demand and/or changes in the money supply. As discussed in Section 14-1, equilibrium in the market for money will be maintained when the changes in the nominal demand for money occurring over any given time period are equal to the changes in the money supply forthcoming over that same period. From equation (1), $\Delta M^D = \Delta M^S$. We find it very convenient to express equilibrium in terms of growth rates, or as

$$\hat{M}^D = \hat{M}^S \tag{15}$$

where $\hat{M}^D \equiv \Delta M^D/M^D$ represents the rate of growth (the proportional change) of money demand, and $\hat{M}^S \equiv \Delta M^S/M^S$ is the rate of growth of money supply over a given period of time. What equation (15) says is that the market for money will remain in equilibrium, $M^D = M^S$, when money demand and money supply grow at the same rate.

We have already studied the money supply process in some detail. We have seen that changes in the money multiplier, external payments imbalances, and Central Bank credit creation can all act upon the money supply. The effects of these variables on the rate of growth of the money supply can be expressed algebraically as[13]

---

[13] From $M^S = \mu H$, one obtains

$$\hat{M}^S = \hat{\mu} + \hat{H} = \hat{\mu} + \frac{B_N + \Delta CBC}{H} = \hat{\mu} + \frac{B_N}{H} + \frac{CBC}{H}\frac{\Delta CBC}{CBC} = \hat{\mu} + \frac{B_N}{H} + \frac{CBC}{H}\widehat{CBC}$$

where $\hat{\mu}$, $\hat{H}$, and $\widehat{CBC}$ represent proportional changes in the respective variables (e.g., $\hat{H} = \Delta H/H$).

$$\hat{M}^S = \hat{\mu} + \frac{B_N}{H} + \frac{CBC}{H}\widehat{CBC} \tag{16}$$

where $\hat{\mu}$ represents the rate of change of the money multiplier ($\hat{\mu} = \Delta\mu/\mu$), B_N is, as before, the balance of payments (so that B_N/H expresses it as a proportion of the monetary base), and $\widehat{CBC}$ represents the proportional rate of change of Central Bank credit ($\widehat{CBC} = \Delta CBC/CBC$). Equation (16) is similar to equation (2a) in Section 14–1. The difference hinges in that we are now allowing for changes in the money multiplier, which were ignored before, and that all variables appear in proportional terms.

Equation (16) can be rewritten as

$$\frac{B_N}{H} = \hat{M}^D - \hat{\mu} - \frac{CBC}{H}\widehat{CBC} \tag{17}$$

where we have substituted the condition of equality of money demand and money supply growth ($\hat{M}^D = \hat{M}^S$). Equation (17) shows the balance of payments (measured as a proportion of high-powered money) as being affected by changes in money demand ($\hat{M}^D$), changes in the money supply multiplier ($\hat{\mu}$), and by changes in Central Bank credit ($\widehat{CBC}$). Observe that factors augmenting the money supply, that is, growth of the money multiplier and Central Bank credit creation, deteriorate the balance of payments (the money account), while factors increasing money demand improve it. What factors affect the nominal demand for money?

The *nominal* demand for money balances, M^D, should be distinguished from the *real* demand for money, L^D. The nominal demand is the demand individuals have for domestic money (dollars if a U.S. resident). The real demand for money represents how much the money you demand—your nominal money balances—is worth in terms of its purchasing power. Symbolically, we find that $L^D = M^D/\bar{P}$, where $\bar{P}$ is the domestic price level used to express the nominal demand for money, M^D, in terms of its purchasing power value. Of course, you demand money for what it buys and so the demand for money is a demand for real money balances. As we saw earlier, the demand for real balances depends on income and on interest rates. Changes in the price level will then give rise to changes in the nominal demand for money. For example, if the price level doubles ($\bar{P}$ doubles), you will have to pay twice as much for everything you buy, and so you will have to double your holdings of nominal balances to be able to buy the same amount of goods as before (M^D doubles). This relationship between the price level and the nominal demand for money can be seen more clearly by observing that

$$M^D = \bar{P}L^D \tag{18}$$

real
money
demand

The higher the price level, the more domestic money (dollars if a U.S. resident) you will need to purchase your consumption basket and the larger the amount of nominal money balances you will demand. Similarly, the higher the demand for real balances, the larger the demand for nominal balances, everything else being constant. Taking percentage changes in equation (18) yields

$$\hat{M}^D = \hat{\bar{P}} + \hat{L}^D \tag{19}$$

where $\hat{\bar{P}} = \Delta\bar{P}/\bar{P}$ is the rate of increase of the domestic price level (domestic inflation), and $\hat{L}^D \equiv \Delta L^D/L^D$ is the rate of growth of real money demand. Desired growth of nominal money balances thus arises from inflation and from growth in real money demand.

The demand for real money balances, L^D, is a function of income, Y, and the interest rate, i, or

$$L^D = L(Y, i)$$

If income rises, holding interest rates constant, transactions increase and so does the demand for money. Increases in interest rates, on the other hand, with income constant, induce a shift toward interest-earning assets, reducing the real demand for money. The effects of changes in income and interest rates on the *growth* of real money demand can be expressed algebraically by

$$\hat{L}^D = \eta_Y \hat{Y} + \eta_r \hat{i} \tag{20}$$

where $\hat{L}_D$, $\hat{Y}$, and $\hat{i}$ are the growth rates of money demand, income, and interest rate, and with

$$\eta_Y = \frac{\Delta L^D/L^D}{\Delta Y/Y}\bigg|_{i=i_0} > 0 \quad \text{and} \quad \eta_r = \frac{\Delta L^D/L^D}{\Delta i/i}\bigg|_{Y=Y_0} < 0$$

The parameter η_Y is the *income elasticity* of the demand for money and represents how responsive money demand is to percentage changes in income, given a fixed level of the interest rate (at $i = i_0$). For example, a value of two for this elasticity ($\eta_Y = 2.0$) means that, keeping interest rates constant, a 1% increase in income raises money demand by 2%.

The parameter η_r, on the other hand, is the *interest rate elasticity* of demand for money and measures the responsiveness of money demand to changes in the interest rate, keeping income constant (at $Y = Y_0$). A value of $\eta_r = -0.5$ means that, keeping income constant, a 1% increase in the interest rate would decrease money demand by one-half a percentage point.

Given these definitions, it is easy to visualize that the first term in equation (20) represents the particular (partial) influence of income growth on money demand (holding fixed interest rates), and the second term represents the partial influence of changes in interest rates on money demand (holding constant the level of income). Combining the effects of these two variables must then give us the overall changes in money demand, $\hat{L}^D$.

Substituting equation (20) into (19) and placing the resulting expression into equation (17), one finally obtains

$$\frac{B_N}{H} = \hat{P} + \eta_Y \hat{Y} + \eta_r \hat{i} - \hat{\mu} - \frac{CBC}{H}\widehat{CBC} \tag{21}$$

Equation (21) is extremely useful for various reasons. First, it conveniently summarizes the influence of growth in various economic variables on the balance of payments; it therefore helps us in reviewing and pulling together many of the points discussed earlier. Second, it can be used as a basic tool of Central Bank financial programming, aiding policymakers in evaluating the balance of payments implications of various policies. Finally, equation (21) has served as a basis for much of the empirical evidence on the monetary approach. Virtually identical equations have been estimated for many countries, providing information on how the monetary approach fares in explaining the balance of payments behavior of actual economies. Each of these facets of equation (21) will now be examined in detail.

Equation (21) provides a concise statement of the influence of growth in various variables on the balance of payments, B_N. As observed, higher inflation, higher income growth rates and greater reductions in interest rates are all positively associated with the balance of payments. These factors increase the rate of growth of (nominal) money demand, inducing higher inflows of international reserves. Similarly, the higher the growth in the money multiplier and in Central Bank credit, the more likely a payments deficit will arise. This reflects the negative relationship between factors leading to excess money supply growth and the balance of payments.

A key aspect of Central Bank financial programming involves the evaluation of the balance of payments impact of Central Bank policies. Equation (21) can serve as a basic tool for such endeavors. If forecasts of inflation, output growth, interest rate changes, and money market multiplier trends exist, equation (21) will tell us what various Central Bank credit growth targets will do to the balance of payments. Suppose, for example, that you were given the figures shown in Table 14–1, and you were asked about the balance of payments impact of a 4% target on the rate of growth of Central Bank credit (i.e., $\widehat{CBC} = 0.04$). Plugging all the numbers quoted into equation (21), you would obtain that $B_N/H = 0.089$, and if the monetary base is $H = \$100$ billion, then $B_N = (0.089)(100) = \$8.9$ billion, which would increase the international reserves of the Central Bank by that amount. A 20% target on the rate of growth of Central Bank credit, however, would lead to a deficit in the balance of payments equal to $B_N = -\$3.1$ billion.

TABLE 14–1. **Hypothetical Values of Crucial Economic Parameters**

$\hat{P}$	$\hat{Y}_F$	η_Y	η_r	$\hat{\imath}$	$\hat{\mu}$	CBC/H
0.10 (10%)	0.04 (4%)	0.50	−0.10	−0.09 (9%)	0.01 (1%)	0.75

Economic Growth and the Money Supply Rule Under Fixed Exchange Rates

In Sections 14–4 and 14–5, we suggested that monetary policy, in the form of a once-and-for-all increase in Central Bank credit, gives rise to a loss of reserves of exactly the same amount. Expansionary monetary policy was consequently associated with balance of payments deficits. The analysis at that point was carried out under the assumption that prices, income, and interest rates were fixed so that money demand was not changing. In this situation, increased Central Bank credit leads to an excessive increase in money balances that is eliminated from the economy by means of payments deficits. When the economy grows, however, expansionary monetary policy may not necessarily lead to balance of payments deficits, but it may actually work to maintain external balance. For example, as income grows, so does the demand for money. As a result, Central Bank credit growth could be used to satisfy these desired increases in money holdings without causing any excess accumulation of money balances. No payments deficit would arise. Just as we saw in the previous subsection that varying rates of Central Bank credit creation can generate persistent balance of payments disequilibria, adequate monetary policy can potentially be used to attain external balance in a growing economy.

What determines the target rate of credit creation that produces external balance in the economy? Setting equation (21) equal to zero, and solving for $\widehat{CBC}$, implies that

$$\widehat{CBC}_o = \frac{H}{CBC} [\hat{P} + \eta_Y \hat{Y} + \eta_r \hat{\imath} - \hat{\mu}] \tag{22}$$

This expression gives us the Central Bank credit growth required to maintain balanced payments over time. A higher rate of credit creation would lead to persistent balance of payments deficits, while a lower rate would lead to persistent surpluses. With the hypothetical values of basic economic parameters given in Table 14–1, the rate of growth that the Central Bank should target for is

$$\widehat{CBC}_o = \frac{1}{0.75} [0.10 + (0.5)(0.04) + (-0.10)(-0.09) - 0.01]$$

$$\cong .135$$

With a 13.5% rate of gr(
would net out to zero a
of international reserves.
13.5% would lead to pe
examples of the last subs(
on the other hand, woul
mented with in the last

The main point ma(
monetary policy in the f(
Bank credit does not n
can potentially help att
would have to know ex;
time, and would also h;
elasticities of money d(
actual values of all the
difficult for the moneta
used are grossly off target, the Central ...
away from balanced payments. In this situation, the best the monetary authorities
may be able to do is to follow long-term trends in prices, income, and so on,
and set a Central Bank credit growth target consistent with those trends, no
matter what happens over the short run. Such a monetary policy, called a
monetary rule, has been advocated by Milton Friedman for a long time. We
should stress, however, that even though the spirit is the same, the nature
and goals of the monetary rule discussed here are different from those of Friedman. Actually, a discussion of the differences between the two brings forth
the divergencies between open economy and closed economy macroeconomics.

The monetary rule proposed by Friedman is that "the *stock of money* be
increased at a fixed rate year-in and year-out without any variation in the rate
of increase to meet cyclical needs."[14] This differs from the monetary rule discussed here, suggesting *Central Bank credit* expansion be maintained at a fixed
rate. In an open economy under fixed exchange rates, the Central Bank has
no complete control over the growth of the stock of money. Changes in international reserves are not under the (direct) handle of the Central Bank and are
in the hands of individuals buying or selling domestic money for foreign exchange. What the Central Bank does control is credit creation, which is the
tool the monetary rule should refer to in such economies.

One of the goals of Friedman's monetary rule is to control the rate of increase
of prices in the economy. In his framework, money supply growth causes inflation
and, accordingly, "the rate of increase [of the money stock] should be chosen
so that on the average it could be expected to correspond with a roughly stable

---

[14] Milton Friedman, *A Program for Monetary Stability* (New York: Fordham Unversity Press,
1960), p. 90 [italics added].

rices."[15] The monetary rule represented by
d, has the goal of maintaining the economy as
balance. It has nothing to do with controlling
open economy under fixed exchange rates, money
clear-cut causal effect on domestic inflation. This was
developed in our general discussion of inflation in Chapter

MPIRICAL EVIDENCE ON THE MONETARY APPROACH TO THE NCE OF PAYMENTS

his section examines the empirical evidence (the studies that have used real data) on the monetary approach to the balance of payments. In an earlier section we derived equation (21), that offers a concise representation of the variables affecting the balance of payments as viewed by the monetary approach.

$$\frac{B}{H} = \hat{P} + \eta_Y \hat{Y} + \eta_r \hat{\imath} - \hat{\mu} - \frac{CBC}{H} \widehat{CBC} \tag{21}$$

What does the evidence show? Does the data for actual countries support the hypothesis of a balance of payments equation such as (21)? To determine whether equation (21) is consistent with the data, we have to consider a general equation, such as:

$$\frac{B}{H} = a_1 \hat{P} + a_2 \hat{Y} + a_3 \hat{\imath} + a_4 \hat{\mu} + a_5 \frac{CBC}{H} \widehat{CBC} \tag{22}$$

and test whether the $a_1, a_2, \ldots, a_5$ coefficients that *best* fit the data in the economy during the period of concern are as postulated by the monetary approach

$$a_1 = -1, \qquad a_2 = \eta_Y > 0, \qquad a_3 = \eta_r < 0, \qquad a_4 = -1, \qquad \text{and} \qquad a_5 = -1$$

A large number of empirical studies exist on the monetary approach, covering a wide range of countries and time periods. The weight of this evidence does not overwhelmingly support or reject the monetary approach. The *signs* of

---

[15] Ibid., p. 91. In all fairness to Friedman, we must state that his monetary rule is really tailored to a flexible exchange rate regime, to which it can apply much better. Within the case of fixed exchange rates, it would also be relevant to large countries whose price level partially determines (rather than is determined by) world inflation; as we show, however, it is not relevant for small countries lacking control of their money supply and for which domestic inflation is heavily determined by world inflation. This point is not often recognized.

the estimated coefficients are generally the same as those postulated by the monetary approach. The data bear out the conclusion that, by themselves (holding all other variables constant), inflation and income growth are associated positively with the balance of payments, while increased interest rates, money multiplier growth, and Central Bank credit creation are negatively associated with the balance of payments. Even though their signs are in the predicted direction, the numerical values of the estimates in the literature are often significantly different from those predicted by the monetary approach through equation (21). There are various possible explanations for this. The first is related to how long it actually takes domestic residents to make monetary adjustments. In other words, just how long is the long run? Studies made on the demand for money[16] indicate that it may take up to 2 years for money demand to adjust to changes in income and interest rates, even though about three-quarters of the adjustment is complete after 1 year. The time period suitable to evaluating the monetary approach would thus have to be at least 1 year, perhaps longer, but most empirical studies examining the approach use quarterly data. Since the monetary adjustments hypothesized by the monetary approach can be expected to take longer, use of quarterly data will tend to give rise to results inconsistent with the approach. When annual data are used, however, the estimated coefficients tend to move closer to those hypothesized by the monetary approach.

A second possibility explaining deviations from the predictions of the monetary approach lies in the money demand function used. As studied up to this point, the demand for money is determined by only two variables: income and interest rates. Analytically, this is a very convenient specification, since it greatly simplifies the discussion. Its simplicity, however, tends to hurt its empirical use, since changes in income and interest rates often fail to explain important changes in money demand. For example, studies of money demand in the United States [17] tend to indicate that since 1973 a downward shift of money demand has occurred that cannot be explained by changes in income and interest rates. Something else has been affecting U.S. money demand that is not taken into account by the simple money demand functions we have been using and that serve as a basis for most of the empirical evidence on the monetary approach. Many variables have been postulated to explain these deviations. Financial management innovations, for example, reduce the amount of money needed by businesses and individuals in their usual volume of transactions. In addition, the formation of expectations, by itself, will have an effect on money demand. For instance, expectations about inflation and/or devaluation may shift money demand down by attaching an expected cost to the holding of domestic money.

---

[16] Such as Stephen M. Goldfeld, "The Demand for Money Revisited," *Brookings Papers on Economic Activity* (1973).

[17] Richard Porter, Thomas Simpson, and Eileen Mauskopf, "Financial Innovation and the Monetary Aggregates," *Brookings Papers on Economic Activity* (1979).

In any case, these examples point out an important source of deviations from the particular balance of payments relationship postulated by equation (21); if money demand is not a stable function of income and interest rates, very little will be explained unless one explicitly incorporates all the many factors impinging on money demand and supply.

A third reason why the monetary approach as described by equation (21) may not fare well regards the so-called simultaneous equations problem, a problem that appears in many disguises and plagues empirical work. The point can be better grasped by observing that equations (21) and (22) showed the balance of payments as explained by prices, income, Central Bank credit, and so on, but did not tackle the question of the determination of these explanatory variables. In general, most of these variables are determined jointly and simultaneously in the economy. As a consequence, one must pay explicit attention to relationships (equations) other than (21) and (22) establishing their connections. It is the task of Section 14.8 to examine the nature of this problem with respect to the monetary approach. Our short-run aggregate demand–aggregate supply framework developed in Part IV will serve as a basis for the discussion.

14–8   Fitting the Pieces Together: The Monetary Approach and Short-Run Balance of Payments Theory

We have now examined in detail the nature, implications, and empirical evidence regarding the monetary approach to the balance of payments. It is time to steer the discussion away from the specifics of the approach and seek some perspective on how it fits into the overall scheme of open economy macroeconomics and balance of payments theory. As the parable goes, we must stop looking at the trees and take a glance at the forest.[18]

How does the monetary approach relate to our analysis of the balance of payments in previous chapters? As can be recalled, our general framework of analysis in Chapter 10 included the following relationships that we have related to equations in Chapter 10:

$$\frac{M^S}{P} = L(Y, i)$$ (money market equilibrium condition)   (10–1)

$$Y^D = \alpha[\bar{A} + \bar{T}(q) - bi]$$ (aggregate demand function)   (10–2a)

$$Y^S = Y_F + \theta\beta\left(\frac{P - P_{-1}}{P_{-1}}\right)$$ (short-run aggregate supply equation)   (10–A4)

---

[18] For an advanced exposition of the points made in this section, see J. Frenkel, T. Gylfason, and J. F. Helliwell, "A Synthesis of Monetary and Keynesian Approaches to Short-Run Balance of Payments Theory," *Economic Journal* (September 1980).

and

$$B = T(q, Y) + K(i) \qquad \text{(balance of payments equation)} \qquad (10\text{--}4)$$

Equations (10–1) and (10–2a) were combined into what we referred to as an aggregate demand equation. The economy's short-run equilibrium was then determined by that point at which aggregate demand equaled aggregate supply, giving rise to a certain short-run balance of payments deficit or surplus, as represented by equation (10–4). In other words, the system of equations (10–1) to (10–4) was used to represent the economy's equilibrium, determining the basic variables of concern (domestic prices, output, interest rates, and the balance of payments).

How does the monetary approach fit into this framework? The monetary approach singles out the money market equilibrium equation (10–1) and focuses its attention on analyzing it. By noting that money market equilibrium is maintained when $\Delta M^D = \Delta M^S$, the monetary approach establishes its basic representation of the balance of payments as follows:

$$B = \frac{B_N}{P} = \frac{1}{P} (\Delta M^D - \Delta CBC) \qquad (3a)$$

The interpretation of equation (3a), a variant of equation (3), has been the main point of this chapter, and its cousin, equation (21), is the basis for most of the empirical work on the monetary approach. Note, however, that the balance of payments expression derived by the monetary approach appears to be different from the explicit representation of the balance of payments stated in equation (10–4). Does this mean that these two balance of payments equations are inconsistent? Take the following example. According to equation (3a), increases in income imply that the balance of payments improves, since the demand for money rises. The balance of payments expression in equation (10–4), however, associates increases in income with increased imports and a deteriorating balance of payments. Does this mean that the two equations provide conflicting views on the balance of payments? Surprisingly, no.

To visualize the fallacy involved, think in terms of the standard demand and supply model of determination of market output, Q, and price, P. In this system, there is a demand curve (or equation) that establishes a negative relationship between P and Q, and a supply curve that establishes a positive relation between P and Q. Clearly, the fact that P and Q are related differently by each curve does not imply that the demand and supply curves are inconsistent. It just suggests that demand and supply curves embody the behavior of different sectors of the market (consumers and producers), and that only their interaction will simultaneously determine the market's *equilibrium* price and output (at that point at which demand and supply meet). Analogously, in our balance of payments example, even though equations (3a) and (10–4) represent two different responses of the balance of payments with respect to income, they are not inconsistent. The two form part of the aggregate demand and supply model shown by equations (10–1) to (10–4) just as demand and supply curves form part of a market model.

Figure 14–5 illustrates the issue. Curve *MM* represents the positive relationship between the balance of payments, *B*, and income, *Y*, established by the monetary equation (3a). The *KK* curve, on the other hand, represents the negative association between income and the balance of payments shown by equation (10–4). In equilibrium, both equations must be satisfied and point *E* would be established, with a short-run *equilibrium* level of income *Y** and a short-run balance of payments surplus equal to *B**. Note that *MM* and *KK* are consistent with each other, even though, when considered in isolation, they appear to be in conflict. This has been the source of enormous controversy regarding the monetary approach. Economists emphasizing an equation such as (10–4) would, for example, point to curve *KK* and stress that *Y* and *B* are negatively related. Monetary economists concentrating on equation (3a), however, would angrily disagree, indicating that the unavoidable monetary equilibrium of the economy implies that income and the balance of payments are positively related, as curve *MM* illustrates. In a sense, both statements are correct, and in another both are incorrect. They are both correct in the sense that they are consistent with a general model of how the economy behaves [both form an integral part of equations (10–1) to (10–4)]. They are both wrong, however, in that each equation is part of a broader system describing the economy; it would be misleading to analyze the actual behavior of the economy (its equilibrium path of *Y**'s and *B**'s) on the basis of one equation alone (i.e., on the basis of either *KK* or *MM* alone). Stating that income and the balance of payments are positively related through their monetary implications says as much as that price and output are positively related through a supply curve. It provides us with information about the money market, but it does not tell us about how the short-run

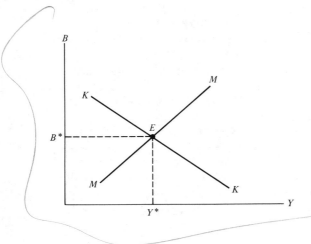

FIGURE 14–5. Simultaneous Determination of Income and the Balance of Payments

equilibrium income and balance of payments of the economy are related, just as a supply curve alone cannot tell us how the equilibrium price and output of a market are related.

Furthermore, estimating one equation alone, such as most of the empirical work on the monetary approach does [by focusing on the money market equation (3a)], may involve a serious statistical problem. Suppose, for example, that the statistician is given the data points shown by A, B, and C in Figure 14–6. These points are the actual, observed combinations of the balance of payments and income of the economy over three time periods (say, 3 years). With only these data, the statistician would estimate the downward-sloping line, $\hat{M}\hat{M}$, which is the one that best fits the observed points. Consequently, the estimate of income on the balance of payments would be negative, apparently contradicting the monetary approach. The problem, however, is that the estimated line $\hat{M}\hat{M}$ does not really provide an estimate of the monetary relationship between the balance of payments and income but only provides an estimate of what the actual behavior of the equilibrium balance of payments and income of the economy has been, which depends not only on monetary considerations, but also on the other aggregate demand–aggregate supply relationships in the economy. The two could be very different. This is depicted in Figure 14–6, where we have drawn possible KK and MM curves consistent with the data. If the curves had been K_1K_1 and M_1M_1 in the first time period, K_2K_2 and M_2M_2 in the second, and K_3K_3 and M_3M_3 in the third, the data points A, B, and C

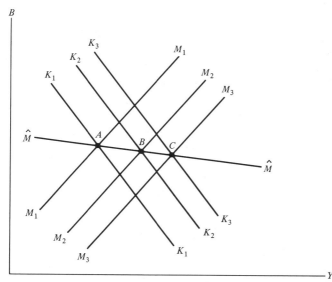

FIGURE 14–6. The Simultaneous Equations Problem of Estimation

would have arisen. Note, however, that these points would be perfectly consistent with a positive monetary connection between income and the balance of payments: They do not say anything about what the *MM* curves look like. One must therefore be very careful in evaluating the results of an equation such as (22), which really forms part of a broader system.[19]

14–9   ELASTICITIES, ABSORPTION, AND MONETARY APPROACHES TO THE BALANCE OF PAYMENTS

The last section showed that different conceptions of the balance of payments are not necessarily inconsistent with each other. Differences in their appearance, however, have given rise to intense controversy and the consequent emergence of competing approaches to the balance of payments. In this section we provide some perspective on these views from a contemporary vantage point.

In the analysis of the balance of payments, one often observes studies that concentrate on discussing either the trade balance or the capital account. Two of the best-known approaches to the balance of payments, the so-called elasticities and absorption approaches, pay special attention to the trade balance.

The *elasticities approach* stresses the need for an explicit analysis of the exports and imports of a country in dissecting the balance of payments. It thus emphasizes the conception of the trade balance as the difference between exports and imports:

$$T = X - M$$

The elasticities approach, for instance, addresses the problem of the impact of devaluation by discerning how exchange rate changes disturb the terms of trade, and how these changes affect exports, imports, and the trade balance. In so doing, many of the initial practitioners of the approach ignored the income effects of a devaluation as well as its monetary implications. The discussion encompassed what in our own treatment we have referred to as the effects of devaluation on the autonomous trade balance. As may be recalled from Chapter 5, the answer to this question involves the specification of the values of the price elasticities of demand for domestic imports and exports. This is the basis, of course, for the name of the approach.

The income effects of a devaluation were emphasized by the *absorption approach* that looked at the trade balance as the difference between income and absorption:

---

[19] This is precisely the simultaneous equations problem mentioned before. There are various statistical methods geared toward dealing with it. For their specific application with respect to the monetary approach, see P. D. Jonson, "Money and Economic Activity in the Open Economy: the United Kingdom, 1880–1970," *Journal of Political Economy* (September–October 1976).

$$T = Y - A$$

In this conception, a devaluation tends to improve the trade balance only insofar as it reduces the level of spending relative to income. In practice, the absorption approach overlooked the long-run monetary adjustments that the monetary approach suggests will prevent a devaluation from having any lasting effect on the trade balance. In addition, many of the initial practitioners of the approach disregarded the relative price effect of a devaluation (its impact on the autonomous trade balance), and its results appeared as being opposed to those of the elasticities approach. In reality, a devaluation involves both income and relative price effects, implying that the elasticities and absorption approaches can be integrated into an overall analysis of devaluation. That was our own approach in Chapter 5 and the one implicit in equation (10–4), in which both income, Y, and relative prices, q, affect the trade balance, T. We must thus stress that, in a well-specified framework, it should not matter if one analyzes the trade balance as the difference between exports and imports or as the gap between income and spending; symbolically,

$$T = X - M = Y - A = T(q, Y) \tag{23}$$

To study the overall balance of payments, one must consider the capital account in addition to the trade balance. Since the elasticities and absorption approaches look essentially at the *trade balance,* we have to add the capital account to the expression in (23) to obtain their representation of the *balance of payments.* Using also equation (3a), one obtains

$$B = (X - M) + K = (Y - A) + K = \frac{1}{P}(\Delta M^D - \Delta CBC)$$

stating that, no matter what the approach to the balance of payments is— elasticities, absorption, or monetary—it should be consistent with the other approaches. The difference between them lies in the way the balance of payments is looked at.

As a practical matter, however, adopting a particular point of view, though providing particular insights, may tend to obscure other possible insights developed by other points of view. Furthermore, in the case in point, many of the supporters of each approach have been associated with different theories and schools of thought about the behavior of the open economy. All of this has generated intense, and often wasteful, disputes and controversy over balance of payments policy. In this book, enjoying the benefits of hindsight, we have synthesized the approaches and studied each of their insights.

14–10   SUMMARY

This chapter provided a detailed account of the key ideas behind the so-called monetary approach to the balance of payments. To highlight the basic, but sometimes subtle, monetary processes characterizing the monetary approach, we have deemphasized the important issues of unemployment and business cycles. We have not, however, completely restricted ourselves to a longer-run view of monetary adjustments. We have also shown how the monetary approach fits into the short-run Keynesian framework developed in earlier chapters. The following conclusions can be drawn:

1. The monetary approach to the balance of payments asserts that the balance of payments involves *essential monetary phenomena*. This does not imply that the balance of payments is uniquely a monetary phenomenon, nor does it propose a *monetarist* view of the economy.

2. In equilibrium, the money account of the balance of payments represents a gap between people's desired accumulation of money and the money forthcoming from monetary injections by the Central Bank or from changes in the money multiplier.

3. In the absence of government meddling with the economy, a purely monetary mechanism exists that can correct payments imbalances automatically, without requiring changes in output, prices, or interest rates.

4. Devaluation tends to increase the domestic price level, reducing the real value of the money stock and triggering a temporary improvement in the money account.

5. Printing money (or its equivalent) leads to a worsening of both the trade and money accounts, and a consequent loss of international reserves. If the government continuously prints money, the balance of payments deficits will be persistent; otherwise, they would subside as domestic residents return their money holdings to their desired level.

6. The monetary effects of higher inflation, higher income growth rates, and greater reductions in interest rates, are all positively associated with the balance of payments. These factors increase the rate of growth of (nominal) money demand, inducing larger inflows of international reserves. Similarly, the higher the growth of the money multiplier and Central Bank credit, the worse the balance of payments will turn. This reflects the negative relationship between factors leading to excess money supply growth and the balance of payments.

7. The formulation of monetary rules for open economies should recognize that neither the price level nor the money supply may be controllable by domestic monetary authorities under a fixed exchange rate regime. Still, a monetary rule specifying a target rate of growth of Central Bank credit can be formulated with the purpose of keeping external balance in the economy.

8. The empirical evidence on the monetary approach yields mixed results. While many studies have confirmed the empirical associations between the balance of payments and income, interest rates, and Central Bank credit postulated by the approach, others have found the hypothesis to be contradicted by the data. This discrepancy may possibly be attributable to problems with the data used, the neglect of relevant variables (like expectations) in the simple versions of the approach tested, the inability to disentangle the impact of government policy on the balance of payments from the reverse effect of the balance of payments on government policy, and statistical problems arising from the difficulty of dealing with a single equation (the monetary equation) that forms part of a bigger structural system determining all relevant variables in the economy simultaneously.

PROBLEMS

1. Within the simple monetary wealth framework examined in Sections 14–1 through 14–4, describe the effects of an increase in full-employment income, Y_F, on the desired real money balances of individuals in the economy. Then trace the short-run and long-run behavior of the trade balance in response to the increase in real income. Does the trade balance worsen or improve over the short run? Is the short-run relationship between income and the trade balance obtained in any way different from that obtained in earlier chapters? If it is, can you explain the reason for the differences? Explain your results using the diagrammatic tools developed in the text.

2. Consider the simple model of monetary wealth examined in Sections 14–1 through 14–4. Suppose that you are given the following numerical parameters: $Y_F = 800$ billion, $\rho = 0.25$, $\bar{A} = 110$ billion, $a = 0.80$, with all variables as defined in the text and with income and absorption measured in terms of units of domestic goods (over a period of a year).

   (a) Calculate the desired real money balances, $(M/P)_e$, of residents in this economy. The income velocity of money, V, is defined as the ratio of real income to real money balances, that is, $V = Y_F/(M/P)$. How much is the value of money velocity in the present case?

   (b) You are told that the country considered is a small open economy producing and consuming only goods traded in world markets. The country faces prices of exportables and importables in world markets equal to $P_x = £5$ and $P_m = £5$, where world prices are expressed in pounds. Assuming that the share of exportables in a domestic resident's consumption basket is 20% and that the exchange rate is currently fixed at $e = \$2.00/£$, then:

      (1) Calculate the domestic price level and the level of nominal money balances (in dollars), using your results in part (a). Assume that the economy is in long-run equilibrium.

      (2) Suppose that the exchange rate increases from $2/£ to $4/£. What would be the effects on the world prices of exportables and importables? On the prices faced by domestic consumers? On the domestic

price level? Assuming that the economy is initially in long-run equilibrium, what would be the impact effect of the devaluation on the level of real money balances (at the original level of nominal balances)? Would external balance be disturbed and by how much? What would be the "new" long-run value of desired nominal money balances in view of the devaluation? Would money velocity change in the short run? All your answers should be numerical and the economic intuition behind the results explained in detail.

3. Utilizing the framework of Sections 14–1 through 14–4, determine what would be the effects of a halving of world market prices on:
   (a) Domestic prices.
   (b) Short-run and long-run desired real money balances.
   (c) The trade balance in the short run and the long run.
   Use diagrams if possible.

4. Open market operations are the bread and butter of Central Bank actions in many of the industrial economies. Suppose that the Central Bank engages in an open market purchase of bonds. Utilizing the monetary approach, what would be the impact of this disturbance on the trade balance, capital flows, and the balance of payments in the short run and in the long run? How does this policy differ from the "printing money" (so-called helicopter operation) examined in Section 14–5? Use diagrams if possible.

5. What would be the effects of a government budget deficit financed by "printing money" on the capital account, the trade balance, and the balance of payments? Suppose that the budget deficit is financed by external borrowing (say, selling government bonds to the rest of the world), would your answers change? Explain.

6. You are in charge of the financial programming of a Central Bank in a small developing country. The following public forecasts for the next year are available: $\hat{P} = 5\%$, $\hat{Y} = 2\%$, $\eta_Y = 0.50$, $\eta_r = -0.10$, $\hat{\mu} = 0$, $\hat{i} = 0$, $CBC = 100$ million pesos, $IR = 10$ million pesos, with all symbols as defined in the text. In addition, the president of the Central Bank tells you (in secrecy) that domestic currency will be devalued by 10% in a few months. Your task is to find next year's CBC growth consistent with balanced payments, for which you use the monetary approach. What would be your recommendation and would you give any warnings regarding its adoption?

APPENDIX: NONTRADED GOODS AND ECONOMIC POLICY

In this appendix we discuss the analytical aspects of modeling nontraded goods in the open economy and explore some of the consequent policy implications. To simplify matters, it is assumed that the economy of concern is a small open economy that takes the prices of traded goods as given by world markets and thus faces fixed terms of trade. This type of economy has been referred to as a *dependent economy* to stress its inability to influence the prices of its export and import products in world markets. The pioneering work in examining the economics of dependent economies was carried out initially by James Meade, W. E. Salter, T. Swan, and W. Corden, among others. It has been developed and popularized by Rudiger Dornbusch in various articles.[20]

First of all, for expositional purposes, let us lump together exportables and importables into a category called internationally traded goods, or, for short, *traded goods*. When we refer to the price of traded goods, P_T, we shall then refer to an index of the prices of exportables, P_X, and importables, P_M. If we let θ be the symbol representing the share of expenditure allocated to exportables, then the price of traded goods is

$$P_T = \theta P_X + (1 - \theta)P_M$$

and assuming, for present purposes, that the domestic prices of importables and exportables are equal to their world prices, translated to domestic currency ($P_X = eP_X^*$ and $P_M = eP_M^*$, where P_X^* and P_M^* are world prices), then

$$P_T = \theta eP_M^* + (1 - \theta)eP_M^*$$
$$= e(\theta P_X^* + (1 - \theta)P_M^*)$$
$$= eP_T^*$$

where P_T^* is the world price (foreign-currency price) of the typical basket of traded goods consumed by a domestic resident. For a small economy that takes P_T^* as given, the domestic prices of traded goods would then be solely determined by prices in world markets, assuming a fixed exchange rate. This does not imply, however, that domestic prices will be completely determined by world prices. Since they are not traded internationally, the prices of nontraded goods are determined by local demand and supply in the country where they are both produced and consumed. With domestic consumers purchasing both traded and nontraded goods, the domestic price level will then be affected by the prices of both of these types of commodities, with the relative importance of each determined by the share of each commodity in the consumers' expenditures. Accordingly, if σ represents the fraction of expenditure on nontraded goods, the domestic price level is given by

$$P = \sigma P_N + (1 - \sigma)P_T$$
$$= \sigma P_N + (1 - \sigma)eP_T^*$$

Observe that were nontraded goods to be unimportant in the consumption patterns of domestic residents, their share of domestic expenditures would be insigni-

---

[20] See his *Open Economy Macroeconomics* (New York: Basic Books, Inc., 1980), Chapters 5 and 6, for an advanced survey of the work on this topic.

ficant, $\sigma = 0$, and the domestic price level would be completely determined by the prices of traded goods in world markets (converted to domestic currency). With nontraded goods an important part of expenditure, however, the prices of nontraded goods form an integral part of the domestic price level. Different countries will have different inflation rates depending on how the prices of nontraded goods behave in each specific country.

Actually, it appears that, for most countries, there has been a systematic tendency over the years for increases in the prices of nontraded goods to exceed increases in the prices of traded goods. The result is an observed increase in the prices of nontraded goods relative to those of traded goods. That is the picture one obtains from Figure 14–7, in which the ratio of a price index of nontraded goods to a price index of traded goods is presented for various countries for the time period of 1950 to 1972. What explains this clear trend? One of the main hypotheses is that postulated by Bela Balassa,[21] who has convincingly argued that the rate of productivity change in the traded goods sector has systematically exceeded that in the nontraded goods sector over the years. Lagging productivity growth in the nontraded goods sector will result in higher relative nontraded goods prices. The upward trend in the prices of nontraded

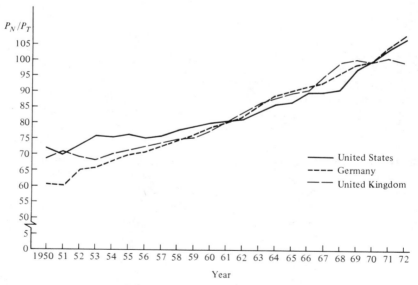

Figure 14–7. Ratio of the Price Index of Nontraded Goods to the Price Index of Traded Goods (1970 = 100). (From M. Goldstein and L. Officer, "New Measures of Prices and Productivity of Tradable and Nontradable Goods," *Review of Income and Wealth,* 1976.)

[21] Bela Balassa, "The Purchasing-Power Parity Doctrine: A Reappraisal," *Journal of Political Economy* (December 1964).

goods will then remain so long as the differential productivity growth persists. A second explanation offered regards the behavior of the demand for nontraded goods as income increases. The hypothesis is that the income elasticity of the demand for nontraded goods exceeds unity. As a consequence, as income grows, the demand for nontraded goods grows at a higher rate, generating the observed increase in the relative price of nontraded goods. Subsequently, we shall refer in more detail to this systematic tendency regarding the prices of traded and nontraded goods and its implications. For the moment, however, let us discuss more fully what are the implications of the presence of nontraded goods with respect to policymaking.

The effects of government policies will be affected by how the nontraded goods sector responds to those policies. Consider the case of monetary policy.

As noted earlier in the chapter, a small open economy under fixed exchange rates has limited scope in using monetary policy to affect domestic prices, provided that the nontraded goods sector is not significant and the economy is closely integrated to world markets. In economies in which the nontraded goods sector is important, however, domestic monetary authorities may affect domestic prices by altering the prices of nontraded goods. The impact effect of a reduction in Central Bank credit on the economy, for instance, will be to reduce real money balances and, consequently, expenditure relative to income. This reduction in expenditure decreases the demand for both traded and nontraded goods, inducing a decline in the prices of nontraded goods relative to traded goods. This is because a decrease in the demand for nontraded goods results in lower nontraded goods prices, but a decrease in the demand for traded goods does not affect the externally given traded goods prices. Similarly, the impact of a monetary expansion will be to increase the prices of nontraded goods relative to the prices of traded goods. Of course, over longer periods of time, decreases in the domestic money supply below their desired level would be eliminated through the hoarding actions of domestic residents. Conversely, increases in the money supply above their desired level would be gradually dishoarded over time until they are eliminated. These adjustments return the domestic money supply to its original, desired level, inducing the relative price of nontraded goods to revert to its initial level also. The monetary adjustment mechanism of the economy makes the effects of monetary policy only temporary. This is a result we have found many times before in other contexts; it is not altered by considering nontraded goods.

The analysis of the effects of devaluation is also affected by the presence of nontraded goods. Devaluation tends to increase the prices of traded goods, thereby reducing real money balances at a given level of the nominal money supply. But a reduction in real money balances decreases expenditure, causing a decrease in the relative price of nontraded goods. This has two effects. First, it switches domestic consumption toward the now relatively cheaper nontraded goods and away from traded goods (like imports), and it shifts production toward the, now relatively more profitable, traded goods (such as export and import-competing products). Both of these effects improve the balance of trade. The suggestion is that devaluation can affect the balance of trade, even if it cannot influence the terms of trade (i.e., even if the prices of traded goods—exports and imports—all increase in the same proportion). This additional effect of devaluation results from its expenditure-reducing effects and from the decrease in the relative price of nontraded goods it causes, an effect not discussed before. Note that this influence of devaluation on the trade balance would be only temporary. Over time, domestic residents will replenish their depleted real money balances, increasing expenditure in the process and returning the relative price of nontraded goods to its predevaluation level.[22]

The empirical work focusing on the responsiveness of the prices of nontraded goods to devaluation and the consequent effects on the trade balance is quite limited and is a topic of current research in the field. The evidence available, however, does suggest that devaluation has a negative impact on the prices of nontraded goods relative to traded goods, making the adjustments mentioned earlier potentially important.

In conclusion, we have seen how the domestic price level can deviate, and can be made to deviate by various policies, from world-determined prices in the presence of a significant nontraded goods sector.

---

[22] Kravis and Lipsey provide such evidence on devaluations and revaluations in various industrial countries during the period 1970 to 1973. See Irving Kravis and Robert Lipsey, "Price Behavior in the Light of Balance of Payments Theories," *Journal of International Economics* (May 1978).

CHAPTER 15

Asset Markets and Exchange Rate Determination

Have you ever asked yourself why is it that over the last 10 years it has always taken between $1.00 and $2.50 to purchase a British pound and not between $3.50 and $4.50? What induces the dollar–pound exchange rate to fluctuate around a value of $2.00 instead of $4.00, or $5.00 for that matter? This chapter examines the factors determining or influencing exchange rates and their behavior over time. It is clear that any adequate theory of exchange rate behavior must face the fact that the values of the major industrial countries' currencies have shown marked turbulence during the recent period of floating exchange rates, a turbulence that often looks perplexing. For instance, why was it that the value of the dollar vis à vis other currencies generally moved downward the day Ronald Reagan was shot in 1982 or during the early weeks of the Iranian hostage crisis of 1980? Can you explain why the dollar brusquely appreciates in value when the Federal Reserve Board announces money supply growth figures above what were anticipated or when the Commerce Department announces unexpectedly large U.S. current account balance surpluses (or surprisingly small deficits)? All these situations involve either sudden events or new information unanticipated by agents in the economy. In this sense, they can all be catalogued as "news." A major task of this chapter is to explain why and how news is related to exchange rate turbulence.

When one observes the day-to-day fluctuations of exchange rates in response to news, one must be obviously reminded of the wild movements in the prices of assets traded on the stock exchange. The gyrations of the price of a share of Eastern, General Motors, and the Tandy Corporation in large part reflect new information, rumors, or announcements made by these companies regarding present or future returns. An unanticipatedly dismal quarter in terms of sales or profits may prompt a rapid downfall of share prices. Growing expectations of economic recovery and increased sales, on the other hand, may start a sudden rise of share prices. Clearly, the bumbling behavior of stock market prices in response to news looks very similar to that of exchange rates, which suggests that exchange rates might be analyzed in a similar framework as stock prices.

471

The asset market approach states that "the exchange rate must adjust instantly to equilibrate the international demand for stocks of national assets."[1] Exchange rate behavior is thus looked at from the point of view of its role in clearing relative demands for stocks of domestic and foreign assets rather than in terms of clearing international trade flows of goods and services. The asset market approach to analyzing exchange rates sprouted during the late 1970s from a variety of intellectual perspectives. As a result of the diversity of origins, there exists a whole range of alternative frameworks of analysis whose common underlying core involves in some way the asset market approach.

The simplest version of the asset market view is referred to as the *monetary approach to the exchange rate*. This approach looks at exchange rate adjustment as equilibrating the domestic and foreign markets for money. Factors affecting supplies and demands for domestic and foreign money—as might arise from the government's monetary policies or from changes in relative income growth among countries—will disturb equilibrium in money markets and will influence exchange rates. We shall examine the various implications of the monetary approach with regard to exchange rate determination and variability. The phenomenon of currency substitution, occurring when residents of a given country hold money balances in foreign currencies in addition to domestic currency, is also examined and its implications for exchange rate determination stated.

In emphasizing the association between exchange rate adjustments and money market equilibrium, the monetary approach assumes that domestic and foreign bonds are perfect substitutes, freely interchangeable in investors' portfolios. On the other hand, the *portfolio balance* approach to the exchange rate relaxes precisely this assumption by focusing on the situation where domestic and foreign bonds are indeed imperfect substitutes. This implies that in addition to considering equilibrium in the money market, one must also pay attention to the association between exchange rate behavior and changes in the relative demands and supplies of domestic and foreign bonds. Factors increasing the relative demand for domestic bonds, for instance, would disturb portfolio equilibrium among domestic and foreign assets and, according to the portfolio balance approach, will influence the exchange rate. The details of these connections are examined later. We start, however, at the beginning, by describing the monetary approach.

15–1   THE MONETARY APPROACH TO THE EXCHANGE RATE

The monetary approach to the exchange rate was developed over the late 1970s in response to the increased exchange rate flexibility faced by most industrial countries after 1973 and the corresponding growth of academic interest in ex-

[1] Jeffrey A. Frankel, "Monetary and Portfolio-Balance Models of Exchange Rate Determination," in J. S. Bhandari and B. H. Putnam, *Economic Interdependence and Flexible Exchange Rates* (Cambridge, Mass.: The M.I.T. Press, 1983), p. 84.

change rate determination. Its sources, though, go as far back as the early writings of Joan Robinson (in the 1930s), Lord Keynes (1924), Gustav Cassel (1916), and even David Ricardo in the early 1800s.[2]

The monetary approach to exchange rates starts at the most basic level, by taking a close look at the definition of an exchange rate. An exchange rate is, by definition, the price at which foreign currency (foreign money) is sold in terms of domestic currency (domestic money). It is the almost obvious intuition of the monetary approach that, as any relative price, the exchange rate should be determined by the forces of demand and supply. And since the relative price involved is that between two moneys, it should relate to the demands and supplies of these two moneys.

More specifically, to sustain domestic money market equilibrium, the existing supply (stock) of money must be willingly held (demanded) or

$$\frac{M}{P} = L(i, Y) \tag{1}$$

where M/P represents the domestic real money supply and $L(i, Y)$ depicts domestic (real) money demand as a function of domestic interest rates, i, and income, Y. Similarly, the foreign money market equilibrium condition is given by

$$\frac{M^*}{P^*} = L^*(i^*, Y^*) \tag{2}$$

where asterisks represent foreign variables (e.g., M^* is the foreign nominal money supply, L^* foreign real money demand). Observe that the money market equilibrium conditions in (1) and (2) do not show explicitly how the equilibrium value of the exchange rate is established. In order to do that, one has to specify an additional relationship determining explicitly how the exchange rate influences money market equilibria. That is, how do exchange rate changes contribute to equilibrate money demands and supplies?

To answer this question, one can utilize the so-called *absolute purchasing power parity* (PPP) relationship, stating the equality between domestic prices, P, and foreign prices converted into domestic currency, eP^*, or

$$P = eP^* \tag{3}$$

which can be transformed into an expression for the exchange rate:

$$e = \frac{P}{P^*} \tag{3a}$$

[2] For details on the origins of the monetary approach to the exchange rate, see J. Frenkel, "A Monetary Approach to the Exchange Rate: Doctrinal Aspects and Empirical Evidence." In Jacob Frenkel and Harry Johnson, *The Economics of Exchange Rates: Selected Studies* (Reading, Mass.: Addison-Wesley Publishing Co., Inc., 1978).

Equation (3a) establishes a relationship between the exchange rate and the domestic price level. Its implication is that the higher the domestic price level relative to foreign prices, the higher the exchange rate must be in order to maintain purchasing power parity between domestic and foreign money. If, for instance, the U.S. price level is twice that in Britain ($P/P^* = 2$), then the exchange rate will have to reflect the lower relative purchasing power of U.S. money vis à vis British money by making U.S. money (the dollar) half as valuable in terms of British money (the pound). The dollar–pound exchange rate should thus equal $2.00 per pound.

The purchasing power parity relationship as stated by (3) implies that exchange rates can influence money market equilibria through their connections to domestic and foreign prices. Transforming equations (1) and (2) to express them in terms of price levels yields $P = M/L \, (i, Y)$ and $P^* = M^*/L^* \, (i^*, Y^*)$, which can be substituted into equation (3) to obtain

$$e = \frac{M}{M^*} \frac{L^*(i^*, Y^*)}{L(i, Y)} \tag{4}$$

showing the exchange rate as being determined by the ratio of the domestic money supply to the foreign money supply, M/M^*, and the ratio of the demand for foreign money to domestic money demand, L^*/L. This version of the monetary approach to the exchange rate succinctly shows the economic interdependence involved in exchange rate determination. Being the relative price of two moneys, the exchange rate depends not only on demand and supply of domestic money, but also on demand and supply of foreign money. Exchange rate adjustments are therefore dependent on changes in both domestic and foreign variables. Even though a given domestic (nominal) money supply increase by itself tends to raise the exchange rate, if there is a simultaneous larger proportional increase in the foreign (nominal) money supply, the result is an excess supply of foreign money relative to domestic money. This requires a reduction in the relative price of foreign money, that is, a lower exchange rate. Exchange rates cannot, therefore, be determined independently of the behavior of foreign economies or the actions of foreign governments. Questions related to the control of exchange rate changes or fluctuations must then be addressed within the context of a common dialogue among the countries involved. This serves well to illustrate that, in general, no single open economy can dissociate itself entirely from foreign influences.

Equation (4) shows that, given relative money supplies, factors increasing domestic money demand relative to foreign money demand will raise the value of domestic currency; that is, they will lower the exchange rate. An increase in domestic income relative to foreign income, Y/Y^*, for instance, will tend to increase relative domestic money demand and appreciate the value of domestic currency. Similarly, lower domestic nominal interest rates relative to foreign nominal interest rates raise relative domestic money demand and will also appreciate the value of domestic currency.

These results stand squarely opposed to those derived from other points of view on exchange rate determination. For example, it is often argued that higher domestic real incomes reduce rather than increase the value of domestic money. Since they tend to increase imports and worsen the current account, the exchange rate would have to increase to assure external balance. This positive connection between depreciation of domestic currency and higher domestic income is often voiced in official circles. The Honorable Paul Volcker, chairman of the Federal Reserve System, has been alleged to argue that in order to support the dollar, the United States must accept a lower standard of living. The monetary approach to the exchange rate suggests an opposite view. The same dichotomy arises with regard to the effects of changes in nominal interest rates on the exchange rate. A popular view is that higher nominal interest rates strengthen the value of domestic currency because they induce incipient capital inflows reflected in a rising capital account surplus that requires a domestic currency appreciation to assure external balance. Again, the Federal Reserve Board has often voiced this view arguing that in order to strengthen the dollar, higher U.S. nominal interest rates are required. The monetary approach suggests the opposite.

What is the evidence on the monetary approach to the exchange rate? Do equations such as (4) explain accurately actual exchange rates? Are changes in relative money supplies, income, and interest rates related to exchange rate changes as predicted by the monetary approach? The next sections wrestle with these questions.

15-2   EMPIRICAL EVIDENCE ON THE MONETARY APPROACH: A FIRST LOOK

This section introduces the data available on the monetary approach to exchange rate determination and, in particular, the question as to whether equation (4) explains accurately actual exchange rates. In order to answer this question, it is apparent that one must deal with the problem of specifying in a precise way the form that the money demand functions, L^* and L, take. Even though the monetary approach asserts in a clear fashion that these money demands are stable functions of certain variables—income, interest rates—it still leaves open the question of exactly how money demands relate to those variables. In a simple version, money demands are assumed to be of the following multiplicative form:

$$L = YK(i)$$

and

$$L^* = Y^* \ K^*(i^*)$$

where the K functions reflect the particular influence of interest rates on money demand. These can be substituted into equation (4) to obtain the following simplified exchange rate determination equation:

$$e = \frac{M}{M^*} \frac{Y^*}{Y} \frac{K^*(i^*)}{K(i)} \tag{4a}$$

It is clear that one must still specify how interest rates are related to money demands through the functions K and K^*. This, however, need not concern us here as different studies generally adopt different versions for the Ks.

Table 15–1 displays the computation of the exchange rates implied by equation (4a) for the dollar vis à vis selected foreign moneys using actual 1978 data for relative money supplies, income, and interest rates (the specific measures of these variables utilized can be found in Table 15–1). The predicted exchange

TABLE 15–1.   The Fundamental Determinants of the Exchange Rate[a]

Country	M($)/M(*)	Q(*)/Q($)	K(*)/K($)	Exchange Rate Prediction	Actual
Australia	1.47	0.78	1.09	1.25	1.15
Austria	0.05	0.85	1.19	0.05	0.07
Belgium	0.03	1.11	1.19	0.04	0.03
Canada	0.93	0.85	1.06	0.85	0.84
France	0.22	0.98	1.10	0.23	0.24
Germany	0.31	1.18	1.75	0.65	0.54
Italy	0.001	0.48	0.51	0.0003	0.0012
Japan	0.003	0.95	1.75	0.005	0.005
Netherlands	0.37	1.06	1.43	0.56	0.51
Norway	0.14	1.02	1.19	0.17	0.20
South Africa	8.33	0.16	0.88	1.18	1.15
Sweden	0.24	1.14	0.92	0.25	0.23
Switzerland	0.14	1.56	2.5	0.56	0.62
United Kingdom	4.55	0.60	0.66	1.79	2.04

Source: International Financial Statistics, International Monetary Fund, (Washington, D.C.). Based on John Bilson, "Comment on Willet and Sweeney," in J. Dreyer, G. Haberler, and T. Willet, eds., *The International Monetary System: A Time of Turbulence* (Washington, D.C.: American Enterprise Institute, 1982).

[a] The predicted exchange rate is the product of the first three columns.

$M(\$)/M(*)$ = the quantity of money per capita in the United States relative to the quantity of money per capita in the sample country.

$Q(*)/Q(\$)$ = U.S. dollar value of GNP per capita in the sample country, relative to the U.S. GNP per capita.

$K(*)/K(\$)$ = 0.84 exp 0.13($i(*)-i(\$)$), where $i(\$)$ is the long-term bond yield in the United States and $i(*)$ is the long-term bond yield in the sample country. The 0.84 adjustment ensures that the geometric mean of the forecast errors is equal to zero.

rates are compared with actual exchange rates prevailing at that time. Notice that in some cases the exchange rates implied by the monetary approach as given by equation (4a) are relatively close to the actual values of the exchange rates, although there are clear substantial deviations in most cases. Other studies following the same or similar strategy yield similar findings.

What causes these deviations? A major factor generating divergencies between the predictions of the monetary approach as embodied in equations (4) and (4a) and actual exchange rates is the fact that, in order to derive equations (4) or (4a), the absolute version of PPP as stated in equation (3a) is used. As a consequence, the predicted exchange rates quoted in Table 15–1 are the joint result not only of the monetary approach hypotheses regarding money market equilibrium, but also of the absolute PPP assumption.

The empirical evidence shows that the absolute PPP hypothesis fails to hold on a systematic basis over time. In the case of the United States, for example, Figure 15–1 shows how the dollar (nominal) effective exchange rate, e, has generally failed to equal the ratio of an index of United States to foreign prices, P/P^*. Therefore, if the relationship between the exchange rate and relative prices used is to have any empirical basis, it must be modified from the one stated by equation (3).

Let us denote the ratio of foreign prices (expressed in domestic currency) to domestic prices by $\tilde{q} = eP^*/P$. Absolute PPP assumes that $\tilde{q}$ is equal to 1 on a systematic basis, which is the basis for equation (3). In general, however, $\tilde{q} > 1$ if domestic prices, P, are lower than comparable foreign prices, eP^*, and $\tilde{q} < 1$ if domestic prices exceed foreign prices converted into domestic currency. The relationship between the exchange rate and relative price levels can then be expressed by

$$e = \tilde{q}\frac{P}{P^*} \tag{5}$$

A modified version of the purchasing power parity hypothesis allows the exchange rate to diverge from relative price levels ($\tilde{q} \neq 1$) but by a fixed margin, implying that $\tilde{q}$ is fixed over time.

Expressing equation (5) in terms of percentage changes yields

$$\hat{e} = \hat{\tilde{q}} + \hat{P} - \hat{P}^* \tag{6}$$

where $\hat{P} \equiv \Delta P/P$ is the rate of increase of domestic prices, $\hat{\tilde{q}} \equiv \Delta \tilde{q}/\tilde{q}$ represents proportional changes in the gap between domestic and foreign prices, $\hat{e}$ is the rate of domestic currency depreciation, and $\hat{P}^*$ is the rate of increase of prices in world markets, over a given time period. Symbolically, the assumption that $\tilde{q}$ remains fixed over time means $\hat{\tilde{q}} = 0$, in which case equation (6) can be expressed as

$$\hat{e} = \hat{P} - \hat{P}^* \tag{7}$$

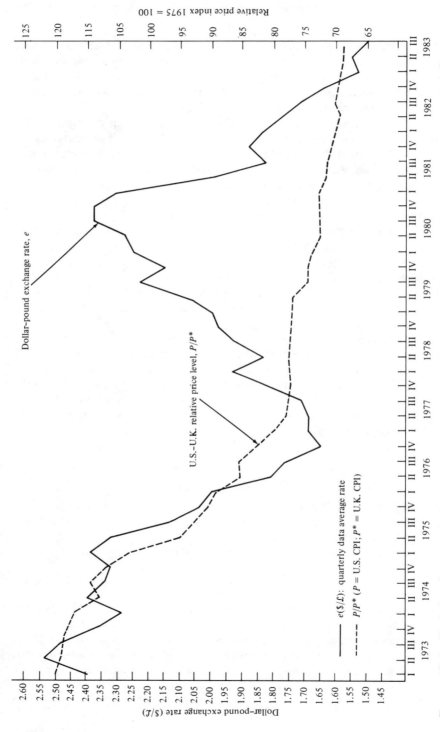

FIGURE 15-1. Deviations from Absolute Purchasing Power Parity. The dollar-pound exchange rate data are for the quarterly, averaged rate; the U.S. and U.K. price levels are the consumer price indexes. (From International Monetary Fund, International Financial Statistics, selected issues.)

referred to as the *relative purchasing power parity* hypothesis, to distinguish it from the *absolute* version of PPP embodied in equation (3). Equation (7) asserts that the rate of domestic currency depreciation or appreciation is equal to the differential rates of inflation among countries. If domestic inflation exceeds foreign inflation, a domestic currency depreciation is required to sustain purchasing power parity between domestic and foreign money. Similarly, if foreign inflation exceeds domestic inflation, this will be associated with a domestic currency appreciation. In summary, equation (7) is less stringent than equation (3) in allowing domestic and foreign prices (in domestic currency) to differ from each other but still sustains the assumption that these deviations will not grow or diminish persistently over time. The relative purchasing power of domestic money vis à vis foreign money will therefore be fixed over time, with exchange rate changes, $\hat{e}$, assuring such parity.

Most studies following the monetary approach have utilized the relative version of PPP in deriving an expression for the determinants of exchange rate changes. The following section derives the monetary approach to exchange rate adjustment on this basis.

15-3   EXCHANGE RATE CHANGES AND THE MONETARY APPROACH

The state of flux in which the world operates implies economic variables will be constantly changing. Interest rates, income, prices, and so on, all change significantly over time. According to the monetary approach, changes in these variables will generally influence exchange rates by affecting money market equilibrium. Formally expressed, taking proportional changes in equations (1) and (2) yields

$$\hat{M} - \hat{P} = \hat{L} \quad \text{and} \quad \hat{M}^* - \hat{P}^* = \hat{L}^*$$

Expressing these relationships in terms of domestic and foreign inflation, $\hat{P} = \hat{M} - \hat{L}$ and $\hat{P}^* = \hat{M}^* - \hat{L}^*$, respectively, and substituting the resulting expression into equation (7), we obtain

$$\hat{e} = \hat{P} - \hat{P}^* = (\hat{M} - \hat{M}^*) + (\hat{L}^* - \hat{L}) \tag{7a}$$

Exchange rate changes, $\hat{e}$, are thus determined by changes in relative money supplies, $\hat{M} - \hat{M}^*$, and changes in relative money demands, $\hat{L}^* - \hat{L}$. Changes in relative money supplies reflect the countries' monetary policies. Changes in relative money demands, in turn, reflect differential changes in the variables affecting money demand, mainly income and interest rates. The specific way through which these variables influence relative money demands depends clearly on the form of the money demand functions and is therefore subject to a degree of discretion. Most studies following the monetary approach, however, assume that

$$\hat{L}^* - \hat{L} = \phi(\hat{Y}^* - \hat{Y}) + \lambda(\hat{i} - \overset{\wedge}{i^*}) \qquad (8)$$

where ϕ and λ are both positive parameters. Equation (8) states, first, that higher foreign income growth relative to domestic growth results in a higher proportional growth of foreign money demand relative to domestic money demand. This reflects the higher rate of increase of transactions abroad, that generates a relatively higher growth of foreign money demand. In addition, an increase in domestic interest rates above foreign interest rates—a positive $(i - i^*)$ term—will also result in a relatively higher growth of foreign money demand vis à vis domestic money demand. The relatively higher domestic interest rate puts a brake on domestic money demand growth relative to foreign demand by inducing domestic residents to shift out of money and into bonds.

Substitution of equation (8) into (7a) yields the following expression showing the determinants of exchange rate changes according to the monetary approach

$$\hat{e} = (\hat{M} - \hat{M}^*) + \phi(\hat{Y} - \hat{Y}^*) + \lambda(\hat{i} - \overset{\wedge}{i^*}) \qquad (9)$$

This is the basic equation used by the monetary approach to examine exchange rate changes. As shown next, it provides us with additional insights on the economics of exchange rate movements, particularly on how expectations influence exchange rates.

Interest Differentials, Expected Inflation, and the Exchange Rate

The role of expectations can be explicitly examined by modifying equation (9) through the use of the uncovered interest rate parity condition:

$$i - i^* = x \qquad (10)$$

establishing the equality of interest rate differentials with anticipated exchange rate changes, x, where exchange risk premia are being momentarily ignored (the role of the latter on exchange rate determination is examined in Section 15–6). In addition, it must be realized that, on the assumption relative PPP holds, agents in the economy would anticipate exchange rates to change according to the anticipated differential in the rates of domestic and foreign inflation, or

$$x = \pi - \pi^* \qquad (11)$$

where π and π^* denote expected domestic and foreign inflation. Equation (11) is essentially the expectational counterpart of equation (7) in the general situation where future inflation rates are not known.

Substitution of equation (11) into equation (10) and then into equation (9) yields

$$\hat{e} = (\hat{M} - \hat{M}^*) + \phi(\hat{Y}^* - \hat{Y}) + \lambda(\overset{\wedge}{\pi} - \overset{\wedge}{\pi}{}^*) \tag{9a}$$

The first two terms of equation (9a) have been basically explained earlier. The last term deserves more attention. It states that, everything else being constant, higher domestic anticipated inflation tends to depreciate the value of domestic currency. The higher anticipated inflation will be associated with higher domestic nominal interest rates, which consequently reduce domestic real money demand and require a reduction in the value of domestic currency to sustain asset market equilibrium.

This point makes clear the important role expectational considerations have according to the monetary approach and serves well to illustrate the monetary approach's view of exchange rate variability. News relevant to the formation of expectations regarding future domestic and foreign inflation will immediately be reflected in spot exchange rate changes. Since such news are sudden and not known beforehand, the changes in exchange rates will also be sudden and unanticipated. Consequently, there is a significant component of exchange rate changes that is uncertain, moving along the bumbling, unpredictable path that new events and information induce it to follow. Exchange rate changes, therefore, appear to follow a "random walk."

Evidence on the Monetary Approach to Exchange Rate Changes

The empirical data on the monetary approach seem to yield mixed results, some studies finding support for the relationships predicted by the monetary approach and others rejecting those hypotheses.[3] For the case of the U.S. dollar, for example, studies[4] using data for the period 1973 to 1978 yield findings consistent with the monetary approach as stated by equation (9), but studies incorporating more recent data have been much less favorable to the monetary approach. A particular problem that has received much attention is shown by Figure 15–2, in which the U.S. dollar–pound sterling exchange rate is plotted against the U.S.–U.K. interest rate differential, $i - i^*$. According to the monetary approach, a higher U.S.–U.K. interest rate differential should be associated with an equivalent U.S. dollar depreciation, ceteris paribus. Such a relationship

---

[3] See M. E. Kreinin and L. H. Officer, "The Monetary Approach to the Balance of Payments: A Survey," *Princeton Studies in International Finance,* No. 43 (November 1978); also, R. Dornbusch, "Exchange Rate Economics: Where Do We Stand?" in J. S. Bhandari and B. H. Putnam, *Economic Interdependence and Flexible Exchange Rates* (Cambridge, Mass.: The M.I.T. Press, 1983).

[4] See J. Bilson, "The Monetary Approach to the Exchange Rate: Some Evidence," *IMF Staff Papers* (March 1978); R. Hodrick, "An Empirical Analysis of the Monetary Approach to the Determination of the Exchange Rate," in Jacob Frenkel and Harry Johnson, eds., *The Economics of Exchange Rates: Selected Studies* (Reading, Mass.: Addison-Wesley Publishing Co., Inc., 1978).

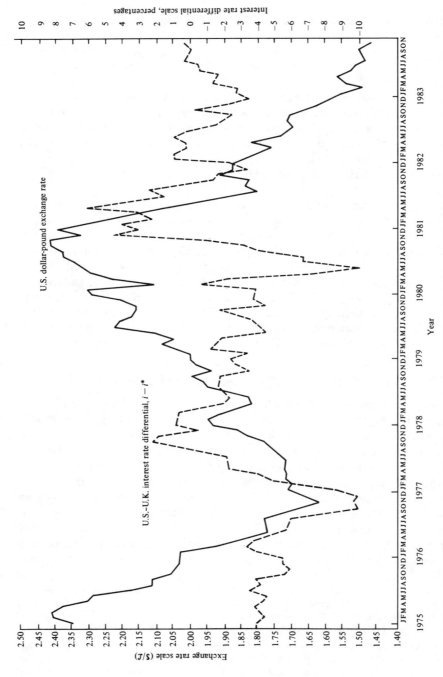

FIGURE 15–2. U.S. Dollar-Pound Sterling Exchange Rate and U.S.–U.K. Interest Differential. (From Bank of England, *Quarterly Bulletin*, selected issues.)

appears to be consistent with most of the data for the 1970s in Figure 15–2. During 1979 to 1980, however, an interest differential increasingly favoring the United Kingdom was associated with a sharp depreciation of the dollar in terms of sterling, seemingly contradicting the presumption of the monetary approach. Furthermore, the different situation during late 1980, when the U.S.– U.K. interest differential favored the United States but was accompanied by a U.S. dollar appreciation, casts further doubts on the robustness of the monetary approach.

However, one must be very careful when evaluating this experience. First, just as the power of equation (4a) in explaining exchange rates is dependent on the accuracy of absolute purchasing power parity, the ability of equation (9) in accounting for exchange rate changes is associated with whether or not the relative version of PPP holds. As a consequence, the failure of some studies to find results consistent with an equation such as (9) might very well be attributable to the breakdown of relative PPPs during the periods examined and thus may not necessarily imply the monetary approach should not be accepted. Other aspects to be considered when evaluating the empirical evidence on the monetary approach regard the phenomenon of currency substitution and the presence of exchange risk, both of which modify drastically the predictions of the monetary approach. The evidence and role of each of these factors in explaining the data will be the subject of the following sections.

15–4   DEVIATIONS FROM PURCHASING POWER PARITY AND EXCHANGE RATE CHANGES

The relative version of PPP does not appear to have held to any significant extent during the recent period of increased exchange rate flexibility. Figure 15–3 illustrates this breakdown of PPPs during the seventies and early eighties for the U.S.–U.K. case. Similar data appear to hold for other currencies as well.[5] However, a close look at Figure 15–3 suggests that even though there are substantial and persistent short-run deviations from relative PPP, on average these deviations tend to even out over time so that over the long run the relative PPP hypothesis is much closer to being satisfied. One might consequently want to think about equation (9a) as being a long-run relationship, toward which exchange rate changes move over time, but from which they deviate in the short run.

Why does relative PPP break down over certain periods of time? Relative PPP involves the assumption that the real exchange rate remains unchanged over time. Factors altering the real exchange rate, whether temporarily or perma-

---

[5] For more details, see J. A. Frenkel, "Flexible Exchange Rates, Prices and the Role of News: Lessons from the 1970's," in J. S. Bhandari and B. H. Putnam, *Economic Interdependence and Flexible Exchange Rates* (Cambridge, Mass.: The M.I.T. Press, 1983); and his "The Collapse of Purchasing Power Parities During the 1970's." *European Economic Review* (May 1981).

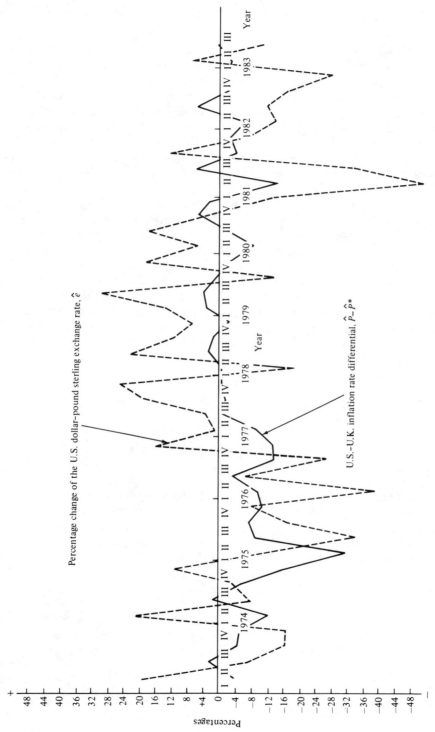

FIGURE 15-3. Breakdown of Relative Purchasing Power Parities in the 1970s and 1980s. Data for U.S. and U.K. inflation: Annualized percentage change in U.S. and U.K. consumer price indexes. Data for the exchange rate is the annualized percentage change of the U.S. dollar-pound exchange rate ($/£). (From International Monetary Fund, International Financial Statistics, selected issues.)

484

nently, will then generate deviations from relative PPP. Algebraically, from equation (6), exchange rate changes are given by

$$\hat{e} = \hat{P} - \hat{P}* + \hat{\bar{q}} \qquad (6)$$

where $\hat{\bar{q}}$ represents changes in the real exchange rate. Relative PPP assumes $\hat{\bar{q}} = 0$, that is, the absence of real exchange rate changes. But more generally, $\hat{\bar{q}}$ will differ from zero.

Various factors generate changes in real exchange rates. Differential changes in taste, technology, factor supplies, and market structures between countries will generally affect their relative costs of production, thereby influencing their relative price competitiveness and, therefore, real exchange rates. These long-term changes in real exchange rates appear as deviations from relative PPP.[6] But even if the long-run real exchange rate is fixed, our analysis in previous chapters should have alerted us to the possibility that disturbances in the economy, particularly unanticipated disturbances, might lead to short-term fluctuations in real exchange rates. Labor and/or goods market rigidities facing the economy generally imply that the economy's adjustment to these disturbances will not occur instantaneously and will have short-run effects on real variables, such as real exchange rates.

To take an extreme example, when domestic and foreign prices are relatively rigid in how much they can change in the short run, domestic currency appreciation or depreciation over that time period will result in deviations from relative PPP. Such was the case analyzed in Chapter 9, where an (unanticipated) increase in the money supply was observed to require a short-run currency depreciation exceeding its longer-term equilibrium depreciation. This overshooting of the exchange rate in the presence of price rigidity is then associated with a short-run real exchange rate change and to deviations from PPP. Note, however, that prices and/or other economic variables will adjust over time in moving the economy to its long-run equilibrium. As a result, the deviations from relative PPP arising from an unanticipated monetary expansion would be gradually eliminated over time. The real exchange rate will therefore decline back toward its long-run value, above which it momentarily moved in response to the disturbance.

To reiterate, over the long run, exchange rate changes generally tend to reflect inflation rate differentials among countries. In the short run, however, fluctuations in real exchange rates give rise to substantial deviations from relative PPP. A number of studies have incorporated deviations from relative PPP into the structure of the monetary approach to the exchange rate, providing it with

---

[6] For more details, see R. Dornbusch, "The Theory of Flexible Exchange Rate Regimes and Macroeconomic Policy," in J. A. Frenkel and H. G. Johnson, *The Economics of Exchange Rates: Selected Studies* (Reading, Mass.: Addison-Wesley Publishing Co., Inc., 1978); and K. W. Clements and J. A. Frenkel, "Exchange Rates, Money, and Relative Prices: The Dollar–Pound in the 1920's," *Journal of International Economics* (May 1980).

a broader basis for empirical support.[7] Still, even in this case, the data often do not seem to provide support for the hypothesized relationships connecting relative money growth and relative income growth to exchange rate changes, as stated by equation (9a), especially when updated to take into account the events of the late seventies and early eighties.[8] For instance, during the years of 1978 and 1979, the dollar depreciated sharply against the deutsche mark, a movement viewed by many at the time as probably resulting from high U.S. monetary growth combined with German monetary restraint. If this had been so, the implications of the monetary approach would have been vindicated: High relative U.S. money growth would have resulted in a declining value of the U.S. dollar. Unfortunately, the reverse was true: German monetary growth during the period was higher than U.S. monetary growth. Of course, according to the monetary approach, as stated by equation (9a), the U.S. dollar depreciation could have been accounted for by higher German income growth relative to the United States or by higher expected inflation in Germany relative to U.S. expected inflation. These factors would have raised German money demand growth relative to the United States, offsetting the higher German money supply growth and leaving an excess relative demand for German money. An appreciation of the mark would then have been indeed called for. However, when one tries to explain the U.S. dollar–deutsche mark exchange rate changes during 1978 and 1979 introducing all the variables in equation (9a), one still finds that the dollar depreciation could not be accounted for by these factors. In other words, the changes in relative money demands postulated by the factors spelled out in equation (9a) do not appear to have been enough to offset the high relative German money supply growth. One would have to posit the presence of an exogenously large increase in German money demand relative to U.S. money demand to explain the dollar depreciation. The next section examines this possibility and its implications in terms of the empirical evidence on the monetary approach to the exchange rate.

15–5   CURRENCY SUBSTITUTION AND THE EXCHANGE RATE

Up to this point it has been assumed that each country's money is held only by its own residents. In other words, only U.S. residents hold dollars and only German residents demand marks. More generally, however, it appears that residents of major industrial countries do hold both domestic and foreign currencies.

[7] See J. A. Frankel, "On the Mark: A Theory of Floating Exchange Rates Based on Real Interest Differentials," *American Economic Review* (September 1979); and R. A. Driskill, "Exchange Rate Dynamics: An Empirical Investigation," *Journal of Political Economy* (April 1981).

[8] See R. Dornbusch, "Exchange Rate Economics: Where Do We Stand?" in J. S. Bhandari and B. H. Putnam, eds., *Economic Interdependence and Flexible Exchange Rates* (Cambridge, Mass.: The M.I.T. Press, 1983); and J. Frankel, "Monetary and Portfolio-Balance Models of Exchange Rate Determination," in Bhandari and Putnam, *ibid.*

The U.S. multinational corporations engaging in frequent transactions abroad, for example, acquire foreign currency deposits to facilitate and reduce the costs of such transactions. Similarly, speculators and/or arbitrageurs seeking to profit from purchases and sales of currencies hold domestic and foreign money so as to have available highly liquid funds that can be quickly transferred across borders or easily exchanged for other currencies. Finally, Central Banks also hold international reserves in the form of foreign currency balances, often used to intervene in foreign exchange markets. Whatever the reason, when residents of different countries hold a portfolio of currencies, changes in economic variables may alter the desired share of each currency in that portfolio, leading to changes in relative money demands. This phenomenon is referred to as *currency substitution*.

What determines the proportion of total money balances that domestic and foreign residents wish to hold in domestic money relative to foreign money? A crucial factor here is the opportunity cost of holding domestic relative to foreign money, often represented by the anticipated rate of depreciation of domestic currency. An increase in the anticipated rate of depreciation of domestic currency raises the expected cost of holding domestic money vis à vis foreign currency and will result in an increase in the share of money balances held in foreign money, *ceteris paribus*. On the other hand, a higher rate of domestic currency appreciation will raise the proportion of domestic money in currency portfolios.

Currency substitution has essential implications for the functioning of both fixed and flexible exchange rates.[9] Under fixed exchange rates, growing expectations of domestic currency devaluation can generate massive currency substitution away from domestic money and could in the process wipe out the international reserves of the Central Bank. The role of currency substitution in foreign exchange crises was evident in the Mexican case of 1982. Currency substitution between Mexican pesos and dollars was to a large extent in the form of dollar deposits at banks located in Mexico, that is, Mexidollars. Being afraid that the banks would export their Mexidollars in the event of a scare regarding possible exchange controls, and given the importance of Mexidollars in financing transactions of firms and individuals trading with Mexico, the Mexican government decided to avoid taking any risks and went ahead and nationalized the banks during the crisis. This created, of course, other types of disruptions in the local financial markets,[10] but it serves well to illustrate the significance of currency substitution in economies under fixed exchange rates.

[9] For details, see G. Calvo and C. Rodriguez, "A Model of Exchange Rate Determination Under Currency Substitution and Rational Expectations," *Journal of Political Economy* (June 1977); M. A. Miles, "Currency Substitution, Flexible Exchange Rates and Monetary Independence," *American Economic Review* (June 1978); and L. Girton and D. Roper, "Theory and Implications of Currency Substitution," *Journal of Money, Credit and Banking* (February 1981).

[10] Currency substitution in Mexico and its interconnections with the crisis of 1982 have been

(*Continued*)

Under flexible exchange rates, expected depreciations of domestic currency may induce money holders to switch their cash holdings from domestic to foreign currency. The concomitant drop in the demand for domestic money relative to foreign money would then induce a depreciation of domestic currency. Observe that this effect of anticipated exchange rate changes in shifting the demand for money out of the domestic and into *foreign currency* operates in addition to the effect of expected exchange rate changes in shifting the demand for money out of domestic currency and into *bonds*.[11] As specified earlier, by raising domestic nominal interest rates relative to foreign rates, a sudden expected depreciation of domestic currency reduces domestic money demand and increases the demand for bonds. The currency substitution effect adds an additional factor affecting relative demands for domestic and foreign money not considered earlier. Introducing currency substitution into the analysis may thus improve upon the ability of equations such as (9a) in explaining exchange rate changes.

Consider the case of the dollar–deutsche mark exchange rate of the late seventies. There is an unexplained decline in the demand for dollars relative to German deutsche marks during that period. One possible explanation[12] is that the expected depreciation of the dollar at the time, associated partly with the intentions of the Carter administration to "talk down" the dollar, gave rise to currency substitution in favor of the deutsche mark and against the dollar. The attendant increased demand for marks relative to dollars could then account for the unexplained depreciation of the dollar vis à vis the mark. As a matter of fact, a significant movement of funds out of dollars and into marks was indeed observed during the period. This was combined with the unsuccessful attempts of the Bundesbank to prevent the appreciation of the mark by purchasing dollars in foreign exchange markets. Since this intervention was nonsterilized, it meant that the acquisition of dollar reserves by the Bundesbank produced an increase of the German money supply. The high rate of growth of the German money supply relative to the U.S. money supply was patently related to these events.

Even though the unexplained shift in relative U.S.–Germany money demands over this time period could be partially accounted for by a currency portfolio shift arising from a heightened preference toward marks relative to dollars, it might have been due to a portfolio balance shift arising from increased preference toward the holding of bonds denominated in marks relative to bonds denominated

---

examined by G. Ortiz, "The Dollarization of Mexico: Causes and Consequences," in P. Aspe, M. Obstfeld, and R. Dornbush, eds., *Financial Policies and the World Capital Market: The Problem of Latin American Countries* (Chicago, Illinois: University of Chicago Press, 1983).

[11] For an analysis of the effects of expected exchange rate changes in generating shifts between money and bonds and among different moneys, see J. T. Cuddington, "Currency Substitution, Capital Mobility and Money Demand," *Journal of International Money and Finance* (1983).

[12] Espoused by R. I. McKinnon, "Currency Substitution and Instability in the World Dollar Standard," *American Economic Review* (June 1982).

in dollars. It is the purpose of the next section to examine the role of portfolio balance considerations on the exchange rate.

15–6   EXCHANGE RISK AND THE PORTFOLIO BALANCE APPROACH

In studying the connections between exchange rates and money market equilibrium, the monetary approach assumes domestic and foreign bonds are perfect substitutes and therefore freely interchangeable in investors' portfolios. However, there are a variety of reasons why domestic and foreign assets might not be perfect substitutes, such as differences in liquidity, government tax laws, default risk, political risk, and exchange risk. The portfolio balance approach to the exchange rate focuses on examining the case where exchange risk makes domestic and foreign bonds imperfect substitutes.[13] Exchange risk is the particular risk associated with holding uncovered investments in foreign-currency-dominated assets relative to domestic investments. Risk-averse investors will generally diversify their asset holdings internationally so as to avoid "placing all their eggs in the same basket" and reduce the risks attached to holding only one type of asset. International portfolio diversification involves assessing the effect of uncovered foreign investments on the risk of the investors' portfolio. If, for example, adding the uncovered foreign investment results in an increase in the overall risk of the investors' portfolios, then they will have to be compensated for the hair-raising and heart-stopping effects of the increased risk. That is, risk-averse investors will require an exchange *risk premium* to compensate them for the increased risk of their uncovered undertakings. Similarly, if investors are already holding high-risk domestic currency-denominated asset portfolios and the uncovered foreign investments reduce their portfolios' overall riskiness, the foreign-currency-denominated assets will be associated with a negative risk premium (a discount) in the sense that investors would be willing to pay a certain amount to obtain the reduced portfolio risk.[14]

The existence of an exchange risk premium (or discount) deeply influences international financial equilibrium and the determination of domestic-foreign interest rates. The existence of an exchange risk premium implies that the uncovered interest parity condition must be modified to

$$i = i^* + x - R \tag{12}$$

[13] For an excellent, although somewhat advanced, exposition of the portfolio balance approach, see J. Frankel, "Monetary and Portfolio-Balance Models of Exchange Rate Determination," in Bhandari and Putnam, op. cit.

[14] The reader may wonder what is the source of real return variability in domestic assets when one is evaluating default-free short-term assets bearing a fixed nominal interest rate. In this case, the source of domestic real return variability is inflation risk. This means that a highly uncertain domestic inflation contributing to portfolio real return variability could make domestic assets riskier than foreign assets. Hence there is no a priori presumption regarding whether domestic assets bear a risk premium or discount.

where R represents the risk premium or discount attached to the addition of foreign investments to asset portfolios in the absence of covering. This foreign exchange premium is positive if foreign investments increase investors' portfolio risk. In that case, the foreign rate of return, as represented by the foreign interest rate, i^*, plus the expected domestic currency depreciation, x, must exceed the domestic interest rate so as to compensate investors for their increased risk taking. Similarly, if the risk premium is negative, foreign investments reduce portfolio risk and domestic interest rates will have to exceed the foreign rate of return, $i^* + x$, to compensate for the relative riskiness of domestic currency-denominated assets.

Obviously, changes in the foreign exchange risk premium will generally influence domestic-foreign interest rate differentials, relative asset demands, and consequently the exchange rate. What factors, then, affect the exchange rate risk premium? One crucial factor[15] is the relative variability of real returns on domestic vis à vis foreign investments. Other things being equal, if foreign real returns become less variable relative to domestic real returns, the risk premium will tend to decline, whereas if foreign real yields become relatively more variable, the risk premium increases. As a matter of fact, one explanation[16] for the appreciation of the German deutsche mark relative to the U.S. dollar during 1978 to 1979 has relied precisely on the presence of a portfolio diversification effect toward the deutsche mark induced by a reduction of real return variability in deutsche-mark-denominated assets relative to U.S. dollar-denominated assets during the mid-1970s. In this situation, investors seeking to minimize risks desired to increase the share of deutsche mark-denominated assets in their portfolios. The consequent capital flows led to an increase in the demand for marks relative to U.S. dollars and a deutsche mark appreciation. Algebraically, this effect appears through a reduction of the exchange risk premium, R. Its influence on exchange rate changes is visualized by noting that equation (12) implies $i - i^* = x - R$, which can be substituted into equation (9) to yield

$$\hat{e} = (\hat{M} - \hat{M}^*) + \phi\,(\hat{Y}^* - \hat{Y}) + \lambda\,(\hat{\pi} - \hat{\pi}^*) - \lambda\,R \qquad (9b)$$

Equation (9b) is identical to equation (9a) except for the additional final term involving the exchange risk premium, R. If equation (9b) is applied to the case of the U.S. dollar–deutsche mark exchange rate, the reduced risk premium, R, associated with the decline of relative real yield variability in favor of deutsche

[15] Details on the determinants of the risk premium are provided by R. Dornbusch, "Exchange Rate Risk and the Macroeconomics of Exchange Rate Determination," in R. Hawkins, R. Levich, and C. Wihlborg, *Internationalization of Financial Markets* (Greenwich, Conn.: JAI Press, 1982); and A. C. Stockman," Risk, Information and Forward Exchange Rates," in J. Frenkel and H. Johnson, eds., *The Economics of Flexible Exchange Rates* (Reading, Mass.: Addison-Wesley Publishing Co., 1978).

[16] As espoused by R. Dornbusch, "Exchange Rate Economics: Where Do We Stand?" in Bhandari and Putnam, op. cit., pp. 61–62.

mark-denominated assets results in an increased U.S. dollar depreciation ($\hat{e}$ increases). The inability of equation (9a) to explain the appreciation of the mark during the period could then be accounted for by the exclusion of the risk premium effect.

A second source of changes in exchange risk premia is changes in the relative net supplies of domestic and foreign bonds. Suppose, for instance, that, due perhaps to relatively high real yield variability, foreign bonds have a positive risk premium attached to them. In this situation, an increase in the net supply of foreign bonds relative to domestic bonds means investors will have to be compensated in order to hold the larger supply of foreign bonds, thus requiring a higher exchange risk premium. It must be understood that the changes in bond supplies influencing the risk premium involve changes in relative net supplies of bonds in the market. If one market participant issues a debt to another, the assets and liabilities will cancel each other out, leaving no net additional supply of bonds. What matters, therefore, is the additional relative supplies of outside assets in the market, such as government bonds.[17] In the example above, with foreign bonds bearing an exchange risk premium, it would be an additional supply of foreign currency-denominated government bonds that would raise the premium. This has crucial implications for the impact of government financing on the economy and, in particular, on the exchange rate. Suppose, for instance, that growing budget deficits have forced foreign authorities to borrow in the market by issuing foreign currency-denominated government bonds. The resulting rise in the relative net supply of foreign bonds increases the foreign exchange risk premium and therefore induces foreign interest rates to rise relative to domestic interest rates; that is, the term R in equation (12) increases. Therefore, as equation (9b) shows, a domestic currency appreciation occurs, or, what is the same, a foreign currency depreciation. From an exchange risk perspective, bigger domestic budget deficits financed by increased borrowing will tend to depreciate domestic currency.

A third way by which the risk premium can be influenced is through changes in relative wealth. In general, assuming that a larger fraction of domestic wealth is held in domestic assets relative to foreign assets, an increase in domestic wealth relative to foreign wealth will raise the demand for domestic securities relative to foreign securities and will increase the risk premium required by investors to hold foreign securities. Similarly, an increase in foreign wealth relative to domestic wealth will result in a decrease of the exchange risk premium. The implication is that rising (or declining) domestic wealth relative to foreign wealth will be associated with an appreciation (or depreciation) of domestic currency. In addition, whenever current account balance surpluses (or deficits) are associated with rising (or declining) domestic wealth relative to foreign

---

[17] This assumes that government bonds are considered net wealth by the private sector. See J. A. Frankel, "The Diversifiability of Exchange Risk," *Journal of International Economics* (August 1979).

wealth, one could then link such surpluses (deficits) with domestic currency appreciation (depreciation). The portfolio balance approach thus "puts back the current account balance into exchange rate determination."[18]

Empirical studies examining the connection between the current account balance and exchange rate changes indeed find surpluses (or deficits) associated with currency appreciation (or depreciation). As a matter of fact, both the depreciation of the U.S. dollar and the appreciations of the deutsche mark and yen during 1978 have been strongly correlated to the U.S. current account balance deficit and the German and Japanese current account surpluses over the period.[19] Apparently, however, it is only unexpected current account surpluses or deficits that influence the exchange rate, with the impact of anticipated surpluses or deficits already embodied in exchange rates. The next section examines the nature and evidence of the effect of unanticipated economic events on the exchange rate.

15–7   NEWS AND ANNOUNCEMENT EFFECTS IN THE FOREIGN EXCHANGE MARKET

The asset market approach asserts that new information affecting expectations regarding future exchange rate changes will immediately influence the current exchange rate. Political events provide a dramatic illustration of this proposition. When President Ronald Reagan was shot in 1982, for instance, the possibility of his death raised serious doubts as to the success and continuation of the tough anti-inflation contractionary monetary policy stance at the time. These doubts sent the U.S. dollar tumbling down in foreign exchange markets. In this particular case, later news eliminated any expectations as to a possible reversal of the government's policies. It is apparent, however, that lasting political events, such as an administration shakeup, or shifting foreign policy stances, will influence economic policy and will therefore have some bearing on the exchange rate.

Our earlier analysis in this chapter—and in earlier discussions—suggests

---

[18] As described in previous chapters, the exchange rate adjusts to eliminate balance of payments disequilibria. Since, under a high degree of capital mobility, the current account will be swamped by international capital movements in the balance of payments, standard short-run open economy macroeconomics developed during the 1950s and 1960s proceeded to emphasize the role of capital mobility in exchange rate adjustment with the consequent neglect of the role of the current account. During the 1970s, however, the asset market approach proceeded to note the association between the current account and wealth adjustments, returning the current account to the picture. See P. Kouri, "The Exchange Rate and the Balance of Payments in the Short-Run and in the Long-Run: A Monetary Approach," *Scandinavian Journal of Economics* (May 1976); R. Dornbusch and S. Fischer, "Exchange Rates and the Current Account," *American Economic Review* (December 1980).

[19] See J. Frankel, "Monetary and Portfolio-Balance Models of Exchange Rate Determination," in Bhandari and Putnam, op. cit., pp. 92–95.

some leading economic variables that can be watched closely to determine possible changes in the economy and, particularly, in exchange rates. News regarding these variables can be expected to give rise to substantial action in foreign exchange markets. First of all, consider the current account balance. As noted in the previous section, current account balance surpluses (deficits) that are associated with rising (declining) domestic wealth relative to foreign wealth will generally give rise to domestic currency appreciation (depreciation). Indeed, substantial foreign exchange market trading and significant exchange rate changes are frequently observed in response to the release by the government of figures on the U.S. current account balance. Furthermore, it seems that it is the unanticipated component of the current account figures that is associated with the exchange rate changes. Unanticipatedly large announced current account deficits are observed to generate immediate U.S. dollar depreciation, while unexpected surpluses are usually connected to U.S. dollar appreciation.[20]

A second factor influencing exchange rate changes regards budget deficits. By increasing net supplies of domestic bonds relative to foreign bonds, increased government borrowing to cover those deficits reduces foreign exchange risk premia and induces domestic currency depreciation. Indeed, U.S. budget deficit announcements or pronouncements tend to have a strong effect on exchange rates, with unanticipatedly large domestic budget deficits—relative to foreign budget deficits—tending to weaken the value of the dollar.[21]

Another variable whose announcements appear to generate substantial action in foreign exchange markets is the growth of the domestic money supply. The Federal Reserve announces on Friday afternoons the Fed's estimates of the money supply growth for the week ending 9 days earlier. Usually, unexpectedly large money supply growth figures tend to be associated with dollar appreciation in foreign exchange markets and with increases of U.S. nominal interest rates. Conversely, unanticipatedly low reported money supply growth figures are usually connected to U.S. dollar depreciation and lower nominal interest rates. Notice that these figures appear to contradict the standard dictum that higher domestic monetary growth should lead to a dollar depreciation and to lower nominal interest rates. This apparent inconsistency has been referred to as the "money supply announcements puzzle." Note, however, that the money supply growth figures reported by the Federal Reserve do not actually change the *current* rate of growth of the money supply but refer to the past rate of money growth. In other words, the announcement must alter economic variables—

---

[20] R. Dornbusch finds that an unanticipated current account surplus in the U.S. of $1 billion is worth half a percent of dollar appreciation; see his "Exchange Rate Economics: Where Do We Stand?" in Bhandari and Putnam, eds., op. cit., pp. 55–60; see also P. Hooper and J. Morton, "Fluctuations in the Dollar: A Model of Nominal and Real Exchange Rate Determination," *Journal of International Money and Finance* (January 1982).

[21] See P. Isard, "An Accounting Framework and Some Issues for Modeling How Exchange Rates Respond to the News," in J. A. Frenkel, ed., *Exchange Rates and International Macroeconomics* (Chicago: University of Chicago Press, 1983).

exchange rates, interest rates—purely through its effects on the expectations that agents form about the future.

One interpretation[22] is that an unexpectedly high rate of growth of the money supply pushes upward the agents' expectations regarding future inflation. This is consistent with the observed rise of domestic nominal interest rates but appears to be inconsistent with the noted appreciation of the dollar: Rising domestic nominal interest rates reduce money demand and would depreciate domestic currency. An alternative explanation is that an unexpectedly high reported rate of growth of the past money supply generates expectations in investors that, in response, the Federal Reserve will tighten future growth of the money supply so as to maintain current target rates of monetary growth to which the Federal Reserve subscribes. Expectations of future monetary tightness then tend to raise domestic real interest rates. This view is consistent with both the observed rise of domestic nominal interest rates and the appreciation of the dollar in response to high money growth figures: A rise in real interest rates induces capital to flow into the economy, and the domestic currency then appreciates in value.

15–8   FITTING THE PIECES TOGETHER: THE ASSET MARKET APPROACH TO THE EXCHANGE RATE AND SHORT-RUN MACROECONOMIC THEORY

We have now dissected in some detail the nature, implications, and empirical evidence regarding the asset market approach to the exchange rate. In this section, we shall gain some perspective on how this approach fits into the overall scheme of open economy macroeconomics and exchange rate theory. To simplify the exposition, we shall concentrate on examining how the monetary approach fits into the structural scheme of macroeconomics.[23]

How does the monetary approach relate to the analysis of exchange rate determination we learned in Part IV?[24] In our general framework of analysis developed earlier, the equilibrium exchange rate was determined jointly with

[22] For a discussion of the "money supply announcements puzzle" and alternative explanations, see C. Engle and J. Frankel, "Why Money Announcements Move Interest Rates: An Answer From the Foreign Exchange Market," Mimeo., 1982; B. Cornell, "The Money Supply Announcements Puzzle: Review and Interpretation," *American Economic Review* (September 1983).

[23] An advanced exposition of the points made in this section is made by T. Gylfason and J. F. Helliwell, "A Synthesis of Keynesian, Monetary, and Portfolio Approaches to Flexible Exchange Rates," National Bureau of Economics Research, Working Paper No. 949 (July 1982). For an integration of monetary and portfolio balance considerations into a comprehensive structural open economy macroeconomics framework, see P. Allen and P. B. Kenen, *Asset Markets and Exchange Rates: Modelling an Open Economy* (Cambridge, England: Cambridge University Press, 1980).

[24] The answer to this question is analogous to the one we provided in our study of the monetary approach to the balance of payments in Section 14–8. The reader may want to refer to it for more details.

equilibrium income, prices, interest rates, and so forth, by means of the following relationships: a money market equilibrium condition, an aggregate demand relationship, an aggregate supply equation, and a balance of payments equilibrium condition

$$B = T(q, Y) + K(r) = 0 \qquad (13)$$

stating that, under a free float, the exchange rate will adjust to guarantee balanced payments. This last condition, however, provides a view of the relationship between, say, domestic income and the exchange rate very different from that stated by the monetary approach. From its perspective, an increase in domestic income, Y, raises imports and tends to deteriorate the trade balance, all else being constant. The exchange rate would then have to increase to assure external balance. In other words, higher U.S. income growth reduces the value of the dollar. The monetary approach to the exchange rate suggests the opposite view: An increase of domestic income raises domestic money demand and tends to raise the value of the dollar. In other words; higher U.S. income strengthens the U.S. dollar. Why this divergence in viewpoints?

It is apparent that what the monetary approach does is to pick one relationship—the money market equilibrium condition—out of a set of relationships establishing the economy's equilibrium. It then proceeds to study in detail the connections between the exchange rate and other economic variables as determined by the money market equilibrium condition. The balance of payments equilibrium equation (13), on the other hand, singles out another particular relationship from the package of conditions required to establish equilibrium in the economy and, again, examines its specific implications as to the connections among exchange rates, income, and so forth. As it turns out, the implications obtained this way are opposite to those yielded by looking at the money market equilibrium condition. This does not mean, however, that the two points of view are mutually exclusive. Just as in the simple demand and supply model of price, P, and output, Q, determination, there is a demand curve (or equation) that establishes a negative relationship between P and Q and a supply curve (or equation) that establishes a positive connection between P and Q without their being mutually inconsistent, so the two relationships between the exchange rate and income implied by the monetary approach as given by equation (4a), and the balance of payments equilibrium equation (13), are not inconsistent with each other.

As a matter of fact, just as we can draw demand and supply curves showing the opposite connections between P and Q implied by the supply and demand relationships, we can also draw curves showing how the monetary approach and equation (13) depict different relationships between income, Y, and the exchange rate, e. In Figure 15–4, the MM curve shows the negative connection between e and Y established by the money market equilibrium condition, while the KK curve shows the positive association between e and Y implied by balance

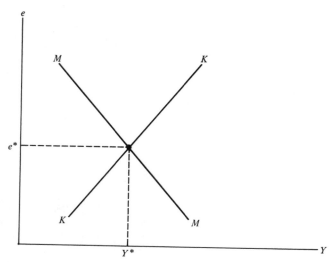

FIGURE 15–4. Simultaneous Determination of Income and the Exchange Rate

of payments equilibrium, equation (13). Now, utilizing again the supply–demand analogy, just as the equilibrium price and output in a market are determined by the intersection of demand and supply curves, one can look at the intersection of the *KK* and *MM* curves as establishing the levels of the exchange rate and income consistent with the general equilibrium of the economy. The equilibrium exchange rate, *e**, and income, *Y**, are consistent with both monetary equilibrium and the balance of payments equilibrium condition (13).

It can now be seen that stating income and the exchange rate are negatively related, as given by the money market equilibrium condition, just refers to the relationship between the exchange rate and income along the *MM* curve. This provides us with information about the money market but does not necessarily show us how equilibrium income and the exchange rate are related in the economy. To determine these relationships, we have to examine not only the money market equilibrium condition, but also the other conditions establishing equilibrium in the economy, one of which is represented by equation (13). Geometrically, the equilibrium *e* and *Y* are determined jointly by *KK* and *MM* and not by *MM* alone. Similarly, the positive relationship between income and the exchange rate postulated by equation (13) corresponds geometrically to how *e* and *Y* are related along the *KK* curve, and again does not tell us how the equilibrium income and the exchange rate are related in the economy.

In a broader context, it can be concluded that, when evaluating the implications of, and the evidence regarding, the asset market approach,[25] the results

---

[25] For further details on the statistical problems involved in estimating one relationship—the monetary or portfolio balance equilibrium—out of a whole structural set of relationships establishing the economy's equilibrium, see Section 14–8.

can shed light on the asset market relationship between exchange rates and other variables but not necessarily on how equilibrium exchange rate changes and income are related in the economy.

15–9 SUMMARY

1. Being the relative price of two moneys, the exchange rate depends not only on the demand and supply of domestic money, but also on the demand and supply of foreign money. Exchange rate adjustments are therefore dependent on changes in both domestic and foreign variables and cannot be determined independently of the behavior of foreign economies or the actions of foreign governments.

2. The monetary approach adopts a point of view in which exchange rates adjust to assure money market equilibrium in the open economy, whereas balance of payments surpluses and deficits carry out that role in a fixed exchange rate economy. The monetary approach to the exchange rate is to a floating exchange regime what the monetary approach to the balance of payments is to a fixed exchange rate system. According to the monetary approach, given fixed relative money supplies, factors increasing (or decreasing) domestic money demand relative to foreign money demand will raise (or lower) the value of domestic currency. For instance, a reduction of domestic interest rates relative to foreign nominal rates raises relative domestic money demand and appreciates the value of domestic currency. Similarly, the higher domestic income is relative to foreign income, the higher the value of domestic currency, ceteris paribus.

3. A key factor accounting for divergencies of the exchange rate predictions of the monetary approach from actual exchange rates is the fact that predicted exchange rates are the joint result not only of the monetary approach's hypothesis regarding money market equilibrium, but also of the purchasing power parity assumption used to relate exchange rates and prices. The empirical evidence available shows that both the absolute and the relative versions of purchasing power parity (PPP) fail to hold on a systematic basis over time. If the relationship between the exchange rate and relative prices utilized is to have any empirical basis, its computation must be modified to allow for deviations from PPP.

4. "News" relevant to the formation of expectations regarding future domestic and foreign inflation will immediately be reflected in changes in the spot exchange rate. As a result, a significant component of exchange rate changes is uncertain, moving along the unpredictable path induced by new events and information. An event leading to higher anticipated inflation, for instance, will be associated with higher domestic interest rates, reducing domestic real money demand and requiring a reduction in the value of domestic currency to sustain market equilibrium.

5. Currency substitution arises when residents of different countries hold a portfolio of currencies. Changes in economic variables may then alter the desired share of each currency in that portfolio, leading to changes in relative money demands. A crucial factor in determining the proportion of total money balances that domestic and foreign residents wish to hold in domestic money relative to foreign money is the opportunity cost of holding domestic money relative to foreign money, represented by the anticipated rate of depreciation of domestic currency.

6. Currency substitution has essential implications for the functioning of both fixed and flexible exchange rates. Under fixed exchange rates, growing expectations of domestic currency devaluation can generate massive currency substitution away from domestic money and could in the process wipe out the international reserves of the Central Bank. Under flexible exchange rates, expected depreciations of domestic currency may induce domestic and foreign residents to switch their cash holdings from domestic to foreign currency. The resulting decline in the demand for domestic money relative to foreign money would then immediately depreciate domestic currency. This effect of anticipated exchange rate changes in shifting the demand for money out of domestic and into foreign currency operates in addition to the effect of expected currency depreciation in increasing domestic interest rates and shifting the demand for money out of domestic money and into bonds.

7. A currency will bear an exchange risk premium or discount depending on whether additional funds invested in assets denominated in that currency increase or decrease the risk of investors' portfolios. The exchange risk premium can change as a result of changes in the distribution of asset returns, in relative supplies of assets denominated in different currencies, and in the relative wealth of domestic and foreign investors.

8. The monetary approach picks one relationship—the money market equilibrium condition—out of a set of relationships establishing the economy's equilibrium and analyzes the connections between the exchange rate and other economic variables as determined by that condition. This does not exclude alternative approaches to the exchange rate based on other equilibrium relationships in the economy.

PROBLEMS

1. Assess the evidence on alternative models of exchange rate behavior and on the monetary approach to the exchange rate in particular. Which factors can account for deviations from the predictions of these models? Support your analysis with specific real-world examples.

2. Royalia is a developing country that trades only with another developing country, Glutonia. Currently, Royalia had a wide range of exchange controls and uses various different exchange rates for different balance of payments transactions. The government is seeking to eliminate all of its controls and to fix an across-the-board exchange rate for all international transactions.

Royalia's governor asks you to tell him at which exchange rate the country should fix the value of the royalian (Royalia's currency) vis à vis the glutonian (Glutonia's currency). You decide, based on your reading of Chapter 15, to calculate the exchange rate predicted by the monetary approach. The following information is provided by the governor's statistical office regarding Royalia's real money demand relative to Glutonia's (Glutonia's variables in asterisks):

$$\frac{L}{L*} = \frac{Y}{Y*} \, 1.5 \, (i - i*)$$

with all symbols as in the text. You also find out the following information:
(a) Royalia's money supply consists of 500 million royalians.
(b) Glutonia's money supply consists of 250 million glutonians.
(c) Royalia's real income is five times that of Glutonia.
(d) Royalia's interest rate is 10%; Glutonia's is 5%.
What exchange rate (in royalians per glutonian) would you recommend be set? With what caveats?

3. You are forecasting exchange rate changes between the dollar and the German deutsche mark over the next year. You are told that, over the period of concern, relative money demand between Germany and the United States will change according to:

$$\hat{L}* - \hat{L} = 0.75 \, (\hat{Y}* - \hat{Y}) + 0.10 \, (i - i*)$$

with all variables as defined in the text and with asterisks denoting German variables. The following next-year forecasts are available:
U.S. money supply growth: 10%.
German money supply growth: 5%.
U.S. real income growth: 2%.
German real income growth: 5%.
U.S nominal interest rate: 12%.
German nominal interest rate: 10%.
(a) By how much, in percentage terms, would you forecast the U.S. dollar–deutsche mark exchange rate will change over the next year? Will the mark depreciate or appreciate? (HINT: Assume that you are a hardened monetarist.)
(b) What factors could make your forecast inaccurate? Explain.

4. Consider a small country that faces exogenously given external prices, $P*$. Assuming that $M/P = L(i, Y)$, obtain the exchange rate as a function of $P*$ and the values of the domestic money supply, income, and interest rate. (HINT: Assume that $P = eP*$.) What is the role of foreign price disturbances, foreign monetary policies, and changes in the levels of foreign income and interest rates on the determination of the exchange rate?

5. "Since exchange rates reflect anticipated future events, they can only change

as a consequence of "news," that is, of new developments and information not already available and incorporated in the exchange rate. Consequently, exchange rates follow a random walk. Algebraically, $P_{t+1} = P_t + U_t$, where U_t reflects new information and is statistically independent of P_t and of its own past values." Evaluate this statement. Consider explicitly the empirical evidence supporting or rejecting it.

6. Private forecasters and government agencies are predicting large and persistent U.S budget deficits during the next 5 years. What is the implication of this prediction for the value of the dollar in foreign exchange markets. In answering the question, consider alternative scenarios regarding the monetization of the debt, foreign monetary policies, and so forth.

7. "If foreign real returns become less variable relative to domestic real returns, the exchange risk premium for foreign assets will tend to decline, while if foreign real yields become relatively more variable, then the risk premium increases." Evaluate this statement.

8. It is often stated that wealth influences money demand. Assuming that it does, in what way would including wealth in money demand functions affect exchange rate determination? In other words, what effects would changes in domestic and foreign wealth have on the exchange rate, holding everything else constant? Try to develop a monetary model of exchange rate determination and to derive an equation that you could estimate statistically to determine the effects of relative wealth on the exchange rate of the dollar vis à vis a foreign currency.

9. Consider the attached clipping (reprinted by permission of *The Wall Street Journal*, © Dow Jones & Company, Inc., All Rights Reserved, New York, Monday, October 4, 1982, p. 36) describing the immediate behavior of the U.S. dollar exchange rate in response to the money supply announcement made by the Federal Reserve the previous Friday. Explain it in detail and give alternative explanations if possible, including the one you believe the most.

Rise in Money Supply Pushes Dollar Higher; Gold Also Increases

A WALL STREET JOURNAL *News Roundup*

An unexpected $400 million rise in the U.S. money supply in the latest week pushed the U.S. dollar sharply higher Friday. Gold also rose, but on the earlier expectations.

Most traders had anticipated a fall in the money supply, which could pave the way for lower American interest rates. But when the increase was announced, the dollar quickly broke out of the narrow range in which it had traded most of the day.

"The number was a real shocker," one New York dealer said. He said it was especially jolting to dealers who had sold the dollar in anticipation that the West German mark would strengthen dramatically with the ousting of the Social Democratic government.

CURRENCY RATES

	New York Fri.	Home Mkt. Fri.	New York Thur.
(In U.S. dollars)			
British pound	1.6925	1.6973	1.6955
Canadian dollar	0.8087	0.8090	0.8089
(In foreign units to U.S. dollar)			
French franc	7.1425	7.1300	7.1325
Japanese yen	269.88	269.00	268.50
Swiss franc	2.1830	2.1700	2.1700
West German mark	2.5358	2.5223	2.5263

Based on average of late buying and selling rates
Home markets: London, Toronto, Paris, Tokyo, Zurich and Frankfort.

GOLD PRICES
(In U.S. dollars per troy ounce)

Camex Fri.	London PM Fri.	London AM Fri.	Camex Thur.
406.80	402.00	397.75	398.50

Camex based on settlement price for gold for delivery in current month on Commodity Exchange in New York.
London based on morning and afternoon price fixing of five major dealers.

The government was removed, but the mark rose only slightly, leading many analysts to conclude that the German currency could be in for more trouble. The mark currently is trading at about a 14-month low against the dollar.

In early trading in Tokyo Monday, the dollar rose against the Japanese currency to 270.775 yen from 269.88 in New York Friday.

Interdependence in the World Economy

PART VI

CHAPTER 16

The International Monetary System: History and Controversies

Economic transactions between residents of different countries require some sort of arrangement to effectuate payments and settle the trade or exchange involved. This is not a trivial task, since the required arrangements have to cut across the diverse political regimes, legal systems, and customary ways of doing business in different countries. In antiquity, trade among reigns was settled in kind through barter. Sovereigns would exchange cattle for wheat or send a shipment of timber for oil or grains. Direct barter of goods gave way to monetary arrangements when some commodities, particularly metals, began to command a general acceptability as a form of payment in different regions, assuming the role of commodity monies. In modern times, the inconvenience of international barter has been avoided by a wide array of monetary arrangements ranging from black markets in foreign exchange operating at the margin of the official or legal framework to multilateral agreements embracing dozens of countries and supervised by international organizations.

It has been said that the international monetary system is like a traffic light network, in that one usually takes it for granted except when it breaks down. The analogy is quite appropriate, since the international monetary system— the collection of conventions, rules, procedures, and institutions that govern financial relations among nations—usually remains in the background of international affairs, with banks, investors, speculators, and other international traders in full control of its day-to-day activities. It is when international monetary arrangements are in disarray that we suddenly become painfully aware of them. On these occasions, as when the dollar ceased to be accepted as payment abroad in 1971, or during the overall 1971 to 1973 period, when the Bretton Woods regime collapsed and was replaced with a new set of international monetary procedures, the international monetary system suddenly becomes visible and makes the headlines. Perhaps because the international monetary system is indeed

505

crisis-prone and is subject to violent shakedowns from time to time it is a recurrent theme in economic history.

Our previous analysis has dealt with specific facets of the international monetary system. Witness our discussion of foreign exchange markets in Chapter 1, international banking and Eurodollars in Chapter 3, and our examination of macroeconomic adjustment under alternative exchange rate regimes in Parts III and IV. Most of the time, however, the international monetary system was taken as exogenously given, and attention was focused on specific aspects of its operation. The present chapter and the following chapter change gear in that the international monetary system finally gets to the center of the stage and becomes the endogenous variable to be explained. In this vein, we offer a broad comparative perspective on alternative monetary regimes that stresses the historical evolution of international monetary arrangements, critically evaluates alternative views on the proper design of an international monetary system, and discusses specific reform proposals regarding the current regime. The role of the main international organizations and agencies facilitating the global operation of the system is also examined. This chapter begins by taking us back in time to the early history of monetary arrangements and up to the final collapse of the Bretton Woods system in early 1973. In Chapter 17 we shall focus on the current set of international monetary arrangements and future prospects.

16-1   COMMODITY STANDARDS AND THE PLIGHT OF BIMETALLISM

From antiquity to modern times, city-states and countries generally operated on a *specie commodity standard,* in which metals—predominantly gold and silver—made up the bulk of the circulating media of the economy. Although gold and silver initially circulated mostly in raw form or in bars and rings, the monetary innovation of standardization and certification by means of official coinage had been introduced by 600 B.C. Coinage facilitated transactions and saved traders the time and effort of weighing and assessing metal values, substituting instead the simple task of counting stamped coins. Coins were stamped according to their metal worth in weight and fineness, and these qualitites were guaranteed by the sovereign.[1]

That gold and silver have been particularly favored relative to other metals throughout history is not surprising when one takes into account the many attributes making them most suitable as commodity money. These include scarcity, durability, transportability, divisibility, homogeneity, and consistency of quality. The acceptability of these metals as money was also aided by the fact that they were widely recognized to have value in nonmonetary uses (e.g., jew-

---

[1] An interesting etymological note is that weight is associated with the names of many of today's currencies. The British *pound sterling* originally denoted a pound of silver of a certain fineness. Similarly, the *mark* was originally a unit of weight, the Italian *lira* derives from the Latin term for pound, and *peso* means weight in Spanish. The word *dollar* is a corruption of the Germanic *thaler,* first coined in Joachims*thal* (Valley of Joachim) during the 16th century.

elry, industrial), they enjoyed a relatively stable value in terms of other commodities, and their quality could be verified or certified by a qualified expert, or by biting them in the absence of better means.

In their purest form, specie commodity standards operated on the basis of full-bodied coins, the monetary value of which equaled the value of the metals they contained.[2] This generally meant that, when the price of gold changed relative to the price of silver, so would the rate at which silver and gold coins were exchanged for each other. Even though sovereigns minted their own coins bearing a particular stamp as evidence of their metallic content, the counterfeiting of coins was frequently undertaken by mixing gold or silver with other, less valuable, metals. Sovereigns themselves frequently reduced the gold (or silver) content of the coins they minted, a practice called *debasement*. Coin debasement, the predecessor of the modern devaluation of a currency, usually led to a loss of the coin's value.

What was the effect, in a monetary system based on commodity monies, of the simultaneous circulation of full-bodied money and debased coins of the same denomination, both often similarly stamped? The British series of debasements during the period 1540 to 1560 clearly illustrates the result: Debased coins drove the fuller-bodied ones out of circulation.[3] The reason for this outcome stemmed directly from the official imposition of the same nominal value to debased and full-bodied coins, even if they differed in metallic content. Debased money was overvalued as a medium of exchange, since it was assigned a higher face value than its metal content justified. Conversely, fuller-bodied money was relatively undervalued as a medium of exchange. For that reason, people holding both types of coins would effectuate payments by means of debased coins, retaining for their own accumulation fuller-bodied ones, whose greater value in metal made them a better store of value. Fuller-bodied coins could also be melted to be sold as metal, exported, or even sent to the coinage to be exchanged or coined into new, debased coins.[4] The end product was that debased money—

---

[2] In practice (specie) commodity standards functioned as a combination of full-bodied and token coins, the monetary value of which exceeds their value as metals. Token coins, often made from copper, bronze, or iron, facilitated everyday transactions in small sums and were a preferred choice for small change. Currently, only token coins are issued by the U.S. government. The American quarter, for instance, is worth 25 cents as a medium of exchange, but its metallic value is far less than that.

[3] Similar to the effects of a devaluation, the debasements over this period were accompanied by substantial price inflation. For more details, see J. D. Gould, *The Great Debasement* (New York: Oxford University Press, Inc., 1970).

[4] Official mints stood ready to accept metals—either bullion or old coins—to be minted or reminted into new, debased coins. Old coins could then be exchanged for a higher number of debased coins, with the precise quantity determined by the metallic content of the old coins vis à vis the new coins. People could therefore exchange their old coins to acquire the new coins, with which they could then carry out transactions. Note, however, that the sovereign would charge a seignorage fee on the creation of the new coins. The revenues so obtained were a gain for the sovereign, a side product of its monopoly over money creation.

overvalued as a medium of exchange—would remain in circulation, while full-bodied coins—undervalued as a medium of exchange—would disappear.

The notion that overvalued money drives undervalued money out of circulaion when they bear the same face value, popularly expressed as "bad money drives out good," has come to us under the heading of *Gresham's law*. This was precisely the reasoning followed by Thomas Gresham (1529–1579) to explain why British circulating media had been reduced to debased money by 1560 (following substantial coin debasements from 1542 to 1551), and to convince Queen Elizabeth I to replace all those debased coins with newly minted full-bodied coins. Actually, a coin reform in which debased coins were retired from circulation and substituted by newly minted full-bodied coins did take effect in 1560 and 1561.

On a quite different front, the U.S. experience under bimetallism from 1792 to 1861 also sheds light on Gresham's law. The Coinage Act of 1792 adopted the dollar as the U.S. monetary unit and gave it a fixed value in terms of both gold and silver, thus officially establishing a *bimetallic standard* in the United States. The dollar was set equal to 24.75 grains of fine gold and 371.25 grains of fine silver, implying that a troy ounce[5] (480 grains) of gold was worth $19.394 and a troy ounce of silver $1.293. Under this system, the U.S. mint stood ready to convert, at a nil seignorage charge, each ounce of gold it was offered into $19.394. Similarly, each ounce of silver would command $1.293 at the mint. This established a mint price of gold in the United States 15 times that of an equivalent amount of silver. The mint ratio of 15:1 was approximately equal to the prevailing ratio of the market values of gold and silver bullion at the time, but toward the end of the century the market price of silver fell. Furthermore, other countries, such as France in 1803, established a bimetallic standard with a mint ratio of 15.5:1. As a result, gold could command more silver abroad than in the United States. One could then gather 15 ounces of silver in the United States, exchange them locally for an ounce of gold, and export the gold so obtained to get $15\frac{1}{2}$ ounces of silver abroad. This operation could yield a net profit of $\frac{1}{2}$ ounce of silver, transaction costs aside, and created an incentive to ship silver into the United States and export gold abroad. Furthermore, Americans effectuating payments abroad found it cheaper to pay in gold (which had a higher relative value abroad), while foreigners found it cheaper to pay in silver for their spending in the United States. In effect, gold was undervalued, and silver overvalued, as means of payments in the United States. Under these conditions Gresham's law operated quite efficiently. Gold disappeared from circulation and the United States, while officially on a bimetallic standard, effectively ended up on a monometallic silver standard. In other words, overvalued silver drove gold out of circulation in the United States. These were

---

[5] A troy ounce equals 480 grains, or one-twelfth of a pound. Troy weights are commonly used for gold, silver, and other metals and should not be confused with the usual avoirdupois ounce, which equals 437.5 grains, or one-sixteenth of a pound.

the conditions prevailing until 1834, when Congress raised the mint price of gold from $19.394 to $20.67 per ounce, leaving the mint price of silver unchanged, in an attempt to reestablish the bimetallic standard. This altered the U.S. mint ratio up to 16:1, but the mint ratios abroad remained at 15.5:1, and this time Gresham's law operated in reverse. Gold was now overvalued in the United States and drove silver out of circulation, placing the United States on a de facto monometallic gold standard.

The United States continued to operate on a de jure bimetallic but de facto monometallic standard up to 1861. Throughout this period, paper money and bank deposits were gradually increasing in importance relative to coins in the U.S. money supply. The rigid link of the monetary system to metals, however, remained untainted as the dollar was defined in terms of, and freely convertible into, gold and silver. If, for instance, you were holding $20.67 in currency, the U.S. government would freely convert that amount into an ounce of gold. This convertibility, however, was suspended in 1861 at the start of the Civil War. After the Civil War, there was a return to gold convertibility but not to silver, effectively obstructing an eventual return to a bimetallic standard in the United States. The decision taken in 1879 to resume convertibility of the U.S. dollar into gold, but not silver, was the major single step in establishing a gold standard in the United States. This move was fraught with great quarrels and intrigue and did not go without the strong opposition of vocal silver proponents. Bimetallism represented a price support scheme for silver, and its replacement by a single gold standard had an obvious negative impact on the powerful silver-mining interests (particularly mine owners) profiting from the scheme. As a result, the issue of bimetallism became a political battleground, partly explaining why in spite of being de facto on a gold standard, the United States did not legally sanction the system until the Gold Standard Act of 1900.

16-2 THE GOLD STANDARD AND ITS RULES

Although Britain operated under a gold standard for most of the nineteenth century, it was not until the 1870s that the gold standard achieved widespread adoption. Most European countries, led by Germany in 1871, moved toward the gold standard during that decade, and the United States followed suit in 1879. By 1880, the gold standard had developed from a domestic standard adopted by a few individual nations to a full-fledged international monetary system with the adherence of major countries. For the next 30 years, until its abandonment after the outbreak of World War I in 1914, the international gold standard reigned supreme and came to incorporate the major trading countries and colonial territories of the time.

The essential features of the operation of a "pure" gold standard can be characterized in terms of three basic rules of the game. First, a country on the gold standard fixes the value of its currency in terms of gold. The government accomplishes this by setting a fixed price of gold in terms of its currency and standing ready to buy or sell gold at that price. This establishes a two-way convertibility between domestic currency or coin and gold. In the case of the United States, for instance, the value of a troy ounce of pure gold was set at $20.67, with the U.S. mint ready to buy or sell gold on demand at that price. With various countries operating under a gold standard, the gold values of any two currencies as set by each country's mints implicitly specify their relative value, referred to as *mint parity* or *mint exchange rate*. Consider, for example, the case of the U.S. dollar and the pound sterling. In the United Kingdom, an ounce of pure gold was set at a value of approximately £4.24. Since the value of an equivalent ounce of gold in the United States was $20.67, the implicit relative value of the dollar in terms of the pound was approximately $4.87 a pound ($20.67/£4.24). In other words, the mint parity between the U.S. dollar and the pound was $4.87 per pound, which remained so throughout the 1880 to 1914 period. Observe that the mint parity exchange rate is an implicit, or imputed, rate of exchange (or relative value) between two currencies. The direct market exchange rate between dollars and pounds, however, did not deviate significantly from mint parities. This was guaranteed by the free flow of gold among countries, as we shall now see.

The second basic rule of a pure gold standard is that imports and exports of gold be allowed to flow freely and unrestricted among countries. Free trade in gold ensured that market exchange rates would not deviate much from the mint exchange rates implied by the gold values of currencies. To illustrate why, let us suppose that the U.S. dollar–pound market exchange rate was equal to $5.00 per pound, which deviates significantly from the mint parity of $4.87 established earlier and determined by a U.S. gold price of $20.67 and a U.K. gold price of £4.24. In this situation, one could buy an ounce of gold in the United States at a cost of $20.67, sell it in the United Kingdom to obtain £4.24, and then exchange these pounds for U.S. dollars in the free market, which yields $21.20. (Multiply £4.24 by the market exchange rate of $5.00 per pound.) In other words, a profit of $1.20 could be made by freely buying and selling an ounce of gold across countries. Of course, such a situation would not be sustainable, as the market exchange rate would decline in response to the flood of profit-seeking arbitrageurs willing to sell pounds in exchange for U.S. dollars. Although the presence of transaction costs, particularly in the shipment of gold, prevented mint parities from precisely fixing market exchange rates, the rates were nevertheless confined within narrow limits—the so-called *gold points*—around mint parities.

The third rule of the pure gold standard specifies that the Central Bank or the monetary authority in charge has to hold gold reserves in a direct relationship to the money notes it issues. These gold reserves allow Central Banks to engage smoothly in their purchases and sales of gold without running into the embarrassing situation of not being able to fulfill a sudden demand for gold on the part of the public. The gold backing provides for a certain amount of gold behind the currency issued, thereby assuring the convertibility of the currency into gold. In its extreme, this rule could take the form of 100% gold backing, in which gold reserves of an amount equal to the domestic currency's worth in gold are held in the monetary authorities' coffers.

The presence of a strict rule connecting gold reserves and money note issues imposes some discipline on monetary expansion in the economy: The Central Bank can issue domestic currency only by acquiring gold from the public. Consequently, the main source of changes in the domestic money supply is given by changes in the amount of gold available to domestic residents. This can arise, first, from production of gold supplied by the domestic mining industry, some of which would be sold directly for the private use of citizens and the rest to the government. In addition, when there is a balance of payments surplus and domestic residents receive gold for their net sales to foreigners, the domestic money supply would also increase. Note that the role of the Central Bank under a pure gold standard is limited to purchasing gold acquired by domestic residents and issuing notes in exchange. It is the discipline imposed on the government by the pure gold standard that has attracted the favor (and candor) of many economists and politicians.[6] At the same time, and for the same reasons, other economists and politicians also oppose the gold standard. Their argument is that to combat the maladies of unemployment and recession, and the ups and downs of the business cycle, an active monetary policy is required—not one that has its hands tied. In spite of all this controversy, when evaluating the real possibility of the reestablishment of the gold standard—or in assessing the actual experience with that regime—one must be aware that the way in which international monetary systems actually operate can differ substantially from the image given by rules or dictums that are never followed in practice. This point must be borne in mind when evaluating the performance of the gold standard, as we do in the next section.

16–3 THE HEYDAY OF THE GOLD STANDARD (1880 TO 1914)

The gold standard regime of 1880 to 1914 is often presented as a smoothly operating system in which countries abided by the key rules of the game mentioned in the previous section. That this was so to a large extent should not

---

[6] As a matter of fact, the return to the gold standard has been a recurrent theme of discussion in both the academic arena and in political circles. See, for instance, L. B. Yeager, *In Search of a Monetary Constitution* (Cambridge, Mass.: Harvard University Press, 1962). More recently, during the 1980s, the interest in the gold standard in political circles (e.g., see Rep. R. Paul and L. Lehrman, *The Case for Gold* (Washington, D.C.: Cato Institute, 1982), was reflected in the appointment of a Commission by the president of the United States to study the possibility of reestablishing to some degree the basic characteristics of a gold standard. The Commission's recommendations were in the negative, although it has been alleged that the members appointed to the Commission might have been stacked against it. The report is available from the U.S. Department of the Treasury, *Report of the Gold Commission,* Washington, D.C., 1982.

be taken to mean that there were no significant exceptions. First, even though the major European countries and the United States adopted and remained on the gold standard during the period, a number of other countries either abandoned the system or otherwise avoided adopting the regime altogether. The turbulent monetary history of Argentina, Mexico, and other Latin American countries at the time, involving shifts in and out of the gold standard with accompanying monetary crises, exchange controls, and exchange rate instability, presents a very different picture from the pastoral image so often displayed of the 1880 to 1914 gold standard regime.

If one takes a world perspective, the gold standard period of 1880 to 1914 was actually characterized by a whole range of international monetary arrangements, all functioning alongside each other. Some countries, for instance, pegged the value of their currencies directly to sterling and held foreign exchange (mostly sterling) reserves to support their parity. Such an arrangement, referred to as a *gold exchange standard,* was based on the convertibility of sterling into gold and the confidence traders had in the use of sterling as an international means of payment. At the time, Great Britain was extremely influential in the world economy (accounting for roughly 10% of world income) and had an even greater role in world trade and investment (e.g., British capital was crucial in financing railroads and industrial development in places as far apart as the United States, Argentina, and India). It is not surprising, then, that sterling became a widely diffused means of payment and the main international reserve of Central Banks in many countries. It was actually possible for Phineas Fogg, Jules Verne's character in *Around the World in Eighty Days,* to pay his expenses with Bank of England notes, which were accepted almost everywhere.

Did countries adhering to the gold standard abide by the rules discussed in the previous section? Consider the fixing of the value of currency in terms of gold. It is impressive that there were no devaluations or revaluations (no changes in mint parities) between the currencies of the United States, United Kingdom, France, and Germany at all during the entire period. This remarkable feat credits the gold standard as being the closest example of a truly fixed exchange rate regime among major countries.[7] As far as the first rule of the gold standard is concerned, the record for the major countries shows it was indeed strictly followed. The second basic rule of a pure gold standard involves the free flow of gold among the participating countries. As far as the period 1880 to 1914 goes, the rule appears to have been followed very closely. Barriers to trade in gold were generally dismantled and exchange or capital controls seldom used. As a matter of fact, a thriving international capital market operated,

---

[7] Although market exchange rates were not fixed directly by these countries and did fluctuate within a narrow band, the efficient operation of the system as well as the numerous improvements in information and communications networks (such as the telegraphic cable) and reductions in transport costs systematically shrank the spread between gold points during the period. The U.S. dollar–sterling market exchange rate, for instance, stayed mostly within the range of $4.84 and $4.90 per pound.

with its nerve center in London, shifting funds across borders quite actively in search of profits.

Contrary to the evidence showing that the first two rules of a pure gold standard were mostly satisfied during the 1880 to 1914 period, the third rule bearing on the connection between gold reserves and the supply of domestic currency does not appear to have been closely followed. Although laws were passed requiring a certain proportion of gold reserves be held to back issues of notes—such as the Bank Act of 1844 in the United States—waivers to the law were frequently drawn. Central Banks often tried to offset the effects of gold flows on the domestic money supply, a venture precisely opposite to the purpose of the laws, and, when necessary, governments would sidestep them in some way. The next section examines the theory of, and evidence on, the connections between gold flows and money supply changes under the gold standard, in addition to relevant macroeconomic issues.

16–4 THE MACROECONOMIC PERFORMANCE OF THE GOLD STANDARD

Proponents of the gold standard argue that, under this regime, the economy has an inherent tendency toward price stability and external balance. First, the requirement that the money created be backed with gold reserves limits the ability of the monetary authorities to print money and puts a brake on the inflationary sprees that undisciplined Central Banks can impose on the economy. As a result, price stability would be more likely. In addition, it is argued, gold flows among countries imply that the system provides an automatic mechanism through which external payments disequilibria can be eliminated. How does this occur?

One of the most discussed aspects of the gold standard is the so-called *price-specie-flow* mechanism proposed by David Hume as a description of the automatic balance of payments adjustment mechanism implicit in the system. Hume's argument rests on the third rule of the pure gold standard in assuming that gold flows are strictly linked to changes in the domestic money supply. Balance of payments deficits associated with net gold payments to foreigners would then reduce the domestic money supply and lead to deflation. With domestic prices declining, the increased competitiveness of domestic products in international markets would result in an improvement of the current account balance and in an eventual elimination of the balance of payments deficit. In other words, the external disequilibrium would be automatically corrected. Similarly, the gold inflows linked to a balance of payments surplus would raise the domestic money supply and lead to inflation. Rising prices of domestic goods would then reduce domestic competitiveness in international markets, deteriorating the current account and eliminating the surplus. Again, the external disequilibria would self-correct.

Hume's price-specie-flow mechanism has the problem of associating balance of payments adjustment with current account balance adjustment. As we have seen many times before, however, the balance of payments is composed of the current account *and* the capital account. As a result, depending on how capital flows behave, the effects of gold flows in adjusting the current account would not necessarily be associated with the elimination of balance of payments disequilibria. Subsidiary mechanisms of capital account adjustment are necessary. One alternative is to connect the changes in the money supply implied by gold flows with interest rate changes. A gold outflow connected to a payments ·deficit would lower the domestic money supply, pressuring domestic interest rates to rise above world levels and inducing incipient capital inflows that offset the initial gold outflows. Similarly, balance of payments surpluses linked to gold inflows would raise the money supply and lower domestic interest rates relative to foreign rates. The consequent capital outflows—and the associated shipment of gold abroad—would then offset the initial inflow of gold.

Clearly, there are various mechanisms through which balance of payments disequilibria under a pure gold standard could be automatically eliminated. Unfortunately, the crucial link in these mechanisms—the link between gold flows and money supplies—does not appear to have held during the actual practice of the gold standard of 1880 to 1914. Laws requiring the backing of currency creation with gold reserves were often waived or not extended to bank deposits, which reduced their effectiveness in controlling money creation. As a matter of fact, the evidence suggests that monetary authorities frequently and actively attempted to offset the contractionary (or expansionary) effect of a gold outflow (or inflow) on the money supply.[8] One way through which this occurred was by sterilization operations in which the Central Bank would decrease its domestic asset holdings in response to acquisitions of gold and increase its domestic assets when gold withdrawals occurred. In general, though, these operations did not result in a full offset of the effects of gold flows on the money supply but only in a partial offset. In addition to sterilization, monetary authorities would frequently use their discount rate—the interest rate charged on loans to private banks or private citizens—to influence domestic credit in the face of the monetary changes associated with gold flows. In conclusion, even though on paper a pure gold standard implies monetary discipline, in actual practice such discipline did not completely materialize during the 1880 to 1914 period. Monetary authorities frequently broke the third rule of the gold standard and engaged in active monetary policy.

It remains true, though, that under the gold standard changes in the supply of gold constituted a major source of variation in the U.S. money supply. Increased domestic production of gold above the level privately demanded was purchased by the monetary authorities and directly increased the money supply.

---

[8] See A. Bloomfield, *Monetary Policy Under the International Gold Standard: 1880–1914* (New York: Arno Press, Inc., 1978) (reprint of 1959 original).

Increased foreign production of gold, however, would also spill over into an increase of the U.S. money supply. Some of the increased expenditures of foreigners in response to their rise in wealth would be spent on domestic goods, resulting in an improvement of the balance of payments. In addition, some of the foreign wealth would end up being invested in the United States, again bringing about an inflow of gold.

The connection between the domestic money supply and the vagaries of gold production under the gold standard means money supply changes are subject to a high degree of uncertainty. Figure 16–1 shows the behavior of the U.S. money supply (M1, as currently defined) growth during the period of 1880 to 1902. As observed, there is a high variability of money supply growth during those years, much of which can be associated with changes in the supply of gold. For instance, the relatively small—even negative—rates of U.S. money growth during the 1890s have been associated with a slow rate of growth of world production during that period, and the higher growth rates after 1896 to the discovery of new gold mines in South Africa in 1895 and the development of new processes for working old gold mines.[9]

The variability of U.S. money supply growth shown in Figure 16–1 suggests that U.S. inflation might also have been highly variable. Still, the picture one obtains from many studies of the gold standard is that it was a period of price stability. Indeed, wholesale commodity prices in Britain and the United States during 1914 were actually slightly lower than those in 1880. Does this mean that, in spite of money growth variability, there was price stability during the period? The answer to this question is obtained by looking at Figure 16–2,

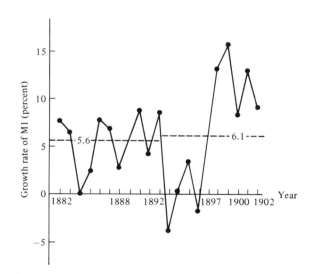

FIGURE 16–1. Money Growth (M1, as currently defined) Under the Gold Standard, 1881 to 1902. (From *Historical Statistics of the World States,* pp. 992–993.)

[9] A. O. Bloomfield, *Monetary Policy Under the International Gold Standard: 1880–1914* (New York: Arno Press, Inc., 1978), p. 21.

FIGURE 16–2.   Behavior of U.S. and U.K. Prices During and After the Gold Standard of 1880–1914 (Wholesale Price Levels). (From R. W. Jastram, *The Golden Constant: The English and American Experience,* New York: John Wiley & Sons, Inc., 1977, reprinted by permission.)

which shows the behavior of an index of U.S. and U.K. wholesale price levels during 1880 to 1935. What is observed is a year-to-year instability of price changes—consistent with the U.S. money growth variability noted earlier—but the absence of a general trend (whether upward or downward) in prices during the 1880 to 1914 period. What can be concluded is that, on the average, the gold standard period of 1880 to 1914 was one of relatively low but highly variable inflation in the United States and the United Kingdom.[10]

Perhaps the strongest case against the popular view on the economic stability of the gold standard period regards the behavior of output growth and employment. On average, the period of 1880 to 1914 was one of respectable growth worldwide. In the United States, for example, the average annual growth rate of GNP was close to 4%. On a per capita basis, though, growth rates were between 1 and 2%. Furthermore, large year-to-year fluctuations were observed. Figure 16–3 shows the striking variability of U.S. unemployment during 1880 to 1914, sinking below 5% during the early 1890s and the mid-1900s yet rising above 15% in-between, during the late 1890s.

The data we have presented on the macroeconomic performance of the gold standard disprove claims that the system was one of remarkable stability. In certain essential economic variables, substantial variability was indeed observed. Still, when assessing the performance of the gold standard as compared to other international monetary systems, what one must evaluate is whether the gold standard performed "better" or "worse" than these other systems. This is a difficult task. First, one has to determine which aspects of the economy are more crucial. The gold standard, for example, generally showed low inflation rates on average as compared with the Bretton Woods system or the current

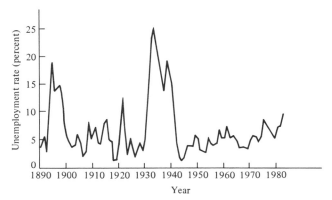

FIGURE 16–3. U.S. Unemployment Rate, 1890 to 1983. (From *Historical Statistics of the United States,* p. 135; and Economic Report of the President, 1984.)

---

[10] For more details on this and other aspects of the classical gold standard, see R. N. Cooper, "The Gold Standard: Historical Facts and Future Prospects," *Brookings Papers on Economic Activity* (1982).

regime of dirty floating. The high unemployment rates of the late 1890s, however, mean the gold standard performed worse on average than the Bretton Woods system in this respect. How does one go about evaluating the relative merits of these accomplishments or failures? Furthermore, undertaking comparisons of this sort makes the mistake of comparing economies whose structure varies significantly among regimes. It is apparent, for example, that the increased role of the government through regulation of the banking system and through government expenditures in the aftermath of the Great Depression made the wild fluctuations in unemployment to which the gold standard was subject less likely.[11] Fiscal policy, as it is known today, was virtually unknown during most of the 1880 to 1914 period of the gold standard. The present fractional reserve banking system was also unknown; even the U.S. Federal Reserve Board was nonexistent for most of the period, being created only in 1913. It is, therefore, not wholly appropriate to compare the gold standard with other regimes through the use of such incomparable situations. Furthermore, in political terms, the 1880 to 1914 period was rather remarkably—and unusually—peaceful, forming part of the so-called Pax Britannica. Comparing the gold standard with other regimes operating in periods of political instability would again result in inappropriate comparisons.

16–5   THE INTERNATIONAL MONETARY SYSTEM DURING THE INTERWAR PERIOD

The outbreak of World War I in 1914 struck a fatal blow to the gold standard, as country after country suspended the convertibility of currency into gold. The system of fixed exchange rates that had operated for almost 35 years gave way to floating exchange rates. The United States maintained gold convertibility of the dollar but, since other currencies were no longer convertible into dollars, the U.S. dollar in effect floated in value against them.

The World War I period saw rising inflation rates as governments oriented their monetary policies toward financing war expenditures. The inflation in Europe, however, was higher than that in the United States, partly because of the delayed formal entrance of the United States into the war (in 1917) and partly because the war was being physically fought in Europe, with obvious disruptive effects on production. The result was increased competitiveness of U.S. products abroad and the rapid growth of U.S. international trade. In addition, the convertibility of the dollar into gold together with the inconvertibility of the European currencies resulted in a growing attractiveness of dollar-dominated assets as a haven for investment purposes. The dollar became increasingly involved in international transactions. Since gold remained at the heart of the

---

[11] See M. Bordo, "The Classical Gold Standard: Lessons from the Past," in M. B. Connolly, ed., *The International Monetary System: Choices for the Future* (New York: Praeger Publishers, Inc. 1982), pp. 251–252.

system, the growing demand for dollars resulted in rising gold inflows to the United States and ballooning U.S. gold reserves.

After World War I, the European countries continued to allow their currencies to float in value; most of them depreciated sharply against the dollar. The float was seen, however, only as a temporary situation and the main question pondered at the time was at which value to reestablish the price of gold in terms of each currency, that is, gold parities. The return to a gold standard at prewar gold prices became a subject of much debate. A number of economists, and prominently Gustav Cassell among them, made use of the idea of purchasing power parity to advocate a return to a price of gold above that prevailing under the prewar (classical) gold standard. They argued that in order to maintain the prewar relationship between gold prices, P_G, and other goods' prices, P, a substantial deflation was necessary. Given that the inflation of the 1910s substantially lowered the price of gold relative to that of other goods' prices (P_G/P declined), an equivalent deflation was necessary to reestablish parity. Otherwise, to spare deflation, the price of gold would have to be reset at a higher level, consistent with the hike in goods market prices.

Contrary to countries that had rapid inflation rates (hyperinflation) during the 1920s—such as Germany and Austria—and eventually set parities of their currencies with gold higher than the prewar levels, the United Kingdom did face some deflation during the early twenties and, when its gold parity was reestablished in the mid-1920s, it was set at its 1913 level. This meant that in spite of the fact that most currencies had been devalued vis-à-vis the dollar, the pound sterling–U.S. dollar exchange rate remained as before the war, $4.8065 per pound.

The reestablishment of gold parities in the mid-1920s led to a rebirth of the gold standard. This 1925 to 1931 version of the gold standard, however, was fraught with difficulties and it was in many ways dissimilar to the classical gold standard. First, goods market prices in the United Kingdom had not returned to prewar levels by 1925 and, as a result, the setting of the prewar gold–sterling parity resulted in an overvalued sterling. By contrast, other countries, such as France, had gone too far in the devaluation of their currency, resulting in undervalued currencies. The established gold parity levels, therefore, did not have the expected stability of those under the classical gold standard. In addition, the 1925 to 1931 gold standard moved much closer to becoming a gold-exchange standard. Many Central Banks no longer maintained the bulk of their international reserves in gold but kept them rather in currencies convertible to gold, especially sterling and, increasingly, dollars. This shift was partly a result of the continued growth of U.S. international trade and investment during the period and the increased use of the dollar in international transactions. It was also associated with a scarcity of gold production relative to demand.

The return to a gold standard during the twenties turned out to be short-lived. The Great Depression of 1929 brought a collapse of banking systems around the world—bankruptcies, panics, and bank closings proliferated—and a grave crisis of confidence in the ability of countries to maintain the convertibility of their currencies into gold. The burden fell especially heavily on the United Kingdom, which went off gold on September 21, 1931. Fixed exchange rates were finally abandoned as other major countries followed suit (the United States in 1933) in suspending gold convertibility. The world monetary system then disintegrated into currency blocs, such as the sterling bloc, dollar bloc, and a bloc of currencies still based on gold, with floating exchange rates among them. What followed was indeed monetary chaos. Dirty floating, nominally pegged exchange rates accompanied by frequent devaluations to improve competitive positions, collapsing currency blocs, multiple agreements directed to reestablish some order to monetary arrangements that were then broken, and so forth, all coexisted. Furthermore, exchange controls, tariffs, and other trade restrictions proliferated. The result was a collapse of international trade and finance that left a deep impression on subsequent generations and established the prevention of such a situation as a main objective of the international monetary system.

16–6   THE BRETTON WOODS SYSTEM (1946 TO 1971)

World War II was still raging in 1941 when the United States and the United Kingdom began a series of bilateral conversations and negotiations that laid the basis for the postwar international monetary order. Alternative plans for reestablishing a workable monetary system were presented and discussed, and differences were gradually settled. The negotiation process culminated in an international monetary conference held in July 1944 at the resort town of Bretton Woods, New Hampshire. This conference, which gathered representatives from 44 countries, turned out to be a major international economic event. It created the International Monetary Fund (IMF),[12] the chief organization in charge of overseeing and monitoring the operation of a new monetary order, and drafted the Articles of Agreement of the IMF, which specified the basic structure and rules of the game of the new regime. The international monetary system so created came to be known as the Bretton Woods system and was to maintain its basic structure until 1971, for almost a quarter of a century after the IMF was organized in 1947.

The IMF's Articles of Agreement stipulated that each participating country would set a fixed value—called *par value*—of its currency in terms of gold (or the U.S. dollar). The par values of two currencies determined the official exchange rate (also called parity) between them. Exchange rate fluctuations were to be limited to a narrow band around the official exchange rate. In other words, participating countries had to adopt a pegged exchange rate regime. However, the Bretton Woods system was not conceived in terms of fixed, immuta-

---

[12] For a detailed discussion of the organization and present role of the IMF in the international monetary system, see Chapter 17.

ble exchange rates in the manner in which the gold standard had operated among major countries from 1880 to 1914. Instead, it was an adjustable-peg system, allowing alterations in official exchange rates—subject to the approval of the IMF—to correct a *fundamental disequilibrium* in the balance of payments. Although the term *fundamental disequilibrium* was never formally defined by the IMF, what was meant in practice was that countries facing chronic payments deficits (or surpluses) and heavy reserve losses (or gains) could alter their exchange rates. The purpose of establishing an adjustable peg system was to attain a balance between the objective of stable exchange rates and the concerns of participating countries with domestic macroeconomic goals. For instance, the expedient of devaluation was left open to correct chronic payments deficits. This, it was hoped, would smooth out the high cost of adjustment toward payments equilibrium in the form of unemployment and recession. The availability of devaluation as a policy tool had also the benefit of reducing the likelihood that exchange controls and other restrictions on trade would be imposed to suppress a payments imbalance, deemed an important objective in light of the experience of the 1930s. Supervision and scrutiny over desired exchange rate changes, on the other hand, tried to prevent competitive devaluations, by means of which some countries attempted to obtain a competitive advantage in international markets at the expense of others.

The key role of gold during the Bretton Woods system was connected to the convertibility of the U.S. dollar into gold at a fixed price. This meant that the United States stood ready to sell gold to foreign Central Banks, but not to private citizens, in exchange for U.S. dollars at a fixed price of $35 per ounce. Aside from the United States, however, countries were not committed to exchanging their money into gold (i.e., their currencies were not convertible into gold). The Bretton Woods system operated on the basis of a *gold-exchange standard.* Under a gold-exchange standard, countries are expected to redeem their currencies into gold-convertible currencies (but not necessarily into gold directly), and Central Bank reserves are held in convertible currencies (but not necessarily in the form of gold itself). Under Bretton Woods, most Central Banks kept a large part of their international reserves in the form of dollar-denominated assets, such as dollar deposits or U.S. Treasury bills. The dollar became the main reserve currency of the system, a role it had been chipping away from the pound sterling ever since World War I.

Exchange rates were maintained within the narrow limits allowed by the International Monetary Fund by means of Central Bank intervention in foreign exchange markets. The U.S. dollar played a predominant role in this respect, since it was used as an intervention currency by foreign Central Banks. For instance, when a depreciating French franc reached the limit allowed by the IMF, the Bank of France would buy francs and sell dollars in exchange so as to support the value of the franc. Conversely, when the franc appreciated relative to the dollar, the Bank of France would sell francs and buy dollars in the foreign exchange markets, supporting the value of the dollar in the process.

In effect, France was in charge of determining the French franc–U.S. dollar exchange rate. The same pattern applied to other foreign countries. The United States, therefore, could not devalue or revalue the dollar vis-à-vis other currencies by itself, that is, the United States was spared the need to intervene in foreign exchange markets in order to keep its exchange rate fixed. Other countries fulfilled that function.

In a nutshell, the Bretton Woods system was an adjustable peg regime operating under a gold exchange standard in which most currencies were convertible into the U.S. dollar and the dollar, in turn, convertible into gold.

16–7   THE ECONOMIC EXPERIENCE UNDER BRETTON WOODS

The aftermath of World War II left the European countries and Japan with both a shortage of international reserves and the need to finance large trade deficits to reconstruct their war-ravaged economies. In 1948 the United States offered the European Recovery Program (ERP)—usually called the Marshall Plan in honor of George C. Marshall, then U.S. Secretary of State—to aid in financing infrastructure, food, basic needs, and the large net exports that the United States incurred abroad (U.S. trade surpluses climbed to 4% of GNP during the later forties).

The generally low levels of international reserves held by the major foreign industrial countries after the war and their large trade deficits with the United States became associated with a massive dollar shortage abroad and with acute balance of payments difficulties for these countries during the late forties and fifties. As a result, most European countries maintained a range of capital controls throughout the fifties, and it was not until 1958 that their currencies really became fully convertible to the dollar.[13] Hence, the Bretton Woods system became fully operational, in the sense of the major countries featuring full convertibility of their currencies into others, particularly U.S. dollars, only during the late fifties.

During the fifties, the United States began to show substantial deficits on an official reserve settlements basis, a pattern that persisted and deteriorated over the next decade. For most of the fifties, U.S. deficits were not generally

[13] The term *convertibility* is used in two different contexts: convertibility into gold and convertibility into other currencies. Only the United States maintained gold convertibility during Bretton Woods. Convertibility into other currencies essentially means that foreign currencies can be freely obtained from Central Banks on demand, at the established exchange rate parities. Convertibility into other currencies for current account transaction purposes was a main goal of Bretton Woods and reached to a large extent early on in the system, but the agreements of the International Monetary Fund allowed more flexibility with regard to the imposition of exchange controls on capital account transactions. This was partly a result of a prevailing feeling that short-run speculative capital flows could be potentially destabilizing and governments should therefore have the freedom to restrict them.

regarded as a problem, since foreign Central Banks desired to accumulate dollar reserves. During the sixties, however, the dollar shortage of the previous decade turned into a dollar glut. Between 1950 and 1970, foreign holdings of dollars rose by $39 billion. The increasing supply of dollars abroad was accompanied by a rapidly shrinking stock of U.S. gold reserves. The gold holdings of the U.S. Treasury declined by $8 billion between 1949 and 1960, a loss whose rate picked up even more during the mid- and late 1960s.

The growth of gold-convertible dollars abroad combined with depletion of U.S. gold reserves gradually eroded confidence in the ability of the United States to sustain sales of gold for dollars in the face of growing purchases of gold on the part of foreign Central Banks and private citizens. The gold convertibility of the U.S. dollar was threatened. Various solutions were proposed, and some actually implemented, to solve this problem. One of them involved restricting the private demand for gold. In general, the post–World War II period saw rising private demand for gold combined with sagging production. If the price of gold had been set in a free market, such events would have led to a rise in the price of gold. With the United States fixing the price of gold at $35, however, the increased demand for gold on the part of the private sector was filled by sales of gold by Central Banks and, in particular, the U.S. Treasury. In order to prevent the continuation of this situation, the U.S. government barred U.S. citizens from buying gold, whether from the U.S. Treasury or from foreign Central Banks. Unfortunately, the same regulations were not adopted by foreign Central Banks, which continued to sell gold to their citizens. The impact of the policy on gold outflows was thus minimal.

An alternative approach would have been to encourage the quantity of gold supplied. To do that, however, an increase in the price of gold relative to the general price level would have been required. With the price of gold fixed at $35, only a deflation—à la gold standard—would have been able to manage a rise in the relative price of gold. Another dead end was reached.

Another experiment was tried in 1968: The so-called *two-tier gold market.* The two-tier gold market consisted of a segmentation of the private and the Central Bank markets for gold. The private market, where the purchases of private citizens and most of the sales of newly mined gold were to be settled, was left free to clear through a flexible price. The Central Bank market for gold, where foreign Central Banks would buy and sell gold from the U.S. Treasury, was to remain transacting at the official $35 price per ounce of gold. The result was that the dollar remained convertible into gold for foreign Central Banks at $35 per ounce, but the private market price rose above that level. Again, the experiment did not stop the outflow of gold from the U.S. Treasury's coffers.

The difficulties faced in controlling the gold shortage and the questions raised by the dollar glut regarding the role of the dollar as an international reserve asset crystallized a movement on the part of some European countries—with

France at the helm—to create an alternative international reserve asset that could serve the functions of the dollar and be as good as gold in international transactions among Central Banks. As early as 1964, France had publicly supported the idea of the creation of a so-called Composite Reserve Unit, which would be made up of major currencies and would be issued by the International Monetary Fund. The original French proposal called for the Composite Reserve Unit to replace the U.S. dollar and sterling as international reserve assets, which was clearly unacceptable to the United States and the United Kingdom. As a result, the proposal was substantially modified before the IMF accepted to create *special drawing rights* (SDRs). When it was created in 1967, an SDR was worth one U.S. dollar and one thirty-fifth ounce of gold. Later on, during the 1970s, the IMF reverted to the original French proposal and assigned a value to the SDR in terms of the currencies of major member countries. The value of SDRs created initially in 1970 was worth $3.1 billion. These were distributed among the Central Banks of member countries, which could use them in their transactions with other Central Banks (SDRs, therefore, did not circulate among the public). Unfortunately, the possible role of SDRs under Bretton Woods could not be determined, as the system collapsed under its feet before SDRs were created to any significant extent.

Even though during 1968 and 1969 the U.S. Official Reserve Settlements balance had been in surplus, the situation brusquely reversed during 1970 to 1971 when the ORS went into deep deficits, including an unheard-of $30 billion in 1971. The Bretton Woods system literally collapsed during 1971. With rampant expectations that an increase in the dollar price of gold was imminent and that a major devaluation of the dollar vis-à-vis most other major currencies was soon forthcoming, the resulting speculative run on the dollar became unsustainable. During May 1971, in the face of massive short-term capital inflows associated with speculation against the dollar, Germany decided to let its currency float against the dollar. The Netherlands followed suit and Switzerland and Austria also both revalued their currencies. Still, the speculative run on the dollar was not abated and on August 15, 1971, President Richard Nixon went on television to announce the closing of the *gold window,* that is, the end of the U.S. Treasury's sales and purchases of gold, in addition to a package of policies referred to as the *New Economic Policy.* In response, the major European countries and Japan decided to let their currencies float in terms of the dollar, with the dollar taking it on the chin through declining values vis-à-vis other currencies.

During the months following the closing of the gold window in August 1971, a substantial amount of discussion and negotiation took place as to how exchange rates were to be realigned and about what role changes in the official price of gold would play. In December, the so-called *Smithsonian Agreement* established a currency realignment with the official dollar price of gold rising to $38 and the exchange rate of the dollar vis-à-vis foreign currencies pegged at a higher level in terms of the major European currencies and the yen. Gold convertibility, however, was not reestablished. The Smithsonian Agreement did not last long. Renewed speculation and capital movements forced foreign Central Banks to abandon any intent to fix exchange rates so that early in 1973 the major European currencies and the Japanese yen started floating vis-à-vis the dollar. They have been bumbling ever after.

The Bretton Woods system operated well while it lasted. It supported a flourishing regime of international trade and finance, with stable and relatively high growth rates by historical standards and with relatively low unemployment and inflation rates. Given this record, and taking into account the fact that the 1971 to 1973 period was not directly connected to any major war involving the European industrial countries, the collapse of the Bretton Woods system appears paradoxical. Nevertheless, its history shows a number of basic problems.

16–8 THE BRETTON WOODS SYSTEM: WHY DID IT FAIL?

Under Bretton Woods, the United States effectively acquired two essential roles in the international monetary system. The first one was to keep the U.S. dollar convertible to gold at a fixed price and to maintain confidence in its ability to do so. This required the United States to hold gold reserves in a high enough proportion so as to confidently back its convertibility commitment. A second role of the United States was to provide adequate supplies of what became the main international reserve asset of the system: the dollar. The United States, as a reserve currency country, was supposed to supply international *liquidity* at an adequate rate.[14] As it turns out, this second role of the United States as supplier of liquidity to the world economy—and to foreign Central Banks in particular—was in conflict with its role of maintaining confidence in the gold convertibility of the dollar at a fixed price of $35 per ounce. The need to incur higher and higher liabilities to foreign Central Banks would gradually reduce U.S. gold reserves as a proportion of total liabilities to foreign Central Banks. This eventually undermined confidence in the ability of the United States to convert dollars into gold on demand: The United States could not fulfill its role in sustaining confidence in the dollar as an international reserve asset. Of course, policy measures could be taken to avoid U.S. external payments deficits and maintain the ratio of U.S. gold reserves to foreign official liabilities at safe levels. In this event, the confidence problem would be solved but not the liquidity problem.

[14] The role of the United States in supplying international liquidity was linked to its role as a world banker, accepting liquid dollar-denominated deposits from foreign Central Banks and lending to foreign countries in the form of long-term investments abroad. See C. P. Kindleberger, "Balance of Payments Deficits and the International Market for Liquidity," in his *Europe and the Dollar* (Cambridge, Mass.: The M.I.T. Press, 1965).

In short, the Bretton Woods system faced a dilemma, the so-called *Triffin Dilemma*, [15] between the role of the United States in solving the world liquidity problem by incurring liabilities to foreigners and its role in maintaining the confidence in the dollar. A major crisis was then bound to arise at some point, the timing of which was dependent on historical circumstances. At that juncture, the confidence crisis would not only give rise to destabilizing speculation, but also would undermine the U.S. role as a supplier of liquidity. As soon as Central Banks lost their confidence in the dollar, they would begin to exchange their dollar assets for gold. For them, this just represents a shift in the composition of international reserves, reducing dollar assets and increasing gold holdings. World international reserves shrink, however, since U.S. international reserves are in the form of gold holdings and these decline. The confidence problem is then compounded by a liquidity problem, as world international reserves contract in the face of dollar conversions into gold.

The Triffin dilemma is depicted in Figure 16–4. As shown, the ratio of U.S. gold reserves to U.S. liabilities to foreign officials declined rapidly during the late fifties and sixties, undermining confidence in the gold convertibility of the dollar. This inherent conflict between the role of the United States as a supplier of liquidity and its role in maintaining gold convertibility was heightened by the massive explosion of international liquidity provided by the United States during 1970 and 1971. The dollar glut of these years was associated with huge U.S. balance of payments deficits and resulted in a drastic increase of world inflation. This episode, a prelude to the breakdown of Bretton Woods, serves well to illustrate some of the other problems of this fixed exchange rate regime.

Given that, by any standards, the liquidity explosion of 1970 and 1971 was excessive, on whom, and by what means, does the burden of correcting the U.S. balance of payments deficits fall? As far as the United States was concerned at the time, the policy was one of benign neglect, that is, of ignoring the effects of external imbalance in the hope that the balance of payments deficits would be accepted in the form of increased dollar holdings by foreign Central Banks. This meant that the United States could worry about its internal economic policy matters without any external balance objectives in mind. As a matter of fact, the growth of defense spending in the United States as a result of the Vietnam war was connected to the balance of payments deficits of 1970 and 1971. The growing budget deficits were associated with rising U.S. inflation, which jumped from 1.9% in 1965 to 4.7% by 1968. When combined with the increased competition, the United States was suffering in world trade, particularly at the hands of West Germany and Japan, the deteriorating competitiveness of U.S. products abroad in response to the rising relative U.S. inflation rate

[15] In honor of Robert Triffin, who spelled it out during the late 1950s. See his *Europe and the Money Muddle: From Bilateralism to Near-Convertibility, 1947–56,* and *Gold and the Dollar Crisis: The Future of Convertibility* (New Haven, Conn.: Yale University Press, 1957 and 1960, respectively).

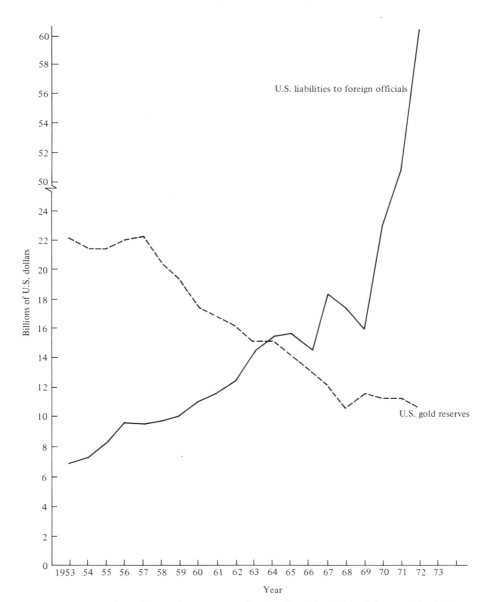

FIGURE 16–4.   The Triffin Dilemma: Growing Dollar World Liquidity and Dwindling U.S. Gold Reserves. (From International Monetary Fund, International Financial Statistics, 1972.)

resulted in a drastic worsening of the current account balance, giving impetus to the payments deficits of 1971 and 1972.

From the U.S. viewpoint, the problem of adjustment to an "excessive" U.S. balance of payments deficit lay in the hands of foreign countries. It was indeed true that adequate policies on the part of foreign governments and/or the automatic adjustment mechanisms inherent in a fixed exchange rate regime would have moved foreign economies toward readjustment. The West German external payments surpluses, for example, would have increased Germany's money supply—under laissez-faire—and consequently its inflation rate. The resulting worsening of West Germany's competitiveness in international markets would then have reduced the U.S. current account deterioration vis-à-vis Germany. A West German policy of increased credit growth would have accelerated this process. The key assumption made, however, was that West German authorities would have tolerated the Bundesbank support of inflationary policies, just for the sake of sustaining external balance. As the years passed after the beginning of the Bretton Woods system, the European countries and Japan became increasingly reluctant to accept the asymmetry of bearing the burden of adjustment regarding external payments disequilibria vis-à-vis the United States. It was felt that the reserve currency country—the United States—had as much responsibility in controlling its external payments situation as nonreserve currency countries.

As early as 1965, Charles de Gaulle had protested and challenged U.S. hegemony by refusing to accept $2 billion in reserves and exchanging them for gold while clamoring for a return to a pure gold standard.[16] The gold standard provides a good basis for comparison with the Bretton Woods system of the late 1960s. Under a pure gold standard, a country like the United States, with growing inflation, current account deficits, and losses of international reserves (gold), would have been forced to reduce its money supply in proportion to the losses of gold. The resulting U.S. deflation would have then increased U.S. competitiveness abroad, reduced net imports, and therefore improved the current account balance. In addition, the inflow of gold into the surplus countries would have resulted in an increase of their inflation rates and in further adjustment of their economies and external payments surpluses. In this situation, adjustment

---

[16] The case of France against the accumulation of dollar reserves at the time also involved the view that the United States was extracting a seignorage gain from its creation of international liquidity at the expense of the nonreserve currency countries. Since in order to acquire dollar-denominated reserves, foreign countries had to release real resources—such as those involved in net exports to the United States—the idea was that the United States was benefiting from its almost costless creation of international money. Nevertheless, a large share of the international reserves acquired by foreign countries were invested in interest-yielding dollar-denominated assets or were exchanged for gold. As a result, even though a seignorage gain was most likely being earned, its absolute magnitude and importance are not easily discernable. See H. G. Grubel, "The Distribution of Seignorage from International Liquidity Creation," in R. A. Mundell and A. K. Swoboda, eds. *Monetary Problems of the International Economy* (Chicago: University of Chicago Press, 1969).

would have been more symmetric than that under Bretton Woods.[17] It must be realized, though, that the link between world liquidity and gold production established by a pure gold standard cuts both ways. It also implies that world liquidity is costly to acquire, since it takes resources (e.g., labor and machinery) to mine gold out of the ground. On the other hand, the creation of dollars, or any other paper money, is virtually costless. In addition, world liquidity under a gold standard would be subject to the vagaries of gold discoveries, which may or may not be superior to the vagaries of U.S. balance of payments deficits.

In summary, the absence of external payments adjustment steps on the part of the United States meant that nonreserve currency countries had the burden of adjustment under Bretton Woods. Whether through internal adjustment involving monetary, price, output, and/or interest rate changes, or through external adjustments involving devaluations or revaluations of their currencies, European countries and Japan had to subjugate their policy attention toward external balance. Even though in the environment of the immediate post-World War II period such a scheme of things was tolerable, it could not be sustained permanently. When the supply of dollars in 1970 and 1971 exploded, straining to its limits the internal goals of price stability in nonreserve currency countries, the latter reacted by converting dollars into gold, sterilizing increases in reserves and, finally, by letting their currencies float vis-à-vis the dollar. The inconsistency of the explosion in international liquidity with the national policy autonomy and goals of nonreserve currency countries finally pushed the Bretton Woods system into collapse. Chapter 17 deals with the international monetary arrangements that gradually emerged after March 1973 and which currently operate in the world economy.

16–9 SUMMARY

1. Since antiquity, and up to modern times, countries generally operated on a specie commodity standard, in which metals—predominantly gold and silver—composed the bulk of the circulating media of the economy.

2. In their purest form, specie commodity standards operated on the basis of full-bodied coins, the monetary value of which equaled the value of the

---

[17] For a discussion of the impact of establishing a gold reserves–money supply rule within a Bretton Woods regime in order to discipline (anchor) both reserve and nonreserve currency countries in their national and international money creation, see R. A. Mundell, "The Case for a Managed International Gold Standard," in M. B. Connolly, ed., *The International Monetary System: Choices for the Future* (New York: Praeger Publishers, Inc., 1982). For a general examination of the issue of asymmetry in external payments adjustment under Bretton Woods, see Marina V. N. Whitman, "The Current and Future Role of the Dollar: How Much Symmetry?," in her *Reflections of Interdependence* (Pittsburgh, Pa.: University of Pittsburgh, 1979).

metals they contained. Sovereigns could reduce the metallic (say, gold) content of the coins they minted, a practice called debasement.

3. In a monetary system based on commodity monies, the simultaneous circulation of full-bodied and debased coins of the same denomination would lead to the operation of Gresham's law, stating that overvalued money drives undervalued money out of circulation.

4. By 1880, the gold standard had developed into a full-fledged international monetary system, having been adopted by a range of major countries. The essential features of the operation of a pure gold standard can be characterized in terms of three basic rules: (1) A country on the gold standard fixes the value of its currency in terms of gold; the gold values of any two countries' currencies then specify their relative value, referred to as mint parity or mint exchange rate; (2) under the pure gold standard, imports and exports of gold among countries are freely allowed; (3) Central Banks or appropriate monetary authorities have to hold gold reserves in relation to paper money in order to assure gold convertibility of paper money and fulfill the public's demand for gold; the amount of gold reserves then controls the amount of money growth in the economy. Even though the first two rules of a pure gold standard were satisfied to a large extent during the heyday of the gold standard during 1880 to 1914, the third rule does not appear to have been closely followed at all.

5. The outbreak of World War I in 1914 struck a fatal blow to the gold standard. Attempts to reestablish it during the interwar period were unsuccessful.

6. The Bretton Woods system was organized in 1947 with the creation of the International Monetary Fund, which was to oversee and monitor the operations of the new international monetary system. The IMF's agreements stipulated that member countries would set a fixed value of their currency in terms of gold (or U.S. dollars). The par value of two currencies then determined the official exchange rate or parity. Exchange rate fluctuations were to be limited to a narrow band around the official exchange rate.

7. Under Bretton Woods, the United States was the reserve currency country, providing world liquidity through a supply of dollars and guaranteeing convertibility of dollars into gold. A major reason for the collapse of Bretton Woods was the so-called Triffin dilemma: The role of the United States in solving world liquidity problems required the United States to incur liabilities to foreigners, but its role in maintaining the confidence in the convertibility of the dollar into gold was undermined as a result of the expansion of dollar liabilities.

8. The Bretton Woods system was an adjustable peg regime, allowing exchange rate changes to correct fundamental disequilibria in the balance of payments, subject to IMF approval. The absence of external payments adjustment constraints on the part of the United States—the reserve currency country—meant that nonreserve currency countries had the burden of adjustment under Bretton Woods. Whether through internal adjustments involving monetary, price, output, and interest rate changes, or through devaluations or revaluations of their currencies, European countries and Japan had to subjugate their policy attention toward external balance.

9. The massive U.S. balance of payments deficits of 1970 and 1971 strained to the limit the ability of European countries and Japan to absorb the increased dollar supply without compromising domestic goals of price stability. As a result, these countries finally allowed their currencies to fluctuate vis-à-vis the dollar in 1971. Later attempts to realign fixed exchange rates failed and in March 1973 all serious efforts to sustain fixed exchange rates among the industrial countries ended.

PROBLEMS

1. Suppose that you were living in London during the 1540s. What effects would you most likely observe on prices, real income, and trade in response to a coin debasement? Assuming that you adopt a monetary approach to the debasement, what would you emphasize as being the effects of the disturbance?

2. Based on the considerations noted in the text, would you make any particular adjustments or qualifications in the official reserve settlements balance to measure fundamental disequilibria in the "balance of payments" of a reserve currency country? If you have any suggestions, how would they alter the popular view that the United States was in fundamental balance of payments disequilibrium in the late 1960s?

3. Evaluate the following statement: "SDRs would have never been widely utilized as an international means of transaction among Central Banks during Bretton Woods because of Gresham's law."

4. "The collapse of Bretton Woods was a reflection of the decline in the economic and political power of the United States over West European countries and Japan obtained during World War II but no longer sustainable." Please evaluate or comment on this statement.

5. At a conference on international monetary economics, an economist assails the monetary approach to the balance of payments as adding nothing new to the adjustment process operating through Hume's price-specie-flow mechanism. Is this correct? Explain.

CHAPTER 17

Economic Policy, Monetary Regimes, and the Current State of the World Economy

The definitive breakdown of the Bretton Woods regime in March 1973 represented a fundamental shift from a system of adjustable pegs to one of wider flexibility in the management of exchange rates. This change in international monetary arrangements was officially sanctioned in 1978, when the International Monetary Fund's Articles of Agreement were amended to take into account the exchange rate flexibility that had already become a fact of life half a decade before. The amended Articles allowed a large degree of freedom to countries in choosing their exchange rate regime. Currencies could float or be pegged to the dollar, Special Drawing Rights (SDRs), or any other basket of currencies.

The present regime, as it has worked since 1973, can be described as being a hybrid system, although its free-for-all nature has led some to refer to it as a nonsystem. The currencies of the major industrial countries have been floating against the dollar. At the same time, about 50 other countries—including most of Latin America—keep adjustable pegs to the U.S. dollar, while still another group pegs to the French franc, the SDR, or other currency baskets. Some countries, particularly developing countries, have adopted a so-called *crawling peg regime,* under which exchange rates are subject to small but frequent adjustments, as opposed to the generally large and infrequent devaluations or revaluations typical of Bretton Woods. Finally, perhaps the best illustration of the hybrid character of the present international monetary regime is the exchange rate arrangement of the European Monetary System, adopted by all members of the European Economic Community except the United Kingdom and Greece. These countries keep a regime of pegged rates among their currencies, which float jointly against other currencies, such as the U.S. dollar, the Canadian dollar, and the Japanese yen. Established in 1979, the EMS is associated with a long-standing tradition of efforts toward European monetary integration since World War II.

This chapter examines in detail these current international monetary arrangements, utilizing a policy approach that explicitly addresses such issues as the degree and appropriate extent of Central Bank intervention in foreign exchange markets, the current role of the IMF, and the international monetary problems of the developing countries and their debt crisis. We start by examining the regime of floating exchange rates followed by the United States vis à vis the major European countries and Japan, which has become one of the major developments of the post-Bretton Woods era.

17–1   OFFICIAL INTERVENTION AND MANAGED FLOATING

The floating exchange rate arrangement followed by most industrial countries after 1973 has been characterized by active intervention of Central Banks in foreign exchange markets. In other words, the regime has been one of managed (or dirty) floating rather than one of free-floating exchange rates. The extent of Central Bank intervention in foreign exchange markets can be illustrated through Figure 17–1, depicting U.S. intervention as measured by changes in U.S. official reserve assets. Foreign Central Banks have also actively intervened in foreign exchange markets. For instance, between June 1973 and May 1975 alone, the United Kingdom spent $7.5 billion in reserves to buy pounds in foreign exchange markets; from that point until October 1976 an additional $7.5 billion were spent. A similar pattern holds for other time periods and for most of the industrial countries, even though the extent of intervention varies considerably.

Paradoxically, the general extent of Central Bank intervention in foreign exchange markets during the period of increased exchange rate flexibility after 1973 has exceeded that under the Bretton Woods' fixed exchange rate regime. This is partly reflected in the growth of official foreign exchange reserves of the industrial countries as a group, which have increased from $65.7 billion in 1973 to $155.1 billion worth in 1983.

What rationale do Central Banks have for intervening in foreign exchange markets? The answer most frequently provided is that intervention is called for in order to smooth-out "excessive" fluctuations in exchange rates so as to avoid the effects of these fluctuations on domestic economic activity. There are three basic links in this argument for intervention. First, it is asserted that exchange rate turbulence can be excessive, setting the basis for possible intervention. Second, it is assumed that these exchange rate fluctuations can have substantial effects on economic activity and are therefore an important economic problem. Finally, it is believed that Central Banks can in practice smooth out excessive turbulence through the purchase and sale of foreign exchange reserves. These three issues are examined next.

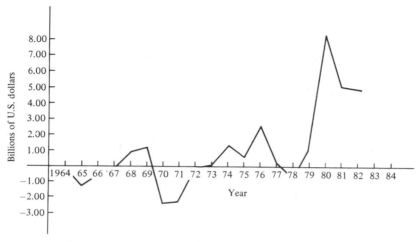

FIGURE 17–1.   Changes in U.S Official Reserve Assets. These include gold, SDRs, U.S. reserve position in the IMF, and foreign currencies. Note that changes in official reserve assets do not necessarily coincide precisely with official intervention in foreign exchange markets. Changes in reserves, for instance, may arise purely from the revaluation of reserve assets (such as changes in the price of gold); intervention in foreign exchange markets, on the other hand, might take place through the use of government foreign assets not formally catalogued as reserve assets. For more details, see D. Taylor, "The Mismanaged Float: Official Intervention by the Industrialized Countries," in M. Connolly, ed., *The International Monetary System,* New York, Praeger Publishers Inc., 1982. (Data are from Economic Report of the President, 1984.)

Has Exchange Rate Turbulence Been Excessive?

When the major European countries and Japan abandoned the Bretton Woods regime of fixed exchange rates and allowed their currencies to float vis-à-vis the dollar, they implicitly accepted that exchange rate flexibility was required to sustain the wide divergences of their national policy goals from those of the United States. In particular, their goal in controlling inflation required that the monetary effects of the massive balance of payments surpluses vis à vis the United States be impeded. A floating exchange rate regime does not completely insulate economies from each other—as was shown in previous chapters and confirmed by the experience since 1973—but it was thought that the increased exchange rate flexibility would aid in sustaining external balance while leaving monetary policy freer to attain the goals of internal balance. Some degree of exchange rate flexibility was, consequently, desirable from their point of view at the time.

The wide gyrations of exchange rates observed during the float, however, have surpassed any of the expectations of academics or policymakers. This has given rise to claims that exchange rate changes have been excessive and that Central Bank intervention in foreign exchange markets is required to smooth them out. But how much can be considered excessive? In other words, what constitutes an excessive exchange rate change?

Exchange rate variability has many sources. Changes in fundamental economic variables, such as real income growth and inflation rates, will alter the fundamental equilibrium values of exchange rates and generate exchange rate variability. The rising U.S. rate of inflation relative to European inflation during the late 1960s and early 1970s, for instance, required an increase in the equilibrium exchange rate of the dollar against most European currencies. During the last years of Bretton Woods, then, the dollar was overvalued, that is, above its fundamental equilibrium value. The float of 1971, and then that of 1973, effectively devalued the dollar moving it toward its equilibrium value at the time. Exchange rate variability can therefore arise from changes in the *equilibrium* value of exchange rates, a simple result of the fact that we live in a dynamic world in which fundamental economic variables are constantly changing.

On the other hand, exchange rate changes may be of the *disequilibrium* type, where the exchange rate deviates from its fundamental equilibrium value. As we have repeatedly noted, expectations about the future exert a major influence on exchange rates. Generally, speculation in foreign exchange markets can be of the *stabilizing* type, accelerating required equilibrium exchange rate changes or smoothing out adjustment in that direction. However, *destabilizing speculation*, which moves exchange rates away from their fundamental, equilibrium values, has been a recurrent source of worry for many supporters of floating exchange rates, generating the above-mentioned statement that such exchange rate movements are excessive and should be offset by government intervention.[1]

What factors are associated with destabilizing speculation? That is, what type of speculative phenomena can generate deviations of exchange rates from their fundamental, equilibrium values?[2] One situation is connected to the presence of speculative bubbles, in which investors get caught in the bandwagon of speculating against, or in favor of, a currency, keeping the exchange rate moving away from its fundamental value. It might also arise from the effects

[1] The debate on the theoretical and actual significance of stabilizing and destabilizing speculation under flexible exchange rates has a long history. Ragnar Nurkse argued strongly against floating exchange rate regimes precisely on the basis of destabilizing speculation; see his *International Currency Experience* (Princeton, N.J.: Princeton University Press, 1946). Milton Friedman, on the other hand, has emphasized the role of stabilizing speculation; see his "The Case for Flexible Exchange Rates," *Essays in Positive Economics* (Chicago: University of Chicago Press, 1953).

[2] An alternative question often asked in this regard is whether speculators will stabilize the exchange rate when the foreign exchange market is rendered unstable because of the failure of the Marshall–Lerner condition to hold or because of any factors generating a *J*-curve response of the trade balance to exchange rate changes. See W. Witte, "Another Case of Profitable Destabilizing Speculation," *Journal of International Economics* (February, 1973); and R. Driskill and S. McCafferty, "Speculation, Rational Expectations, and the Stability of the Foreign Exchange Market," *Journal of International Economics* (May 1982).

of extraneous (unsubstantiated) exchange rate expectations on exchange rates. By inducing a run on domestic currency, expectations of domestic currency depreciation will be associated with an immediate exchange rate depreciation, even if the expectations are based on unsubstantiated rumors or beliefs that do not turn out to actually occur and are, therefore, completely reversed ex-post. Examples of both of these phenomena have been frequently noted.[3]

The possibility that speculative influences on exchange rates might lead to excessive exchange rate movements in the sense of cumulative deviations from fundamental, equilibrium exchange rates does not automatically call for intervention. One must first answer the question of how significant these deviations are in influencing the economy. That is, do deviations of exchange rates from their fundamental equilibrium value have any negative impact on the economy?

Exchange Rate Variability and Real Economic Activity

A major channel through which exchange rate variability can affect economic activity is through its effects on real exchange rates. Real exchange rates are equal to nominal exchange rates weighted by the ratio of foreign to domestic prices and can be used to measure the relative price of foreign goods in terms of domestic goods. Rising real exchange rates can be associated with increased price competitiveness of domestic products relative to foreign products and declining real exchange rates with worsening domestic competitiveness. As a result, if fluctuations in nominal exchange rates are connected to changes in real exchange rates, they will have a crucial effect on domestic net exports, production, employment, and so forth. As a matter of fact, the flexibility of nominal exchange rates in the 1970s and 1980s has generally revealed an association between swings in real and nominal exchange rates. The basic reason is that nominal exchange rates adjust more rapidly than goods market prices, which change sluggishly. Accordingly, nominal exchange rate turbulence is closely related to real exchange rate turbulence.[4]

One of the traditional arguments against flexible exchange rates as a regime is that the presumably greater real exchange rate (or terms of trade) uncertainty present in that system discourages international commerce. Even though the evidence is not conclusive, and world trade has definitely not stagnated during the post-1973 period, recent work suggests that real exchange rate uncertainty has had a negative impact on international trade among several industrial

---

[3] See, e.g., R. Dornbusch, "Equilibrium and Disequilibrium Exchange Rates," *Zeitschrift Fur Wirtschafts-und Sozialwissenshaffen*, 583–589 (1982); and M. Moffitt, *The World's Money* (New York: Simon & Schuster, Inc., 1983). See also our earlier discussion in Chapter 9.

[4] For measures of turbulence in nominal exchange rates relative to price level turbulence, see J. Frenkel and M. Mussa, "The Efficiency of Foreign Exchange Markets and Measures of Turbulence," *American Economic Review* (May 1980).

countries.[5] Deviations of exchange rates from their fundamental, equilibrium levels then imply real economic activity is similarly disturbed from equilibrium.

If we assume that excessive exchange rate changes arise, and given the potential disruptive effects of such changes on real economic activity, is it desirable for the Central Bank to intervene in an effort to smooth them out?

Can Intervention Smooth Out Exchange Rate Fluctuations

Central Bank intervention geared toward smoothing out excessive exchange rate fluctuations takes the form of leaning against the wind. When domestic currency starts to depreciate, the Central Bank will buy domestic currency and sell international reserves so as to prevent the currency's value from declining further. Consequently, when the currency starts to appreciate, the Central Bank will sell domestic currency (and purchase foreign exchange) with the intention of preventing further rises in value. The obvious question that arises—and a tough one, for that matter—is: How does the Central Bank determine when to intervene? If the intention of the authorities is to limit disequilibrium movements in exchange rates, how do they distinguish between equilibrium and disequilibrium movements? This problem is crucial as errors made by mistakenly intervening to prevent changes in the fundamental level of the exchange rate might result in delays of such equilibrium adjustments and can be quite costly both for the Central Bank and for society.

The problems involved in Central Bank intervention when the authorities lack knowledge of the source of a disturbance to the exchange rate (i.e., when they do not know whether it represents a destabilizing speculative movement or a change in the equilibrium exchange rate) are illustrated by Figure 17–2. Two disturbances are depicted—one purely speculative and destabilizing, occurring at time t_0, and one representing an equilibrium change in the fundamental level of the exchange rate from its initial value of $\bar{e} = \$1.50$ per pound to $\bar{\bar{e}} = \$2.00$, occurring at time t_1. It is assumed the United States is intervening in the foreign exchange market in order to smooth out fluctuations in the dollar–pound exchange rate. The behavior of the exchange rate in the absence of Central Bank intervention would be the one illustrated by means of the continuous tracing in the diagram. If the Central Bank had perfect information about the sources of disturbance to the exchange rate, it could choose to intervene only during the first, destabilizing, disturbance at time t_0. In general, however, there is no clear-cut, foolproof way of determining on the spot whether a certain exchange rate movement represents a change of the fundamental, equilibrium value of the exchange rate or whether it is a destabilizing speculative disturbance.

[5] D. Cushman, "The Effects of Real Exchange Rate Risk on International Trade," *Journal of International Economics* (August 1983). For a different view, see "Exchange Rate Variability and World Trade," International Monetary Fund, Washington, D.C., 1984.

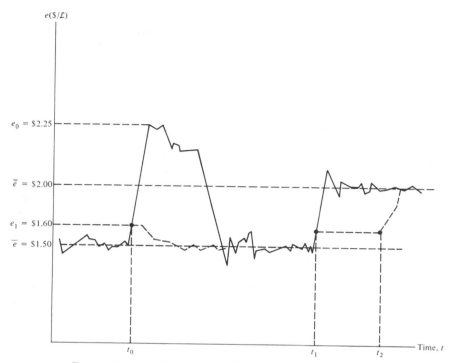

FIGURE 17–2.   The Problems of Central Bank Intervention

As a result, having no way to select among them, it is assumed the U.S. authorities intervene in both instances. During the speculative disturbance the Central Bank prevents the bubble from deviating the exchange rate upward to $e_0 = \$2.25$, instead bursting it apart and inducing a rapid movement back toward the initial equilibrium level of the exchange rate. The dotted line indicates how the exchange rate would behave in the presence of intervention.

In the case where the disturbance involves a permanent increase of the equilibrium exchange rate from $\bar{e} = \$1.50$ to $\bar{\bar{e}} = \$2.00$, occurring at time t_1, intervention will prevent the currency from depreciating. The U.S. authorities would support the dollar, keeping the exchange rate at a level, say, equal to $e_1 = \$1.60$. The Central Bank can do this by selling pounds in exchange for dollars in foreign exchange markets. Given the equilibrium nature of the disturbance at t_1, however, the upward pressure on the exchange rate will continue and the U.S. authorities would have to maintain their dollar support operations. Usually, in a situation such as this, the authorities will eventually give up defending the currency and allow the exchange rate to increase. Figure 17–2 shows this to occur at time t_2. During the period over which the Central Bank has intervened to avoid the domestic currency depreciation, however, the exchange rate has been prevented from adjusting to its higher equilibrium level, generating socially costly, government-induced deviations from equilibrium.

Foreign exchange market intervention can stabilize or destabilize the exchange rate depending on the source of the disturbance. Stabilizing intervention usually provides a revenue gain to monetary authorities, while destabilizing intervention will result in losses. This can be explained using the cases illustrated in Figure 17–2. Central Banks will frequently sell a substantial portion of their international reserves during their operations supporting a depreciating currency. They correspondingly replenish their reserves at some point. Now, consider first a stabilizing intervention, such as that occurring at t_0. In that situation, the domestic authorities sell pounds at an exchange rate of $e_1 = \$1.60$ in order to burst open the exchange rate bubble. Immediately after the situation settles down, the Central Bank will replenish its lost international reserves and will therefore buy pounds at the prevailing exchange rate, which would be around $\bar{e} = \$1.50$. In other words, the Central Bank, in its sale and purchase of foreign exchange, has made a profit of approximately \$0.10 per pound. Consider, on the other hand, the case of destabilizing intervention, such as it would occur at time t_1 in Figure 17–2. In this case, the Central Bank sells pounds at the rate of \$1.60 during the time period between t_1 and t_2, losing a certain portion of its pound sterling reserves in the process. When the authorities abandon the intervention, the exchange rate jumps upward to approximately \$2.00. This is the rate at which the Central Bank would have to replenish its reserves of sterling. The result is a loss of close to \$0.40 per pound sold and purchased.

In summary, as Milton Friedman has remarked:[6]

> it would do little harm for a government agency to speculate in the exchange market provided it held to the objective of smoothing out temporary fluctuations and not interfering with fundamental adjustments. And there should be a simple criterion of success—whether the agency makes or loses money.

The available evidence on whether the intervention carried out by the Central Banks of industrial countries during the managed floating regime has been profitable or not suggests that some Central Banks have in some periods made profits and in others lost from their intervention in foreign exchange markets.[7]

The present analysis is consistent with the view that there is an inherent difficulty in intervention: The authorities must determine whether the disturbance to be potentially offset is associated with a change in the fundamental value

---

[6] M. Friedman, "The Case for Flexible Exchange Rates," *Essays in Positive Economics* (Chicago: University of Chicago Press, 1953).

[7] Evidence on losses from official intervention is provided by D. Taylor, "The Mismanaged Float: Official Intervention by the Industrialized Countries," in M. Connolly, ed., *The International Monetary System* (New York: Praeger Publishers, Inc., 1982). Evidence on profits is provided by J. Williamson, *The Exchange Rate System* (Washington, D.C.: Institute for International Economics, 1983). See also V. Argy, "Exchange Rate Management in Theory and Practice," *Princeton Studies in International Finance* (October 1982).

of the exchange rate or whether it represents a deviation from fundamentals. Given the presumption that, at the present, such a differentiation cannot be made to any degree of accuracy casts dark shadows on the ability of intervention to be predominantly stabilizing.

Even if the source of a disturbance is known, however, and intervention is called for, this does not mean that intervention can in effect prevent exchange rate changes from occurring. In other words, there is the further question as to whether intervention could prevent a growing exchange rate bubble or strong extraneous beliefs in the foreign exchange market from influencing the exchange rate.

Central Bank intervention in foreign exchange markets can be of two types: *sterilized* and *nonsterilized intervention.* Sterilized intervention occurs when the Central Bank buys or sells foreign exchange reserves but does not allow these changes in reserves to affect the domestic money supply. It does this by engaging in offsetting changes of domestic credit through open market operations. Nonsterilized intervention, on the other hand, means that the Central Bank allows its purchases and sales of foreign exchange to alter the domestic money supply. In general, nonsterilized intervention tends to be more effective than sterilized intervention in influencing exchange rates, since it is associated with changes in the domestic money supply. For instance, adopting a monetary approach to the exchange rate, nonsterilized intervention will directly affect exchange rates by changing relative money supplies, whereas sterilized intervention will affect the exchange rate only in so far as it affects relative money demands (say through influencing exchange rate expectations or through portfolio balance effects). Available evidence indeed suggests the relative ineffectiveness of sterilized intervention—and the effectiveness of nonsterilized intervention—in affecting exchange rates.[8]

In conclusion, Central Bank intervention in foreign exchange markets can in principle be called for in situations in which exchange rates tend to deviate substantially from fundamentals. Unfortunately, in practice it is extremely difficult to discern the sources of sudden changes in exchange rates, making Central Bank intervention to smooth out fluctuations in exchange rates more difficult to justify.

17-2   PERFORMANCE OF THE MANAGED FLOAT IN PERSPECTIVE

The current managed floating regime followed by the major industrial countries is unique in that it provides a case in which major currencies have been floating in value against each other over a substantial time interval. Before the present

---

[8] See M. Obstfeld, "Exchange Rates, Inflation, and the Sterilization Problem: Germany 1975–81," *European Economic Review* (March/April 1983), and K. Rogoff, "On the Effects of Sterilized Intervention, An Analysis of Weekly Data," International Monetary Fund, Working Paper (May 1983).

experience, most analyses of floating regimes were based on either theoretical speculation or the analysis of limited experiences with floating rates, such as the Canadian float of 1952 to 1961 and the interwar experience during 1918 to 1925. The present regime of managed floating provides us with a richer basis on which to evaluate alternative exchange rate regimes. Unfortunately, just as comparisons between the classic gold standard and Bretton Woods could be highly inappropriate, so comparisons between the fixed exchange rate regime of Bretton Woods and the current managed floating regime can be inadequate. For instance, the post-1973 time interval has been characterized by inflation and unemployment rates that, on average, have been well above those under Bretton Woods. Output growth after 1973 has also been slower than the Bretton Woods average. These data, however, should not be taken to indicate a clear superiority of the performance of Bretton Woods over that of managed floating. The explanation is that, in contrast to the relative global economic stability of Bretton Woods, the post-1973 period has involved massive external shocks to the economies of the industrial countries. The oil crises of 1973 and 1979 were major exogenous disturbances to the world economy, with no comparable shocks under Bretton Woods. Since, ideally, to compare the performance of alternative international monetary regimes requires controlled comparisons, evaluations based on a casual look at the behavior of the industrial economies are wholly inappropriate. It might very well be that exchange rate flexibility has not contributed to accentuate economic instability but that, on the contrary, the apparent massive global economic disturbances occurring in the seventies have contributed to accentuate exchange rate instability. The question of the relative economic performance of Bretton Woods and managed floating must thus remain, at the present time, an open question.

Besides giving rise to a few "I told you so" comments, the significance of the performance of the current regime of floating dollar exchange rates to the debate on fixed versus flexible exchange rates is greatly eclipsed by the extent of Central Bank intervention. The fact is that the current regime is one of managed floating and, as such, it cannot be considered to be either free floating or fixed exchange rates but a hybrid regime. Indeed, the nature of the present system has led to recasting the debate between fixed and flexible exchange rates from one involving irreconcilable adversaries to one involving what is the desirable or optimal degree of exchange rate flexibility. The point has been made that whether the economy should peg or float exchange rates depends on the particular economic environment or the specific economic disturbance facing the country.[9] As a matter of fact, the country could find it optimal to adopt

---

[9] See, for instance, J. Frenkel and J. Aizenman, "Aspects of the Optimal Management of Exchange Rates," *Journal of International Economics* (November 1982); D. Henderson, "The Role of Intervention Policy in Open Economy Financial Policy: A Macroeconomic Perspective," International Finance Discussion Paper No. 202, Federal Reserve, Washington, D.C. (February 1982); and E. Helpman and M. June Flanders, "On Exchange Rate Policies for a Small Country," *The Economic Journal* (March 1978).

a fixed exchange rate vis-à-vis some countries and a flexible exchange rate against others. This type of regime is what European countries have chosen under the European Monetary System, as we shall discuss in the following section.

17–3 MONETARY UNION AND THE EUROPEAN MONETARY SYSTEM

At a meeting in Bremen in 1978, the European Community agreed to promote tighter monetary cooperation through the creation of the European Monetary System (EMS), which started operations during March of 1979. The EMS replaced the so-called snake agreement developed during the twilight of the Bretton Woods regime. The Smithsonian Agreement of December 1971 had established a realignment of exchange rates among the United States, the major European countries, and Japan (the so-called Group of Ten) after the earlier months of generalized floating. The exchange rate arrangement among the European countries that emerged out of the Agreement and through negotiations during the following months was one in which (1) the bilateral exchange rates of the European currencies involved would be maintained within close margins (the so-called *snake*), while (2) the exchange rates against the dollar would be maintained within twice those margins (the so-called *tunnel*). The resulting regime was referred to as the "snake within the tunnel," and its membership dwindled during the years as European countries abandoned their pegging margins vis-à-vis the U.S. dollar or other European currencies (the United Kingdom and Ireland abandoned the snake by mid-1972, Italy in 1973). The EMS represented a move back toward a history of close exchange rate monitoring and monetary integration on the part of the European Economic Community (EEC). Established in 1957, the EEC now consists of Belgium, Britain, France, Germany, Greece, Italy, Luxembourg, and the Netherlands, with the associate membership of Denmark and Ireland. The EEC members grant each other preferences facilitating factor movements and trade among each other while engaging and coordinating common policies toward the rest of the world.

The European monetary system is basically a variant of the snake as it regards exchange rate arrangements. Each currency has a peg (a central rate) expressed in terms of the European currency unit (ECU), where the ECU is a composite currency composed of a basket of nine European currencies (the deutsche mark, French franc, Italian lira, Belgian franc, Dutch guilder, Danish krone, Luxembourg franc, Irish pound, and British pound[10]) and gold. With each currency having a central rate peg, a grid of bilateral central rates is determined. Fluctuations around these bilateral pegs are allowed in a margin of ±2.25% (except for the Italian lira, which is allowed a 6% margin). However, if a currency's exchange rate reaches 75% of this margin—the so-called *threshold*

---

[10] Even though the pound forms part of the ECU and the United Kingdom is a member of the EMS, Great Britain does not participate in the currency arrangements of the EMS. For more details on the EMS, see H. Ungerer et al., "The European Monetary System: The Experience, 1979–82," IMF Occasional Paper No. 19 (May 1983).

of divergence—the country is presumed, under the agreements, to engage in either foreign exchange intervention or in domestic policies intended to correct the situation. In cases where the margins are reached and cannot be sustained, a realignment of the central rate pegs may be in order. Several such exchange rate realignments have occurred since 1979. The EMS is therefore a regime of fixed but adjustable exchange rates among member countries. At the same time, the EMS countries engage in a joint currency float against the U.S. dollar. That is, even though each country's exchange rate is fixed vis-à-vis the ECU, the ECU itself floats against the dollar, as the behavior of the exchange rate of the ECU in terms of the dollar in Figure 17–3 shows.

A *monetary union* represents a group of countries that fix their exchange rates vis-à-vis each other and abdicate the active use of domestic monetary policy, leaving such tasks to a central organization or Fund that coordinates the monetary actions of the union's members. The extreme case of a monetary union would be a *common currency area,* in which states or countries arrange to utilize a common currency. In this case the exchange rates among the area's members are permanently fixed while monetary policy is under the control of a joint, coordinating monetary agency or bank. The EMS is obviously far from being a common currency area but it is certainly an experiment in monetary union. For instance, even though each country has complete autonomy in domestic monetary affairs, the European Monetary Cooperation Fund—the EEC's counterpart of the IMF—serves the function of a joint central monetary organization in the EMS. In addition, even though each country has retained use of its own currency, exchange rates among them are indeed pegged (within a

FIGURE 17–3. Exchange Rate of the ECU Against the U.S. Dollar. (From H. Ungerer, "The European Monetary System: The Experience, 1979–1982," International Monetary Fund Occasional Paper, May 1983, p. 6.)

band), and the ECU has become a major international currency through its use as a unit of account and as international reserve and intervention currency of member countries. The increasing role of the ECU as an international money has been reflected in the growing use of ECU-denominated debt in many European financial markets.

What factors have encouraged monetary integration in Europe, so difficult to achieve among other groups of countries?

Factors Promoting Monetary Unions

What are the conditions for a well-functioning monetary union? A well-functioning monetary union should contribute to stabilize income and prices and facilitate payments adjustment among participating countries. Robert Mundell[11] has stressed the need for substantial factor (capital and labor) mobility as a precondition for a successful monetary union. He argued that regions or countries featuring high factor mobility should join together in a single currency area or a multicurrency area with fixed exchange rates (to which he referred as an optimum currency area), while those whose factors are relatively immobile should adopt flexible exchange rates vis-à-vis each other. The issues can best be appreciated by analyzing how two regions, say West and East, adjust to an exogenous shift in demand away from Western, and toward Eastern, goods. This disturbance, would—everything else being constant—tend to generate a trade surplus and inflationary pressures in the East and a trade deficit and stagnation in the West. A depreciation of the Western currency in terms of the Eastern currency, however, could switch back demand toward the West, offsetting the aggregate demand effects of the initial disturbance. This stabilizing property is one of the main arguments for exchange rate flexibility. Exchange rate changes, however, will not always be necessary for adjustment to occur. A high degree of factor mobility would result in migration from the West to the East, increasing the supply of factors of production and output and alleviating the inflationary pressures in the East, while relieving unemployment in the Western region. Factor mobility, then, acts as a substitute for exchange rate changes in achieving equilibrium and improving welfare in both regions, suggesting that it is an important condition contributing to a successful monetary union. Indeed, the considerable promotion of European factor market integration after World War II must have paved the way to the monetary union experiments in that region.

Factor mobility is not, though, a necessary or sufficient condition for a successful monetary union. Ronald McKinnon[12] has argued, for example, that small open economies will not be able to use exchange rate flexibility effectively, since in such economies domestic prices would react quickly to exchange rate

[11] R. A. Mundell, "A Theory of Optimum Currency Areas," *American Economic Review* (September 1961); for a survey of the literature on the subject, see F. Machlup, *A History of Thought on Economic Integration* (New York: Columbia University Press, 1977).

[12] R. I. McKinnon, "Optimum Currency Areas," *American Economic Review* (September 1963).

changes, nullifying any impact the exchange rate changes would otherwise have on the relative price of domestic and foreign goods. A high share of traded goods relative to nontraded goods in the economy would then essentially mean that the country faces externally given prices and cannot alter relative prices through exchange rate changes. It is in countries with a significant nontraded goods sector that exchange rate changes can have a substantial impact on the economy by altering the relative price of traded and nontraded goods. In conclusion, even if there is zero factor mobility, countries might be advised to peg their currencies if they are small and open and produce an insignificant amount of nontraded goods.

Other factors can also affect the choice of a monetary union. When different countries join under the head of a single monetary authority, complications might arise regarding the financing of fiscal deficits. The usual interaction between the economy's Central Bank and Treasury in the financing of government activities would have to be subordinated to the jurisdiction of the currency area's monetary authorities, something that might be objectionable to domestic policymakers.[13] As a matter of fact, the nature of a monetary union or a common currency area strongly suggests that the regions or countries involved must have some common political interests and/or a willingness to adopt fiscal and monetary policies consistent with those of the other countries in the union. This requires close similarity of political and/or economic interests. It would be naïve to assume that countries with long-standing sociopolitical conflicts, such as Greece and Turkey or Iran and Iraq, would convene to form a monetary union. Similarly, countries desiring different policy mixes would have difficulty in agreeing on a common monetary policy. If countries A and B form a common currency area but country A feels that a 15% growth of the money supply is more consistent with its booming, developing economy, while country B considers a 5% money growth more appropriate to contain its high inflation rate, then there is little chance a consensus will be reached on the growth of the common currency supply and the less likely the common currency area between the countries will be successful. Similarity and/or affinity in sociopolitical and economic spheres might then be the deciding factor contributing to the success of a monetary union.

17–4   THE EXCHANGE RATE POLICIES OF THE DEVELOPING COUNTRIES AND THE CRAWLING PEG

In spite of the post-Bretton Woods flexibility of the exchange rates of the dollar against the currencies of major European countries and Japan, a substantial number of the developing countries have generally pegged the value of their

[13] See P. B. Kenen, "The Theory of Optimum Currency Areas: An Eclectic View," in R. A. Mundell and A. K. Swoboda, eds., *Monetary Problems of the International Economy* (Chicago: University of Chicago Press, 1969).

currencies to the dollar or a major European currency (or to a basket of those currencies). Latin American countries such as Bolivia, Chile, Ecuador, Guatemala, Honduras, Venezuela, and many others have generally pegged their currencies, within narrow limits, to the dollar, while African nations such as Cameroon, Congo, Nigeria, and Senegal, have pegged vis-à-vis the French franc. In contrast to the general situation under Bretton Woods, however, many developing countries have resorted to frequent, marginal adjustments of their exchange rates. Such an exchange rate regime has been called a *crawling peg system,* although it has been referred to by many other names, such as trotting peg, sliding or moving peg, and creeping devaluation or minidevaluations.

Under the crawling peg, the country sets a peg or par value for its currency, while at the same time allowing the peg to change gradually, in small steps, over time. The crawling peg is therefore an adjustable peg regime, as the Bretton Woods system was; the main difference lies in the exchange rate adjustments, which under Bretton Woods were supposed to be less frequent and of larger magnitude. In a sense, the crawling peg is another hybrid between fixed and flexible exchange rates as it embodies aspects of both regimes: External balance adjustments now involve both changes in international reserves as well as exchange rate changes.[14]

Key aspects in setting up a crawling peg regard to which currency (or basket of currencies) to peg and what rule, if any, to follow in making exchange rate adjustments, that is, by how much and how fast exchange rates will change. For instance, a possible exchange rate rule is to set monthly changes in the exchange rate based on the differential between domestic and foreign inflation rates during previous months. Such a purchasing power parity rule would allow domestic inflation to diverge from world inflation without major effects on real exchange rates and, therefore, on domestic competitiveness. One disadvantage[15] of such a rule is that, since future exchange rate changes are not determined much in advance, speculation based on inflationary expectations might arise as to future exchange rate adjustments, generating instability. An alternative rule would be to set a preannounced path of exchange rate changes, such as Chile instituted by means of its "tablita" (a table of pre-set exchange rate changes) during the late seventies and Argentina from 1978 to 1981. One of the possible advantages of this type of crawling is that it tends to reduce the instability surrounding speculation about exchange rate changes and thereby the possibility of foreign exchange crises. At the same time, in practice, governments frequently

[14] For an economic analysis of the simultaneous determination of the balance of payments (or changes in international reserves) and the exchange rate under a crawling peg with application to the case of Brazil, see M. Blejer and L. Leiderman," A Monetary Approach to the Crawling Peg System: Theory and Evidence," *Journal of Political Economy* (February 1981).

[15] Arguments for and against the crawling peg and various exchange rate rules may be found in J. Williamson, *Exchange Rate Rules: The Theory, Performance, and Prospects of the Crawling Peg* (New York: St. Martin's Press, Inc., 1981).

alter exchange rate rules, by reducing, say, the rate of devaluation of domestic currency, and therefore destabilizing speculation might still arise.

Another postulated advantage of the crawling peg lies in the possibility that Central Banks might be able to hold a smaller volume of international reserves as a buffer to finance balance of payments deficits. The explanation lies in that, everything else being constant, the heightened use of exchange rate changes as a device for external balance under a crawling peg regime might reduce the level of reserves below those required in a regime where only expenditure-changing policies are used to solve balance of payments problems. Recent empirical work by Sebastian Edwards,[16] using a sample of developing countries, tends to provide support for such a conclusion. This last point suggests broader questions regarding international reserves: What determines their optimal level and what effect has the wider degree of exchange rate flexibility after 1973 had on the level of international reserves of developing countries?

17–5   CENTRAL BANKS AND THE DEMAND FOR INTERNATIONAL RESERVES

Table 17–1 presents data for selected years on the international reserves of groups of countries. It can be observed that, overall since 1973, international reserves have increased at a faster rate than in previous periods.

Accounting for a large chunk of the increase in the value of international reserves during the 1970s and 1980s is the rise in the price of gold over that period. The rise in the price of gold from the original $35-per-ounce sustained by the United States under Bretton Woods to a price fluctuating around $400.00 at the present time, has implied a massive explosion in the value of gold reserves. Even at constant gold prices, however, international reserves quadrupled over the period of 1969 to 1979. How can we explain that international reserves have risen rather than declined after 1973?

International reserves are to a country what cash balances are to a household: They constitute widely acceptable means of payments and serve to settle transactions with the rest of the world. They provide liquidity, that is, funds in a form that can easily be spent or exchanged for goods or other assets at low transaction costs and with no capital losses. What factors determine the demand for international reserves by a Central Bank? The analogy between a household and a country suggests some of the possible factors involved.[17] In the same

[16] S. Edwards, "The Demand for International Reserves and Exchange Rate Adjustments: The Case of LDCs, 1964–1972," *Economica* (August 1983).

[17] For a discussion of the factors affecting the optimal level of international reserves, see B. J. Cohen, "International Reserves and Liquidity," in P. B. Kenen, ed., *International Trade and Finance, Frontiers for Research* (New York: Cambridge University Press, 1975); and J. A. Frenkel, "The Demand for International Reserves by Developed and Less-Developed Countries," *Economica* (February 1974).

TABLE 17–1.   **International Reserves for Selected Years. (Millions of SDRs, end of period)**

Area and Country	1952	1962	1972	1979	1980	1982	1983 November
All countries	49,391[a]	62,851	147,443	307,149	355,100	364,202	400,135
Industrial countries	38,582	52,535	110,282	180,791	211,904	211,918	231,194
United States	24,714	17,220	12,112	15,170	21,479	29,918	30,668
Oil-exporting countries	1,699	2,030	10,071	56,318	69,508	70,031	75,847
Non-oil-developing countries	8,576	8,171	26,132	68,842	71,850	74,388	82,067
Africa	1,202	1,635	3,168	4,311	4,480	3,846	4,371
Asia	3,407	2,550	6,640	23,232	24,968	34,395	40,671
Europe	966	1,346	6,428	7,400	8,060	6,874	7,227
Middle East	825	940	2,402	7,442	8,311	10,132	9,206
Western Hemisphere	2,175	1,700	7,494	26,457	26.031	19,143	20,545

Source: Economic Report of the President (1984).
[a] Includes Cuba.
Notes: International reserves is comprised of monetary authorities' holdings of gold, special drawing rights (SDRs), reserve positions in the International Monetary Fund, and foreign exchange. Data exclude U.S.S.R., other Eastern European countries, and Cuba (after 1960).
   U.S. dollars per SDR (end of period) are 1952 and 1962: 1.00000; 1972: 1.08571; 1977: 1.21471; 1978: 1.30279; 1979: 1.31733; 1980: 1.27541; 1981: 1.6396; 1982: 1.10311; and November 1983: 1.05058.

way that a household holds cash as a precautionary measure against the need to incur in sudden payments not matched by receipts, the demand for international reserves is influenced by the variability of the economy's international payments and receipts. The higher (or lower) the variability, the larger (or smaller) the optimal precautionary amount of international reserves by the Central Bank. In addition, just as individuals hold cash for transaction purposes, a country can hold reserves for the same reason. The higher the degree of openness of the economy, frequently measured in empirical work by the domestic propensity to import, the larger the volume of transactions with the rest of the world and the larger the level of reserves required to sustain such transactions. A relatively closed economy, on the other hand, could get away with holding a relatively small proportion of reserves. A final major factor affecting the demand for international reserves is the level of income of the economy, which reflects the size of the country and influences positively the absolute amount of reserves demanded.

   The sustained increase in the demand for international reserves[18] observed

   [18] See J. Frenkel, "International Liquidity and Monetary Control, "National Bureau of Economic Research, Working Paper 1118 (May 1983).

during the post-Bretton Woods era can be largely explained by the increased openness, real income, and variability of international payments and receipts faced by most countries during the period. As a matter of fact, it has been found that, after adjusting for these factors, the demand for international reserves shows a decline during the current period of floating vis-à-vis Bretton Woods. Still, the estimated differences are relatively minor. This partly reflects the fact that the developing countries and many developed countries continue to use pegged exchange rates, whether against each other or against the dollar, requiring international reserves in their foreign exchange operations. It also reflects the managed nature of the post-1973 float against the dollar and the fact that discretionary Central Bank intervention requires holdings of international reserves with which to carry the intervention.

One trend that can be discerned from Table 17–1 is that the non-oil developing countries sustained a rate of accumulation of international reserves in the 1970s in spite of the well-known massive current account deficits they faced during the period. The explanation lies in the fact that the current account deficits were largely financed through capital inflows particularly in the form of debt financing. The nature and implications of this phenomenon are examined next.

17–6   INTERNATIONAL FINANCIAL MARKETS AND THE EXTERNAL DEBT OF DEVELOPING COUNTRIES

One of the most important developments in international financial markets during the seventies was the drastic increase in the participation of developing countries in these markets. This increased participation originated during the late sixties and boomed after the 1973 quadrupling of oil prices. Two groups of Third World countries have been particularly involved: the oil-exporting countries and the so-called middle-income developing countries, with GNP per capita above $400. The richer oil-exporting countries, such as Saudi Arabia, Kuwait, and Libya, have become heavy lenders as a result of their huge oil revenues. For instance, by the end of 1980, the external assets of the oil-exporting lending countries were equal to $300 billion, most of which was invested in time deposits, equities, government securities, and other financial instruments in industrial countries. The middle-income developing countries, such as Argentina, Mexico, and South Korea, on the other hand, have borrowed heavily in international financial markets. This borrowing is sharply reflected by Table 17–2, which shows net capital inflows to oil-importing developing countries broken down according to source. The increased relative importance of commercial loans as a source of international finance for the middle-income developing countries stands out above anything else. We should also mention that, for the low-income developing countries, access to international financial markets has remained quite limited, with official development assistance through loans

TABLE 17–2. Oil-Importing Developing Countries' Current Account Deficit and Finance Sources, 1970 to 1980 (Billions of 1978 Dollars)

Item	Low-Income Oil Importers					Middle-Income Oil Importers				
	1970	1973	1975	1978	1980	1970	1973	1975	1978	1980
Current account deficit[a]	3.6	4.9	7.0	5.1	9.1	14.9	6.7	42.8	20.4	48.9
Financed by										
Net capital flows										
Official Development Assistance	3.4	4.1	6.6	5.1	5.7	3.3	5.3	5.3	6.5	7.9
Private direct investment	0.3	0.2	0.4	0.2	0.2	3.4	5.1	3.9	4.6	4.5
Commercial loans	0.5	0.6	0.8	0.9	0.7	8.9	13.7	21.0	29.4	27.1
Changes in reserves and short-term borrowing[b]	-0.5	-1.1	-0.7	-1.1	2.4	-0.8	-11.7	12.7	-20.1	9.5
Memorandum item										
Current account deficit as percentage of GNP	1.9	2.4	3.9	2.6	4.5	2.6	1.0	5.5	2.3	5.0

Source: The World Bank, *World Development Report 1981*, 49. Copyright © 1981 by the International Bank for Reconstruction and Development/The World Bank. Reprinted by permission of Oxford University Press, Inc.

[a] Excludes net official transfers (grants), which are included in capital flows.
[b] A minus sign (−) indicates an increase in reserves.

and grants from governments and official organizations in industrial countries remaining the most important source of external capital.

The rising overall participation of non-oil developing countries in international financial markets has been accompanied by a sharp increase in their external debt. External debt refers to all the fixed-income foreign claims to which a debtor country is subject. For most developing countries, however, external debt is essentially bank debt. Bond indebtedness is rarely used as a source of financing in developing countries. Table 17–3 shows the growth of the external bank debt of non-oil developing countries. Note that the eight countries pinpointed (Argentina, Brazil, Chile, Mexico, Peru, Philippines, South Korea, and Thailand) account for more than 75% of the external bank debt of all non-oil developing countries.

The spiraling external debt of the developing countries has raised serious concerns about the possibility of a default on these debts and of the ability of the heavily indebted countries to finance even the scheduled interest payments on their debts. The specter of a default from the major LDC debtors, and of a consequent 1930s-like worldwide financial collapse, haunts the sleepless nights

TABLE 17–3. **External Bank Debt, Selected Years, 1975–1982 (Billions of Dollars, End of Period)**

	Bank Debt				
Country	1975	1978	1979	1980	1982
Argentina	3.2	6.7	13.1	18.9	25.7
Brazil	14.8	31.7	36.9	43.3	60.5
Chile	0.8	2.7	4.5	6.7	14.6
Mexico	13.5	23.2	30.7	41.0	62.8
Peru	2.3	3.4	3.6	3.9	5.4
Philippines	2.0	4.0	5.4	7.0	12.6
South Korea	3.3	6.9	10.3	14.0	23.3
Thailand	1.2	2.7	3.0	3.2	4.9
Total	41.1	81.3	107.5	138.0	209.8
Addenda					
All non-OPEC LDCs[a]	63.0	120.8	155.9	193.5	263.3
Eight countries as a proportion of all non-OPEC LDCs	0.65	0.67	0.69	0.71	0.78
Brazil as a proportion of all non-OPEC LDCs	0.23	0.26	.024	0.22	0.23
Brazil plus Mexico as a proportion of all non-OPEC LDCs	0.44	0.45	0.44	0.43	0.47

Sources: Bank for International Settlements, "International Banking Developments: Second Quarter 1981," November 1981, Tables 6 and 7, and preceding issues. For 1982 data, International Monetary Fund, "International Capital Markets: Developments and Prospects, 1983," IMF Occasional Paper no. 23 (July 1983), Table 7.

[a] Non-oil developing countries excluding South Africa and European countries.

of finance ministers, bankers, and presidents in both developed and developing countries alike. To understand whether there are grounds for such fears, one must first analyze the role and functions of the increased external debt in the indebted countries. That is the task of the following sections.

17–7 ROLES AND FUNCTIONS OF EXTERNAL DEBT IN DEVELOPING COUNTRIES

To examine the role external debt plays in developing countries, it is useful to recall some of our earlier accounting identities. From the balance of payments accounts (see Chapter 4),

$$\text{CAB deficit} = \text{total capital inflows} + \text{IRs lost} \tag{1}$$

which states that a current account balance (CAB) deficit can be financed through capital inflows and/or through losses of international reserves. Given a certain current account balance deficit, external borrowing can provide the capital inflows required to finance that deficit without the Central Bank's level of international reserves declining. In a certain sense, capital inflows and losses in reserves are substitutes for each other. The increased access of non-oil developing countries to world financial markets allowed them to sustain large current account deficits, while at the same time increasing (or preventing huge decreases of) their overall level of international reserves. Actually, the oil shocks of 1973 to 1974 and of 1979 to 1980 both led to sudden huge increases in the current account deficits of these countries, deficits that were not able to be completely financed immediately through increased debt and other capital inflows. As a result, in the year immediately following the oil shocks, overall losses of international reserves were clearly observed. In the ensuing years, however, one finds increased reliance on indebtedness and a replenishing of the lost reserves. For example, in 1975, right after the oil shock of 1973 to 1974, the overall current account deficits of oil-importing developing countries were more than triple the amount they were in 1973 (in constant 1978 dollars). There were also overall losses of international reserves. During the period of 1976 to 1978, however, the current account deficits declined while indebtedness continued to increase. In 1978 there was a net accumulation of reserves equal to $21.2 billion.

In conclusion, during the 1970s external indebtedness increasingly financed the current account deficits of the developing countries. For these countries, the predominant item on the right-hand side of equation (1) became private financial capital inflows, rather than official capital inflows or losses of international reserves. How were the funds available from this borrowing used exactly? In other words, what particular items made up the current account balance deficit of the developing countries during the seventies? Was it increasing bills on the consumption of imported oil, or was it increased investment spending, arising perhaps from private and public capital accumulation projects, or what? Clearly, this is one of the major questions regarding the role of external debt in the developing countries as well as the issue of repayment of the debt.

From our introductory discussion of the balance of payments and national income in Chapter 5 [see equations (1) and (3)], we know that a current account deficit is associated with an excess of domestic spending over national income, namely,

$$CAB \text{ deficit} \equiv (I_N + C_N + G_N) - Y_N \tag{2}$$

Where CAB is our symbol for current account balance, I_N represents private domestic investment, C_N refers to private consumption expenditures, G_N is equal to total government spending, and Y_N is gross national product. Now, breaking down government expenditures into public investment spending, I_N^G (which includes such expenditures as the public construction of roads or oil wells), and public consumption expenditures, C_N^G (which includes expenses on public health, education, and other services), we can modify equation (2) to yield

$$CAB \text{ deficit} = (I_N + I_N^G) + [(C_N + C_N^G) - Y_N] \tag{2a}$$

$$= \text{total domestic investment} - \text{total domestic savings}$$

where total domestic investment includes both private and public domestic investment, and total domestic savings is the difference between GNP and the aggregate of private and public consumption.

What equation (2) says is that increased indebtedness financing CAB deficits can be associated with an excess of domestic investments over savings. Consequently, the increased external borrowing of developing countries is associated with a persistent and growing shortfall of domestic savings below investment in these countries. This gap may have arisen through two main routes: through sustained and increasing expenditures with relatively fixed savings, or through decreased savings (increasing consumption relative to income) with relatively fixed investment spending. The first possibility implies that countries borrow in order to accumulate capital with which to increase future income, while the second possibility implies that countries borrow to finance current consumption expenditures that have no clear-cut effect on economic growth or future income. Accordingly, the first possibility seems less likely to give rise to problems involving the repayment of the debt. As long as the investment projects undertaken are profitable, increased future income streams should provide enough funds for repayment of the principal plus interest. Borrowing for consumption purposes, however, does not provide such a clear-cut future repayment potential and seems likely to require a reduction of consumption some time in the future by means of which funds can be obtained to pay the debt without crippling reductions in domestic wealth.

What evidence exists on the links between spending and external borrowing in developing countries? The overall behavior of gross domestic savings, gross domestic investment,[19] and the current account balance (all as fractions of GNP) for groups of developing and developed countries is presented in Table 17–4.

The breakdown of the current account balance into its components varies from country to country and on the specific years considered. Still, some trends can be discerned. First of all, for the developing countries considered, the increased current account balance deficits of the 1970s were associated with rising investment (as a fraction of GNP) combined with relatively stable (or slightly rising) savings rates. The matter is very different for the developed countries, whose current account deficits during the 1970s have been associated with declines in savings (as a fraction of GNP) combined with relatively stable (or slightly falling) investment rates. Of course, these generalizations cannot be applied without qualification to every country. In the case of Chile, for example, the seventies were associated with a sharp decline in savings and investment relative to GNP. In 1975 alone, savings as a fraction of GNP plummeted to 2.8%, down from a 14.9% level in the previous year. Investment also declined but at a slower rate. Among the developed countries, Canada offers a picture very different from that above. Its ratio of investment to GNP rose from an average of 21.8% during 1963 to 1973 to an average of 23.2% during the 1974 to 1979 period; savings as a fraction of GNP, on the other hand, remained virtually unchanged (on average) between the two periods.

Perhaps the baffling story of the seventies as shown in Table 17–4 was the marked shift of investment spending from the (non-oil) developed countries to the developing countries. What factors can account for this shift? One cause has been attributed[20] to the general worsening of investment opportunities in the developed countries during the seventies attributable to widespread recession and declining productivity coupled with growth of real wage rates,[21] all of which combined to cause a sharp squeeze on profits. Another factor involved the increased receptiveness to foreign investment in many developing countries

---

[19] The investment figures presented in Table 17–4 consider only fixed investment and ignore inventory investment. Therefore, the gap between investment and savings will not coincide with the current account balance.

[20] See J. Sachs, "The Current Account and Macroeconomic Adjustment in the 1970s," *Brookings Papers on Economic Activity* (1981). See also A. Fishlow, "Latin American External Debt: The Case of Uncertain Development," in M. Syrquin and S. Teitel, *Trade Stability, Technology, and Equity in Latin America* (New York: Academic Press, Inc., 1982).

[21] The general growth of real wage rates in the developed countries during the seventies has been examined by Jeffrey Sachs in his article "Wages, Profits and Macroeconomic Adjustment: A Comparative Study," *Brookings Papers on Economic Activity,* 219–319 (1977). There are, of course, exceptions, the United States being a particularly significant one.

TABLE 17–4. The Current Account, Savings, and Investment, 1965 to 1979

Item	Period	
(Average over period)	1965–1973	1974–1979
Debt-ridden developing countries (selected)[a]		
Investment/GNP	20.4	22.6
Savings/GNP	20.6	21.9
CAB/GNP	−1.8	−3.1
Developed countries (selected)[b]		
Investment/GNP	21.6	21.3
Savings/GNP	23.1	22.0
CAB/GNP	0.3	−0.2

Source: Jeffrey Sachs, "The Current Account and Macroeconomic Adjustment in the 1970s," *Brookings Papers on Economic Activity* (1981), Tables 8 and 9.

[a] The selected debt-ridden countries in the sample are Brazil, Chile, Colombia, Mexico, Peru, Philippines, South Korea, Taiwan, and Thailand.

[b] The selected developed countries in the sample are the United States, the United Kingdom, Austria, Belgium, Denmark, France, Italy, Norway, Sweden, Canada, Japan, Finland, Australia, and the Netherlands.

and the heightened attractiveness offered by investments in raw materials and manufactured industries in these countries.

With widely available funds represented by the capital account surpluses of OPEC countries (especially through the Eurobanks), the world financial markets turned to the developing countries for their investments during the seventies. Offering low real interest rates (often negative, depending on the measure of inflation used), external borrowing became in effect an irresistible bargain. The subsequent explosion of the external debt of the developing countries is now history. Its most recent episode involves the previously mentioned scare regarding a possible default on the debt. With East-Bloc and Third World countries owing foreign commercial banks more than $500 billion, the payment of interest and repayment of principal (the so-called debt-service problem) has grown into an uncontrollable monster. As a group, developing countries had to pay (or roll over) more than $250 billion alone in debt-service payments during 1982. As a result, many countries have had to reschedule their debts. For example, Chile, Zaire, Peru, Turkey, and others had to reschedule their debts as early as 1976 and 1977. The resulting uncertainty and the rising fear of default has led to significant tightening of the lending offered to developing countries by the international financial markets. The extensive long-term lending of the seventies has been giving way to a shift toward short-term lending at high interest rates and, more recently, to set credit constraints on all lending. In addition, real interest rates have risen to levels much higher than in the seventies. The terms of external borrowing have thus become more stringent. This has placed the finance ministers of many developing countries in a difficult position, which generates the following kind of comment, made by a Mexican government official: "Those bastards [foreign bankers] got us into this hole. Now they are trying to bleed us for everything we have."[22]

One apparent conclusion from our discussion relating to Table 17–4 is that the external debt of developing countries has been associated with increased investment rather than increased consumption. This tends to suggest a rather optimistic view regarding the repayment of the debt. As Sachs concludes from a 1982 vantage point: "Both the ability to repay debt and the disincentives to default rise to the extent that indebtedness reflects high levels of domestic investment rather than low levels of savings. And at least for the major borrowing countries such a pattern is evident in the 1970s."[23]

A main problem of analyzing external borrowing by focusing on the aggregate investment and savings behavior of the economy is that it ignores the issues relating to the composition of these aggregates into their public and private components. An alternative expression for a current account deficit, also established in Chapter 5 [see equation (4)], is

$$\text{CAB deficit} = (I_N - S_N) + (G_N - TX_N) \qquad (3)$$

where TX_N refers to tax revenues so that $(G_N - TX_N)$ is the government budget deficit. This means that when external indebtedness finances a current account balance deficit, it is financing that part of domestic investment which is not accounted for by domestic savings and/or that part of government expenditures which is not financed by government revenues.

The measured size of budget deficits is clearly dependent on the particular country and time period considered and is complicated by the intricacies of the various government and public enterprise accounts (and government statistics on the matter) and by the general problems of measuring public sector deficits.[24] Generally, however, budget deficits in the debt-ridden developing countries were relatively high during the seventies. In Argentina, for instance, the fiscal deficit in 1975 reached more than 12% of GNP and revenue less than 25% of government expenditure[25]; in Mexico the government deficit gradually increased over

---

[22] *The Wall Street Journal,* "Bank Responsibility for Mexico's Woes" (October 22, 1982).

[23] J. Sachs, "LDC Debt in the 1980s: Risk and Reforms," National Bureau of Economic Research Working Paper No. 861, 68 (February 1982).

[24] For a debate on the issues regarding the proper measure of public sector deficits and their connection to external borrowing, see the contributions by E. Bacha and R. Dornbusch, in J. Williamson, eds., *Prospects for Adjustment in Argentina, Brazil, and Mexico: Responding to the Debt Crisis,* (Washington, D.C.: Institute for International Economics, 1983).

[25] As stated by G. Calvo, "Trying to Stabilize: Some Theoretical Reflections Based on the Case of Argentina," in P. Aspe, R. Dornbusch, and M. Obstfeld, eds., *Financial Policies and the World Capital Markets: The Problem of Latin American Countries* (Chicago: University of Chicago Press, 1983), p. 201.

the early seventies reaching close to 10% of GDP by 1976. A large fraction of these deficits has been financed by borrowing from the local financial community or from the Central Bank (by printing money), but a substantial fraction has been associated with external public borrowing. The next section examines and documents the importance of the growth of the public external debt of the developing countries.

17–8   BUDGET DEFICITS AND PUBLIC EXTERNAL DEBT

Public external borrowing has been an increasingly important source of revenues for the governments of the developing countries and has consistently comprised a major part of their external borrowing. Table 17–5 shows how the external public debt of the developing countries (as a percentage of GNP) increased during the 1970s. This growth continued unabated until 1982, keeping pace with a growth of the overall debt of (non-oil) developing countries of more than 30% from 1980 to 1982. After 1982, new lending to these countries has been sharply curtailed.

The rise of public external borrowing as a means of financing budget deficits during the 1970s was directly connected to the relatively low real interest rates and easy terms widely available in international financial markets at the time.

TABLE 17–5.   The External Public Debt of the Developing Countries

Country	External Public Debt (Outstanding and Disbursed) as a Percentage of GNP	
	1970	*1982*
Algeria	19.3	31.9
Argentina	8.7	29.5
Brazil	7.1	16.9
Chile	25.8	23.7
Costa Rica	13.8	111.7
Egypt	23.8	52.8
Mexico	9.1	31.1
Peru	12.6	33.5
Philippines	8.1	22.5
South Korea	20.4	28.3
Thailand	4.9	17.4
Venezuela	6.6	17.8

Source: World Bank, *World Development Report 1984,* Table 15. Copyright © 1984 by the International Bank for Reconstruction and Development/The World Bank. Reprinted by permission of Oxford University Press, Inc.

It was also due to the relative attractiveness external borrowing offered to the governments of developing countries at the time. In contrast to raising taxes and printing money, external debt does not immediately generate the outrage of taxpayers (although it may now raise some eyebrows), nor does it give rise either to the losses of international reserves to which monetization of the debt would lead. As a matter of fact, the immediate effects of external borrowing is to generate capital inflows and avoid losses of international reserves. Consequently, developing countries relied more and more heavily on external borrowing to finance their huge deficit expenditures on investment projects and other consumption and subsidy programs.

The apparent short-run attractiveness of external borrowing, however, hides the potential longer-term problems associated with persistent borrowing. First of all, borrowing usually involves interest payments. As a result, accumulating debt will give rise to accumulating *interest payments*. In addition, even though much of the external borrowing of the 1970s involved long-term debt, borrowing is borrowing and, even if slowly, the debt principal has to be repaid. Accumulating debt means accumulation of these *amortization payments*. The addition of interest and amortization payments is what is called the *debt service*, which involves a negative item on the balance of payments and, thus, losses of international reserves. Consequently, accumulating debt will eventually generate balance of payments deficits intended to finance its repayment. Furthermore, unless the budget deficits are used to finance growth-inducing expenditures that can raise future revenues (such as capital accumulation, oil-reserves exploration, or research and development), future taxes will have to finance government debt engaged today. Growing debt thus implies higher future taxes to service it. This is the so-called *burden of the debt*. When the external public debt of the economy is important, this burden falls on domestic taxpayers paying foreign banks, and it can become a sticky international problem. Since the burden of the debt may not be politically (if economically) possible to exert effectively after the debt has accumulated to a certain point, the government may be forced to roll it over and borrow even more to pay for debt servicing. Accumulating debt-service payments, however, may impose a heavy burden on the public sector. When external debt service payments reach 64.1% and 34.6% of the exports of a country, as in Mexico and Brazil in 1979, the government starts playing with default and bankruptcy.[26]

The case of Mexico, more than any other case, illustrates the problems of large, persistent budget deficits. In 1976, Mexico faced one of its worse economic crises, threatening the financial stability of the country as well as its fiscal and political system. The symptoms of the disease surfaced through rumors and speculation on the dwindling international reserves of the Central Bank, the

---

[26] The financial aspects of the current debt crisis are thoroughly discussed by Donald Lessard, "North-South: The Implications for Multinational Banking," *Journal of Banking and Finance* (1983). See also Larry Sjaastad, "International Debt Quagmire—To Whom Do We Owe It?," *The World Economy* (March 1984).

devaluation of the Mexican peso (which did actually occur) and the possible fiscal bankruptcy of the government and default on its debts. One of the primary sources of the 1976 crisis lay in the increased budget deficits the government accrued during the previous years. The overall public sector deficit, which had averaged 2.5% of GDP annually between 1965 and 1970, averaged 5.7% during the 1971 to 1976 period, being 9.5% in 1976.[27] A large fraction of these deficits was financed by printing money, but there was also an increase in external borrowing: The government's foreign borrowings increased from $6.5 billion in 1973 to more than $10.0 billion in 1974 and up to $20 billion by 1976. Since most of the increased government revenues went to finance current expenditures and subsidies to government-owned industries, rather than government-revenue-producing activities, the borrowing did not give rise to any significant additional revenues. The accumulating external debt thus gave rise to an acute debt-service problem. Combined with huge balance of payments deficits arising from the monetization of the debt and speculative capital flight, this problem led to massive losses in international reserves. The outcome was the eventual crisis.

The 1976 crisis was resolved through a number of emergency measures, which included agreements among the International Monetary Fund, the United States, and Mexico. Through these agreements, temporary financing facilities were made available to the Bank of Mexico, thereby easing the strain on the dwindling international reserves. In exchange, the government agreed to undertake a number of policy measures intended to reduce its budget deficits, its external borrowing, and so on. The stabilization program seemed to ease the sense of impending disaster at the time, especially when it coincided with the discovery of large oil and gas reserves and increased earnings from petroleum exports. An excessive optimism, however, was generated by the return of economic stability and the ballooning expectations of renewed economic growth through oil exports. As a result, the fiscal excesses that generated the 1976 crisis gradually erupted again. Even though the growth of the budget deficit was contained for a short period of time after the 1976 crisis, it gradually crept up again. By 1980, the budget deficit, as a percentage of GDP, was 6.7%; in 1981 it grew to 12.6% and much higher during 1982.

A new crisis became imminent during the early eighties, heightened and compounded by a shifting environment in world financial markets. In contrast to the relatively low interest rates of the early seventies, the eighties brought about rising interest rates in both nominal and real terms. Consequently, the government's new borrowings and the refinancing of maturing debt through short-term borrowing had to be undertaken at relatively high interest rates. Debt service payments increased dramatically and the government's liquidity problems started to look quite bleak. When combined with less-than-expected

[27] Sidney Weintraub, "Case Study of Economic Stabilization: Mexico," in S. Weintraub and W. R. Cline, eds., *Economic Stabilization in Developing Countries* (Washington, D.C., The Brookings Institution, 1981), p. 276.

oil revenues (facing sagging demand in world markets, Mexico was forced to slash oil prices by $4.00 per barrel in early 1981), persistent current account deficits, and recession, rumors and speculation arose once again about the financial situation of the government and the likelihood of a devaluation. The massive capital flight induced by the expected devaluation led to unsustainable losses of international reserves. In February 1982, the Mexican government allowed the peso to float, which resulted in a 40% effective devaluation. The episode culminated with the nationalization of the Mexican banking sector in September 1982.

The depreciation of the peso stopped the loss of international reserves, but their depleted levels were hardly sufficient to support the balance of payments deficits required by the continued current accounts deficits and the increasing external debt-servicing payments. Trying to avoid further reductions in the value of the peso, during 1982 to 1984, the Mexican government engaged in new rounds of agreements with the International Monetary Fund, the Federal Reserve, and other Western Central Banks to delay debt-service payments and to obtain temporary increases in its foreign exchange holdings.

The Mexican case clearly illustrates the role of the public sector in the so-called problem of the external debt of the developing countries. Using aggregate figures, Table 17–4 showed us how the external borrowings of the heavily indebted developing countries have been associated with significant increases in investment rates and relatively small (if any) decreases in domestic savings. Much of this investment, however, has been undertaken by the government. Roughly 50% of gross domestic fixed investment in Mexico in 1978 was public investment, a fraction representative of the government investment expenditures during the seventies. Now, as long as domestic investment projects are profitable, one can expect the payment of external borrowings to cause no serious dilemmas. Eventually, the increased income reaped from the projects would more than pay for the borrowings. Three factors, however, may give rise to problems. First, the existence of a lengthy gestation period before which the projects come to fruition may generate a short-term liquidity problem, especially when, as we have seen, the international financial climate of the eighties is not so friendly. Even if temporarily bothersome, however, this type of problem should not be of much concern over the long run.

The second major factor causing problems in the payment of the external public debt lies in the lack of revenues generally provided by the public investments engaged by developing countries during the eighties. There are various reasons for this. The first one regards unfulfilled expectations: Investments that appear profitable at one point in time may face very different prospects after they have been undertaken. The commodity and raw materials price boom of the early seventies is one case in point. The increased relative profitability of these sectors at the time generated much investment spending on them by developing countries. These projects may now face difficult times given the recent downward trend in the relative price of raw materials. In the case of Mexico, the current declining price of oil may have hurt its development projects (and their financing) as much as anything else. Another factor that causes a lack of income from public investment projects is the entrenched government practice of subsidizing publicly produced goods and services. A large share of the investments of the developing countries have indeed gone into public enterprises whose services are heavily subsidized when provided to the public (such as electricity or gasoline). The prices of these goods and services are often not sufficiently high to cover the costs of production, inclusive of the interest on the debt and depreciation. This happens even when the investments are physically productive, and it is often compounded by the presence of technological and managerial inefficiency.

The general conclusion of this section is the importance government finances have had on the so-called external debt crisis of the developing countries. Government budget deficits are closely related to the problem, and any sort of solution would certainly involve some belt tightening; public enterprise pricing may play a major role in this process. This is, of course, one of the primary conditions imposed by the IMF on the granting of loans to countries with major debt problems. Actually, the role of the IMF, both through its function as international lender of last resort and through intermediating activities between international lenders and borrowers, must be extremely important if the existing external debt mess is to be resolved without a major shake-up of the international financial system. The next section examines the functions and role of the IMF in the current world economic juncture.

17–9 THE INTERNATIONAL MONETARY FUND AND ITS CURRENT ROLE IN THE WORLD ECONOMY

The International Monetary Fund is a membership organization of nations.[28] It is open to countries that consent to abide by its Articles of Agreement— the IMF's basic constitution—and contribute an assigned *subscription or quota,* a sort of entry fee, 75% of which is to be paid in the currency of the member country and the remaining 25% in SDRs or a currency acceptable to the IMF (originally this portion was payable in gold). The quotas are determined by a formula that takes into account the size of the country and its importance in international trade. The voting power of a member country is directly related to its quota and is thus unevenly distributed among countries. For instance, the United States commands about 20% of the total number of votes, while the smaller countries' voting power is indeed negligible.

The Board of Governors, in which every member has a representative casting the votes assigned to the country, is the senior decision-making body of the

---

[28] A full description of the IMF can be obtained from A. W. Hooke, *The International Monetary Fund: Its Evolution, Organization, and Activities,* 2nd ed., Pamphlet Series No. 37 (Washington, D.C., International Monetary Fund, 1982).

IMF. It approves all Amendments to the Articles of Agreement and decides on such matters as the acceptance of new members and the allocation of SDRs. The Board of Governors only meets from time to time; actually, a Governor is typically a minister of finance or the head of the central bank of a member country, having a full set of commitments besides being on the Board of Governors. The responsibility for the day-to-day operation of the IMF falls on the Executive Board, consisting of executive directors representing member countries and headed by a managing director, the IMF's Chief Executive Officer.

Created originally to monitor and oversee the operation of the Bretton Woods system, the IMF has proved to be a survivor in international monetary affairs. More than a decade after Bretton Woods passed away, it operates in full capacity and remains a pivotal international financial institution. From an original membership of less than 50 countries, the IMF currently embraces almost 150 countries (a substantial number of them excolonial territories that did not exist as independent nations when the IMF was created). These comprise most countries in the world except Russia, which has never joined the Fund, and a few other— mostly communist—countries.

The Current Role of the International Monetary Fund

Although the rules and operations of the Fund have changed over time to adapt to drastically altered circumstances, its basic objectives have remained unchanged: to contribute to maintaining a stable and workable international payments system that stimulates international trade and promotes worldwide economic growth. How the Fund works toward attaining these objectives is best shown by examining its current functions in international monetary affairs.

Perhaps the foremost current role of the IMF, and the main reason it has reached the headlines lately, is its lending to member countries. Counting with financial assets reaching $80 billion in 1983, the IMF is a major leaguer among financial institutions and an important supplier of funds to member countries. The main source of funds the IMF itself has available is provided by its member countries in the form of member country subscriptions or quotas, but also through their lending to the IMF.

The IMF provides last-resort financing to those countries with short-term balance of payments difficulties. In doing so, it contributes toward speeding up the balance of payments adjustment process in these countries and prevents disruptive monetary crises. The loans usually serve to finance directly the replenishing of international reserves, external debt repayments, and so on. Most Fund lending is made on a conditional basis; that is, the Fund imposes conditions on the countries to which it lends. These include restrictions on economic policies, like reductions in government budget deficits or monetary contractionism, that are deemed by many to be undue foreign intervention in the countries involved, particularly in the LDCs, which represent a substantial portion of the Fund's clientele. The issue of conditionality has strong political connotations, especially in light of the fact that the Fund is effectively controlled by a small number of large industrial countries.[29] The restrictions on economic policies imposed by IMF conditions are themselves the subject of controversy, as we have repeatedly shown in previous chapters (particularly Chapters 10 and 13).

The role of the IMF in the international monetary system has come to the forefront lately when the IMF emerged as a main negotiator, collaborator, and intermediary in the negotiations between creditor and debtor countries during the debt crisis of the 1980s. Its coordinator's role in this respect is generally considered as having been crucial in the successful completion of many negotiations.

Finally, the IMF is the organism in charge of creating SDRs, an international reserve asset. In this respect, it fulfills some of the functions of a world central bank, but only partially, since SDRs comprise less than 5% of world international reserves, and furthermore, the SDR does not generally circulate as a currency and has a limited commercial use. Other functions of the IMF include providing a code of conduct in international trade and financial matters (it condemns competitive devaluations and other beggar-thy-neighbor policies), and surveillance over member exchange controls and other restrictions that obstruct international trade (although countries do not have any commitment or obligation to follow IMF guidelines any more).

17-10 REFORM AND EVOLUTION OF INTERNATIONAL MONETARY ARRANGEMENTS: A SUMMING UP AND A LOOK AHEAD

We have now completed an overview of the main international monetary arrangements currently prevailing in the world economy. We conclude by venturing some comments on where we stand and on where to go in terms of international monetary reform.

In the present context, there are three major international economic developments associated predominantly with the post-Bretton Woods era that have drastically modified the world economy. The first one regards the higher degree of exchange rate flexibility faced by the industrial countries; the second is the growth of international financial markets—including the Eurocurrency markets—and the enhanced degree of international capital mobility; and the third is the decline in the role of gold and the dollar in international reserve transactions among Central Banks. In addition, there is a common thread running along

---

[29] For a full analysis of conditionality, see J. Williamson, *Fund Conditionality* (Washington, D.C.: Institute of International Economics, 1983). From yet another point of view, IMF lending has been criticized for being destabilizing and counter-productive in the resolution of the debt problems of developing countries. The argument is that IMF lending generates a moral hazard by providing cheap bailouts to economic mismanagement, reducing the incentives for a country to remain solvent and keep its house in order. See R. Vaubel, "The Moral Hazard of IMF Lending," *The World Economy* (January, 1984).

the many events occurring during the post-Bretton Woods era: the substantial variability observed of certain fundamental economic variables. Although not a general rule, it is widely recognized—as documented in this and previous chapters—that the last decade has witnessed substantial variability of real exchange rates, nominal and real interest rates, inflation rates, and so forth. There are two schools of thought interpreting these observations. One argues that the marked turbulence of economic variables has been the product of the inherent uncertainty connected to the economic and political events of recent years and that the current set of international monetary arrangements, if anything, has contributed to ameliorate the effects of such exogenous shocks. In an extreme version of this viewpoint, there is no major problem with the state of current international monetary affairs.

An alternative approach postulates that, in spite of the shocks to the system, the turbulence of economic variables has been excessive by any measure, and therefore the current state of international monetary arrangements requires some basic modifications to promote greater stability. From this point of view, for instance, the greater degree of capital mobility of the seventies has been associated with destabilizing speculative movements, generating sustained deviations of real exchange rates from fundamentals and resulting in distortionary effects on domestic inflation, output, and employment. It is implied that capital mobility has resulted in a system that is too oiled or greased, too easily and drastically influenced by purely speculative disturbances. It is from this vantage point that Nobel Prize winner James Tobin has argued[30] that controls or disincentives on capital movements should be imposed—in the form of, say, interest rate equalization taxes—so as to "throw some sand on the wheels" of the system and stabilize its response to disturbances. Opponents of such a proposal have noted its potentially distortionary effects if it channels capital to areas of low marginal productivity and out of higher productivity regions. Still, the proposal could be advocated as a second-best policy: Its stabilization benefits might more than offset the efficiency costs.

The future of the international monetary system seems uncertain at this point. The recent proposals for modifying or reforming international monetary arrangements are baffling in their diversity. Each politician or economist seems to have his or her own pet proposal, whether it is a return to the gold standard, a pegged exchange rate regime, full flexibility of currency values, managed floating, managed floating with cooperation and coordination among countries, or other hybrid systems. Behind these proposals is a whole range of arguments for or against alternative exchange rate regimes, arguments that have a long history of debate. For many years, the controversies centered on the relative merits of fixed and flexible exchange rate regimes in leading to economic stability and an efficient use of money in society. On the one hand, fixed exchange

---

[30] See J. Tobin, "A Proposal for International Monetary Reform," *Eastern Economic Journal* (July/October 1978).

rates were hailed by some because, under free currency convertibility, they mimic a single world money—promoting monetary efficiency—and impose some controls or discipline on the use of economic policy instruments. On the other hand, it was recognized that fixed exchange rates could impose a severe constraint on the ability of a country to choose its inflation rate, since the latter was closely linked to world inflationary conditions. Individual countries could thus be prevented from attaining their optimal inflation rate, as determined by their particular circumstances. In addition, pro-free market economists claimed that a fixed exchange rate regime, as a price (exchange rate) fixing mechanism, interferes with market determination of exchange rates and forces domestic economic policy, particularly monetary policy, to be geared toward keeping the exchange rate fixed.

The business cycle insulation properties of a flexible exchange rate regime were stressed by pro-flexible-rates economists, though opponents pointed out the possibility of wildly fluctuating or badly behaving exchange rates, and to the likelihood that destabilizing speculation would move exchange rates away from their fundamental equilibrium values with a deleterious effect on world trade and income. In spite of these misgivings, most academic experts in the late sixties were inclined to favor floating exchange rates as an international payments system, though there were prominent exceptions such as C. P. Kindleberger, A. B. Laffer, and R. A. Mundell.

The experience since 1973 shattered the belief in the insulation properties of exchange rate flexibility, as well as the hope that real exchange rate variability would not be much higher than under Bretton Woods. As a matter of fact, the increased awareness of interdependence in the world economy and the absence of rules governing Central Bank intervention in foreign exchange markets have led to a reformulation of the controversies on exchange rate regimes. The emphasis has shifted to the question of what is the optimal degree of foreign exchange market intervention and, more recently, to the problem of policy coordination among countries. Some economists currently propose a coordinated, managed floating regime as a better alternative to fixed and floating regimes as well as to the current managed floating regime, which lacks a coordinating authority or general rules of intervention.

Inconsistency of policy goals in a world lacking coordination can indeed be a source of difficulty for the current regime of managed floating. For instance, if the intervention of the United States in foreign exchange markets is to keep the dollar from appreciating in value while that of other countries is aimed at preventing a depreciation of their currencies against the dollar, inconsistency and conflict will arise on a global scale, since these objectives cannot be realized simultaneously. Likewise, conflict arises if all countries try to achieve trade surpluses. Since the world trade surplus has to be zero, at least one country will find its efforts frustrated. The problems connected to the presence of global constraints on national economic policies are often referred collectively as the consistency, or $n - 1$, problem: Once $n - 1$ national authorities, in a set of *n* countries, have attained a certain trade balance or exchange rate target, the remaining country's trade balance or exchange rate is automatically determined. This last country's goal is redundant in that it cannot be attained without frustrating other countries' targets. Since *n* independent goals may conflict and be impossible to attain, either one country gives in and abandons its own targets, or some agreement is made by all countries so as to coordinate their policies to make them consistent. Otherwise, if countries try to pursue their own policies, the ensuing conflict might lead to losses for all, such as when the attempt to improve the trade balance in one country through protection results in reduced world trade but no improvement in each country's trade balance. The same type of issue arises with respect to exchange rate determination and the intervention policies of *n* countries trying to achieve targets regarding the value of their currencies. Still, the issue of policy coordination and harmonization is not settled yet due to the enormous practical difficulties in formulating and implementing coordinated intervention policies.

Two specific proposals that have been widely discussed recently are a return to a classical gold standard and the expansion of the SDR as an international reserve currency. In our discussion of the gold standard in Chapter 16, we noted the advantages and disadvantages of such a regime. Still, a basic problem with such a proposal is its political infeasibility. Rearranging international monetary arrangements at the present time requires the consent and coordination of the major industrial countries. Unilateral moves seem doomed to failure. The gold standard, however, imposes substantial constraints on the autonomy of domestic monetary authorities, something most industrial countries would probably be unwilling to accept. Besides, in a world in which gold supplies are largely monopolized by Russia and the Republic of South Africa, the return to a gold-determined world money supply seems politically infeasible.

An alternative set of proposals encourage the expansion of the SDR as an international reserve currency.[31] The proposals here include making the SDR more prominent by trying to induce voluntary substitution from dollars or other reserve assets to SDRs. One possibility is for the IMF to issue a so-called substitution account by means of which the IMF would accept deposits owned by Central Banks and issue in exchange an equivalent amount in SDRs. The payment of interest on such account would then encourage the substitution. Although it has been widely discussed in IMF meetings, the future of this proposal is still an open question.

It appears that the international monetary system is slowly moving toward one of *multiple reserve currencies,* with a decline in the role of gold and the dollar as international reserves. Even though the dollar continues to be a major reserve currency (from the end of 1976 to the end of 1983, the percentage of

---

[31] See P. B. Kenen, "The Use of the SDR to Supplement or Substitute for Other Means of Finance," in G. M. von Furstenberg, ed., *International Money and Credit: The Policy Roles* (Washington, D.C.: International Monetary Fund, 1983) and D. M. Sobol, "A Substitution Account: Precedents and Issues," *Federal Reserve Bank of New York Quarterly Review* (Summer 1979).

official foreign exchange holdings in dollars has been reduced from 76.5 to 69.1%), the fact that Central Banks keep diversified currency portfolios, holding ECUs, deutsche marks, yen, and Swiss francs as reserve currencies, is seen by some as a destabilizing force. The fear is that, in such a multiple reserve currency regime, Central Banks will shift among reserve currencies in response to actual or anticipated changes in economic variables, amplifying exchange rate movements in much the same manner as private speculators would (in the presence of currency substitution).[32] Proposals in this area usually promote a single reserve currency asset as international money, such as the SDR or a composite currency involving the dollar, the German mark, and other currencies.

This chapter has surveyed a substantial number of proposals for reform of the international monetary system, most of them—as can be expected—plagued by controversy. As long as they continue to generate heat, it is clear that international monetary reform will continue to be in the headlines and remain at the center of the current international dialogue.

17–11 SUMMARY

1. The floating exchange rate regime followed by most industrial countries vis-à-vis the dollar after 1973 has been characterized by active intervention of Central Banks in foreign exchange markets. The system has thus been one of managed floating.

2. Central Bank intervention can in principle be called for in situations where exchange rates tend to diverge considerably from fundamentals. In practice, however, it is difficult to discern the sources of sudden changes in exchange rates, making Central Bank intervention more difficult to justify.

3. Whether an economy should peg or float the exchange rate depends on the particular environment or the specific economic disturbances facing the country. A country could find it optimal to adopt a fixed exchange rate against some currency and a flexible exchange rate against others.

4. Under the European Monetary System (EMS), member countries peg their currencies in term of the European currency unit (ECU). Bilateral pegs are then determined and fluctuations of $\pm 2.25\%$ allowed around them. Since the ECU floats against the dollar, the EMS currencies float together against the U.S. dollar. The system is therefore a joint currency float.

5. A monetary union represents a group of countries that fix their exchange rates vis-à-vis each other and abdicate the active use of monetary policy. If a country is a small open economy with a minor nontraded goods sector and faces a high degree of factor mobility with another country, it will be more likely that a monetary union with that country will be successful.

[32] This is suggested by the evidence provided by C. F. Bergsten and J. Williamson, *The Multiple Reserve Currency System: Evolution, Consequences, and Alternatives* (Washington, D.C.: Institute for International Economics, 1983).

6. The crawling peg is a regime in which the country sets a peg for its currency while allowing the peg to change gradually.

7. The sustained increase in the demand for international reserves observed during the post-Bretton Woods era can be largely explained by the increased openness, real income, and variability of receipts and payments faced by most countries during the period. All these factors raise the demand for international reserves. The fact that the demand for international reserves has not significantly declined during the seventies (holding these factors constant) reflects the adoption of pegged exchange rates by some countries and Central Bank intervention in foreign exchange markets.

8. The rising overall participation of the non-oil developing countries in international financial markets during the 1970s has been accompanied by a sharp increase in their external debt. This external debt has been associated with increased investment rather than increased consumption. A large share of the investments involved, however, has been undertaken by the public sector. Short-run liquidity problems, rising real interest rates, unfulfilled expectations regarding investments in raw materials sectors, unrealistic public pricing policies, and government willingness to guarantee or take over private debt have combined to generate developing-country public sector difficulties in the repayment of their external borrowings.

9. The International Monetary Fund (IMF) has had a major role in international monetary affairs recently because of its function as a lender to developing countries and as an intermediary between debtor countries and their lenders.

PROBLEMS

1. Two countries, A and B, trade only with each other. They operate under a managed float. Country A engages in a nonsterilized purchase of the other country's currency. What would be the effect on the exchange rate? Suppose the purchase of foreign currency is sterilized. What operation must the Central Bank of country A engage in to sterilize and what would be the impact on the exchange rate? What actions could country B undertake to offset the effects of country A's intervention on the exchange rate, if any? (H I N T : Assume first a monetary approach to exchange rate determination, as in Chapter 15, and then a portfolio balance approach, determining the effects of intervention on the risk premium.)

2. A developing country has decided to adopt fixed exchange rates. What factors determine to which currency—or basket of currencies—the country should peg?

3. According to Mundell's analysis, if two neighboring regions face zero factor movements among them, adopting flexible exchange rates might be the best regime, rather than a monetary union. However, in their article, "Exchange Rate Policies for Developing Countries" [in S. Grassman and E. Lundberg,

eds., *The World Economic Order: Past and Prospects* (New York: St. Martin's Press, 1981)], W. Branson and L. Katseli-Papaefstratiou argue that for countries with zero international trade in assets and facing short-run *J*-curve effects, this result breaks down. Why?

4. Monetary integration is typically established in stages. Some experts suggest that a system of fixed exchange rates among participating countries should be introduced first, even while factor mobility and effective policy coordination and harmonization have not yet been promoted. Others argue for the opposite path—that is, attain freer movement of labor and capital and coordinate policies before establishing fixed exchange rates and consummating the union. Discuss the arguments for and against each position and evaluate them. Provide, if possible, historical examples of how monetary integration has proceeded in practice.

5. Would it aid Pennsylvania to be endowed with a separate currency, with a floating exchange rate against the dollar, in solving the problems of unemployed steel workers?

6. Suppose that the U.S. government wants the world to return to a classical gold standard. (a) Could it do so without coordination with other industrial countries? (b) Assuming that the system was agreed upon by all countries concerned, could it be feasible; that is, would the regime be able to operate at all?

7. Some economists have suggested that industrial countries return to a gold exchange standard as an alternative to the current regime of floating exchange rates. Assume that the United States decides to fix the dollar price of gold. What problems, economic and political, do you foresee arising from such a move?

8. Examine the advantages and disadvantages of a group of countries fixing their currency values in terms of each other versus setting up a single currency area.

9. Could the state of Illinois suffer from balance of payments deficits? Could Illinois face an external debt crisis? Explain.

10. Using the framework developed in Chapters 10 and 11, analyze the short-run and long-run effects of a Central Bank credit expansion in an economy under a crawling peg. Assume that the exchange rate rule followed is to raise the exchange rate in the same proportion as the last period's increase in domestic prices. For the sake of simplicity, assume no capital mobility and fixed foreign prices.

Author Index

Subject Index

$$q = \frac{e\rho *}{\rho \uparrow} \Big\} \downarrow$$

$\rightarrow$